The World Bank Legal Review

Volume 3

The World Bank Legal Review
Volume 3
International Financial Institutions and Global Legal Governance

The World Bank Legal Review is a publication for policy makers and their advisers, judges, attorneys, and other professionals engaged in the field of international development with a particular focus on law, justice, and development. It offers a combination of legal scholarship, lessons from experience, legal developments, and recent research on the many ways in which the application of the law and the improvement of justice systems promote poverty reduction, economic development, and the rule of law.

The World Bank Legal Review is part of the World Bank Law, Justice, and Development Series managed by the Research and Editorial Board of the World Bank's Legal Vice Presidency, composed of Hassane Cissé, Editor in Chief; Kenneth Mwenda and Alberto Ninio, Co-chairs; Christina Biebesheimer, Charles di Leva, Laurence Folliot Laulliot, Vikram Raghavan, Vijay Tata, and Kishor Uprety, Members.

The present volume of *The World Bank Legal Review* benefited from inputs from members of the World Bank's Legal Vice Presidency and other units of the World Bank Group, including Alexis Albion, Luiz Henrique Alcoforado, Evarist Baimu, Christina Biebesheimer, Anna Chytla, Adrian di Giovanni, Frank Fariello, Rowena Gorospe, Zoe Kolovou, Siobhan McInerney-Lankford, Patricia Miranda, Marco Nicoli, Alberto Ninio, Aristeidis Panou, Maurizio Ragazzi, Vikram Raghavan, Elena Segura, Barry Walsh, and Yesha Yadav. The preparation of this volume was made possible with the invaluable help of Paola Scalabrin and Nigel Quinney.

The World Bank Legal Review

Volume 3

International Financial Institutions and Global Legal Governance

Hassane Cissé

Daniel D. Bradlow

Benedict Kingsbury

Editors

THE WORLD BANK

1 2 3 4 15 14 13 12 11

ISBN: 978-0-8213-8863-1

e-ISBN: 978-0-8213-8864-8

DOI: 10.1596/978-0-8213-8863-1

Library of Congress Cataloging-in-Publication data has been requested.

The World Bank Legal Review

Volume 3

International Financial Institutions and Global Legal Governance

EDITORS

Hassane Cissé

Deputy General Counsel, Knowledge and Research, World Bank

Daniel D. Bradlow

SARCHI Professor of International Development Law and African Economic Relations, University of Pretoria, and Professor of Law, American University Washington College of Law

Benedict Kingsbury

Murry and Ida Becker Professor of Law and Director of the Institute for International Law and Justice at New York University School of Law; Visiting Professor of Law, University of Utah

PRODUCTION EDITOR

Aristeidis Panou

Legal Associate, World Bank

Contents

Foreword

Robert B. Zoellick

The global financial crisis encouraged a major rethinking of our global financial architecture, policies, and institutions. But it also reminded us that effective rule of law, including respect for property rights and access to justice, remains fundamental for inclusive and sustainable globalization. This was clearly demonstrated earlier this year: The frustration of a fruit vendor when his weighing scales were confiscated and he was mistreated by police—which led him to set himself on fire in public—ignited a firestorm that engulfed Tunisia and the wider Middle East, and led to a demand for justice, rules, and laws that are fair, predictable, and transparent.

The rule of law is not just a set of rules and their judicial application. As the third volume of *The World Bank Legal Review* makes clear in its subtitle, *International Financial Institutions and Global Legal Governance,* the law is also about policy making, institutional frameworks, international politics, development, and—ultimately—freedom. The law broadens the scope of the questions that people ask, and so helps policy makers find solutions to complex, multifaceted problems. To do that effectively, however, legal research and legal practitioners must focus on how the law can support innovative and pragmatic responses to development challenges.

One such challenge is how we can link international norms with local laws and customs. For example, today fighting corruption is a key part of development projects and programs. We know that corruption is a drag on economies, taxes the poor, and strangles opportunity. But anticorruption legislation and conventions can be effective only if they are linked with the needs of developing economies and are seen as enabling rather than hampering.

This linkage is particularly important for states affected by fragility and conflict, which struggle to break free from vicious cycles of violence. Effective justice and justice administration—both formal justice institutions and local legal institutions—are key factors in breaking that cycle. Legal research and legal practitioners need to focus on exploring and promoting the linkages between the formal justice institutions and local mechanisms.

The law also has a role to play at the microlevel of community-driven development. Ethiopia, for example, has used intellectual property tools to renegotiate the distribution and selling arrangements of its coffee production with multinational enterprises. The results have benefited both local farmers and traders.

Legal research and practice need to identify, and make full use of, the law's potential to encourage innovation in the development process and empower otherwise marginalized groups so that they can play a key role in development interventions. We need to develop a global platform to facilitate this kind of knowledge exchange in the field of law.

I hope that legal practitioners will take up this challenge and invest in a more innovative use of law for the benefit of development. *The World Bank Legal Review* can be a useful guide.

Preface

ANNE-MARIE LEROY

Even today, the aftershocks of the global financial crisis of 2008 continue to be felt throughout the world. Economists wisely warn us that a global recovery remains fragile and uneven, and progress needs to be made in dealing with some of the underlying legal and regulatory failures that led to the crisis in the first place. In addition, the World Bank's member countries continue to experience a myriad of other food, financial, and economic crises, as well as natural disasters.

At the same time, demand for World Bank assistance continues to be high, especially from the poorest countries, which need help to move beyond the crisis and make progress in their quest for development. In this respect, I am certain that our legal expertise will continue to play a crucial role in helping our institution design effective, innovative, and legally sound responses to the variety of crises faced by our member countries.

However, our legal expertise needs to constantly evolve and be enriched by the knowledge and experience of outside partners. We need to continue learning from others, and to let others benefit from our own experiences. In particular, given the global and multidisciplinary nature of the crisis, we would be remiss not to listen to as many different perspectives as possible, whether from academia, civil society, government, or the private sector.

For this reason, the World Bank's Legal Vice Presidency greatly values collaborative initiatives and openness, and we have strived to forge close links with institutions around the world. Such North-South and South-South linkages are central elements in the broader knowledge creation and exchange agenda of the Bank, and we will continue to widen and strengthen them.

A variety of perspectives and partnerships can create a critical mass of thought-provoking and imaginative ideas with the potential to generate new solutions to the legal problems that confront development.

The third volume of *The World Bank Legal Review,* subtitled *International Financial Institutions and Global Legal Governance,* exemplifies our commitment to partnerships in the area of knowledge development.

In November 2010, the Legal Vice Presidency held the first Law, Justice and Development Week, "International Financial Institutions in a Post-crisis World: Legal Challenges and Opportunities." Organized in close cooperation with leading law schools and policy institutes, this event took stock of the role and record of these institutions and analyzed their future, focusing on their legal mandates, competencies, and operations. The golden strand that ran through and linked all the discussions and debates was a shared commitment to good governance and the rule of law at national and international levels. While the law should continue to give different actors in the international community access to globalization, the law should also provide incentives for good global citizenship, as well as sanctions against those that offend it.

Much of this volume of *The World Bank Legal Review* consists of contributions by speakers at the 2010 Law, Justice and Development Week. The volume examines international financial institutions as international organizations and development agencies, and explores international regulatory governance. This multiplicity of topics and perspectives has been developed by two distinguished law professors, Daniel D. Bradlow and Benedict Kingsbury, and our Deputy General Counsel for Knowledge and Research, Hassane Cissé. Touching on current and cutting-edge issues, this volume presents incisive analyses and stimulating recommendations that will interest policy makers, practitioners, academics, and, indeed, anyone interested in the interplay of global legal governance and international financial institutions.

Contributors

Evarist Baimu is Senior Counsel in the World Bank's Legal Vice Presidency. He received his legal education in Tanzania (LL.B. from University of Dar es Salaam), South Africa (LL.M. and LL.D. from University of Pretoria), and the United States (LL.M. from Harvard Law School). Before joining the Bank in 2004, Mr. Baimu worked for four years in government, academia, and international organizations in Dar es Salaam and Pretoria. Since joining the World Bank, he has worked in various practice groups of the Legal Vice Presidency, including Operations Policy, Corporate Finance, and Africa.

William M. Berenson is currently Chief of Litigation in the Department of Legal Services of the Secretary General of the Organization of American States, where he has served in a number of legal positions since 1980, including General Counsel. He is also an adjunct professor at American University's Washington College of Law, where since 1984 he has taught a survey course in United States law for foreign lawyers in the LL.M. international legal studies program. He has authored articles on a wide range of legal topics, which reflect the diversity of his practice. Mr. Berenson received his J.D. from Boston University (1978). He has both M.A. and Ph.D. degrees in political science from Vanderbilt University (1972 and 1975) and an A.B. from Dartmouth College (1969). He is admitted to the practice of law in the District of Columbia, Virginia, and Massachusetts.

Daniel D. Bradlow is SARCHI Professor of International Development Law and African Economic Relations, University of Pretoria, and Professor of Law, American University Washington College of Law. He is the Chair of the Roster of Experts for the Independent Review Mechanism at the African Development Bank, and is a member of the Executive Council of the American Society of International Law, the Board of Directors of New Rules for Global Finance Coalition, and the High Level Panel on Governance of the Financial Stability Board. His current scholarship focuses on international financial institutions, legal aspects of global economic governance, and international legal aspects of sustainable and equitable development.

Chris Brummer is an expert in international financial regulation whose research interests concern globalization and its impact on financial markets and financial market regulation. Prior to joining Georgetown University's faculty with tenure in 2009, he was an assistant professor of law at Vanderbilt Law School. In 2008, he served as the Securities and Exchange Commission's first Academic Fellow in the agency's Office of International Affairs. Professor Brummer lectures widely on finance and international governance, as well as on public and private international law, market microstructure, and international trade. His writings have appeared, or are slated to appear, in several leading journals. He earned his J.D. from Columbia Law School, where he graduated with honors, and he holds a Ph.D. in Germanic studies from the University of Chicago. Before becoming a professor, he practiced law in the New York and London offices of Cravath, Swaine & Moore. In 2011 he joined the Milken Institute as a Senior Fellow.

Thiago Chagas is a Legal Counsel at Climate Focus. He has provided legal and regulatory advice on climate finance to a number of international institutions and governmental and nongovernmental agencies. He has also assisted many companies in establishing an optimal legal structure for greenhouse gas mitigation activities, as well as in adjusting to key climate and energy policies. He holds an LL.B. from Pontificia Universidade Catolica de São Paulo and an LL.M. in international law from the University of Edinburgh.

Hassane Cissé, a national of Senegal, is presently Deputy General Counsel, Knowledge and Research, of the World Bank. Before holding this position, he served for six years as Chief Counsel for Operations Policy. Since 2007, he has been a member of the World Bank's Sanctions Board. Before joining the World Bank in 1997, Mr. Cissé served for seven years as Counsel at the International Monetary Fund. He is a member of the World Economic Forum Global Agenda Council on the Rule of Law and has authored reports and publications on international economic law topics. Mr. Cissé obtained his LL.B. from Dakar University in Senegal; he also holds a LL.M. degree from Harvard Law School, as well as graduate degrees in international law from the universities of Paris I Panthéon–Sorbonne and Paris II Panthéon–Assas and a graduate degree in history from Paris I Panthéon–Sorbonne University.

Laurence Boisson de Chazournes is Professor of International Law at the University of Geneva. She was the Director of the Department of International Law and International Organization from 1999 until 2009. Her areas of expertise include the law of international organizations, international environmental law, international economic law, and international dispute settlement. She was a Senior Counsel to the World Bank (1995–99) and is an adviser to various international organizations, including the World Bank, the World Health Organization, the United Nations Development Programme, and the International Labour Organization. She is a member of the Permanent Court of Arbitration's list of arbitrators, has served as chairperson of World Trade Organization arbitration panels on pre-shipment inspections, and is counsel in cases before the International Court of Justice and other dispute-settlement procedures.

Deval Desai is a Research Associate with the Faculty of Law at the School of Oriental and African Studies (University of London) and an Honorary Fellow at the School of Environment and Development at the University of Manchester. He was previously a justice and conflict specialist at the World Bank, where he jointly established the Justice and Conflict Program. His research encompasses building and strengthening justice institutions in fragile and conflict-affected states, with a particular emphasis on demand-side accountability and on extractive industries in sub-Saharan Africa. He has worked on these issues across West Africa (including in Nigeria) and South Asia, with a focus on building community voice and empowering communities to hold public and private actors to account. He has published widely on these issues in a range of academic and policy forums.

Alexandre Pinheiro dos Santos is Attorney General of the Brazilian Securities Commission (CVM), Professor of Business Law and Capital Market, and a former lawyer of Rio de Janeiro Stock Exchange. He is also a member of the Forum of Attorneys General of Brazilian Regulators; Co-Chairman of the Committee on Emerging Markets Issues, Follow-Up and Implementation of the Convention on Substantive Rules Regarding Intermediated Securities; and one of the five Vice-Presidents of the Final Session of the Diplomatic Conference for the adoption of the Convention on Substantive Rules Regarding Intermediated Securities. He coordinated the cooperation agreement between CVM and the Brazilian Federal Public Prosecutor's Office, and acted directly on their joint work in the first civil and criminal cases related to insider trading in Brazil. He has also worked directly for the conclusion of a cooperation agreement between CVM and the Brazilian Federal Police.

Frank A. Fariello Jr. a graduate of Brown University and New York University School of Law, is currently Lead Counsel, Operations Policy, in the World Bank's Legal Vice Presidency (LEG). He is LEG's primary focal point for the Bank's sanctions regime and governance and anticorruption policies. In that capacity, he coordinated the recent comprehensive reforms of the Bank's sanctions process and advised INT in connection with the Agreement on Mutual Enforcement of Debarment Decisions among Multilateral Development Banks. Before joining the Bank in 2005, Mr. Frank worked for nine years at the International Fund for Agricultural Development (IFAD) as Senior Counsel and subsequently as Special Advisor to the Vice President. For the first ten years of his career, prior to his service at IFAD, he practiced corporate law, with an emphasis on international financial transactions, at a number of New York firms, including Skadden, Arps, Slate, Meagher & Flor.

Chiara Giorgetti is an Associate at White & Case, LLP (International Arbitration Group) and Adjunct Professor of Law at Georgetown University Law Center, where she teaches classes on international courts and tribunals and international transitional justice. Dr. Giorgetti's work focuses on international dispute resolution and postconflict issues. Her practice includes states representation at the Permanent Court of Arbitration and United Nations Claims Commission, as well as acting as co-counsel for both claimants and respondents in international investment disputes. She clerked at the International Court of Justice and worked for the United Nations in New York and Kenya. She holds a degree in law from Bologna University, an M.Sc. from the London School of Economics, and an LL.M. and JSD from Yale Law School. She has written extensively on various aspects of international law. Her book, *A Principled Approach to State Failure*, was published in 2010.

Deborah Isser is Senior Counsel and Global Program Manager of the Justice for the Poor program (J4P) at the World Bank. J4P promotes the development of legitimate and effective institutions for managing disputes and promoting equity in development processes, especially in contexts marked by fragility and legal pluralism. Formerly, she was Senior Rule of Law Advisor at the United States Institute of Peace, Senior Policy Advisor at the Office of the High Representative of Bosnia and Herzegovina, and Special Advisor at the United States Mission to the United Nations. She is the editor of *Customary Justice and the Rule of Law in War-Torn Societies* (2011) and author of numerous publications on justice in fragile and conflict-affected states.

Benedict Kingsbury is Murry and Ida Becker Professor of Law and Director of the Institute for International Law and Justice at New York University School of Law (iilj.org), and Visiting Professor of Law at the University of Utah. With Richard Stewart, Kingsbury initiated and directs the IILJ's Global Administrative Law Research Project, a pioneering approach to issues of accountability, transparency, participation, and review in global governance, focused especially on developing countries. His coedited volumes in that project include *Climate Finance: Regulatory and Funding Strategies for Climate Change and Global Development* (2009) and *El nuevo derecho administrativo global en América Latina* (2009). With Kevin Davis and Sally Merry, Kingsbury leads an IILJ project, Indicators as a Technology of Global Governance, including a forthcoming book, *Governance by Indicators: Global Power through Quantification and Rankings*. Kingsbury works also on the history and theory of international law.

Rutsel Silvestre J. Martha has been the General Counsel of the International Fund for Agricultural Development (Rome, Italy) since 2008. He was the Minister of Justice of the Netherlands Antilles and Minister Plenipotentiary in the Netherlands Permanent Representation to the European Union. He also worked as Counsellor in the Legal Department of the International Monetary Fund and, prior to this, as Legal Advisor of the Central Bank of the Netherlands Antilles. Dr. Martha is a Visiting Professor of Law in the NYU@NUS Programme at the National University of Singapore and was Adjunct Professor of Law at the Washington College of Law of the American University. He has published extensively on international law, including *Tax Treatment of International Civil Servants* (2009), *The Jurisdiction to Tax in International Law* (1989), and *The Legal Foundations of INTERPOL* (2010).

Kiri Mattes is currently working as a Senior Solicitor specializing in constitutional law at the New South Wales Crown Solicitor's Office. She graduated from the University of Sydney with a Bachelor of Commerce in 2000, an LL.B. with first-class honors in 2002, and a Graduate Diploma of Law in 2009. In 2010 she completed her LL.M. at New York University as an Arthur T. Vanderbilt Scholar, with a focus in public international law and constitutional law. In 2010–11, she worked as a Fellow at NYU Law's Global Climate Finance project.

Aristeidis Panou is Legal Associate in the World Bank's Legal Vice Presidency. He holds degrees from NYU School of Law (LL.M. in international legal studies) and from the National and Kapodistrian University of Athens School of Law (LL.B. and LL.M. in public international law).

Annie Petsonk is International Counsel with the Environmental Defense Fund (EDF), an 800,000-member nonprofit, nonpartisan, nongovernmental organization that develops innovative, economically sensible, and scientifically sound solutions to environmental challenges. Ms. Petsonk works to create legal frameworks that deliver economic incentives for companies, countries, and communities to cut pollution while they grow their economies. She has worked in the private bar, the United Nations Environment Programme, and the administrations of Presidents George H. W. Bush and Bill Clinton, including in the Office of the U.S. Trade Representative in the Executive Office of the President. A graduate of The Colorado College and Harvard Law School, she has published extensively. At the George Washington University Law School, she teaches international trade and sustainable development law.

Bryce Rudyk is Coordinator of the Global Climate Finance Project at the New York University School of Law and Fellow at the Center for Environmental and Land Use Law at New York University School of Law. His research focuses on the institutional regime for climate finance. He has previously worked as a lawyer in transnational litigation.

Richard B. Stewart is University Professor and John Edward Sexton Professor of Law at New York University School of Law, where he directs the school's Center on Environmental and Land Use Law and Global Law School Program. He has formerly served as Assistant Attorney General for Environment and Natural Resources, U.S. Department of Justice, and Chairman, Environmental Defense Fund.

Charlotte Streck is Director of Climate Focus and a former Senior Counsel with the World Bank in Washington, D.C. Dr. Streck serves as an adviser to numerous governments, private companies, foundations, and nonprofit organizations and is actively involved in the debate around the development of new carbon finance mechanisms in the areas of reducing emissions from deforestation, climate-resilient agriculture, national and international climate frameworks, and reform of the current Kyoto Mechanisms. She serves on the Board of the Rainforest Partnership, is an associate editor of *Climate Policy,* and is lead counsel for climate change with the Center for International Sustainable Development Law with McGill University. She holds a J.D. and Ph.D. from Humboldt University in Berlin and an M.Sc. from the University of Regensburg, Germany.

Michael Trebilcock is University Professor and Professor of Law and Economics at the University of Toronto. In 1999, Professor Trebilcock received an Honorary Doctorate in Laws from McGill University and was awarded the Canada Council Molson Prize in the Humanities and Social Sciences. In the same year, he was elected an Honorary Foreign Fellow of the American Academy of Arts and Sciences. In 2003, he received an Honorary Doctorate in Law from the Law Society of Upper Canada and in 2007 he was the recipient of the Ontario Attorney General's Mundell Medal for contributions to Law and Letters. In 2010, he was the recipient of the Ontario Premier's Discovery Award in the Social Sciences. He has published widely in contract law, economic and social regulation, competition law, international trade law, law and development, and immigration law and policy.

Michael Woolcock is Lead Social Development Specialist in the World Bank's Development Research Group, where he was worked since 1998. He has been a visiting fellow at Cambridge University and in 2007–09 he was the founding Research Director of the Brooks World Poverty Institute at the University of Manchester, where he was also Professor of Social Science and Development Policy. He has also taught part-time at the Harvard Kennedy School for many years. At the World Bank, he has been on two *World Development Report* teams ("Poverty" in 2000, and "Equity" in 2005) and is the cofounder of the global Justice for the Poor program, working on marginalized groups' engagement with customary and formal justice systems. He is also the coauthor or coeditor of six books, the most recent being *Contesting Development: Participatory Projects and Local Conflict Dynamics in Indonesia* (2011).

Stephen S. Zimmermann is the Director of Operations for the World Bank's Integrity Vice Presidency, where he directs a multidisciplinary team charged with detecting, investigating, sanctioning, and preventing fraud and corruption in Bank-financed activities around the world. He has had a leading role in developing and implementing an expanded strategy for the World Bank's integrity agenda, including the introduction of negotiated resolutions of investigations and enhancements to the Voluntary Disclosure Program, as well as leading efforts to reach the historic Cross-Debarment Agreement. Before joining the World Bank Group, Mr. Zimmermann was the Chief of the Office of Institutional Integrity for the Inter-American Development Bank and also served as the interim Chief of Staff for the Independent Inquiry Committee into the United Nations Oil for Food Program. He was an Assistant United States Attorney in the District of Maryland from 1991 until 1999, and an attorney with Wilmer, Cutler & Pickering from 1987 to 1991.

The World Bank
Legal Review

Volume 3

Introduction

Global Administrative Law in the Institutional Practice of Global Regulatory Governance

Benedict Kingsbury[*]

Introduction

Long-term changes in the nature of global political and social order include the use of increasingly fine-grained regulatory arrangements intended to overcome collective action problems and market failures and to take advantage of global cooperation. Although framing the changes in these politico-economic terms suggests that the key drivers are the maximization by each actor of achievement of its own (self-defined) interests within the constraints of the prevailing constellation of power, any global order model must also address values conflicts and cultural diversity, on the one hand, and the implications of dramatic but shifting inequalities of power, on the other.

Two long-standing state-based models of global order blending these considerations provide the framework for standard approaches to international law: minimal interstate pluralism and more ambitious and moralistic interstate solidarism.[1] Global regulatory governance (GRG) can be framed as a third model of global order, dependent on and layered over the existing models and grappling in distinctive ways with the considerations of power, value conflicts, and inequality. This introduction surveys some specific roles of law in the emerging GRG model, with particular attention to the present and future roles of global administrative law (GAL).

GRG involves the increasingly dense and politically significant exercise of power beyond the state. New understandings of law and its roles are emerging through the practice of GRG. Several features of GRG have distinctive legal implications:

- GRG employs an array of distinctive regulatory techniques, including disclosure and reporting requirements; "reg-neg" negotiations between the regulator and the regulated entity; use of private monitoring and enforcement; peer review; and governance by information. GRG regimes are often designed to create incentives or costs for private actors even when the formal legal regime and regulatory structure are interstate. Some of these techniques seek to shift behavior at the margins, rather than

*   This chapter reflects close collaboration with Richard B. Stewart and draws on joint work with Megan Donaldson. Conversations with Danny Bradlow and Hassane Cissé and suggestions from Vikram Raghavan, Aristeidis Panou, Estefania Ponce, and Florencia Lebensohn are gratefully acknowledged.

1   Andrew Hurrell, *On Global Order* (Oxford U. Press 2007).

aiming to change behavior of all regulated entities. Regulation frequently involves cost-benefit calculations, not only in rule making but also in the processes of supervision and in determining consequences of breaches. Regulation depends on an intricate mesh of institutions, market and political forces, social and cultural features, historic experiences, and path dependencies. The relevant institutions and regimes may not be designed or operated in close coordination—indeed, they may have redundancies or run in opposing directions, which can create arbitrage opportunities and problematic externalities, although redundancy and checking structures sometimes can have positive value. Much regulatory design is premised on informational uncertainty, the definition of tolerable and nontolerable levels of risk, management of risk, planning for contingencies, and rapid adaptation. GRG is probabilistic rather than closely determinate. It may be designed to encourage experimentation rather than uniformity of approaches, and to foster and incorporate learning through feedback loops, benchmarking, and revision processes. Regulation, like other governance arrangements, is dynamic and responsive to interactions and to changes in external conditions. These elements of regulation are often not captured in the simple legal binaries of obligation/no obligation, violation/no violation (or breach/no breach), and liability (or responsibility) *vel non*. Nor are they exactly aligned with precepts incorporated into some definitions of rule of law, such as requirements that every comparable case be addressed in the same way.[2]

• The organizational forms of the international institutions with significant roles in GRG are highly diverse, and they vary greatly in the breadth and publicness of their purposes, membership, reach, and the interests or expertise they embody. They extend far beyond the range of traditional treaty-based intergovernmental institutions to include entities that under traditional analysis are not subjects of international law. Yet many such entities set formal or informal standards that determine practice and expectations in markets, and in some cases are incorporated into other sets of standards or supervisory mechanisms or made binding or cognizable by formal agreements or national law. Some such entities also exercise decisional powers, directly or through their participation in other GRG entities. Many play significant specialist governance roles, for example, in certification or in generation and control of information. Examples of such extrastate institutions in global financial regulation include,[3]

---

2   Michael Trebilcock, *The Rule of Law and Development: In Search of the Holy Grail*, in this volume, discusses the model of legal liberalism, according to which rules are made to achieve the purposes of the society as a whole, not of limited groups within it, and the rules are enforced equally for all citizens.

3   *See* the discussion of these actors in Chris Brummer, *Networks In(-)Action? The Transgovernmental Origins of, and Responses to, the Financial Crisis*, in this volume.

- Formal intergovernmental bodies created by treaties, such as the International Monetary Fund (IMF), the World Bank, and the regional development banks.

- Networks of government or regulatory officials in particular sectors, sometimes with membership that is deliberately restricted by the founding states to like-minded states they select or to the most important states as regards the issues involved.[4] Participants may directly represent the national political leadership, such as in meetings of the group of 20 (G20) state leaders or governmental ministers, or they may represent national regulatory agencies with varying degrees of independence from the national political leadership, such as the Basel Committee of banking supervisors or regulators, the International Organization of Securities Commissions, and the International Association of Insurance Supervisors. In some cases, such as the Financial Stability Board, representatives of other GRG institutions such as the World Bank and IMF join with national regulators.

- Hybrid bodies involving both public and private actors, such as the International Financial Reporting Standards (IFRS) structure, under which the International Accounting Standards Board, consisting of private individuals with relevant commercial and professional experience (including some former regulators), produces the standards and consults with and reports to a monitoring board comprising public capital market authorities whose decisions may be essential if the IFRS are to be required or accepted from businesses as meeting national regulatory standards for financial reporting.

- Purely private actors, such as the International Swaps and Derivatives Association, which consists of participants in over-the-counter derivatives markets and associated service providers.

- GRG blends formal and informal instruments in highly varying concoctions. This combination creates many challenges for traditional international law analysis. International legal doctrine addresses rules on the conclusion, entry into force, and legal effects of formal interstate treaties. In many countries, national law also sets detailed formal requirements relating to treaties, including approval by the legislature and conditions for application within the national legal system. But informal instruments used in GRG are made through rule-making processes with few established legal controls. Such instruments may have substantial practical effects and sometimes legal effects, for example, when they are incorporated by reference into a legal text or weighed by a body exercising a

---

4   *Coalitions of the Willing: Avant-Garde or Threat?* (Christian Calliess, Georg Nolte, & Peter-Tobias Stoll ed., Heymann 2007), particularly Eyal Benvenisti, *Coalitions of the Willing and the Evolution of Informal International Law*, 1–24.

law-governed discretion, yet only sparse international or national legal doctrines squarely address these effects.[5]

- Much GRG rule making and decision making takes place within institutions operating under distinctive processes that are largely beyond the reach of national public law or the traditional law of international organizations, which has focused mainly on questions of legal competence or mandate. Even in formal intergovernmental institutions with broad global or regional membership, the controlling governance arrangements may be problematic for many states and nonstate groups. These institutions may have tenuous structures of representation of under-represented states and rules or practices of decision making that date from earlier eras and do not align with current geopolitical or economic distributions of power, let alone with demands for justice or equality.[6] Efforts to reform IMF and World Bank governance have sought to respond to some such concerns, although many critics do not regard the reforms as sufficient.[7]

The rapid growth of GRG has posed sharp challenges to traditional international law, to standard approaches to the law of international organizations, and to some elements of national legal systems that struggle to grapple with

---

5   The French Ministry of Foreign Affairs, in its general note on the international engagements of France issued on May 3, 2010, asserts that administrative arrangements concluded between ministers of different national governments are not recognized by international law and ought to be avoided as much as possible because of uncertainty about their effects: "Les arrangements administratifs conclus par un ministre français avec son homologue étranger ne sont pas répertoriés dans la base de données documentaire. En effet, il ne s'agit pas de traités ou d'accords internationaux. Les arrangements administratifs sont conclus par un ministre avec son homologue étranger pour compléter ou préciser un accord existant ou, à la rigueur, pour organiser une coopération administrative de portée limitée dans la stricte limite de ses attributions. Cette catégorie n'est pas reconnue par le droit international. La circulaire du 30 mai 1997 relative à l'élaboration et à la conclusion des accords internationaux recommande aux négociateurs français de ne recourir à ce type d'arrangements qu'exceptionnellement et souligne que les effets qu'ils produisent sont incertains." Available at <http://www.doc.diplomatie.fr/pacte/>. This statement is somewhat less sanguine than the view taken in the French Prime Minister's circular of May 30, 1997, that such agreements can be made on matters entirely within the purview of a single minister but are in a category unknown to international law. *Circulaire du 30 mai 1997 relative à l'élaboration et à la conclusion des accords internationaux*, Journal official de la République Francais 8415 (May 31, 1997), available at <http://www.doc.diplomatie.fr/pacte/pdf/circul.pdf>. The German government takes a more favorable approach to the use of such instruments in its Collective Standing Order for all federal ministries of 2000, §72 Gemeinsame Geschäftsordnung der Bundesministerien of 2000: "Before the planning and the conclusion of international agreements (international treaties, agreements, interministerial or interagency agreements, notes and exchanges of letters) the responsible federal ministry must always inquire whether the conclusion of the international undertaking is indeed required, or whether the same goal may also be attained through other means, especially through understandings which are below the threshold of an international agreement." *See* Benvenisti, *supra* note 4.

6   Ngaire Woods, *Multilateralism and Building Strong International Institutions*, in *Global Accountabilities: Participation, Pluralism, and Public Ethics* 27 (Alnoor Ebrahim & Edward Weisband ed., Cambridge U. Press 2007).

7   Daniel D. Bradlow, *The Reform of the Governance of the IFIs: A Critical Assessment*, in this volume.

external sources of regulation and regulatory decision making. How does law fit into a GRG model of global order?

The role of law is modest (although not negligible) in the overall configurations of power for GRG, the stocks and flows of resources and capabilities, and the organizational forms these take, which are key variables determining who shapes agendas and who gets what in GRG.[8] Law contributes appreciably, but generally only in limited ways, alongside political, economic, social, and historical factors in explaining why certain institutions exist in the global administrative space with particular memberships and structures, why these have the mandates and decision rules they do, and why other institutions, mandates, or rules do not exist.

Basic legal concepts and principles of a constitutional or systemic nature play a significant role in instantiating, and to some extent in constituting, interstate pluralist and solidarist order. These basic legal concepts and principles of global order include the juridical conception of the state and its representation and contracting capacity; core principles of imperium such as the entitlements of the state to control its territory and monopolize violence there; fundamental human rights; some emerging principles limiting environmental harm; and rights relating to dominium, including property rights. Public international law and national public law together do this legal work in interstate orders.[9] In relation to GRG, scholars have proposed that general principles of public law, or international public law, might play a comparable role,[10] but the practical influence of these proposals has not yet been great.

For purposes of GRG, the roles of law are of rapidly growing importance. Some of these roles are explicated in work on GAL. This chapter explores specific issues arising for the legal and governance work of intergovernmental international financial institutions (IFIs). It introduces and draws out themes developed by contributors to this volume of the *World Bank Legal Review*.[11]

---

8   *See,* for example, Miles Kahler & David Lake, *Economic Integration and Global Governance: Why So Little Supranationalism?*, in *The Politics of Global Regulation* 242 (Walter Mattli & Ngaire Woods ed., Princeton U. Press 2009).

9   Several relevant international law principles are surveyed in Chiara Giorgetti, *International Norms and Standards Applicable to Situations of State Fragility and Failure: An Overview*, in this volume.

10   *The Exercise of Public Authority by International Institutions* (Armin von Bogdandy, et al. ed., Springer 2010); Benedict Kingsbury, *International Law as Inter-Public Law*, in *Moral Universalism and Pluralism: NOMOS XLIX* 167 (Henry R. Richardson & Melissa S. Williams ed., N.Y.U. Press 2008); Giacinto della Cananea, *The Genesis and Structure of General Principles of Global Public Law*, in *Global Administrative Law and EU Administrative Law* 89 (Edoardo Chiti & Bernardo Mattarella ed., Springer 2011).

11   This volume is based on papers presented and themes discussed at the 2010 Law, Justice and Development Week, organized by the Legal Vice Presidency of the World Bank and cosponsored by several academic institutions, including the Global Administrative Law Network convened by the Institute for International Law and Justice at New York University Law School. The website of the Global Administrative Law Project, which includes papers and symposia, is <http://www.iilj.org/GAL>. Symposia on GAL have been published in 68:(3–4) L. & Contemp. Probs. (2005); 37(4) N.Y.U. J. Intl. & Pol. (2005); 17 Eur. J. Intl. L. 1 (2006). *See*

GAL is based on the insight that much of global regulatory governance can be understood as "administration." Intergovernmental organizations and other institutions engage in this activity beyond the reach of controls imposed by the public law, democratic apparatus, or other review structures of individual states. The term "administration" in this context encompasses bureaucratic or routine adjudicative decisions on individual situations short of major interstate dispute settlement, general rule making short of treaty making, and other important managerial actions affecting voice and outcomes—all of which bear a resemblance to what is considered administration in domestic legal systems. This administrative component of global governance is undertaken by a wide array of actors.

These actors frequently overlap in their domains of activity, and the regulatory processes in which any particular actor is engaged are often influenced by, and perhaps in tension with, activities of other global (extrastate) institutions and national or subnational institutions. [12] For some purposes, it is distortionary to separate global from national/subnational processes of regulatory administration. Extranational actors and regimes (both global actors and other states) shape domestic administrative practices, and domestic actors play a

---

also *Global Administrative Law in the Operations of International Organizations* (Laurence Boisson de Chazournes, Lorenzo Casini, & Benedict Kingsbury ed.), 6 International Organizations L. Rev. (2009). Books from this project include *El Nuevo Derecho Administrativo Global en América Latina* (Benedict Kingsbury et al. ed., Ediciones Rap 2009); *Global Administrative Law: Development and Innovation* (Hugh Corder ed., Juta 2009); *Climate Finance: Regulatory and Funding Strategies for Climate Change and Global Development* (Richard Stewart, Benedict Kingsbury, & Bryce Rudyk ed., N.Y.U. Press 2009). The GAL Project, jointly with leading law schools and research institutes in Africa, Asia, Europe, and Latin America, has convened research and policy conferences with San Andrés University and the University of Buenos Aires, the Centre for Policy Research in New Delhi, the University of Cape Town, FGV Law School in São Paulo, Tsinghua Law School in Beijing, Los Andes University in Bogotá, and the University of Toronto. Together these institutions form the Global Administrative Network, which has completed innovative joint research projects on relations between foreign and local anticorruption activities in Brazil and Argentina; access to essential medicines under TRIPS regimes in Latin America; procedures used by national and supranational competition authorities; and the Regulatory State of the South (a project on models and experience of water, electricity and telecommunications regulations in developing countries, directed by Navroz Dubash and Bronwen Morgan). Publications from these projects are forthcoming; research reports are at <http://www.iilj.org/GAL>.

12   A modest point on terminology concerns the term "global," which is frequently used in GAL to refer to all regulatory or other administrative structures that extend beyond a single state. In many cases (for example, a binational mutual recognition regulatory arrangement), this use stretches the ordinary meaning of "global." However, these regulatory structures typically do not operate in isolation; they may be part of a network of other comparable regulatory arrangements, or they may be nested in or influenced by a regional (for example, Mercosur) or worldwide (such as the WTO GATS) regulatory structure, and the relevant commercial actors and even consumer or public interest groups involved are often transnational. Moreover, many regulatory structures, whether purporting to span the globe or not, are highly exclusionary, and not "global" in the sense of being inclusive. Nonetheless, although it can be important to differentiate truly worldwide structures from more local structures, and to distinguish between more and less inclusive structures, for the purpose of understanding the exercise of governance power beyond the state, a stretched use of "global" is practical.

role in global and foreign regimes. There thus exists an uneven but discernible "global administrative space."[13]

International institutions have increasingly sought to shore up their legitimacy, and to enhance the effectiveness of their regulatory activities, by applying to (and between) themselves procedural norms (referred to here as "GAL norms") of transparency, participation, reasoned decision making, and legality, and by establishing mechanisms of review and accountability.[14] These procedural norms and mechanisms resemble, at least in their general orientation, administrative law as applied to regulatory agencies and other executive bodies within some national legal systems. GRG institutions frequently incorporate GAL norms and mechanisms (in varying mixes) when they alter structures for control and conduct of operations as wider forces of change reshape the activities and missions of these institutions. The law bearing on these operational features and dynamics can have considerable significance for on-the-ground outcomes and for normative evaluation of these institutions (for example, in terms of justice or of political acceptability).

Four forms of legal development prompted by the dynamic requirements of GRG and the global administrative space are highlighted in this volume.

- *The operational law of specific intergovernmental institutions.* Stretching and adapting principles of the established law of international organizations, and crafting newer regulatory modalities and mechanisms, are characteristic of efforts to structure and control the operations of IFIs in GRG and to meet the intensifying demands for procedural specification of, and compliance with, the emerging principles of GAL.

- *Interinstitutional governance arrangements.* Effective GRG depends more and more on interinstitutional arrangements and structures. The capacity of intergovernmental institutions to make such arrangements and adapt their policies and culture to work effectively with other institutions is one measure of their quality and success. Increasingly, GAL considerations are significant in the crafting and operation of interinstitutional arrangements.

- *Internationally prescribed national administrative law.* A third strand of GAL, in which IFIs are very involved, comprises the norms and mechanisms that international bodies urge or impose on states as prescriptions for good administration within the state. Some such norms and mechanisms are requirements intended to support the state's adherence to a specific international legal regime; for example, the World Trade Organization requires states to meet requirements of transparency, notice, and reason

---

13   Benedict Kingsbury, Nico Krisch, & Richard Stewart, *The Emergence of Global Administrative Law*, 68(3–4) L. & Contemp. Probs. 15 (2005). *See* also Sabino Cassese, *Lo spazio giuridico globale* (Laterza 2003).

14   Kingsbury, Krisch, & Stewart, *supra* note 13; Sabino Cassese, *Administrative Law without the State? The Challenge of Global Regulation*, 37 N.Y.U. J. Intl. L. & Pol. 663 (2005); Benedict Kingsbury, *The Concept of "Law" in Global Administrative Law*, 20 Eur. J. Intl. L. 23 (2009).

giving when they restrict trade in goods and services with another state. Comparable requirements are set for particular states as part of programmatic obligations of "good governance" or "rule of law" that may be prescribed as conditions for funding from international development agencies. International organizations promote such norms and mechanisms through funding, capacity building, and epistemic influences, including rankings of states based in part on such criteria (for example, the World Bank's Governance Indicators and Ease of Doing Business Indicators).[15]

* *New GRG regimes.* New or deepened GRG regimes are being crafted in vital fields such as financial market supervision, forests, and climate regulation. Typically, these new regimes incorporate different mixes of the three kinds of legal development already mentioned: operations of existing intergovernmental institutions, interinstitutional arrangements, and international standards for coordinated national regulation. But these new regimes are dependent on behavior in markets as well as other forms of private conduct. Private and hybrid governance bodies play major roles, and innovative governance mechanisms and techniques are deployed.

This chapter discusses these four kinds of legal development in the global administrative space, using the topics covered in this volume of the *World Bank Legal Review* as illustrations. Although the relatively new terminology of "global administrative law" is used in only some of the chapters in this volume, all can be read through the lens of GAL.

Danny Bradlow, in a critical assessment of what has been achieved and remains to be achieved in reforms of governance of the World Bank and the IMF, deploys an evaluative structure that integrates these four kinds of legal development into a wider set of political-economy dimensions of GRG. He assesses their governance arrangements in five dimensions: "voice and vote" (decision rules, allocation of voting power, and representation of different groups of states by executive directors); political requirements that the IMF be headed by a European and the World Bank by a U.S. national, with further allocative arrangements for other senior management positions; accountability of member states and affected persons and publics; transparency (particularly disclosure of information publicly); and adequacy of operational policies and of public consultations in making the arrangements.[16] Bradlow proposes a set of normative criteria to use as metrics in evaluating governance arrangements of these IFIs: a holistic understanding of development; flexibility of management arrangements to meet expectations of diverse stakeholders; implementation of relevant international law principles (respect for national sovereignty; nondiscrimination, including special attention to participation of low-capacity states; ensuring respect for customary international law human rights and

---

15   Kevin Davis, Benedict Kingsbury, & Sally Engle Merry, *Indicators as a Technology of Global Governance*, IILJ Working Paper 2010/2 Rev. (Jul. 2011).

16   Bradlow, *supra* note 7. *See* also the contributions to *International Financial Institutions and International Law* (Daniel Bradlow & David Hunter ed., Kluwer Law International 2010).

rights of foreign legal persons; respect for international environmental law); adequate and meaningful coordination with other relevant institutions; and adherence to GAL principles in operations. These criteria integrate a substantive standard (a holistic approach to development), basic principles of international law, a management standard concerning suppleness and effectiveness, and two criteria to which GAL is directly relevant: GAL within the IFI and interinstitutional arrangements. One might argue the addition of a further criterion concerning relations between IFI governance and approaches the IFI takes and promotes toward governance issues (including GAL issues) within member states. Thus, it might be asked, can the governance arrangements of the World Bank and the IMF contribute to the advancement within states of human rights, environmental standards, and equity and nondiscrimination in development; policies and practices of governmental transparency and anticorruption; or enumerated features of rule of law, good governance, or democratic national governance?

Each of these issues is either addressed as an objective or deliberately not addressed in poverty reduction strategy papers (PRSPs) negotiated jointly by the World Bank and the IMF with recipient countries.[17] What requirements are set in each PRSP, and what processes of participation and consultation within the country were required in order for the country to be deemed in negotiating the PRSP to have taken "national ownership" of it, may in some measure reflect governance processes within the World Bank and IMF.

Adapting Traditional International Organizations Law to Contemporary Operations of GRG Institutions: The Political Prohibition, Mandate, Immunities, Review, and Responsibility

Adaptation, stretching, and even reconstruction of existing concepts in the traditional law of international organizations have been the dominant strategy of IFI lawyers as they deal with changes generated by GRG and demands for adherence to GAL principles. The long-established concepts of the law of international organizations subject to these processes include the "political prohibition" applicable to some IFIs, more general mandate issues connected with the "principle of speciality," the law of immunities, and the law of responsibility. Whether these traditional concepts for mobilizing, channeling, limiting, controlling, and legitimizing the power of intergovernmental institutions are sufficient for functional GRG or to meet GAL requirements is questionable. Newer legal strategies include structures of review, principles of accountability (or "soft responsibility"), and the coalescing of substantive and procedural policies into what may become a droit commun for specialist institutions or part of a more general law of global governance.

---

17   For a critical assessment, *see* Celine Tan, *Governance through Development: Poverty Reduction Strategies, International Law and the Disciplining of Third World States* (Routledge 2011).

The Political Prohibition

The powers and mandate conferred on an organization by its constitutive instruments are the basis for its action and for limiting its action, but these can be subject to extension through the legal doctrines of inherent and attributed and implied powers,[18] through creative interpretation of the mandate,[19] and through practice as supported by or acquiesced to by member states or other relevant actors.[20]

The political prohibition (a categorical term for a highly variegated practice) in the World Bank's Articles of Agreement raises a concern regarding mandates. The articles specify that the Bank "shall not interfere in the political affairs of any member [state]," and that "only economic considerations shall be relevant" to its decisions. These principles are accompanied by other mandate-related restrictions, such as that the Bank finance only expenditures for "productive purposes," and by limits on the substantive mandates of the various organizations of the World Bank Group. The ways in which the political prohibition and the other restrictions have worked are analyzed in Hassane Cissé's account of how lines are drawn and adjusted in specific policy areas.[21]

For example, with its adoption of OP 7.30 (2001), the Bank can consider attitudes of regional organizations in deciding on its financial dealings with a government that came to power through a military coup or other unconstitutional means; this consideration has enabled the Bank to avoid undermining prodemocratic norms such as those of the Inter-American Democratic Charter of 2000 or the African Charter on Democracy, Elections and Governance of 2007,[22] without itself articulating a prodemocratic or even an anticoup normative stance. The Bank has pursued the policy articulated in OP 2.30 (1997) of not financing peacemaking, peacekeeping, and humanitarian relief, but it has delicately nuanced its practice in order to support some activities related to peace processes (for example, making presentations to delegates to peace negotiations in Burundi and Sierra Leone in 1999). The Bank continues not to finance military expenditures, but it has assisted with demobilization and landmine clearance projects. Its long-standing refusal to finance criminal justice projects, on the basis that these might involve political activities, is gradually being eased, with ongoing debate as to financing police, prosecutors, and prisons, but the Bank likely will not finance specific actions against ter

---

18 Jan Klabbers, *An Introduction to International Institutional Law* ch. 4 (2d ed., Cambridge U. Press 2009).

19 Rutsel Martha, *Mandate Issues in the Activities of the International Fund for Agricultural Development (IFAD)*, 6 International Organizations L. Rev. 447 (2009).

20 Jan Klabbers, *Global Governance before the ICJ: Re-reading the WHA Opinion*, 13 Max Planck Yearbook of United Nations Law 1 (2009).

21 Hassane Cissé, *Should the Political Prohibition in Charters of International Financial Institutions be Revisited? The Case of the World Bank*, in this volume.

22 Alison Duxbury, *The Participation of States in International Organisations: The Role of Human Rights and Democracy* (Cambridge U. Press 2011).

rorism and crimes of state. Its articulated positions on taking account of human rights considerations have become more permissive, but without a major cultural shift or a comprehensive human rights policy.[23] The Bank partners with donors who set political conditions for recipients, such as the inclusion of marginalized groups, but it does not join these partners in threatening to withhold funds for breach of such conditions, and it seeks humanitarian or other exemptions in UN sanctions so as not to face dilemmas about whether to honor such sanctions. The Bank supports anticorruption measures, including recovery of proceeds of corruption from other countries, but it does not finance work on individual cases.

All this line drawing operates as a shield for the Bank and its staff against pressures from borrowing states and their allies, other donors, nongovernmental organizations (NGOs), and national legislatures. It may help retain the confidence of lenders to the Bank, it may improve the effectiveness of the Bank by narrowing its focus, and it may boost the professional self-esteem of Bank staff and their sense of having a mission that is insulated from politics. Yet, the question can be asked whether the evidence for (or against) such results from the political prohibition is conclusive. (The European Bank for Reconstruction and Development may provide informative counterpoint experiences, because its constitutive instruments do not include any political prohibition, but the European regional context makes it a special case.) There is a risk of decoupling when some parts of the Bank's processes, such as the reduction of lending to India and Pakistan after they inducted nuclear weapons into their arsenals in 1998, are readily construed by commentators as the Bank being brought into interstate geopolitics.

Even in more quotidian work, much of what the IFIs do within their own rules can be characterized as highly political and open to denunciation. However, the drawing, nudging, and redrawing of the lines are themselves a significant form of governance. Such actions may empower IFI legal counsels;[24] but, from a broader legal standpoint, they constitute a law-based governance with some connection to principles and rules, and require some reason giving and internal review and contestation.

A case for the value of law-based governance is made in the account given by a former IMF lawyer of what he considered improvements in outcomes that resulted from IMF staff adhering to policies. These included the IMF's insistence that if it was to be involved in anti-money-laundering assessments, these assessments must be applied to all countries on the basis of preset standards and methodologies, effectively bringing to an end the Financial Action Task Force strategy of evaluating nonmember states and denouncing some of

---

23 Galit Sarfaty, *Why Culture Matters in International Institutions: The Marginality of Human Rights at the World Bank*, 103 Am J. Intl. L. 647 (2009).

24 *Cf.* Treasa Dunworth, *The Legal Adviser in International Organizations: Technician or Guardian?*, 46 Alberta L. Rev. 869 (2009).

them as "noncooperating countries and territories" who were then potentially subject to sanctions from member states.[25]

Mandate

The main control mechanisms for the political prohibition, as for other mandate restrictions in most intergovernmental institutions, are the intergovernmental organs such as the institution's executive board or general assembly, and the legal counsel; these bodies may be prompted to act, or be assertively augmented, by legal arguments or unilateral policies made by governments of particular member states. National courts have addressed mandate issues in cases directly involving intergovernmental institutions, such as in rulings that functional immunity is not available to an organization because it has acted outside its mandate.[26] A few international institutions, including regional organizations such as the European Union, have their own courts with powers of judicial review. Mandate issues may arise collaterally in national or international courts, typically in cases to which the institution is not itself a party.[27]

The International Court of Justice (ICJ, and its predecessor, the Permanent Court of International Justice) has addressed some questions concerning the powers of international organizations in global regulatory governance. Notable was the announcement by the ICJ of a new framing of a principle of speciality, according to which the responsibilities of the World Health Organization (WHO) could not be extended (in the absence of an express textual commitment in its mandate) to peace and security because this would "encroach on the responsibilities of other parts of the United Nations system."[28] The ICJ's opinion in this case was self-enforcing, as the only immediate legal consequence was that the WHO could not get an opinion from the ICJ on the question it had asked, relating to whether the use of nuclear weapons by a state in armed conflict would be a breach of the state's obligations under international law. If the ICJ's principle of speciality were to be amplified into a major principle of the law of GRG, it would have significant consequences, including for IFIs. Its benefits in curbing wasteful duplication and overextension may be difficult to capture without generating other, larger problems.

---

25   Richard Gordon, *On the Use and Abuse of Standards for Law: Global Governance and Offshore Financial Centers*, 88 N.C. L. Rev. 502, 577–84, 588 (2010).

26   In *INTERSIDE v. Ministerio de Agricultura y Secretaría Ejecutiva del Convenio Andrés Bello*, Sala de lo Contencioso Administrativo del Consejo de Estado (Mar. 26, 2009), the Colombian Council of State denied functional immunity to the Convenio Andrés Bello (an intergovernmental institution) in a contract case on the basis that the purposes stated in its charter did not even remotely include administering government-financed agricultural subsidies.

27   Such issues have been raised in interstate cases under the ICJ's contentious jurisdiction, for example in the *Lockerbie* cases (Libya v. UK; Libya v. USA), ICJ Reports 1992 p. 3 and p. 114, with regard to the powers of the UN Security Council.

28   *Legality of the Use by a State of Nuclear Weapons in Armed Conflict*, Advisory Op., 1996 I.C.J. Reports, paragraph 26. *See* generally Klabbers, *supra* note 20.

Overlapping mandates and competences are a feature of the increasingly dense institutionalization of GRG. Although the concept of a functional delineation under which one global organization exists for each field of activity is attractive, GRG is not organized in such a way. Much of the architecture of GRG is pluralist by design; for example, the Cartagena Protocol to the Biodiversity Convention of 1992 purposefully created a second normativity, more accommodating of public anxieties about genetically modified foods, that weakened the exclusivity of WTO Sanitary and Phyto-Sanitary rules on this issue.[29] Powerful states encountering obstacles to the pursuit of their objectives (including interests of particular private sector constituencies) on a particular topic within one institution may expand the range and reach of another institution in which the set of members or the decision rules or the culture is more favorable.[30] They may create new treaty-based intergovernmental institutions, as is likely to happen in the development of a climate finance regime, although political objections to the cost, cumbersomeness, and potential intractability of new formal intergovernmental institutions have been a brake on the drivers for such institutionalization. States may instead create intergovernmental network institutions, or support hybrid public-private institutions, or leave the terrain to privately constituted institutions of global governance in which states play significant roles.

Immunity and Remedies

The issue of increased judicial review of GRG institutions, particularly formal intergovernmental institutions, arises when considering whether intergovernmental organizations should have immunity before national courts and what legal forums should be available for persons seeking remedies against intergovernmental organizations. The stakes can be high, as in proceedings in Swiss courts seeking to force the Bank for International Settlements, which since the 2000–2001 Argentine financial crisis had come to hold a high proportion (reportedly reaching 99 percent) of Argentina's total foreign reserves, to make available funds to satisfy monetary awards secured by bondholders against Argentina.[31]

Intergovernmental organizations' legal counsel tend to favor sweeping immunities for their organizations and personnel in national courts. Most recognize that a quid pro quo for immunity is that the institution ensures that alternative venues are available in which claims against the organization can be brought and fairly adjudicated and remediated. This formalized bargain— for claims by third parties and staff—is embodied in the 1994 Headquarters

---

29   Nico Krisch, *Beyond Constitutionalism: The Pluralist Structure of Postnational Law* 189–220 (Oxford U. Press 2010).

30   Eyal Benvenisti & George Downs, *The Empire's New Clothes: Political Economy and the Fragmentation of International Law*, 60 Stanford L. Rev. 595 (2007).

31   *NML Capital Ltd, EM Limited v. Bank für Internationalen Zahlungsausgleich (BIZ)*, (Swiss Federal Tribunal, Basel), Jul. 12, 2010, upholding immunity, and subsequent developments.

Agreement between the United States and the Organization of American States (OAS).[32] The OAS has absolute immunity from suit and execution in U.S. courts, but must provide arbitration for any claims not within the jurisdiction of its Administrative Tribunal (which deals largely with claims by staff).[33] Even when no explicit agreement has been made, many international organizations have strengthened the due process qualities and remedies powers of staff administrative tribunals, partly under the shadow of national courts that have threatened to deny immunity to international organizations in employment-related cases brought by staff members.[34]

Most international organizations also provide for arbitration of contractual disputes with private parties. Much weaker, however, are their provisions and policies in relation to third-party claims, that is, noncontract claims by nonstaff.[35] Although some such claims are arbitrated by agreement or settled by negotiation, international civil servants face difficulties in committing an organization to binding arbitration or to making financial settlements in the absence of a legal obligation to do so. It can be difficult to persuade interstate organs to entertain such expenditures. A commitment to binding arbitration of all third-party claims could entail exposure to huge financial risks and might have a chilling effect on the activities of the organization, especially in risky settings. Adequate insurance of such risks ensures financial predictability and that recalcitrance or grandstanding by member states will not block payment of liabilities. Prohibitions of punitive damages in the arbitrations, ceilings on awards, and some limits to the range of arbitrable claims can all help cabin such risks.[36]

---

32   William M. Berenson, *Squaring the Concept of Immunity with the Fundamental Right to a Fair Trial: The Case of the OAS*, in this volume.

33   The US-OAS agreement may be compared, as Martha suggests, with an agreement between Interpol and France. Rutsel Silvestre J. Martha, *International Financial Institutions and Claims of Private Parties: Immunity Obliges*, in this volume. Interpol, the International Criminal Police Organization, reached a similar arrangement with the French government in 1982 over Interpol's exemption from laws on databases otherwise applicable in France. Interpol established a Commission on the Control of Files (CFF), which receives and potentially acts on petitions by individuals who believe data held about them in Interpol databases is erroneous, or that Interpol should not have issued a "red notice" asking other countries to arrest that person as requested by the police of a member state. Mario Savino, *Global Administrative Law Meets "Soft" Powers: The Uncomfortable Case of Interpol Red Notices*, 43 N.Y.U. J. Intl. L. & Pol. 263 (2011); Allan Brewer-Carías, *Global Administrative Law on International Police Cooperation: A Case of Global Administrative Law Procedure*, in *Global Administrative Law: Towards a Lex Administrativa* 341 (Javier Robalino-Orellana & Jaime Rodríguez-Arana Muñoz ed., Cameron 2010); Wui Ling Cheah, *Policing Interpol: The Commission for the Control of Interpol's Files and the Right to a Remedy*, 7 International Organizations L. Rev. 375 (2010). The most controversial disputes concerning red notices, such as those relating to a leader of the Kazakhstan opposition or to prominent Iranian officials accused by Argentine authorities of involvement in bombings in Buenos Aires, have been addressed, not in the CFF, but in the Executive Committee and General Assembly of Interpol (Savino, 301–21).

34   Martha, *supra* note 33, discusses cases in European and Argentine courts, as well as a perplexing decision of a court in Dacca, Bangladesh. Berenson, *supra* note 32, adds discussion of several cases in Brazilian and U.S. courts.

35   Martha, *supra* note 33.

36   Berenson, *supra* note 32.

If sweeping immunities from national jurisdiction and enforcement are as essential to the operation of intergovernmental institutions as their legal counsel suggest, one may wonder how private and hybrid institutions are able to exercise significant powers in global governance without the benefits of such immunity. Some private institutions do have immunity, for example, the International Committee of the Red Cross (ICRC). The Global Fund to Fight TB, HIV/AIDS, and Malaria, although constituted as a private foundation under Swiss law, has immunity in Switzerland, where it is based, and in the United States, where its funds are mainly held, and it has undertaken an energetic campaign to be accorded immunities in other countries. The ICRC and the Global Fund are comparable to major intergovernmental institutions in some functional respects: they engage in activities that might risk liability and operate all over the world, often in dangerous conditions and in countries where judicial or state power might be exercised arbitrarily. Nonetheless, most major private and hybrid operational and standard-setting institutions operate without generalized immunity arrangements. Detailed empirical studies of the consequences of different regimes of immunity and nonimmunity for particular kinds of operations of specific types of institutions may make a valuable contribution to future policy and practice.

Responsibility, Accountability, and Review

The principle that intergovernmental institutions are responsible for breaches of rules of international law applicable to them, along with the related principle that these institutions are liable to victims for harm caused by their breaches of such rules, has achieved considerable prominence with the efforts of the UN International Law Commission (ILC) to codify the legal elements of such responsibility. The ILC draft has been the subject of academic criticism, as well as submissions by international institutions eager to clarify limits to their exposure, as exemplified by the World Bank's request that the ILC clarify limits on responsibility arising from the provision to a state of financial assistance.[37] The extensive literature on this form of legal responsibility of intergovernmental institutions is out of proportion to the amount of practice of such responsibility, which remains modest for most institutions other than in employment and contract matters or preset arrangements, such as compensation for death or injury of personnel in UN peacekeeping operations.

The normative demands that have accompanied GRG, including demands framed in terms of GAL principles and procedures, have prompted exploration in the practice of GRG institutions of review mechanisms with distinctive rules and practices concerning participation, transparency, and remedies.

---

37   ILC, Responsibility of International Organizations: Comments and Observations Received from International Organizations, at 28, UN Doc. A/CN.4/637 (Feb. 14, 2011). This and other comments and criticisms relating to the ILC draft articles are noted in Evarist Baimu & Aristeidis Panou, *Responsibility of International Organizations and the World Bank Inspection Panel: Parallel Tracks Unlikely to Converge?* in this volume.

These are associated with extension of (or sidestepping from) issues of mandate and responsibility to broader concepts of accountability.[38]

The term "accountability" is used in many different ways in political discourse and academic writing,[39] and is often underspecified for any operational purpose. Richard B. Stewart proposes that the term be confined to

> institutionalized mechanisms under which an identified account holder has the right to obtain an accounting from an identified accountor for [the accountor's] conduct, evaluate that conduct, and impose a sanction or obtain another appropriate remedy for deficient performance. . . . Such mechanisms are of two basic types. The first is where the account holder delegates or grants authority or resources to the accountor; it includes electoral, fiscal, hierarchical, and supervisory accountability mechanisms. The second is legal accountability, where the account holder seeks redress for infringement by the accountor of [the account holder's] legally protected interests.[40]

The World Bank Inspection Panel, although clearly a mechanism of review, is not so clearly on its own a mechanism of accountability under Stewart's definition. The Bank's Executive Board must approve a full inspection of a Bank project. The Inspection Panel has powers in relation to management-proposed remedial action plans, but these powers depend on the Board; the Inspection Panel cannot impose remedies or sanctions on the Bank's management other than naming and shaming (although for individual staff, that prospect can operate as a strong and potentially disproportionate sanction). When combined with the Bank's Executive Board, however, the panel can be viewed as a composite accountability mechanism vis-à-vis management. The accountor is the Bank's management. The account holders are those persons or groups who trigger the inspection request and are able to participate in the panel's investigation and in any remedial arrangements made.

What are the parallels and divergences between the Inspection Panel's mandate and practice and the principles of responsibility set forth by the International Law Commission?[41] The panel investigates actions or omissions of the Bank that are inconsistent with Bank policies. Because of the

---

38   A thoughtful analysis of the genesis, features, and limitations in relation to international organizations of different approaches to responsibility and accountability is provided by Jan Klabbers, *Autonomy, Constitutionalism and Virtue in International Institutional Law*, in *International Organizations and the Idea of Autonomy: Institutional Independence in the International Legal Order* 120 (Richard Collins & Nigel D. White ed., Routledge 2011).

39   Some of the different usages are reviewed in Mark Bovens, *Two Concepts of Accountability: Accountability as a Virtue and as a Mechanism*, 33 West European Politics 946 (2010).

40   Richard B. Stewart, *Accountability, Participation, and the Problem of Disregard in Global Regulatory Governance* 5 (unpublished draft of Jan. 2008, subject to revision). Electoral, fiscal, hierarchical, supervisory, and legal accountability are among the eight categories specified in Ruth W. Grant & Robert O. Keohane, *Accountability and Abuses of Power in World Politics*, 99 Am. Pol. Sci. Rev. 29 (2005).

41   This question is creatively posed and addressed by Baimu & Panou, *supra* note 37. This paragraph summarizes arguments they make.

way Bank policies are written, with Bank staff as addressees, the panel is un-likely to investigate actions or omissions of the Board, or indeed of itself (quite apart from the improbability of such an investigation being proposed or au-thorized). As Evarist Baimu and Aristeidis Panou point out, the primary rules (here, the Bank's policies) set a narrower limit on the actors whose conduct is actually investigated than do the ILC's rules on attribution, under which the acts or omissions of the Board of Governors and the Executive Board as well as different units of Bank management could all entail responsibility of the Bank. The obligations in relation to which the panel can investigate breaches are the Bank's policies. The panel does not generally have jurisdiction to ad-dress any other primary rules of international law that a project may infringe, many of which would be rules applicable to the borrowing state, although some may be rules applicable to the Bank. However, some such rules may be made relevant by the terms of the Bank's policies, and the panel has in some cases found other bases to treat such rules as relevant.[42] The panel is able to investigate Bank action or inaction in situations where the Bank would not bear responsibility under the ILC draft articles (because, for example, only the borrowing state is responsible). But the panel can only investigate where harm has occurred or will occur,[43] and its investigations do not necessarily result in remedies that are the same as what the responsibility regime would theoreti-cally entail.

The creation of mechanisms of investigation and review within intergov-ernmental institutions in response to the dynamics of GRG may be related not only to responsibility but also to other traditional public international law doc-trines, such as immunity. For example, Ibrahim Shihata, while general counsel of the World Bank, emphasized that the reports of the World Bank Inspection Panel, even if highly critical of particular Bank conduct, were unlikely to be used in evidence in cases against the Bank in national courts because of the Bank's immunity.[44] It seems plausible that investigative mechanisms, espe-cially those that produce detailed and reasoned reports made widely available under a principle of transparency, are more likely to be established or to oper-ate effectively when the IFI creating the mechanism is largely shielded from li-ability. Thus, immunity may make possible the increased use of investigation, review, transparency, and some other GAL procedures within IFIs.

Operational Policies and Other Normative Instruments for GRG

GAL comprises some "hard law" obligations (including in international trea-ties and the juridical output of international organizations) and a body of more

---

42   Baimu & Panou, *supra* note 37, point to the *Chad Petroleum Development and Pipeline Project* case (2002), and the *Honduras—Land Administration Project* case (2007).

43   In theory, the harm must be caused by the Bank's failures to follow its own policies; but the panel has in practice moved away from treating this nexus as a requirement for investigation or remediation.

44   Ibrahim Shihata, *The World Bank Inspection Panel: In Practice* 243–53 (2d ed., Oxford U. Press 2000).

general normative principles, many of which mirror requirements and qualities set by domestic administrative law. The hard international law obligations
tend to be most developed in specific areas, particularly trade, investment,
and environmental law, and to apply primarily to states and state agencies
engaging in functions pursuant to global regimes rather than to international
institutions themselves.

More general normative principles emerge reflexively from practice, often
prompted by contestation of an institution's authority or legitimacy and borrowing from other institutions or domestic administrative law traditions. The
World Bank's 2010 reform of its transparency arrangements is an example of
this process. One of the main motivations for reform appears to have been
long-standing criticism from NGOs, including the Global Transparency Initiative (GTI), an alliance formed to press for greater transparency in the IFIs,
coupled with a sense within the Bank that its own protocols fell short of what
it urged on client countries. The Bank issued a draft policy and embarked on
consultations, relying on NGO interlocutors to help organize this outreach,
and reprinting a "scorecard" prepared by the GTI rating different IFIs as "acceptable," "needs improvement," or "unacceptable" based on principles of
access to information. During the policy redrafting, Bank officials declined to
articulate transparency as a human right, a position the NGOs urged on them,
but in some consultations, officials did say that they understood the Bank as
a "public institution" and had drawn on state freedom of information policies
in approaching questions of institutional transparency. Once the broad Access
to Information Policy was adopted, the Bank promoted it extensively. NGOs
proclaimed the World Bank as a "leader" on transparency and inaugurated a
campaign to spread these new, more extensive transparency mechanisms to
other IFIs. Moreover, the Bank's reformed policy, inspired by domestic freedom of information laws, extends to information that client countries share
with the World Bank when doing business with it.

The World Bank and the various regional development banks have
adopted broadly similar sets of operational policies and supervisory mechanisms. This cross-institutional normativity might eventually assume qualities
of a *droit commun*.[45] The mechanisms by which policy convergence and insti-

---

45 Laurence Boisson de Chazournes, *Partnerships, Emulation, and Coordination: Toward the Emer-
    gence of a* Droit Commun *in the Field of Development Finance*, in this volume. The evidence for
    the World Bank as first mover is strong in some cases. For example, the World Bank's Inspec-
    tion Panel, created in 1993, was the first independent accountability mechanism (IAM); by
    2010, all multilateral development banks had IAMs in some form, although with differences
    in design and powers (Bradlow, *supra* note 7). However, the IMF does not have an IAM; nor
    do many other international organizations whose operations directly affect vast numbers
    of identifiable individuals, such as the Office of the United Nations High Commissioner for
    Refugees. Further research may contribute to mapping and explaining these discontinuities
    in diffusion patterns even when the demand and the functional case for comparable inno-
    vations seem strong. Even among MDBs, more unevenness is evident in practices concern-
    ing public consultation before adoption of substantive institutional policies on some topics
    of particular public interest; and the IMF engages in such consultation much less than the
    World Bank does.

tutional similarity occur among international institutions have been the subjects of little recent study (whereas diffusion, convergence, and differentiation among states, economies, firms, and nonstate institutions have been extensively investigated across different issue areas). One model suggests that innovations that are diffused are typically those first initiated in the World Bank.[46] This might be due to the World Bank's large size, meaning it has greater resources for innovation. Subsequent uptake by regional institutions could then be due to learning as the results of the innovation are assessed and the methods for implementing it are refined. Widespread adoption of the innovation makes it more cost-effective for institutions to align to the new norm and more costly to be an outlier, and often these institutions also wish to be regarded as up-to-date. Another driver of uptake could be pressure (or coercion), probably not usually exerted by the World Bank on regional development banks but perhaps exerted by powerful states (that is, lenders, or the biggest borrowers). The size, global mandate, and location of the World Bank may lead to external pressures for reform so that political bargains struck there are in effect also bargains for the regional multilateral development banks (MDBs), in which many of the major lenders are the same countries. Whether the World Bank is always the first mover, as this model implies, may be questioned.

It is to be expected that innovations on some issues will originate in diverse experimentation by regional development banks, with promising experiences then drawn upon by the World Bank, which could learn from these experiences so as not to incur political and resource costs for untried innovations. This seems to have occurred, for example, in policies promoting transparency, where innovations, particularly in the Asian Development Bank, preceded the 2010 World Bank reforms. The incorporation of a problem-solving function into the mandate of MDB independent accountability mechanisms, along with the policy-compliance function, is an innovation developed in several regional MDBs that has not been incorporated into the mandate of the World Bank Inspection Panel. Fine-grained and robust studies of pathways of diffusion and reasons for variation and nonadoption of specific GAL principles and mechanisms among IFIs and among other GRG institutions are needed to understand how and why change occurs in GAL and GRG.

Interinstitutional Relations

GRG has been likened to polysynody,[47] the system in which a 10-person council took the place of each government minister that was introduced in France by the regent in 1715 and eloquently defended by the Abbé Saint-Pierre.[48]

---

46   Boisson de Chazournes, *supra* note 45.

47   The parallel is drawn by Cassese, *supra* note 14.

48   Charles-Irénée Castel (Abbé) de Saint-Pierre, *Discours sur la polysynodie* [1718] (Du Villard and Changuion 1719). This work is an argument for constitutional monarchy and against despotism, including excessive powers of the king's ministers. The councils were introduced after the death of King Louis XIV in response to complaints about ministerial power, but

Organizing the relations between collective entities in global governance, or between different legal regimes of which different entities are part, has been tortuous, with much less systematicity and coherence than French polysynody envisaged. Nonetheless, institutions are in increasingly intricate relationships with each other, including in structures of interagency coordination, prioritization (for example, appointment of a lead agency to deal with a specific government receiving humanitarian aid), and representation.

Isomorphism among clusters of institutions with similar missions, taking informal mimetic steps to resemble each other institutionally or to adopt similar operational policies, might provide a foundation for interinstitutional relations. However, similitude is not sufficient—cultural differences and sheer inequality may weigh heavily against interinstitutional arrangements. Staff in some agencies believe that the World Bank, because of its size and culture, is unwilling to adjust its policies or practices to conform to those of other institutions or to easily enable interoperability or greater speed and cost-effectiveness through harmonization in joint activities.

One clear modality for organizing change is through interinstitutional agreements harmonizing policies or linking institutional responses in pre-specified classes of cases. The cross-debarment regime, established in the Agreement for Mutual Enforcement of Debarment Decisions among a group of MDBs in 2010, illustrates this modality.[49] Each participating institution adopted a harmonized definition of fraud and corruption. An institution investigating such phenomena in a project it has financed follows the IFI Principles and Guidelines for Investigations. Its sanctions decision must be made by a distinct body and conform to requirements of due process, publicity, and proportionality. If a debarment from further contracting is imposed for more than one year, a debarment for the same period is automatically applied by the other participating institutions unless they give written notice (albeit without a requirement to state reasons) that they are opting out due to institutional or legal considerations. This agreement required a considerable amount of harmonization. The step of creating a single unified body to decide on and impose debarment sanctions, while potentially advantageous in unifying the jurisprudence and the length of sanctions imposed, proved impossible to achieve. Partly this was due to a divide between MDBs that consider economic actors to have a right to bid and contract with the MDB, and thus insist on robust due process before interfering in that right, and MDBs that consider it their prerogative to decide on contracts subject only to more modest requirements of nonarbitrariness.

---

they proved ineffective, partly due to the delinquency of their aristocratic members, and they were dissolved over the period 1718–23.

49   Stephen S. Zimmermann & Frank A. Fariello Jr., *Coordinating the Fight against Fraud and Corruption: Agreement on Cross-Debarment among Multilateral Development Banks*, in this volume. This paragraph summarizes points they make.

The difficulties for IFIs in achieving interinstitutional integration even on fundamentally shared objectives are manifest in relation to an anticorruption strategy operated by the World Bank since 2006.[50] The Voluntary Disclosure Program (VDP), which was approved by the Board of Executive Directors, aims to encourage disclosure to the Bank of corrupt or fraudulent practices. Any entity or individual involved in contracts or projects financed by the World Bank Group (excluding World Bank Group staff) that is not already under active investigation by the Bank may request entry into the VDP by providing preliminary background details. Once the Bank confirms the entity's eligibility, the entity commits to cease all corrupt and fraudulent practices and to disclose all details of impropriety to the Bank. The requirement that an entity not already be under investigation sets up a clear incentive for wrongdoers to come forward, because there is otherwise a risk that accomplices will come forward first, leaving later disclosers ineligible for the VDP and exposed to the sanctions that would usually follow an investigation (including debarment from bidding for future Bank projects and sanctions imposed by state authorities alerted by the Bank). Once the VDP begins, the participating entity completes an internal investigation (subject to Bank verification), implements a compliance plan, and is subject to external monitoring of adherence to that plan for three years. In exchange, the Bank does not debar the participating entity (as it may do if the corruption or fraud is discovered by the Bank's own investigations) and, although the Bank does not confer immunity of any kind on the participating entity, the Bank has the discretion not to disclose the conduct or the entity's participation in the VDP to third parties (including host countries and other MDBs).[51] To some extent, this nontransparency is necessitated by the logic of the program, including the risk in some countries that transparency about the fact that a participating entity has come forward might compromise the safety of individuals involved with the participating entity.

The Bank's creation of the program reflects a judgment that major drawbacks such as nontransparency are outweighed by the benefits of using this kind of regulatory technique for reducing corruption. It was hoped that the VDP would give the Bank fine-grained information on how corruption operates so that system vulnerabilities could be attenuated and prevention and detection efforts could be focused on specific areas. Bank or state-initiated investigations alone might not produce this information, and major investigations are so expensive (as well as facing other challenges) that they cannot cover nearly as many situations as the VDP. In theory, the Bank can use this information in working with member states and other agencies on forward-looking anticorruption programs. These forward-looking elements, and the

---

50 This paragraph, and the discussion of the World Bank's Access to Information Policy, draws on joint work with Megan Donaldson.

51 World Bank, Department of Institutional Integrity, VDP Guidelines for Participants (2011), available at <http://siteresources.worldbank.org/INTVOLDISPRO/Resources/VDP_Guidelines_2011.pdf>. Redacted reports of the misconduct, not identifying the participating entity, may be provided to member countries and to other international organizations or civil society.

general deterrence effects of these measures and of the VDP, were given considerable weight in the decision to create the VDP, on top of the possible roles of the VDP in detecting specific corruption and reducing risks of repetition.

At the same time, the VDP may have undesirable consequences.[52] The VDP puts the Bank's VDP unit in the position of keeping wrongdoing secret from other Bank staff and from other MDBs working with the wrongdoers. Perhaps most problematic, the VDP means the Bank may keep secret from citizens of the host state wrongdoing affecting projects in that state funded by loans that will be repaid from public monies and possibly also wrongdoing by that state's officials.[53] The VDP differs from similar programs within states, where the agency to which the wrongdoing is disclosed is itself an arm of the state acting (at least theoretically) in the interests of its citizens. Under the VDP, there is a risk that the Bank may be seen as keeping secrets from the state and the public. Moreover, the VDP process is triggered by the decision of wrongdoers to disclose. This decision is not contingent on any evidence that host state authorities would be unable to investigate or prosecute wrongdoing, or that disclosing the confession to the host country would result in some conceivable risk of retaliation to personnel of the participating entity. Obvious tensions arise with GAL principles of transparency: secrecy can be a necessary part of good administration and can advance accountability and the rule of law.

Attempts to curb corruption in projects funded by IFIs illustrate three points. First, different institutional mechanisms directed toward the same goals may vary significantly in their deployment of specific GAL principles. In regard to transparency, the World Bank's Sanctions Board process accomplishes highly public performative acts against corruption,[54] the cross-debarment process is public but not so performative, and the VDP is non-public and nontransparent. Second, each specific institutional mechanism is nested in, or connected with, several others. The substantive significance of one mechanism cannot be evaluated without studying the whole regime. Some mechanisms are deliberately designed to mesh together, as in the case of the cross-debarment system meshing with the sanctions board system to impose costs on a wrongdoer and reduce incoherence between different IFIs. Among meshed mechanisms, differences in levels of adherence to GAL principles may result in the displacement of an activity from one mechanism to another. Other

---

52 For example, by favoring larger (and more likely Western) contractors because it privileges the first party to disclose wrongdoing; larger contractors are likely to be in the best position to understand and make use of the VDP process. It may also be easier for larger contractors to comply with the VDP requirements, although the Bank offers technical assistance to reduce the costs of compliance for smaller contractors; see Sarah B. Rogers, *The World Bank Voluntary Disclosure Program: A Distributive Justice Critique*, 46 Colum. J. Transnatl. L. 709 (2008).

53 However, if the World Bank determines that it has a legal obligation or receives a judicial notice, it can disclose the name of the participating entity after providing notice to it.

54 World Bank Group Sanctions Regime—An Overview (Oct. 8, 2010), available at <http://siteresources.worldbank.org/EXTOFFEVASUS/Resources/Overview-SecM2010-0543.pdf>.

key parts of the regime may be designed separately and controlled by different actors. Thus, IFI sanctions processes may be influenced by investigatory and sanctions practices of national institutions, which may precipitate an entrant into the VDP or provide material for an IFI sanctions investigation. Across the gamut of meshed and unmeshed mechanisms, regulatory and institutional competition and arbitrage may occur, including over levels of adherence to different GAL principles. Third, differences of culture and values and great disparities in capacity are highly relevant to these GRG processes and their GAL dimensions.

The anticorruption field illustrates some of the difficulties of creating joint institutions. The dense and variegated institutional environment is nonetheless increasingly populated by institutions that were themselves created by existing institutions. Some are subsidiaries of a single existing entity, but many are interinstitutional structures.[55] Their governing authorities might consist of both state institutions and international institutions,[56] multiple intergovernmental institutions,[57] or hybrid and private organizations. These institutions may create further institutions, and they themselves are frequently part of complex interinstitutional and inter-regime arrangements. The substantive nature and importance of these phenomena in global governance has not been fully investigated;[58] the relevance and potential value of applying GAL principles to this organogenesis and to the operations of these complexes have scarcely been studied.

Prescriptions of International Institutions for Governance within States

Formal and informal international institutions have long been in the business of promoting good governance within states.[59] Among the myriad prescriptions by different international agencies for governance within states, few have provoked more introspection among lawyers in recent decades than those in

---

55 Edoardo Chiti & Ramses Wessel, *The Emergence of International Agencies in the Global Administrative Space*, in *International Organizations and the Idea of Autonomy: Institutional Independence in the International Legal Order* 142 (Richard Collins & Nigel D. White ed., Routledge 2011).

56 Edoardo Chiti, *EU and Global Administrative Organizations*, in *Global Administrative Law and EU Administrative Law* 13 (Edoardo Chiti & Bernardo Mattarella ed., Springer 2011).

57 Boisson de Chazournes, *supra* note 45, discussing the Global Environmental Facility (GEF) and other examples.

58 Many works bear on this vast topic. *See*, for example, Margaret Young, *Trading Fish, Saving Fish: The Interaction between Regimes in International Law* 241–305 (Cambridge U. Press 2011); Robert Keohane & David Victor, *The Regime Complex for Climate Change* (Harvard Project on International Climate Agreements, Discussion Paper 10-33, Jan. 2010), available at <http://belfercenter.ksg.harvard.edu/files/Keohane_Victor_Final_2.pdf>.

59 For critical assessment, *see* Antony Anghie, *Civilization and Commerce: The Concept of Governance in Historical Perspective*, 45 Vill. L. Rev. 887 (2000); Antony Anghie, *International Financial Institutions*, in *The Politics of International Law* 217 (Christian Reus-Smit ed., Cambridge U. Press 2004).

the field of law and development. Efforts by international institutions and bilateral aid agencies to promote justice sector reform or rule of law within recipient countries are premised on a view of what is good practice in the administration of particular activities by state institutions in these sectors.

Critiques in the early 1970s of such reform efforts focused on societal differences as reasons why ethnocentric Western liberal-legalist interventions aimed at enabling "them" to be like "us" were unlikely to succeed. Third world societies, David Trubek and Mark Galanter wrote, tend to be stratified and divided, with political governance that is authoritarian or totalitarian.[60] State institutions are less important to social control than tribal or other structures. Legal rules are made not by and for the whole society but by small elites or power groups, and in any case are often not observed, nor are state courts very independent or very important. Efforts to apply a liberal-legalist model in such contexts are thus, these authors suggest, likely to be misguided.

Similar perceptions led some Western scholars and institutions into a reaction akin to Montaigne's quietist focus on cultivating his own garden. This reticence was overwhelmed by the resurgence of rule-of-law interventionism from the late 1980s onward. This resurgence was a manifestation of several starkly different agendas arising from postconflict state building, conflict prevention, waves of democratic transitions, and a new interest among development economists in law and legal institutions as contributors to prosperity. Some modest convergence may be occurring among these agendas, although they pull in competing directions. Hence, much current work is devoted to the renovation of some central tenets discernible in this convergence. These more recent development interventions have been guilty, it is argued, of excessive state centrism and "skipping straight to Weber" in assuming that rules-based meritocratic politically accountable public agencies can be built and perform well in desperately poor and divided fragile states,[61] where many local people may see these as just another manifestation of the power and interests of a small elite in the capital city.[62]

Concerns are also raised about persisting tendencies of foreign actors to advocate isomorphic transplantation of institutional models from one setting to another, and about short time horizons driven by budget or election cycles or by career paths of task managers, when in fact 30 or 40 years may be needed for transformations to take root.[63] A fundamental issue is the theory of change used by external actors. The rhetoric of rule-of-law interventions

---

60   David Trubek & Marc Galanter, *Scholars and Self-Estrangement: Some Reflections on the Crisis in Law and Development Studies in the United States*, 4 Wis. L. Rev. 1062 (1974).

61   Lant Pritchett & Michael Woolcock, *Solutions Where the Solution Is the Problem: Arraying the Disarray in Development*, 32 World Development 191 (2004).

62   Deval Desai, Deborah Isser, & Michael Woolcock, *Rethinking Justice Reform in Fragile and Conflict-Affected States: The Capacity of Development Agencies and Lessons from Liberia and Afghanistan*, in this volume.

63   *Id.*

has often assumed that the trajectory of change in a country's institution will be linear (more or less).[64] Experience demonstrates, however, that change occurs in many other trajectories, including j curves (deterioration followed eventually by improvement), f curves (rapid early gains followed by some deterioration), n curves (short-term improvements but an eventual return to baseline), and punctuated equilibria or step functions (periods of stasis or incremental change, punctuated by moments of major change).

Understanding of circumstances and trajectories under which change occurs, or does not occur, in societies or institutions can be sought through the locally specific perspective and expertise of change-agents or astute observers within the society, or through more detached general models.

Rational-actor models emphasize the weights against change that arise from self-reinforcing mechanisms built into the status quo and from switching costs.[65] Reforms may thus have better prospects of success when existing ways of doing things can be grandfathered in or allowed a long transition; new constituencies with proreform interests can be empowered on the demand side; extensive education and retraining are provided to enable job holders to work successfully in reformed institutions; and traditional institutions (with adaptations) are accorded significant roles in the reformed system to minimize cultural dissonance.[66] The embeddedness of any specific national regulatory or justice institution in a wider set of practices and understandings and a matrix of other institutions can make lasting and effective reform of any single institution difficult to achieve. The aggregate of all of this means that reforms must usually be modest in aspiration and carefully sequenced across institutions; critical junctures at which wholesale reform across a whole society might succeed are extremely rare and pass quickly. Reform efforts in ordinary times might thus focus on relatively autonomous, separable, or wholly new institutions, in the hope of demonstrating for other institutions that switching costs are lower and benefits higher than constituencies of resistance expect.[67] Uneven results have been attained in reforms of courts, police, prisons, independent regulatory agencies for utilities, tax administrations, and competition authorities.[68]

What might GAL contribute to contextualized or generalized understandings of national reform?[69] A starting point is to study closely the connections between national (or subnational) public or public-private governance in these sectors and extranational sources of norms, practices, ideas, funding, expertise, and assessment. When sufficiently dense and interdependent, these

---

64   *Id.*

65   Trebilcock, *supra* note 2.

66   *Id.*

67   *Id.*; Mariana Mota Prado & Michael Trebilcock, *Path Dependence, Development, and the Dynamics of Institutional Reform*, 59 U. Toronto L.J. 341 (2009).

68   Trebilcock, *supra* note 2; Desai, Isser, & Woolcock, *supra* note 63.

69   This discussion draws on work with Megan Donaldson.

connections bring the national and extranational governance together in the loosely unified global administrative space. Local and extralocal programs and sites of specific activities can be integrated through GAL norms and mechanisms.

This integrative process is continuous, iterative, and reflexive. It begins with abstractions from broad normative principles and mechanisms found in national public law systems, which are given abstract or more specific expression in the internal and external practice of international agencies; these abstractions or more specific prescriptions are then invoked in the concretization of practices at national and transnational institutional sites.

For example, an IFI may have a broad program of promoting good governance and rule of law for states.[70] In dealing with a borrowing state on a specific project, the IFI may urge that state to establish particular national institutions (such as an insurance industry supervisory body or an electricity regulator) that follow principles of transparency, participation, reason giving, review, and accountability in forms distilled as best practices from the same sector in other countries. This advocacy may be represented by the IFI as a vindication of the broad program of good governance and rule of law. Such practices then influence a further round of abstractions as the process continues. Moreover, these abstract norms are likely to find some application and be given weight in the internal practices of the relevant international institutions and in their interinstitutional arrangements, partly to avoid cognitive dissonance. Intrastate and extrastate programs and practices are thus brought into unity through common framings, normativities, mechanisms, and metrics.

Much research is required on the implications and consequences of adoption of particular GAL mechanisms by national or subnational regulators and other agencies. Further work could also be done tracing the way in which GAL mechanisms diffuse within a state. There is often an assumption that GAL mechanisms have positive externalities beyond a specific sector, for example, acting as a beachhead or best practices standard for procedural norms that can then be applied to other sectors and areas of government. Yet, depending on how they operate in practice, GAL mechanisms in one sector could have negative impacts beyond that sector; for example, if the mechanisms do not work or prove unwieldy, the failure might discourage governments from implementing similar measures in other areas. These theories might be tested by more detailed qualitative work tracking the evolution of particular ideas among policy makers.

---

70   The distinction is between a broad program identified in the discourse of leading decision makers and a more specific practice or technology that, although described by participants as simply a means to advance the program, is in fact likely to be decoupled from it. Peter Miller & Nikolas Rose, *Governing Economic Life*, 19 Economy and Society 1 (1990). GAL, at least as it applies to the design and operation of regulatory structures and institutions, can be understood as a technology for the pursuit of, or as congruent with, sweeping programmatic ideas of "good governance" and "rule of law" that are proclaimed and promoted by many global institutions for states and, to some extent, for themselves.

Empirical law and development work on theories of change and differential uptake or success of reforms is likely to provide valuable insights as the questions are addressed in relation to GAL in national or subnational institutions. For example, modes of regulation in authoritarian or centralized regimes may simply not accommodate many GAL mechanisms; conversely, more populist modes of regulation, in which there is a significant measure of public participation or regulation is conducted in a corporatist framework by unions or municipal governments, may accommodate some GAL mechanisms (public participation) but not others (legality). If GAL is dependent on a particular political order—liberal capitalism—then regimes that reject liberalism in favor of some more comprehensive and substantive account of value (religious or otherwise) might be expected to reject GAL as irrelevant, except insofar as it fosters the particular ends to which the regime is committed.

New Forms of Global Regulatory Governance

Three major areas in which some but not all necessary elements of political agreement have come into place for newly crafted GRG arrangements are financial markets supervision, forest governance, and climate finance. In each area, existing or proposed governance arrangements feature significant but varied uptake of GAL principles and mechanisms. Little research has been done, however, on the impacts or consequences of these uses of GAL or on the reasons for and consequences of the variations.

National regulators of capital markets, including in some of the most successful emerging markets, place considerable emphasis on the conformity of regulatory rules and practices with the increasingly dense bodies of standards set by international bodies and on the effectiveness of rules, enforcement, and educational initiatives.[71] These include provisions aimed at ensuring transparency and accountability among market participants. Although some models exist for central bank independence or the design of governmental securities regulatory institutions, and significant arrangements exist for transnational cooperation among counterpart institutions, there appears to be less prescription for the design and procedures of national market regulatory institutions than there is with regard to the standards they ought to apply.

Global bodies in this sector vary considerably with regard to their own institutional design features (such as general or restricted membership) and their norms of process and procedure. To give one example of variation in uptake of GAL norms, the International Accounting Standards Board and associated bodies producing the International Financial Reporting Standards have given a high priority to public transparency and to enabling interested groups to make comments before drafts are finalized. The IFRS Foundation Trustees have a prominent Due Process Oversight Committee devoted to such

---

71   Alexandre Pinheiro dos Santos, *Mitigating the Impact of Financial Crises on the Brazilian Capital Market*, in this volume.

matters. A contrast is the Committee on Payment and Settlement Systems (CPSS), hosted by the Bank for International Settlements in Basel. The membership of CPSS, initially a very small club, was expanded in 2009 and now comprises representatives of 25 national central banks, with a further program of outreach to other central banks. The committee, which produces principles and recommendations, meets three times per year. Its website informs the public that "No public releases of the meeting agendas or discussions are made. Regular reports on the Committee meetings are made by the Chairman to the Governors of the Global Economy Meeting."[72] Why does such great variation exist between the IFRS bodies and the CPSS with regard to GAL principles of transparency and participation?

There may be differences on the demand side, with narrower interest in CPSS work and little pressure to change from a historic model of operating in private. CPSS has as members many of the key public and governmental actors needed to implement its recommendations, whereas the IFRS bodies must persuade government regulators to accept or require the use of IFRS in nationally regulated markets. The IFRS bodies thus need greater nonmember buy-in and face greater risk of challenges to their legitimacy, which is linked to their private or nongovernmental character. This comparison suggests a few of many possible hypotheses to explain differential uptake of GAL norms. Such hypotheses, and hypotheses concerning the effects of application of GAL norms by different bodies, are only now being systematically developed and tested.

From the standpoint of forest preservation, national governmental performance has varied greatly, and existing intergovernmental arrangements for forest governance are not adequate. Institutional solutions have not been able to overcome the fundamental incentives to tropical deforestation that arise from the market price of timber (and in some cases the value of cleared land), producing returns that far outweigh monetary returns from the use of intact forests. Governance initiatives for conservation easements or protected areas, benefit sharing from plant genetic resources, curbing of forest-destructive lending and conditionality by IFIs, partnerships to improve enforcement and curb trade in tropic timber, recognition of indigenous peoples' land and resource rights, and forest certification by entities such as the Forest Stewardship Council have all produced some positive results,[73] and debates about the contributions of GAL norms to effectiveness or legitimacy have been prominent in several of these regimes. In aggregate, however, these initiatives have not provided a solution. Many advocates hope that financial mechanisms aimed at mitigating climate change will provide, through initiatives such as Reducing Emissions from Deforestation and Forest Degradation (REDD+) with associated national reforestation and forest management modalities, sufficient economic incentives to keep forests standing. The administration of forests

---

72   <http://www.bis.org/about/factcpss.htm>.

73   Annie Petsonk, *Legal Obligations and Institutions of Developing Countries: Rethinking Approaches to Forest Governance*, in this volume.

under REDD+ will largely be national, but under conditions of monitoring, reporting, and verification that are likely to entail substantial international prescription of both substantive and process standards. National administration will in many cases be dependent also on international administration of a climate finance regime—GAL procedures will play an essential role in making these different administrative structures transparent to each other and to market actors and in ensuring that they are subject to adequate processes for review and accountability.

The scale of fund flows and of projects envisaged in an effective global climate finance regime, albeit a decentralized regime with numerous different carbon markets and significant powers of initiation and control exercised by national agencies, [74] will necessitate a sophisticated global administrative apparatus with intricate relations between national and international institutions.[75] GAL issues have become increasingly central in debates about the clean development mechanism and its reform and viability.[76] Although they have not featured as much in evaluations of the work of some of the special-purpose climate funds, such as those administered by the World Bank,[77] GAL issues have loomed larger in relation to the Global Environmental Facility (GEF), especially in response to proposals that the GEF be a significant vehicle for climate finance in the future. GAL issues are likely to feature prominently in the work of the Green Climate Fund and its associated board and implementing agencies, in compliance mechanisms, and perhaps also in the work of the nationally appropriate mitigation action (NAMA) registry.[78] GAL principles are likely also to play a significant role in the intricate set of interinstitutional governance arrangements that the emerging climate finance regime will entail.

---

74 For thoughtful advocacy of a bottom-up approach, *see* Navroz Dubash, *Climate Change and Development: A Bottom-Up Approach to Mitigation for Developing Countries?*, in *Climate Finance: Regulatory and Funding Strategies for Climate Change and Global Development* 172 (Richard B. Stewart, Benedict Kingsbury, & Bryce Rudyk ed., N.Y.U. Press 2009).

75 Charlotte Streck & Thiago Chagas, *Developments in Climate Finance from Rio to Cancun*, in this volume; Arunabha Ghosh, *Harnessing the Power Shift: Governance Options for International Climate Financing* (Oxfam Research Report 2010).

76 *See*, for example, Charlotte Streck & Jolene Lin, *Making Markets Work: A Review of CDM Performance and the Need for Reform*, 19 Eur. J. Intl. L. 409 (2008); Moritz von Unger & Charlotte Streck, *An Appellate Body for the Clean Development Mechanism: A Due Process Requirement*, 3 Carbon & Climate L. Rev. 31 (2009).

77 *See*, however, the critique of such funds in Sophie Smyth, *Agency and Accountability in Multilateral Development Finance*, 4(1) L. & Dev. Rev. (Article No. 3) (2011); also Ilias Bantekas, *Trust Funds under International Law: Trustee Obligations of the United Nations and International Development Banks* (TMC Asser Press 2009).

78 Richard B. Stewart, Bryce Rudyk, & Kiri Mattes, *Governing a Fragmented Climate Finance Regime*, in this volume.

Conclusion

The stakes involved in GRG regimes are high. Too little is yet known about the differences law makes in such regimes. Enough evidence is now available, however, to suggest that it is unwise to be sanguine about GAL. GAL has winners and losers. GAL can provide substantial net benefits. But in some contexts it can legitimize the highly unjust, and mask or divert substantive critique. Requirements of process can blunt the effectiveness of institutions. Moreover, GAL operates mainly where institutional forms exist or are being created; the lens of GAL may provide little insight into power that is not exercised in such institutional forms, or into ways in which formal institutions can draw gaze and effort away from dynamics or basic structures that ought to be at the center of inquiry and challenge.[79]

GAL can and frequently does serve the interests of powerful actors—a central reason for the rapid uptake of GAL norms, mechanisms, and rhetoric.[80] One major strand of GAL, oriented to stability and due process for foreign investors and for businesses engaged in trade, includes economic-liberal requirements concerning transparency, participation, review, and (to some extent) reason giving in trade institutions and in investor-state arbitration.[81] These norms align closely with those urged on, or required of, developing countries by international institutions.[82]

Some GAL norms, although fulfilling such purposes, are oriented more toward enhancing the rights of a wider public. These include the norms prescribed in the Convention on Access to Information, Public Participation in Decision-Making and Access to Justice in Environmental Matters of 1998 (the Aarhus Convention), developed under the auspices of the United Nations Economic Commission for Europe. This convention requires public authorities to make available environmental information to the public on request and to provide certain types of information on a routine and proactive basis; it also requires structures for public participation in various stages of environmental decision making. These norms have informed and been woven into policies of the World Bank and other IFIs, and the Aarhus Convention Compliance Committee processes have overlapped with World Bank Inspection Panel proceedings in relation to the Vlora power plant in Albania.[83]

---

79   David Kennedy, *The Mystery of Global Governance*, 34 Ohio N.U.L. Rev. 827 (2008).

80   This and the following paragraphs draw on work with Megan Donaldson.

81   Gus van Harten & Martin Loughlin, *Investment Treaty Arbitration as a Species of Global Administrative Law*, 17 Eur. J. Intl. L. 121 (2006); Benedict Kingsbury & Stephan Schill, *Investor-State Arbitration as Governance: Fair and Equitable Treatment, Proportionality and the Emerging Global Administrative Law*, IILJ Working Paper No. 2009/6 (2009).

82   Rene Urueña, *Espejismos constitucionales: La promesa incumplida del constitucionalismo global*, 24 Revista de Derecho Público (Bogotá 2010).

83   World Bank Inspection Panel Investigation Report No. 49504-AL, Albania-Power Sector Generation and Restructuring Project (IDA Credit No. 3872-ALB) (Aug. 7, 2009), available at <http://siteresources.worldbank.org/EXTINSPECTIONPANEL/Resources/ALB_Power_Investigation_Report_whole.pdf>. There were 44 states parties to the Aarhus Convention in August 2011.

GAL serves other agendas of IFIs. The World Bank is exemplary of IFIs positioning themselves as "knowledge banks" and sources of expertise.[84] GAL processes and procedures have been mobilized by the IFIs in this endeavor. Extensive external consultations and reason giving on proposed "safeguards" policies and other normative instruments, requirements that the public and affected groups receive adequate information and have opportunities to comment before a project proposed by a state is approved for financing, mechanisms for review of the institutions' compliance with their own policies, and Access to Information policies may all facilitate greater public access to, and contestation of, ideas espoused by IFIs. Reporting and inspection or review can bring feedback about on-the-ground experience into the renovation or creation of global regulatory regimes. Some of these mechanisms shape knowledge dissemination and interaction, and they may tip these processes toward being more inclusive and less "top-down" than in the past.

GAL can be state buttressing. In its orientation to a strong if vague sense of "publicness" and public interest,[85] not only may it influence extrastate public authority, but it may also articulate a distinctive role for the state. In areas such as investment and trade law, GAL may have a potential, only glimpsed so far, to strengthen the sense that states and state authorities have a responsibility to the public that in some situations overrides commercial or other obligations to private actors.

At the same time, GAL may facilitate critique, contestation, resistance, and reform in GRG.[86] The extent to which GAL norms, processes, and mechanisms have been significant in opening space for disregarded groups and interests or in advancing the realization of different conceptions of substantive justice is unknown. Vignettes and anecdotes suggest, however, that such effects are more than de minimis and may be increasing.

New legal ideas are required in the work of IFIs as in the work of other key institutional actors in global governance. GAL may provide one conceptual resource in this regard. At the same time, innovative work in or relating to GRG institutions and to national practices may inform and shape some aspects of GAL.

---

84 A nomenclature popular in Bank rhetoric from World Bank, *World Development Report 1998–99: Knowledge for Development* (World Bank 1999). *Cf.* David Kennedy, *Challenging Expert Rule: The Politics of Global Governance*, 27 Sydney L. Rev. 5 (2005).

85 Kingsbury, *supra* note 14; Benedict Kingsbury & Megan Donaldson, *From Bilateralism to Publicness in International Law*, in *From Bilateralism to Community Interest: Essays in Honour of Bruno Simma* 79 (Ulrich Fastenrath et al. ed., Oxford U. Press, 2011).

86 Bhupinder S. Chimni, *Co-option and Resistance: Two Faces of Global Administrative Law*, 37 N.Y.U. J. Intl. L. & Pol. 799 (2005); Bronwen Morgan, *Turning Off the Tap: Urban Water Service Delivery and the Social Construction of Global Administrative Law*, 17 Eur. J. Intl. L. 216 (2006); Doreen Lustig & Benedict Kingsbury, *Displacement and Relocation from Protected Areas: International Law Perspectives on Rights, Risks and Resistance*, 4 Conservation and Society 404 (2006).

PART I

LAW OF INTERNATIONAL ORGANIZATIONS: ISSUES CONFRONTING IFIs

The Reform of the Governance of the IFIs

A Critical Assessment

Daniel D. Bradlow[*]

The first two global international financial institutions (IFIs), the International Monetary Fund (IMF) and the International Bank for Reconstruction and Development (IBRD), were created at the Bretton Woods Conference in 1944. Their governance, their functions, and, ultimately, their membership were shaped by the geopolitical realities of the time.[1] The IMF's function was to use its financial resources to create and support a rules-based international monetary system based on stable exchange rates and relatively free payments for current transactions.[2] The IMF was expected to use its surveillance authority to oversee the operation of the international monetary system and advise members on their balance of payments and the maintenance of the par value of their currencies.[3] The founding states anticipated that the IMF would use its financial resources to help member states correct their balance-of-payments problems in ways that were not destructive to international or domestic prosperity. The Articles of Agreement of the IMF made clear that, although member states were surrendering some control over their exchange rates and their policy discretion in regard to current transactions, they retained full authority to regulate capital transfers as they saw fit.[4] Thus, the founding member states did not anticipate that the IMF would play any direct role in the regulation or oversight of either national or international financial markets or in the international allocation of credit. At the time, this made good sense because very few banks operated across national boundaries, all financial regulation was national, and international financial activity was a relatively small part of the global financial scene.

---

[*] The views in this chapter are the author's own and should not be attributed to any institution with which he is affiliated. The author would like to thank Veronique Lendresse for her research assistance.

1 For a history of these institutions, *see*, for example, Devesh Kapur, John P. Lewis, & Richard Webb, *The World Bank: Its First Half Century* (Brookings Institute 1997); Margaret Garritsen De Vries, *The IMF in a Changing World, 1945–85* (Intl. Monetary Fund 1986).

2 Articles of Agreement of the IMF, Article I, available at <http://www.imf.org/external/pubs/ft/aa/>.

3 Under the system established with the creation of the IMF, each state was expected to establish the value of its currency in terms of the U.S. dollar, which would be fixed in terms of gold. The member state was expected to maintain this value, known as the "par value of the currency," within narrow limits. It could change the par value only with the consent of the IMF.

4 Articles of Agreement of the IMF, Article VI.

The IBRD's role was to help finance the reconstruction of Europe and the economic development of its erstwhile colonies and a few independent states in Africa, Asia, and Latin America.[5] At the time this was understood to mean that the IBRD would provide financial support primarily for physical infrastructure projects in member states that were not able to raise sufficient financing from private sources.

Since the IMF and the IBRD were established, the world has changed dramatically. The number of states participating in the global monetary and financial system has increased; the IMF and the institutions in the World Bank Group[6] each now have more than 180 member states. In addition, many more IFIs have been created. There are now IFIs such as the International Development Association (IDA), which provides concessional financing to the poorest states; regional and subregional development banks; and institutions dedicated to funding the private sector, such as the International Finance Corporation (IFC). The par value system of exchange rates has broken down; we now live in a world with freely fluctuating exchange rates and liberalized financial flows. In this environment, international financial flows exceed by several orders of magnitude annual international trade volumes; international capital markets are a key component of the global financial order; and, in a number of cases, the IFIs either compete or cooperate with the private sector and other official creditors in funding projects in their member states.

In addition, no financial regulator in a major economic power can effectively regulate its financial industry without addressing the international aspects of that industry's operations and without collaborating in some way with its counterparts in other key countries. As a result, the IMF has become involved in international financial market oversight and in reviewing its member states' financial regulatory frameworks.[7] It is supported in these efforts by a broad range of relatively new international forums and bodies involved in the various aspects of international financial governance. These include the Financial Stability Board (FSB), the Basel Committee of Banking Supervision, the International Organization of Securities Commissions, and the International Association of Insurance Administrators.[8] The IMF also plays a leading role when a member state needs support in dealing with its international debt problems.

---

5   IBRD Articles of Agreement, Article I, available at <http://go.worldbank.org/0FICOZQLQ0.>

6   The members of the World Bank Group are the International Bank for Reconstruction and Development (IBRD), the International Development Association (IDA), the International Finance Corporation (IFC), the Multilateral Investment Guarantee Agency (MIGA), and the International Centre for the Settlement of Investment Disputes (ICSID).

7   The IMF's website provides a useful overview of the diversity of its activities; see <http://www.imf.org>.

8   For a useful overview of these institutions and their functions, see, generally, Howard Davies & David Green, Global Financial Regulation: The Essential Guide (Polity Press 2008); Kern Alexander, Rahul Dhumale, & John Eatwell, Global Governance of Financial Systems: The International Regulation of Systemic Risk (Oxford U. Press 2006).

The various entities in the World Bank Group and the regional development banks are involved in helping their member states develop the institutional and technical capacity to effectively regulate, supervise, and manage their evolving financial systems and to develop capital markets. The growing complexity of the international financial and economic system and our deepening understanding of the complexities of poverty and development are also changing the ways in which these multilateral development banks (MDBs) operate. They can no longer limit their operations to funding physical infrastructure projects. They are now involved in helping their member states improve various aspects of their governance arrangements; deal with such complex social issues as legal and judicial reform, education reform, vulnerable population groups, and health care; confront such environment-related challenges as climate change, sustainable energy and water strategies, and food security; manage their public finances; and fund physical infrastructure projects.[9]

These changes are occurring at the same time that the global political economy is undergoing a shift in power. This process of change is not yet over, and its final outcome is not yet clear. Currently, the rising powers are powerful enough to demand changes in some aspects of the existing international economic governance arrangements but not powerful enough to shape the global economic governance agenda, including reforming the key institutions in global financial governance. The existing powers, primarily the Group of Seven (G7) countries, still control the global agenda and can still block reform efforts that they oppose. This situation has two implications for governance reforms. First, it suggests that reform any faster or more extensive than the existing powers are willing to accept is not feasible in the short run. This situation may change over time as power shifts more toward newly rising powers, but at the moment, this is an important constraint on governance reform. Second, the current governance reforms are unlikely to produce sustainable and stable governance arrangements in the IFIs until the process of change in the balance of global power plays itself out.

One effect of these changes has been to produce differences in the relationships between the IFIs and their member states. Today, the major IFIs, de facto, are important actors in the policy-making processes of many of the member states that rely on their financial services. The IFIs have become more sensitive to the interests of those member states that use their financial services and are gaining international power and influence while remaining subject to the influence of the IFI's richer and more powerful member states.

As is clear from the number of financial crises that the world has experienced since the 1980s, international governance arrangements do not always

---

9　The websites of the MDBs provide a useful overview of the diversity of their activities. *See,* for example, World Bank Group, <http://www.worldbank.org>; African Development Bank, <http://www.afdb.org>; Asian Development Bank, <http://www.adb.org>; European Bank for Reconstruction and Development, <http://www.ebrd.org>; Inter-American Development Bank, <http://www.iadb.org>; International Finance Corporation, <http://www.ifc.org>.

function effectively. In fact, even though some significant reforms in IFIs' governance occurred before then, the 1997 Asian financial crisis resulted in a general agreement that both the existing arrangements for international financial governance, often referred to as the global financial architecture, and the governance of the key IFIs needed to be reformed. However, since that time, the attention paid to this topic has been inversely proportional to the well-being of the global financial system. Consequently, during the early years of the millennium, the topic was not high on the international agenda and some commentators even began to question the need for the IFIs, particularly the IMF.

As signs that the global political economy could be running into problems appeared and accelerated after the financial crisis fully erupted in 2008, there were significant efforts to reform the governance of the IFIs. These efforts resulted in changes in voting arrangements, representation on boards of directors, and the selection of top management.[10] These reforms were complemented by a strengthening of the role of some of the IFIs, most notably the IMF.

Given all the governance changes that the IFIs have undergone in recent years, now is an opportune time to assess the actual significance of these reforms. Such an evaluation asks three questions: What has been achieved in terms of reforming the governance of the IFIs? What standards should one use in assessing the adequacy of these reforms? How well do these reforms measure up to these assessment standards?

The thesis of this chapter is that, despite all the governance changes that the IFIs have undergone, they still do not have adequate governance arrangements and will need to undergo further reform if they are to perform their mandates effectively. In order to establish this thesis, this chapter is divided into four parts. First, it describes the reforms the IFIs have agreed to and have implemented. Second, it sets out some benchmarks against which these governance reforms can be measured. Third, it assesses the adequacy of the reforms undertaken based on the benchmarks identified in the second section. The final section is a conclusion.

The Governance Reform of the IFIs

Over the past twenty years, the IFIs, particularly the World Bank[11] and the IMF,[12] have undergone more substantial changes in their governance and

---

10   The recent election of another European, Christine Lagarde, as the management director of the IMF suggests that these reforms may not be as solid as they first appeared.

11   For a useful overview of the reforms at the World Bank Group, *see* <http://www.worldbank .org/html/extdr/worldbankreform/>.

12   For a useful overview of the reforms at the IMF, *see* IMF Finance, Legal and Strategy, Policy and Review Departments, IMF Quota and Governance Reform—Elements of an Agreement (IMF, Oct. 31, 2010); IMF, Factsheet: A Changing IMF—Responding to the Crisis (Mar. 16, 2011), available at <http://www.imf.org/external/np/exr/facts/changing.htm>.

operational practices than have other international organizations.[13] As a result, they are more transparent and more open to interactions with their external stakeholders than are other international organizations. The World Bank is also more accountable to its various stakeholders than are other international organizations.

Voice and Vote

One of the most persistent complaints about the governance of the IFIs, particularly the World Bank and the IMF, was that they were not representing their membership very effectively and they needed to realign both their voting arrangements and the way in which their member states were represented on their boards of executive directors. In the past few years, both the World Bank and the IMF have made efforts to address this issue. The IMF has increased its member states' basic votes in order to enhance the representation of its smallest and poorest member states in its total vote. It also increased and redistributed the quotas of some of its member states to ensure that formerly underrepresented states are now more appropriately represented in the total votes of the organization. As a result, a number of the major emerging markets now have some of the biggest quotas in the IMF. In addition, the IMF membership agreed to reassess the formula used in assigning quotas (and therefore votes) to its member states so that the counts more accurately reflect the role of its member states in the global financial and economic system.[14]

The membership of the IMF has also agreed to reform the structure of its board of executive directors. In particular, it has agreed to appoint a second alternative executive director to support those executive directors who represent large numbers of states. There will also be a reduction in the European representation on the board and a concomitant increase in the developing-country representatives on the board. Finally, the membership has also agreed to move to an all-elected board, thereby eliminating the privileged position that its five largest shareholders held on the board.[15]

The World Bank has made similar reforms. Its member states have agreed to increase the share of its developing and transitional member states in its total vote.[16] Following the implementation of these changes, these countries will constitute 47.19 percent of the total vote in the Bank. This represents an

---

13 It should be noted that the regional development banks have also undertaken substantial governance reforms. However, they tend to follow the lead of the World Bank in their reform efforts. Consequently, it can be assumed that these banks have implemented roughly analogous reforms to those that the World Bank has undertaken and described in this section.

14 For a general overview of these reforms, see IMF Press Release No. 08/64, IMF Executive Board Recommends Reforms to Overhaul Quota and Voice (Mar. 28, 2008), available at <http://www.imf.org/external/np/sec/pr/2008/pr0864.htm>.

15 Id.

16 For an overview of these voting reforms, see <http://web.worldbank.org/WBSITE/EXTERNAL/NEWS/0,,contentMDK:22556192~menuPK:34457~pagePK:34370~piPK:34424~theSitePK:4607,00.html>.

increase of 4.59 percent in their share of the total vote since 2008. In addition, within these totals, there will be some realignment of voting shares so that the most dynamic emerging markets increase their share of the votes and have a vote in the Bank that is more commensurate with their role in the global economy. The member states have also increased the size of the Bank's Board from 24 to 35 members, with the new member being a third African executive director.

Senior Management

Historically, the selection of the chief executive officers of the IMF and the World Bank has been governed by a "gentlemen's agreement" according to which the managing director of the IMF was a European and the president of the World Bank was an American. In addition, the process through which this person was selected was opaque and closed to outside participation. The member states have now agreed that the process should be transparent and understandable to outsiders and that it should be based on merit without regard to national origin.[17] Analogous procedures should also apply to the selection of other senior management officials. It is important to note that the IMF failed to fully implement this reform and followed the old "gentlemen's agreement" in its recent selection of a new managing director. Despite their commitments to the contrary, the leading member states banded together to elect another European as the IMF's managing director.[18]

Accountability

Over the past 20 years, the World Bank and the other MDBs have made significant efforts to become more accountable. In 1993, the World Bank created the Inspection Panel, the first mechanism in any international organization through which nonstate actors that believed that they had been harmed by the failure of the Bank to comply with its own policies and procedures could have their concerns investigated by an independent body that reports to the Board of the Bank. This was an important breakthrough for all international organizations; subsequently, most MDBs created similar mechanisms, known

---

17   See, for example, Development Committee, Strengthening Governance and Accountability: Shareholder Stewardship and Oversight, DC2011-0006 (Apr. 4, 2011) (discussing selection process for World Bank president), available at <http://siteresources.worldbank.org/DEVCOMMINT/Documentation/22885978/DC2011-0006%28E%29Governance.pdf>; G20, Declaration on Strengthening the Financial System (Apr. 2, 2009), available at <http://www.g20.org/Documents/Fin_Deps_Fin_Reg_Annex_020409_-_1615_final.pdf>; G20, Declaration Summit on Financial Markets and the World Economy (Nov. 15, 2008), available at <https://www.g20.org/Documents/g20_summit_declaration.pdf>.

18   See "IMF Executive Board Selects Christine Lagarde as Managing Director," Press Release No. 11/259 (Jun. 28, 2011), available at: <http://www.imf.org/external/np/sec/pr/2011/pr11259.htm>.

collectively as independent accountability mechanisms.[19] Interestingly, the one IFI that has not created such a mechanism is the IMF.[20]

The IFIs have taken other steps to improve their accountability to their member states and to the public, who ultimately provide their funding. Significantly, the World Bank has agreed that it will establish dual performance reviews of its president by its Board and of the Board by the president and senior management. The goal of these reviews will be to ensure more effective performance by both parties. The World Bank is also working to create a corporate governance scorecard that will allow for more effective assessment of its governance and the efficacy of its operations.[21]

Transparency

The most substantial and far-reaching change in the operations of the IFIs has been in regard to transparency. All the IFIs have adopted information-disclosure policies.[22] These policies, many of which have been revised over time, have steadily increased the amount of information that the IFIs disclose. As a result, they are rapidly establishing as a standard operating procedure that all their documents and information be publicly available unless specifically decreed not to be so. It is important to note that this does not mean that all information is disclosed. In a number of cases, the clients of the IFIs—either the member state or the private sector borrower—claim that the information belongs to them and cannot be disclosed due to market sensitivities.

Operational Policies

The MDBs have always had policies to guide their staff in the complex operations that they undertake.[23] However, initially these policies were viewed as internal documents of no interest to anyone other than the staff. Over time, this perception changed, and the policies are now publicly available. One consequence of this development is that the policies, particularly those dealing with

---

19   For overviews of these various independent accountability mechanisms and comparisons of their structures and mandates, *see* Richard E. Bissell & Suresh Nanwani, *Multilateral Development Bank Accountability Mechanisms: Developments and Challenges*, 6(1) Manchester J. Intl. Econ. L., 2 (2009); Daniel D. Bradlow, *Private Complaints and International Organizations: A Comparative Study of the Independent Inspection Mechanisms in International Financial Institutions*, 36 Geo. J. Intl. L. 403 (2005).

20   *See* Daniel D. Bradlow, *Operational Policies and Procedures and an Ombudsman*, in *Accountability of the International Monetary Fund* 88 (Barry Carin & Angela Wood ed., Ashgate 2005).

21   *See,* for example, Development Committee, *supra* note 17, at 2 (discussing the creation of a corporate scorecard for the World Bank Group).

22   *See,* for example, IMF, FactSheet Transparency at the IMF (Mar. 24, 2011), available at <http://www.imf.org/external/np/exr/facts/trans.htm>; World Bank Policy on Access to Information (Jul. 1, 2010), available at <http://www-wds.worldbank.org/external/default/WDSContentServer/WDSP/IB/2010/06/03/000112742_20100603084843/Rendered/PDF/548730Access0I1y0Statement01Final1.pdf>.

23   *See,* for example, the World Bank Operational Manual, available at <http://web.worldbank.org/WBSITE/EXTERNAL/PROJECTS/EXTPOLICIES/EXTOPMANUAL/0,,menuPK:6470 1637~pagePK:51628525~piPK:64857279~theSitePK:502184,00.html>.

the controversial social and environmental aspects of the MDB operations, have become the subject of great public interest and public debate. These policies have also tended to be the ones most often invoked in the requests for inspection to the independent accountability mechanisms.

One consequence of this development is that the MDBs have recognized that their policies have significance and relevance outside the institutions and that their external stakeholders have the capacity to influence the content of these policies. As a result, the MDBs have begun to develop informal, transparent, and participatory procedures for making these policies.[24] The World Bank Group, in particular, has used such informal procedures with sufficient frequency that it is developing an implicit rule-making procedure that involves disclosure of policy drafts, opportunities for public comment on these drafts, and explanations of how the public comments have been addressed by the institution in formulating the final versions of the policy.

Interestingly, the other IFIs have not followed this practice in a consistent way. Most of the regional MDBs have occasionally provided opportunities for public consultation on drafts of policies and practices, particularly in regard to the structuring or amending of their independent accountability mechanisms. However, they have not regularly done so in regard to their substantive operational policies. The IMF has not developed such an implicit policy, partly because it does not have a comparable set of publicly available operational policies. It does, however, have some policies that are publicly available and, in at least one case—its policy on conditionality—it followed a process similar to the evolving process in the World Bank:[25] the policy was developed in a relatively transparent and participatory process.

Principles for Assessing the Governance of the MDBs

This section formulates five principles that can help assess the efficacy of the governance reforms undertaken by the IFIs: a holistic approach to development; flexible management; respect for applicable international law; coordinated specialization; and good administrative practice.

Holistic Approach to Development

The original vision of development as an economic process that focuses on growth, as measured by gross domestic product (GDP) per capita, is no longer seen as sufficient. It is now recognized that the development of individuals and societies is influenced by both noneconomic factors and economic criteria.[26] This insight has led to a new understanding of development as a

---

24   *See* David B. Hunter, *International Law and Public Participation in Policy-Making at the International Financial Institutions*, in *International Financial Institutions and International Law* 199 (Daniel D. Bradlow & David B. Hunter ed., Kluwer Law International 2010).

25   *See*, Bradlow, *supra* note 20.

26   UNDP, *Human Development Report 1990* (Oxford U. Press 1990); Amartya Sen, *Development*

comprehensive and holistic process that involves intertwined economic, environmental, social, cultural, political, and even ethical dimensions. According to this view, the economic aspects of development and its social, political, environmental, and cultural aspects are all components of one dynamically integrated process. Thus, one measure of the performance of the IFIs should be the extent to which their own governance arrangements support their institutions' ability to implement this holistic vision of development.

Flexible Management

The principle of flexible management means that the governance and operations of the IFIs must be sufficiently flexible and dynamic that they can adapt to the differing and changing needs, circumstances, and activities of their diverse stakeholders. For example, the IFIs must have the ability to assist member states with the technical, institutional, and economic capacity to design, implement, and manage large, complex operations, often with substantial social, environmental, and cultural impacts and policy implications; to help countries with limited technical, institutional, and economic capacity undertake infrastructure projects and governance reform projects that are both commensurate with their management capacity and appropriately scaled to meet their needs; and to finance and support smaller-scale operations that are more focused on directly meeting the needs of the poor and other vulnerable population groups in their member states.

Two corollaries follow from the principle of flexible management. First, the IFIs themselves need to have personnel and the management systems that enable them to effectively respond to the broad range of needs of their member states; they need to ensure that their staff has both the social and the cultural background necessary to understand the people and countries in which they operate and the technical expertise and professional experience to meet the demands of their member states. In addition, the IFIs need to have effective feedback mechanisms so that they can understand all the impacts of their operations in their borrower countries. Without such capacity to learn lessons from their operations, the IFIs are unlikely to fully understand their successes and failures and are more likely to repeat the failures. In addition, they are less likely to be able to identify problems in their operations in a timely manner and to mitigate any unintended or unanticipated adverse consequences of these operations.

Second, given the broad range and diversity of the demands on IFI's services, no IFI can fully meet the needs of its member states. Consequently, the IMF, the World Bank, and the other MDBs need some mechanism for coordinating their operations and ensuring that together the organizations can effectively address their member states' demands. One possible approach for

---

as *Freedom* (Alfred Knopf 1999); Declaration on the Right to Development, GA Res. 41/128, UN GAOR, 41st Sess./UN Doc. A/RES/41/128 (Dec. 4, 1986). *See* also, Daniel D. Bradlow, *Differing Conceptions of Development and the Content of International Development Law,* 21S. Afr. J. Hum. Rights 47 (2005).

ensuring that overall these institutions function in a flexible, efficient, and not unduly centralized manner is based on the principle of subsidiarity,[27] which holds that all decisions should be taken at the lowest level in the system compatible with effective decision making. This principle is complicated to implement because it must apply both in standard operating conditions and in crisis situations, which may require that decision-making authority be moved to a different level in the system or institution than is the case during standard operating conditions.

Respect for Applicable International Law

All the IFIs are formal international organizations created by treaties. Consequently, they are subjects of international law and should comply with applicable international legal principles.[28] Although international law does not offer many detailed standards that the IFIs can apply to international financial transactions, it does provide general principles that they can use in structuring their governance arrangements.[29] In particular, the IFIs' governance structures and decision-making principles should conform to universally applicable customary and treaty-based international legal principles. Four sets of principles are pertinent in this regard.[30]

Sovereignty

The first is the principle of respect for national sovereignty, which must be respected even though, by joining an IFI, a state agrees to surrender some decision-making autonomy in return for the benefits of participation in the IFI. This means that, even though their different power and wealth characteristics and the particular voting rules in the various IFIs mean, de facto, that the amount of independence the member states give up on joining the IFI will be related to their power and wealth and their need for the services of the particular IFI, all member states remain sovereign states with equal international

---

27 The principle of subsidiarity is defined in Article 5 of the treaty establishing the European Community. It is intended to ensure that decisions are made as closely as possible to the citizen and that constant checks are made as to whether action at the community level is justified in light of the possibilities available at the national, regional, or local level. Specifically, it is the principle whereby the union does not take action (except in the areas that fall within its exclusive competence) unless the potential action would be more effective than action taken at a national, regional, or local level. This principle is closely bound up with the principles of proportionality and necessity, which require that any action by the union not go beyond what is necessary to achieve the objectives of the treaty. *See* the definition of subsidiarity at <http://europa.eu/scadplus/glossary/subsidiarity_en.htm>.

28 *See*, for example, Philippe Sands & Pierre Klein, *Bowett's: Law of International Institutions* (6th ed., Sweet & Maxwell 2009); Jan Klabbers, *An Introduction to International Institutional Law* (Cambridge U. Press 2007); Henry G. Schermers & Niels M. Blokker, *International Institutional Law: Unity within Diversity* (4th ed., Martinus Nijhoff 2003).

29 Daniel D. Bradlow, *International Law and the Operations of the IFIs*, in *International Financial Institutions and International Law* 1 (Daniel D. Bradlow & David B. Hunter ed., Kluwer Law International 2010).

30 *See*, generally, Ian Brownlie, *Principles of Public International Law* (7th ed., Oxford U. Press 2008).

legal status. Thus, the principle of national sovereignty imposes some constraint on the demands that an IFI can place on a particular member state and should help each member state preserve as much independence and policy space as is practicable in its relation with each IFI and consistent with the demands of overall effective global financial governance.

Nondiscrimination

The principle of nondiscrimination applies to both the member states of the IFIs and all those nonstate actors with which the IFIs interact or which are directly affected by their operations. The principle of nondiscrimination means that all similarly situated states and nonstate actors should receive similar treatment in their dealings with the IFIs and that those who are differently situated should receive differential treatment that reflects the differences in their situations. The key question thus becomes what standards can be used for ensuring that all stakeholders receive treatment that is fair and reasonable.

Although the IFIs should base their treatment of all states on the same principles, they should apply these principles in a way that is responsive to the similarities and differences in the situations of each member state and of the affected nonstate actors.

Recognition should be given to the fact that weaker and poorer states are significantly different in capacities from rich and powerful nations. One way of implementing this standard could be to apply the general principle of special and differential treatment that is applicable in a number of international legal contexts, for example, in international environment and international trade law, to international financial governance. In the IFI governance context, this principle means that special attention is paid to ensuring that weak and poor countries are able to enjoy a meaningful level of participation in international financial decision-making structures, even when their participation is based on principles such as weighted voting. For example, in cases where it is not possible to offer states a full seat at the decision-making table,[31] one alternative could be that the organization create a mechanism through which these states and their citizens can raise concerns in connection with any decisions that adversely affect them and that they do not believe are receiving adequate attention at the relevant decision-making level in the IFI.

The relevant principles applicable to how IFIs should treat natural persons are derived largely from customary international law. This means that they should be derived from the Universal Declaration of Human Rights, which is now considered to be part of customary international law.[32] Pursuant to

---

31 For example, boards of executive directors at the IFIs would become too large and unwieldy if all poor and weak member states were full participants in the boards' deliberations that directly affect them.

32 Universal Declaration of Human Rights, GA Res. 217(III), UN GAOR, 3d Sess., Supp. No. 13, UN Doc. A/810 (1948); Report of the Special Representative of the Secretary-General on the Issue of Human Rights and Transnational Corporations and Other Business

this document, individuals, at a minimum, are entitled to expect that the IFIs respect and protect their social, economic, and cultural rights, such as rights to housing, health care, education, jobs, and social security. The IFIs should also ensure that member states' operations do not de facto undermine respect for or protection of their civil and political rights, such as rights to freedom of speech and association.[33]

The situation of juridical persons is more complex because judicial persons are not clearly covered by the Universal Declaration of Human Rights. However, the treatment of foreign juridical persons is covered by the customary international law on state responsibility.

State Responsibility

Pursuant to the principles applicable to state responsibility for treatment of foreigners located in the sovereign's home territory,[34] states have an obligation to provide foreign legal persons who are present in the state with fair and equitable treatment. This means that foreign entities should receive treatment that conforms to certain minimum standards, a term not clearly defined in international law, but that at least must be comparable to the treatment of similarly situated domestic institutions. This principle does not necessarily mean that foreign entities should receive the same treatment received by domestic institutions that, because of the particular roles they play in the domestic political economy, have different relations to the state and the market than the foreign entities.

International Environmental Law

The principles derived from international environmental law[35] impose on financial regulators an obligation to insist that financial institutions fully understand the environmental and social impacts of their policies and procedures and of their individual transactions.

The principle of respect for applicable international law, therefore, establishes a third test for good governance, namely, to what extent the governance arrangements of the IFIs promote respect for national sovereignty,

---

Enterprises, paragraph 38, UN Doc. A/HRC/4/35 (2007); also, see, generally, Hurst Hannum, *The UDHR in National and International Law*, 3(2) Health and Human Rights 144 (1998).

33   For an overview of the World Bank's approach to human rights, see Robert Danino, *Legal Opinion on Human Rights and the Work of the World Bank* (Jan. 27, 2006), available at <http://www.ifiwatchnet.org/sites/ifiwatchnet.org/files/DaninoLegalOpinion0106.pd>; Siobhán McInerney-Lankford, *International Financial Institutions and Human Rights*, in *International Financial Institutions and International Law* 239 (Daniel D. Bradlow & David B. Hunter ed., Kluwer Law International 2010).

34   *See,* generally, GA Res. 62/61, UN GAOR, 61st Sess., UN Doc. A/RES/62/61 (Jan. 8, 2008); Report of the International Law Commission on the Work of Its Fifty-Third Session, UN GAOR, 56th Sess., at 43, Supp. No. 10, UN Doc. A/56/10 (2001).

35   *See,* generally, David Hunter, James Salzman, & Durwood Zaelke, *International Environmental Law and Policy* (Foundation Press 2006).

the environment, and the rights of all natural and legal stakeholders in the international financial system.

Coordinated Specialization

The principle of coordinated specialization acknowledges that, even though development is holistic and all aspects of international governance are interconnected, IFIs cannot function efficiently without a limited mandate and without the officials in these institutions having the requisite specialist knowledge to implement these mandates. Thus, the principle of coordinated specialization has two requirements in regard to the governance of the IFIs. First, the IFIs' mandates must be clearly defined and limited to their areas of expertise, while not being insensitive to how their specialization fits into a holistic vision of development. Second, the IFIs cannot ignore the fact that other international organizations have expertise in and responsibility for other aspects of development. Consequently, to ensure that all these organizations help their member states implement a holistic vision of development, IFIs need to ensure some form of coordination between themselves and other international organizations. An effective mechanism for ensuring such coordination must be transparent and predictable. It may also need some dispute-settlement mechanism.

In this respect, it is important to keep in mind that the IFIs are not free actors. In some cases, they are subject to receiving "direction" from other intergovernmental entities in which their member states are active. For example, the IMF, together with the World Bank Group and the FSB, is subject to "guidance" from the Group of Twenty (G20). Previously the IMF and the World Bank would receive such "guidance" from the G7.

This principle, therefore, establishes a fourth standard for measuring the adequacy of the IFIs' governance arrangements: the extent to which the IFIs coordinate their policies and operations with other relevant international institutions, each of which has its own limited mandate. At a minimum, this principle should ensure that the IFIs offer other international institutions with relevant areas of expertise a meaningful and timely opportunity to raise their concerns with them. It should also offer both the IFIs and all other relevant international organizations a mechanism for resolving tensions between them.

Good Administrative Practice

The basic principles of good administrative practice in global governance are the same as those applicable to any public institution:[36] transparency, predictability, participation, accountability, and clear and predictable rule making. In the case of IFIs, these principles have the following meanings:

---

36   *See,* generally, Benedict Kingsbury, Nico Krisch, & Richard B. Stewart, *The Emergence of Global Administrative Law,* 68 Law & Contemp. Probs. 15 (2005), and the materials available on the Institute for International Law and Justice website at <http://iilj.org/publications>.

- *Transparency:* This term refers to the degree to which an IFI discloses information about its operational policies and procedures, operations, and decisions.[37]

- *Predictability:* IFIs should conduct their operations in a manner that is sufficiently open so that their procedures, decisions, and actions are predictable and understandable to all stakeholders. An aspect of predictability is that decisions should be made in a timely manner.

- *Participation:* Mechanisms exist for allowing all stakeholders to participate in the decisions of the IFIs that directly affect them. Important factors to consider are both the extent to which member states are able to express their views and have their votes factored into the decisions of the IFIs and the extent to which nonstate actors can participate in those operational and policy decisions that affect them.[38]

- *Accountability:* Mechanisms are available to both member states and nonstate actors to hold the IFIs accountable for their actions.[39] These mechanisms include the channels through which member states can raise their concerns to the highest levels of the institution and the means that nonstate actors can use to have claims that they have been harmed by the actions and decisions of the IFIs heard by the institution. These claims can arise from the contractual relations between these actors and the IFIs as well as from noncontractual claims.

- *Clear and predictable rule making:* IFIs follow certain procedures in formulating and adopting their operational policies and procedures. Best practice in IFI rule making means that the IFIs provide all stakeholders who have an interest in a proposed policy with an opportunity to comment on the proposed policy, to submit comments on it, and to receive feedback on their comments and submissions. Ideally, the procedures to follow in developing these policies and procedures should be based on clear and predictable rules and should not be ad hoc.[40]

Thus, the final standard against which the IFI governance reforms can be measured is the extent to which they comply with the five principles of good administrative practice stated above.

Summary of the Standards for Evaluating the Governance of the MDBs

Based on the five principles, following are questions that can be used for assessing the adequacy of the IFIs' governance arrangements:

---

37 *See supra* note 23.

38 *See,* for example, Hunter, *supra* note 24.

39 *See* Bissell & Nanwani, *supra* note 19; Bradlow, *supra* note 19.

40 *See* Hunter, *supra* note 24.

- Are the governance arrangements based on a holistic understanding of development?

- Are the management arrangements sufficiently flexible to deal with the full range of demands that the IFIs can expect from their diverse collection of stakeholders?

- Do the mechanisms for IFI governance implement and comply with all applicable international law standards, including respect for national sovereignty, the rights of all natural and legal persons, and responsible environmental law practices?

- Do the decision-making procedures in the IFIs provide adequate and meaningful opportunities for coordination with other international institutions with relevant expertise?

- Do IFI governance arrangements comply with the principles of good administrative practice, namely, transparency, predictability, participation, accountability, and clear and predictable rule making?

An Assessment of the IFI Governance Reforms against the Principles of Good Governance

This section evaluates the extent to which the reforms that have been undertaken in the governance of the IFIs conform to the principles of good governance set out above.

Approach to Holistic Development

The MDBs have substantially expanded their view of development over the past twenty years. They all recognize that development is not purely an economic process and that it involves social, cultural, political, and environmental aspects. This recognition is reflected, for example, in the safeguard policies of the IBRD and IDA, the performance standards of the IFC, and the comparable social, poverty, gender, and environmental policies at the other MDBs. In addition, the MDBs recognize that political factors are an integral part of the development process, as evidenced by their work in postconflict states and on governance issues and in their statements on such sensitive development issues as gender and indigenous people. However, the IMF, although not denying that development involves more than purely economic matters, has not explicitly incorporated a more holistic vision of development into its operations. This is in part a reflection of its specific monetary and macroeconomic focus. It may also be due, in part, to the fact that the IMF lacks the publicly available operational policies in which the MDBs tend to express their visions of specific aspects of the development process.

Despite the MDBs' impressive efforts in regard to this principle of good governance, one aspect of their approach to development is deficient. They have been slow to link their operational policies and procedures explicitly to applicable international legal treaties and conventions and to the declarations, standards, and norms developed in other international organizations and forums. This can be seen, for example, in the policies on involuntary resettlement and indigenous people at the World Bank and the regional MDBs, which are silent about the applicable human rights conventions, declarations, and norms and do not discuss how they should be applied in their operations. This deficiency in the policies of the MDBs, particularly in regard to human rights, may be related to the political prohibitions in their articles, to the fact that the MDBs are not signatories to the relevant international legal instruments, and to the fact that often the applicable standards provide limited guidance on how they should be implemented in dealing with such complex issues as the appropriate standard of compensation in cases of involuntary resettlement or the nature of consent required from indigenous people. Nevertheless, it is striking that the MDBs' policies do not explicitly reference either the applicable international legal standards or the applicable decisions, declarations, or other legal instruments of those institutions and bodies that have the expertise and the mandate to develop the standards and norms in these areas that are outside the scope of the MDBs' assigned areas of expertise. In this sense, the MDBs' implementation of a holistic vision of development is linked to their performance under the coordinated specialization criteria.

Flexible Management

Although the IFIs have often worked together in specific projects or programs in a country, their interactions have grown more intense over the past twenty years. As a result, they are making greater efforts to ensure better coordination between their operations within specific member states. For example, the MDBs now work to ensure cross-debarments for contractors found to be involved in fraudulent and corrupt practices.[41] In addition, the independent accountability mechanisms of these institutions have begun to cooperate in joint investigations of projects for which they have received requests for investigations.[42]

The IFIs have enhanced their ability to respond flexibly to developments in their member states by increasing the voice and vote of underrepresented member states in their governance. For example, the World Bank, by increasing the share of the total votes of their developing- and emerging-market member states and by agreeing to a third African chair on its Board of Executive Directors, has enhanced the ability of at least some of these countries to have their voices heard in its decision-making process. In theory, these changes should result in the World Bank being more responsive to the needs and concerns of these countries.

---

41   See Stephen S. Zimmerman & Frank A. Fariello, Jr., *Coordinating the Fight against Fraud and Corruption: Agreement on Cross-Debarment among Multilateral Development Banks* in this volume.

42   For example, the independent review mechanism of the African Development Bank and the World Bank Inspection Panel conducted a joint investigation of the Bujagali Dam Project in Uganda in 2007.

In addition, the World Bank, with the encouragement of the Development Committee, has initiated a number of organizational reforms designed to enhance its responsiveness to the needs of its member states.[43] It is actively working to improve the diversity of its workforce so that it is more representative of its full membership. The Bank is also actively working to devolve more management authority from its headquarters to its field staff, which is expected to grow as a portion of the total staff. This effort has been slowed down because of budgetary constraints and the complexities of this change. Finally, and more controversially, the Bank is working to make the formulation of its country assistance strategies a more participatory process that is more responsive to the development priorities of its member states. Some external observers of the Bank are concerned that this effort is intended more to weaken the Bank's current operational policies and standards than to enhance each member state's influence in the Bank's assistance strategy for that country.

These developments could result in a more responsive Bank and in more effective allocations of responsibilities between the World Bank and the other IFIs working in a particular country or region. This in turn would suggest greater compliance with the principle of flexible management. However, these reforms are relatively new, and it is too soon to predict how successful they will be.

Respect for Applicable International Law

It is clear that all the IFIs respect and work to comply fully with the requirements of their constituent treaties and with the customary international law and general principles of law applicable to them as international organizations. However, it is also clear that it is easier for the IFIs to enunciate these principles than to apply them in the day-to-day management of their operations and in their governance.

In this regard, it is particularly noteworthy how few of the MDBs' operational policies mention relevant international legal principles or explain how management and staff are expected to ensure that operations comply with applicable international law. To some extent, this can be explained by the fact that the applicable international legal principles, standards, and norms are not easy to implement, particularly within the contexts of complex development projects. However, the MDBs cannot avoid dealing with the issues addressed by these international legal principles in their operations, particularly those that raise safeguard issues.[44] Consequently, the fact that there is no reference to these principles, standards, and norms in their policies means, in effect, that

---

43   *See* Development Committee, Enhancing Voice and Participation of Developing and Transitional Countries in the World Bank Group: Update and Proposal for Discussion, paragraphs 26–27(a–c), DC2009-0011 (Sep. 29, 2009), available at <http://siteresources.worldbank.org/DEVCOMMINT/Documentation/22335196/DC2009-0011%28E%29Voice.pdf>.

44   World Bank, Safeguard Policies, available at <http://go.worldbank.org/WTA1ODE7T0>; International Finance Corporation, Performance Standards, available at <http://www.ifc.org/ifcext/sustainability.nsf/Content/PerformanceStandards>.

the MDBs are leaving to their staff and management the responsibility of deciding whether or not to utilize applicable legal principles in their implementation of MDB policies and how to interpret these principles when they do use them. Staff decisions in regard to the applicability and the interpretation of these principles may then be reviewed by the independent accountability mechanisms during their review of the complaints that they receive and the investigations that they conduct of staff and management compliance with the applicable policies, in particular MDB-funded operations.

The decisions of the MDB staff and management and the reports of the independent accountability mechanisms, therefore, amount to precedents of how various international actors are determining the applicability and the interpretation of particular principles, norms, and standards of international law in specific cases. Thus, the MDBs are helping to make the international law in regard to complex issues such as the rights of indigenous people, involuntarily resettled people, treatment of physical cultural property, women in development, and environmental issues such as impact assessments, responsibilities to mitigate adverse impacts, and the nonnavigable uses of international waterways.

Unfortunately, the MDBs appear reluctant to accept the concept that they are de facto establishing precedents on important legal issues that can influence the evolution of these legal principles. As a result, they have not accepted the responsibilities that go with performing law-making functions and so are not effectively meeting their obligations in terms of transparency, participation, and reasoned decision making in this regard. Thus, the MDBs cannot be viewed as being fully compliant with this principle of good governance.

Coordinated Specialization

The issue of IFIs' relationships with other international organizations has become more important because the scope of their missions has expanded so dramatically.[45] As a result, IFIs are now undertaking work that involves the specialized competence of other international organizations.[46] For example, the World Bank funds public health projects that overlap with the expertise and responsibility of the World Health Organization; it funds agricultural projects that may "trespass" into the jurisdiction of the Food and Agricultural Organization or the International Fund for Agricultural Development. However, although they may do so on an ad hoc basis, IFIs are not formally obligated to consult with other international organizations or to ensure that there is effective coordination among them. Given this situation, it is noteworthy

---

45   Claudio Grossman & Daniel Bradlow, *Limited Mandates and Intertwined Problems: A New Challenge for the World Bank and the IMF,* 17(3) H. Rig. Quar. 411, 412 (Aug. 1995) (also available at <http://papers.ssrn.com/sol3/papers.cfm?abstract_id=1365257>).

46   In this regard, it is important to recall that the World Bank and the IMF are, de jure, specialized agencies of the UN system. Thus, they are expected to report to the UN Economic and Social Council, and their relationships with the United Nations are governed by the terms of their relationship agreement.

that the Bank is making a concerted effort to coordinate its operations in crises and emergencies with other international organizations. In this regard, the Bank has updated its operational policies so that they acknowledge the leadership role of other international organizations, particularly the United Nations, in certain aspects of this work.[47]

One consequence of this development is that, because IFIs tends to be better resourced than most other international organizations, they are able to more effectively influence their member states' approaches to issues in which they are interested, even when other organizations have expertise in those issues and the mandate to operate in regard to them. Thus the IFIs tend to become de facto, although not de jure, the primary international bodies for dealing with these issues.

Because their role in these issues is not consistent with the division of responsibility inherent in having international organizations with limited mandates, the IFIs have a distorting effect on the overall global governance architecture. In particular, the MDBs' assertion of influence in a particular area tends to undermine the authority and effectiveness of any other international organization with responsibility in that area. In addition, it creates governance challenges for the IFIs because it means that they have assumed responsibilities in regard to issues and activities for which their governance structures were not necessarily designed.

One possible channel for mitigating this distortion could be through the international bodies in which either the IFIs and these other international organizations or their member states are represented. This is particularly applicable to bodies such as the United Nations Economic and Social Council, the International Monetary and Finance Committee, the Development Committee, and the G20. Although these bodies are not unaware of these governance challenges, they have not yet effectively addressed the global governance distortions that result from the IFIs asserting authority over issues that fall within the expertise and mandate of other international organizations.

Good Administrative Practice

The best way for determining how well the IFIs are complying with this principle of good global governance is to assess their performance in regard to four aspects of good administrative practice.

Transparency

Over the past 20 years, MDBs have gone from being closed institutions to being probably the most open international organizations. During this time,

---

47   *See* OP 2.30—Development Cooperation and Conflict and OP 8.00—Rapid Response to Crises and Emergencies, available at <http://web.worldbank.org/WBSITE/EXTERNAL/PROJECTS/EXTPOLICIES/EXTOPMANUAL/0,,menuPK:64701637~pagePK:51628525~piPK:64857279~theSitePK:502184,00.html>. Also *see,* generally, *Towards a New Framework for a Rapid Bank Response to Crises and Emergencies* (World Bank Jan. 12, 2007).

they have developed, amended, and redrafted information-disclosure policies so that today their basic operational assumption is the opposite of what it used to be: today all information is presumed to be disclosable unless there is a good reason not to disclose the information.[48] The primary exceptions to this operating assumption are categories of information that do not technically belong to the organization or could have market implications for the institution, the member state, or other actors in the transaction. This is particularly an issue in regard to IFI transactions that involve the private sector. As a result, the IFIs are in substantial compliance with this principle of good governance.

Participation

The MDBs have made an effort to encourage consultations with all affected peoples in their particular operations. Thus, under the safeguard policies of the IBRD and the IDA, the performance standards of the IFC, and the social and environmental policies of other MDBs, the MDBs are all required to consult with indigenous people, those who will feel the impacts of the MDBs' operations, and those who will be adversely affected by these operations.[49] In addition, as indicated above, the World Bank has made substantial efforts to incorporate, albeit informally, greater public participation into its rule-making procedures, at least for those rules of greatest interest to nonstate actors.[50] Given these developments, the IFIs can be deemed to have made significant progress toward meeting the applicable standards for good governance but are not as yet fully compliant with them.

Accountability

The IFIs have made significant progress in promoting accountability to nonstate stakeholders in their operations. By 2010, all the MDBs had established independent accountability mechanisms that were authorized to investigate claims from nonstate actors that they had been harmed or threatened with harm by the failure of the MDBs to comply with their operational policies and procedures in regard to a particular project.[51] These mechanisms usually are independent of the management and staff of the MDBs and report directly to the boards of executive directors of these institutions.

The IMF is the only IFI that has not created an independent accountability mechanism. Although the nature of its operations is different from that of the other IFIs, the IMF could establish some form of independent accountability mechanism.[52] In fact, given that its operations have important impacts on nonstate actors in its member countries and that these impacts are not necessarily well understood by the institution, the creation of such a mechanism

---

48   *See supra* note 22.

49   *See supra* note 44.

50   *See* Hunter, *supra* note 24.

51   *See* Bissell & Nanwani, *supra* note 19; Bradlow, *supra* note 19.

52   For one model of such a mechanism for the IMF, *see* Bradlow, *supra* note 20.

could have a positive impact on the IMF and thus improve the quality of its operations. In this regard, it should be noted that the IMF's board of executive directors can introduce such a mechanism on its own authority without any decision by its board of governors or amendment to its articles of agreement.

The IFIs have made less progress in promoting accountability to those member states that use their financial services but are not directly represented on their boards. These states, in principle, can use the executive director representing them on the board of the particular IFI to raise issues of concern to the board. However, the current constituency system of representation at the board level makes this difficult in practice. The reason is that the executive director may not believe it is an opportune time to raise a claim to his or her board colleagues; there are only limited ways for a frustrated state to hold the executive director accountable for this decision. In this regard, the recent efforts of the World Bank and the IMF to hold their boards more accountable for their performance is a positive development that has the potential to result in more accountable IFIs.

Clear and Predictable Rule Making

Over the past twenty years, the World Bank Group has evolved an informal practice of participatory rule making. The practice has not yet been formalized into a "policy on policies," but it has evolved from the practice the Bank has followed in connection with important Bank Group policies. Thus, the practice of consulting interested stakeholders, providing opportunities for interested parties to submit comments on draft policies, and responding to these comments was a prominent feature of the development of the indigenous people's policy and the information-disclosure policy in the IBRD and the IDA and of the review of the performance standards in the IFC. This practice has also been used in the reviews of the independent accountability mechanisms of the IBRD and IDA, the European Bank for Reconstruction and Development, the Inter-American Development Bank, the Asian Development Bank, and the African Development Bank. A version of it was followed by the IMF in its review of its conditionality policy. However, this practice remains informal and at the discretion of an IFI. It is not yet consistent practice, and the process followed in each policy review is a matter for discussion and negotiation. Therefore, while the IFIs have made substantial progress toward meeting this principle of good governance, they are not yet fully compliant with it.

Conclusion

This chapter has set out a framework for assessing efforts to reform the governance of the IFIs. Based on this framework, it is clear that, while the recent reform efforts, despite the setback in the selection of the current IMF managing director, have the potential to produce substantial changes in the operations and governance of the IFIs, they do not fully comply with the principles of good governance. However, the international community, in light of the problems in Europe, the uncertain state of the global economy, and the ongoing shifts in global power, seems to have exhausted its interest in reforming IFI governance. Consequently, there is little reason to expect the additional reforms that are required for full compliance to be undertaken in the short run. Nevertheless, it is to be hoped that in the medium term the shift in the balance of global political and economic power will create the conditions for another round of significant IFI governance reforms.

Should the Political Prohibition in Charters of International Financial Institutions Be Revisited?

The Case of the World Bank

HASSANE CISSÉ

The World Bank Articles of Agreement[1] prohibit the Bank from interfering in the political affairs of its members and from taking political considerations into account in its decision making.[2] Three principal clauses in the articles enshrine the prohibition on interference with the political affairs of Bank members. First, Article IV, Section 10, of the IBRD articles stipulates that "the Bank and its officers *shall not interfere in the political affairs of any member*; nor *shall they be influenced in their decisions by the political character of [a] member. . . . only economic considerations* shall be relevant to their decisions, and these . . . shall be weighed impartially in order to achieve the purposes stated in Article I" [emphasis added].[3] Article III, Section 5(b), of the IBRD articles provides that the Bank's loan proceeds *must be used only for their intended purposes and "with due attention" to economy "without regard to political or other non-economic influences or considerations"* [emphasis added].[4] Finally, Article V, Section 5(c), of the IBRD articles states that "the President, officers and staff . . . owe their duty entirely to the Bank," and each member is obliged to respect that duty and "[r]efrain from all attempts to influence any of them in the discharge of their duties."

In essence, these provisions allow the Bank to make decisions based only on economic considerations and impose a mutual obligation on the member states and the Bank's president, officers, and staff to respect the independence of each other.[5]

---

1   In this chapter, unless the context otherwise requires, the terms "Bank" and "the World Bank" include both the International Bank for Reconstruction and Development (IBRD) and the International Development Association (IDA), and the term "articles" denotes the Articles of Agreement of the IBRD and the IDA.

2   The author would like to thank Evarist Baimu and Aristeidis Panou for their invaluable assistance in the preparation of this article. Useful comments were also provided by Frank A. Fariello, Vikram Raghavan, Adrian Di Giovanni, Siobhán McInerney-Lankford, and Jonathan Heath. Responsibility for any errors or omissions remains with the author.

3   IDA Articles of Agreement, Article V, Section 6.

4   IDA Articles of Agreement, Article V, Section 1(g).

5   Aron Broches, *International Legal Aspects of the Operations of the World Bank*, 98 Recueil des Cours 297, 327–28 (1959).

The political prohibition provisions were enshrined in the articles for two reasons that have to do with the nature of the Bank as an international financial institution and as a cooperative international organization with membership from all over the world.[6] A financial intermediary, the Bank borrows funds from capital markets to finance its lending operations. If political consider- ations were to drive decisions, the smooth operation of the Bank's business model might be affected, because the Bank might have difficulty maintain- ing the confidence of the capital markets where it sources its funds as well as the member countries to which it lends the borrowed funds.[7] In addition, given the diversity of political beliefs and approaches of its membership, the "Bank's broad acceptability and its continuity required depoliticization of its decisions and impartiality in weighting the economic considerations which alone were to be taken into account."[8] Indeed one explanation of the political prohibition provision is that it was adopted "with the Soviet Union princi- pally in mind."[9]

The nonpolitical[10] mandate of the Bank can be also explained as a char- acteristic of the functionalist approach to international organizations,[11] which was widely accepted at the time.[12] This approach is reflected in the technical and focused mandate of other international organizations that came to life before or after World War II (e.g., the International Labour Organization; the United Nations Educational, Scientific and Cultural Organization; the Food and Agriculture Organization, the World Health Organization, and the Inter- national Civil Aviation Organization). In the case of the Bank, the functionalist approach reflected deeper views about development and prevailing economic

------

6   The political prohibition provisions, especially Article IV, Section 10, do not seem to have
     been adopted with the purpose of protecting the sovereign equality of member states. How-
     ever, given the use of similar language in Article 15(8) of the Covenant of the League of
     Nations and Article 2(7) of the UN Charter, one could argue that an incidental function of
     Article IV, Section 10, is to protect and retain the sovereignty of states; *see* Bartram S. Brown,
     The United States and the Politicization of the World Bank: Issues of International Law and Policy
     103 (Kegan Paul International 1992).

7   Ibrahim F. I. Shihata, *World Bank Legal Papers* 226 (Kluwer Law International 2000).

8   *Id.*

9   Edward S. Mason & Robert E. Asher, *The World Bank since Bretton Woods* 27 (Brookings Insti-
     tution Press 1973). The Soviet Union never became a member of the Bank. In addition, Soviet
     scholars viewed the Bank as an organization that was used by the United States to pursue
     its own policy; *see* Grigori I. Tunkin, *Theory of International Law* 315 (William Butler trans.,
     Harvard U. Press 1974).

10   The Bank's mandate could be characterized as nonpolitical but not apolitical. The word
     "apolitical" is defined as "unconcerned *with* or detached from politics"; the word "nonpo-
     litical" is defined as "not involved in politics"; *see New Shorter Oxford English Dictionary* 94,
     1935 (Lesley Brown ed., 3d ed., Oxford U. Press 1993).

11   David Mitrany, *The Functional Approach to World Organization*, 24 Intl. Aff. 350 (1948).

12   Philippe Sands & Pierre Klein, *Bowett's Law of International Institutions* 76 (6th ed., Sweet and
     Maxwell 2009). For an overview of the intellectual theory of international organizations, *see*
     José E. Alvarez, *International Organizations as Law-Makers* 17–57 (Oxford U. Press 2005).

thought in the post–World War II period. From this perspective, development was seen primarily as an economic endeavor, aimed at increasing gross domestic product and productivity of economies, which in turn could be achieved through technical, nonpolitical solutions. Interestingly, no sooner did the functionalist approach diminish than instances of politicization became apparent in international organizations.[13]

The political prohibition clause played a significant role in the development of the Bank's governance in the mid-1940s.[14] The British vision of creating technical and expert organizations, free of political control, informed the UK position about the role of the executive directors in both the Bank and the International Monetary Fund (IMF).[15] The British had argued for part-time executive directors with financial expertise, but the American preference for full-time directors prevailed.[16]

The political prohibition clause has continued to shape the Bank's policy decisions over the years. On the one hand, the Bank has declined to predicate its lending on the human rights record of the governments of member countries or the form of political governance found in such states (whether a monarchy or a republic, a single-party or multiparty state). At the same time, with the Board-endorsed general counsel's legal opinions, the Bank has been able to expand to new areas previously regarded as lying outside the

---

13   Gene M. Lyons, David A. Baldwin, & Donald W. Mcnemar, *The "Politicization" Issue in the UN Specialized Agencies*, in *The Changing United Nations: Options for the United States* 81 (David A. Kay ed., Praeger 1978), and Victor-Yves Ghebali, *The Politicisation of UN Specialised Agencies: A Preliminary Analysis*, 14 Millennium: J. of Intl. Studs. 317 (1985). These studies note that the Bank was at the time one of the least "politicized" specialized agencies of the UN.

14   The Bretton Woods institutions were established in 1944, but several issues—such as the seat of the institutions, the adoption of bylaws, and the relations between Management and the executive directors—were resolved at the inaugural meeting of the Board of Governors at Savannah, Georgia, in March 1946.

15   The British delegation argued, early in the negotiations, that "so far as practicable . . . we want to aim at a governing structure doing a technical job and developing a sense of corporate responsibility to all members, and not the need to guard the interests of particular countries," quoted in Kenneth W. Dam, *The Rules of the Game: Reform and Evolution in the International Monetary System* 111 (U. of Chicago Press 1982).

16   These decisions earned the skepticism of Lord Keynes, one of the main architects of the Bretton Woods institutions, who eloquently warned the Board of Governors in Savannah about the dangers of politicization: "I hope that Mr. Kelchner [chief of the Division of International Conferences, U.S. Department of State] has not made any mistake and that there is no malicious fairy, no Carabosse, whom he has overlooked and forgotten to ask to the party. For if so, the curses which that bad fairy will pronounce will, I feel sure, run as follows: 'You two brats shall grow up politicians; your every thought and act shall have an arrière-pensée; everything you determine shall not be for its own merits but because of something else.' If this should happen, then the best that could befall—and that is how it might turn out— would be for the children to fall into an eternal slumber, never to waken or be heard in the courts and markets of mankind." *Id.*, at 114.

boundaries of the political prohibition clause, including legal and judicial re-form and governance[17] issues.[18]

Although the language of the political prohibition clause appears to be absolute and does not permit any exceptions,[19] from early on "certain political circumstances were recognized" in Bank practice as being "clearly relevant to the Bank's work" and could not be disregarded.[20] For example, a World Bank document dated April 1968 acknowledges that the Bank "cannot ignore conditions of obvious internal political instability or uncertainty which may directly affect the economic prospects of a borrower."[21]

This chapter traces and evaluates the development and the controversies of the political prohibition provision. More specifically, it discusses the evolution of application of the political prohibition clause in Bank practice. It then notes that contemporary criticism of the political prohibition takes two forms, with some critics expressing concern about the extent of the Bank's mission creep while others worry that the Bank's sense of responsibility has not kept pace with its expanding role. It evaluates the tools available for evolving, through amendment or interpretation, the political prohibition and explores in greater depth the arguments for and against retaining the prohibition. It concludes with the suggestion that the Bank's business might be best served by continuing the institutional practice of adapting political prohibition through creative but responsible interpretation.

Evolving Practice: Overview of Current Frontier Issues

The drafters of the IBRD articles in 1944 and the IDA articles in the 1950s were mindful of the needs of their time. It is unlikely that they could have anticipated all evolving challenges and the changing operating environment that the Bank and its member countries would face. Some of these contemporary challenges and the changing political, social, and economic landscape might have a bearing on the political prohibition clause. These challenges include

---

17 Governance is defined as "the traditions and institutions by which authority in a country is exercised. This includes (a) the process by which governments are selected, monitored and replaced; (b) the capacity of the government to effectively formulate and implement sound policies; and (c) the respect of citizens and the state for the institutions that govern economic and social interactions among them." *See* Daniel Kaufmann, Aart Kraay, & Massimo Mastruzzi, *The Worldwide Governance Indicators: Methodology and Analytical Issues,* World Bank Policy Research Working Paper No. 5430 (Sep. 2010).

18 Ibrahim F. I. Shihata, *The Creative Role of the Lawyer—Example: The Office of the World Bank's General Counsel,* 48 Cath. U.L. Rev. 1041, 1048 (1998–99). Because the authority to interpret the articles is vested in the Board of Executive Directors of the Bank, the legal opinion of the general counsel does not constitute an authoritative interpretation of the articles. Nevertheless, the Board's endorsement (or concurrence) grants such opinions the authority that allow for their incorporation into the Bank's practice.

19 Shihata, *supra* note 7, at 227.

20 *Id.,* at 228.

21 *Id.,* quoting World Bank, IDA and IFC—Policies and Operations 43.

- Increasingly more intense and violent conflict within states, which is creating an environment quite different in nature from the post–World War II European landscape that the Bank was established to address. The resultant weak postconflict states of today are in need of enhanced support to prevent recurrence of conflict.[22] There is also a need for a different approach to the growing number of "fragile pockets"—territory outside government control or under a government's weakening control leading to illicit trade in drugs and gang warfare and raising issues of criminal justice.

- Evolving demands of member countries, including a growing share of development policy lending relative to specific investment lending and a growing number of requests for fee-based services.

- Unconstitutional changes in government and the evolving response of regional organizations to such changes.

- Increased complexity of the international aid architecture at the global level, creating growing pressure to achieve harmonization and coordination among bilateral and multilateral donors in the Bank's member countries, which brings up its own challenges, because most of these bilateral donors do not have constraints such as the Bank's political prohibition.

- Increased impact of and challenges posed by emerging problems such as climate change, compounding threats such as overpopulation pressures, increased scarcity of resources, and environmental degradation faced by vulnerable societies.

- Growing recognition that many challenges of development stem from poor governance and a failure to achieve the participation of citizens in government and to develop a sense of public ownership of government. This recognition requires, in turn, engagement with actors at all levels of society, not just within the executive.

The Bank's response to the challenges over the years is a story of an incremental, measured opening of space for the Bank to intervene[23] in ways that may not have been envisaged in 1944.[24] This trend is illustrated in the examples discussed below, which are drawn from some of the most pressing and challenging issues faced by the Bank in recent years.

---

22 Paul Collier, *The Bottom Billion: Why the Poorest Countries Are Failing and What Can Be Done about It* 177–78 (Oxford U. Press 2007).

23 The terms "intervene" and "intervention"—as used with reference to the Bank in this chapter—include all Bank activities, including lending, grants, trust funds, donor and aid coordination, research, and economic and sector work, all of which are subject to the provision of the articles.

24 Some key terms in the articles that are of relevance to political prohibition, including "development," "political considerations," "economic considerations," "productive purposes," and "political affairs," are not defined in the articles. Their meaning has thus been subject to interpretation and has evolved.

Dealing with Extraconstitutional Governments

The Bank's operational framework restricts it from operating in the territory of a member without the approval of that member state. In situations where there is no government, the Bank operates upon the request of the internat-ional community and with the approval of its Board.[25] A challenge arises when more than one government purports to represent a member country or when a government comes to power through means that are unconstitutional. This is a common phenomenon in many states that borrow from the Bank.

The Bank's early approach was that it recognized the political situation, that is, the existence of a de facto government, but it took into account only the economic effects of this situation. The IBRD/IDA report on the economic po-sition and prospects of Greece in 1969 acknowledged that a military govern-ment was installed in 1967 and noted that "certain constitutional provisions on civil rights remain in abeyance, to be made effective at the discretion of the military authorities."[26] The report evaluated only the economic implications of this situation, and stated that the economic slowdown that emerged at the end of 1966 was significantly reinforced by political uncertainties in 1967–68.[27] The way the situation in Greece was treated by the Bank is characteristic of how the Bank's staff understood the political prohibition provisions, realizing that a political situation cannot be taken into account per se but that its economic implications can be factored into the Bank's decision making.

In the mid-1960s, the Bank codified certain legal and policy principles for dealing with de facto governments.[28] It subsequently issued more compre-hensive policies,[29] including the current framework provided by Operational Policy (OP)/Bank Procedure (BP) 7.30—Dealings with de Facto Governments, issued in July 2001.

---

25 Consistent with this practice, in 2008, the Bank provided resources drawn from its Food Price Crisis Trust Fund to finance a project in Somalia implemented by the Food and Agri-culture Organization following a request by the UN resident representative in Somalia, and with the approval of the Bank's Board.

26 Greece was condemned by the European Commission on Human Rights for violations of human rights enshrined in the European Convention on Human Rights (ECHR); to avoid embarrassment, Greece withdrew from the Council of Europe and denounced the ECHR.

27 During the seven years of the military regime, the Bank offered a number of loans to Greece.

28 During the early years of its existence, the Bank took a rather strict attitude and in certain cases took the position that it could not properly enter into agreements with the de facto governments because of their extraconstitutional nature and the absence of parliaments. As experience with de facto governments accumulated, the Bank's attitude became more prag-matic, and loans were made to de facto governments.

29 The first principles were issued in 1964; these were revised and restated in Operational Man-ual Statement (OMS) No. 1.27, issued in June 1978. In 1991, Operational Directive (OD) 7.30 superseded OMS No. 1.27. In November 1994, the Bank replaced OD 7.30 with OP/BP 7.30.

In determining its attitude toward de facto governments,[30] the Bank has been concerned with the establishment of a proper legal framework for its loans. Consequently, OP/BP 7.30 states that the Bank's decision to make a loan to a de facto government does not constitute "approval," nor does the Bank's refusal to make a loan indicate "disapproval" of the government.[31] According to the policy framework, immediately upon the emergence of a de facto government, the Bank takes three actions. First, it avoids processing any further withdrawal requests under existing loans, with certain limited exceptions, pending consultations with the de facto government.[32] Second, it gathers all relevant information about the status, policies, and public acceptance of the new government. Third, it initiates an internal process to determine whether to continue or suspend disbursements under existing loans and whether to process new operations.[33]

Under the existing policy, the Bank cannot stop disbursements under existing loans unless there are grounds for such suspension or termination based on existing agreements or pragmatic concerns about the de facto government's ability and willingness to honor its obligations under the loan agreements. The situation seems more perplexing with respect to new operations. In this case, the policy requires that the Bank weigh (a) whether a new lending would expose the Bank to additional legal or political risks; (b) whether the government is in effective control of the country and enjoys a reasonable degree of stability and public acceptance; (c) whether the government generally recognizes the country's past international obligations; (d) the number of countries that have recognized the government or dealt with it as the government of the country; and (e) the position of other international organizations toward the government.[34]

Since 2001, the Bank has applied OP/BP 7.30 to a number of situations involving coups and other extraconstitutional changes in governments. Most of these situations arose from military coups, and the Bank's operational response varied from case to case.[35]

In the context of dealing with de facto governments, the Bank has developed an approach that allows it to take into account a number of factors that

---

30   Under the current framework, a government is de facto if it comes into, or remains in, power "by means not provided for in the country's constitution, such as a coup d'état, revolution, usurpation, abrogation, or suspension of the constitution."

31   OP 7.30, paragraph 2. In this connection, the policy notes that the Bank, under its articles, is required to refrain from interference in the political affairs of any member and may not be influenced in its decision by the political character of the member or members served.

32   BP 7.30, paragraph 2. The Bank may also reach an informal agreement with the new regime to withhold disbursements until a decision has been made on dealing with it.

33   *Id.*, at paragraph 1.

34   *See* OP 7.30, paragraph 5.

35   In some instances, the emergence of de facto governments caused certain institutional and governance implications, especially in connection with the appointment of governors and executive directors and annual meeting representation.

might seem to go beyond its obligation to evaluate only economic considerations but are consistent with the Bank's will to act as a good and responsible
international citizen.[36] OP 7.30 elevates the role of other international organizations, an approach that appears to fit with subsequent regional efforts to
deal with the problem of unconstitutional governments.[37] In this respect, it
gives the Bank grounds to consider (formally or informally, implicitly or explicitly) the decisions of these organizations with respect to unconstitutional
changes occurring in their region.[38]

Security, Conflicts, and Postconflict Situations

The World Bank was originally established to support the reconstruction of
Europe in the post–World War II period. Although, it quickly moved from reconstruction to development,[39] conflicts continued to occur and acquired new
forms. Thus, the operations of the Bank proliferated in countries affected by
conflict. The "R" in IBRD started to obtain a new meaning.[40]

For many years, the Bank did not have a comprehensive policy on how to
deal with hostilities. It took a case-by-case approach. In deciding whether it
could lend or continue lending to conflict-affected countries, the Bank would
take into account the extent to which (a) the expected benefits from the project
would be realized; (b) the borrowing country would be in a position to repay
the loan; (c) the borrowing country could effectively carry out the project; and
(d) Bank staff could safely and regularly visit project areas for purposes of supervision. In that respect, only economic factors appeared to guide the Bank's
approach toward conflict-affected countries.

In 1997, the Bank endorsed A Framework for World Bank Involvement in
Post-conflict Reconstruction to guide work in postconflict countries, followed
by the adoption of OP 2.30—Development Cooperation and Conflict. Three
main principles guide the Bank's involvement in conflict-affected areas.[41] The
first principle is that the Bank should act within the limits of its mandate,
without aspiring to be the "world government" and leaving peacemaking,
peacekeeping, and humanitarian relief to other organizations or donors.[42] The
second principle is a reminder of the political prohibition provisions, which

---

36   OP 7.30, paragraph 2, serves as a reminder of the political prohibition in the Bank's articles.

37   *See* Inter-American Democratic Charter (2001); the Declaration on Unconstitutional Changes
      of Government (2000)—Lomé Declaration; and the African Charter on Democracy, Elections,
      and Governance (2007).

38   This could also be interpreted as an adequate division of core competencies.

39   Mason & Asher, *supra* note 9, at 52–53. This was mainly due to the development of the
      Marshall Plan by the United States, which aimed to support the reconstruction of Europe.

40   Robert B. Zoellick, Speech, *Fragile States: Securing Development* (International Institute for
      Strategic Studies, Geneva, Switzerland, Sep. 12, 2008), available at <http://go.worldbank
      .org/QS00KKG8A0>.

41   Maurizio Ragazzi, *The Role of the World Bank in Conflict-Afflicted Areas*, 95 Am. Socy. Intl. L.
      Proc. 240, 243 (2001).

42   OP 2.30, paragraph 3(a).

require that the Bank refrain from interfering "in the domestic affairs of a member or from questioning the political character of a member."[43] Although a corollary of the principle of noninterference is that the Bank cannot operate in the territory of a member state without its consent, this OP goes a step further, allowing the international community to invite the Bank to provide assistance if is no government in power. The third principle is that the resources and facilities of the World Bank may be used only for the benefit of its member states.[44]

Besides OP 2.30, the Bank adopted an operational policy (OP/BP 8.50) to deal with emergencies and crises in 1995.[45] This policy was replaced by OP 8.00—Rapid Response to Crises and Emergencies in 2007; it provides that the Bank, at the request of the borrower state,[46] can "support, in partnership with other donors, an integrated emergency recovery program that includes activities outside the Bank's traditional areas, such as relief, security, and specialized peace-building."[47]

It is important to note that, although OP 8.00 expands the Bank's work compared with OP 2.30, the two policies are to be considered together. In addition, the Bank recognizes the comparative advantage of other organizations in providing support in the areas of security and political governance (and humanitarian relief).[48] Following are some specific examples of the activities that the Bank has financed in postconflict situations.

In relation to peacekeeping, the Bank does not finance negotiations of peace accords, political reconciliation processes, or the organization of elections. However, four specific areas within the broader realm of peacebuilding are eligible for the Bank's support: contributions to peace processes, contributions to peacebuilding and social and economic stabilization programs, leadership training, and state building.[49]

---

43 *Id.*, at paragraph 3(b). Interestingly, this OP uses slightly different language than IBRD Articles of Agreement, Article IV, Section 10; OP 2.30 uses the phrase "domestic affairs," the IBRD article, the term "political affairs." Although the articles are the "constitution" of the Bank, the choice of different wording in OP 2.30 might constitute a subsequent interpretation of Article IV, Section 10, endorsed by the Board; *see* Article 31(3) of the Vienna Convention on the Law of Treaties.

44 OP 2.30, paragraph 3(c). Under certain requirements, the Bank can and has provided assistance to nonmember states, but this goes beyond the scope of this chapter.

45 OP/BP 8.50—Emergency Recovery Assistance (Aug. 1995).

46 The request could come from the international community if there is no government in power.

47 OP 8.00, paragraph 5.

48 *Id.*, at endnote 7.

49 Examples of involvement in peace processes include Bosnia and Herzegovina and the Dayton peace process, Burundi (1999), Sierra Leone (1999), Democratic Republic of Congo and Rwanda (2002–03), West Bank and Gaza (2005), Kosovo (2005–07). Examples of Bank contributions to integrated peacebuilding and social and economic stabilization programs include Bosnia and Herzegovina (1994), Timor-Leste (1999), Democratic Republic of Congo (2006), Afghanistan, Liberia (2006), Haiti, Rwanda (1996), the Greater Lakes Regional Strategy for Demobilization and Reintegration, and the Democratic Republic of Congo Emergency Ur-

With respect to humanitarian relief, the Bank generally refrains from providing support because of the constraints imposed by its mandate and out of respect for the existing division of powers and the comparative advantage of other international organizations.[50] However, there are no strict divisions between but rather a continuum in the postemergency phases of recovery from relief to development. The Bank may thus have a comparative expertise and may respond to requests for assistance from governments and international partners, requests that could otherwise be characterized as requests for relief, where such assistance is in support of affected persons, including cash transfers and other livelihood support to refugees, internally displaced persons, and demobilized ex-combatants.[51]

The Bank does not finance peacekeeping operations, expenditures incurred by a recipient for military purposes (including the security-related elements of security sector reform), or the disarmament of combatants. These activities are left to national governments, bilateral donors, and, where appropriate, the United Nations. In this regard, the Bank refrains from establishing specialized trust funds that would finance *only* police or other security expenditures.[52] However, in responding to requests from member states, donors, and international organizations, the Bank has provided financial support or administered donor contributions for demobilization and reintegration programs; undertaken the responsibilities of a fiscal agent to manage trust fund resources intended for certain police-related expenditures; supported the development of veterans' policy and pensions; and carried out analytic work relating to the security sector. The Bank has undertaken these activities in partnership with other donors or international agencies with expertise in peace and security matters and within the legal and policy parameters relating to postconflict and reconstruction assistance.[53]

Overall, the Bank has developed an active role in conflict and postconflict situations, with two significant caveats.

---

ban and Social Rehabilitation Project. Examples of leadership capacity-building activities include Central African Republic (2004) and Liberia (2006). Examples of Bank involvement in state building include Sudan and Afghanistan.

50   Legal Opinion from Ana Palacio, senior vice president and group general counsel, *Peace-Building, Security, and Relief Issues under the Bank's Policy Framework for Rapid Response to Crises and Emergencies*, at paragraph 25 (Mar. 22, 2007).

51   Examples include Turkey's response to the Marmara earthquake, the Sri Lanka Tsunami Emergency Recovery Program, and the Pakistan Earthquake Emergency Recovery Credit.

52   According to OP 14.40—Trust Funds, activities financed from trust funds should be in keeping with the IBRD and IDA Articles of Agreement.

53   Relevant examples are the Sierra Leone Disarmament, Demobilization, and Reintegration (DDR) Program (multidonor trust fund), the Rwanda Demobilization and Reintegration Program, support to the police through the Afghanistan Reconstruction Trust Fund, the Timor-Leste Transition Support Program, the West Bank and Gaza Public Financial Management, the Reform Trust Fund, the Veterans Policy Preparation in Timor-Leste, the Cambodia Public Expenditure Review, the Central African Republic Public Financial Management Review of the Security Sector, and the Croatia Social and Economic Recovery Project.

The first is the articulation of activities that the Bank explicitly refuses to support because it cannot reconcile them with its legitimate mandate and the requirement to finance expenditures only for "productive purposes."[54] For example, the Bank explicitly does not finance military expenditures.[55] Although the Bank has declined to finance military expenditures, it has established guidelines under which it can intervene in landmine–clearing activities. As in other frontier areas of support, the Bank intervention is permitted if the landmine–clearance activity can be justified on economic grounds, taking into account the scarcity of financial resources; is an integral part of a development project or a prelude to a future development project or program to be adopted by the recipient; and is carried out under the responsibility of civilian authorities.

The Bank's activities in these areas must be triggered either by the member states or by other donors and international organizations. The Bank is a member-driven organization responsive to the necessities and the realities of the contemporary world, trying to preserve its character as an impartial and technical financial institution.

Criminal Justice Reform

The Bank is increasingly requested to intervene in countries, especially countries emerging from conflict,[56] undertaking reforms in the criminal justice sector.[57] Often recipient countries request the Bank to assist in restructuring police or prison forces or customs enforcement agencies, supporting specialized units that deal with unique problems such as gangs, narcotics, and illegal fishing. In other instances, the Bank has been requested to intervene in activities aimed at addressing the issue of urban violence. In considering these requests, the Bank has to draw the line between permissible and nonpermissible interventions, considering its political prohibition constraints.

---

54 IBRD Articles of Agreement, Article I.

55 "The Bank does not finance . . . military expenditures, nor does it provide direct support for disarming combatants." *See* OP 6.00—Bank Financing, April 2004, footnote 2. Indeed, the Bank cannot even consider whether military expenditures at a certain level are appropriate. In his oral statement at the Board meeting on December 13, 1991, the Bank general counsel opined that the Bank should not determine the appropriate level of military expenditures for a country because this is "a matter which is typically based on security and political considerations, and as such falls . . . outside the Bank's legally authorized powers, let alone its competence." *See* Shihata, *supra* note 7, at 218.

56 The importance of strengthening the criminal justice sector so as to assist fragile and conflict-affected states to break the cycle of violence was highlighted in the 2011 World Development Report on Conflict, Security, and Development; available at <http://wdr2011.worldbank .org/fulltext>.

57 The criminal justice sector comprises all the institutions, processes, and services responsible for the prevention, investigation, adjudication, treatment, and response to illegal behaviors. The sector includes the institutions traditionally associated with it, such as police, prosecutors, public defenders, courts, and prisons, as well as a wide range of other institutions such as private police, victim services, private lawyers and bar associations, human rights and ombudsman's offices, addiction treatment programs, and community service programs.

In at least two instances, Sudan and Afghanistan, the Bank has been involved in supporting police and prisons-related activities carried out by other agencies. In both cases, funds were provided by donors through multidonor trust funds administered by the Bank, whereby the Bank agreed to serve in a limited capacity as a fiscal agent and played no appraisal, supervision, or monitoring and evaluation role with respect to those activities. In Afghanistan, the Bank channeled funds contributed by various donors to the Afghanistan Reconstruction Trust Fund, administered by the Bank, to the United Nations Development Programme (UNDP) for financing certain police-related expenses, including salaries, uniforms, and vehicles of Afghan police.[58]

The Bank has historically refrained from involvement in criminal justice because criminal justice is considered to be an exercise of sovereign power, and thus any involvement would require the Bank to make political judgments. However, selective interventions in the criminal justice sector may fall within the development purpose of the Bank and thus can be legally permissible if the Bank is satisfied that the proposed intervention is grounded in an appropriate and objective economic rationale showing that the intervention is relevant to the overall economic development of the country in which it is to be carried out; the risk of political interference is properly assessed; and any potential risks are appropriately mitigated. The Bank is in the process of developing an approach to engaging in the criminal justice sector.

In order to mitigate the risks of political interference that any involvement in the criminal justice sector might entail, the Bank generally uses a risk-management approach. Under this approach, the Bank distinguishes three categories of activities:

- Activities that likely pose no serious legal issues, for example, public health activities that target the general population and may include participants in the criminal justice sector, such as the prison population or police, as risk groups; case management systems for courts of general jurisdiction; research on crime or criminal justice; and support to help poor and vulnerable people to deal with the effects of crime.

- Activities that pose serious legal issues, for example, financing the purchase of weapons and other lethal equipment and antinarcotics law enforcement campaigns, and supporting specific law enforcement cases. Furthermore, this category likely includes areas of criminal justice that entail inherently high risks of political involvement, such as political crimes or crimes against the state, as well as the investigation, prosecution, and judgment of persons suspected of terrorist activities.

- "Gray areas" that merit particular attention, for example, the financing of policing, prosecutors, and prisons.

---

58   Legal Note from Ko-Yung Tung, vice president and general counsel, *Police-Related Activities under the Afghanistan Reconstruction Trust Fund* (Mar. 26, 2002) (copy on file with the author).

Human Rights

The debate about human rights in the Bank's policies and operations is not new, and much has been written about this issue.[59] In the early years, both the Bank and the IMF took the position that human rights fall outside their field of work.[60] However, two instances forced the Bank to seriously reflect upon its position toward human rights.[61]

The first one was in the 1960s, when the UN General Assembly recommended that the Bank suspend lending to Portugal and South Africa because of their colonial and apartheid policies.[62] The legal dispute that followed was centered on the interpretation of the Bank's political prohibition and the Relationship Agreement between the Bank and the United Nations.[63] The Bank at that time adopted a very narrow interpretation of its Articles of Agreement, arguing that the "policies and the conduct which are being condemned by the General Assembly constitute an essential element of the 'political character' of those States" and the Bank "may and does take into consideration, and is influenced in its lending decisions by, the economic effects which stem from the political character of a member and from the censures and condemnations of that member by United Nations organs." The Bank also stressed that it "must consider such economic effects together with all other relevant economic factors, in the light of the purposes of the Organization. What it is precluded from considering is the political character of a member as an independent criterion for decision."[64]

---

59   For one of the first comprehensive approaches to this issue, *see* Victoria E. Marmorstein, *World Bank Power to Consider Human Rights Factors in Loan Decisions*, 13 J. Intl. L. & Econ. 113 (1978). *See* also John D. Ciorciari, *The Lawful Scope of Human Rights Criteria in World Bank Credit Decisions: An Interpretive Analysis of the IBRD and IDA Articles of Agreement*, 33 Cornell Intl. L.J. 331 (2000); Sigrun Skogly, *The Human Rights Obligations of the World Bank and the International Monetary Fund* (Cavendish 2001); Dana L. Clark, *The World Bank and Human Rights: The Need for Greater Accountability*, 15 Harv. Hum. Rights J. 205 (2002); Korinna Horta, *Rhetoric and Reality: Human Rights and the World Bank*, 15 Harv. Hum. Rights J. 227 (2002); Mac Darrow, *Between Light and Shadow: The World Bank, the International Monetary Fund and International Human Rights Law* (Hart 2003); Bahram Ghazi, *The IMF, the World Bank Group and the Question of Human Rights* (Transnational 2005); Margot E. Salomon, *International Economic Governance and Human Rights Accountability*, in *Casting the Net Wider: Human Rights, Development and New Duty-Bearers* 153 (Margot E. Salomon, Arne Tostensen, & Wouter Vandenhole ed., Intersentia 2007).

60   It is characteristic that the Bretton Woods institutions refused to participate at the negotiations of the International Covenant on Economic, Social, and Cultural Rights in the early 1950s, even though they constitute UN specialized agencies; *see* François Gianviti, *Economic, Social and Cultural Human Rights and the International Monetary Fund*, in *Non-state Actors and Human Rights* 113, 114 (Philip Alston ed., Oxford U. Press 2005).

61   Ibrahim F. I. Shihata, *The World Bank and Human Rights: An Analysis of the Legal Issues and the Records of Achievements*, 17 Denv. J. Int. L. & Policy 39, 40–48 (1988).

62   For an overview of the UN-Bank dispute, *see* Samuel A. Bleicher, *UN v. IBRD: A Dilemma of Functionalism*, 24 Intl. Org. 31 (1970).

63   Agreement between the United Nations and the International Bank for Reconstruction and Development, November 15, 1947, 16 U.N.T.S. 346.

64   Comments of the Legal Department on the United Nations Confidential Memorandum on "The International Bank for Reconstruction and Development and Implementation of

Although the debate was not framed in terms of a possible obligation of the Bank to respect human rights, the Bank believed that it was not allowed under its mandate to use the human rights record of a government as a criterion for making loan decisions. It did, however, stop lending to South Africa and Portugal, invoking reasons not related to the political situation of these countries.[65]

A decade after this controversy, the Bank was again confronted with the issue of human rights in its borrowing countries when the United States enacted legislation that authorized and instructed the U.S. executive director to oppose any loan agreement to a country with a consistent pattern of gross human rights violations. This legislation posed the question of whether the Bank's political prohibition covers the activities of the executive directors. Although the Legal Department answered this question in the affirmative, it noted that there was no legal sanction to challenge the vote of an executive director motivated by political considerations.[66]

In the above two instances, the Bank was clearly reluctant to include human rights considerations in its mandate. However, it has not been indifferent to these concerns. Indeed, the Bank has long funded studies and operations that promote social, economic, and cultural rights such as health, education, freedom from poverty, and employment. It has also influenced the status of vulnerable groups such as women, children, indigenous people, and refugees.[67] Some critics of the Bank's record on human rights acknowledge that the Bank's role has been focused more on promoting social and economic rights and less on promoting civil and political rights;[68] these critics have expressed concern about the lack of a consistent and comprehensive human rights policy in the Bank's practice.[69]

United Nations General Assembly Resolutions to Withhold Assistance of Any Kind to the Governments of Portugal and South Africa" (May 4, 1967), available at United Nations Juridical Y.B. 108, 124 (1967).

65   Shihata, *supra* note 61, at 44.

66   *Id.*, at 45–46. This argument highlights the fact that the Bank could implicitly take into account human rights considerations, if that was the true will of its member states.

67   *Id.*, at 48–65.

68   However, there is research showing that substantial violations of political and civil rights are related to lower economic growth; *see* Robert J. Barro, *Determinants of Economic Growth: A Cross-Country Empirical Study* (MIT Press 1997). In addition, the distinction between the two sets of rights is not accepted under the principles of indivisibility, interdependency, and interrelatedness; *see* Vienna Declaration and Programme for Action, UN Doc. A/CONF.157/ 23 (1993).

69   Daniel D. Bradlow, *The World Bank, the IMF, and Human Rights*, 6 Transnatl. L. & Contemp. Probs. 47 (1996).

Ibrahim Shihata argues that "the Bank may even take political human rights violations into account if they are so pervasive and repugnant as to clearly affect the country's investment climate and its economic performance."[70] In line with this more "careful" approach toward civil and political rights, Shihata suggests that the Bank "may not pursue the financing of a project if the freedom of speech and assembly required" for the purposes of "consultation with the local NGOs and participation of affected people in the design of many projects to be financed by the Bank" is lacking.[71]

The above developments, the debate over the relationship between human rights and development,[72] and the fact that some bilateral donors and other multilateral agencies have adopted human rights "as the normative foundation of their aid policies"[73] have led the World Bank to reexamine its views on these issues and inquire to what extent it should follow this trend.

Indeed, in the past decade, the Bank's officials have been more active in speaking openly about human rights. James Wolfensohn, president of the World Bank at the time, said in a paper published in 2005 that the Bank might need to mention more often the "R" word: "rights."[74] The Bank's general counsel at the time also promoted human rights inside the Bank.[75] In 2005, he was asked by senior management to explore the extent to which human rights considerations would be consistent with the Bank's mandate. This request resulted in a January 2006 note, *Legal Opinion on Human Rights and the Work of the World Bank*, which concluded that "the Articles of Agreement permit, and in some cases require, the Bank to recognize the human rights dimensions of its development policies and activities, since it is now evident that human rights are an intrinsic part of the Bank's mission."[76]

Although outsiders considered that this opinion had a limited impact inside the Bank,[77] a former bank general counsel, Ana Palacio, has acknowledged that the above-mentioned legal opinion

---

70 Ibrahim F. I. Shihata, *The Dynamic Evolution of International Organizations: The Case of the World Bank*, 2 J. of the Hist. of Intl. L. 217, 246 (2000).

71 *Id.*

72 Philip Alston, *Ships Passing in the Night: The Current State of the Human Rights and Development Debate Seen through the Lens of the Millennium Development Goals*, 27 Hum. Rights Q. 755 (2005).

73 Arne Tostensen, *The Bretton Woods Institutions: Human Rights and the PRSPs*, in *Casting the Net Wider: Human Rights, Development and New Duty-Bearers* 185, 185 (Margot E. Salomon, Arne Tostensen, & Wouter Vandenhole ed., Intersentia 2007).

74 James D. Wolfensohn, *Some Reflections on Human Rights and Development*, in *Human Rights and Development: Towards Mutual Enforcement* 19, 22 (Philip Alston & Mary Robinson ed., Oxford U. Press 2005).

75 Roberto Dañino, *Legal Aspects of the World Bank's Work on Human Rights*, in *Human Rights and Development: Towards Mutual Enforcement* 509 (Philip Alston & Mary Robinson ed., Oxford U. Press 2005).

76 This legal note was never adopted by the Board. For this reason, it does not represent an official policy of the Bank.

77 Galit A. Sarfaty, *Why Culture Matters in International Institutions: The Marginality of Human Rights at the World Bank*, 103 Am. J. Intl. L. 647, 665 (2009).

marks a clear evolution from the pre-existing restrictive legal interpretation of the Bank's explicit consideration of human rights. It is
"permissive": allowing, but not mandating, action on the part of the
Bank in relation to human rights. It clarifies "the state of the law,"
and gives the Bank the necessary leeway to explore its proper role
in relation to human rights, updating the legal stance adopted internally to accord with the Bank's practice and the current international
legal context. It facilitates a more comprehensive understanding of
human rights in development, and enables the Bank to take these
issues into account where they are relevant. Finally, it represents a
point of departure for future legal analysis on human rights by the
Legal Vice-Presidency as well as my own thinking on this matter as
General Counsel of the World Bank Group.[78]

In addition, the Bank established the Nordic Trust Fund, which stands
as a first major initiative, at the programmatic level, of the Bank in the area
of human rights. To reconcile this development with the Bank's obligation of
noninterference, the Bank argued that there is scope for the Bank to engage in
human rights provided that engagement is undertaken in a nonpartisan, non-
ideological, and neutral manner and the reason for the engagement is related
to activities the Bank aims to support. This thinking reflects mainstream views
that the notion of sovereignty has evolved under international law and that
certain norms penetrate national boundaries (e.g., corruption, environmental
hazards, and war crimes).[79]

Despite the recent developments, the official approach of the Bank toward
human rights

is based on outlining the substantive and factual ways in which its
activities overlap with the human rights through the reach of Bank
projects and program areas touching upon human rights . . . the approach acknowledges the substantive interrelatedness of human
rights and development but remains non explicit in terms of the
direct or formal relevance of specific duties or international treaty
obligations.[80]

As an interim conclusion, one could argue that the political prohibition
is an important hurdle, but not the only hurdle, on a case-by-case or
project-by-project basis to the Bank's engagement with human rights. What
remains to be seen is the potential reaction of the member states if the Bank
were to take a position on human rights at a corporate level, for instance,
should there be a proposal for the adoption of a comprehensive Bank human

---

78 Ana Palacio, *The Way Forward: Human Rights and the World Bank* (Oct. 2006), available at
    <http://go.worldbank.org/RR8FOU4RG0>.

79 Dañino, *supra* note 75, at 517–20.

80 Siobhán McInerney-Lankford & Hans-Otto Sano, *Human Rights Indicators in Development: An
    Introduction* 6 (World Bank 2010).

rights policy.[81] It is important to note that states are bound by their treaty-based human rights obligations even when they act as members of the World Bank.[82] In this respect, some critics have argued that it is important to achieve "international policy coherence," which demands "coherence across policies governing different issues, as well as coherence in terms of their engagement with and participation in international organizations and processes."[83]

Governance, Participation, and Engagement with Bilateral Donors, Multilateral Agencies, and NGOs

Another issue connected to human rights is that of promoting democracy.[84] The Bank has been extremely cautious in addressing this issue. Although it is accepted that there is a link between democracy and development, the actual involvement of the Bank in the promotion of democracy could lead the Bank into politically charged areas that go beyond its mandate and competence.[85]

Indeed, the Bank explicitly does not support activities such as organizing or assisting political parties or setting up, monitoring, and running elections because these endeavors could collectively be seen as promoting democracy, and are thus considered to imply an inherently high risk of political interference.[86]

However, the Bank and its member countries have recognized the links between governance, corruption, growth, and poverty reduction.[87] In that context, the Bank has recently sought to strengthen its engagement on the demand side of governance,[88] requiring engagement with government and a

---

81   President Wolfensohn has said that "to some of our shareholders the very mention of human rights is inflammatory language"; James D. Wolfensohn, *Some Reflections on Human Rights and Development*, in *Human Rights and Development: Towards Mutual Enforcement* 19, 21 (Philip Alston & Mary Robinson ed., Oxford U. Press 2005).

82   *See* Article 60 of the Draft Articles on the Responsibility of International Organizations; *see* International Law Commission Report on the Work of Its Sixty-First Session (May 4–Jun. 5 and Jul. 6–Aug. 7, 2009) UN GAOR, 64th Sess., Supp. No. 10, at paragraph 50, UN Doc. A/64/10 (2009).

83   Siobhán McInerney-Lankford, *International Financial Institutions and Human Rights*, in *International Financial Institutions and International Law* 239, 265 (Daniel D. Bradlow & David B. Hunter ed., Kluwer Law International 2010).

84   There is an interesting discussion on whether there is a human right to democracy that goes beyond the scope of this chapter; *see*, inter alia, Thomas Franck, *The Emerging Right to Democratic Governance*, 86 Am. J. Intl. L. 46 (1992), and *Democratic Governance and International Law* (Gregory H. Fox & Brad R. Roth ed., Cambridge U. Press 2000).

85   Ibrahim F. I. Shihata, *Democracy and Development*, 46 Intl. & Comp. L.Q. 635 (1997).

86   World Bank Group, *Guidance Note on Bank Multi-stakeholder Engagement*, at paragraph 16 (Jun. 2009).

87   World Bank Group, Operations Policy and Country Services, *Implementation Plan for Strengthening World Bank Group Engagement on Governance and Anticorruption*, at paragraph 4 (Sep. 28, 2007).

88   "A governance system comprises a wide variety of processes, systems, organizations, and rules (that is, institutions) on the public bureaucracy 'supply' side and on the 'demand' side through which non-executive oversight institutions and citizens hold the bureaucracy accountable for performance"; *id.*, at paragraph 1.

wide range of other stakeholders, including parliaments, the media sector, and civil society, but always inside the limits of the political prohibition clause.

More specifically, the Bank has been engaged with parliaments in helping to strengthen responses to the poverty reduction strategy process and to understand the Bank's policies and practices. It has provided nonpartisan, technical capacity building and training to parliaments and parliamentary staff to help them fulfill their responsibilities, for instance, with regard to public accountability committees, their oversight role over government policy implementation, the budgetary process, and ensuring greater transparency in decision making.[89] This support is provided on a nonpartisan basis to the parliament as an institution and does not, either by design or in practice, alter the existing division of power or favor particular political members or forces within the institution.[90]

The main guidance in all these activities is that the Bank seek to avoid any involvement in partisan politics, which could be seen as the outer limit of the political prohibition clause.[91]

Moving away from the domestic level toward the field of cooperation between international actors, the Bank has been working with other donors in the spirit of the Paris Declaration on Aid Effectiveness (2005) in coordinating its development assistance to member countries. The mechanism is captured in a memorandum of understanding (MoU) or other nonbinding instruments—however designated. These instruments commit the donors to provide assistance, often in the form of budget support,[92] over the course of years. Occasionally, donors want certain principles that seem to fly in the face

---

89   For example, members of parliament from Ghana and Kiribati, building on their participation in training activities organized by the World Bank Institute and its partner institutions, have developed action plans and introduced new oversight mechanisms in their national system that have strengthened the capacity of government institutions.

90   World Bank Group, *Guidance Note on Bank Multi-stakeholder Engagement*, at paragraph 30 (Jun. 2009).

91   *Id.*, at paragraph 15.

92   From designation in the articles, as lending provided in special circumstances (as opposed to more standard investment lending), development policy lending (DPL, previously known as structural adjustment lending) has assumed a growing importance in the institution, particularly following the oil crisis of 1979 and debt crisis of the 1980s. *See* Andres Rigo Sureda, *Informality and Effectiveness in the Operation of the World Bank*, 6 J. Intl. Econ. L. 565, 570 (2003). The growth of DPL coincided with a growing involvement of the Bank in policy decision making in the member countries. In effect, DPL involves loans provided in exchange for good policies as defined by the lending institution. Occasionally, a policy action that has political overtones (touching on such subjects as governance, corruption, public participation) will slip in as conditionality; to avoid having to include conditionality with political overtone, the Bank has insisted on picking from a matrix of conditionalities agreed to with other donors only those conditionalities that are relevant to its economic development mandate. In this connection, the former general counsel of the Bank acknowledges that in their attempt to do what in their judgment is "essential for effective [development policy] lending" Bank staff often "find it relevant or useful to take certain political considerations into account" and indeed "[a]t times, they are blamed if they fail to do so." Shihata, *supra* note 7, at 220.

of the Bank's political prohibition constraints. In other instances, bilateral donors demand that the recipient government include previously marginalized
groups as a prerequisite for resumption of financial assistance, particularly in
countries emerging from (or at risk of falling into) violent civil conflict. Another challenge arises when donors seek to invoke the clause of the MoU to
suspend disbursement and expect the Bank to do the same, notwithstanding
its political prohibition clause.

The Bank response has been to sign these MoUs but to invoke the political
prohibition clause in seeking to free itself from provisions of these memoranda that involve interference with political affairs of member countries. It
has likewise insisted on refraining from exercising its remedies on the basis of
political considerations; the Bank would not, for example, suspend disbursement because the new government came into power through an election that,
in the overwhelming opinion of the international community, was not free
and fair. The Bank is required to exercise caution "when supporting broad or
integrated programs and participating in donor partnerships" to avoid being perceived as "encouraging other donors to take particular positions on
matters that are outside the Bank's mandate" and to ensure that it does not
endorse or appear to endorse "controversial program components or activities . . . that are inconsistent with the political prohibition."[93] In this regard,
in instances in which the Bank has found itself chairing donor meetings in
a country, the Bank has declined from serving as a conduit for political mes-
sages from bilateral donors to recipient governments.

The need to coordinate with other agencies is relevant when a multilateral
agency or regional organization adopts a decision imposing economic sanctions on countries where the Bank has operations. As a legal matter, the Bank
is an independent international organization not bound by decisions of any
other multilateral entity. However, it is required to pay due regard to the UN
Security Council's decisions made under Chapter VII of the UN Charter and
to take note of its members' obligations to comply with those decisions.[94]

Several UN Security Council resolutions have been made under Chapter VII of the UN Charter that target the Bank's member countries. However,
few refer specifically to the Bank or international financial institutions.[95] The
resolutions that do, tend not to articulate clear and specific action that the Bank
needs to take to comply with the resolution or direct the Bank to act in a manner inconsistent with its developmental mandate.[96] In any event, if the Bank

---

93 Legal Opinion from Ana Palacio, senior vice president and group general counsel, *Peace-
   Building, Security, and Relief Issues under the Bank's Policy Framework for Rapid Response to Crises
   and Emergencies*, at paragraph 19 (Mar. 22, 2007).

94 Article VI of Agreement between the United Nations and the International Bank for Reconstruction and Development, 16 United Nations Treaty Series 346 (1948).

95 *See*, for example, UN SCOR, 58th Sess., 4761st mtg., UN Doc. S/RES/1483 (2003).

96 *See*, for example, UN SCOR, 62d Sess., 5647th mtg., UN Doc. S/RES/1747 (2007), which
   called upon international financial institutions not to provide new financial assistance to
   Iran except for humanitarian and developmental purposes.

were to take action pursuant to its obligation to pay due regard to a Security Council decision, it would also have the obligation to ensure that its action was consistent with its articles, in particular the purposes provision and the political prohibition.

Fraud, Corruption, and Stolen Asset Recovery

The Bank's engagement with corruption is a long and interesting story. President Wolfensohn said that the general counsel once informed him that he was not allowed to use the "C" word.[97] Although prevention of corruption seems to have always been a legitimate objective of the Bank with respect to its lending operations,[98] it became a major issue in the Bank's development agenda only in 1996.[99] Because corruption is widely perceived as a matter of governance,[100] and the Bank had already been involved in the governance sector,[101] the Bank did not provoke great controversy when it explained why it was legitimate for the Bank to deal with the "cancer of corruption."

When explaining the Bank's involvement in addressing corruption issues, the general counsel cautioned that the Bank is not a "world government": "its role as a world reformer" should not go beyond its defined purposes, and should avoid "complex political considerations." However, the Bank did develop the operational experience "to deal with a large number of governance and institutional issues which have direct relevance to its development mandate, without entanglement in partisan domestic politics and corruption had become a

---

97   Wolfensohn, *supra* note 81, at 22.

98   *See* IBRD Articles of Agreement, Article III, Section 5(b). In 1966, in the context of the dispute with the UN over the loans to Portugal and South Africa, when the Bank adopted a very restrictive interpretation of the political prohibition provision, the general counsel hinted that corruption could be taken into account when making loan decisions. Responding to an observation by the representative of Zambia, who had heard "of countries applying for loans which had not been forthcoming because of alleged extravagance, corruption or bad planning," the general counsel said that "the extravagance mentioned might have been caused by a policy of national or military prestige, or might have been merely a way of life. Corruption would, of course, cut down on the use of resources. Some countries could obviously afford to sin a little, economically, and still progress, while others were forced to make the most, in every sense, of what they had. The situation was that all factors were taken into consideration and a judgment reached with which an observer was then free to agree or disagree."

99   In the 1996 annual meetings address, President Wolfensohn publicly committed to "deal with the cancer of corruption." The 1997 World Development Report entitled "The State in a Changing World" contains a chapter on corruption; it was followed by the influential publication "Helping Countries Combat Corruption: The Role of the World Bank."

100 Joel S. Hellman et al., *Measuring Governance, Corruption, and State Capture: How Firms and Bureaucrats Shape the Business Environment in Transition Economies*, World Bank Policy Research Working Paper No. 2312, at 4 (Apr. 2000); Susan Rose-Ackerman, *Governance and Corruption*, in *Global Crises, Global Solutions* 301 (Bjørn Lomborg ed., Cambridge U. Press 2004).

101 One of the first Bank reports to mention the issue of governance was "Sub-Saharan Africa—From Crisis to Sustainable Growth: A Long Term Perspective Study" (first published in Nov. 1989).

major issue of development policy, the Bank could take action in relation to the fight against corruption."[102]

This evolution has been viewed as an example of reconciling the Bank's mandate with a politically charged issue. Susan Rose-Ackerman argues that "an explicit concern with corruption is consistent with a focus on economic rationality and is one way to *counter* some of the political pressures faced by the Bank."[103]

The Bank developed both remedial measures to investigate and sanction activities involving fraud and corruption and preventive measures aimed at fostering an environment in which instances of fraud and corruption are reduced.[104] A recent development in the Bank's fight against corruption that appears to be in tension with the political prohibition is the Stolen Asset Recovery (StAR) Initiative.

This joint initiative between the Bank and the UN Office on Drugs and Crime (UNODC) focuses on helping developing countries recover assets stolen by corrupt officials and hidden abroad. The initiative was launched on September 17, 2007, in recognition of the concept that asset recovery is a critical component of anticorruption efforts and is strongly linked to development.[105]

The key risk related to the StAR Initiative arises from the fact that asset recovery is pursued by national authorities in a highly politicized environment. Often a new government pursues corruption charges (and asset recovery efforts) against individuals linked with a predecessor government dominated by an opposing political party or faction. This means that sometimes political vendetta—rather than commitment to rule of law—is a key motivating factor for such prosecutions. Thus, the Bank's involvement in the StAR Initiative could expose it to interfering, or being perceived as interfering, with domestic partisan politics in violation of the political prohibition clause. Equally significant, the Bank could risk interfering with the foreign political affairs of a member if it takes sides (or appears to do so) with one member country (or group of countries) against another country (or group of countries).

To manage these risks, the Bank has operational guidelines for country assistance in support of asset recovery activities at the country level. The guidelines limit the Bank's involvement in asset recovery to activities of a preparatory nature (mostly fact finding and advice) and require that staff refrain from

---

102 Ibrahim F. I. Shihata, *Corruption: A General Review with an Emphasis on the Role of the World Bank*, 15 Dick. J. Intl. L. 451, 475–76 (1997).

103 Susan Rose-Ackerman, *The Role of the World Bank in Controlling Corruption*, 29 L. & Policy Intl. Bus. 93, 94 (1997–98).

104 For a recent Bank initiative in sanctioning fraud and corruption, *see* Stephen S. Zimmermann & Frank A. Fariello, Jr., *Coordinating the Fight against Fraud and Corruption: Agreement on Cross-Debarment among Multilateral Development Banks*, this volume.

105 For an overview of the StAR Initiative, *see* Theodore S. Greenberg et al., *Stolen Asset Recovery: A Good Practices Guide for Non-conviction Based Asset Forfeiture* (World Bank 2009).

getting involved in any case-specific law enforcement activities. In addition, the initiative was designed such that certain activities that pose unacceptable political interference risks for the Bank are carried out exclusively by UNODC, with the Bank playing a limited fiscal agency role.

Nonlending Decisions

There have been several cases in which the Bank decided not to lend to countries for factors that do not appear to be purely economic, referred to in Bank parlance as "nonlending." Examples of nonlending due to noneconomic considerations can be found in the early practice of the Bank. In the first years of its operations, the Bank denied lending to Poland, despite the fact that economic considerations seemed favorable, because the U.S. executive director informed the Bank's president that he would vote against the loan proposal. The *Third Annual Report (1947–48)* stated with regard to the nonlending decision in regard to Poland that

> the Bank is fully cognizant of the injunction in its Articles of Agreement that its decisions shall be based only on economic considerations. Political tensions and uncertainties in or among its member countries, however, have a direct effect on economic and financial conditions in those countries and upon their credit position.

This led to the subsequent withdrawal of Poland from the institution.[106]

The reduction of lending to both India and Pakistan after the 1998 nuclear weapons tests is also a case in point. The distinction between various forms of nonlending decisions and their relationship to political prohibition is well articulated by Andres Rigo Sureda:

> Non-lending has been seized by commentators as an indication of the politicization of decision making in the Bank. While in general non-lending or diminished lending would be for economic reasons, *the non-presentation to the Board of operations which have been prepared and that in the Management's judgment are sound, may be prompted by shareholders' politically motivated pressure on Management.* [emphasis added][107]

Summary of Bank Practice

Bank practice with respect to political prohibition can be summarized as follows: The political prohibition clause imposes two broad constraints on Bank operations. First, the Bank is prohibited from interfering in the internal affairs of a member. This means the Bank must refrain from interfering in partisan

---

106 A similar story occurred with respect to a loan proposal from Czechoslovakia; *see* Mason & Asher, *supra* note 9, at 170–71. In the early 1970s, after Salvador Allende won the presidential elections of Chile, the Bank did not approve any new loans to this country during his presidency. The Bank was criticized for aligning with the U.S. policy, but there is no conclusive evidence to support this claim; *see* Brown, *supra* note 6, at 157–70.

107 Rigo Sureda, *supra* note 92, at 588.

political affairs. It cannot favor, or appear to favor, one side in political or ideological disputes. Second, the Bank is required to ensure that only economic considerations (weighed impartially in order to achieve the Bank's purposes) are relevant to its decisions. This means that all activities that the Bank undertakes must be grounded on an appropriate and objective economic rationale. Relying on this two-part test, the Bank has refrained from financing military expenditures and direct law enforcement, including investigation and prosecution of specific individual cases.

The Criticism of the Political Prohibition Clause

The decades-long practice of the Bank and its position on the political prohibition clause have triggered two-pronged criticism. On the one hand, the Bank has been accused of creeping politicization because of the expansion of its mandate. On the other hand, the Bank has been accused of invoking political prohibition as a constraint. Both criticisms are based on the "mission creep" of the Bank, but there is a distinction between those arguing against the mission creep per se and those arguing against the direction of the mission creep.[108]

The Creeping Politicization of the World Bank

Critics have claimed that the Bank has added too many tasks to its agenda. It has, the critics allege, moved too far beyond its original mandate, hampering its effectiveness. The prescribed remedy is for the Bank to reverse direction and return to its basic mandate.[109]

Mission creep affects not only the Bank's effectiveness but also its technical and nonpolitical character. In other words, mission creep results in a creeping politicization. This has been argued particularly with respect to the Bank's work in the fight against corruption.[110] In this respect, the Bank has been perceived, through its activities in governance and anticorruption, to make recommendations on democratization.[111] The main argument is that the Bank promotes "the idea that good governance was a precondition for economic growth, including accountable and transparent decision-making, an independent judiciary, a free press, increased popular participation through a vital civil society and, finally, a commitment to combating corruption," but "has stopped short of calling this 'democracy.'"[112]

The mission creep of the Bank, which has been made possible by the expansive interpretation of the political prohibition clause, has also been criticized

---

108 John Head, *Law and Policy in International Financial Institutions: The Changing Role of Law in the IMF and the Multilateral Development Banks*, 17 Kan. J.L. & Pub. Pol. 194, 205 (2007/08).

109 Jessica Einhorn, *The World Bank's Mission Creep*, 80(5) Foreign Affairs 22 (Sep.–Oct. 2001).

110 Heather Marquette, *The Creeping Politicisation of the World Bank: The Case of Corruption*, 52 Pol. Studs. 413 (2004).

111   *Id.*, at 427.

112 *Id.*, at 419.

by advocates of the Third World Approaches to International Law (TWAIL). For instance, Bhupinder Chimni has argued that

> through the different interpretative moves, the Bank's actions give meaning to the term "political" in a way that serves the purpose of the powerful Member States. First, it defines "political" in a manner that the "non-economic" interests of advanced capitalist states are subsumed under the rubric of "economic" decision-making. Second, the term "political" is assigned a meaning that disregards the implications of the Bank agenda and the conditionalities prescribed for principles of sovereignty and non-intervention in the internal affairs of states.[113]

The creeping politicization has been seen as a deviation from the Bank's mandate and from the perception that it acts as an independent and technocratic organization. In this respect, critics argue, politicization leads to a legitimacy crisis for the Bank.[114]

The criticism of creeping politicization implies two different things. First, it means that the Bank takes political factors into account when making decisions about lending, and due to the existence of a weighted voting system is seen as promoting the interests of powerful states.[115] Second, it implies that some of the Bank's activities extend to areas that affect the political affairs of its borrowing states.

The Political Prohibition Invoked as a Constraint

Other critics are more concerned about the content of the mission creep and about the fact that the expansion of the Bank's activities is not accompanied by a similar expansion of its responsibilities.[116] This criticism is mostly related to the Bank's refusal to take human rights considerations into account when deciding to make loans. This position has resulted in some rather uncomfortable situations. For example, the World Bank issued a report on development in Rwanda in 1994 as the genocide was ongoing. The report took note of the massacres, but went on with specific recommendations.[117]

---

113 Bhupinder S. Chimni, *IFIs and International Law: A Third World Perspective*, in *International Financial Institutions and International Law* 30, 40 (Daniel D. Bradlow & David B. Hunter ed., Kluwer Law International 2010).

114 Antony Anghie, *International Financial Institutions*, in *The Politics of International Law* 217, 235 (Christian Reus-Smit ed., Cambridge U. Press, 2004).

115 It is interesting to note that President McNamara signed a letter to the U.S. Congress making a commitment that the Bank would not provide any loan to Vietnam for the fiscal year 1980, in light of a proposed bill that would impose restrictions on the use of the U.S. contributions; *see* Brown, *supra* note 6, at 173–90; Devesh Hapur, John P. Lewis, & Richard Webb, *The World Bank: Its First Half Century* vol. 1, 1150 (Brookings Institute 1997).

116 Daniel D. Bradlow, *International Law and Operations of the IFIs*, in *International Financial Institutions and International Law* 1, 16 (Daniel D. Bradlow & David B. Hunter ed., Kluwer Law International 2010).

117 William Easterly, *The White Man's Burden: Why the West's Efforts to Aid the Rest Have Done So Much Ill and So Little Good* 151 (Penguin Press 2006).

The main criticism from this camp is that, due to the ambiguity of the political prohibition clause, the Bank's decisions as to whether to finance particular projects appear to be arbitrary.[118] This ambiguity is enhanced by the imprecise way in which the political prohibition clause is interpreted by the Bank's general counsel.[119]

Although the political prohibition clause is often invoked as the rationale for the Bank's reluctance to explicitly take into account human rights when it finances a project, it does not constitute the only explanation of the Bank's position. In the first place, as an international organization with a separate legal personality, the Bank is not a party to any human rights treaty, and its human rights obligations under customary international law remain unclear.[120] In addition, financing decisions might be affected by the Bank's capacity to address human rights matters, given the comparative advantage and the specificity of functions of different international organizations operating in a complementary fashion.

Human rights is not the only area in which the Bank has been reluctant to engage fully. The Bank is not involved in peacekeeping, mainly because of the political prohibition clause. Thus, some critics argue that the Bank should adopt a narrow interpretation of the term "political" that will allow early engagement with peace operations.[121]

These two types of criticism have led scholars to argue that the political prohibition clause in the Bank's articles is an "organizational myth" and that "the point about such a myth is not whether it is true or false, but that it plays an essential role in an institution's self-conception and quest for legitimacy."[122]

Tools for Evolving the Political Prohibition Clause

Changing Bank practice with respect to the political prohibition would require either amending the Articles of Agreement or expanding the interpretation (whether formal or informal) of the clause.

Challenges of Following an Unexplored Path: Amendment

At first glance, amendment appears to be the appropriate way to deal with the matter. Amending the Bank's articles is not a simple process, however. To amend the IBRD articles, the approval by the Board of Governors is required,

---

118 Daniel D. Bradlow, *The World Bank, the IMF, and Human Rights*, 6 Transnatl. L. & Contemp. Probs. 47, 61 (1996).

119 Bradlow, *supra* note 116, at 14.

120 For a discussion of the human rights obligations of the Bank, which falls outside the purview of the present study, *see* Bradlow, *supra* note 116, at 17–23.

121 John D. Ciorciari, *A Prospective Enlargement of the Roles of the Bretton Woods Financial Institutions in International Peace Operations*, 22 Fordham Intl. L.J. 292 (1998–99).

122 Michelle Miller-Adams, *The World Bank: New Agendas in a Changing World* 22 (Routledge 1999).

as well as acceptance by 60 percent of IBRD members holding 80 percent of the total voting power.[123] Given these stringent requirements, it is not surprising that only two sets of amendments have been approved with respect to the IBRD articles and none for the IDA articles. Considering that the political prohibition clause touches on an issue on which little consensus seems to exist among member countries, it is doubtful whether sufficient votes could be mustered to effect the requisite amendment. Even if they could, there is a danger that introducing amendments to the articles of both institutions might encourage shareholders to introduce their own amendments, with unforeseen implications for the institution.[124]

The Long-Standing Practice but Limited Option: Interpretation

Likewise, there are limits to the desirability and practicability of expanding the scope of the Bank's mandate through Board-endorsed interpretations of its mandate issued by the Bank's general counsel. Article 31 of the Vienna Convention on the Law of Treaties, which is widely held as reflecting customary international law on the question of interpretation of treaties, requires treaties to be interpreted "in good faith in accordance with the ordinary meaning to be given to the terms of the treaty in their context."[125] One would thus find it difficult to develop a legally defensible basis for the general counsel to reinterpret a provision of a treaty whose language is clearly prohibitive. To paraphrase Heribert Golsong, a former general counsel of the Bank who has weighed in on this issue, any decision under a provision of the IBRD articles dealing with interpretation that would lead to a change in the ordinary meaning of the articles would constitute an abuse of the power of interpretation and should be made subject to the formal amendment procedure.[126] Moreover, as a practical matter, even in cases where the provisions of the articles could plausibly be read in a more expansive and permissive manner, such an interpretation could nonetheless face pushback from the country members (viz., executive directors) who have the ultimate say in how the articles should be interpreted.[127]

Using interpretation as a tool to effect changes in the text that would ignore or contradict the ordinary meaning of the words used in the text does not seem appropriate. In rare and unusual instances, however, interpretation

---

123   Article VIII of IBRD Articles; Article VII of IDA Articles.

124   Rigo Sureda, *supra* note 92, at 569.

125   According to the ICJ, "some of the rules laid down in [the Vienna Convention on the Law of Treaties] might be considered as a codification of existing customary law"; *see Gabčíkovo-Nagymaros Project Case (Hungary v. Slovakia)* 1997 I.C.J. 7, 38. The same provision is found in the Vienna Convention on the Law between States and International Organizations or between International Organizations.

126   Legal Opinion from Heribert Golsong, vice president and general counsel, *Valuation of the Bank's Capital* (May 1, 1981) (copy on file with the author).

127   Andres Rigo Sureda, *The Law Applicable to the Activities of International Development Banks*, 308 Recueil des Cours 1, 48–53 (2004).

that contradicts the ordinary meaning of the terms of a text may be warranted.[128] To respond to Golsong's point, there may be cases in which interpretation does not function as a means that will "lead to a change in the ordinary meaning" of the words used in a text, but merely formalizes or confirms changes in the meaning of a text that have been brought about by obsolescence or incremental interpretations that modify the ordinary meaning of these words.

An Assessment of the Available Tools

Despite the challenges associated with the process of amendment, if the Bank decides to move away from the political prohibition clause, the option of amendment will be more consistent with three fundamental general principles of law: rule of law, transparency, and equitable treatment of members.

Rule of Law

As for an organization committed in letter and spirit to the rule of law, the Bank's organs must operate, and must be perceived to operate, within certain proper and predefined legal limits set out in its constituent document. This is important not only for the sake of the rule of law but also because of the close relationship between the "proper adherence to applicable legal rules and principles" and "the financial strength that the [Bank] enjoys."[129] The Board does not have unfettered discretion to modify the provisions of the articles as it pleases. As noted by Ibrahim Shihata:

> In interpreting the Articles, the Executive Directors . . . should weigh carefully both the requirements of legal interpretation as well as the policy requirements dictated by the Bank's objectives and its changing environment. *They should not, however, amend existing provisions under the guise of interpreting them. Amendment is a separate process to be undertaken under the different requirements of Article VIII.* [emphasis added][130]

Modifying such a fundamental clause without a formal process could constitute an ultra vires act for failing to follow the predefined procedures, improperly appropriating the powers of the Board of Governors and ultimately of member states. To apply a principle derived from municipal administrative law—as ultra vires actions—these attempts at interpretations are *void ab initio*.

---

128 *See* John L. Taylor, *Legal Challenges at the Start of a New International Financial Institution*, 17 Kan. J.L. & Pub. Pol. 349, 361 (2007/08). Taylor, a former general counsel of EBRD, discussing the merits of interpretations over amendment, argues: "In some cases, proposed interpretations proved controversial, but for the most part this process served as an efficient method for bringing clarity to the meaning that should be ascribed to the charter in uncertain cases, without going through the laborious exercise required for actually amending the charter. This increased clarity, in turn . . . contributed to the process of developing . . . a shared understanding, particularly among the shareholder countries, as to the meaning of the EBRD's nature, powers, and mission."

129 *See* Head, *supra* note 108, at 217.

130 Shihata, *supra* note 7, at xlviii.

Transparency

Amending the constituent document and other steps to reshape the Bank's mission are so far-reaching in nature that they should be undertaken only in a proper transparent process. Informal interpretation is certainly *not* a model of transparency.

Equitable Treatment of Members

Because a simple majority of Board members can effect certain changes to the articles if "amendment through interpretation" is adopted, small shareholders stand to be deprived of "protection of their interests guaranteed by the high majority required for formal amendment."

However, interpretation, which is consistent with the "overall tendency to informality that has pervaded [the Bank] throughout its history," might continue to be useful if the political prohibition is still meaningful despite the accumulation of changes in the Bank's activities. [131] After all, it seems that the preferred interpretation of the Bank's articles is teleological, because a multilateral institution "by the nature of its mandate must be able to respond to the changing needs of its members."[132] This type of interpretation is generally considered the most dynamic and the most adequate for international organizations because it "can take account of the living charter of an international organization . . . in a rapidly changing world."[133]

Should the Political Prohibition Clause Be Retained?

This section elaborates various arguments for and against retaining the political prohibition clause.

A Case against Retaining the Political Prohibition Clause

The arguments against retaining the political prohibition are related to the evolution of development thinking, the interrelationship between politics and economics, and the existence of competing sources of financing.

The Evolution in Development Thinking and the Establishment of the EBRD

Development is a concept that has evolved greatly over the past sixty years. In the 1950s and the 1960s, the focus of development policy was on the role of the state in managing the economy and transforming traditional societies.[134] In the

---

131　Rigo Sureda, *supra* note 92, at 595.

132　Andres Rigo Sureda, *The Law Applicable to the Activities of International Development Banks*, 308 Recueil des Cours 1, 157 (2004).

133　Henry G. Schermers & Niels M. Blokker, *International Institutional Law: Unity within Diversity* 844 (4th ed., Martinus Nijhoff 2003).

134　David M. Trubek & Alvaro Santos, *Introduction: The Third Moment in Law and Development Theory and the Emergence of a New Critical Practice*, in *The New Law and Economic Development: A Critical Appraisal* 1, 2 (David M. Trubek & Alvaro Santos ed., Cambridge U. Press 2006).

1980s, a neoliberal agenda took over and the so- called Washington consensus emerged.[135] The neoliberal development policy viewed the government as a facilitator to participation in the market, and the focus was on property rights, free trade, and foreign investment.[136] The transition in the countries of Eastern Europe proved the limits of the neoliberal agenda and coincided with the newly emerged theory of institutional economics that put emphasis on the institutions.[137] Another watershed event in the evolution of development thinking is the work of Amartya Sen, who viewed development "as a process of expanding the real freedoms that people enjoy."[138]

This evolution in development thinking could not but have an impact on development agencies and multilateral development banks (MDBs).[139] The EBRD, a third-generation MDB established in 1990, is the most characteristic example. Established during the apogee of the Washington consensus, the EBRD is not subject to political prohibition, and indeed is directed to factor in environmental considerations as well as to help foster multiparty democracy, pluralism, and market economies. These goals have been incorporated into other institutions, including the Bank, through practice.[140]

Intertwined Economics and Politics and the Bank's Effectiveness

The increasing extent to which economics and politics are intertwined might mean that retaining the clause has the effect of tying the Bank's hands and thus adversely affecting its effectiveness. If the Bank had the ability to make decisions for political reasons, it would be easily exposed to reputational risks, which in turn could affect its ability to raise funds in capital markets.[141] The IBRD has

---

135 Tor Krever, *The Legal Turn in Late Development Theory: The Rule of Law and the World Bank's Development Model*, 52 Harv. J. Intl. L. 287, 297 (2011).

136 David Kennedy, *Political Choices and Development Common Sense*, in *The New Law and Economic Development: A Critical Appraisal* 95, 128–50 (David M. Trubek & Alvaro Santos ed., Cambridge U. Press 2006).

137 Douglass C. North, *Institutions, Institutional Change, and Economic Performance* (Cambridge U. Press 1990).

138 Amartya Sen, *Development as Freedom* 3 (Alfred Knopf 1999).

139 For the impact on the World Bank, *see* Alvaro Santos, *The World Bank's Uses of the "Rule of Law" Promise*, in *The New Law and Economic Development: A Critical Appraisal* 253 (David M. Trubek & Alvaro Santos ed., Cambridge U. Press 2006).

140 *See* Head, *supra* note 108, at 206.

141 This argument applies to the IBRD and is less relevant to the IDA. For an interesting discussion on how confusion about the Bank's role results from the Bank's dual nature, which supports dual-model thinking (the Bank as financial intermediary—the Bank as a bank model) that is linked with IBRD and the Bank as a mechanism for the transfer of resources from wealthier to poorer countries in its membership, *see* Moises Naim, *The World Bank: Its Role, Governance and Organizational Culture* (Apr. 1994), available at <http://www.carnegieendowment.org/publications/index.cfm?fa=view&id=759>. According to Naim, the differing assumptions about the "basic role of the World Bank not only engender very different visions about its goals and policies" but also engender "standards with which to judge the organization's performance [and] changes needed to respond to new problems."

begun to position itself in the capital market as an appealing, socially responsible investment for both retail and institutional investors. By putting itself in this position, the IBRD hopes to widen and diversify the investor base of its debt instruments by tapping into the growing number of investors who incorporate environmental, social, and governance criteria into their investment decisions.[142] The downside of this is that the IBRD has opened itself to scrutiny of its "social responsibility record." If its actions are perceived as being inconsistent with its rhetoric and image[143] (e.g., if it continues to fund projects in countries where human rights violations are pervasive), its ability to raise funds from socially responsible investors could be impaired. More broadly, political risk assessments are being used ever more frequently within private capital and investment sectors to help guide investment decisions. The Bank needs to keep up with best practices in capital markets, which in this case means that the Bank must be increasingly attuned to political considerations.

As a socially responsible actor, the Bank may find that its expertise or funds are required for more extensive and enduring interventions than the ones that exist today in support of governments or state building. Numerous types of flaws in a political system can make it impossible for an honest government to come to power through a political process. Campaign finance reform "nudged" by the Bank, in coordination with other bilateral donors, may be warranted in some cases because it may help to create a more equitable political arena from which an honest government can emerge. In cases of state collapse where temporary administration of the state by the international community may be needed (as was the case in East Timor and Kosovo), the Bank could use its expertise to help a nascent state establish its financial institutions.

---

142 Heike Reichelt, *Green Bonds: A Model to Mobilize Private Capital to Fund Climate Change Mitigation and Adaptation Projects,* in *The Euromoney Environmental Finance Handbook 2010,* available at <http://treasury.worldbank.org/web/Euromoney_2010_Handbook_Environmental_Finance.pdf>.

143 Borrowing a page from the Apartheid South Africa disinvestment campaign, some activist organizations that have been seeking for years to get institutional investors to boycott the World Bank bonds. *See,* for example, Jubilee 2000 campaign at <http://www.jubileeusa.org/fileadmin/user_upload/Resources/Education_Action_Packet/boycott.pdf>. There is hardly any evidence that these organizations had a detrimental effect on the ability of the Bank to raise funds. However, it is worth recalling that the Bank made hardly any efforts to appeal to socially responsible investors in the past as it has been doing lately.

Competing Sources of Financing

Competing sources of financing in countries can effectively discipline the Bank in its application of political considerations. Many Bank member countries can obtain funding and investments from other sources, including capital markets;[144] bilateral lenders;[145] international financial institutions, including multilateral development banks; sovereign wealth funds; and charitable organizations.[146] The member countries may opt to turn to one or more of these alternative sources of funding if those countries adjudge the Bank to be factoring inappropriate political considerations into its decision making. Additionally, the Bank might be seen by its clients as irrelevant or misguided if, because it is constrained by its political prohibition clause, it fails to factor political issues into its decision making while other donors do incorporate those factors into their decisions.

A Case for Retaining the Political Prohibition Clause

Despite the above arguments against the political prohibition, one could argue that this clause should be retained, because its underlying rationale remains relevant and it has served the Bank as both a financing and a knowledge institution.

The Rationale for the Prohibition Remains Relevant Today

The political prohibition helps the Bank focus on its core competence. Importantly, the Bank is viewed as a neutral arbiter on many sensitive and technical issues and is able to provide an independent and mediating voice on those issues to the extent that the Bank's decisions are seen primarily to be based on empirical data and guided by technical and nonpolitical considerations.

Ibrahim Shihata wrote with respect to the political mandate of the EBRD that "it will also be interesting to note the extent to which the new provisions in the EBRD Agreement may influence the practice of other MDBs or inspire calls for the amendment of their constituent instruments."[147] The fact that twenty years after the creation of the EBRD nothing has changed in the

---

144   Many middle-income countries, including most countries in Latin America and a few African countries (notably South Africa, Morocco, and Egypt), can and do borrow from international capital markets by issuing debt instruments. Even poorer countries have shown interest in accessing capital markets—Ghana and Gabon issued their debut Eurobond in 2007. Since then, several other countries in Africa, including Nigeria, Kenya, Tanzania, and Uganda, have demonstrated interest in doing the same.

145   In addition to traditional bilateral donors, mostly European countries, and North America, there are "new" bilateral donors such as Brazil, India, China, and South Korea.

146   The Bill and Melinda Gates Foundation, for example, has over US $33 billion in an assets trust endowment and operations in over a hundred, and made grant payments of over $3 billion in 2009. Compare these figures with the IBRD, which had net disbursements of $8.3 billion in the fiscal year ending in June 2009.

147   Ibrahim F. Shihata, *The European Bank for Reconstruction and Development: A Comparative Analysis of the Constituent Agreement* 4 (Graham & Trotman/Martinus Nijhoff 1990).

Bank and the other international financial institutions might indicate that the EBRD will remain the exception with respect to this issue and that the political prohibition continues to serve these institutions.[148]

The Interpretation of This Clause Has Served the Organization Well

By allowing certain political considerations that have a direct and obvious relation to economic considerations to be factored into its decisions, Bank Management has some leeway, thus obviating the need to dispense with the political prohibition.[149] It is significant that the Bank can get involved in many activities related to governance—including many that were previously considered outside its mandate, such as civil service reform, legal, regulatory and judicial reform, accountability for public finance, and efficiency in public functions[150]—as long as the recipient government requests such assistance and areas of governance "fall reasonably within its developmental mandate."[151] Because development is not defined in the Articles of Agreement, the meaning of the term can evolve in such a manner that more activities can be interpreted as falling within the Bank's mandate.[152]

In addition, the political prohibition could be seen as a protection or a shield for the Bank. It has permitted the Bank to make decisions that in other organizations would have been too controversial to contemplate.[153] The political prohibition and the absence of Soviet countries among its membership allowed the Bank to be insulated from the debates of the Cold War and to focus on its development mandate.[154]

---

148 It is noteworthy that the amendment of the African Development Bank Articles of Agreement in 2002 was not seen as an opportunity to introduce the principles, which characterize the EBRD's mandate; *see* Rigo Sureda, *supra* note 132, at 193.

149 *See* Shihata, *supra* note 70, at 241, where he argues that "the limitations on the Bank's interference in the political affairs of its members, cannot, however, be interpreted away or treated as if they did not exist. These are legal limitations that have been reasonably and flexibly applied and have served the Bank well through the years."

150 Discussing this point in the context of EBRD, John Taylor argues, "with legal reform so closely aligned, certainly in the minds of national government officials, with national sovereignty, any involvement—much less pressure—by an IFI in the area of "legal reform" is highly suspect, especially in view of the fact that all of the IFIs created *before* the EBRD included specific "political prohibition provisions." *See* Taylor, *supra* note 128, at 357.

151 *See* Shihata, *supra* note 70, at 242.

152 The need for an evolving understanding of development has become even more compelling in light of recent events in the Middle East and North Africa. According to the president of the World Bank, "it is vital that the World Bank Group continually challenges itself to refresh our development thinking"; *see* Robert B. Zoellick, Speech, *The Middle East and North Africa: A New Social Contract for Development* (Peterson Institute for International Economics, Washington, D.C., Apr. 6, 2006), available at <http://go.worldbank.org/277S26D030>.

153 For example, the Bank has been able to extend lending to entities that are not recognized as states, such as the West Bank and Gaza, and to accept Kosovo as a member state.

154 Perhaps it is not irrelevant that the expansion of the Bank's activities coincided with the end of the Cold War and the emergence of the Washington consensus.

The Importance of Prohibition for the Knowledge Products of the Bank

The World Bank has learned that its knowledge services are just as important as—for some of its clients, increasingly more than—the financing that it provides. However, the significance of the political prohibition clause for the knowledge services of the Bank has rarely been noted.[155]

The Bank has been transformed over the past twenty years into a knowledge institution, and it has assumed the responsibility not only to collect and produce knowledge but also to share it. But if others are to want to mine this rich resource, they must be convinced that the Bank's knowledge is objective and stands on a firm technical, rather than political, basis. By extending its political prohibition provisions to its research and analytical work, the Bank has thus endowed its knowledge base with special authority.

Conclusion

The purpose of this chapter is to give an overview of the practice of the Bank with respect to the political prohibition clause, to present the criticism raised against this provision, and to outline the arguments against and in favor of this clause. In this respect, this chapter can be seen as check on the sustainability of a fundamental provision of the Bank's Articles of Agreement. This check is necessary because of the changing environment in which the Bank operates. Other international organizations have engaged in similar exercises. For example, it has been argued that Article 2(7) of the UN Charter—a provision similar to the Bank's Article IV, Section 10—has become obsolete, but the UN secretary-general has opined that it is still as relevant as it was in 1945.[156]

The same conclusion could be reached with respect to the political prohibition clause: it continues to remain as relevant as it was in 1944. Back then the dangers for the newly established institution and the difficulties of distinguishing between politics and economics were obvious to everyone. For this reason, a "Questions and Answers" paper prepared by the U.S. Treasury tried to answer the question of whether the Bank could avoid making loans based chiefly on political considerations.

The paper concluded that "no set of rules will of itself completely eliminate political considerations and that proper limitation of the Bank's activities depends ultimately on the character of the men responsible for its operations." Besides the men (and women) responsible for the Bank's operations, there are also men and women responsible for providing legal advice

---

155 Anghie, *supra* note 114, at 223.

156 Georg Noelte, *Article 2(7)*, in *The Charter of the United Nations: A Commentary* 148, 149–50 (Bruno Simma ed., 2d ed., Oxford U. Press 2002).

on the interpretation of the Bank's articles. It is upon the latter that falls the task of providing not only legally correct advice but also advice that will allow the executive directors and the senior management to perform their responsibilities in a manner that best suits the requirements of the Bank's business.[157] What seems to suit the requirements of the Bank's business, as long its articles are not amended, is to continue the "constructive and creative stretching" of the political prohibition provisions, without breaking them.[158]

---

157 Shihata, *supra* note 18, at 1049.

158 This term was coined by Joachim von Amsberg, World Bank vice president, Operations Policy and Country Services, during the discussion on the political prohibition on November 9, 2010, during the 2010 Law, Justice, and Development Week.

International Financial Institutions and Claims of Private Parties

Immunity Obliges

Rutsel Silvestre J. Martha[*]

Writing in 1997, Judge Kooijmans of the International Court of Justice (ICJ) observed that although the system of judicial protection of the European Union (EU) is unique, much can be learned from the European Court of Justice's case law concerning the noncontractual liability of the European Communities (currently the European Union) and the provision of effective remedy for third parties seeking compensation for damages.[1] A primary lesson is that the immunity from domestic legal process enjoyed by the European institutions pursuant to the (predecessors of the) Protocol on the Privileges and Immunities of the European Union is not questioned because it is accompanied by a system that provides for protection against unlawful acts of the institutions. Central to the European system is the division of tasks between the national courts, the European Court of Justice, and the General Court (formerly the Court of First Instance), in particular the preliminary ruling procedure. The combination of preliminary ruling proceedings brought in the national courts (which may by themselves grant sufficient protection) and proceedings under which protection is sought directly before the General Court and the Court of Justice enables the European Court to safeguard the independent functioning of the EU while affording adequate means for redress to private parties.[2]

Unlike in the case of the European Union, the immunity from domestic legal process of the other international organizations, in particular multilateral financial institutions, is being attacked for being anachronistic or excessive. The mounting pressure from a range of observers (scholars, private sector actors, and civil society) to strip international organizations of their immunity,[3] or at a minimum to restrict such immunity,[4] is directly linked to the actual

---

[*]   This paper represents the author's personal views. He is thankful to Sarah Dadush.

1   Peter H. Kooijmans, *Foreword*, in *The Action for Damages in Community Law* v (Ton Heukels & Alison McDonnel ed., Kluwer Law International 1997).

2   *See* Henry G. Schermers & Denis F. Waelbroeck, *Judicial Protection in the European Union* (6th ed., Kluwer Law International 2000).

3   *See*, for example, Steven Herz, *Rethinking International Financial Institution Immunity*, in *International Financial Institutions and International Law* 137 (Daniel D. Bradlow & David B. Hunter ed., Kluwer Law International 2010).

4   *See*, arguing that absolute immunity is an anachronism, *McElhinney v. Ireland*, App. No. 31253/96, 2001-XI, Eur. Ct. Hum. Rights 37 (2001) (Dissenting Opinion of Judge Loucaides), Stephen Herz, *International Organization in U.S. Courts: Reconsidering the Anachronism of Absolute Immunity*, 31 Suffolk Transnatl. L. Rev. 471 (2007–08), and Gerhard Thallinger, *Piercing*

or perceived absence of adequate means to facilitate the resolution of mostly noncontractual private claims against such organizations.[5]

This chapter demonstrates that international financial institutions' immunity from domestic legal process is neither an anachronism nor unnecessary nor excessive, but that, as in the European Union, full attention ought to be given to implementing the obligation of international organizations to provide appropriate modes for the settlement of disputes with private parties. Specifically, the establishment of a default mechanism for the settlement of disputes between international organizations and private parties seems to be the way to go.

The chapter also discusses the link between the reason for the existence of international financial institutions and their immunity from legal domestic process. When there is no longer an international public need for an organization, its privileges and immunities serve no purpose. Only in such cases could it validly be argued that immunity from domestic legal process is unnecessary and should be rescinded. Subsequently, the chapter addresses the fundamental differences between states and international organizations that render the restrictive immunity theory that applies to states in respect of their commercial operations inapplicable to international financial institutions. Membership in international organizations requires states to abstain from interfering with the functioning of these organizations, including through the states' courts, which in and of itself severely limits any role domestic courts could play in this field.

This chapter then examines the inherent jurisdictional limitations of domestic legal orders under international law that entail categorical impediments to the role that domestic courts could play in the settlement of claims against international financial institutions. The relevant international legal instruments exclude a role for domestic courts in the settlement of disputes between private parties and international organizations. However, the enjoyment of immunity comes with responsibilities. In other words, immunity obliges. Accordingly, the aforementioned instruments require international organizations to provide appropriate modes for the settlement of claims of private parties. Although usually mechanisms are put into place to deal with contractual claims of private parties, unfortunately, too often international financial institutions fail to make arrangements for dealing with noncontractual claims. Drawing on examples from the practice of international organizations (the Bank for International Settlements, BIS; the International Fund for Agricultural Development, IFAD; INTERPOL; and the Organization of American States, OAS), the chapter discusses the default mechanisms that could and should be put into place by international financial institutions in order to address the legitimate complaint that immunity from domestic legal process

---

Jurisdictional Immunity: The Possible Role of Domestic Courts in Enhancing World Bank Accountability, 1 Vienna Online J. Intl. Const. L. 4 (2008), (available at <http://www.icl-journal.com>).

5   Emmanuel Gaillard & Isabelle Pingel-Lenuzza, *International Organisations and Immunity from Jurisdiction: To Restrict or to Bypass*, 51 Intl. Comp. L.Q. 1 (2002).

would otherwise infringe on the right of private parties to effective remedies against international organizations.

Why Do International Financial Institutions Exist?

The discussion about the desirability and the extent of multilateral financial institutions' immunity from domestic legal process is linked to the raison d'être of these institutions. Yet this important aspect is often relegated to the background. This is regrettable because the reasons for the existence of international organizations, international financial institutions in particular, hold clues for understanding the continued need for and relevance of their immunities as well as for contextualizing the limited role—if any—that domestic courts could play in settling disputes between private parties and international organizations.

Consider the trajectory of the International Telecommunications Satellite Organization (INTELSAT), from its inception as a public international organization to its conversion into a private organization. INTELSAT was formed by a 1964 treaty to improve global communication, particularly between developing and developed economies. In response to the 1960 launch of the first telecommunications satellite, Echo I, a 1962 UN resolution called for a system of "communications by means of satellite" that would be "available to the nations of the world . . . on a global and nondiscriminatory basis."[6] Accordingly, as a public international organization, INTELSAT was set up to provide reliable, high-quality international public telephony on a nondiscriminatory basis to all areas of the world through the development and operation of a global commercial telecommunications satellite system. However, dramatic changes took place over the years, especially the growing popularity of fiber-optic cable as a substitute for satellites in providing telephone links and the emergence of private satellite providers, that rendered the global public-good function of the organization unnecessary.[7] This development led to the privatization of the organization and the attendant removal of its privileges and immunities.[8] What this story shows is that when the international public function for which an international organization has been set up is no longer necessary, the reason for its immunity disappears.

Unfortunately, in a discussion about jurisdictional immunity, one often forgets that unlike states, which are created on the principle of self-determination, international organizations are usually created out of functional

---

6   GA Res. 1721 (XVI), UNGAOR, 16th Sess., Supp. No. 17, U.N. Doc. A/5100 (1962).

7   *See* The White House, *Towards Competition in International Satellite Services: Rethinking the Role of INTELSAT*, available at <http://clinton4.nara.gov/WH/EOP/CEA/html/paper.html>.

8   *See* Rutsel Silvestre J. Martha, *The Tax Treatment of International Civil Servants* 192–94 (Martinus Nijhoff 2010), and the sources cited there.

necessity.[9] As the example of INTELSAT confirms, in the case of international financial institutions, that functional need is captured by the concept of "capital market imperfections."[10] According to this concept, international capital markets tend to discriminate among borrowers; more specifically, countries whose ability to repay is perceived as being uncertain are typically forced to pay a premium when they borrow. Considerations of creditworthiness—whether or not based on economic fundamentals[11]—often affect not only the cost of credit in international financial markets but also its availability. The perception that a country's creditworthiness has deteriorated or is about to deteriorate can lead to an abrupt curtailment of funding to all domestic borrowers, public and private,[12] and can thus impair the allocation of needed resources for matters such as postconflict reconstruction and social and economic development. Hence the decision by states (and sometimes international organizations) to establish international financial institutions in order to rectify this and other related capital market imperfections.[13] It is for this reason that the constitutional instruments of institutions such as the World Bank Group and regional development banks invariably contain certain operational principles, including the specific condition that, when deciding on loans, the institution must be satisfied that the borrower would be unable to obtain credit under prevailing market conditions. Because of these clauses, the World Bank Group (and the regional development banks) was required to adopt a graduation policy.[14] In the same vein, several institutions have been created to remedy the conditions that stand in the way of access to capital for private sector growth in developing countries,[15] as well as the problems with dispute settlement between investors and developing-country governments,[16] the need for resources to facilitate transition from planned economies to market economies,[17] and sectoral

---

9   Rutsel Silvestre J. Martha, *Mandate Issues in the Activities of the International Fund for Agricultural Development (IFAD)*, 6 Intl. Organizations L. Rev. 447, 450–52 (2009).

10   *See* Yilmaz Akyüz, *Rectifying Capital Market Imperfections: The Continuing Rationales for Multilateral Lending*, in *The New Public Finance: Responding to Global Challenges* 486 (Inge Kaul & Pedro Conceição ed., Oxford U. Press 2006). *See* also Daniel Cohen, Pierre Jacquet, & Helmut Reisen, *Beyond "Grants versus Loans": How to Use Debt for Development?* (Dec. 15, 2005), available at <http://www.pierrejacquet.fr/IMG/pdf/Cohen_Jacquet_Reisen_EUDN_final.pdf>.

11   *See* Georges Ugeux, *Are Sovereign Ratings a Legacy of Colonialism?* Huffington Post (Oct. 16, 2009), available at <http://www.huffingtonpost.com/georges-ugeux/are-sovereign-ratings-a-l_b_323870.html>.

12   For example, on April 27, 2010, the Greek debt rating was decreased to BB+ (a "junk" status) by Standard & Poor's amid fears of default by the Greek government.

13   Koen de Feyter, *World Development Law—Sharing Responsibility for Development* 78 (Intersentia 2001).

14   *See* Ibrahim F. I. Shihata, *The World Bank Legal Papers* 493–507 (Martinus Nijhoff 2000).

15   *See* Aron Broches, *International Legal Aspects of the Operations of the World Bank*, in *Selected Essays—World Bank, ICSID, and Other Subjects of Public and Private International Law* 3, 28–29 (Martinus Nijhoff 1995).

16   Aron Broches, *Settlement of Investment Disputes*, in *Selected Essays*, at 161–63.

17   *See* Ibrahim F. I. Shihata, *The European Bank for Reconstruction and Development* (Martinus Nijhoff 1990).

needs such as agriculture[18] and the environment.[19] In the case of monetary institutions, balance-of-payments needs are a critical condition for accessing their resources.[20]

An important conclusion to draw is that as long as there is a functional need for international financial institutions to address market imperfections, such entities must be regarded and treated as what they are, namely, providers of international public goods. Their privileges and immunities cannot be properly discussed without keeping this in mind.

Functional Need to Operate in a Domestic Market

The conflicts that arise when the function of an international organization collides with the demands of national law can be attributed to the fact that national courts tend to see international organizations through the prism of their legal personality under domestic law. From this perspective, it is easy to assume that international organizations should not be treated any differently than other market participants. Yet this perception is misguided, because "the legal position of international organizations is governed by the fact that their competences in every field are restricted by their purposes. . . . In other words, every act performed by an international organization must be compatible with the purposes which the organization is supposed to pursue."[21] The basic premise here is that unless international organizations expressly undertake actions that are not compatible with their purposes, they should receive different treatment from that accorded to ordinary market participants.

Aside from the matters beyond national jurisdiction discussed below, which underscore the special status of international organizations, one should remain mindful of the fact that, unlike other foreign participants in the market, in order to execute their mandates and administer their resources, international organizations—both legally and factually—cannot avoid operating in domestic markets. Thus, whereas foreign states and foreign private parties can be required to bear the consequences of their choice to operate in the domestic market of another country, an international organization's presence in the domestic market of its members is a matter not of choice but of necessity. Some critics might argue that the claim that international organizations have no choice but to operate within states, whereas foreign states do have a choice, is overdrawn because in reality, many foreign states do not see any option but to engage in capital markets, give and receive aid in foreign curren-

---

18   Martha, *supra* note 9, at 450–52.

19   Stephen A. Silard, *The Global Environment Facility: A New Development in International Law and Organization*, 28 Geo. Wash. J. Intl. L. & Econ. 607 (1995).

20   *See* Richard W. Edwards Jr., *International Monetary Collaboration* 240–41 (Transnational Publishers 1985).

21   Pieter H. F. Bekker, *The Legal Position of Intergovernmental Organizations: A Functional Necessity Analysis of Their Legal Status and Immunities* 157 (Martinus Nijhoff 1994).

cies, conduct diplomacy abroad, and the like. The proponents of this theory believe that the financial operations and commercial transactions of international organizations are ordinary market operations that deserve no special treatment; further, international organizations should not receive immunities that states acting alone do not receive.[22] The proponents of this theory[23] must have celebrated the 2010 judgment of the court of appeals in *OSS Nokalva v. European Space Agency*,[24] in which the U.S. Court of Appeals for the Third Circuit expressly broke with the often-followed interpretation of *Atkinson v. Inter-American Development Bank*,[25] adopted by the District of Columbia Court of Appeals, and found that the U.S. International Organizations Immunities Act (IOIA) grants international organizations only limited immunity, consistent with the contemporary understanding and application of the U.S. Foreign Sovereign Immunities Act (FSIA).

The case came to the court under the collateral order doctrine on appeal from the district court's order denying the European Space Agency's (ESA) motion to dismiss a breach-of-contract claim by OSS Nokalva (OSSN). In its motion to dismiss, ESA asserted absolute immunity from suit under the IOIA based on ESA's status as an international organization. The court noted that Congress had not included any language to convey an intent to tether the IOIA to the law of foreign sovereign immunity as it existed in 1945, and that allowing international organizations to enjoy absolute immunity while foreign sovereigns were subject to the immunity limitations of the FSIA could create an incentive for foreign governments to evade legal obligations by acting through international organizations. In the end, the court saw no compelling reason to accord the international organization any kind of special treatment, and concluded that the ESA was not entitled to absolute immunity.[26] This holding reveals the fundamental misunderstanding that fuels the argument for restricting the immunity of international organizations:

> If a foreign government, such as Germany, had contracted with OSSN, it would not be immune from suit because the FSIA provides that a foreign government involved in a commercial arrangement such as that in this case may be sued, as ESA acknowledged at oral argument. We find no compelling reason why a group of states acting through an international organization is entitled to broader immunity than its member states enjoy when acting alone. Indeed, such a policy may create an incentive for foreign governments to evade legal obligations by acting through international organizations.[27]

---

22   Herz, *supra* note 3, at 159.

23   *See* Herz, *supra* note 4.

24   *OSS Nokalva, Inc. v. European Space Agency*, 617 F.3d 756 (3d Cir. 2010).

25   *Atkinson v. Inter-American Development Bank*, 156 F.3d 1335 (D.C. Cir. 1998).

26   Matthew Parish, *U.S. Courts Chip Away at the Crumbling Edifice of Legal Immunity* (Sep. 29, 2010), available at <http://www.unjustice.org/blog/?p=316>.

27   *Id.*

Although one may agree with the view that where international organizations and states are comparable, they should be subject to comparable treatment, the flaws in the reasoning are obvious. Irrespective of their considerable size, stature, and influence, international organizations differ from states exactly on the points that are relevant for the question of immunity from domestic legal process. Both the Permanent Court of International Justice and the ICJ clearly state that although international organizations are subjects of international law, they cannot be compared with states. The argument that an international organization's operation in the domestic market should be treated in the same way as that of states for the purpose of jurisdictional immunity is therefore flawed in four ways.

Functional Gaps in the International Legal Order

The presence of certain functional gaps in the international legal order compels reliance on domestic markets in order to perform organizational functions. This is particularly evident in relation to the resources of international organizations. Take the issue of the currency for the remuneration of staff members of international organizations, a recognized problem for international organizations.[28] Unlike states, with the exception of a few regional organizations that constitute a monetary union (for example, the Eastern Caribbean States and the European Union), international organizations do not have their own currency and must rely on the currency of some country.[29] With respect to the operational cash of international organizations, applicable international law typically requires the organization's executive to designate the banks in which the organization's funds will be kept and to establish bank accounts for the transaction of the organization's business.[30] Although the resources of international organizations are inherently international and as such beyond national jurisdiction,[31] once these resources are converted into assets, namely, through the acquisition of bank holdings, securities, real property, and the like, they become at least in part subject to national law.[32] For instance, the national legislation that regulates the currency in which assets are denominated (the *lex monetae*) will also govern the valuation of these assets. Real property owned by the organization is subject to the principle of *lex rei sitae*, that is, the law where the property is situated, including zoning and safety regulations.

---

28   Henry G. Schermers & Niels M. Blokker, *International Institutional Law* 357–58 (4th ed., Martinus Nijhoff 2004).

29   *See Mann on the Legal Aspect of Money* 587–88 (Charles Proctor ed., 6th ed., Oxford U. Press 2005).

30   *See*, for example, ICC Financial Regulation 8; INTERPOL Financial Regulation 3.9; ILO Financial Regulations, Article 22; ICAO Financial Regulations, Article X, 10.1; and WMO Financial Regulations, Article 11.

31   Rutsel Silvestre J. Martha, *International Organizations and the Global Financial Crisis: The Status of Their Assets in Insolvency and Forced Liquidation Proceedings*, 6 Intl. Organizations L. Rev. 117, 118–20 (2009).

32   *See* James Fawcett, *Trade and Finance in International Law*, 128 Recueil des Cours 215, 237–39 (1968).

Similarly, the foreign exchange laws of the jurisdictions involved affect the transfer of funds across borders.[33] With respect to the management of international organization assets, the division of tasks and responsibilities between the custodian and the entity issuing the securities is likely to be governed by a national legal system, unless the parties agree otherwise. Finally, the laws regulating domestic financial institutions and the insolvency laws that apply in the country of a debtor of an international organization will impact the assets of an international organization.[34]

Thus, there is simply no way for any international organization to avoid entanglement with at least one domestic market of a member state. Two domestic court rulings prove the point that failure to acknowledge the unavoidability of international organizations operating in domestic markets can lead to the misappropriation of international resources. Imagine the following situation: States come together and set up an international fund to combat the effects of climate change on agriculture. They pay contributions, and the fund sets aside the resources that are not immediately needed for operations in demand accounts and time deposits. Then, for whatever reason, the bank holding the deposits is liquidated. In such a situation, would the organization's assets be frozen? The Court of Appeals of Paris ruled in the affirmative in *ECOWAS v. BCCI* (1993).

The Economic Community of West African States (ECOWAS), a regional group of fifteen West African countries whose mission is to promote economic integration, learned an important lesson when a portion of its deposits and those of the ECOWAS Fund were placed under the control of the Bank of Credit and Commerce International (BCCI) and subsequently liquidated. On July 5, 1991, what was then described as the biggest bank fraud in history came to light when regulators in seven countries raided and took control of the branch offices of the BCCI. An administrator appointed by the French Banking Commission suspended BCCI's operations and froze its accounts. The bank was subsequently put into liquidation by a French court. The Paris branches of BCCI, whose operations were effectively suspended as of July 5, 1991, held a total amount of US$12.6 million of resources that belonged to the ECOWAS Fund.[35] In the lawsuit against BCCI to unfreeze the assets, the claims of ECOWAS and the ECOWAS Fund were rejected on the first hearing by the Tribunal de commerce of Paris. On appeal, the Court of Appeals of Paris maintained that international organizations could invoke immunities in France only if the entitlement to immunity resulted from either an inter-

---

33   *See* William Blair, *Interference of Public Law in the Performance of International Monetary Obligations*, in *International Monetary Law—Issues for the New Millennium* 395 (Mario Giovanoli ed., Oxford U. Press 2000).

34   *See,* generally on the application of national law to international organizations, August Reinisch, *Accountability of International Organizations According to National Law*, 36 Neth. Y.B. Intl. L. 119 (2005).

35   Chibuike U. Uche, *Can African Institutions Finance African Development? Evidence from the ECOWAS Fund*, in *Africa and Development Challenges in the New Millennium: The NEPAD Debate* 235 (Jimi O. Adesina, Yao Graham, & Adebayo Olukoshi ed., Codesria 2005).

national agreement to which France was party or from a rule of customary international law relevant to the case.

The principal grounds for rejection of immunity were articulated around two arguments: first, that France neither was a member country of ECOWAS nor had entered into any agreement with ECOWAS and the ECOWAS Fund; and second, that there was no established applicable rule of customary international law. The Court of Appeals of Paris thus contended that ECOWAS and the ECOWAS Fund were not entitled to immunity. Moreover, the court of appeals reasoned that by initiating the proceedings, the ECOWAS and the ECOWAS Fund waived the jurisdictional immunity that they might otherwise have enjoyed. Finally, the court argued that immunity was inapplicable because no measure had been taken against the ECOWAS or the ECOWAS Fund. According to the court of appeals, the assets belonging to ECOWAS and the ECOWAS Fund could no longer be (re)claimed due to French private law peremptory rules, which are a matter of public policy.[36]

By depositing its cash in a nonmember state with which the organization had no agreement on privileges and immunities, ECOWAS exposed its funds to serious risk. ECOWAS could have been more diligent in choosing where to place its resources, and one could argue that it brought this outcome on itself. Taking additional measures to protect resources doesn't necessarily mitigate risk, however. A 1996 decision of the D.C. Court of Appeals in *U.S. v. BCCI*[37] affirms this assertion. In that case, the general secretariat of the OAS appealed the district court's dismissal of its petition for adjudication of its interest in funds deposited with the BCCI. The funds had been ordered forfeited under U.S. law. The court of appeals affirmed the district court's dismissal on the ground that, notwithstanding its status as an international organization, OAS was, like any other bank depositor, a general creditor of BCCI, with no legal interest in any specific forfeited property. The effect of this ruling is that one member of the organization allowed its bankruptcy court to appropriate international resources that were destined to support the operations of the organization.

If the above two cases represent the state of international law on the control over international organizations' financial resources held in domestic banks, then there is a sizable risk that the funds pooled by sovereign states to finance international public goods may be made unavailable to serve their intended purpose. This deviation could occur when national laws permit an international organization's funds to be frozen and distributed among the creditors of bankrupt banks or banks in liquidation. Clearly, allowing national courts to apply national bankruptcy or forced-liquidation laws, or any national law for that matter, can deprive an international organization of the funding supplied by its member states, which is tantamount to allowing a single member state

---

36 *Economic Community of West African States v. Bank of Credit and Commerce International* (Paris Court of Appeals, 1993), 113 Intl. L. Rep. 473.

37 *United States v. BCCI Holdings (Luxembourg), S.A.*, 73 F.3d 403 (D.C. Cir. 1996).

to undermine the very purpose for which the funds were pooled. By ignoring the exclusive international nature of the international organizations' resources and the fact that, unlike other market participants, international organizations cannot avoid operating in the domestic market of the forum, both the Court of Appeals of Paris and the D.C. Court of Appeals condoned a situation whereby France and the United States essentially misappropriated funds that had been assembled in the service of international public welfare.

Need to Engage Services of Private Parties

The most frequent source of legal matters brought to national courts for settlement concerns natural persons who work at or have rendered to international organizations.[38] Unlike states, international organizations have neither their own citizens nor their own residents.[39] International organizations are abstract (fictional) entities that cannot act in the physical world. The same is true for corporate entities established under domestic law and for the state itself. Conduct always originates in individuals, that is, natural persons. As acknowledged in the *Reparation for Injuries* case,[40] because international organizations do not have citizens or residents, the link between international organizations and individuals is not a nationality link but a functionality link. Whereas states have citizens and residents from whom they can recruit civil servants and thus exclude exposure to foreign legal orders, international civil servants must be recruited from among citizens of the organization's members. The natural persons the organizations engage, whether staff members, service providers, or vendors, are necessarily the nationals and residents of some state. Thus, the contracting of individuals by international organizations establishes links with the domestic legal orders of at least one country.

Lack Territory of Their Own

As Judge Ago wrote in his opinion in the *WHO/Egypt* case, an international organization is, like a state, a subject of international law, but one that enjoys limited international legal capacity and, unlike a state, a subject of law that lacks territorial bases. An international organization's "establishment" in the territory of a given state is therefore a condition sine qua non of its functioning as an organization, carrying on its activities and fulfilling its objects and purposes.[41] In other words, unlike foreign states, when international organizations operate in the territory of a state, they do so not out of

---

38 August Reinisch, *International Organizations before National Courts* 25–26 (Cambridge U. Press 2000). Also Finn Seyersted, *Common Law of International Organizations* 449–50 (Martinus Nijhoff 2008).

39 When an international organization governs an inhabited territory, which is exceptional, it normally also exercises jurisdiction over the residents and nationals of the territory in question. *See* Seyersted, *supra* note 38, at 208.

40 *Reparation for Injuries Suffered in the Service of the United Nations, Advisory Op.,* 1949 I.C.J. 174.

41 *Interpretation of the Agreement of 25 March 1951 between the World Health Organization and Egypt, Advisory Op.,* 1980 I.C.J. 73, 155 (Separate Opinion, Judge Ago). *Cf.* Felice Morgenstern, *Legal Problems of International Organizations* 5 (Cambridge U. Press 1986).

volition but because they have no alternative. According to special rapporteur Díaz-González, this fact provides the rationale for the unrestricted immunity accorded to international organizations:

> Being unable to enjoy the protection conferred by territorial sover-eignty, as States can, international organizations have as their sole protection the immunities granted to them. The ample immunity afforded them is fully justified, in contrast to the increasingly restricted immunity of States, for the good reason that States are political entities pursuing their own interests while international organizations are service agencies operating on behalf of all their member States.[42]

The Functional Nature of Their Powers

In the *Legality of Nuclear Weapons* case, citing *European Commission of the Danube*,[43] the ICJ stated that

> international organizations are subjects of international law which do not, unlike states, possess a general competence like States. Inter-national organizations are governed by the "principle of speciality," that is to say, they are invested by the States which create them with powers, the limits of which are a function of the common interests whose promotion those States entrust to them.[44]

Due to this principle of specialty, unlike with states, the activities of inter-national organizations can be divided not between public activities (*acta iure imperii*) and commercial activities (*acta iure gestionis*) but rather by whether the activities are functional or not.[45] It must be stressed, however, that the fact that an act is functional does not necessarily mean that it cannot engage the re-sponsibility of the actor. The point here is that because the distinction between *acta iure imperii* and *acta iure gestionis* cannot be made in respect to the actions of international organizations, the restrictive immunity doctrine that applies to states cannot be applied to international organizations.

The conclusions to draw from the foregoing are that the activities of inter-national organizations are determined on the basis of their functionality; the absence of certain functions at the international level compels international

---

42   Leonardo Díaz-González, special rapporteur, *Fourth Report on Relations between States and International Organizations (Second Part of the Topic)*, 2 Y.B. Intl. L. Commn. (part 1) 153, 158 (1989).

43   *Jurisdiction of the European Commission of the Danube, Advisory Op.*, 1927 P.C.I.J. Series B, No. 14, at 64.

44   *Legality of the Use by a State of Nuclear Weapons in Armed Conflict, Advisory Op.*, 1996 I.C.J. 66, 78. See also Elihu Lauterpacht, *The Development of the Law of International Organizations by the Decisions of International Tribunals*, 152 Recueil des Cours 377, 414 (1976) (noting that interna-tional organizations are artificial and deliberate creations that owe their existence not only to the instrument on which they are founded but also to their ability to act).

45   Felice Morgenstern, *Legal Problems of International Organizations*, Hersh Lauterpacht Memorial Lectures 6 (Grotius 1986).

organizations to rely on and expose themselves to domestic markets; and international organizations have no territory, nationals, or residents of their own, which compels further exposure. These aspects render any comparison of international organizations and states for the purpose of the application of the principles of immunity from legal process utterly misguided.[46]

Functional Need of Noninterference by Domestic Authorities

Given the functional needs of international organizations to operate in domestic markets, it is necessary to establish safeguards against interference at the national level, a principle that is captured in the phrase *ne impediatur officia*. This basic principle was articulated by the IV/2 Committee of the United Nations Conference as follows: "No Member state may hinder in any way the working of the Organization or take measures the effect of which might increase its burdens, financial or other."[47] It has been argued that the obligation not to intervene is inherent in the status of a member of an international organization. As succinctly articulated by Judge Rezek in *Cumaraswamy*:

> There is no obligation on sovereign States to found international organizations, or to remain Members of them against their will. However, the fact of membership—even in the case of an organization whose objectives are less essential than those of the United Nations, and in fields less salient than that of human rights—requires that every State, in its relations with the Organization and its agents, display an attitude at least as constructive as that which characterizes diplomatic relations between States.[48]

In line with the principle of *ne impediatur officia*, the parties to the constituent instrument of an international organization undertake the obligation to recognize the privileges and immunities necessary for the exercise of the entity's functions and the fulfillment of its objectives. This obligation is often expressed in a general clause that can be found in the constituent instrument itself and is further defined in special agreements on privileges and immunities.[49] In the case of the United Nations, its specialized agencies (which includes, inter alia, the World Bank Group; the International Monetary Fund,

---

46   *Cf.* Christian Dominicé, *La nature et l'étendue de l'immunité de juridiction des organisations internationales*, in *Law of Nations, Law of International Organizations, World's Economic Law—Liber amicorum Honouring Ignaz Seidl-Hohenveldern* 77, 85 (Hans-Ernst Folz, Jörg Manfred Mössner, & Karl Zemanek ed., Kluwer Law International 1988).

47   UNCIO, Report of the Rapporteur of Committee IV/2, Doc. 933, IV/2/42, at 3.

48   *Difference Relating to Immunity from Legal Process of a Special Rapporteur of the Commission on Human Rights, Advisory Op.*, 1999 I.C.J. 62, 109–10.

49   For example, UN Charter, Article 105; Agreement Establishing IFAD, Article 10, Section 2(a); WHO Constitution, Article 67; ILO Constitution, Article 40.

IMF; and the International Fund for Agricultural Development, IFAD), and their related organizations, two general conventions are relevant. Article II of the Convention on the Privileges and Immunities of the United Nations (1946) and Article III of the Convention on the Privileges and Immunities of the Specialized Agencies (1947) both stipulate that the United Nations and the specialized agencies, their property, and their assets, wherever located and by whomsoever held, shall enjoy immunity from every form of legal process, except insofar as in any particular case it has expressly waived its immunity.[50] These and similar stipulations in other conventions often provide the basis for domestic court rulings that decline to exercise jurisdiction over international organizations.

A case in point is the decision of the D.C. Court of Appeals in the landmark case of *Broadbent v. OAS*, where the court upheld the doctrine of noninterference and held that OAS was immune from suit. The use of the term "absolute immunity" in *Broadbent*, inspired by the national legislation that the court was interpreting in that case, should not be understood as meaning that the scope of the immunity is unlimited. As Bekker explains, strictly speaking, immunities of international organizations are neither absolute nor restrictive, but functional.[51] In this sense, absolute immunity from domestic legal process merely means that the answer to the question of whether the claimed immunity is functionally necessary is reserved for the competent international body. This was explained by Judge Weeramanty in *Cumaraswamy*:

> The Secretary-General's determination as to whether a particular action is within an official's or rapporteur's sphere of authority should therefore be binding on the domestic tribunal, unless compelling reasons can be established for displacing that weighty presumption ... if a State disputes such a ruling by the Secretary General, there is always room for the matter to be brought to the Court.[52]

---

50 The property and assets of the United Nations and the specialized agencies, wherever located and by whomsoever held, shall also be immune from search, requisition, confiscation, expropriation, and any other form of interference, whether by executive, administrative, judicial, or legislative action. Moreover, the United Nations and its specialized agencies may, without being restricted by financial controls, regulations, or moratoria of any kind, hold funds, gold, or currency of any kind and operate accounts in any currency; and freely transfer its funds, gold, or currency from one country to another or within any country and convert any currency held by it into any other currency. The rationale for conferring immunity in these provisions can be attributed to the fact that without immunity, states could interfere with or affect the functioning of an international organization, for instance, by impounding its assets.

51 Bekker, *supra* note 21, at 156–59.

52 *Difference Relating to Immunity from Legal Process of a Special Rapporteur of the Commission on Human Rights, supra* note 48, at 97.

International practice reveals that such bodies sometimes agree with the organization that it entitled to immunity,[53] but not always.[54] In the latter cases, the organization will have to accept the consequences of the operation of domestic law in accordance with the terms of the international decision.

Jurisdictional Limitations of Domestic Courts

Much of the discussion around the desirability and the extent of multilateral financial institutions' immunity from legal process fails to consider the fact that certain matters involving international organizations are simply beyond the powers of national courts. This fact imposes significant limitations on the role that domestic courts can play in the settlement of private-party claims against international financial institutions. It also makes the legal viability of removing or restricting immunity from legal process a highly questionable proposition. Although it may be obvious at a theoretical level that certain matters specifically fall to international organizations and are beyond national competence, both scholars and national courts struggle with this issue. Much of the debate and judicial musings about the purported anachronism of the immunity of international organizations, at least in its absolute version, is conducted without considering the threshold question of whether national courts even have jurisdiction over international organizations. Such approaches tend to overlook the fact that, from an international law perspective, the answer to this question is not found in domestic law: "The existence of a State's right to exercise jurisdiction," whether regulation, adjudication, or enforcement related, "is exclusively determined by public international law."[55]

Scholars and national courts that look at international organizations through the lens of immunity from jurisdiction are likely to limit their examination to the exemption from the powers of courts and tribunals. Given that in most cases, international instruments contain provisions on organizational immunity, such an approach is tempting. However, as stated by the ICJ in the *Arrest Warrant* case: "It is only where a State has jurisdiction under international law in relation to a particular matter that there can be any question of immunities in regard to the exercise of that jurisdiction."[56] According to the

---

53　*Applicability of Article VI, Section 22, of the Convention on the Privileges and Immunities of the United Nations, Advisory Op.,* 1989 I.C.J. 177; *Difference Relating to Immunity from Legal Process of a Special Rapporteur of the Commission on Human Rights, supra* note 48; *Case Concerning the Taxation Liability of Euratom Employees between the Commission of the European Atomic Energy Community (Euratom) and the United Kingdom Atomic Energy Authority,* decision of February 25, 1967, XVIII UNRIAA 467.

54　*European Molecular Biology Laboratory* case *(v. Germany)* (Arbitration Tribunal, 1990) 105 Intl. L. Rep. 1; *Question of the Tax Regime Governing Pensions Paid to Retired UNESCO Officials Residing in France (France v. UNESCO),* decision of January 14, 2003, XXV UNRIAA 231.

55　Frederick A. Mann, *The Doctrine of Jurisdiction in International Law,* 111 Recueil des Cours 9, 96 (1964).

56　*Arrest Warrant of 11 April 2000 (Democratic Republic of the Congo v. Belgium),* 2002 I.C.J. 3, 19, paragraph 46.

then president of the court, Judge G. Guillaume, this means that "a domestic court's jurisdiction is a question which it must decide before considering the immunity of those before it. In other words, there can only be immunity from jurisdiction where there is jurisdiction."[57] This view was shared by judges Higgins, Kooijmans, and Buergenthal who stated in their joint separate opinion: "If there is no jurisdiction *en principe*, then the question of immunity from a jurisdiction which would otherwise exist simply does not arise."[58] This confirms what Lalive pointed out in 1953: "L'immunité présuppose un tribunal territorial qui serait normalement compétent" (Immunity presupposes a tribunal that is otherwise competent to deal with the matter).[59]

The far-reaching implications of this statement cannot be overstated: because most issues concerning international organizations, including international financial institutions, involve matters that are beyond domestic jurisdiction, many cases could be disposed of by domestic courts on lack of jurisdiction *rationae materiae* grounds, without requiring inquiry into immunity issues.

The Exclusive International Nature of the Corporate Life of International Organizations

As Kelsen asserts, "certain subject matters cannot be regulated by national law but only by international law."[60] The categorical nature of this assertion, which cannot be reduced to dogmatic postulation, has occasionally been recognized by national courts. Aware of the inherent dangers of exercising national jurisdiction over international organizations, some national courts have resorted to a wide array of means and procedural devices in order to avoid doing so.[61] It took the International Tin Council (ITC) litigations in British courts to make visible the logical extreme of accepting national jurisdiction over international organizations.[62]

Established in 1956 by a treaty, the ITC was an international organization that acted on behalf of large tin producers and bought surplus tin stocks to maintain prices. However, with the advent of aluminum containers, the use of protective polymer lacquers inside cans, and increased recycling by industry, the demand for tin had decreased considerably by the early 1980s; in October 1985, the ITC could no longer carry out its price-maintaining function. It

---

57   *Id.*, at 35, paragraph 1.

58   *Id.*, at 64, paragraph 3. *Cf.* Rutsel Silvestre J. Martha, *The Jurisdiction to Tax in International Law* 17–18 (Kluwer Law and Taxation 1989).

59   Jean-Flavien Lalive, *L'immunité de juridiction des états et des organisations internationales* 84 Recueil des Cours 205, 293 (1953).

60   Hans Kelsen, *Principles of International Law* 241 (Rinehart 1952); also Hans Kelsen, *General Theory of Law and State* 365 (Harvard U. Press 1945).

61   *See* Reinisch, *supra* note 38, and *Challenging Acts of International Organizations before National Courts* (August Reinisch ed., Oxford U. Press 2010).

62   Philippe Sands, *The Tin Council Litigation in the English Courts*, 34 Neth. Intl. L. Rev. 367 (1987); Christopher Greenwood, *The Tin Council Litigation in the House of Lords*, 49 Cambridge L.J. 8 (Mar. 1990).

eventually ran out of money, accumulating a staggering debt of nine hundred million pounds sterling through borrowings from the capital market.[63] Faced with the insolvency of the organization, the creditors filed suits, inter alia, in British courts seeking the appointment of a receiver for the purpose of winding up the organization in accordance with English bankruptcy laws. In other words, a national court was asked to use domestic law to liquidate an organization that was created under international law by a group of sovereign states. Not much imagination is needed to understand the legal, political, and practical unattractiveness of this proposition. To the disappointment of the creditors, the national courts politely declined the honor. Starting from the premise that international organizations are created not by the territorial enactments of any single state but by an international legal instrument, and finding that they are, as a consequence, not subject to any territorial system of law,[64] Justice Millet reasoned in the following way:

> An international organisation . . . is merely the means by which a collective enterprise of the member States is carried on, and through which their relations with each other in a particular sphere of common interest are regulated. Any attempt by one of the member States to assume responsibility for the administration and winding up of the organisation would be inconsistent with the arrangements made by them as to the manner in which the enterprise is to be carried on and their relations with each other in that sphere regulated. Sovereign States are free, if they wish, to carry on a collective company incorporated in the territory of one of their number. But if they choose instead to carry it on through the medium of an international organisation, no one member State, by executive, legislative or judicial action, can assume the management of the enterprise and subject it to its own domestic law.[65]

Because international organizations are creatures of international law that cannot be regulated by domestic law, "the court has no jurisdiction to wind up the ITC"; further, "this makes it unnecessary to consider the question of immunity, for there is no need for immunity from jurisdiction which does not exist."[66]

Indeed, the charters of international organizations, embodied in international agreements, are multilateral treaties according to the ICJ, albeit of a particular type.[67] One of these particularities is that the constituent instruments

63   Sandhya Chandrasekhar, *Cartel in a Can: The Financial Collapse of the International Tin Council*, 10 Nw. J. Intl. L. & Bus. 309 (1989–90); Ian A. Mallory, *Conduct Unbecoming: The Collapse of the International Tin Agreement*, 5 Am. U.J. Intl. L. & Policy 835 (1989–90).

64   *Re International Tin Council* (England High Court, 1987), 77 Intl. L. Rep. 18, 28.

65   *Id.*, at 36.

66   *Id.*

67   *See*, for example, *Legality of the Use by a State of Nuclear Weapons in Armed Conflict supra* note 44, at 74–75; and, more comprehensively, Tetsuo Sato, *Evolving Constitutions of International Organizations* (Kluwer Law International 1996).

create new subjects of law endowed with certain autonomy.[68] The ICJ says that international organizations "are subjects of international law and, as such, are bound by any obligation incumbent upon them under general rules of international law."[69] In other words, the legal existence and operations of international organizations are, by definition, governed by international law.[70] More recently, the Hague Arbitration Tribunal confirmed in its partial award in the *Bank for International Settlements* (BIS) case[71] that any matter that implicates the organic principles or internal governance of international organizations shall be governed by international law. By consequence, the question of whether the BIS was authorized to squeeze out certain shareholders by recalling the privately held shares in the organization was to be answered not by any system of national law but by international law.[72]

The obligations of international organizations that emanate from their constitutional instruments and from the secondary law of international organizations are international legal norms, just as the obligations emanating from treaties to which an organization is a party are legal norms; the same can also be said of customary international law.[73] By definition, then, the operations of international organizations are governed by international law.[74] International tribunals have often declared that the laws of member states of international organizations, whether statutory or judicial, do not govern the organizations or any of their organs. Otherwise, operations could be encumbered by entanglements and (possible) conflicts created by domestic laws and regulations and by the (possibly) divergent rulings of its many member states.[75]

---

68 Paul Reuter, *Introduction to the Law of Treaties* 85–86, paragraph 169 (Pinter 1989).

69 *Interpretation of the Agreement of 25 March 1951 between WHO and Egypt, supra* note 41, at 89, paragraph 37. For a discussion of ICJ's case law applicable to international organizations, *see* Hugh Thirlway, *The Law and Procedure of the International Court of Justice, 1960–1989, Part Eight*, 67 British Y.B. Intl. L. 1, 4–36 (1996).

70 *Cf. Westland Helicopters Ltd. v. Arab Organisation for Industrialization et al.*, 23 Intl. Leg. Materials 1071 (1984) and Broches, *supra* note 15.

71 *Dr. Horst Reineccius et al. v. Bank for International Settlement*, Hague Arbitral Tribunal, Partial Award of November 22, 2002, available at <http://www.pca-cpa.org/upload/files/EPA .pdf>. This case stems from a decision on January 8, 2001, of the extraordinary general meeting of the BIS to restrict the right to hold shares in the BIS exclusively to central banks and approve the mandatory repurchase of all BIS shares held by private shareholders against payment of compensation of 16,000 Swiss francs per share. Three former private shareholders had challenged the repurchase by initiating proceedings before the Hague Arbitral Tribunal, which has sole jurisdiction in this matter. The Hague Arbitral Tribunal confirmed that the compulsory repurchase by the BIS was legally valid and consistent with its public interest mandate as an international organization.

72 *Id.*, at paragraph 123.

73 *See* Chittharanjan F. Amerasinghe, *Principles of the Institutional Law of International Organisations* 326 (2nd ed., Cambridge U. Press 2005). *See* also Philippe Sands & Pierre Klein, *Bowett's Law of International Institutions* 441 (5th ed., Sweet & Maxwell 2001).

74 *Cf. Westland Helicopters* case, *supra* note 70, and Broches, *supra* note 15.

75 *See* World Bank Administrative Tribunal (WBAT): *de Merode*, Decision No. 1 (1981), paragraph 36; *Mould*, Decision No. 210 (1999), paragraphs 23–24; *Cissé*, Decision No. 242 (2001),

Such a view is illustrated by an event in 2000 in which a South Korean court rejected a lawsuit filed by a group of labor unions against the IMF for alleged policy mistakes. The unions were suing the IMF for 480 million won (US$426,000) in compensation for job losses caused by austerity measures adopted by the Korean government as conditions for a US$57 billion IMF balance-of-payments credit. The unions claimed that the IMF had given bad advice—including maintaining high interest rates and pushing for corporate restructuring—that had caused businesses to fail and unemployment to rise. The judge accepted the IMF's defense that no signatory country can hold the IMF civilly or criminally liable over its policy implementation.[76] This is entirely different from saying that the IMF—and, for that matter, international financial institutions—cannot be held responsible internationally for its policy implementation; it merely means that such responsibility can only be established by a competent international body—whether ad hoc or standing—applying governing international norms.

The Exclusive International Nature of Financial Resources

The problem manifests itself also in relation to the ability of domestic courts to dispose of the financial resources of international financial institutions. International organizations typically derive the financial resources needed to fund their operations from contributions by their member states. The funding so obtained in effect constitutes a common international fund, the exclusive use of which is to support and sustain organizational functioning. Members transfer resources to international organizations through legal transactions governed by international law,[77] namely, by using the constituent instrument of a given organization as the appropriate legal vehicle. These transactions may consist of the payment of assessed contributions, the discharge of pledges to contribute to the replenishment of the organization, the payment for quotas or shares in the capital of an organization, and loans from member states to the organization.[78] Such loans are governed by international law.[79] The fact that these legal transactions are governed by international law signifies that an international organization's property title over its resources does not hail from any system of national law.[80] This in turn explains why international organizations

---

paragraph 23; *Rodriguez-Sawyer*, Decision No. 330 (2005), paragraph 14; and *Aida Shekib*, Decision No. 358 (2007).

76   *Korean Workers Lawsuit against IMF Thrown Out*, available at <http://www .brettonwoodsproject.org/art-15638>.

77   *Cf.* Frederick A. Mann, *Money in Public International Law*, 96 Recueil des Cours 99–104 (1959) (discussing the monetary law of interstate obligations).

78   For example, IFAD, *Establishment of the Spanish Food Security Co-financing Facility Trust Fund*, IFAD Doc. EB 2010/100/R.29/Rev.2, available at <http://www.ifad.org/gbdocs/eb/100/e/ EB-2010-100-R-29-Rev-2.pdf>.

79   On the legal implications of the possibility of IMF borrowing from other than official sources, *see* Joseph Gold, *Borrowing by the International Monetary Fund from Nonofficial Lenders*, 20 Intl. Law. 455 (1986).

80   *See* Ian Brownlie, *Principles of Public International Law* 416 (6th ed., Oxford U. Press 2003).

can be liquidated only through the operation of a rule of international law,[81] which for most organizations is a decision reserved for the institution's highest governing body. Once such a body decides to liquidate the organization, it must also make decisions concerning the orderly collection and liquidation of the organization's assets and the settlement of its liabilities. Thus, the property rights that international organizations hold over the financial resources made available to them by their member states belong to the realm of matters that cannot be regulated by any national legal order. As stated in *Maclaine Watson v. International Tin Council*, "it is axiomatic that municipal courts have not and cannot have the competence to adjudicate upon or to enforce the rights arising out of transactions entered into by independent sovereign states between themselves on the plane of international law."[82]

The Exclusive International Nature of Employment Relations

A third area that is beyond domestic jurisdiction concerns the employment relations between international organizations and their international civil servants. To avoid conflicting norms, international administrative tribunals have often declared that domestic laws, whether statutory or judicial, do not govern the international organizations or any of their organs.[83] Although this declaration should suffice to explain the nonapplicability of national laws, another persuasive reason is that an autonomous system of law is necessary for preserving the independence of international civil servants from national pressures and thus to protect the organizations from unilateral control by a member over the activities in its territory.[84]

According to Amerasinghe, this "principle is basic for the operation of international organizations."[85] Taking a softer approach, others caution against using national rules and laws in the practice of international courts and international administrative tribunals unless the organization in question has specifically submitted to such rules to a limited degree and in a limited context, meaning that these rules amount to customary international law.[86] In this respect, mention is made of *Saunoi v. INTERPOL*, in which the International Labour Organization Administrative Tribunal (ILOAT) based its dismissal of the complaint on the plaintiff's reliance on the legislation and case law of the host state by stating that as an international organization, INTERPOL is not subject to national law and that the claims that the plaintiff sought to support using

---

81   *Re International Tin Council, supra* note 64, at 27–36.

82   *Maclaine Watson & Co. Ltd. v. International Tin Council*, 3 All Eng. L. Rep. 523 (1989).

83   *See* WBAT: *de Merode*, Decision No. 1 (1981), paragraph 36; *Mould*, Decision No. 210 (1999), paragraphs 23–24; *Cissé*, Decision No. 242 (2001), paragraph 23; *Rodriguez-Sawyer*, Decision No. 330 (2005), paragraph 14; and *Aida Shekib*, Decision No. 358 (2007).

84   *Cf. Mendaro v. World Bank*, 717 F.2d 610 at 615 (D.C. Cir. 1983).

85   Chittharanjan F. Amerasinghe, *The Law of the International Civil Service* vol. I, 7 (2d ed., Oxford U. Press 1994); *see also* Reinisch, *supra* note 38, at 242–43.

86   Finn Seyersted, *Applicable Law in Relations between Intergovernmental Organizations and Private Parties*, 122 Recueil des Cours 427 (1967).

French law had to be set aside because the complainant was not able to refer to any INTERPOL text that would warrant taking such law into account.[87] According to the tribunal, therefore, the application of national law must be justified and cannot be presumed.[88] It should be noted that in *Kock, N'Diaye and Silbereiss*, the ILOAT clarified that it never ruled out municipal law a priori. Affirming its competence in international law contexts, the tribunal acknowledged that under certain circumstances, it could benefit from drawing upon municipal law provisions, particularly where there is a *renvoi* to such law in a contract of service or in an organization's rules. Precedent further illustrates that reference to municipal law can be made for comparative purposes in order to deduce certain general principles of law that apply to the international civil service.[89] Such *renvoi* to national law is inherently limited, however, and can never lead to the total submission of an international organization to a national legal order unless the organization ceases to be a creature of international law.

The reverse would imply that national courts would be able to apply national standards to international organizations and impose national remedies in handling complaints. This scenario is firmly rejected in the decision of the D.C. Court of Appeals in *Broadbent v. OAS*, an appeal of a district court judgment that had dismissed an action by appellants who claimed that they had been improperly discharged by the OAS:

> The United States has accepted without qualification the principles that international organizations must be free to perform their functions and that no member state may take action to hinder the organization. . . . Denial of immunity opens the door to divided decisions of the courts of different member states passing judgment on the rules, regulations, and decisions of the international bodies. Undercutting uniformity in the application of staff rules or regulations would undermine the ability of the organization to function effectively.[90]

The World Bank's epic journey through the Bangladeshi courts further renders testimony to the undesirability of domestic courts sitting in judgment over disputes between international organizations and their staff.[91] Ismet Zerin Khan, who challenged the Bank's decision not to confirm her probationary appointment on the grounds of abuse of discretion and failure to apply the staff rules, had exhausted all the internal administrative grievance recourses of the World Bank, including the appeals committee and the administrative

---

87   ILOAT Judgment 1020 (1990).

88   ILOAT Judgment 1080 (1991), paragraph 13.

89   ILOAT Judgment 1451 (1995). *See* also ILOAT Judgments 1311 (1994) and 1369 (1994).

90   *See* the reasoning of the D.C. Court of Appeals in *Broadbent v. OAS*, 628 F.2d 27, 35 (D.C. Cir. 1980) (references omitted).

91   IFI WATCH Bangladesh, Bangladesh Working Group on International Financial Institutions and Trade Organizations, *The World Bank and the Question of Immunity* (Sep. 4, 2004), available at <http://www.unnayan.org/Other/IFI_Watch_Bangladesh_Vol_1 %20No_1.pdf>.

tribunal. An advertisement for recruitment to the disputed position while Kahn's application was pending review in the appeals committee led her to file a case in the court of Dhaka. After ignoring several summons, the Bank filed an application for rejection of the complaint. The primary ground cited was that the Bank enjoyed immunity from legal process and could therefore not be sued in Bangladesh. In the meantime, a judgment favorable to Khan was rendered by the World Bank Administrative Tribunal. The tribunal did not accede to Khan's request for reinstatement, however, awarding only pecuniary compensation (one year's salary plus costs).[92] This development did not end the proceedings in Dhaka. Instead, on the critical issue of immunity, the court observed, "no Establishment Agreement existed between the World Bank and Bangladesh." The court also determined that the provision of immunity is in opposition to the Constitution of Bangladesh and that immunity in this setting is fundamentally contrary to the spirit of the constitution. As to the merits, the court ruled that the plaintiff was entitled to be reinstated and receive arrear salaries and benefits[93] and

> that the instant suit be decreed against the defendants on contest without any order as to costs and further declared that the letter dated 03/05/2001 terminating the plaintiff from service is illegal, malafide, arbitrary and not binding upon the plaintiff. The plaintiff is entitled to be reinstated in her post and get all arrear salaries and benefits. Defendants are directed to pay the salaries and other benefits to the plaintiff deducting the compensation money which the plaintiff has received earlier as she is still now in service as External Affairs Officer of the defendant.[94]

Thus, a domestic court of a World Bank member state asserted jurisdiction to ignore a final decision (*res judicata*) of the World Bank Administrative Tribunal; set aside an employment decision of the chief administrative officer; and expressly issued an order to the World Bank to reinstate the claimant. This ruling is unprecedented, and it illustrates why domestic courts cannot be given a role in examining the legality of decisions of international organizations. Recall that "from the standpoint of international law . . . municipal laws are merely facts which express the will and constitute the activities of the States, in the same manner as do legal decisions or administrative measures."[95] As a result, no decision of a national court can invalidate an act or conduct that owes its existence and validity to international law.[96]

---

92   WBAT Decision No. 293, *Khan* (2003).

93   News from Bangladesh, *Termination of WB Employee Declared Illegal: Dhaka Court*, available at <http://bangladesh-web.com/view.php?hidRecord=321074>.

94   *Ismet Zerin Khan v. World Bank and Others*, High Court of Dhaka, April 28, 2010, Suit/Case No. 48.

95   *Certain German Interests in Polish Upper Silesia (Merits) (Germany v. Poland)*, 1926 P.C.I.J. Series A, No. 7, at 19.

96   Cf. *Chorzow Factory (Merits) (Germany v. Poland)*, 1928 P.C.I.J. Series A, No. 17, at 33–34.

By ignoring this principle, the Dhaka High Court contributed to a situation in which the World Bank was confronted with two conflicting judgments dealing with the same matter: one rendered by an incompetent domestic court that ordered reinstatement and compensation, and another decided by a competent international tribunal that awarded only compensation. Even though this ruling clearly exceeded Bangladesh's jurisdictional authority under international law, relegating it to little more than *brutum fulnem* at the international level, the undesirability of its outcome remains problematic: it is compelling evidence against the argument favoring a role for domestic courts in the settlement of disputes between private parties and international organizations.

The foregoing analysis shows that the issue of inherent constraints on domestic legal orders—that is, that domestic law cannot regulate matters that are essentially international by their nature—poses limitations on the role domestic courts can play in settling claims of private parties against international organizations. Domestic courts will have to declare that they are incompetent to deal with such questions without having to expressly address the issue of immunity from legal process:

> chacun sait qu'il y a des litiges qui, par leur nature même, relevant exclusivement d'une ordre juridique determiné . . . et à l'égard desquels un juge est radicalement incompétent [anyone knows that there are cases which, by their nature, relate to only a given legal order . . . and in respect of which the judge is manifestly incompetent].[97]

The Exclusion of a Role for Domestic Courts by International Law

When considering the argument for allowing domestic courts to deal with private claims against international organizations, one should not forget that, given the principle of the unity of the state, domestic courts are no more than organs of states whose conduct—notwithstanding their independence from the executive power—is attributable to the state for the purposes of international responsibility.[98] As a matter of fact, at the time of the writing of this chapter, a case is pending before the ICJ on the very question of whether the denial of immunity to Germany by Italian courts was lawful under international law.[99] As regards the immunity from legal process of international organizations, this was confirmed by the *Cumaraswamy* case in 1999, when the ICJ ruled that any decision by a domestic court that denies or restricts its immunity can be ruled wrongful by a competent international authority.[100] In the same

---

97   Dominicé, *supra* note 46, at 83.

98   James Crawford, *The International Law Commission's Article on State Responsibility—Introduction, Text and Commentaries* 95 (Cambridge U. Press 2002).

99   ICJ Press Release No. 2008/44, *Germany Institutes Proceedings against Italy for Failing to Respect Its Jurisdictional Immunity as a Sovereign State* (Dec. 23, 2008), available at <http://www.icj-cij.org/docket/files/143/14925.pdf>.

100 *Difference Relating to Immunity from Legal Process of a Special Rapporteur of the Commission on Human Rights, supra* note 48, at 88. *See also* Rosalyn Higgins, *The Changing Position of Domestic*

case, the ICJ stated that international organizations should not go free when their actions harm private parties, clarifying that "the question of immunity from legal process is distinct from the issue of compensation for any damages incurred as a result of acts performed" by an international organization.[101] In other words, "an international organization which deals with private parties cannot use its jurisdictional immunity to hide from its responsibilities."[102] The court continued, "the United Nations may be required to bear responsibility for the damage arising from such acts. However, as is clear from Article VIII, Section 29, of the General Convention, any such claims against the United Nations shall not be dealt with by national courts but shall be settled in accordance with the appropriate modes of settlement that "the United Nations shall make provisions for" pursuant to Section 29.[103]

In other words, as confirmed by the Brussels Civil Tribunal in *Manderlier* (1966), there is no role to be played by national courts in resolving private-party claims against international organizations: "it is for the United Nations, and for it alone, to set up courts that could produce an appropriate method of settlement for disputes which it may have with third parties (*sic*)."[104] More recently, in *Cynthia Brzak v. United Nations*, the U.S. Court of Appeals for the Second Circuit confirmed that the convention "unequivocally grants the United Nations absolute immunity without exception."[105]

An identical obligation is found in Article IX, Section 31, of the Convention on the Privileges and Immunities of the Specialized Agencies,[106] which means that this obligation applies as well to the International Bank for Reconstruction and Development (IBRD), International Development Association (IDA), International Finance Corporation (IFC), IMF, and International Fund for Agricultural Development (IFAD) by virtue of their status as specialized agencies of the United Nations. As a result, in the territories of the member-state parties to the Convention on the Privileges and Immunities of the Specialized Agencies that have not made a reservation in respect of that provision,

---

Courts in the International Legal Order, in *Themes & Theories: Selected Essays, Speeches, and Writings in International Law* vol. 2, 1340, 1344 (Oxford U. Press 2009).

101 *Difference Relating to Immunity from Legal Process of a Special Rapporteur of the Commission on Human Rights, supra* note 48, at 88.

102 Alexander S. Muller, *International Organizations and Their Host States: Aspects of Their Legal Relationship* (Kluwer Law International 1995), at 177.

103 *Difference Relating to Immunity from Legal Process of a Special Rapporteur of the Commission on Human Rights, supra* note 48, at 88–89.

104 *Manderlier v. United Nations and the Belgian State*, Civil Tribunal of Brussels, May 11, 1966, 45 Intl. L. Rep. 446, 452. For a discussion, *see* Jan Wouters & Pierre Schmidt, *Challenging Acts of Other United Nations Organs, Subsidiary Organs and Officials*, in *Challenging Acts of International Organizations before National Courts* 76, 102, 105 (August Reinisch ed., Oxford U. Press 2010).

105 *Cynthia Brzak, Nasr Ishak, Plaintiffs v. United Nations, Kofi Annan, Ruud Lubbers, Wendy Chamberlin*, 597 F.3d 107 (2010), *cert. denied*.

106 Convention on the Privileges and Immunities of the Specialized Agencies (Nov. 21, 1947), 33 U.N.T.S. 261.

domestic courts have no role to play in the settlement of disputes between private parties and these international financial institutions unless the immunity has expressly been waived in respect to the claim or qualified by a special rule contained in the charters of the organizations concerned or another relevant international instrument, such as a headquarters agreement.

In the case of the World Bank Group and the IMF, a provision in their respective annexes[107] to the convention restricts the authority of the ICJ to "differences arising out of the interpretation and application of privileges and immunities solely derived from the Convention and which are not included in the privileges and immunities that these agencies can claim under their Articles of Agreement or otherwise."[108] The only real question is whether in light of Section 34—which stipulates that the provisions of the convention in relation to any specialized agency must be interpreted in light of the functions with which that agency is entrusted by its constitutional instrument—the qualified amenability to domestic legal process contained in the Articles of Agreement of the IBRD and IFC must be deemed to limit the scope of Section 4. This question is a matter on which ultimately the ICJ will have the final say pursuant to Section 32: "it is . . . *for the Court* to exercise the authority vested in it to make a determination . . . on the applicability of the Convention, and on . . . entitlement to immunity."[109]

Article 35.2 of the Statute of the European System of Central Banks and of the European Central Bank (ECB) states that the European Court of Justice shall have jurisdiction in any dispute between the ECB and its servants within the limits and under the conditions laid down in the terms of employment. In other words, disputes between the ECB and its staff fall under the exclusive competence of the court of justice, specifically the European Union Civil Service Tribunal, and must not be brought before a national court. Similarly, Article 28.5 of the EIB statute stipulates that the European Court of Justice shall have jurisdiction in disputes concerning measures adopted by organs of a body incorporated under European Union law.

Thus, even where the charters of the international financial institutions contain a special arrangement concerning the position of the institution with regard to legal process, as is the case with the IBRD, IDA, and IFC, the role

---

107 Section 33 of the convention states that in their application to each specialized agency, the standard clauses shall operate subject to any modification set forth in the final (or revised) text of the annex relating to that agency, as provided in Sections 36 and 38.

108 *The Practice of the United Nations, the Specialized Agencies and the International Atomic Energy Agency Concerning Their Status, Privileges and Immunities: Study Prepared by the Secretariat*, 2 Y.B. Intl. L. Commn. 154, 322 (1967).

109 *Difference Relating to Immunity from Legal Process of a Special Rapporteur of the Commission on Human Rights, supra* note 48, at 99, 102 (Separate Opinion, Judge Oda). *See* also Charles N. Brower & Pieter H. F. Bekker, *Understanding "Binding" Advisory Opinions of the International Court of Justice*, in *Liber amicorum Judge Shigeru Oda* vol. 1, 351 (Nisuke Ando, Edward McWhinney, & Rudiger Wolfrum ed., Kluwer Law International 2002).

accorded to domestic courts is restricted to specified dealings.[110] Domestic courts cannot deny or narrowly interpret the scope of existing immunities under the Specialized Agencies Convention and thereby vest themselves with the jurisdiction to adjudicate suits against the global international financial institutions. The same is true with respect to the immunity clauses in the charters of these institutions as well as in the constituent instruments of the regional development banks. These charters contain provisions reserving the right to provide authoritative interpretation to an organ of such institutions (often the executive board);[111] learned opinion[112] and at least one domestic quasi-judicial body[113] hold that there is an obligation to defer to the competent executive board on matters concerning the interpretation of charters of international financial institutions.

Seen in this light, the choice of whether immunity from domestic legal process of international financial institutions is obsolete or should be restricted must be understood to be proffered as a possible new direction of the law (*lege ferenda*). The remainder of this chapter clarifies that, in order to ensure that claims of private parties against international financial institutions are afforded (procedural and substantive) due process, it is not necessary to eliminate or restrict their immunity from domestic legal process.

Immunity Obliges

It has been established that

- The relevant international legal instruments reserve the final authority to determine the scope of the immunity from legal process to designated international bodies.

---

110 For a discussion of those provisions *see* August Reinisch & Jakub Wurm, *International Financial Institutions before National Courts*, in *International Financial Institutions and International Law* 103, 104–07 (Daniel D. Bradlow & David B. Hunter ed., Kluwer Law International 2010).

111 Andres Rigo Sureda, *The Law Applicable to the Activities of International Development Banks*, 308 Recueil des Cours 9, 48–52 (2005).

112 For example, Joseph Gold, *Interpretation: The IMF and International Law* 32, 38, & 39 (Kluwer Law International 1996), and Christoph C. Schreuer, *Decisions of International Institutions before Domestic Courts* 67–70 (Oceana 1981). *Contra*, but not going as far as saying that national courts are competent, Frederick A. Mann, *The "Interpretation" of the Constitutions of International Financial Organizations*, in *Studies in International Law* 591, 606–08 (Oxford U. Press 1973).

113 *IBRD, IMF v. All American Cables et al.*, 22 Intl. L. Rep. 705. For discussions, *see* Joseph Gold, *The Fund Agreement in the Courts* vol. I, 20–27 (IMF 1962); Ervin P. Hexner, *Interpretation by Public International Organizations of Their Basic Instruments*, 53 Am. J. Intl. L. 341, 354–55 (1959); and Lester Nurick, *Certain Aspects of the Law and Practice of the International Bank for Reconstruction and Development*, in *The Effectiveness of International Decisions: Papers of a Conference of the American Society of International Law and the Proceedings of the Conference* 100, 123–26 (Stephen M. Schwebel ed., Sijthoff/Oceana 1971).

- Some of the international instruments expressly exclude any role of domestic courts in the settlement of private claims against international organizations.

- The potential role of domestic courts in the settlement of private claims against international financial institutions is inherently limited due to the fact that certain matters cannot be regulated by domestic law.

- Unlike states, international organizations operate in domestic markets out of functional necessity, rather than choice, and therefore they cannot be treated in the same way as states for the purpose of the application of the doctrine of immunity.

- Given the responsibility of international financial institutions to mitigate, if not eliminate, the imperfections of the capital market as it relates to the developing needs of the eligible countries, noninterference by domestic legal order, including immunity from domestic legal process, is a *conditio sine qua non* for their functioning.

The Obligation to Provide an Appropriate Mode of Settlement

However, the conversation does not end with the conclusion that the immunities of international organizations are not anachronistic or that they are a *conditio sine qua non* for their functioning. The ICJ confirmed in *Cumaraswamy* that this is only a part of the story. The rest of the story is equally important. The court made it crystal clear that immunity from national legal process does not mean impunity; it further explained that international organizations are required to adopt appropriate modes of settlement for resolving disputes between international organizations and private claimants.[114] Thus, although the court underscored that issues concerning the responsibility of international organizations, whether contractual or noncontractual, are not to be dealt with by domestic courts, the court also emphasized that the settlement of disputes with private parties through appropriate means is mandatory.[115] This is in line with the court's 1954 advisory opinion in the *Effect of Awards* case, in which it upheld the legality of the creation of the UN Administrative Tribunal (UNAT). According to the court,

> it would … hardly be consistent with the expressed aim of the Charter to promote freedom and justice for individuals … that it [the UN] should afford no judicial or arbitral remedy to its own staff for the settlement of any disputes which may arise between it and them.[116]

The court's ruling indicates that both the immunity of international organizations from domestic legal process *and* the duty to establish an adequate

---

114 *Difference Relating to Immunity from Legal Process of a Special Rapporteur of the Commission on Human Rights, supra* note 48, at 88–89.

115 *See* Muller, *supra* note 102, at 176–77.

116 *Effect of Awards of Compensation Made by the U.N. Administrative Tribunal, Advisory Op.*, 1954 I.C.J. 57.

dispute settlement system are absolute.[117] In other words, immunity obliges! Unlike suggestions by William Berenson in this volume,[118] there is no inherent conflict between immunity from national legal process and the right to a fair trial, and the concept of immunity is in no way anathema to the concept of fair play and substantial justice. A clear expression of this dual obligation can be found in Article VIII, Section 29, of the Convention on the Privileges and Immunities of the United Nations[119] and in Article IX, Section 31, the Convention on the Privileges and Immunities of the Specialized Agencies.[120] The latter convention applies to the global multilateral financial institutions—that is, the World Bank Group, the IMF, and the IFAD—by virtue of their status as specialized agencies of the United Nations. This fact is important because Section 31 requires those institutions to establish appropriate modes of settling disputes with private parties.

In *Cabrera* (1983), the Argentine Supreme Court took the position that when a treaty containing immunity from domestic legal process is not paired with alternative means to settle disputes with private parties, such a clause is not valid under international law. The court declared unconstitutional Article 4 of the headquarters agreement between Argentina and the Comisión Técnica Mixta de Salto Grande, which accorded immunity from domestic judicial process to this bi-national organization. The court reasoned that the absence in the agreement of an obligation for the organization to set up dispute settlement mechanisms for private claims infringed on the right to judicial protection enshrined in the Argentine Constitution and in international law. Most striking about this decision is that in the eyes of the court, this omission rendered the immunity from legal process invalid on account of Article 53 of the 1969 Vienna Convention on the Law of Treaties, that is, for breach of a peremptory norm of international law (*ius cogens*): the right of access to justice.[121] Interestingly, the court based this qualification of the right of access to justice, inter alia, on Articles 8 and 10 of the Universal Declaration of Human Rights, and on Section 31 of the Convention on the Privileges and Immunities of the Specialized Agencies.

---

117 *Cf.* Karel Wellens, *Remedies against International Organizations* 125 (Cambridge U. Press 2002).

118 William M. Berenson, *Squaring the Concept of Immunity with the Fundamental Right to a Fair Trial: The Case of the OAS*, in this volume.

119 Convention on the Privileges and Immunities of the United Nations (Feb. 13, 1946), 1 U.N.T.S. 15.

120 Convention on the Privileges and Immunities of the Specialized Agencies (Nov. 21, 1947), 33 U.N.T.S. 261.

121 *Cabrera, Washington J. E. c. Comisión Técnica Mixta de Salto Grande*, Corte Suprema de Justicia de la Nación (CS) (1983), available at <http://www.planetaius.com.ar/fallos/jurisprudencia-c/caso-Cabrera-Washington-JE-c-Comision-Tecnica-Mixta-de-Salto-Grande .htm>. For a discussion, *see* Zlata Drnas de Clément & Marta Susana Sartori, *La aplicación del Derecho Internacional en los fallos de la Corte Suprema de Justicia de la Nación Argentina* 161 (Lerner 2010). *See also* Christian Dominicé, *Morgan v. World Bank (Ten Years Later)*, in *Liber amicorum Ibrahim F. I. Shihata—International Finance and Development Law* 155, 166 (Sabine Schlemmer-Schulte & Ko-Yung Tung ed., Kluwer Law International 2001) (supporting the view that the right to access to court is *jus cogens*).

In reaching this decision, the court took into account that the Comisión Técnica Mixta de Salto Grande had established its Tribunal Arbitral Internacional de Salto Grande, which had jurisdiction over private claims against the organization. However, because the case started before the establishment of said tribunal, the tribunal did not have jurisdiction over the case and was not deemed sufficient to remedy the situation confronted in that case. In a subsequent judgment, *Fibraca Constructora* (1993),[122] the Argentine Supreme Court took the opportunity to clarify that *Cabrera* does not apply in cases in which the organization has established an adequate dispute-settlement mechanism. What was at stake was the immunity of the Comisión Técnica Mixta de Salto Grande. The court ruled that due to the availability of the Tribunal Arbitral Internacional de Salto Grande, *Cabrera* did not apply. A few years later, in *Duhalde* (1999),[123] the court underscored this view. The case involved the immunity from legal process of the World Health Organization (WHO) and the Pan-American Health Organization. The court upheld WHO's immunity given the existence of appropriate alternative remedies for WHO employees (in particular the ILOAT), but only after recalling that without such remedies, the treaty-based immunity would be struck down by operation of a *jus cogens* norm.

The *Cabrera* jurisprudence failed to garner international attention, but its assertion of a synallagmatic relationship between international organizations' immunity and the duty to provide means of redress to private parties was catapulted to the forefront by the European Court of Human Rights in 1999.[124] Less than three months prior to the ICJ's ruling in *Cumarasawamy*, in *Waite and Kennedy*, by unanimous judgment, a grand chamber of the European Court of Human Rights rejected attempts to question the compatibility of absolute immunity with human rights obligations.

In a case arising from domestic litigation before the German labor court, instituted by the applicants against the European Space Agency (ESA), the court held that Germany had not violated Article 6(1) of the European Convention on Human Rights by granting the ESA immunity from suit. The court reiterated the principle that Article 6(1) secures the right to have any claim relating to civil rights and obligations brought before a court or tribunal. In this way, the article embodies the "right to a court," of which the right of access or the right to institute proceedings before a court in civil matters constitutes only one aspect. The court deemed that the reasons advanced by the German labor court to give effect to the immunity from legal process of the ESA could

---

122 *Fibraca Constructora S.C.A. c. Comisión Técnica Mixta de Salto Grande,* Fallo de la Corte Suprema: Buenos Aires (Jul. 7, 1993), available at <http://federacionuniversitaria23.blogspot.com/2008/05/fibraca-constructora-sca-vs-la-comisin.html>.

123 *Duhalde, Mario Alfredo c. Demandado: Organizacion Panamericana de la Salud Organizacion Mundial de la Salud Oficina Sanitaria Panamericana,* Dictamen n° D. 73. XXXIV de Corte Suprema de Justicia de la Nación (Mar. 31, 1999), available at <http://ar.vlex.com/vid/-39899405>.

124 Wellens, *supra* note 117, at 13–14.

not be regarded as arbitrary. It examined whether access, when limited to a preliminary issue, was sufficient to secure the applicants' right to a court in light of its case law, and in particular in light of the principle that such restricted access be in pursuit of a legitimate aim and the principle that there is a reasonable relationship of proportionality between the means employed and the aim.

According to the court, the rule of immunity of international organizations from domestic legal process as applied to the ESA by the German courts had a legitimate objective. The court noted that the attribution of privileges and immunities to international organizations was an essential means of ensuring the proper functioning of such organizations free from unilateral interference by individual governments. Rather than invoking *jus cogens*, as was done in *Cabrera*, the European Court of Human Rights analyzed the issue in terms of proportionality. A material factor in determining whether granting ESA immunity from German jurisdiction was permissible was whether the applicants had available reasonable alternative means to protect their rights under the convention. The court opined that, because the applicants had claimed the existence of an employment relationship with ESA, they could and should have had recourse to the ESA Appeals Board, which is "independent of the Agency" and has jurisdiction "to hear disputes relating to any explicit or implicit decision taken by the Agency and arising between it and a staff member" (Regulation 33.1 of the ESA Staff Regulations). The court also considered the possibility for temporary workers to seek redress from the firms that had employed them and contracted with them. It concluded that the test of proportionality could not be applied in such a way as to compel an international organization to submit itself to national litigation for matters concerning employment conditions prescribed under national labor law. Such an interpretation of Article 6(1) would thwart the proper functioning of international organizations:

> The Court shares the Commission's conclusion that, bearing in mind the legitimate aim of immunities of international organisations (see paragraph 63 above), the test of proportionality cannot be applied in such a way as to compel an international organisation to submit itself to national litigation in relation to employment conditions prescribed under national labour law. To read Article 6 § 1 of the Convention and its guarantee of access to court as necessarily requiring the application of national legislation in such matters would, in the Court's view, thwart the proper functioning of international organisations and run counter to the current trend towards extending and strengthening international cooperation.[125]

Yet, except in Switzerland, the court's unequivocal assertion did not resonate. Rather, the decision in *Waite and Kennedy* is understood to state that an alternative means of redress is a precondition for the enjoyment of immunity

---

125 *Waite and Kennedy v. Germany*, App. No. 26083/94, 30 Eur. Ct. Hum. Rights 261 (1999).

from national legal process.[126] More important, some domestic courts read into *Waite and Kennedy* a license to examine the presence and adequacy of the alternative means of redress offered by international organizations and to deny immunity where they deem the means not to be adequate.[127] This development feeds the controversy and uncertainty about jurisdictional immunity beyond the shores of Europe.[128] However, as the Swiss Federal Tribunal held in *NML Capital Ltd.*, to read into the right of access to court an entitlement to deny immunity when an alternative means is deemed to exist would thwart the proper functioning of international organizations and run counter to the trend toward extending and strengthening international cooperation.[129]

None of the foregoing judicial rulings recognized any link between the obligation to provide appropriate means to deal with claims of private parties and the question of whether the immunity should be restricted or absolute. According to Wellens, the "obligation to establish such a (judicial) remedial system for the settlement of conflicts or disputes in which international organisations may become involved does not disappear when the immunity is restrictive, rather than absolute."[130] Be that as it may, these rulings contain important advice that should be heeded by any international organization in light of its duty to guard its own independent functioning against interference by national authorities.

Discharging the Obligation

Qualified Amenability to Domestic Legal Process

The position of international financial institutions with regard to judicial process, as stated in their constituent instruments, generally does not assert uncompromised immunity from legal process, but rather entails a regime of qualified amenability to lawsuits. In fact, only Article IX, Section 3, of the Articles of Agreement of the IMF is as uncompromising as the Convention on the Privileges and Immunities of the Specialized Agencies. It provides that the IMF, its property, and its assets, wherever located and by whomsoever held, shall enjoy immunity from every form of judicial process except to the extent that it expressly waives its immunity for the purpose of any proceedings or

---

126   *See* discussion at August Reinisch, *The Immunity of International Organizations and the Jurisdiction of Their Administrative Tribunals,* 7 Chinese J. Intl. L. 285 (2008).

127   Cedric Ryngaert, *The Immunity of International Organizations before Domestic Courts: Some Recent Trends,* 7 Intl. Organizations L. Rev. 121 (2010).

128   For example, a letter dated February 6, 2009, from the chair of the Senate economic affairs committee (Miriam Defensor Santiago) to the Philippine Country Director of the World Bank, available at <http://www.senate.gov.ph/press_release/2009/0206_santiago2.asp>.

129   *NML Capital Ltd., EM Limited v. Bank für Internationalen Zahlungsausgleich (BIZ), Betreibungsamt Basel-Stadt,* Bundesgericht, July 12, 2010, Consideration 4.5.3. available at <http://www.bger.ch/index/jurisdiction/jurisdiction-inherit-template/jurisdiction-recht/jurisdiction-recht-urteile2000.htm.>

130   Wellens, *supra* note 117, at 125.

by the terms of any contract. The position of the other international financial institutions is much more nuanced. For example, Section 4 of Article VII of the IBRD Articles of Agreement states:

> Actions may be brought against the Bank only in a court of competent jurisdiction in the territories of a member in which the Bank has an office, has appointed an agent for the purpose of accepting service of process, or has issued or guaranteed securities. No action shall, however, be brought by members or persons acting for or deriving claims from members.[131]

The regime established by this provision entails that the World Bank may be subjected to legal process only in a competent court in a member country, provided that it either has an office in the territory concerned or has appointed an agent to accept service or notice of process, or has issued or guaranteed securities.[132] This regime, which is replicated in the charters of the IDA,[133] the IFC,[134] the Nordic Investment Bank,[135] the European Bank for Reconstruction and Development (EBRD),[136] and the Inter-American Development Bank,[137] differs from the one established in the constituent instruments of the Caribbean Development Bank,[138] the Asian Development Bank,[139] the Black Sea Trade and Development Bank,[140] the African Development Bank,[141] and the African Development Fund.[142] In the latter cases, amenability to legal process is provided as an express exception to the immunity that otherwise applies. The attendant provisions typically state that an institution shall enjoy immunity from every form of legal process, except in cases arising out of or in connection with the exercise of its powers to borrow money, guarantee obligations, or buy, sell, or underwrite the sale of securities, in which cases actions may be brought against the institution in a court of competent jurisdiction in the territory of a country in which it has its principal or a branch office, or has

---

131 U.S. courts have held that Article VII does not constitute a waiver of Bank immunity with regard to employment-related suits under the immunities conferred upon the Bank by the U.S. International Organizations Immunities Act of 1945. *See*, for example, *Mendaro v. World Bank, supra* note 84; *Chiriboga v. International Bank for Reconstruction and Development*, 616 F. Supp. 963 (D.D.C. 1985); *Morgan v. International Bank for Reconstruction and Development*, 752 F. Supp. 492 (D.C. Cir. 1990).

132 Broches, *supra* note 15, at 9.

133 IDA Articles of Agreement, Article VIII, Section 3.

134 IFC Articles of Agreement, Article VI, Section 3.

135 Article 5, Agreement on the Nordic Investment Bank.

136 Article 46, Agreement Establishing the European Bank for Reconstruction and Development.

137 Article XI, Section 3, Agreement Establishing the Inter-American Development Bank.

138 Article 49.1, Agreement Establishing the Caribbean Development Bank.

139 Article 50.1, Agreement Establishing the Asian Development Bank.

140 Article 45.1, Establishing Agreement of the Black Sea Trade and Development Bank.

141 Article 52.1, Agreement Establishing the African Development Bank.

142 Article 43.1, Agreement Establishing the African Development Fund.

appointed an agent for the purpose of accepting service or notice of process, or has issued or guaranteed securities. Although stated in substantially different terms, the qualified amenability to domestic legal process is also followed by the EIB and the ECB. Article 27 (ex Article 29) of the Statute of the European Investment Bank provides that disputes between the bank, on the one hand, and its creditors, debtors, or any other person, on the other, shall be decided by the competent national courts, save where jurisdiction has been conferred on the Court of Justice of the European Union. The same rule applies to the ECB.[143] This means that the EIB and the ECB enjoy immunity from national jurisdiction only for those cases that fall under the exclusive jurisdiction of the European Court of Justice as laid down in the European Union Treaty, the EIB statute and EC treaty, and the ESCB statute. In particular, the European Court's exclusive competence relates to actions against the foregoing institutions aimed at reviewing their acts and omissions as well as claims for damages.

Noncontractual Claims

In light of the above, the problem of adequate means for dealing with claims of private parties against international financial institutions exists mainly in the relatively narrow area of noncontractual liability of non-EU international financial institutions. In addition to the international administrative tribunals that have been conferred jurisdiction over employment disputes involving international financial institutions, contracts between those institutions and private parties invariably contain provisions designating arbitration as a manner for resolving the disputes arising out of such contracts. Although arbitration is deemed acceptable for contractual disputes, no standard mode of settlement exists for disputes concerning noncontractual claims against international financial institutions, such as tort, promissory estoppel, and other quasi-contractual claims.[144]

As shown in *Morgan*,[145] too often the litigation strategy of international financial institutions in noncontractual cases brought in domestic courts invites criticism about their immunity. The plaintiff in *Morgan* sought compensatory and punitive damages for intentional infliction of emotional distress, false imprisonment, libel, and slander. Although no alternative means for settling the dispute was offered, the World Bank asserted that it was immune from suit, and the court agreed. Ten years later, Christian Dominicé revisited the case in light of evolving views about the fundamental right to access courts and

---

143 Article 35.2 of the Statute of the European System of Central Banks.

144 *Cf.* August Reinisch, *Immunity of International Organizations and Alternative Remedies against International Organizations*, Seminar on State Immunity (2006), available at <http://intlaw .univie.ac.at/fileadmin/user_upload/int_beziehungen/Internetpubl/neumann.pdf>.

145 *Morgan v. IBRD*, 752 F. Supp. 492 (D.D.C. 1990). For a discussion, *see* Daniel Hammerschlag, *Morgan v. International Bank for Reconstruction and Development*, 16 Md. J. Intl. L. & Trade 279 (1992).

pointed out that it was unlikely that the outcome in *Morgan* would have been the same in 2000, given the absence of an alternative means for the dispute settlement.[146]

However, if international financial institutions were to adopt a different strategy with respect to private noncontractual liability claims, they would likely silence the growing call for the limitation or even elimination of their immunity from domestic legal process. The 2009 D.C. Court of Appeals judgment in *Jorge Vila v. Inter-American Investment Corporation,* involving a consultant's claim of unjust enrichment, underscores that courts will be tempted to side with claimants in these cases. Indeed, most of the calls for eliminating or restricting the immunities of international organizations invoke the absence of alternative dispute-settlement mechanisms for noncontractual disputes in order to justify why the concept of immunity is anathema to the concept of fair play and substantial justice. [147]

Outside the realm of risk-bearing activities of international organizations, the noncontractual claims of private parties cannot easily be anticipated.[148] Because of this, when engaging in risk-bearing activities (for example, debarring of vendors),[149] organizations would do well to accompany those activities with default arbitration clauses or other provisions having equivalent effect. Such default arbitration provisions are used by the IFAD with respect to the debarment of vendors on account of violations of the organization's policy on fraud and corruption. The IFAD's debarment decisions contain a suspension clause and are communicated to the affected vendor. An affected vendor is offered the possibility of initiating arbitration against the IFAD, within a specified period, under the Permanent Court of Arbitration Optional Rules for Arbitration between International Organizations and Private Parties. Debarment decisions become effective either upon expiration of the time limit for appeal or on the date of the final award.

There is no reason why arbitration cannot serve as the required alternative default mechanism for dealing with the noncontractual claims of private parties against international financial institutions. Availability of arbitration in such cases would shift the debate away from the legitimacy of immunity and draw attention instead to the lack of subject matter jurisdiction of the domestic

---

146 Dominicé, *supra* note 121.

147 *Jorge Vila v. Inter-American Investment Corporation,* 2009 U.S. App. LEXIS 13279 (D.C. Cir. 2009).

148 For instance, an unfortunate event involving renowned economist Jacques Polak at the eighth annual meeting of the IMF institute named after him led to an action against the IMF for alleged negligence and negligence per se in the construction and maintenance of stairs on the IMF's premises. Holding that a functional necessity analysis is called for only in cases where the immunity has been waived, the court ruled that the plaintiff's reliance on the functional necessity test was misplaced. As a result, the court concluded that the IMF is immune and dismissed the suit for want of subject matter jurisdiction. *See Jacques Polak v. International Monetary Fund,* 657 F. Supp. 2d 116 (D.D.C. 2009).

149 *See* Scope Williams, *The Debarment of Corrupt Contractors from World Bank–Financed Contracts,* 36 Pub. Contract L.J. 277 (2006–07).

court, which should defer decision making to the established dispute-settlement mechanism. An example of such a deferral can be found in the memorandum order of Judge Green of the U.S. District Court of Pennsylvania in *Bro Tech Corporation v. EBRD*.[150] The EBRD filed a motion to dismiss for lack of subject matter jurisdiction, pursuant to Rule 12(b)(1) of the U.S. Federal Rules of Civil Procedure. In addition to the subject matter jurisdiction arguments posited by the organization, the motion invoked lack of personal jurisdiction, improper venue, and insufficiency of process. The court concluded that the EBRD had absolute immunity but had waived that immunity in its dealings with the plaintiffs. More important, the court found that the EBRD's waiver was limited, and that the EBRD had waived its immunity only with respect to the resolution of disputes through arbitration. This led to the conclusion that all plaintiffs' claims were controlled by the arbitration clauses in their agreements with the EBRD. Accordingly, the court held that it did not have subject matter jurisdiction over the dispute and dismissed the claims.

Although the result in *Bro Tech* can be relied upon to support the notion of deferral, because the court based its conclusion on an analysis of the effects of commercial arbitration clauses, the ruling invites reflection on the viability of a default arbitration provision unilaterally declared by an international organization. This issue was addressed in *First Eagle* in respect to Article 54 of the BIS statutes, which specifies that any dispute concerning the interpretation or application of the statutes—including an amendment such as the one at issue here—"shall be referred for final decision" to the arbitration tribunal established by the Hague Agreement of 1930. The plaintiff, a private shareholder, moved for a temporary restraining order against the BIS to prevent the buyback of privately held shares. This action was prompted by the fact that in September 2000, the bank announced that it would hold a meeting of its central bank members on January 8, 2001, to vote on an amendment to its statutes allowing a mandatory redemption of all public shares. The mandatory redemption was apparently motivated by problems inherent in the restricted market for public bank shares and by the tension between the bank's purpose of promoting international financial cooperation and a publicly owned company's goal of maximizing profit to shareholders. The plan called for the bank to cancel the registrations of all of the public shares, redistribute these shares to the central banks, and then issue a statutory right of payment of 16,000 Swiss francs per share to the public shareholders. The U.S. District Court for the Southern District of New York denied the motion on the ground that no irreparable harm was threatened. On appeal, a consideration on which the confirmation was based was that

> the primary complaint advanced by First Eagle appears to be that the valuation methods employed by J.P. Morgan and Arthur Andersen undervalued the privately held shares. Should First Eagle succeed in

---

150 *Bro Tech v. EBRD*, 2000 U.S. Dist. LEXIS 75626 (E.D. Pa. 2000).

this complaint, its injury can be fully compensated by an award in the district court or in the mandatory arbitration forum designated by the Bank's statutes plan.

The appeal was thus dismissed for lack of appellate jurisdiction.

Two points spring to the fore in this ruling. First, the fact that the arbitration clause is statutory—thus unilateral—rather than contractual did not seem to constitute a problem for the domestic court. Second, the fact that the fully competent international arbitral tribunal would deal with the substance of the claim and provide the appropriate substantive remedies was a decisive factor in the court's decision to defer. At the international level, this was further underscored by the Hague Arbitral Tribunal's subscription to BIS's assertion that the costs of access to justice must be regulated in such a way that the exercise of the right is not rendered impossible for those affected private parties who lack the resources of large corporate entities.[151] Furthermore, the Hague Tribunal, in awarding BIS's claim to recover the costs of its defense in the case filed in the United States, pointed to the combination of BIS's immunity from domestic legal processes and the mandatory arbitration in order to assert the exclusive character of its own jurisdiction.[152] Admittedly, the tribunal hedged its argument by emphasizing the declaration of acceptance of shares, which contained the acceptance of the mandatory arbitration; however, if an international organization is required to provide alternative means for the settlement of disputes, there is no way to avoid a certain degree of unilateralism.

Learning from INTERPOL

The way INTERPOL handled the matter of noncontractual claims related to its operations is exemplary. Long before the World Bank Inspection Panel saw the light of day, INTERPOL responded to the requirement that international organizations whose actions directly affect individuals establish a forum in which individuals may bring claims.[153] The establishment of the Commission for Control of INTERPOL Files (CCF[154]), an implementation of this requirement,[155] arose out of need. As technology evolved and INTERPOL became more and more effective, the calls for remedies against the organization became louder;[156] this, combined with the French data protection authority's

---

151 *Dr. Horst Reinecius et al. v. Bank for International Settlement,* Hague Arbitral Tribunal, Final Award of September 19, 2003, paragraph 126, at <http://www.pca-cpa.org/upload/files/BIS%20Final%20Award.pdf>.

152 *Id.,* at paragraphs 113–15.

153 *See* Daniel D. Bradlow & Sabine Schlemmer-Schulte, *The World Bank New Inspection Panel,* 45 Recht der Internationales Wirtschaft 175, 179 (1999).

154 *See* Claude Valleix, *INTERPOL,* 88 Revue Générale de Droit International Public 621 (1984), and S. El Zein, *Nature juridique de la Commission de contrôle des fichiers de l'OIPC-INTERPOL,* 480 Revue Internationale de Police Criminelle 2 (2000).

155 *See* Wellens, *supra* note 117, at 209–12.

156 C. Eick & A. Tritel, *Verfassungsrechtliche bedenken gegen deutsche Mitarbeit bei INTERPOL,* EurGRZ 1985/Seite 81 (12. Jg. Heft 4); and James Sheptycki, *The Accountability of*

attempt to assert jurisdiction over INTERPOL's files, triggered the creation of the commission.

France argued that individuals should have access to data concerning them, a right that could be exercised through its Commission Nationale de l'Informatique et des Libertés, which had been established under the above-mentioned law and given power to control computerized files in France. To accept the French view would have meant that INTERPOL no longer had autonomy from the authority of any one country. INTERPOL therefore countered that this law could not apply to the police information processed by the general secretariat because information sent by member countries does not belong to INTERPOL, which merely acts as a depository, and applying the law of 1978 to INTERPOL's files could hamper international police cooperation, because certain countries would prefer not to communicate police information that could be disclosed to French bodies.

Acknowledging these powerful arguments, France was nevertheless unwilling to strengthen INTERPOL's status on its territory without some kind of guarantee concerning the processing of personal data protected by the law of 1978. INTERPOL, meanwhile, was keen to ensure the smooth functioning of international police cooperation through its channels.[157] These conflicting aims were reconciled as a result of both parties' commitment to data protection, in order to protect both international police cooperation and individual rights, and the commission was thus established.[158]

The implication of these developments for domestic courts with respect to INTERPOL is alluded to in *Balkir v. INTERPOL* (1993).[159] The High Court of Lyon found that it lacked subject matter jurisdiction over INTERPOL's activities due to a combination of factors derived from the headquarters agreement between France and INTERPOL, including INTERPOL's system of internal control of the processing of police information. In *X & Y v. INTERPOL* (2009) the District Court of Jerusalem went a step farther by explaining (*obiter*) that declining to hear the case would not deprive the applicants of a remedy:

> The Plaintiffs approached to Defendant and their approach was transferred for the attendance of the CCF on 4.4.07. The CCF (Commission for Control of Interpol's Files) is a specialized body *established* by Interpol whose purpose and specialization is the examination of complaints by individuals regarding the information stored at the Organization's information databases, including red

---

Transnational Policing Institutions: The Strange Case of INTERPOL, 19 Can. J.L. & Society 107 (2004).

157 *Cf.* Rutsel Silvestre J. Martha, *Remedies against INTERPOL: Role and Practice of Defence Lawyers*, Address to the European Criminal Bar Association, Autumn Conference 2007, available at <http://www.ecba.org/extdocserv/conferences/lyon2007/remedies_against_interpol.pdf>.

158 *See* Valleix, *supra* note 154, Alice Pezard, *L'organisation internationale de police criminelle et son nouvel accord de siège*, 29 Annuaire Français de Droit International 564, 572–75 (1983), and El Zein, *supra* note 154.

159 *Balkir v. INTERPOL*, Tribunal de Grande Instance de Lyon, Premier Chambre, March 17, 1993 (unpublished).

notices published against some individuals. This body is authorized to ensure that the transfer of the information inside and outside the Organisation is carried out in accordance to the Organization's rules. The CCF has a supervising role regarding the use, processing and storing of the information, it is given the authority to examine any file and to request clarifications from the information sources which were transferred to the Organization. The CCF updates the INTERPOL General Secretariat of its findings, and to the measure its findings determine that a notice was published in negation to the Organization's rules, this notice will be removed.[160]

As far as staff disputes are concerned, INTERPOL recognized the jurisdiction of the ILOAT. For any residual dispute with private parties, INTERPOL agreed to a default mechanism. Effective September 1, 2009, Article 24(1) of the new headquarters agreement between France and INTERPOL[161] provides that unless the parties to the dispute decide otherwise, any dispute between the organization and a private party shall be settled in accordance with the Optional Rules for Arbitration between International Organizations and Private Parties of the Permanent Court of Arbitration.[162] These new arrangements were clearly inspired by the 1994 revision of the headquarters agreement between the United States and the OAS, which clarified that the immunities enjoyed by the OAS were absolute, not qualified, and that its officials enjoyed immunity in relation to the performance of their official functions. Like INTERPOL, the 1994 USA-OAS headquarters agreement clearly identified viable alternative dispute-resolution mechanisms for persons with grievances against the organization.[163]

The case of INTERPOL is of particular interest because the organization is based on an agreement that has not been formally celebrated, as have those of most international organizations.[164] In the absence of a formal conventional foundation, which would contain a clause equivalent to Article 105 of the UN

---

160 *X & Y v. INTERPOL*, District Court of Jerusalem, March 31, 2009, paragraph 9 (unpublished).

161 The agreement between INTERPOL and the government of the French Republic came into force on September 1, 2009, and replaced the headquarters agreement of February 14, 1984; it is available at <http://www.interpol.int/Public/ICPO/LegalMaterials/constitution/hqagreement/AccordSiegeRevise2008.pdf>.

162 Permanent Court of Arbitration, *Optional Rules for Arbitration between International Organizations and Private Parties of the Permanent Court of Arbitration*, available at <http://www.pca-cpa.org/upload/files/IGO1ENG.pdf>. By virtue of Article 24(3) of the Agreement between INTERPOL and the Government of the French Republic, the procedure specified in paragraph 1 is not applicable to disputes whose origins lie in the application or interpretation of the INTERPOL Constitution or its appendices, which include the staff regulations and the rules concerning the processing of police information and the publication of notices. *See* also Agreement between the Republic of Austria and the International Criminal Police Organisation (ICPO-INTERPOL) regarding the seat of the INTERPOL Anti-Corruption Academy in Austria, available at <http://www.parlament.gv.at/PAKT/VHG/XXIII/BNR/BNR_00191/imfname_100182.pdf>.

163 *See* Berenson, *supra* note 118; also, Muller, *supra* note 102, at 180–81.

164 *See* Rutsel Silvestre J. Martha, *The Legal Foundations of INTERPOL* (Hart 2010).

Charter detailing a general arrangement, INTERPOL is left to find bilateral solutions for the "privileges and immunities" needed for its operation. Nevertheless, INTERPOL has been highly successful in averting domestic lawsuits. The organization's assurance that aggrieved individuals have recourse to a forum competent to hear their cases has reduced the incentive for courts to deny immunity to the organization or to interfere with its operations.[165]

Conclusions

Leaving the European Union aside, with the exception of their suppliers, service providers, staff, and—where applicable—nongovernmental creditors and beneficiaries (of grants and loans), international organizations do not normally have direct relations with private parties; their interlocutors are states and other international organizations.[166] In most cases, the multilateral financial institutions provide for mechanisms to settle claims of such private parties, including qualified amenability to the jurisdiction of domestic courts with respect to disputes with bondholders. A blind side exists with regard to noncontractual claims of private parties in the case of most international organizations, with the exception of the European Union, the OAS, and INTERPOL. The habit of international organizations to claim immunity even in those cases without offering alternative means to deal with such claims seems to be the main feeder of the argument against the continued need and scope of the judicial immunity.

This chapter argues that although the unrestricted immunity from domestic legal process cannot be dispensed with without scarifying the independent functioning of the multilateral financial institutions, international financial institutions are obliged to provide appropriate means for the settlement of all private claims, not only contractual ones. That exercise produces the following conclusions:

- It cannot be said that the immunities of international organizations are either unnecessary or out-of-date.

- The suggestion that domestic courts would be capable of dealing with all or most of the issues that may be involved in disputes between international organizations and private parties ignores the fact that certain matters are simply beyond national jurisdiction. In other words, such disputes may involve issues that can be adequately handled only by an international forum.

---

165 Rutsel Silvestre J. Martha, *Challenging Acts of INTERPOL in Domestic Courts*, in *Challenging Acts of International Organizations before National Courts* 206 (August Reinisch ed., Oxford U. Press 2010). *See* also Martha, *supra* note 164, at 92–105 and 131–36.

166 *Cf.* Giorgio Malinverni, *Le règlement des différends dans le cadre des organisations internationales*, in *Droit International: Bilan et perspectives* tome 1, 571 (Mohammed Bedjaoui ed., Éditions A. Pedone 1991).

- The argument that the doctrine of restrictive foreign sovereign immunity should apply to international organizations ignores the fact that, unlike states, international organizations have no territory or citizens. They are therefore functionally required to operate in the domestic market of a state. This functional necessity implies that rules that apply to free choices of foreign states to operate in the territories of other states cannot apply to international organizations without interfering with their independent functioning.

- The resultant obligation to respect the immunities of international organizations does not mean that international organizations escape accountability. Rather, inherent in the immunity of international organizations is their duty to establish a dispute settlement mechanism to handle complaints of private parties.

- Many organizations do not observe this obligation diligently—in particular with regard to noncontractual claims—which has contributed to the increased calls for limitation or denial of immunity of international organizations before national courts.

- As demonstrated by the experiences of certain international organizations—notably the European Union, the IFAD, INTERPOL and the OAS—the only way for international organizations to remedy this situation is to establish either unilateral or collective default mechanisms to deal with any dispute that may arise between them and private parties.

Squaring the Concept of Immunity with the Fundamental Right to a Fair Trial

The Case of the OAS

WILLIAM M. BERENSON[*]

The Inherent Conflict between Immunity and the Right to a Fair Trial

In many respects, the concept of immunity is anathema to the American concept of fair play and substantial justice. The granting of immunity to international organizations and their officials,[1] in those cases where reasonable alternative dispute-resolution mechanisms are unavailable, likely deprives their victims of the right to a fair trial for the redress of their grievances and compensation for their injuries. The right to a fair trial is a fundamental human right under the American Convention on Human Rights,[2] Article 8 of which defines the right to a fair trial as "the right to a hearing with due guarantees and within a reasonable time by a competent and impartial tribunal previously established by law . . . for the determination of [a person's] rights, and obligations of a civil, labor, fiscal, or any other nature."

Possible Rationalization of the Conflict through Substantive Due Process Analysis

How can one square the right to a fair trial guaranteed under the American Convention on Human Rights with the concept of immunity? Perhaps the simple answer is that in a perfect world, one cannot. Nonetheless, in attempting to reconcile these two conflicting interests, jurists and lawyers have sought rationales for balancing one against the other in the search for "reasonable accommodation."

One rationale that can serve the purpose of reasonable accommodation well is substantive due process analysis, as developed by the U.S. courts. This rationale provides a framework for determining under what circumstances a government may limit a fundamental right and to what extent.

---

[*]   This chapter was the basis for remarks made by the author at the World Bank's Law, Justice, and Development Week 2010, held in Washington, D.C. The views expressed herein are not necessarily shared by the institutions with which the author is associated.

[1]   In this chapter, the term "officials" connotes both the employees, also known as "staff," "staff members," or "personnel," and other officers of those organizations.

[2]   *See* American Convention on Human Rights, Article 8 (Nov. 22, 1969), available at <http://www.oas.org/juridico/english/treaties/b-32.html>.

The doctrine of substantive due process accepts that no fundamental right is absolute. That is, when the government has a "compelling state" interest, the government may limit or trim that right, but only by way of the "least restrictive means." Of all the possible measures that the government may adopt to achieve its compelling state interest, the measure selected must be the least restrictive of the affected fundamental right. If it is not the least restrictive or at least "carefully tailored" to be the least restrictive, the measure restricting the fundamental right is illegal.

Immunity for International Organizations as a Compelling State Interest for Their Member States

When looking at immunity through the lens of substantive due process analysis, one must ask whether the interest member governments have in granting international organizations and their officials immunities is "compelling." Those who truly appreciate the mission of international organizations would answer "yes." For most member states, international organizations offer compelling services relating to development, finance, security, and the conduct of foreign policy. Without immunity, international organizations would be reticent to establish offices, implement projects, and conduct other operations in their member states. Immunity is a sine qua non for doing business in those states.

Why is that? There are several reasons. First, immunity prevents any single member state from exercising undue influence on an international organization and thwarting the will of the majority by way of its courts. Certainly, for example, adjudication by the courts of one country declaring the activities of an international organization illegal or arresting or detaining its officials in penal facilities on trumped-up charges could frustrate the objectives of that organization. An injunction from the court of one member state or a multi-million-dollar judgment, particularly in the courts of the host country where the organization's accounts are maintained, could virtually cripple an organization if it is not shielded by immunity. Moreover, in the absence of immunity, a member state wishing to obstruct the activities of an organization in pursuit of its own political designs could simply urge its citizens to bring suit against the organization, thus tying up the organization's resources in litigation, to the prejudice of its other member states and its noble objectives.

In addition, in disputes between a member state and an international organization, the member state may become both judge and party in the dispute if the matter is adjudicated in its own courts or administrative forum. Separation of powers is more an ideal in many countries rather than a reality: the independence of the judiciary from the other branches of government cannot be presumed. Immunity guarantees protection for international organizations and their officials from those instances in which reality strays from the ideal.

Scholars may list a dozen or more additional reasons why international organizations generally demand immunity as a condition for operating in or doing business within their member states.[3] But in the end, they boil down to the two basic reasons stated above:

- Preventing any one state from gaining an unfair advantage in or crippling an international organization by way of its courts or administrative agencies with adjudicative authority

- Providing a guarantee that a member state, in disputes with international organizations, is not likely to become both judge and party, thereby denying the organization a mechanism for the fair and independent adjudication of the dispute in accordance with due process

Measures That Restrict the Adverse Impact of Immunity on the Right to a Fair Trial

Under substantive due process analysis, the conclusion that member states have a compelling state interest in providing immunity to international organizations is not enough, by itself, to justify the limitation immunity poses on the fundamental right to a fair trial for persons who have disputes with those organizations. The issue persists of whether the immunity, as granted, is the least restrictive means for obtaining the compelling state interest in having international organizations operate within member states. If that question can be answered affirmatively, then the conflict between the internationally recognized right to a fair trial and the immunities evaporates (at best) or becomes tolerable both intellectually and in practice (at worst).

Certainly, a member state and an international organization can employ measures to minimize the adverse impact of immunity upon the right to a fair trial in disputes with international organizations. None of these measures is mutually exclusive.

One such measure is limiting the scope of immunity by granting functional immunity instead of absolute immunity. That is, the organization and its officials are immune only with regard to those activities they engage in with respect to the organization's functions stated in its charter or constituent treaty. They have no immunity for acts they commit not within the scope of those functions. The Council of State of Colombia, a high-level court in Colombia, recently took this position when it denied immunity to an international organization sued over activities that clearly did not fall within its objectives and functions under its charter.[4]

---

3   *See,* for example, August Reinisch, *International Organizations before National Courts* 233–51 (Cambridge U. Press 2000); Richard J. Oparil, *Immunity of International Organizations in United States Courts: Absolute or Restrictive?* 24 V. and J. Transnatl L. 689, 709–10. *See* also Rutsel Silvestre J. Martha, *International Financial Institutions and Claims of Private Parties: Immunity Obliges,* in this volume.

4   *INTERSIDE v. Ministerio de Agricultura y Secretaría Ejecutiva del Convenio Andrés Bello,* Sala de lo Contencioso Administrativo del Consejo de Estado (Mar. 26, 2009) (defendant organization not immune with regard to claims of breach of contract with subcontractor arising out of the organization's administration of agricultural subsidies financed by government because its purposes under its charter are strictly educational and cultural).

Another measure to minimize the adverse impact of immunity is to deny immunity to organizations with respect to their pursuit of activities of a commercial nature, as opposed to their political or "sovereign" functions. Under international law, this measure is often referred to as "restrictive immunity"; under the modern doctrine of sovereign immunity applied to states, it is prevalent.[5] With regard to international organizations such as the United Nations (UN) and the Organization of American States (OAS), this distinction makes little sense because, unlike many sovereign states, those organizations do not engage in commercial enterprises.[6] Nonetheless, this distinction does make some sense with regard to lending institutions, insofar as lending money is a commercial activity.

Another means states may use for limiting the exposure of international organizations to crippling or otherwise seemingly unfair judgments in national courts is limiting the amount of damages that may be awarded against an international organization in any civil case or excluding international organizations for liability for punitive damages.[7] Such a limitation provides, in effect, immunity from those claims. But it leaves open the possibility that national courts or mutually agreed-on arbitration tribunals may adjudicate disputes and compensate the aggrieved party with actual damages.

Still another means is the language set out in the charters for the World Bank Group, which grant immunity from suits by member states but leave open the possibility of actions against the World Bank (but not against its officials) brought by other possible plaintiffs. Compliance with the resulting judgments, however, is left largely to the will of the defendant institution due to the immunity of its assets from seizure and confiscation under those charters.[8]

---

5   Beginning in 1952, the concept of sovereign immunity was adopted by the U.S. Department of State (the *Tate* Letter, 26 Dep't State Bull. 984 (1952); in 1976, it was codified by Congress in the Foreign Sovereign Immunities Act, 28 U.S.C. paragraphs 1602–11.

6   See *Restatement of the Foreign Relations Law of the United States,* paragraph 467 cmt. d (1987), which states: "It appears that the restrictive theory that limits the immunity of a state from legal process (Sec. 451) does not apply to the United Nations, to most of its Specialized Agencies, or to the Organization of American States. These organizations enjoy immunity from jurisdiction to adjudicate in all cases, both under their charters and other international agreements (comment b) and under the law of the United States."

7   For example, in the Foreign Sovereign Immunities Act (FSIA) and the 1994 Headquarters Agreement with the Organization of American States (OAS), available at <http://www.oas .org/legal/english/docs/BilateralAgree/us/sedeusa.htm>, the United States exempts foreign sovereigns and the OAS from claims for punitive damages. In the case of the OAS, which enjoys absolute immunity subject to its agreement to arbitrate all civil disputes, the limitation applies to the arbitration tribunal.

8   For example, International Bank for Reconstruction and Development (IBRD) Articles of Agreement, Article VII, Section 4, states: "Actions may be brought against the Bank only in a court of competent jurisdiction in the territories of a member in which the Bank has an office, has appointed an agent for the purpose of accepting service of process, or has issued or guaranteed securities. No action shall, however, be brought by members or persons acting for or deriving claims from members. The property and assets of the Bank, wherever located and by whomever held, shall be immune from all forms of seizure, attachment, or execution before the delivery of final judgment against the Bank." Section 4 continues: "Property

In legislation or a treaty recognizing immunity, perhaps the most effective measure for curtailing the adverse impact of immunity on the right to a fair trial is to include a provision that requires the international organization to provide alternative measures for the resolution of its disputes with others. Generally, those alternative measures include establishing or providing access to a specialized labor court, called an "administrative tribunal," for the adjudication of employment-related claims against the organization, and providing for independent binding arbitration in all commercial agreements or for the settlement of tort claims that cannot be reasonably settled by negotiation with the organization's insurers.

Of course, the effectiveness of alternative measures as a substitute for a fair trial in the national courts and in the administrative agencies with adjudicatory functions of the member states depends on the degree of independence and accessibility of these courts and agencies. Courts in Europe, North America, and Latin America have examined that issue in considering whether to recognize the immunities of international organizations.[9] In other words, the comfort level of today's nations with the concept of immunity depends on how effective alternative dispute mechanisms provided by international organizations are in limiting the adverse effect of immunity upon the fundamental right to a fair trial.

Governments may cushion the impact of immunity on the right to a fair trial by including in their agreements with international organizations a provision that requires the legal representative of an organization to waive privileges and immunities when, in his or her judgment, justice so demands and the waiver will not necessarily thwart the organization in the pursuit of its objectives. Under such a provision, the waiver is not mandatory. It depends on the opinion or discretion of the legal representative, who is usually the

---

and assets of the Bank, wherever located and by whomsoever held, shall be immune from all from search, requisition, confiscation, expropriation, or any other form of seizure by executive or legislative action." Note, however, that the 116 countries that are parties to the Convention on Privileges and Immunities of the United Nations Specialized Agencies have, under Article III(4) of the convention, accorded broader immunities to the World Bank as one of those agencies. The United States is not a party to that convention; however, the World Bank, as a public international organization, enjoys in the United States functional immunities under the International Organizations Immunities Act of 1945, 22 U.S.C. Section 288a (IOIA). U.S. courts have held that the more limited immunities granted under Article VII, which appears to permit suits by nonbank members against the Bank, do not constitute a waiver of the broader immunity accorded the Bank under the IOIA as a shield against such suits in the United States. *See*, for example, *Mendaro v. World Bank*, 717 F.2d 610, 612 (D.C. Cir. 1983); *Chiriboga v. International Bank for Reconstruction and Development*, 616 F. Supp. 963 (D.D.C. 1985); *Morgan v. International Bank for Reconstruction and Development*, 752 F. Supp. 492 (D.C.C. 1990).

9 *See*, for example, cases discussed by R. S. J. Martha, *supra* note at 26–34, including *Waite and Kennedy v. Germany*, App. No. 26083/94, 30 Eur. Ct. Hum. Rights 261 (1999); *Dulhalde v. Organización Panamericana de Salud*, Dictámen No. D.73, XXXIV de Corte Suprema de Justicia de la Nación (Argentina, Mar. 31, 1999). See also *In re Illemassene v. OECD*, Cour de Cassation, Chambre Sociale (France, Sep. 29, 2010).

secretary general, director general, or president. But it does imply their obligation to consider the waiver option in good faith.

The Case of the OAS

First established in 1889 as the International Union of American Republics and later known as the Pan American Union, the OAS is the oldest of the major international organizations.[10] The mission of the OAS is to promote peace and security in the Americas by promoting representative democracy; facilitating integral development; providing mechanisms for the common defense, as well as for the peaceful settlement of disputes among its members; and eradicating extreme poverty.

As described more fully below, the OAS member states have recognized, in the OAS Charter,[11] national legislation, and a host of bilateral and multilateral agreements, that to achieve the OAS mission, the OAS and its personnel must have immunity from national courts and the adjudicative jurisdiction of national administrative agencies. Nonetheless, in order to sustain political support for that immunity in many of its member states, the OAS has had to agree to provide or otherwise submit to reasonable alternative dispute-resolution mechanisms.

The OAS Charter

Article 133 of the OAS Charter provides that the OAS shall have "such legal capacity and privileges and immunities necessary for the exercise of its functions and the accomplishment of its purposes." That immunity is clearly functional in scope.

Broader language is used for defining the privileges and immunities of the secretary general, the assistant secretary general, and member-state delegations to the OAS and their personnel. It suggests that the kind of absolute immunity conveyed under the 1961 Vienna Convention on Diplomatic Relations to "diplomatic agents" may be appropriate for those individuals so as to guarantee their independence of action in the interest of the organization.[12]

---

10   *Conferencias Internacionales Americanas, 1889-1936* (Washington 1938), at 36.

11   The OAS Charter is a multilateral treaty first adopted in 1948. Since then, it has been amended four times by the member states. *See* <http://www.oas.org/dil/treaties_A-41 _Charter_of_the_Organization_of_American_States.htm>. *See* also W. Berenson, *The Structure of the Organization of American States: A Summary,* <http://www.oas.org/legal/english /WMB%20Structure%20of%20OAS,%20Eng.doc>, originally published as *La estructura de la organización de los Estados Americanos: Una reseña in el sistema interamericana frente el nuevo siglo* (Antioquia, Colombia 2002).

12   Article 134 of the charter states: "The representatives of the Member States on the organs of the Organization, the personnel of their delegations as well as the Secretary General and the Assistant Secretary General, shall enjoy the privileges and immunities corresponding to their position and necessary for the independent performance of their duties." *See* also Articles 29–37 of the Vienna Convention on Diplomatic Relations (Apr. 18, 1961), 500 U.N.T.S. 95.

Article 135 of the charter leaves the elaboration of the specific immunities to be enjoyed by the staff members of the OAS General Secretariat and other organs to further agreement between the member states in the general secretariat or those organs.[13] Pursuant to Article 135, the OAS opened a multilateral agreement for signature in 1949 that entered into force in 1951. Since then, 13 member states have ratified it. All the other OAS member states have subscribed to bilateral agreements with the OAS General Secretariat extending functional immunity to the OAS, the general secretariat, and its rank-and-file staff. Some member states have extended diplomatic immunities to the secretary general, assistant chief of mission, and director of the office of the general secretariat in country.[14]

The Multilateral and Bilateral Agreements

The multilateral and bilateral agreements that the OAS has concluded with its member states contain language requiring the OAS to establish alternative dispute-resolution mechanisms for disputes arising under contract and tort law, as well as for disputes between third parties and OAS officials.[15] Most agreements also provide that the secretary general may waive the immunities, when in his or her discretion they will not have an adverse effect upon the goals and objectives of the organization and it is in the interest of justice to do so.[16]

---

13   Article 135 of the charter states: "The juridical status of the Specialized Organizations and the privileges and immunities that should be granted to them and to their personnel, as well as to the officials of the General Secretariat, shall be determined in a multilateral agreement. The foregoing shall not preclude, when it is considered necessary, the concluding of bilateral agreements."

14   Pursuant to Article 135, several other OAS organs have entered into separate agreements for privileges and immunities with member states. They include the Inter-American Institute for Cooperation on Agriculture, with headquarters in Costa Rica; the Inter-American Children's Institute, headquartered in Uruguay; and the Inter-American Human Rights Court, in Costa Rica.

15   For example, Article 12 of the Agreement on Privileges and Immunities of the OAS (the multilateral agreement), provides: "The Pan American Union [now the OAS General Secretariat under the 1967 Protocol of Buenos Aires to the OAS Charter] shall make provisions for appropriate modes of settlement of: (a) disputes arising out of contracts or other disputes of a private law character to which the Pan American Union is a party; (b) disputes involving any official or member of the staff of the Pan American Union with reference to which immunity is enjoyed, if immunity has not been waived by the Secretary General in accordance with Article 14." *See* Agreement on Privileges and Immunities of the Organization of American States (May 15, 1949), available at <http://www.oas.org/dil / treaties _ C - 13 _ Agreement_on_ Privileges_and_Immunities_ of _ the _ Organization _of_American_States_htm>. Similar language is included in the bilateral agreements on privileges and immunities that the OAS has negotiated with its other member states.

16   Regarding the obligation of the secretary general to consider waiving immunities, Article 14 of the multilateral agreement specifies: "Privileges and immunities are granted to officials and personnel of the Pan American Union in the interests of the Organization only. Consequently, the Secretary General shall waive the privileges and immunities of any official or member of the staff in the case where, in the judgment of the Secretary General, the exercise thereof would impede the course of justice and the waiver can be made without prejudice to the interests of the Organization. In the case of the Secretary General or of the Assistant Secretary General, the Council of the Organization shall have the right to waive the immunity."

Alternative Dispute Mechanisms Established by the OAS

Over the years the OAS has adopted a panoply of dispute-resolution mechanisms as an alternative to national justice systems. As described more fully below, they include the OAS Administrative Tribunal, established by the OAS General Assembly in 1971 for the resolution of disputes with its employees; arbitration pursuant to agreements with contractors and other aggrieved persons; maintenance of adequate insurance policies to cover reasonable potential liability; and the occasional waiver of immunity when justice so demands and it can be done without substantial damage to the organization.

The Administrative Tribunal

Like most other major international organizations, the OAS has established an administrative tribunal for handling disputes between its organs and their employees. The tribunal judges are elected by the general assembly. Judges must all be lawyers and cannot hold positions within the OAS or serve on the member-state delegations to the organization. All staff members and others claiming entitlement to the rights of staff members have access to the tribunal once they have exhausted the corresponding internal grievance procedures.[17]

Arbitration

Regarding all other disputes with contractors and others, the OAS has adopted a policy of providing for arbitration in accordance with generally recognized rules. In the case of contracts, the arbitration authority and rules to be used are usually established from among several options. They include the American Arbitration Association (AAA), the Inter-American Commercial Arbitration Commission (IACAC), and the United Nations Commission on International Trade Law (UNCITRAL).

The OAS's most extensive agreement on immunities is its Headquarters Agreement with the United States of America, which entered into force in November 1994 ("Headquarters Agreement").[18] In exchange for recognition of absolute immunity from the jurisdiction of the courts and administrative proceedings in the United States, the OAS agreed under Article VIII of the Headquarters Agreement to provide arbitration for all disputes that do not fall under the jurisdiction of its administrative tribunal. The arbitration

---

17   *See* Statute of the Administrative Tribunal of the Organization of American States, Article VI, available at <http://www.oas.org/tribadm/estatuto_en.asp>. No filing fees are required of current staff members; however, all others are required to post a bond to cover possible attorneys' fees and costs if the reconsideration committee, which must consider the case before the case goes to the tribunal, does not find in favor of the staff member. The reconsideration committee, which advises the secretary general on the disposition of employment-related grievances, is made up of a representative of the staff association, a representative of the secretary general, and a chair appointed by both of them.

18   There is a separate March 20, 1975, agreement between the OAS and the United States that recognizes diplomatic immunity for representatives of the member-state and permanent-observer missions to the OAS, available at <http://www.oas.org/legal/english/docs/BilateralAgree/US/sedeusa1.htm>.

must proceed in accordance with the rules of either the AAA or the IACAC, or such other rules to which the parties may agree. Article VIII of the Headquarters Agreement prohibits the arbitration tribunal from entertaining claims for punitive damages.

In the case of small claims, the OAS provides a special arbitration procedure under rules attached to the Headquarters Agreement and under which it is obligated to pay the cost. The agreement fixed the amount of a small claim at $2,000 in 1994, and provided that after five years, the amount could be increased by agreement with the U.S. secretary of state or, in the absence of such agreement, the amount would increase automatically each year in accordance with the consumer price index for the District of Columbia.[19]

Insurance

As for satisfying claims, the OAS General Secretariat maintains insurance policies at a responsible level. The availability of these policies has facilitated the resolution of most reasonable claims against the organization arising out of contract disputes or torts with third parties and has obviated the need for frequent recourse to arbitration and other dispute-resolution mechanisms.

Waivers of Immunity

Pursuant to its obligation to waive immunity when, at the discretion of the secretary general, the interests of justice so demand and the interests of the organization are not impaired, the OAS General Secretariat generally complies with orders for the garnishment of staff wages for payment of delinquent child support and alimony. It may also, depending on the facts in each case, comply with bankruptcy garnishment orders, and its pension committee will voluntarily comply with qualified domestic support orders in divorce actions. In so doing, however, the general secretariat or the pension committee, as the case may be, usually sends a note back to the court underscoring that its compliance is voluntary and should in no way be considered a waiver of its immunities.

In rare instances, the OAS General Secretariat has waived its immunities in order to obtain mortgage financing for the purchase of real estate.[20] In doing so, however, it has insisted that the waiver be limited to the value of the facility being mortgaged and not extend to all other assets. The secretariat has also occasionally waived immunities in order to recover past-due payments from delinquent recipients of OAS student loans or to pursue commercial claims

---

19 Headquarters Agreement, Section 2(b). *See* also W. Berenson, *Privilegios e Inmunidades de organizaciones internacionales: El acuerdo de sede entre la Organización de los Estados Americanos y los Estados Unidos; Apuntes* (1995), available at <http://www.oas.org/legal/english/PrivilegioseInmunidadesBerenson.doc>, also published in *XXII Curso de Derecho Internacional, Comite Jurídico Interamericano, 1995* 235–50 (Ediciones Jurídicas de las Américas 1997).

20 Those waivers, under both common and civil law, have been construed to require the approval of the OAS General Assembly or, when it is not meeting, the OAS Permanent Council, because a mortgage constitutes an encumbrance upon real property.

it may have in contract or tort where no arbitration provision is binding the adverse party. The secretariat will not, however, waive immunities by initiating an adverse action in the courts of a member state unless it is reasonably assured that the possibilities of a meaningful counterclaim by the defendant are minimal.

Cases Challenging OAS Immunities

Since the OAS Headquarters Agreement entered into effect in 1994, there have been no cases in the United States challenging the immunities of the organization, its general secretariat, or its staff. The Headquarters Agreement definitively clarified that the immunities enjoyed by the organization are absolute, not qualified, and that its officials enjoy immunity in relation to the performance of their official functions. Moreover, the Headquarters Agreement clearly identified viable alternative dispute-resolution mechanisms for persons with grievances against the organization, thereby reducing the need to challenge the organization's immunities.

During the early 1980s, however, the extent of those immunities was challenged in two cases before the U.S. Court of Appeals for the District of Columbia Circuit. In *Broadbent v. OAS*,[21] the plaintiffs, who had received a ruling in their favor at the OAS Administrative Tribunal for wrongful discharge, brought another claim for wrongful discharge and significantly higher damages in the federal courts. The court of appeals reaffirmed a lower district court decision holding that the organization was immune from employment-related claims, and it suggested in a footnote that the immunities that the OAS then enjoyed under the International Organizations Immunity Act were absolute immunities, rather than the restricted immunities enjoyed by foreign sovereigns under the Foreign Sovereign Immunities Act (FSIA).[22]

In another wrongful-discharge case previously adjudicated by the OAS Administrative Tribunal in the plaintiff's favor, *Donald v. Orfila*,[23] the plaintiff sued the former secretary general in the federal courts. The amount was for $1 million, instead of the maximum of three years' basic salary he had been awarded under the Administrative Tribunal Statute. The court concluded that the secretary general was entitled to immunity "to the extent that the acts alleged in the complaint relate to his functions as director," and that the termination of the plaintiff "unquestionably relates" to the secretary general's official functions. It further observed that it would be improper for the court to investigate the appropriateness of the motive for the secretary general's decision to terminate the plaintiff, because if it were to do so, "the

---

21   628 F.2d 27 (D.C. Cir. 1980).

22   *Id.*, at footnote 20. Moreover, the court held: "the relationship of an international organization with its internal administrative staff is noncommercial, and absent a waiver, activities defining or arising out of that relationship may not be the basis of an action against the organization, regardless of whether international organizations enjoy absolute or restrictive immunity." *Id.*, at 35.

23   618 F. Supp. 545 (D.D.C. 1985), aff'd per curiam, 788 F.2d 36 (D.C. Cir. 1986).

immunity shield which Congress intended to afford solid protection would indeed be evanescent."

In another pre–Headquarters Agreement case, *In re Lopez Cayzedo*, a bankruptcy trustee petitioned the bankruptcy court to order the secretary treasurer of the OAS Retirement and Pension Fund to turn over to the trustee the bankrupt's OAS pension fund account for distribution to creditors. The court agreed with the secretary treasurer that his functional immunities as an OAS General Secretariat staff member shielded him from the jurisdiction of the court and dismissed the trustee's petition.[24]

In other OAS member states, the secretariat has had to defend its immunities against claims alleging violation of the local labor laws. In most instances, the organization has reached reasonable settlements with the plaintiffs, resulting in the abandonment or dismissal of those claims prior to judgment.

In Brazil, however, courts were reluctant in the years immediately following the adoption of the 1988 constitution to recognize the immunities of the OAS and other international organizations from employment-related claims. That reluctance was based on Article 114 of Brazil's constitution, which extended jurisdiction over employment-related disputes arising between "entities of public international law" and their employees to Brazilian labor tribunals. They used Article 114 to support the thesis that when it came to questions of immunity, international organizations were identical to foreign sovereigns, which under modern customary international law, as embodied in the FSIA, were entitled to only restrictive immunities. The Brazilian courts went on to assume that the contracting of the staff of international organizations, like the contracting of staff for foreign sovereigns, was a commercial activity, and therefore immunity did not apply to labor disputes between international organizations and their employees. The OAS appealed those judgments, asserting that the agreements approved by the executive and legislative authorities were valid under the doctrine of separation of powers and also noting that, due to the differences between international organizations and foreign sovereigns, the Brazilian courts were mistaken in assuming that the contracting of staff was a commercial activity for international organizations. Initially, the results of those appeals were mixed.

In 2004, the momentum turned in favor of the OAS and other international organizations. In March, Brazil's federal supreme court reaffirmed a

---

24 *See* Memorandum Decision Granting Motion to Dismiss, Case No. 88-4-1546SD, Chapter 7, Adversary No. 90A-0333SD (unpublished, on file with the author). The OAS Retirement and Pension Fund is a qualified pension fund under the U.S. Internal Revenue Code, and as such it should have been excluded from the bankrupt estate under Maryland and federal law. Nonetheless, because of the erroneous testimony of a witness in a proceeding in which the OAS did not participate, the fund was mistakenly characterized as nonqualified by the witness and included in the bankrupt estate. Thus, it was necessary to assert the immunity defense, which the court endorsed without having to recall the confused witness. Section 7 of Article I and Section 2 of Article IV of the Headquarters Agreement now make it clear that the OAS Retirement and Pension Plan, for purposes of OAS immunities, is an asset of the organization and therefore exempt from confiscation and seizure by U.S. authorities.

2002 supreme labor court judgment in *Orlando da Silva v. OEA*[25] holding that, although Brazilian courts could take jurisdiction of cases against the OAS under Article 114 of its constitution, they could not enforce a judgment in favor of the plaintiff due to the immunity from confiscation and seizure conferred upon OAS assets under the organization's agreements with Brazil. That same month, the Appellate Labor Tribunal for the Tenth Region (Brasilia) issued a judgment in the case of *Fernandez Duarte v. OEA*[26] recognizing immunity from subject matter jurisdiction in labor disputes based on the doctrine of separation of powers under the constitution. That doctrine, asserted the court in *Duarte*, requires courts to respect the agreements with the OAS on immunities signed by the executive branch and ratified by the legislature. Since then, most courts have adopted the position taken by the appellate court in *Duarte*, and in 2009, the supreme labor tribunal, in a case brought by a former employee of the Inter-American Institute for Cooperation in Agriculture (IICA), a specialized organization of the OAS, upheld the IICA's immunities on that same rationale.[27]

Concluding Observations

What conclusions might one draw from all of this?

First, in returning to the lens of substantive due process analysis, the OAS and its member states have gone a long way toward restricting the adverse impact of OAS immunities on the right to a fair trial. What they have come up with may not be considered by all to be the ideal "least restrictive means." But it cannot be denied that significant "tailoring" has taken place over the years, particularly by way of the Headquarters Agreement, to define the scope of the immunities and provide reasonable independent alternative dispute-resolution mechanisms and insurance for the purpose of satisfying claims.

Second, international organizations that do not follow a similar path are destined, in a world of ever-increasing consciousness and advocacy of fundamental human rights, to have their immunities challenged and scrutinized by national courts through a lens similar to that of the substantive due process. The analysis may not go by that name, but it is the kind of process many courts use in attempting to balance one vital interest against another and to find a reasonable accommodation between the two.

Third, in the Americas, for the most part, national courts are still inclined to respect the functional immunities of international organizations with noncommercial objectives, such as the OAS and the United Nations. Those

---

25   Supremo Tribunal Federal, No. 468.498-6 Distrito Federal (Mar. 16, 2004).

26   *See,* for example, Tribunal Regional do Trabalho, 10 Regiao, Proceso 00101 2004-006-10-00-6 (2004).

27   *See Judiciário não pode afastar imunidade de organismo internacional* (Nov. 24, 2009), at <http://jornal.jurid.com.br / materias / noticias / judiciario-nao-pode-afastar-imunidade-organismo -internacional>.

immunities are considered to be absolute with regard to all claims relating to the official functions of those organizations and their officials.

Fourth, the general wisdom regarding immunities is that if you abuse them, you will eventually lose them. Abuse occurs when international organizations and their officials do not provide alternative independent means for recourse for claims against them—that is, when they infringe upon the fundamental right to a fair trial.

All the active member states of the OAS and governments in most other parts of the world are representative democracies. The elected officials of those democracies will be called upon to explain to the citizens who elected them why they cannot pursue a cause of action against an international organization or its officials in their national courts when they have been harmed by them. Unless those elected officials can satisfactorily demonstrate that other reasonable means of pursuing those claims are available, their explanations will fall on deaf ears, and it will be politically inconvenient for those officials to continue to support the legislation and treaties that confer immunities on international organizations. Thus, in those cases where immunity denies a path of redress through the courts, the onus is upon governments, working with international organizations, to assure that other means are available.

Responsibility of International Organizations and the World Bank Inspection Panel

Parallel Tracks Unlikely to Converge?

EVARIST BAIMU AND ARISTEIDIS PANOU[*]

Following the adoption of the articles on state responsibility in 2001, the International Law Commission (ILC) took on the momentous task of addressing the issue of the responsibility of international organizations.[1] This chapter reviews the preliminary outcome of these efforts, and the draft articles on responsibility of international organizations adopted on first reading in 2009 (and on second reading in 2011), in light of the particular features and challenges of international financial institutions (IFIs),[2] specifically the World Bank.[3]

IFIs, including the Bank, have a variety of legal relationships with a variety of actors, including their employees and investors, as well as member and nonmember states that receive funds or technical assistance from the IFIs. In addition, IFIs have legal relationships with other international organizations and legal persons (other than states) with whom IFIs enter into lending agreements in support of developmental projects. In all instances, legal agreements define the reciprocal rights and obligations of the parties. There have been calls to extend the reach of responsibility beyond contractually defined obligations under these agreements,[4] so that international organizations including IFIs are held responsible for, inter alia, acts or omissions in relation to tortious

---

[*] The authors are grateful to Alberto Ninio, Maurizio Ragazzi, and Adrian Di Giovanni for their invaluable comments. This chapter represents personal views of the authors and should not be attributed to the institution with which they are associated.

1 GA Res. 56/82, UN GAOR, 56th Sess., UN Doc. A/56/82 (2002).

2 On IFIs, *see* Maurizio Ragazzi, *Financial Institutions, International*, in *The Max Planck Encyclopedia of Public International Law* (Rüdiger Wolfrum ed., Oxford U. Press 2008), available at <http://www.mpepil.com>.

3 In this chapter, unless noted otherwise, the terms "Bank" and "World Bank" include the International Bank for Reconstruction and Development (IBRD) and the International Development Association (IDA).

4 As international organizations, IFIs are obliged to act consistently with peremptory norms of international law and applicable rules of customary international law. *See* Henry G. Schermers & Niels M. Blokker, *International Institutional Law: Unity within Diversity* 832–35 (4th ed., Martinus Nijhoff 2003).

acts,[5] human rights violations,[6] financial leakages on projects,[7] and actions that harm or threaten to harm the environment.[8]

It is a well-accepted tenet today that responsibility is not reserved for states but is an attribution of the international legal personality of all subjects of international law, including international organizations.[9] However, the mere recognition of responsibility of international organizations is useless without a framework to regulate the occurrence and the consequences of responsibility. The ILC work provides this general framework, but uncertainty persists about how this one-size-fits-all framework will be compatible with the characteristics of every organization.[10]

In the area of state responsibility, there has been a significant discussion about the relation between the general rules of state responsibility and special or self-contained regimes.[11] With the exception of the European Union,[12] a similar discussion has not happened for international organizations. This

---

5   Steven Herz, *Rethinking International Financial Institution Immunity*, in *International Financial Institutions and International Law* 137, 158 (Daniel D. Bradlow & David B. Hunter ed., Kluwer Law International 2010).

6   Daniel D. Bradlow, *The World Bank, the IMF, and Human Rights*, 6 Transnational Law and Contemporary Problems 47, 64–66 (1996); Margot E. Salomon, *International Economic Governance and Human Rights Accountability*, in *Casting the Net Wider: Human Rights, Development and New Duty-Bearers* 153, 174–81 (Margot E. Salomon, Arne Tostensen, & Wouter Vandenhole ed., Intersentia 2007).

7   Fatma Marouf, *Holding the World Bank Accountable for Leakage of Funds from Africa's Health Sector*, 12 (1) Health and Human Rights in Practice 95 (2010).

8   The Independent Evaluation Group, an oversight body of the World Bank, has observed that the Bank "needs to do a better job of measuring the environmental performance and impacts of its activities"; *see* IEG-World Bank, *Environmental Sustainability: An Evaluation of World Bank Group Support* 89 (2008), available at <http://siteresources.worldbank.org/EXTENVIRONMENT/Resources/environ_eval.pdf>.

9   *See Reparation for Injuries Suffered in the Service of the United Nations, Advisory Op.,* 1949 I.C.J. 174, 179; Giorgio Gaja, special rapporteur, *First Report on Responsibility of International Organizations*, at paragraph 15, UN Doc. A/CN.4/532 (Mar. 26, 2003); Alain Pellet, *The Definition of Responsibility in International Law*, in *The Law of International Responsibility* 3, 6 (James Crawford, Alain Pellet, & Simon Olleson ed., Oxford U. Press 2010).

10 After the adoption of the draft articles on first reading, almost all international organizations and states that sent comments to the ILC commented on Article 63 on *lex specialis*; *see* ILC, Responsibility of International Organizations: Comments and Observations Received from International Organizations, at 37–41, UN Doc. A/CN.4/637 (Feb. 14, 2011); ILC, Responsibility of International Organizations: Comments and Observations Received from International Organizations, at 34–35, UN Doc. A/CN.4/637/Add.1 (Feb. 17, 2011); ILC, Responsibility of International Organizations: Comments and Observations Received from International Organizations, at 41, UN Doc. A/CN.4/636 (Feb. 14, 2011).

11 For an overview of this topic, *see* Bruno Simma & Dirk Pulkowski, *Leges Speciales and Self-Contained Regimes*, in *The Law of International Responsibility* 139 (James Crawford, Alain Pellet, & Simon Olleson ed., Oxford U. Press 2010).

12 Stefan Talmon, *Responsibility of International Organizations: Does the European Community Require Special Treatment?* in *International Responsibility Today: Essays in Memory of Oscar Schachter* 405 (Maurizio Ragazzi ed., Martinus Nijhoff 2005).

discussion might be particularly necessary for organizations that have put into place a framework and a mechanism for addressing violations of their obligations.

One such organization is the World Bank, which has established the Inspection Panel as an accountability mechanism to address failures to abide by its policies and procedures. It is instructive to examine the interaction between the ILC work on the responsibility of international organizations and the accountability regime of the Inspection Panel to evaluate[13] the added value that general international law of responsibility could bring to the panel.[14]

Before discussing the international legal responsibility of IFIs from the perspective of their compatibility with the World Bank Inspection Panel, this chapter provides a discussion of some key features that characterize the World Bank and sets it apart from other international organizations.

Setting the Context: Unique Features of the World Bank

The unique features of the World Bank relate to the fact that it is a financial institution with similarities to a private corporation and an actor in the capital market. At the same time, it has a development mandate, is accountable to its member states, and has gradually established a spectrum of accountability and review mechanisms.

A Global Credit Union with a Mandate to Finance Development

The Bank is an international financial cooperative institution[15] "whose resources are available only for the benefit of members"[16] that is required to "act prudently in the interests both of the particular member in whose territories the project is located and of the members as a whole" when making or guaranteeing a loan.[17]

---

13 This chapter touches upon the interrelated but distinct concepts of responsibility, accountability, and liability. The relationships among these concepts have been explored extensively in the literature; see William E. Holder, *Can International Organizations Be Controlled? Accountability and Responsibility*, 97 Am. Socy. Intl. L. Procs. 231 (2003); Jutta Brunnée, *International Legal Accountability through the Lens of the Law of State Responsibility*, 36 Netherlands Y.B. Intl. Law 21 (2005); Malgosia Fitzmaurice, *International Responsibility and Liability*, in *The Oxford Handbook of International Environmental Law* 1010 (Daniel Bodansky, Jutta Brunnée, & Ellen Hey ed., Oxford U. Press 2007). *See* also the discussion and the references in footnotes 35 and 120.

14 Simma & Pulkowski, *supra* note 11, at 148.

15 *See* Salman M. A. Salman, *Downstream Riparians Can Also Harm Upstream Riparians: The Concept of Foreclosure of Future Uses*, 35 (4) Water International 350, 358 (2010) (describing the Bank as an "international financial cooperative institution").

16 IBRD Articles of Agreement, Article III, Section 1(a). This limitation does not preclude assistance to nonmembers when the World Bank Board of Executive Directors has deemed this assistance to be in the interest of membership.

17 IBRD Articles of Agreement, Article III, Section 4(v).

This characterization is buttressed by the corporate structure of the Bank, which, like other corporations, comprises shareholders whose interests are represented by a Board of Governors and a Board of Executive Directors.[18] The executive directors exercise both executive and oversight powers over the Bank. The ultimate control of the Bank's operations rests with the Bank's members, which are also its shareholders and exercise such control through the Board of Governors and Board of Executive Directors.[19] The executive directors function in continuous session and exercise substantially all the Bank's powers related to operations.[20] The resident Board of Executive Directors has exclusive jurisdiction on the question of interpretation of the constituent instrument of the organization.[21]

The purposes of the Bank as set forth in its Articles of Agreement are, inter alia, to assist in the reconstruction and development of territories of its members, to promote private foreign investment, and to promote the long-range balanced growth of international trade and the maintenance of an equilibrium in balances of payments by encouraging international investment for the development of the productive resources of members.[22]

Broadly put, the Bank has a mandate to assist in development through financing investment or technical assistance projects and policy reform programs. Clear delineation of the role of the Bank in projects (the Bank does not get involved in implementing the projects it finances—the borrower or recipient of Bank financing does) is critical in evaluating the Bank's exposure to responsibility.[23]

---

18 *See* Tobias M. C. Asser, *The World Bank,* 7 J. Intl. L. & Econ. 207, 211 (1972) (stating that "the relationship between the World Bank and its clients is a very special one which approaches partnership. This quality of businesslike cooperation which permeates the Bank operations calls for more than what sometimes appear to be conflicting interests").

19 IBRD Articles of Agreement, Article V, Section 4(a).

20 Aron Broches, *International Bank for Reconstruction and Development,* in *Legal Advisers and International Organizations* 83, 85 (Herbert C. L. Merillat ed., Oceana Publications 1966). *See* also IBRD Articles of Agreement, Article V, Section 4(a), providing that the "Executive Directors shall be responsible for the conduct of the general operations of the Bank, and for this purpose, shall exercise all the powers delegated to them by the Board of Governors."

21 Under IBRD Articles of Agreement, Article IX, any question of interpretation of provisions of the Articles of Agreement must be submitted to the executive directors of the IBRD for their decision.

22 IBRD Articles of Agreement, Article I. The purpose of the IDA is to promote economic development and to increase productivity and thus raise standards of living in the less-developed areas of the world included within its membership—in particular by providing finance to meet their developmental requirements on terms that are more flexible and bear less heavily on the balance of payments than those of conventional loans—thereby furthering the IBRD developmental objectives and supplementing the IBRD activities. *See* IDA Articles of Agreement, Article I. IDA Articles of Agreement, Article V, Section I, states: "The Association shall provide financing to further development in the less-developed areas of the world included within the Association's membership."

23 That said, the Bank has an obligation under its Articles of Agreement to "make arrangements to ensure that the proceeds of any loan are used only for the purposes for which the loan was granted, with due attention to considerations of economy and efficiency and without

The World Bank and, more generally, IFIs are entities created by states with limited mandates and competence.[24] Unlike sovereign states, which have sovereign powers, IFIs have limited powers by virtue of their constituent documents.[25] Additional constraints through broad-based concepts such as international responsibility may have unintended consequences by limiting the capacity of these institutions to discharge their mandate.

IBRD as an Actor in Capital Markets

Some IFIs, including the International Bank for Reconstruction and Development (IBRD), the European Investment Bank, and other multilateral development banks, operate according to a business model that uses capital markets to source funds used to finance loans to borrowers. These institutions rely on access to relatively cheap financing from the capital markets to operate effectively in fulfillment of their mandate. Unlike states, IFIs cannot raise taxes to fulfill unexpected financial payouts resulting from being held responsible for harmful actions attributable to them.[26]

In this respect, IFIs face a dual challenge. On the one hand, as financial entities, they may be assumed to possess the financial wherewithal to make payouts if financial liability follows international responsibility for wrongful acts. On the other hand, IFIs that are also actors in capital markets are perhaps more sensitive to such contingent liability to make payments than international organizations that rely on voluntary contributions as the basis of their financing, because contingent risks may impair these IFIs' risk profile and therefore the attractiveness of their bonds as investments.

Accountability Mechanisms

The Bank has created a spectrum of accountability and review mechanisms with an oversight function over the Bank's operations. In addition to the Inspection Panel, the principal accountability and supervisory mechanisms are the Administrative Tribunal, the Internal Auditing Department (IAD), the Independent Evaluations Group (IEG), and the Integrity Vice Presidency (INT).

---

regard to political or other non-economic influences or considerations" (IBRD Articles of Agreement, Article III, Section 5{b}). The Bank discharges this obligation by agreeing with the borrower on certain disbursement, procurement, financial management, monitoring, and supervision provisions for each project that it finances. The borrower is responsible for ensuring that the proceeds of the financing are used for their intended purposes.

24   The Bank plays a specific role in relation to projects, namely, that of a financier. *See* Asser, *supra* note 18, at 210.

25   Unlike a state, "an international organization represents not a subject of international law that has a continuing base of resources in a given population and territory, but a subject that is the creation of other subjects" with "a life and influence of its own" but that "can move only as far and as fast as the leading strings of member states permit." *See* Herbert C. L. Merillat, *Preface*, in *Legal Advisers and International Organizations* vii, viii (Herbert C. L. Merillat ed., Oceana Publications 1966).

26   This is crucial for the IBRD because the liability of its member states is limited to the unpaid portion of the issue price of the shares; *see* IBRD Articles of Agreement, Article II, Section 6.

These mechanisms operate under various mandates and cover different aspects of the Bank's operations. The Administrative Tribunal is entrusted with hearing and deciding complaints by staff members, or persons claiming through them, that a decision or action taken by the Bank has violated the staff member's terms of appointment or contract of employment.[27] The IAD is responsible for auditing operational, financial, administrative, personnel, and information resource management systems and other activities with the objective of assessing their efficiency, compliance with policies, and effectiveness.[28] The IEG's mandate extends to the assessment of the relevance, efficacy, and efficiency of World Bank operational programs and activities and their contribution to development effectiveness.[29] The INT is primarily responsible for investigating allegations of fraud or corruption at the World Bank or in connection with Bank-related projects and allegations of misconduct by Bank staff members.[30]

Accountability is pursued not only through oversight mechanisms but also through the promotion of transparency.[31] In July 2010, the World Bank adopted a policy on access to information that is based on the principle of maximizing access to information.[32] Under this policy, the Bank allows access to any information in its possession unless such information falls under a list of exceptions;[33] an oversight mechanism, consisting of the access to information committee and the appeals board, has been established.[34]

---

27 World Bank Administrative Tribunal Statute, Article II, paragraph 1.

28 Ibrahim F. I. Shihata, *The World Bank Inspection Panel: In Practice* 15–16 (2d ed., Oxford U. Press 2000).

29 IEG, *Mandate of the Director-General, Evaluation,* available at <http://siteresources.worldbank.org/EXTDIRGEN/Resources/dge_mandate_tor.pdf>.

30 *See* World Bank Sanctions Procedures (as adopted by the World Bank as of Jan. 1, 2011), available at <http://siteresources.worldbank.org/EXTOFFEVASUS/Resources/WBG SanctionsProceduresJan2011.pdf>. After completing an investigation in which firms or individuals are found to have engaged in a sanctionable practice, the INT will initiate the sanctions process by preparing a Notice of Sanctions Proceedings. The appropriate sanctions are determined first by the suspension and evaluation officer; if the sanctions are challenged, they are reviewed by the sanctions board.

31 Benedict Kingsbury, *The Concept of "Law" in Global Administrative Law,* 20 Eur. J. Intl. L. 23, 25 (2009).

32 World Bank, *Policy on Access to Information,* paragraph 5 (Jul. 2010), available at <http://go.worldbank.org/LN06W7ZCB0>.

33 *Id.,* at paragraph 6.

34 The committee serves as the first stage of appeal for appeals alleging a violation of the policy. It also serves as the first and final stage of appeal for appeals making a public interest case, and its decisions in these cases are final. The appeals board hears only appeals alleging a violation of the policy. It serves as the second stage of appeal if requesters whose appeal has been denied by the committee wish to file a second appeal. *Id.,* at paragraphs 35–40.

Thus, it is clear that accountability is "a multifaceted phenomenon."[35] Among the accountability mechanisms of the Bank, the Inspection Panel stands out for two reasons: its subject matter extends to almost all aspects of the principal activity of the institution, namely, financing projects; and the Inspection Panel can examine ongoing projects and provide the possibility of a remedial action, not just an ex post evaluation. In this respect, the Inspection Panel offers the most comprehensive and more "binding" review of the Bank's activities.

The Two Regimes

Before examining the interaction between the ILC work on the responsibility of international organizations and the Inspection Panel, it is helpful to briefly introduce these two regimes and discuss the links that exist between their respective rules.

ILC Work on the Responsibility of International Organizations

The ILC completed the first reading of the draft articles on the responsibility of international organizations in 2009.[36] The ILC decided to deal with this topic after it concluded its consideration of the topic of state responsibility, which had been under discussion for almost half a century, in 2001.[37] The working method adopted by the ILC for the new topic was to use the articles on state responsibility as the starting point and build similar provisions on the responsibility of international organizations.[38]

The decision of the ILC to deal with this topic, and its working method, has met considerable criticism. The main points of criticism have been the wide variety of international organizations, which impedes the development

---

35 International Law Association, *Final Report on Accountability of International Organizations* 5 (2004), available at <http://www.ila-hq.org/en/committees/index.cfm/cid/9>. According to this report, depending on the particular circumstances surrounding the acts or omissions of international organizations, their member states, or third parties, accountability can take different forms: legal, political, administrative, or financial. *See* also Rekha Oleschak-Pillai, *Accountability of International Organizations: An Analysis of the World Bank's Inspection Panel*, in *Accountability for Human Rights Violations by International Organizations* 401, 402–08 (Jan Wouters et al. ed., Intersentia 2010).

36 UNGA Resolution 64/114, January 15, 2010, UN Doc. A/RES/64/114 (2010). For an assessment of the draft articles, *see* Kristen E. Boon, *New Directions in Responsibility: Assessing the International Law Commission's Draft Articles on the Responsibility of International Organizations*, 37 Yale J. Intl. L. Online 1 (Spring 2011), available at <http://www.yjil.org/docs/pub/o-37-boon-new-directions-in-responsibility.pdf>.

37 The ILC began discussing the issue of state responsibility in 1949 and concluded it with the adoption of the draft articles on responsibility of states for internationally wrongful acts in 2001. For an account of the ILC's work on this topic, *see* James Crawford, *International Law Commission's Articles on State Responsibility: Introduction, Text and Commentaries* 1–61 (Cambridge U. Press 2002).

38 Giorgio Gaja, special rapporteur, *First Report on Responsibility of International Organizations*, at paragraph 11, UN Doc. A/CN.4/532 (Mar. 26, 2003).

of uniform principles; the lack of available practice from international organizations; and the ambiguity concerning the primary rules applicable to international organizations.[39] Another factor that may undermine the effectiveness of the ILC's work on this topic is the immunities accorded to international organizations.[40]

Although there is a trend to restrict the immunities accorded to international organizations,[41] and the draft articles may contribute to this trend, there is an additional problem. No international judicial or quasi-judicial bodies have direct jurisdiction over the acts or omissions of international organizations.[42] Most multilateral treaties, which set forth international obligations and establish international judicial or quasi-judicial bodies to ensure compliance with those obligations, can have only states as parties to these treaties.[43] Moreover, only states can institute contentious proceedings before the International Court of Justice.[44]

World Bank Inspection Panel

Several international organizations have established internal accountability mechanisms, the most notable of which is the World Bank's Inspection Panel. The rationale behind the panel's establishment was twofold: to enhance the efficiency of the Bank's operations and to meet the demand for greater transparency and accountability.[45] Linked to these two factors is the question of institutional reputation; although it is an elusive concept in the case of international

---

39   Jose Alvarez, *International Organizations: Accountability or Responsibility?* Luncheon Address, Canadian Council of International Law, Thirty-Fifth Annual Conference on Responsibility of Individuals, States and Organizations (Oct. 27, 2006).

40   Eisuke Suzuki, *Responsibility of IFIs under International Law*, in *International Financial Institutions and International Law* 61, 67–69 (Daniel D. Bradlow & David B. Hunter ed., Kluwer Law International 2010).

41   August Reinisch, *International Organizations before National Courts* (Cambridge U. Press 2000); Stephen Hertz, *International Organization in U.S. Courts: Reconsidering the Anachronism of Absolute Immunity*, 31 Suffolk Transnatl. L. Rev. 471 (2007–08). For a discussion of the immunity of international organizations, *see* also William Berenson, *Squaring the Concept of Immunity with the Fundamental Right to a Fair Trial: The Case of the OAS*, and Rutsel Silvestre J. Martha, *International Financial Institutions and Claims of Private Parties: Immunity Obliges*; both in this volume.

42   Shihata, *supra* note 28, at 263–64. The various administrative tribunals of international organizations have exclusive jurisdiction for matters related to the staff of the organizations. For an overview of the administrative tribunals of international organizations, *see* Chittharanjan F. Amerasinghe, *The Law of the International Civil Service: As Applied by International Administrative Tribunals* (2d ed., Oxford U. Press 1994). The judicial organs of the European Union have jurisdiction over actions of the European Union.

43   Where international organizations have become parties to multilateral treaties, the relevant adjudicatory bodies under these treaties have acquired jurisdiction over these organizations (for example, the WTO Dispute Settlement Body has jurisdiction over the European Union, and the European Court of Human Rights will acquire jurisdiction over the European Union if the EU accedes to the European Convention on Human Rights).

44   *See* Article 34, paragraph 1, of the Statute of the International Court of Justice. International organizations may request only advisory opinions; *see* Article 96(2) of the UN Charter.

45   Shihata, *supra* note 28, at 1–5.

organizations, reputation appears to have played no insignificant role in the circumstances leading to the creation of the Inspection Panel.[46]

The panel was established by a resolution[47] of the Bank's executive directors in September 1993 and has since served as a model for instituting inspection functions in other IFIs.[48] The resolution and two subsequent Board clarifications constitute the legal framework that regulates the panel's mandate and procedure.[49] Based on this framework, the panel examines requests for inspection by an affected party,[50] which should allege that "its rights or interests have been or are likely to be directly affected by an action or omission of the Bank as a result of a failure of the Bank to follow the Bank's operational policies and procedures" in projects financed or to be financed by the Bank (including development policy operations).[51] The resolution sets forth three preliminary requirements to be met before the panel can consider a request for inspection.

First, the subject matter of the request must have been dealt with by Bank Management and the Management must have failed to demonstrate that it followed, or is taking adequate steps to follow, the Bank's policies and procedures. Second, the alleged violation of the Bank's policies and procedures must be, in the view of the panel, of a serious character.[52] Third, the act or the omission should have—or be likely to have—a materially adverse effect on the rights or interests of the affected person.[53]

---

46   In the mid-1980s, the Bank decided to partially finance two major projects on the Narmada River in India. The projects caused environmental impacts and were expected to require the resettlement of a large number of people. The criticism from civil society led the president of the Bank to commission an independent review. The Narmada case fueled the debate on the Bank's accountability, which resulted in the establishment of the panel. *See* Shihata, *supra* note 28, at 5-8. *See* also Ian Johnstone, *Do International Organizations Have Reputations?* 7 Intl. Organizations L. Rev. 235 (2011) (arguing that the reputation can be a strong factor in inducing compliance with the law).

47   *Resolution of the Executive Directors Establishing the World Bank Inspection Panel* (No. 93-10 for the IBRD and No. 93-6 for IDA), SecM93-988 (IBRD) and SecM93-313 (IDA) (Sep. 23, 1993).

48   For an overview of the inspection mechanisms of the various IFIs, *see* Daniel D. Bradlow, *Private Complaints and International Organizations: A Comparative Study of the Independent Inspection Mechanisms in International Financial Institutions*, 36 Geo. J. Intl. L. 403 (2005).

49   The inspection function was subsequently reviewed by the Board in 1996. The first review resulted in the adoption of clarifications to the resolution establishing the panel. These clarifications did not solve all the problems in the operation of the panel, and thus a second review took place in 1998–99. This review ended with the Board issuing a statement entitled "Conclusions of the Board's Second Review of the Inspection Panel"; *see* Shihata, *supra* note 28, at 155–203. On August 19, 1994, the Inspection Panel adopted operating procedures that elaborate on certain aspects of its constituent resolution. Bank Procedure (BP) 17.55—Inspection Panel clarifies internal steps that Bank staff are required to follow when responding to a request for inspection.

50   A request for inspection can also be submitted by an executive director.

51   Resolution, paragraph 12.

52   *Id.*, at paragraph 13.

53   *Id.*, at paragraph 12.

Nature of Draft Articles and Panel Regimes

In the course of its work on the topic of state responsibility, the ILC introduced a distinction between primary and secondary rules. This distinction allowed the ILC to limit its focus on rules specifically regulating international responsibility (secondary rules), excluding those rules whose violations give rise to responsibility (primary rules).[54] The ILC did not see a reason to depart from the approach adopted on the topic of state responsibility when it decided to tackle the responsibility of international organizations. In fact, the ILC has explicitly stated that "the meaning of 'responsibility' in the new topic at least comprises the same concept," namely, the "consequences under international law of internationally wrongful acts."[55]

However, the distinction between the two sets of rules has at times been characterized as "artificial."[56] In particular, with respect to international organizations whose international obligations are not defined with the same clarity as the obligations of states,[57] the lines between the two sets of rules can become easily blurred.[58] Commentators have also noted that the draft articles introduce some primary obligations for international organizations.[59]

The panel's framework also sets secondary rules. The obligations of the Bank are found not in the panel's resolution but in the Bank's policies and procedures. In addition, the panel is not mandated to examine or make recommendations on the adequacy or the underlying merits of the policies themselves.[60] The resolution determines only the consequences of violations

---

54 Roberto Ago first proposed to focus only on responsibility; Herbert Briggs first used the expression "primary and secondary" rules; *see* Eric David, *Primary and Secondary Rules*, in *The Law of International Responsibility* 27, 28 (James Crawford, Alain Pellet, & Simon Olleson ed., Oxford U. Press 2010). According to ILC commentary on articles on state responsibility, "The emphasis is on the secondary rules of State responsibility: that is to say, the general conditions under international law for the State to be considered responsible for wrongful actions or omissions, and the legal consequences which flow therefrom. The articles do not attempt to define the content of the international obligations, the breach of which gives rise to responsibility. This is the function of the primary rules, whose codification would involve restating most of substantive customary and conventional international law." Report of the International Law Commission on the Work of Its Fifty-Third Session, UN GAOR, 56th Sess., at 31, paragraph (1), Supp. No. 10, UN Doc. A/56/10 (2001).

55 Report of the International Law Commission on the Work of Its Fifty-Fourth Session, UN GAOR, 57th Sess., at 228, paragraph 465, Supp. No. 10, UN Doc. A/57/10 (2002).

56 David, *supra* note 54, at 29–33 (discussing mainly the provisions on the circumstances precluding wrongfulness as an example of primary rules embedded in the articles on state responsibility).

57 Alvarez, *supra* note 39.

58 This risk has been pointed out to the ILC by international organizations. *See* ILC, Responsibility of International Organizations: Comments and Observations Received from International Organizations, at 14, UN Doc. A/CN.4/637 (Feb. 14, 2011).

59 Pieter J. Kuijper, *Introduction to the Symposium on Responsibility of International Organizations and of (Member) States: Attributed or Direct Responsibility or Both?* 7 Intl. Organizations L. Rev. 9, 22 (2010) (arguing that draft articles 13–16 contain primary obligations for international organizations); and Boon *supra* note 36, at 5, footnote 26.

60 Shihata, *supra* note 28, at 54.

of these policies and the procedure of bringing to the panel and processing a request for inspection.

In that respect, both the draft articles and the panel's framework "spell out consequences of a deviation from normative expectations."[61]

The next part of this chapter reviews specific provisions of the panel's legal framework as well as those of the draft articles to identify the relations between the two sets of rules.[62]

An Overview of the Panel's Mandate through the Lens of the Draft Articles

The general principle relating to the concept of international responsibility of an international organization is found in draft article 3:[63]

> Every internationally wrongful act of an international organization entails the international responsibility of the international organization.

Because an "internationally wrongful act" triggers the responsibility of an international organization, the elements of an internationally wrongful act must be identified. These elements are presented in draft article 4, which states:

> There is an internationally wrongful act of an international organization when conduct consisting of an action or omission:
>
> (*a*) Is attributable to the international organization under international law; and
>
> (*b*) Constitutes a breach of an international obligation of that international organization.

This section discusses how these two basic elements of the internationally wrongful act fit together, whether they are consistent with the panel's legal

---

61   Simma & Pulkowski, *supra* note 11, at 141.

62   The ILC has identified four types of relationships between norms: relations between special and general law; relations between prior and subsequent law; relations between laws at different hierarchical levels; and relations of law to its "normative environment" more generally; *see* Report of the Study Group of the International Law Commission, Fragmentation of International Law: Difficulties Arising from the Diversification and Expansion of International Law, at paragraph 18, UN Doc. A/CN.4/L.682 (2006).

63   The text of the draft articles is found in the Report of the International Law Commission on the Work of Its Sixty-First Session, GAOR, 64th Sess., at paragraph 50, Supp. No. 10, UN Doc. A/64/10 (2009) (ILC Report). On June 3, 2011, the ILC adopted the draft articles on the responsibility of international organizations, on second reading; *see* ILC, Responsibility of International Organizations: Texts and Titles of Draft Articles 1 to 67 Adopted by the Drafting Committee on Second Reading in 2011, UN Doc. A/CN.4/L.778 (2011). Although there are some substantive and stylistic changes between the draft articles adopted on first reading and the ones adopted on second reading, these changes do not affect the analysis of this chapter, and so reference is made only to the draft articles adopted on first reading.

framework, and the main discrepancies, if any, between the draft articles and the panel's legal framework.

Attribution

The rules of attribution of conduct are set forth in draft articles 5–8. The term "conduct" is intended to cover both acts and omissions on the part of international organizations.[64] In the same vein, the Inspection Panel has competence to examine both acts and omissions of the Bank.[65]

The general rule on attribution is in draft article 5, which states:

> 1. The conduct of an organ or agent of an international organization in the performance of functions of that organ or agent shall be considered as an act of that organization under international law whatever position the organ or agent holds in respect of the organization.
>
> 2. Rules of the organization shall apply to the determination of the functions of its organs and agents.

Although the term "agent" is defined in draft article 2(c), the term "organ" has no corresponding definition in the draft articles.[66] According to the ILC, the distinction between the two terms is not relevant, because "when persons or entities are characterized as organs or agents by the rules of the organization, there is no doubt that the conduct of those persons or entities has to be attributed, in principle, to the organization."[67]

Because international organizations have adopted divergent interpretations of draft article 5, it is interesting to consider how the panel might define the terms "organ" and "agent."[68] According to the resolution, the panel covers only the activities of IBRD and the IDA.[69] Furthermore, unlike constituent instruments of other international organizations,[70] neither the IBRD nor the IDA

---

64   ILC Report, at 54, paragraph (1).

65   Resolution, paragraph 12.

66   Several international organizations have noted this discrepancy. *See* ILC, Responsibility of International Organizations: Comments and Observations Received from International Organizations, at 17–19, UN Doc. A/CN.4/637 (Feb. 14, 2011).

67   ILC Report, at 60, paragraph (5).

68   Kuijper, *supra* note 59, at 14–15.

69   Resolution, paragraph 28. The panel's mandate does not extend to actions or omissions of two other affiliates of the World Bank Group, namely, the International Financial Corporation (IFC) and the Multilateral Guarantee Agency (MIGA); *see* Shihata, *supra* note 28, at 33. One of the first requests to the panel involved a project financed by the IFC. The panel refused to register the request because its mandate did not extend to the IFC; *id.*, at 114–15. On the World Bank Group, *see* Maurizio Ragazzi, *World Bank Group*, in *The Max Planck Encyclopedia of Public International Law* (Rüdiger Wolfrum ed., Oxford U. Press 2008), available at <http://www.mpepil.com>.

70   *Cf.* Article 7 of the UN Charter.

articles of agreement use the term "organ" or "agent."[71] However, the IBRD Articles of Agreement state that "[t]he Bank shall have a Board of Governors, Executive Directors, a President and such other officers and staff to perform such duties as the Bank may determine."[72] From this clause, one may infer that the Bank's organs are the Board of Governors, the executive directors, and Management.

The draft articles do not make a distinction between the position and the functions of organs and agents of an international organization.[73] Similarly, the resolution refers to actions and omissions of the Bank resulting from failure of the Bank to follow its own policies and procedures, without indicating whether it matters which organ acted or failed to act in the particular circumstances. In this respect, the position adopted by the resolution appears to correspond to the position of the draft articles.[74] The diversity of international obligations may explain this position of making no distinction among organs for the purpose of assigning responsibility. As the ILC observed when commenting on the corresponding provision of the articles on state responsibility:

> There is no category of organs specially designated for the commission of international wrongful acts, and virtually any State organ may be the author of such an act. The diversity of international obligations does not permit any general distinction between organs which can commit internationally wrongful acts and those which cannot.[75]

Despite the broad wording of the resolution, the panel examines actions and omissions of Bank staff because the Bank's policies, the observance of which the panel reviews, are addressed to Bank staff.[76] This reality suggests that the specialty of primary obligations of international organizations can diminish the scope of secondary obligations of such organizations.[77]

---

71   The term "agent" is used in the IBRD Articles of Agreement, Article VII, Section 3 (and IDA Articles of Agreement, Article VIII, Section 3), but these provisions refer to privileges and immunities.

72   IBRD Articles of Agreement, Article V, Section I. Article V is entitled "Organization and Structure."

73   ILC Report, at 61, paragraph (7).

74   Resolution, paragraph 12.

75   Report of the International Law Commission on the Work of Its Fifty-Third Session, *supra* note 54, at 40, paragraph (5).

76   Shihata, *supra* note 28, at 47.

77   Although the distinction between primary and secondary rules is well established, Kelsen provides a compelling account of the unity between the primary and the secondary norms; *see* Hans Kelsen, *General Theory of Norms* 142 (Clarendon Press 1991).

Breach of an International Obligation

The second element for an internationally wrongful act of an international organization to arise is that the conduct constitutes a breach of an international obligation of that organization. This issue is covered in chapter 3 of the draft articles, the main provision (draft article 9) of which is:

> 1. There is a breach of an international obligation by an international organization when an act of that international organization is not in conformity with what is required of it by that obligation, regardless of its origin and character.
>
> 2. Paragraph 1 includes the breach of an international obligation that may arise under the rules of the organization.

The ILC acknowledges that "for an international organization most obligations are likely to arise from the rules of the organization."[78] The "rules of the organization" are defined in draft article 2(c) as "the constituent instruments, decisions, resolutions and other acts of the organization adopted in accordance with those instruments, and established practice of the organization."[79] Thus, the panel can review whether the Bank has followed its operational policies, procedures,[80] and operational directives (as well as similar documents issued before these series were implemented) and exclude guidelines,[81] best practices, or similar documents or statements. These operational policies and procedures[82] are consistent with the Bank's Articles of Agreement.[83]

---

78   ILC Report, at 78, paragraph (4).

79   However, it is contested whether "all the obligations arising from rules of the organization are to be considered as international obligations"; *see id.*, at 78–79, paragraphs (5)–(6).

80   Resolution, paragraph 12, clarifies the content of operational policies and procedures. Shihata, the World Bank's General Counsel at the time of the establishment of the panel, observed that the definition of the operational policies and procedures in the resolution is not exhaustive. The fact that an operational rule incorporated into the Bank's Articles of Agreement or in any decision of the Board of Executive Directors is not reflected in the operational policies and procedures does not preclude the panel from examining its alleged violation. *See* Shihata, *supra* note 28, at 45. On this basis, one could argue that unless explicitly prohibited from doing so by the Board, the panel can review any violation of the rules of the Bank.

81   Certain Bank rules were explicitly taken out of the panel's purview. For example, the panel cannot review compliance with the Bank's guidelines on procurement; *see* resolution, paragraph 14(b) and Shihata, *supra* note 28, at 52–54.

82   Although the operational policies and procedures are primarily internal rules of the Bank, they become legally binding conditions when incorporated into loan or credit agreements between the Bank and a borrowing state; *see* Benedict Kingsbury, *Operational Policies of International Institutions as Part of the Lawmaking Process: The World Bank and Indigenous Peoples*, in *The Reality of International Law: Essays in Honour of Ian Brownlie* 323, 338 (Guy Goodwin-Gill & Stefan Talmon ed., Clarendon Press 1999).

83   Shihata, *supra* note 28, at 42. This approach is consistent with the position taken by the ILC in defining the "rules of the organization." The ILC notes: "The rules of the organization concerned will provide, expressly or implicitly, for a hierarchy among the different kinds of rules. For instance, the acts adopted by an international organization will generally not be able to derogate from its constituent instruments"; *see* ILC Report, at 50.

According to the ILC, the responsibility of an international organization is not limited to cases where there is a violation of the rules of the organization. Draft article 9, paragraph 1, refers to a breach of international obligations, regardless of their origin or character. In its commentary on this provision, the ILC alludes to its commentary on the corresponding provision in the articles on state responsibility and suggests that the obligations of international organizations "may be established by a customary rule of international law, by a treaty or by a general principle applicable within the international legal order."[84] This comment triggers two distinct questions: Which of the obligations of the Bank are based on treaty law, international custom, or general principles of international law, and is the panel competent to examine alleged violations of these obligations?

The question on the source and nature of international obligations of the Bank is outside the scope of this chapter, which focuses on the secondary rules. Considerable literature seeks to identify these obligations, especially in relation to human rights and environmental law.[85] Can the panel review Bank compliance with these obligations? The text of the resolution is clear that the panel's mandate covers only the Bank's policies and procedures, which are defined in an exclusive way. In other words, there is no indication in the resolution and the two subsequent reviews that the panel can apply international legal norms beyond the Bank's legal framework.[86]

Two examples drawn from the panel's practice illustrate how the panel has navigated the difficult issue of the application of international legal norms

---

84   Report of the International Law Commission on the Work of Its Fifty-Third Session, *supra* note 54, at 55, paragraph (3).

85   For a comprehensive overview of the general principles of international law applicable to IFIs, *see* Daniel D. Bradlow, *International Law and Operations of the IFIs*, in *International Financial Institutions and International Law* 1, 11–25 (Daniel D. Bradlow & David B. Hunter ed., Kluwer Law International 2010). Being a nonparty to international environmental treaties has not prevented the Bank from reflecting international law principles derived from some of these treaties in its own environmental policies. The content of these policies is translated into specific obligations that are incorporated into agreements that the Bank enters with borrowing states. As Di Leva observes, "OP 4.01 and other safeguard policies provide the Bank with tools that support environmental and social principles that can be found in the 1992 Rio Declaration on Environment and Development, the 1991 Convention on Environmental Impact Assessment in the Transboundary Context (Espoo Convention), and the 1998 Convention on Access to Information, Public Participation in Decision Making and Access to Justice in Environmental Matters (Aarhus Convention), among other international environmental instruments." *See* Charles Di Leva, *Transboundary Management of Natural Resources: A Brief Overview of World Bank Policies and Projects*, in *Shared Resources: Issues of Governance* 33, 39 (Sharell Hart ed., IUCN 2008).

86   There have been proposals that the panel broaden the scope of its mandate; *see* Gudmundur Alfredsson, *Introduction: Broadening the Scope of the Applicable Standards*, in *The Inspection Panel of the World Bank: A Different Complaints Procedure* 47 (Gudmundur Alfredsson and Rolf Ring ed., Martinus Nijhoff 2001).

other than the Bank's "rules of the organization." In the *Chad Petroleum* case,[87] the requesters alleged, inter alia, violations of the Bank's "directives on respect for human rights."[88] In response, Bank Management emphasized that the Bank's Articles of Agreement require the Bank to focus on economic considerations—not on political or other noneconomic influences—as the basis of its decisions.[89] This line of argument, although reflective of the official Bank position toward human rights,[90] was not persuasive to the panel. The panel took issue "with the Management's narrow view" and drew attention "in this connection to the UN Universal Declaration of Human Rights adopted in December 1948, three years after the Bank's articles of agreement entered into effect."[91] It also clarified:

> It is not within the Panel's mandate to assess the status of governance and human rights in Chad in general or in isolation, and the Panel acknowledges that there are several institutions (including UN bodies) specifically in charge of this subject. **However, the Panel felt obliged to examine whether the issues of proper governance or human rights violations in Chad were such as to impede the implementation of the Project in a manner compatible with the Bank's policies.** (emphasis in the original)[92]

It is noteworthy that the panel felt compelled to declare that it was not broadening its mandate and to argue that specific human rights considerations are included in the Bank's policies. In that respect, the panel did not argue that the Bank has human rights obligations under international customs or general principles of international law. The panel is mindful of the imperative to operate within the confines of the rules of the organization, even when it tries to expand its mandate.

In the *Honduras–Land Administration Project* case, the panel was asked to examine the relevance of International Labor Organization (ILO) Convention No. 169, concerning indigenous and tribal peoples in independent countries, to the Bank policies. In that respect, the panel observed that

> the Bank is responsible for compliance with its own policies and procedures. But it also notes that Honduras is a party to ILO Convention No. 169. The General Counsel's Response indicates that OD [Operational Directive] 4.20 does not require compliance with ILO

---

87 World Bank Inspection Panel Investigation Report, Chad: Petroleum Development and Pipeline Project (Loan No. 4558-CD); Management of the Petroleum Economy Project (Credit No. 3316-CD); Petroleum Sector Management Capacity-Building Project (Credit No. 3373-CD) (Jul. 17, 2002) (*Chad Petroleum* case), available at <http://siteresources.worldbank.org/EXTINSPECTIONPANEL/Resources/ChadInvestigationReporFinal.pdf>.

88 *Chad Petroleum* case, at paragraph 210.

89 *Id.,* at paragraph 212.

90 Siobhán McInerney-Lankford & Hans Otto-Sano, *Human Rights Indicators in Development: An Introduction* 6 (World Bank Study 2010).

91 *Chad Petroleum* case, at paragraph 214.

92 *Id.,* at paragraph 215.

Convention No. 169. The Panel observes that OD 4.20 broadly reflects the spirit and provisions of ILO Convention No. 169.[93]

The panel then added that

> it is a matter for Honduras to implement the obligations of an international agreement to which it is party and does not comment on this matter. However, the Panel is concerned that the Bank, consistently with OMS [Operational Manual Statement] 2.20, did not adequately consider whether the proposed Project plan and its implementation would be consistent with ILO Convention No. 169.[94]

In conclusion, for the World Bank Inspection Panel, there is a breach of an international obligation by the Bank *only* when an act of the Bank is not in conformity with its rules. In other words, although the Bank's policies may reference, for example, international environmental obligations,[95] the panel can render judgment only upon the Bank's compliance with its own rules.

Concurrent Responsibility

An issue of particular interest for the Bank and other IFIs is that of the responsibility of international organizations in connection with the acts of a state (or an international organization).[96] According to draft articles 13–16, an international organization is responsible when (a) it aids or assists a state in the commission of an internationally wrongful act by the state; (b) it directs and controls a state in the commission of an internationally wrongful act by the state; (c) it coerces a state to commit an internationally wrongful act; and (d) it adopts a decision binding a member state or authorizes a member state to commit an act that would be internationally wrongful if committed by the former organization and would circumvent an international obligation of the former organization.

The ILC did not find a compelling reason not to follow the respective provisions of the articles on state responsibility, even though it had to rely on

---

93   World Bank Inspection Panel Investigation Report No. 39933-HN, Honduras: Land Administration Project (IDA Credit 3858-HO), at paragraph 256 (Jun. 12, 2007), avail-able at <http://siteresources.worldbank.org/EXTINSPECTIONPANEL/Resources/Honduras FINALINVESTIGATIONREPORTrevised.pdf>.

94   *Id.*, at paragraph 257.

95   *See* also Operational Policy (OP) 4.01—Environmental Assessment, paragraph 4, which requires the Bank not to finance project activities that would contravene states' obligations "under relevant international environmental treaties and agreements." However, the policy adds that such obligations must have been identified during an environmental assessment, which is an activity for which the borrowing state, not the Bank, is responsible.

96   ILC, Responsibility of International Organizations: Comments and Observations Received from International Organizations, at 27–28, UN Doc. A/CN.4/637 (Feb. 14, 2011). For previous comments by the International Monetary Fund, *see* ILC, Responsibility of International Organizations, Comments and Observations Received from International Organizations, UN Doc. A/CN.4/582 (May 1, 2007).

limited practice of international organizations in this matter.[97] With respect to aid and assistance, the special rapporteur observed that "an international organization could incur responsibility for assisting a State, through financial support or otherwise, in a project that would entail an infringement of human rights of certain affected individuals."[98]

Although the text of draft article 13 does not explicitly exclude financial aid and assistance,[99] there are two additional conditions for the responsibility of the international organization to occur: the organization provides aid or assistance with knowledge of the circumstances of the internationally wrongful act; and the act would be internationally wrongful if committed by the organization. It has been argued that, on the basis of the commentary to the articles on state responsibility,[100] there might be an additional condition, namely, that the aid or assistance must have a certain level of severity.[101]

These explicitly mentioned conditions pose problems. It is unclear what level of knowledge is required. Some authors have remarked that, if one seeks guidance in the commentary to the articles on state responsibility,[102] knowledge may include intent.[103] Furthermore, the requirement that the act be internationally wrongful by the organization leads us back to the determination of primary obligations. These two considerations would likewise apply to draft article 14 on direction and control, because it contains the same conditions as draft article 13.

The crucial question is whether and how the panel addresses issues of concurrent responsibility between the Bank and the borrowing state. The resolution is explicit that the panel will examine

---

97   ILC Report, at 82, paragraph (1).

98   Giorgio Gaja, special rapporteur, *Third Report on Responsibility of International Organizations*, at paragraph 28, UN Doc. A/CN.4/553 (May 13, 2005).

99   The World Bank has asked the ILC to "consider expressly indicating, in its commentary to draft article 13, that organizations providing financial assistance do not, as a rule, assume the risk that assistance will be used to carry out an international wrong, as the commentary to the articles on the responsibility of States for internationally wrongful acts clearly provides"; *see* ILC, Responsibility of International Organizations: Comments and Observations Received from International Organizations, at 28, UN Doc. A/CN.4/637 (Feb. 14, 2011).

100 "There is no requirement that the aid or assistance should have been essential to the performance of the internationally wrongful act; it is sufficient if it contributed significantly to that act"; *see* Report of the International Law Commission on the Work of Its Fifty-Third Session, *supra* note 54, at 66, paragraph (5).

101 August Reinisch, *Aid or Assistance and Direction and Control between States and International Organizations in the Commission of Internationally Wrongful Acts*, 7 Intl. Organizations L. Rev. 63, 70–71 (2010).

102 "Where the allegation is that the assistance of a State has facilitated human rights abuses by another State, the particular circumstances of each case must be carefully examined to determine whether the aiding State by its aid was aware of and intended to facilitate the commission of the internationally wrongful conduct"; *see* Report of the International Law Commission on the Work of Its Fifty-Third Session, *supra* note 54, at 67, paragraph (9).

103 Reinisch, *supra* note 101, at 72.

> action[s] or omission[s] of the Bank as a result of a failure of the
> Bank to follow its operational policies and procedures with respect
> to the design, appraisal and/or implementation of a project financed
> by the Bank (including situations where the Bank is alleged to have
> failed in its follow-up on the borrower's obligations under loan
> agreements with respect to such policies and procedures).[104]

During the design, appraisal, and implementation of projects, the Bank
and the borrowing state have different roles and obligations. For example,
project preparation is a task for the borrowing state, whereas the Bank's role
includes making sure that the borrower understands the Bank's requirements
and standards and helping the borrower find the financing and the technical
assistance for preparatory work. The project's implementation is the responsibility of the borrowing state, whereas supervision rests with the Bank.

The distinct roles of the Bank and the borrowing state are reflected in the
Bank's policies and procedures. For example, under Operational Policy (OP)
4.12—Involuntary Resettlement, the borrowing state is responsible for, inter
alia, preparing the resettlement plan, carrying out a census to identify the persons who will be affected by the project, determining who will be eligible for
assistance, discouraging the inflow of people ineligible for assistance, and developing a procedure for establishing the criteria by which displaced persons
will be deemed eligible for compensation and other resettlement assistance.[105]
All these actions must be acceptable to the Bank.

The panel is concerned only with the Bank's role. In the *Albania–Power
Sector Generation and Restructuring Project* case,[106] the requesters had—prior to
submitting a request to the panel—approached the Compliance Committee
of the Aarhus Convention[107] to allege that Albania was not complying with
its obligations concerning public access to information and participation in
the construction of a Bank-financed thermal power plant project and an
energy park. The committee accepted the request and found the allegation
to be justified.[108] The panel considered the decision of the committee and
observed that

> the Aarhus Convention Compliance Committee's review focused on
> the actions of Albania (Party), not on the Bank. However, the conclu-
> sions of the Committee are relevant because Bank policy gives the

---

104 Resolution, paragraph 12.

105 *See* OP 4.10—Involuntary Resettlement, paragraphs 7 and 14.

106 World Bank Inspection Panel Investigation Report No. 49504-AL, Albania–Power Sector
Generation and Restructuring Project (IDA Credit No. 3872-ALB) (Aug. 7, 2009) (*Alba-
nia* case), available at <http://siteresources.worldbank.org/EXTINSPECTIONPANEL/
Resources/ALB_Power_Investigation_Report_whole.pdf>.

107 Convention on Access to Information, Public Participation in Decision-Making and Access
to Justice in Environmental Matters (Jun. 25, 1998), 38 ILM 517.

108 *Albania* case, at ix.

main responsibility for consultation to the borrower and requires the Bank to ensure that the borrower fulfills this requirement.[109]

The panel concluded that the Bank did not ensure that the project preparation activities complied with the consultation and public participation requirements of the Aarhus Convention, and thus did not comply with OP 4.01—Environmental Assessment.[110]

This case could be analyzed through the prism of the draft articles as follows: the Bank omitted to direct Albania to conduct consultations in accordance with the Aarhus Convention and therefore it incurred responsibility for Albania's internationally wrongful act. However, this interpretation would have to consider the additional conditions under draft article 14. In particular, Albania's act, namely, noncompliance with the Aarhus Convention, would have constituted an internationally wrongful act if it had been committed by the Bank. Because the Bank was not a party to the Aarhus Convention, it was not under a legal obligation to comply with that convention.

Overall, the panel's provisions seem to create a flexible framework to deal with issues of concurrent responsibility, whereas the draft articles impose conditions that, if applied in this context, might lead to the dismissal of many requests for inspection.

The Requirement of Harm

The ILC has clarified that "as in the case of States, damage does not appear to be an element necessary for international responsibility of an international organization to arise."[111] With respect to state responsibility, the ILC has noted:

> It is sometimes said that international responsibility is not engaged by conduct of a State in disregard of its obligations unless some further element exists, in particular, "damage" to another State. But whether such elements are required depends on the content of the primary obligation, and there is no general rule in this respect.[112]

On the contrary, the panel's resolution requires a request for inspection to state "the harm suffered by or threatened to such party or parties by the alleged action or omission of the Bank."[113] The party submitting a request is required to prove the existence of harm and a causal link between the Bank's alleged failure to follow its policies and procedures and such harm.[114] Harm resulting from actions or omissions of parties other than the Bank (such as

---

109 *Id.,* at paragraph 323.

110 *Id.,* at paragraph 332.

111 ILC Report, at 54, paragraph (3).

112 Report of the International Law Commission on the Work of Its Fifty-Third Session, *supra* note 54, at 36, paragraph (3).

113 Resolution, paragraph 16.

114 Shihata, *supra* note 28, at 58.

harm caused by the borrower alone) cannot be the subject of the panel's investigation.[115]

The regime of the Inspection Panel straddles the classic concept of responsibility and the more dynamic concept of liability for transboundary environmental harm.[116] On the one hand, for a case to be considered, there must be a violation of the Bank's policies and procedures (the activity should be prohibited by the rules of the organization). On the other hand, the activity should result—or threaten to result—in harm to the affected party, since the primary obligation of the Bank is to avoid or minimize harm that may afflict people and the environment as a result of its financing. This duality illustrates that the responsibility under the panel regime is close to the idea of responsibility as conceived by the ILC in the early years of its work on the topic of state responsibility.[117]

It is noteworthy that harm is a requirement even when an executive director or board member submits a request.[118] Harm is not only an eligibility requirement when a request is brought by an affected party but a condition for responsibility under the panel's regime.

Consequently, the idea of responsibility as liability—which, as explained by Crawford and Watkins, relates to the principles that determine the legal

---

115 Resolution, paragraph 14(a). There has been a feeling among Bank staff that the panel was more concerned with the issue of harm, regardless of its cause, than with material harm resulting from the Bank's violation of its operational policies and procedures; *see* Shihata, *supra* note 28, at 259.

116 This topic, which focuses on the consequences of the specific activities and not their lawfulness, is outside the scope of this chapter. Suffice it to point out that the concept of liability for nonwrongful activities consists of four elements: (a) activities are not prohibited by international law; (b) activities involve a risk of causing significant harm; (c) such harm must be transboundary; and (d) the transboundary harm must be caused by such activities through their physical consequences. In relation to this topic, the ILC produced draft articles on the prevention of transboundary harm from hazardous activities and draft principles on the allocation of loss in the case of transboundary harm arising out of hazardous activities. *See* Report of the International Law Commission on the Work of Its Fifty-Third Session, *supra* note 54, at 150–51, paragraphs (6)–(17). The ILC dealt only with the liability of states for transboundary environmental harm and not international organizations, but nothing precludes a mutatis mutandis application. For more information on this topic, *see* Alan E. Boyle, *State Responsibility and International Liability for Injurious Consequences of Acts Not Prohibited by International Law: A Necessary Distinction?* 39 Intl. Comp. L. Quarterly 1 (1990), and Patricia Birnie & Alan Boyle, *International Law and the Environment* 181–200 (2d ed., Oxford U. Press 2002).

117 The traditional understanding of responsibility included damage as a condition for responsibility; *see* Pellet, *supra* note 9, at 9. However, certain commentators support the reintroduction of the requirement of damage; *see* Brigitte Stern, *A Plea for "Reconstruction" of International Responsibility Based on the Notion of Legal Injury*, in *International Responsibility Today: Essays in Memory of Oscar Schachter* 93 (Maurizio Ragazzi ed., Martinus Nijhoff 2005).

118 The Board indirectly exercised this authority once, in a request regarding the China Western Poverty Reduction Project. However, even in that instance, the request was initially presented to the panel by an international NGO acting on behalf of people affected by the project. See World Bank Inspection Panel, *Accountability at the World Bank: The Inspection Panel 10 Years On* 71–72 (2003), available at <http://siteresources.worldbank.org/EXTINSPECTIONPANEL/Resources/TenYear8_07.pdf>.

consequences following from the violation of an international obligation—requires an additional element, namely, the occurrence of or the risk of harm. Responsibility as liability is contrasted to the idea of responsibility as answerability, which is "at work at the point in the legal process *before* it has been decided one way or another whether a breach of international law has taken place" and "finds expression, for example, in the rules that determine *locus standi* and the admissibility of claims."[119]

The primary rule applicable to the Bank, as simplified, is "do no harm,"[120] and for this reason, the requirement of the existence of harm or the threat of harm in addition to a mere violation of the Bank's policies and procedures makes sense. Under this approach, harm is not only a requirement of standing but also an intrinsic element of responsibility under the Bank's rules. Accordingly, the ILC's position that the inclusion of damage as an element of the internationally wrongful act depends on the primary rule is vindicated. Moreover, this approach underlines the interdependence between primary and secondary rules, irrespective of the fact that the rules may be captured in distinct responsibility regimes in specific instances.

Remedies

Having examined the main elements of responsibility of international organizations and the main requirements for an inspection under the panel's legal framework, what remain to be discussed are the consequences of assigning responsibility under the two regimes.

The legal consequences of internationally wrongful acts of international organizations are provided in part III of the draft articles. There are four basic principles.

- The organization continues to have a duty to perform the obligation breached (draft article 28).

- The organization must cease the internationally wrongful act and provide guarantees of nonrepetition (draft article 29).

- The organization must make full reparation for the injury caused by the internationally wrongful act (draft article 30). The draft articles further specify that reparation can take the form of restitution, compensation, or satisfaction (draft article 33).

- The organization may not rely on its rules as justification for failure to comply with the previous obligations (draft article 31).

---

119 "These rules organize the lines of international legal accountability, determining who is answerable to whom, and in respect of what contact." *See* James Crawford & Jeremy Watkins, *International Responsibility* in *The Philosophy of International Law* 283, 284 (Samantha Besson & John Tasioulas ed., Oxford U. Press 2010).

120 Shihata, *supra* note 28, at 241.

The fundamental principle behind these provisions is that "reparation must, so far as possible, wipe out all the consequences of the illegal act and re-establish the situation that would, in all probability, have existed if that act had not been committed."[121]

Under the panel's legal framework, once the investigation phase is complete, the panel submits its findings through an investigation report to the Board of Executive Directors of the Bank.[122] Bank Management then submits to the Board its report and recommendation in response to the panel's findings.[123] The recommendations are intended to bring the project into compliance with Bank policies and procedures. The Board meets to consider both the panel's investigation report and Management's recommendations, and decides whether to approve Management's recommendations.

The panel's process does not provide legal remedies per se. In other words, resort to the panel does not by itself give affected people rights of redress from the Bank, such as the right to seek financial compensation.[124] However, the panel's process leads to the adoption of an action plan, which seeks to bring the project into compliance with Bank policies and addresses related findings of harm or potential harm. This action plan is developed in agreement with the borrowing state and in consultation with the requesters.[125] In that respect, the panel does not make specific recommendations for actions that should be taken by Management, which means that it does not provide specific remedies. Rather, the result of the entire process is to reestablish the situation that would, in all probability, have existed if the violation of the Bank's policies and procedures had not occurred. In addition, Bank Management is required to monitor the implementation of the action plan.[126] This could correspond to the requirement under draft article 29, paragraph 2, that an international organization offer appropriate assurances and guarantees of nonrepetition after the violation has ceased.

Overall, one could argue that the remedial regime under the panel's legal framework is consistent with the main principles of the draft articles, but it is also in some ways distinct from the draft articles because of the Bank's specific supervisory role at various project cycle stages, including design, appraisal, and implementation. Supervision rests with the Bank, whereas project

---

121 *Factory at Chorzow, Jurisdiction*, PCIJ Series A, No. 9 (1927), 47.

122 Resolution, at paragraph 22.

123 *Id.*, at paragraph 23.

124 Shihata, *supra* note 28, at 240.

125 World Bank Inspection Panel, *Accountability at the World Bank: The Inspection Panel at 15 Years* 41 (2009), available at <http://siteresources.worldbank.org/EXTINSPECTIONPANEL/Resources/380793-1254158345788/InspectionPanel2009.pdf>.

126 The Board may ask Management to subsequently submit progress reports either on implementation of the action plan or, more generally, on addressing panel findings on noncompliance and harm; on a few occasions, it has requested the panel to take on a formal follow-up role. *Id.*, at 44.

implementation is the responsibility of the borrowing state. Additionally, in all these stages of project cycle, the Bank, as an international financial cooperative institution, acts in cooperation with the borrowing state, including designing and carrying out measures to address challenges related to compliance with Bank policies and procedures that the panel may have unearthed in the course of its investigations.

Conclusion

The creation of the Inspection Panel was seen as an opportunity to influence the issue of an international organization's responsibility.[127] This prediction never materialized. The "jurisprudence" of the Inspection Panel appears neither in the ILC's commentary on the draft articles nor in any of the reports of the special rapporteur.[128] The ILC may have ignored the rules and jurisprudence of the Inspection Panel, but that does not mean that there is no relation between the draft articles and the panel's legal framework, which regulates aspects of responsibility of the Bank. One could argue that the panel's regime constitutes *lex specialis* that, according to draft article 63, could preclude the application of the remainder of the draft articles' provisions.[129] In addition, this chapter has shown that the panel's legal framework is broadly consistent with the main principles of the draft articles.

Yet there are discrepancies between the panel and the draft articles regimes. First, the panel's resolution refers only to violations of the Bank's policies and procedures—and the panel itself has been reluctant to explore the obligations of the Bank under international law, unless the obligation is anchored in the Bank's policies. Second, under the panel's legal framework, evidence of harm (in addition to a mere violation of Bank policy) is required for the question of Bank responsibility to arise. The draft articles do not contain such a

---

127 Daniel D. Bradlow & Sabine Schlemmer-Schulte, *The World Bank's New Inspection Panel: A Constructive Step in the Transformation of the International Legal Order*, 54 ZaöRV 392, 409 (1994).

128 In his eighth report, the special rapporteur made reference to the West African Gas Pipeline Project, which was brought before the Inspection Panel; *see* Giorgio Gaja, special rapporteur, *Eighth Report on Responsibility of International Organizations*, at paragraph 46, footnote 43, UN Doc. A/CN.4/640 (Mar. 14, 2011). However, this reference is slightly misleading because it relates to the primary obligations of the World Bank, which fall outside the scope of work of the ILC. In that respect, this reference does not alter our conclusion that the panel's "jurisprudence" was not taken into account in order to identify secondary rules, which might have been developed by this accountability mechanism of the World Bank.

129 Draft article 63 provides:

These articles do not apply where and to the extent that the conditions for the existence of an internationally wrongful act or the content or implementation of the international responsibility of an international organization, or a State for an internationally wrongful act of an international organization, are governed by special rules of international law, including rules of the organization applicable to the relations between the international organization and its members.

requirement. Third, the draft articles on the responsibility of international orga-nizations in connection with acts of states appear to be inadequately equipped to deal with the specific relationship between the Bank and a borrowing state in the project cycle—the relationship that forms the basis of the panel's legal framework. Finally, the panel's procedure leads to a remedy that is limited to a Bank Management-proposed action plan to restore compliance with the Bank's policies and procedures. The draft articles have a much broader array of remedies in their toolbox.

What could be the added value of the draft articles on the panel's special regime? According to Simma and Pulkowski, "added value" exists when "a fallback on general international law is expedient to serve the purposes of the special regime."[130] One area where the general law on responsibility might be useful for the panel's regime could be the provisions on the circumstances pre-cluding wrongfulness. A situation could occur in which the Bank could invoke necessity in order to justify its failure to comply with its rules.[131]

Moving beyond the comparison and interaction of the two regimes, there remains a more fundamental issue. The draft articles are inadequate for an institution like the World Bank. The law of responsibility is a constituent char-acteristic of the international legal system, since *ubi responsabilitas, ibi jus.*[132] The panel regime, on the contrary, is usually described as a compliance mech-anism.[133] However, because there is no forum to invoke claims of violations of the Bank's policies and there is uncertainty about the Bank's international obligations—with the exception of its obligation to respect peremptory norms of international law and applicable rules of customary international law—the panel's regime is probably the "hardest" mechanism in existence for enforc-ing, albeit indirectly, the Bank's obligations under its internal rules.

In addition, the draft articles provide that only states or international or-ganizations can invoke the responsibility of an international organization.[134] To the contrary, the panel offers a mechanism through which the grievances of individuals harmed by the Bank's action or omission can be addressed.[135]

This leads to the same conclusion reached by Jean-Marc Sorel, namely, that "the recognition of 'soft responsibility' remains a timely subject, particularly

---

130 Simma & Pulkowski, *supra* note 11, at 148.

131 The World Bank has supported the inclusion of necessity in the draft articles; *see* ILC, Responsibility of International Organizations: Comments and Observations Received from International Organizations, at 8, UN Doc. A/CN.4/568 (Mar. 17, 2006).

132 Pellet, *supra* note 9, at 1–2.

133 Laurence Boisson de Chazournes, *Policy Guidance and Compliance: The World Bank Operational Standards,* in *Commitment and Compliance: The Role of Non-binding Norms in the International Legal System* 281, 292 (Dinah Shelton ed., Oxford U. Press 2000).

134 *See* draft articles 42–49.

135 Under the law of responsibility, the grievances of the individual can be vindicated only through the exercise of diplomatic protection; *see* Kingsbury, *supra* note 84, at 327.

regarding the legal framework that needs to be created for the implementation of the responsibility of international organizations."[136] This conclusion is all the more important for an international organization, such as the Bank, that is concerned not only with its legal accountability but equally—if not more—with its public reputational accountability.[137]

---

136 Jean-Marc Sorel, *The Concept of "Soft Responsibility"?* in *The Law of International Responsibility* 165, 171 (James Crawford, Alain Pellet, & Simon Olleson ed., Oxford U. Press 2010). The inefficiency of a hard law of responsibility for international organizations is stressed by Ian Johnstone, who notes that "one of the concerns about the rulings of the European Court of Human Rights in *Behrami* and *Saramati* is that, by attributing responsibility for the acts committed by peacekeepers to the United Nations and NATO (as opposed to the States contributing to the operations), the remedies available to the complainants are limited." Johnstone, *supra* note 46, at 237.

137 According to Grant and Keohane, "the category of public reputational accountability is meant to apply to situations in which reputation, widely and publicly known, provides a mechanism for accountability even in the absence of other mechanisms as well as in conjunction with them," whereas "[l]egal accountability refers to the requirement that agents abide by formal rules and be prepared to justify their actions in those terms, in courts or quasi-judicial arenas." *See* Ruth W. Grant & Robert O. Keohane, *Accountability and Abuses of Power in World Politics*, 99 Am. Pol. Sci. Rev. 29, 36–37 (2005).

Partnerships, Emulation, and Coordination

Toward the Emergence of a *Droit Commun* in the Field of Development Finance

LAURENCE BOISSON DE CHAZOURNES

Cooperation among international organizations has developed in various ways. The need for cooperation was foreseen at their inception and is reflected in their constitutive agreements. The articles of the International Bank for Reconstruction and Development (IBRD), for example, state that "the Bank, within the terms of this Agreement, shall cooperate with any general international organization and with public organizations having specialized responsibilities in related fields."[1] An example in this context of such means for cooperation is the agreement that the IBRD concluded with the United Nations (UN) in 1947.[2]

In addition to this type of cooperative relationship, the IBRD and the other institutions of the World Bank Group[3] (hereinafter, the "World Bank") have developed relationships with regional development banks. This chapter focuses on these relationships and the legal consequences that arise from them. Because of the institutional features that the World Bank and regional development banks have in common (for example, their capital-based structure and their mandate),[4] there is sometimes an emulation phenomenon in their legal

---

1   IBRD Articles of Agreement, Article V, Section 8(a), adopted at Bretton Woods, July 22, 1944, 2 U.N.T.S. 135 (1944) as amended February 16, 1989; amended version available at <http://go.worldbank.org/SHVKXP10W0>.

2   Agreement between the United Nations and the International Bank for Reconstruction and Development, 16 U.N.T.S. 346 (1947) (entered into force on Nov. 15, 1947).

3   The International Bank for Reconstruction and Development was established in July 1944 at the Monetary and Financial Conference at Bretton Woods. Since then, four other institutions have been established: the International Finance Corporation (IFC) in 1956, the International Development Association (IDA) in 1960, the International Centre for the Settlement of Investment Disputes (ICSID) in 1966, and the Multilateral Investment Guarantee (MIGA) in 1988. These five institutions form the World Bank Group.

4   The IBRD Articles of Agreement, for example, contain a provision that states that "the Bank and its officers shall not interfere in the political affairs of any member; nor shall they be influenced in their decisions by the political character of the member or members concerned" (Article IV, Section 10); see also IDA Articles of Agreement, which contain an identical provision (Article V, Section 6). Almost identical provisions are contained in the Agreement Establishing the Inter-American Development Bank (Article VIII, paragraph 5[f], the Articles of Agreement of the Asian Development Bank (Chapter VI, Article 36), and the Agreement Establishing the African Development Bank (Chapter V, Article 38), as mentioned by Stephen S. Zimmermann & Frank A. Fariello Jr., *Coordinating the Fight against Fraud and Corruption: Agreement on Cross-Debarment among Multilateral Development Banks*, this volume. **173**

and institutional practices. By emulation, what is meant is that the regional development banks emulate the policies, rules, and procedures in place at the World Bank. Emulation may also more broadly refer to the willingness of these regional organizations to put into place procedures framed around similar policies and rules, although the latter may present specific features. In some instances, this process can be multidirectional, with the World Bank and other regional financial institutions emulating the practice followed by a regional institution. These various practices often give rise to a harmonization trend around a standard, a policy, or a rule first developed by one of the concerned organizations. In some cases, this trend is complemented by organized coordination around common procedures. Based on this emulation phenomenon and the harmonization and coordination endeavors, one might wonder if a *droit commun* in the area of development finance is emerging.

In the context of this chapter, the notion of a *droit commun* is defined as a process through which various organizations develop and implement similar standards, rules, or procedures. A *droit commun* allows for the emergence of a distinct legal corpus of the harmonized standards, rules, and procedures that the institutions have in common.

The emergence of *droit commun* indicates that international financial institutions (IFIs) and other actors feel the need to use policy instruments and a legal language presenting similar features in areas of common concern. Although efforts to obtain greater market share might be a reason for replicating the normative and institutional features of another institution and thus attract more interest, the need for increased cooperation and partnerships among these institutions appears to be a key driver in this direction. Decision makers in groups such as the Group of Seven (G7), Group of Eight (G8), and Group of Twenty (G20), or within the executive organs of financial institutions, often advocate the promotion of similar objectives, such as transparency and accountability by all concerned institutions.[5] Civil society is also moving in this direction through domestic and transnational strategies.

These trends do not follow from rules laid down in the articles of agreement of the concerned institutions, but rather are developed from practice and necessity. The institutions are involved in similar types of business activities, that is, development finance and assistance, and thus face similar challenges, such as the promotion of sustainable development.

It should also be stressed that the emulation of the World Bank's practices by regional development banks is in part due to the gravitational force of the World Bank and the links that exist between the regional banks and the World

---

5   *See*, for example, the Anti-Corruption Action Plan issued in November 2010 by the G20 Seoul Summit, which states that "the G20 will exercise its voice in the governance of international organizations to encourage that they operate with transparency, high ethical standards, effective internal safeguards and the highest standard of integrity. To that end, we call for continued dialogue among international organizations and national authorities on defining good practices and ways forward on this objective"; available at <http://media.seoulsummit.kr/contents/dlobo/E5._ANNEX3.pdf>.

Bank. The World Bank's gravitational force can be explained by the fact that the Bank was established earlier than the other institutions,[6] as well as by its size and financial power. The representative power of the World Bank is also partly attributable to the desire of regional development banks to use the World Bank as a proxy for access to forums such as the G8 and the G20. For example, the ten international organizations that were invited to the G20 Seoul Summit in November 2010 (the African Union, the Association of Southeast Asian Nations, the Financial Stability Board, the International Labour Organization, the International Monetary Fund [IMF], the New Partnership for Africa's Development, the Organisation for Economic Co-operation and Development, the United Nations, the World Bank Group, and the World Trade Organization) did not include one regional financial institution.[7] The emulative process is therefore based, not on any formal or informal hierarchy between the institutions, but simply on political and economic dynamics.

This emulation and these cooperative and coordination processes have led to harmonization and mutual recognition, thereby cultivating the development of common practices in both normative and institutional terms. Three examples are discussed in this chapter. Before addressing them, the chapter presents the various types of partnerships that may develop among these institutions; partnerships that help forge an increasingly close relationship between the World Bank and regional development banks.

Partnerships among IFIs

Partnerships among IFIs are manifold. IFIs may receive logistical, material, or financial aid from each other in order to carry out their activities. Sometimes, these institutions participate in discussions and negotiations held in their respective forums. On other occasions, they put into place institutional partnerships aimed at the implementation of a certain activity or the pursuit of a given objective.

Partnerships between international organizations have blossomed in the field of environmental protection and, more generally, in the area of sustainable development. For instance, Agenda 21, the action plan adopted in 1992

---

6   The World Bank was created at the Bretton Woods Conference in 1944. Four other institutions are examined in this chapter. The Inter-American Development Bank (IDB) was established in 1959. It has 48 member countries, including 26 Latin American and Caribbean borrowing members. The African Development Bank (AfDB) was founded in 1964. It is composed of 77 member countries; 53 are African countries and 24 are non-African countries. The Asian Development Bank (ADB) was established in 1966 and is composed of 67 members, of which 48 are from the region and 19 are from other parts of the globe. The European Bank for Reconstruction and Development (EBRD) was established in 1991. It is composed of 61 member countries, of which 16 are non-European countries, the European Union, and the European Investment Bank.

7   *See* <http://www.seoulsummit.kr/eng/boardDetailView.g20?boardDTO.board_seq=201009 0000002320&boardDTO.board_category=BD02&boardDTO.menu_seq=#>.

during the UN Conference on the Environment and Development, calls on several actors—namely, the United Nations Environment Programme (UNEP), the World Bank, and regional development banks—to establish programs and take action for the promotion of developing countries' capacities in environmental protection.[8] Within this framework, some of these institutions may rely on other organizations for carrying out activities in the field. The primary goal of such partnerships is to enhance the overall effectiveness of operations jointly managed by them.

The Global Environment Facility (GEF) constitutes another type of partnership.[9] Established in 1991 and restructured in 1994 with the World Bank, the United Nations Development Programme, and UNEP as implementing agencies, it provides financing to developing countries for projects dealing with the protection of the global environment (including, inter alia, climate change and biodiversity issues). Moreover, institutions such as the African Development Bank (AfDB), the Asian Development Bank (ADB), the European Bank for Reconstruction and Development (ERDB), and the Inter-American Development Bank (IDB) have also been given the option of acting as executing agencies and thus being directly involved with projects of the GEF.

Crucial to these initiatives and, more generally, to the relations between international organizations is the issue of financing. The granting of financial aid by one organization to another may be foreseen in treaty provisions or in other types of legal instruments.[10] Such assistance is intended to strengthen an organization and to provide guaranteed support for its activity.

In this context, it is interesting to recall that the statute of the International Development Agency (IDA), a member of the World Bank Group, provides:

> The Association shall not provide financing for any project if the member in whose territories the project is located objects to such financing, except that it shall not be necessary for the Association to assure itself that individual members do not object in the case of financing provided to a public international or regional organization.[11]

---

8 *See* Agenda 21, Chapter 37.11.

9 See Laurence Boisson de Chazournes, *The Global Environment Facility Galaxy: On Linkages among Institutions*, 3 Max Planck United Nations Y.B. 243 (1999); and Laurence Boisson de Chazournes, *The Global Environment Facility (GEF): A Unique and Crucial Institution*, 14(3) Rev. European Community & Intl. Envl. L. 193 (2005).

10 *See*, for example, the European Development Fund; Council Regulation (EC) No. 617/2007 of May 14, 2007, on the implementation of the 10th European Development Fund under the ACP-EC Partnership Agreement, JO L 152/1, June 13, 2007.

11 IDA Articles of Agreement, Article V, Section 1(e), available at <http://siteresources .worldbank.org/IDA/Resources/ida-articlesofagreement.pdf>.

On this basis, the IDA has granted loans at privileged rates to the West African Development Bank (WADB) and to the Caribbean Development Bank.[12] In 2004, the World Bank approved a financing plan in favor of the WADB as part of the project for market integration among West African countries engaged in by the West African Economic and Monetary Union (WAEMU). Some World Bank financing has been aimed at consolidating the WADB's position as a regional player, transforming it into an institution capable of independently acquiring its own resources.

In addition to the above-mentioned types of partnerships, IFIs have undertaken further forms of multilateral collaboration, such as the Heavily Indebted Poor Countries (HIPC) Initiative, set up by the IMF and the World Bank in 1996 and aimed at avoiding situations in which poor countries may be faced with an unsustainable debt.[13] In 2005, the objectives of the HIPC were reiterated through the creation of the Multilateral Debt Relief Initiative (MDRI), a G8-promoted initiative taken in view of the UN Millennium Development Goals.[14]

The objective of the MDRI is the cancellation of 100 percent of the claims of three multilateral institutions—the IMF, the IDA, and the AfDB—on countries that have reached, or will reach, the completion point under the enhanced HIPC Initiative. This initiative is managed through a fully fledged partnership between the three international organizations. In 2007, the IDB joined the MDRI and then to canceled the debt of five Latin American countries.

Partnerships of this type entail close cooperation among the organizations, and some pragmatism is necessary for meeting the desired operational objectives. The same is true when IFIs cofinance projects. There is a need to find a common approach in the appraisal and monitoring of a project.[15] The search for consistency among social and environmental policies helps direct this common approach.

The quest for effectiveness is central to the effort to achieve mutual collaboration among IFIs. This quest has given rise to various types of emulative practices by IFIs and caused these institutions to forge new forms of institutional and normative relationships.

---

12   *See* Ibrahim F. I. Shihata, *The World Bank Legal Papers* 812 (Kluwer Law International 2000).

13   *See* Leonie F. Guder, *The Administration of Debt Relief by the International Financial Institutions: A Legal Reconstruction of the HIPC Initiative* (Springer 2009).

14   For more details, *see* <http://www.imf.org/external/np/exr/facts/fre/mdrif.htm>.

15   *See* EBRD, *Environmental and Social Policy* paragraph 10 (May 12, 2008), available at <http://www.ebrd.com/downloads/research/policies/2008enviropolicy.pdf>.

Emulation in the Harmonization of Operational Policies and Procedures

Emulation may take the form of a harmonization of operational policies and procedures. Regional development banks have adopted certain rules and procedures that had earlier been developed and adopted by the World Bank.[16] One example is social and environmental policies adopted by the World Bank that are intended to apply to operational activities. These policies, called "safeguard policies," are a set of rules and procedures that must be followed by personnel of the World Bank in the design, implementation, and monitoring of projects by the Bank. Such operational policies are important tools. By requiring an environmental assessment of projects, consultation with affected communities, the publication of information, compensation for any impact, and the restoration of the living environment or biodiversity protection, safeguard policies reduce the negative impacts of projects funded by the Bank.[17]

The adoption of safeguard policies by the World Bank in the 1990s and their subsequent revision have given rise to the adoption of operational rules by regional development banks. Regional banks have developed policies providing for similar standards of behavior in the areas of impact assessment and the protection of indigenous populations.[18] For example, the ADB adopted bank policies in the field of environmental protection; these policies are included in its operations manual.[19] In a recent review of its safeguard policies, the ADB took account of other financial institutions' social and environmental policies so to ensure that its policies are consistent with those of the World Bank Group and also those of regional institutions.[20] The fact that the ADB was involved in cofinancing projects with these institutions was stressed as a reason for this harmonization process.

Similarly, the IDB developed a series of social and environmental policies in line with the World Bank's approach. Taking into account the widespread recognition of the rights of indigenous people in different countries' constitutional and legislative acts, as well as the international practice of international financial and donor institutions, the IDB adopted the Operational Policy on Indigenous Peoples and Strategy for Indigenous Development (OP-765) in

---

16 On the influence of the World Bank in this area, see David Hunter, *Civil Society Networks and the Development of Environmental Standards at International Financial Institutions*, 8 Chi. J. Intl. L. 437, 442 (2008).

17 Laurence Boisson de Chazournes, *Policy Guidance and Compliance Issues: The World Bank Operational Standards, in Commitment and Compliance—The Role of Non Binding Norms in the International Legal System* 281 (Dinah Shelton ed., Oxford U. Press 2000).

18 Benedict Kingsbury, *Operational Policies of International Institutions as Part of the Law-Making Process: The World Bank and Indigenous People, in The Reality of International Law Essays in Honour of Ian Brownlie* 323 (Guy S. Goodwin-Gill and Stefan Talmon ed., Clarendon Press 1999).

19 Available at <http://www.adb.org/documents/manuals/operations/OMB01.pdf>.

20 ADB, *Policy Paper: Safeguard Policy Statement* (June 2009), available at <http://www.adb.org/Documents/Policies/Safeguards/Safeguard-Policy-Statement-June2009.pdf>.

February 2006.[21] Regarding the phenomenon of emulation, it is interesting to note that the Profile of the Operational Policy on Indigenous Peoples (March 2004), approved by the Policy Committee and the Assessment Council of the IDB, indicated that

> many international financial institutions including the World Bank Group, the Asian Development Bank, the European Commission as well as bilateral donors and the private sector, have adopted specific safeguard policies regarding indigenous peoples.[22]

The EBRD undertook a review of many of its policies and strategies, and in May 2008, the EBRD board of directors approved the revision of the Environment Policy of 2003 into an Environment and Social Policy,[23] more in line with challenges in terms of protecting the global environment and with the policies of other financial institutions.

It is noteworthy that at the level of the United Nations, the need for a systemwide strategy for environmental and social safeguards has been identified. There is agreement that a common framework would build confidence through cooperation and the sharing of resources and would make the implementation of safeguards easier.[24]

These developments underline the emergence of common practices in the international financing of development projects. Regional development banks' emulation of World Bank approaches to issues of environmental and social protection, even if they retain some aspects of each regional bank's identity in their precise formulation and sometimes differ in their scope, has led to the emergence of common normative practices among IFIs operating in the field of environmental and social protection. These harmonized practices constitute a first step toward the emergence of a *droit commun*. The policies adopted by the regional development banks may present some specific features. This is in great part due to the fact that these institutions finance both public and private sector projects, a fact that their rules and practices need to take into account.

Institutional Emulation

Institutional emulation refers to situations in which regional development banks establish bodies and mechanisms similar to those set up within the World Bank. In this context, the most illustrative example of institutional emulation is the establishment of independent inspection and compliance

---

21   Available at <http://idbdocs.iadb.org/wsdocs/getdocument.aspx?docnum=1442299>.

22   Available at <http://idbdocs.iadb.org/wsdocs/getdocument.aspx?docnum=1481949>.

23   Available at <http://www.ebrd.com/downloads/about/sustainability/2008policy.pdf> .

24   *See* UNEP, Environment Management Group, Drafting Group on Environmental and Social Safeguards, Progress Report on Options for a System-Wide Approach to Environmental and Social Safeguards (Feb. 2011), available at <http://www.unemg.org/Portals/27/Documents/IMG/Safeguards/SecondMeeting/progress_report_options_for_ES_safeguards_for_second_meeting_14-15_March.pdf>.

mechanisms. These mechanisms respond to the demand for more transparency on the part of financial institutions and the call for them to be more accountable.

In September 1993, the directors of the World Bank created an independent inspection panel to ensure that the Bank meets its own operational policies and procedures during the design, preparation, and implementation of projects. Any group of individuals whose rights or interests are affected or likely to be affected as a result of a failure by the World Bank to follow its operational policies and procedures with respect to a project may institute a request with the inspection panel alleging that the institution has not complied with its operational or procedural policies. The directors then decide, on the basis of recommendations put forward by the panel, whether or not to proceed with an inspection.[25]

Building on the experience of the World Bank Inspection Panel, regional development banks put into place similar types of accountability mechanisms. Each of these mechanisms is different in its structure, procedure, and practice.[26] Yet all the banks are participating in broader efforts to render IFIs more accountable and more participatory.[27] The IDB was the first institution to follow the example of the World Bank Inspection Panel with the creation, in 1994, of an independent investigation mechanism. This mechanism was revised in 2010 and became the "independent consultation and investigation mechanism."[28] Similarly, the ADB revised its inspection procedure, originally set up in 1995, in 2003. The new procedure is based on an accountability mechanism comprising a consultation phase and an inspection phase administered by a compliance review panel.[29]

The AfDB established an independent review mechanism in June 2004. The mechanism includes aspects of monitoring and compliance with policies as well as mediation (problem solving) for projects in the public and private sectors.[30]

---

25   Laurence Boisson de Chazournes, *The World Bank Inspection Panel: About Public Participation and Dispute Settlement, in Civil Society, International Courts and Compliance Bodies* 187, 198 (Tulio Treves et al. ed., T. M. C. Asser Press 2005).

26   Daniel Bradlow, *Private Complainants and International Organizations: A Comparative Study of the Independent Inspection Mechanisms in International Financial Institutions,* 36 Geo. J. Intl. L. 403 (2005).

27   World Bank Inspection Panel, *Accountability at the World Bank: The Inspection Panel at 15 Years* (2009), available at <http://siteresources.worldbank.org/EXTINSPECTIONPANEL/Resources/380793-1254158345788/InspectionPanel2009.pdf>.

28   *See* IDB, *Policy Establishing the Independent Consultation and Investigation Mechanism* (Feb. 17, 2010), available at <http://idbdocs.iadb.org/wsdocs/getdocumentaspx?docnum=35074768>.

29   In May 2010, the ADB announced a review of the mechanism. *See* ADB, *Review of the Accountability Mechanism Policy* (April 2011), available at <http://www.adb.org/Documents/Policies/Accountability-Mechanism-Review/Review-Accountability-Mechanism-Policy-W-Paper-2011-04.pdf>.

30   Available at <http://www.afdb.org/en/about-us/structure/independent-review-mechanism>.

Mention should also be made of the project complaint mechanism established by the EBRD in 2010 to replace the independent recourse mechanism of 2004.[31]

Finally, the Office of the Compliance Advisor/Ombudsman (CAO), established in 1999 by the International Finance Corporation (IFC), was the first mechanism to comprise a two-phase approach: a consultation phase, which involves an ombudsman or an adviser, and a compliance review phase.[32] Other IFIs, such as the ADB, subsequently implemented a two-phase approach.[33]

Even though each of these mechanisms has its own distinctive features, they were all created in the same spirit and with the same objectives as the World Bank Inspection Panel, that is, to increase the transparency and accountability of the organizations that established them. In other words, the establishment of the World Bank Inspection Panel initiated a movement in favor of the creation of such kinds of mechanisms and procedures.

The degree of cooperation and harmonization among these mechanisms is demonstrated by the relationships between them and how they interact in practice.

The existence of inspection panels and compliance mechanisms in development banks can lead to these panels and mechanisms being seized at the same time as those of the World Bank in connection with projects that are cofinanced by the World Bank and a regional development bank. Coordination in such instances can lead to further harmonization practices. One such situation arose during the inspection request concerning the Yacyreta Hydroelectric Project in Argentina and Paraguay. The World Bank Inspection Panel stated:

> it may be noted that a Request for Inspection relating to the same Project had been simultaneously filed with the IDB inspection mechanism. The President of that institution recommended and the Board of Executive Directors likewise agreed to a review of the project under similar terms of reference. Collaboration with the IDB inspection mechanism included a joint visit to the project area in July 1997 as well as an exchange of views on the main findings.[34]

In his report on this matter, the chairman of the Organization, Human Resources and Board Matters Committee of the IDB Board of Executive Directors said that

---

31   Available at <http://www.ebrd.com/pages/project/pcm/about.shtml>.

32   Available at <http://www.cao-ombudsman.org/howwework>.

33   *Id.*

34   Memorandum to the Executive Directors and Alternates, *Request for Inspection—Argentina/Paraguay: Yacyretá Hydroelectric Project—Panel Review and Assessment*, IPN Request RQ96/2, at paragraph 2 (Sep. 16, 1997), available at <http://siteresources.worldbank.org/EXTINSPECTIONPANEL/Resources/PanelReviewandAssessment.pdf>.

> in light of the Bank's interest in harmonizing its efforts with those of
> its co-lender, the World Bank, the Board also instructed Management
> to report on any measures taken with respect to this project by the
> World Bank.[35]

As one can see, a desire to harmonize institutional practices is clearly a priority for both institutions.

The inspection request concerning the Bujagali Hydropower Project in Uganda also shows cooperation between two multilateral development banks. The project, cofinanced by the World Bank and the AfDB, was brought before the inspection mechanisms of both institutions.[36] The Bujagali project, the first case brought before the inspection mechanism of the AfDB, laid the foundation for cooperation between that institution and the World Bank. The World Bank Inspection Panel underlined "its appreciation to the CRMU [Compliance Review and Mediation Unit] for this fruitful and precedent-setting cooperation."[37]

Meanwhile, in its investigation report, the AfDB panel stated:

> The Compliance Review Panel and the World Bank Inspection Panel
> coordinated their field investigations of the Bujagali projects and
> shared consultants and technical information during this investigation in order to enhance the efficiency and cost effectiveness of each
> of their investigations.[38]

The World Bank Inspection Panel and the AfDB panel agreed to a memorandum of understanding to define the conditions for their cooperation and information exchange regarding the project.[39]

---

35   Available at <http://www.iadb.org/iim/pr191719eng.pdf>.

36   The AfDB, the World Bank, and other donors finance the Bujagali Hydropower Project, while the African Development Fund and the Japan Bank for International Cooperation financed the Bujagali Interconnection Project. World Bank Inspection Panel Investigation Report No. 44977-UG, Uganda: Private Power Generation (Bujagali) Project (Guarantee n° B0130-UG) (Aug. 29, 2008), available at <http://siteresources.worldbank.org/EXTINSPECTIONPANEL/Resources/FULL_September_2_2008_FINAL_Red.pdf>.

37   Id., at xix.

38   AfDB Independent Review Panel, Compliance Review Report on the Bujagali Hydropower and Interconnection Projects (Jun. 20, 2008), available at <http://www.afdb.org/fileadmin/uploads/afdb/Documents/Compliance-Review/30740990-EN-BUJAGALI-FINAL-REPORT-17-06-08.PDF>.

39   See Memorandum of Understanding, The World Bank Inspection Panel and the Compliance Review and Mediation Unit of the African Development Bank (Nov. 28, 2007) in World Bank Inspection Panel, supra note 27, at 214–16.

The 2005 Paris Declaration on Aid Effectiveness further supported this harmonization trend.[40] This declaration highlights the need to, inter alia, implement common arrangements, increase complementarity, and strengthen incentives for collaborative behavior. The donors committed to harmonizing standards in order to increase the effectiveness of aid programs[41]—legal harmonization is undoubtedly one way to avoid duplication.[42]

In this context, the Legal Harmonization Initiative (LHI) is a step in this direction. It is a joint undertaking of several IFIs, including the World Bank, regional financial institutions, bilateral aid agencies, and UN agencies, in support of the implementation of commitments expressed in the Paris Declaration to improve aid effectiveness through harmonization and alignment. The LHI is aimed at harmonizing and streamlining legal tools among donors and partner countries. It is conceived of as a forum for legal, operational, and policy advisers to discuss and share knowledge across institutions on legal and policy issues relevant to the harmonization and alignment agenda.[43]

Cooperation and Coordination in the Fight against Corruption

Another step in terms of cooperative practices among institutions has been the establishment of mechanisms for cooperation and mutual recognition between the World Bank and regional development banks. In the fight against corruption, the actions undertaken and policies adopted by the World Bank and the regional development banks have inspired cooperation. In this respect, in September 2006, the Uniform Framework for Preventing and Combating Fraud and Corruption was put into place by the leaders of the AfDB Group, the ADB, the EBRD, the EIB Group, the IMF, the IDB, and the World Bank Group.[44] The uniform framework has two main components: the adoption of common definitions of fraud and corruption and the development of common investigatory principles. It was developed by the International Financial Institutions Anti-Corruption Task Force.[45] The goal of the task force

---

40   Organisation for Economic Co-operation and Development (OECD), the Paris Declaration on Aid Effectiveness (2005), and the Accra Agenda for Action (2008), available at <http://www.oecd.org/dataoecd/30/63/43911948.pdf>. The international organizations adhering to the Paris Declaration and the Accra Agenda for Action include the World Bank, the IDB, the ADB, the AfDB, the EBRD, and the EIB.

41   OECD, Summary—Paris Declaration, available at <http://www.oecd.org/document/18/0,2340,en_2649_201185_35401554_1_1_1_1,00.html>.

42   *See* also Working Party on Aid Effectiveness, *Aid Effectiveness: A Progress Report on Implementing the Paris Declaration* (2008), available at <http://siteresources.worldbank.org/ACCRAEXT/Resources/Progress_Report-Full-EN.pdf>.

43   Additional information is available at <http://goo.gl/UvqXG>.

44   Available at <http://www.afdb.org/fileadmin/uploads/afdb/Documents/Generic-Documents/30716700-EN-UNIFORM-FRAMEWORK-FOR-COMBATTING-FRAUD-V6.PDF>.

45   The IFI task force was established to develop the framework and was afterward disbanded.

was to work toward developing a coherent and harmonized strategy in the fight against corruption in respect to the activities and operations of participating regional and universal financial institutions.

Each member institution of the IFI task force has a distinct mechanism for addressing and sanctioning violations of its anticorruption policies. The task force laid the groundwork for the mutual recognition of decisions made by each of the enforcement mechanisms. Similarly, the IFI task force recommended that each participating institution require that all bidders taking part in the activities financed by a participating institution disclose any penalty imposed on a corporation or an individual by a participating institution, although this recommendation was not put into practice. The task force adopted principles and guidelines for investigations[46] applicable to the integrity offices of the IFIs when executing their investigative mandate.

An additional step was taken by ensuring the mutual recognition and enforcement of decisions made by competent bodies within these institutions.[47] The AfDB Group, the ADB, the EBRD, the IDB Group, and the World Bank Group affirmed their mutual commitment to implementing each other's decisions in an agreement concluded on April 9, 2010.[48] The agreement states:

> 1. Each Participating Institution will enforce debarment decisions made by another Participating Institution, in accordance with the terms and conditions of this Agreement.

To this end, the concerned institutions—having undertaken, under the unified framework in 2006, to adopt harmonized definitions of sanctionable practices and to establish investigation procedures that meet common due process principles to conduct fair, impartial, and thorough investigations[49]—agreed to implement decisions made by each of them, except in circumstances "where such enforcement would be inconsistent with the institution's legal or other institutional considerations."[50] The enforcement of the decisions is subject to the conditions that

> a) the decision was based, in whole or in part, on a finding of a commission of one or more of the sanctionable practices defined in the Uniform Framework;
>
> b) the decision is made public by the Sanctioning Institution;
>
> c) the initial period of debarment exceeds one year;

---

46   *See supra* note 44.

47   A common debarment regime in the form of a joint sanctions board, as advocated by the World Bank, did not get off the ground. It was argued that it would facilitate a unified approach. Zimmermann & Fariello, *supra* note 4.

48   Agreement for Mutual Enforcement of Debarment Decisions (Apr. 9, 2009), available at <http://siteresources.worldbank.org/NEWS/Resources/AgreementForMutualEnforce mentofDebarmentDecisions.pdf>.

49   *Id.*, at paragraph 2(b).

50   *Id.*, at paragraph 7.

d) the decision was made after this Agreement has entered into force with respect to the Sanctioning Institution;

e) the decision by the Sanctioning Institution was made within ten years of the date of commission of the sanctionable practice; and

f) the decision of the Sanctioning Institution was not made in recognition of a decision made in a national or other international forum.[51]

Although each organization generally carries out its own investigation, in some cases, an organization may need to share information with another one. In fact, financial institutions share information routinely on matters of common interest, such as in cases of cofinanced projects. In this context, rather than duplicating efforts through parallel investigations, the institutions may coordinate investigations or one financial institution may take the lead in an investigation.[52] These situations, as well as the cross-debarment regime itself, call for enhancing common approaches such as the harmonization of policies and practices in relation to sanctions.[53] This harmonization aspect has not yet taken shape, although discussions are currently taking place.[54]

The adoption of harmonized definitions and investigation procedures that meet common due process principles coupled with a system of mutual recognition and enforcement is seen by the different development banks as helping win the battle against corruption. In the end, this trend may lead to an even more inclusive harmonization of anticorruption safeguards;[55] that is, although each institution maintains its own rules, the essential elements of these rules are fundamentally the same and pursue the same objective. This trend will also simplify and enhance cooperation among the institutions in the suppression of corruption.

The Development of a *Droit Commun* in the Field of Development Finance

The practices that have been identified in this chapter relate to situations that were not envisaged when the IFIs were created. The World Bank, because of its political and economic status, has played an influential role in the formation and dissemination of many of these common practices; the other IFIs have contributed to the elaboration of the practices. The resulting emulation effects

---

51 *Id.*, at paragraph 4.

52 *See* World Bank Group, *The World Bank Group: Mutual Enforcement of Debarment Decisions among Multilateral Development Banks* 3, paragraph 9 (Mar. 3, 2010), available at <http://siteresources.worldbank.org/INTDOII/Resources/Bank_paper_cross_debar.pdf>.

53 Zimmermann & Fariello, *supra* note 4.

54 *Id.*

55 Due to differences among financial institutions, as for example with respect to the nature of sanctions, a trend toward the adoption of common rules is unlikely in the short term. *Id.*

have led to harmonization practices among these institutions. They have adopted similar standards. Rules on mutual recognition and on the enforcement of decisions are also appearing. All these actions promote the emergence of a *droit commun* in the field of development finance.

This common body of law includes procedures of conformity with the various standards and practices that are put into place. Although differentiation and refinement by individual organizations might occur, a new body of law common to all such institutions is emerging. These converging trends are reinforced through meetings of the legal advisers or compliance officers of the various IFIs that allow for exchanges on respective practices. Insights can be drawn and practical problems can be solved in the context of these networks. The same can be said about electronic exchanges, which allow for comments from the various partners. These various elements contribute to the elaboration of a common legal and policy language among financial institutions.

The legal consequences of this emerging body of law remain to be assessed. Once rules and standards have been harmonized, their respective interpretation, albeit decentralized and in the hands of each institution, will be informed by the others' interpretative approaches. In terms of enforcement measures, procedures such as those of mutual recognition and enforcement in the fight against corruption are but one step in the direction of a common action. The same can be said about the cooperative arrangements put into place by the inspection and compliance mechanisms with respect to information exchange and collaborative practices.

In a decentralized system, the various practices bear witness to the close links that have been established between the various institutions. Such practices are remarkable, and their importance should not be lessened by assessing them in the light of the establishment or the nonestablishment of joint bodies. The existence of joint bodies is intrinsically dependent on the willingness of the member states and organizations to move toward greater political integration. Another avenue can be one institution granting competence to an organ of another institution. The Administrative Tribunal of the International Labor Organization, which by its statute allows other international organizations to recognize its jurisdiction, is an example of this phenomenon.[56] This opens up another path toward the emergence of a *droit commun* in this area that could be further explored.

Various types of relationships have developed between IFIs. The relations between these organizations are forged in a variety of ways both for the sake of better cooperation and as a matter of pragmatism and efficiency. The new legal practices and rules form part of an emerging *corpus juris* that interacts

---

56 At the 32d session of the International Labour Conference in 1949, Article II of the Statute of the ILO Tribunal was amended to permit other international organizations approved by the ILO's governing body to recognize the jurisdiction of the tribunal. *See* <http://www.ilo .org/public/english/tribunal/about/index.htm>.

with, and benefits from,[57] the emergence of the global administrative law approach, especially from the principles of transparency, public participation, and accountability.[58] These principles provide the basis for, and ground the legitimacy of, the decision-making and implementation processes of rules and procedures developed through emulation and coordination.

---

57 For a similar opinion, see Pascale Hélène Dubois & Aileen Elizabeth Nowlan, *Global Administrative Law and the Legitimacy of Sanctions Regimes in International Law*, 36 Yale J. Intl. L. Online 15 (2010), available at <http://www.yjil.org/docs/pub/o-36-dubois-nowlan-global-administrative-law-sanctions.pdf>.

58 On these principles *see* Symposium, *Global Administrative Law in the Operations of International Organizations* (Laurence Boisson de Chazournes, Lorenzo Casini, & Benedict Kingsbury ed.), 6 Intl Organizations L. Rev. 315 (2009).

Coordinating the Fight against Fraud and Corruption

Agreement on Cross-Debarment among Multilateral Development Banks

STEPHEN S. ZIMMERMANN AND FRANK A. FARIELLO, JR.[*]

The fight against fraud and corruption took a major step forward in April 2010 when the heads of five leading multilateral development banks (MDBs)—the African Development Bank Group[1] (AfDB), the Asian Development Bank (ADB), the European Bank for Reconstruction and Development (EBRD), the Inter-American Development Bank Group[2] (IDB), and the World Bank Group[3]—signed the Agreement for Mutual Enforcement of Debarment Decisions. As of this writing (August 2011), the agreement has become effective for four of the five signatories—ADB, EBRD, IDB, and the World Bank Group—after they put into place the required changes to their respective policies and procedures. It is anticipated that AfDB will be in a position to begin implementation of the agreement by the end of 2011.

This chapter examines the policy rationale behind the agreement, the history that led up to it, its principal provisions, and some key issues and challenges faced by MDBs in crafting the agreement. The chapter concludes by looking at the prospects for deeper and wider harmonization in the near- to medium-term future.

In principle, aggressively tackling fraud and corruption in development projects should be a central part of the common agenda of MDBs. The "cancer of corruption" undermines efforts to combat poverty and wastes the scarce resources of the international aid community. But until relatively recently, a number of obstacles had made it difficult for international organizations to move forward. For many years, corruption was seen as primarily, if not exclusively, a political problem with little or no relevance to economic development. Moreover, work on corruption was felt to contravene the so-called

---

[*] The authors would like to thank Roman Majtan, LEG consultant, for his valuable assistance in the preparation of this article.

1   The African Development Bank Group consists of the African Development Bank, the African Development Fund, and the Nigeria Trust Fund.

2   The Inter-American Bank Group consists of the Inter-American Development Bank, the Inter-American Investment Corporation, and the Multilateral Investment Fund.

3   In this article, the term "World Bank Group" means, collectively, the International Bank for Research and Development (IBRD), the International Development Association (IDA), the International Finance Corporation (IFC), and the Multilateral Investment Guarantee Agency (MIGA). The term "World Bank" refers to the IBRD and the IDA alone.

political prohibition that is hardwired into the constituent documents of most (but not all) MDBs, barring them from interfering in the political affairs of their members.[4] Recently, however, the nexus between corruption and governance issues, on the one hand, and development, including economic development, on the other, has become clear.[5] It has also become clear that, if done right, governance issues may be addressed without violating the political prohibition.[6]

When it comes to sanctions, the MDBs owe a fiduciary duty to their stakeholders, enshrined in the MDBs' constituent documents, to safeguard the proper use of the stakeholders' funds.[7] It is that fiduciary duty that underlies sanctions, which operate as a key disincentive against the misuse of MDB funds. Although the MDBs will never be able to investigate and sanction every instance of misuse, sanctions—in particular public sanctions—can leverage a relatively small number of cases to create broader deterrence.

Application of this tool is not always straightforward. On a political level, for example, the MDBs face challenges due to their cooperative governance structures, in which their shareholders—member countries—may face pressures from their private sector "champions" that may be subject to MDB

---

4 The IBRD Articles of Agreement, for example, contain a provision that states that "the Bank and its officers shall not interfere in the political affairs of any member; nor shall they be influenced in their decisions by the political character of the member or members concerned." See IBRD Articles of Agreement, Article IV, Section 10 (as amended Feb. 18, 1989). The IDA Articles of Agreement contain an identical provision. See IDA Articles of Agreement, Article V, Section 6 (Sep. 24, 1960). Almost identical provisions are contained in the Agreement Establishing the Inter-American Development Bank, Article VIII, Section 5(f) (last amended Jul. 31, 1995); the Articles of Agreement of the Asian Development Bank, Chapter VI, Article 36 (Aug. 22, 1966); and the Agreement Establishing the African Development Bank, Chapter V, Article 38 (Jul. 2002). In contrast, the constituent documents of the EBRD and EIB do not contain any such restriction. See also Hassane Cissé, Should the Political Prohibition in Charters of International Financial Institutions Be Revisited? The Case of the World Bank, in this volume.

5 Ibrahim Shihata, Corruption: A General Review with an Emphasis on the Role of the World Bank, 15 Dick. J. Intl. L. 451, 455 (1997) (noting that "the vested interests established through corrupt practices tend to weaken public institutions and delay attempts to reform the system, thus inhibiting the development of new activities and reducing economic growth"); Claes Sandgren, Combating Corruption: The Misunderstood Role of Law, 39 Intl. Law 717, 718 (2005) (suggesting that corruption reduces economic growth).

6 Ibrahim Shihata, The World Bank Legal Papers ch. 9, 219–44 (Kluwer Law International 2000), sets out points made earlier in the legal opinion from Ibrahim Shihata, senior vice president and general counsel, Prohibition of Political Activities in the Bank's Work, July 12, 1995 (internal doc. SecM95-707).

7 The IBRD Articles of Agreement, for example, state that "the Bank shall make arrangements to ensure that the proceeds of any loan are used only for the purposes for which the loan was granted, with due attention to considerations of economy and efficiency." See IBRD Articles of Agreement, Article III, Section 5(b), supra note 5. The IDA articles contain an identical provision. See IDA Articles of Agreement, Article V, Section 1(g), supra note 5. See also Agreement Establishing the Inter-American Development Bank, Article III, Section 1, supra note 5; Articles of Agreement of the Asian Development Bank, Chapter III, Article 8, supra note 5; Agreement Establishing the African Development Bank, Chapter V, Article 14, supra note 5; and Agreement Establishing the European Bank for Reconstruction and Development, Chapter III, Article 8.

sanction. And, although sanctions are not aimed at government, the investigations that lead to sanctions often uncover wrongdoing by government officials, which can be a sensitive issue for the MDBs' member countries.

Notwithstanding these challenges, by the early 2000s, the leading MDBs had established mechanisms to investigate and possibly sanction fraud and corruption in the projects they financed. Although similar in purpose and with generally common goals, these mechanisms were each developed separately, drawing on the distinct institutional cultures and political tolerances of the individual MDBs. Although the MDBs have similar business models, little effort was made to harmonize the specific provisions of these fairly novel programs.

Certain core elements were common to most of these sanctions mechanisms. Rather than rely on local law in each country, each MDB decided to create a "level playing field" by adopting a single set of anticorruption policies applicable in all of its projects. Each MDB created an "integrity" office to investigate allegations of violations of these anticorruption policies. Each MDB also created its own adjudicative mechanism to determine when the policy had, in fact, been violated. And, finally, each MDB settled on ineligibility, aka debarment, as the most likely sanction to be imposed.[8]

As the sanctions mechanisms were implemented, it became clear that the devil was in the details. How should fraud and corruption be defined? What rules should govern the investigative process? How much due process must or should be afforded to an accused party? Collectively, the MDBs came to realize that uniformity among them would allow them to set the standard for best practices. Each MDB would then be able to point to the policies of the others as a basis on how to proceed. Moreover, while the MDBs did often compete for business on price and product among their client countries, there was recognition that flexibility on issues of integrity should not be used to win business. Setting a single standard would allow the MDBs to draw a line that none should cross.

Rationale and Background for the Agreement

In February 2006, a Joint International Financial Institution Anti-corruption Task Force (the "IFI Task Force"), including the AfDB, ADB, EBRD, IDB, and World Bank Group, as well the European Investment Bank (EIB) and the International Monetary Fund (IMF), was formed to work toward a

---

8   The World Bank, for example, defines debarment as a declaration that the debarred firm or individual is "ineligible, either indefinitely or for a stated period of time (x) to be awarded a contract . . . for any Bank Project; (y) to be a nominated sub-contractor, consultant, manufacturer or supplier, or service provided of an otherwise eligible firm being awarded a Bank-financed contract; and (z) to receive the proceeds of any loan made by the Bank or otherwise participate in the preparation or implementation of any Bank Project." *See* World Bank Sanctions Procedures, Section 9.01(c)(i) (Jan. 1, 2011), available at <http://siteresources .worldbank.org/EXTOFFEVASUS/Resources/WBGSanctionsProceduresJan2011.pdf>.

"consistent and harmonized approach to combat corruption in the activities and operations of the member institutions,"[9] recognizing that "a unified and coordinated approach is critical to the success of the shared effort to fight corruption and prevent it from undermining the effectiveness of their work."[10] The work of the IFI Task Force culminated in September 2006 with the signing of a Uniform Framework for Preventing and Combating Corruption (Uniform Framework), which included two key components: a common set of definitions of sanctionable conduct and a common set of principles and guidelines for investigations.

The members of the IFI Task Force agreed that, as a threshold matter, consensus needed to be reached on harmonized definitions of the types of illicit conduct they would consider sanctionable. Each member institution had already established four sanctionable offenses: corrupt practice, fraudulent practice, collusive practice, and coercive practice. The task before them therefore was to align their respective definitions of these practices. After much debate, the IFI Task Force agreed on definitions, thus creating a single set of violations applicable in every project financed by participating institutions.[11] The adoption of these harmonized definitions would not only provide uniformity to governments and firms executing development projects financed by different IFIs but also create a single benchmark by which all the IFIs could judge whether a sanctionable practice had occurred.

Attention then turned to the creation of a unified set of principles and guidelines (the IFI Principles and Guidelines for Investigations) to govern how the integrity offices of the respective MDBs would execute their investigative mandates. Starting with the investigative guidelines adopted by the Third International Investigators Conference,[12] the IFI Task Force was able to agree on a set of core elements: definitions of misconduct and the standard of proof; rights and obligations of witnesses, subjects, and investigative office staff; procedural guidelines on sources of complaints, receipt of complaint,

---

9   International Financial Institutions Anti-Corruption Task Force, Uniform Framework for Preventing and Combating Fraud and Corruption (Sep. 2006).

10   World Bank, Mutual Enforcement of Debarment Decisions among Multilateral Development Banks (Mar. 3, 2010).

11   The World Bank Group subsequently adopted a fifth definition for "obstructive practices," as did the IDB and ADB. *See* IDB, Integrity Principles and Guidelines 4 *et seq.* (May 2010). For more information on integrity at the IDB, *see* <http://www.iadb.org/en/topics/transparency/integrity-at-the-idb-group/integrity,1291.html>. Some MDBs have also adopted other sanctionable practices. The ADB, for example, may sanction for conflict of interest and retaliation against whistleblowers. The IDB does not consider its list of enumerated sanctionable practices to be exclusive; it may sanction any conduct that it deems to constitute fraud or corruption. *See* IDB, Policies for the Procurement of Goods and Works Financed by the Inter-American Development Bank, Section 1.14. The World Bank Group, by contrast, sanctions only the five practices enumerated in this article.

12   The International Investigators Conference is an annual gathering of the investigative offices from more than 35 international organizations to discuss issues of common interest, explore opportunities for harmonization, and identify best practices in the detection, investigation, and sanctioning of misconduct in the execution of development projects.

preliminary evaluation, case prioritization, and investigative activity; investigative findings; referrals to national authorities; review and amendment; and publication.

During the final meetings of the IFI Task Force in 2006, discussion turned to whether institutions were prepared to recognize and enforce each other's sanction decisions. It became clear that the work to reach agreement on definitions and guidelines had expended available political will; the MDBs were not yet willing to surrender the independence and "sovereignty" of decision making that would be implicit in accepting mutual recognition of each other's debarment systems. Each MDB firmly believed that it must maintain control over whom the institution would sanction and the terms of the sanction. The initial agreements would have to take root before further agreement could be reached. Indeed, the initiatives agreed to by the IFI Task Force required the approval of both the respective heads and, on some matters, the boards of the MDBs.

In September 2006, the heads of the institutions represented on the IFI Task Force met at the annual meetings of the World Bank and IMF in Singapore and signed the Uniform Framework, laying down the cornerstone for future harmonization among the banks in the area of fraud and corruption. The Uniform Framework included not only an agreement on harmonized definitions and investigative guidelines but also a placeholder for future discussions on cross-debarment, by stating that the institutions would "explore further how compliance and enforcement actions taken by one institution can be supported by the others," an undertaking predicated on the understanding that "mutual recognition of . . . enforcement actions would substantially assist in deterring and preventing corrupt practices."[13]

Over the next several years, each MDB successfully won approval from its management and governing bodies for the harmonized definitions and implemented the Uniform Framework. Their new partnership fostered closer ties in responding to integrity issues and due diligence in private sector financing activities as well. Constant communication and frequent contact led to an increase in trust and confidence among and between the maturing integrity offices. This sense of community was further supported by the movement of staff from one office to leadership positions in others, building a shared understanding of the issues each institution faced.

Harmonization took another step forward when, in early 2009, some of the MDBs that had been part of the IFI Task Force in 2006 expressed an interest in reopening a dialogue as to the possibility of setting up arrangements for the mutual enforcement of sanctions.

The first proposal on the table, advocated principally by the World Bank, was the establishment of a joint sanctions board (JSB) that would act as an autonomous body that would hear sanctions cases from each of the

---

13   *See* Uniform Framework, *supra* note 9.

participating MDBs using a uniform set of procedures. The internal procedures for the initial vetting of cases would be left to each MDB to work out,
although some MDBs expressed an interest in a figure along the lines of the
World Bank Group's evaluation and suspension officers.[14] The proponents
of the JSB believed that the JSB would play an important role in facilitating
a unified approach to decreasing fraud and corruption in MDB-supported
projects.

However, the JSB idea quickly ran into a number of stumbling blocks,
driven primarily by the wide variance in adjudicative mechanisms employed
by the MDBs.[15] The World Bank Group sat at one end of the spectrum, with
a quasi-judicial two-tiered system that included an oral hearing, an appeals
mechanism, and detailed procedures governing the proceedings. None of
the other MDBs was employing systems as elaborate as those of the World
Bank Group, and none was prepared to move significantly in that direction.
Although all recognized the need to provide adequate notice and some due
process to the accused parties, each believed that its own mechanisms were
sufficient. Moreover, each institution continued to feel strongly that it should
have sole control over who the decision makers would be.

The debate raised some fundamental issues on which the MDBs diverged:
should the sanctions process of the MDBs be viewed simply as a business
decisions as to whom the MDB chooses to do business with, or, given that the
focus is on acts of fraud and corruption that are traditionally crimes, as well as
the consequences of sanctions that go beyond the economic, should the sanctions process be treated as a judicial or quasi-judicial action requiring more
robust due process? Are anticorruption policies more akin to due diligence by
traditional investment banks, or have the MDBs taken on a role and therefore
the responsibilities of an international regulator? Underlying the questions is
a more fundamental point: do firms and individuals have a *right* to do business with the MDBs under the open procurement principles that each MDB
has embraced? If so, then it follows that those firms and individuals should
not be deprived of their rights without robust due process. If not, then the

---

14   The World Bank Group has a two-tiered sanctions process. The first tier consists of a review
      of the case by a Bank officer called the Evaluation and Suspension Officer (EO). The Bank
      EO reviews the case for sufficiency of evidence and recommends a sanction, if any, to be
      imposed. If the respondent does not wish to accept the EO's determination, it may refer the
      case to the World Bank Group Sanctions Board, an autonomous body consisting of seven
      members, four of whom are external to the Bank, for de novo consideration. *See* World Bank
      Sanctions Procedures, *supra* note 8, at Sections 3.01, 5.01, 8.01.

15   There was also a belief that a joint sanctions process might have a negative impact on the
      privileges and immunities of individual MDBs. In reality, the opposite was probably true. In
      deciding whether to uphold the immunities of international organizations, national courts
      (particularly in Europe) often look to whether alternative forms of redress that conform with
      fundamental notions of due process are available. One key feature of these notions of due
      process is independent decision making. *See* Article 10 of the Universal Declaration of Hu-
      man Rights, GA Res. 217(III), UN GAOR, 3d Sess., Supp. No. 13, UN Doc. A/810 (1948)
      ("Everyone is entitled in full equality to a fair and public hearing by an independent and
      impartial tribunal, in the determination of his rights and obligations").

decision to debar is essentially a unilateral business decision by the MDB, and the only due process required is that which is sufficient to ensure that the decision itself is not arbitrary. A JSB would therefore make good sense under the former view, but would be excessively burdensome under the latter.

Each MDB addressed these issues indirectly through the manner in which it chose to implement its anticorruption programs. And although all the MDBs' systems rely on the same central precepts, none of the MDBs was yet ready to sacrifice the nuances of, and the policy assumptions underlying, its own decision-making mechanisms in favor of the others.

In light of these thorny issues, the MDBs agreed that the JSB was a "bridge too far," and that the most logical next step in the harmonization of sanctions processes would be the creation of an effective cross-debarment regime. Therefore, representatives of the six MDBs that had met in early 2009—AfDB, ADB, EBRD, EIB,[16] IDB, and World Bank Group—met regularly to discuss and agree on the key elements of a cross-debarment regime based not on common rules or procedures but on common core principles of due process that they all shared.

It was expected that cross-debarment would serve many of the same purposes as a JSB while preserving each MDB's autonomy of policy and decision making. As stated in the Uniform Framework, cross-debarment among MDBs would greatly enhance deterrence and thus prevention of corrupt practices, advancing and strengthening integrity efforts and safeguarding development resources from corrupt participants. Cross-debarment would also significantly enhance the deterrent effect of sanctions by any one MDB, effectively multiplying the impact of a debarment on a firm or individual by foreclosing the possibility of the firm or individual winning contracts with the other MDBs.

Cross-debarment would also address some of the significant fiduciary and reputational risks associated with the financing of contracts with firms and individuals sanctioned by other MDBs. Other than the EBRD,[17] none of the MDBs had previously had a process in place for cross-debarment. Thus, under the open procurement principles that were adopted, each of the MDBs, firms, and individuals sanctioned by one MDB are free to continue doing business with other MDBs, potentially engaging in further misconduct in relation

---

16   In the end, the EIB did not join the agreement. Its sanctions system is still in the development stage and, when the EIB does impose sanctions, its debarment decisions will be subject to review by courts and institutional bodies within the European Union (EU). Therefore, if the EIB were to cross-debar based on the debarments of another MDB, including the World Bank Group, the debarment could be subject to review by an EU court or institutional body. Because of these circumstances, including the EIB in the cross-debarment regime seemed premature. The EIB is continuing to participate in the discussions among the MDBs on sanctions harmonization and is reviewing how it might join the agreement at a later time.

17   In February 2007, the first instance of cross-debarment occurred when the EBRD debarred Lahmeyer International following debarment by the World Bank as a result of its involvement in the Lesotho Highland Waters Project. *See* Transparency International, *Transparency Watch* (Apr. 2007).

to contracts financed by such other MDBs.[18] This situation exposed the MDBs' borrowers and donors and, most important, the beneficiaries of the projects they finance to further prejudice, while at the same time leaving the MDBs open to serious reputational risks for continuing to engage with firms and individuals found by a sister institution to have committed acts of fraud or corruption.[19]

In addition, although each MDB would retain its own sanctions process and standards within the core principles, it was hoped that cross-debarment would facilitate and encourage deeper harmonization among the MDBs. The logic of cross-debarment would lead the MDBs toward consistency of sanctions across MDBs, in both their level (that is, the length of debarment) and scope (for example, which affiliates are subject to sanction). Further, it was anticipated that cross-debarment would facilitate broader harmonization beyond the circle of the major MDBs. It was felt that smaller, regional MDBs would likely be more willing to take part in a cross-debarment regime than a JSB, for the same reasons that made the JSB proposal problematic for the larger MDBs. Similarly, the desire to join the cross-debarment regime should serve as an incentive for regional MDBs to put the core principles in place.

Key Terms of the Agreement

The agreement is based on representation by each signatory MDB that its sanctions regime meets certain common core principles. *First,* that the MDB has adopted the four harmonized definitions of fraud and corruption in the Uniform Framework. *Second,* that the MDB follows the IFI Principles and Guidelines for Investigations. *Third,* that the MDB has sanctions processes with certain key due process elements, including an internal investigative authority and a *distinct* decision-making authority, written and publicly available procedures that require notice to accused parties and an opportunity to respond, a "more probably than not" standard of proof or equivalent, and a range of sanctions that take into account the principle of proportionality, including aggravating and mitigating factors.

In relying on these representations, each signatory MDB agrees to recognize and enforce any debarment decisions of the other signatories that meet the following criteria:

---

18   The term "open procurement" refers to the fact that the MDBs' borrowers, not the MDBs, carry out the procurement of goods, works, and services financed by the MDBs. To ensure an open and competitive process, borrowers are allowed to exclude bidders based on specific enumerated criteria for ineligibility—one of which is debarment by the MDB. Without cross-debarment, there was no legal basis for firms not debarred by the financing MDBs to be excluded simply because another MDB had debarred them.

19   Knowledge that a firm or individual has been debarred by another MDB for fraud and corruption could be used as a basis for further due diligence, but unless the due diligence finds independent reasons not to do business with the debarred party, an MDB is obliged to finance contracts with that party under open procurement principles.

- The debarment is for fraud and corruption under one or more of the four harmonized definitions (that is, fraudulent, corrupt, coercive, or collusive practices).
- The debarment is made public.
- The debarment period exceeds one year.
- The conduct that gave rise to the debarment occurred no more than ten years prior to the debarment decision.
- The decision to debar is made after the agreement takes effect with respect to that MDB.

If the debarment decision meets these criteria, cross-debarment by the other MDBs is essentially automatic. There is no review by the other MDBs of the underlying decision or the reasons for it. The original debarring MDB determines the period of debarment and, where there are conditions for release from debarment, when the firm is released from debarment. However, each MDB has a right to "opt out" of a particular debarment if it determines that the debarment is inconsistent with "institutional or legal considerations."

The agreement provides that other IFIs[20] can join if they sign a letter of adherence and meet the core principles and standards and all existing signatories consent to their adherence. Signatories are free to leave the arrangement by written notice to the other signatories.

Key Issues and Challenges

The proposal for a mutual enforcement regime raised a number of issues and challenges that needed to be ironed out among the signatory MDBs. Some of the key issues and challenges that the MDBs faced and their resolution are described below.

Why Is Cross-Debarment Automatic?

The MDBs considered but rejected a system whereby each MDB would be able to engage in a de novo review of a sanctions decision before agreeing to cross-debarment in a particular case. The working group concluded that allowing de novo reviews would not only be costly and laborious, because each case from each participating MDB would have to be reviewed again on its merits, but could well result in inconsistent decisions among participating MDBs, exposing both the original debarring MDB and the non-cross-debarring MDB to reputational risks. Moreover, inconsistent results might encourage litigation by sanctioned entities or individuals against the organization that imposed

---

20 Several other regional MDBs have expressed an interest in joining a mutual-recognition-of-debarment regime. *See* Mutual Enforcement of Debarment Decisions, *supra* note 10, at paragraph 35.

the strictest sanction. The MDBs agreed that the more effective form of cross-debarment would be one that is triggered automatically, subject only to the specified criteria and the opt-out.

Why Insist on Cross-Debarring for Public Debarments Only?

The MDBs agreed that it would be essential that only public debarments (i.e., those announced publicly, typically by a listing on the MDBs' websites) would be cross-debarred, even though this effectively excluded most sanctions imposed by the ADB.[21] There were several reasons for this approach. Although a degree of transparency is not stated explicitly as a core principle, most MDBs believe that a degree of transparency is an essential element of due process. The duty to cross-debar a nonpublic debarment would oblige the other MDBs to adopt nonpublic debarments, something they were not willing to do on policy grounds as well as on practical ones: it is through publication that the MDB borrowers' implementing agencies and other interested parties are made aware of debarments so that they may enforce them in their own procurement decisions.[22] Moreover, public debarments maximize the deterrent impact; an insistence on publicity reinforces this effect.

Was the Creation of a Safe Harbor for Debarments of One Year or Less the Right Thing to Do?

The MDBs recognized that some case-specific circumstances may not warrant the onerous impact of cross-debarment. After all, for firms that are heavily reliant on MDB-financed business, cross-debarment could put them out of business. Although this would most certainly be a strong deterrent to engaging in sanctionable practices, it might also be viewed as being a disproportionate consequence for lesser offenses. In an effort to balance these competing concerns, the agreement allows for a "safe harbor" in that cross-debarment is applicable only to debarments exceeding one year. It is hoped that this safe harbor will incentivize firms under investigation to cooperate with the MDBs with a view to mitigating their sanctions enough to avoid cross-debarment.

The Opt-Out Clause: A Giant Loophole or a Necessary Escape Valve?

The MDBs wanted to allow for exceptional situations in which individual MDBs might need to opt out of the cross-debarment regime when there are overriding "legal or other institutional considerations." For example, the World Bank Group would normally not sanction a firm that is participating in its Voluntary Disclosure Program (VDP).[23] Similarly, the World

---

21   The ADB discloses debarments only in two cases: violation by a debarred firm of the terms of its debarment by bidding on ADB-financed contracts and repeat offenses. *See* ADB, Anticorruption and Integrity, Integrity Principles and Guidelines, paragraph 98 (Oct. 2010).

22   On the other hand, ADB nonpublic debarments rely on voluntary restraint by the debarred party. *Id.*

23   Under the VDP, a firm is required to disclose misconduct on World Bank Group–supported projects. If the firm is sanctioned by another MDB for misconduct unrelated to a World Bank

Bank Group would not be able to enforce a sanction through cross-debarment against a firm with which the World Bank Group has resolved a case through negotiation (aka settlement) if the terms of the negotiated resolution related, in whole or in part, to the conduct for which the other MDB debarred the firm. Given the current lack of common sanctioning guidelines among the MDBs, this opt-out right also allows MDBs to decline enforcement of a debarment decision that may be egregiously sweeping in scope or duration, significantly impairing the development missions of the other MDBs. It also allows for "one-off" exceptions, as when a debarred party is playing a crucial development role, particularly in emergency situations.

Any decision to opt out does not affect the decision of the other participating MDBs to cross-debar in the same case. If an MDB chooses to exercise this clause, it is required to provide written notice of its decision to each of the other participating MDBs. Although the MDB is not required to supply the reasons for its decision, which would be based on "sovereign" matters of internal policy, this notification requirement alone should incentivize MDBs to make only exceptional use of the clause. In any event, the participating MDBs know that anything other than highly exceptional use of the opt-out clause would endanger the credibility of the system as a whole, to the detriment of all of the participating MDBs.

Opt-out clauses are a common feature of bilateral and multilateral agreements. The inclusion of such clauses is not a statement of expectation that the clause will be used, but rather an acknowledgment of the reality that exceptional circumstances do in fact arise from time to time.[24] As of this writing, none of the MDBs has invoked its opt-out right.

In the absence of an opt-out clause, an MDB confronted with a legal or institutional matter that would preclude the imposition of a particular cross-debarment would be faced with a Hobson's choice of either committing a breach of or having to withdraw from the agreement. Given this alternative, the opt-out clause can be seen as the lesser of two evils.

Group–supported project, the firm is still protected by the VDP vis-à-vis the World Bank Group. See World Bank Department of Institutional Integrity, Voluntary Disclosure Program: Terms & Conditions, Article 3.

24   See Jeffrey L. Friesen, The Distribution of Treaty-Implementing Powers in Constitutional Federations: Thoughts on the American and Canadian Models, 94 Colum. L. Rev. 1415, 1445 (1994) (noting that "the opt-out provisions provide some safeguard for the autonomy of the nation that has the option to exercise it, while the agreement or standard is otherwise presumptively in force. The burden to opt out is on the nation seeking to exercise the option, and it will presumably do so only when it perceives a genuine threat to its interests"); Ariel M. Ezrahi, Opting Out of Opt-Out Clauses: Removing Obstacles to International Trade and International Peace, 31 L. & Policy Intl. Bus. 123, 142 (Fall 1999) (referring to Article XI of the General Agreement on Tariffs and Trade, which provides for exceptions to the general prohibition on quotas under certain circumstances, such as the need to relieve shortages of food and other essential products).

A Special Challenge for the World Bank:
Applying Cross-Debarment to Existing Projects

MDB cross-debarment required a change in World Bank procurement policy, which in turn necessitated amendments to the relevant legal framework for the World Bank's loans and grants, including the procurement, consultant, and anticorruption guidelines, as well as the general conditions.[25] Unlike other MDBs, the World Bank customarily applies changes in policies only to *new* loans and grants. The existing portfolio—even if there is new procurement—is not affected by changes in policy unless the Bank and its borrowers agree otherwise.

The Bank has traditionally declined to apply policy changes to its existing portfolio on fairness grounds. Once the Bank and its borrower have agreed to apply a certain set of policy-based rules to govern a particular project, it has been felt that it would not be fair for the Bank to unilaterally change the "rules of the game" in midcourse.

In the case of MDB cross-debarment, however, the Bank's usual prospective application posed at least two problems:

- The other MDBs intended to apply cross-debarment to new contracts in both new and existing projects. At least one MBD found it unacceptable that the Bank would not apply cross-debarment in this same way and viewed nonapplication of the regime to the Bank's existing projects as a potential deal breaker because the nonapplication violated the principle of reciprocity that was central to the agreement.

- The Bank itself faced major reputational risk, because the Bank would have been hard-pressed to explain to the press and public at large why it was continuing to finance contracts with cross-debarred firms on some—and, in the short term, most—of its projects.

A consensus formed that the World Bank needed to find a way to apply cross-debarment to its existing portfolio. The Bank's lawyers concluded that the only legally valid way to do so was to amend all existing legal agreements with the Bank's borrowers. International law principles did not allow the Bank to do this unilaterally, but the task of undertaking individual amendments to hundreds of agreements, cosigned by borrowers, seemed onerous at best. The Bank therefore adopted a somewhat novel approach: it drew up omnibus amendments to the legal agreements with each borrower on an absence–of–objection basis, so that unless the borrower objected within a defined period of time, the Bank would consider the amendment to take effect automatically.

---

25 Guidelines Procurement under IBRD Loans and IDA Credits, paragraph 1.8 and 1.14 (May 1, 2010); Guidelines Selection and Employment of Consultants under IBRD Loans and IDA Credits & Grants by World Bank Borrowers, paragraph 23 (Jan. 2011); Guidelines on Preventing and Combating Fraud and Corruption in Projects Financed by IBRD Loans and IDA Credits and Grants, paragraph 11 (Jan. 2011); General Conditions for Loans, Article VII (Jul. 31, 2010).

This approach was not without controversy. A relatively small number of borrowers did, in fact, object or ask for more time to consider the amendment. The Bank allowed more time for those borrowers who asked for it, and actively engaged those borrowers that objected; as of this writing, only a handful of borrowers have continued to object to the amendments.

This issue brought out an interesting point: none of the other MDBs needed to go through this exercise in order to effect the policy changes needed to implement the cross-debarment regime. In some cases, the MDBs' policies were broadly enough stated to allow for cross-debarment without a change in procurement policy. In other cases, changes in policy were automatically applied to existing projects because their legal agreements incorporated their policies "as amended from time to time."

This experience has led some at the World Bank to question why the World Bank takes such a different approach to policy changes than its sister institutions. The "fairness" argument that underlies the Bank's current practice is open to challenge, and not simply because other MDBs do not share the practice. Bank policies are adopted only after extensive consultation with member countries and other stakeholders. Moreover, the Bank, like its sister MDBs, is a cooperative institution; its borrowers are also its member countries, represented in the Bank's governing bodies. Any amendments to Bank policies require the approval of those bodies, and it is not immediately obvious that changes in policy should always be assumed to redound to the detriment of the Bank's borrowers.

More often than not, in fact, the opposite is true, which is why many borrowers agree with the Bank, either formally or informally, to apply new policies to ongoing projects. The Bank's position that the loan agreement requires formal amendment, however, means that there is often a mismatch between the formal legal framework for a project and the reality in the field. And, ironically, even if the Bank's approach to policy changes is fairer in substance, it does not always appear so to the Bank's borrowers. In this case, for example, the Bank was perceived by some borrowers as *imposing* a change, when it was actually asking borrowers to consent to a change that other MDBs were implementing automatically.

What Is the Likely Impact of Cross-Debarment on the Private Sector?

There is some concern that cross-debarment could have a "chilling effect" on bidders in MDB-financed procurement. However, we believe that the chilling effect would likely apply mainly to those firms and individuals whose practices are already questionable. In this sense, "chilling effect" is just another way to talk about deterrence. Honest firms with effective integrity compliance programs should have nothing to fear from cross-debarment.

The risk of cross-debarment should incentivize firms to reevaluate their governance and compliance systems in an effort to mitigate the risk of sanction and cross-debarment. In the wake of the adoption of model compliance principles as part of the reform of its own sanctions process, the World Bank Group intends to engage in outreach with the business community and other stakeholders to explain the cross-debarment regime and what steps they can take to mitigate the risk of cross-debarment. Cross-debarment should also serve to further incentivize company managers to come forward voluntarily as soon as they learn of misconduct in their operations, leading to expansion of the VDP and the use of negotiated resolutions. And although it is difficult at this point to assess the impact on corporate behavior overall, debarment decisions by the MDBs are beginning to have an impact outside the development arena; private firms have begun to include a review of debarment decisions by the MDBs as part of their integrity research.[26]

Experience with Cross-Debarment So Far

As of this writing, the agreement has become effective with respect to four out of the five signatory MDBs. The ADB and EBRD were the first signatories to implement the cross-debarment regime; they signed the agreement on June 9, 2010. The World Bank Group followed, announcing its implementation of the accord on July 19, 2010, and the IDB announced implementation in May 2011. Implementation by the AfDB is anticipated by the end of 2011.

As of August 1, 2011, the World Bank had cross-debarred 16 firms and individuals, all of which were originally debarred by the ADB. The ADB, in turn, has cross-debarred 21 entities originally debarred by the World Bank. The EBRD has recognized all of these debarments issued by the World Bank and the ADB. In line with expectations, no debarment by any of the signatories was subject to an opt-out by another signatory.

Next Steps for Harmonization among MDBs and Beyond

As significant as it is, the harmonization of sanctions policies among MDBs should not, and will not, stop with their agreement on cross-debarment. The future is likely to see deeper and broader harmonization among MDBs and other international organizations.

Further Harmonization among the MDBs

Cross-debarment should further cement the MDBs' role as a leader in the global effort to combat corruption. By encouraging MDBs to work together, cross-debarment should reinforce the momentum behind their anticorruption

---

26   The Bank is planning to undertake a review of its sanctions regime. One of the issues that the Bank will attempt to assess will be the deterrent effect of the system. Recognizing that any direct or precise measurements are virtually impossible, the Bank hopes it will find "proxies" that will provide some useful, if rough, appraisal of the regime's effectiveness.

efforts and provide an "enabling environment" that will help them overcome the ever-present challenges discussed at the outset of this chapter.

We hope and expect that Agreement for Mutual Enforcement of Debarment Decisions will lead to deeper and wider harmonization of sanctions policies and practices. Already, there are discussions under way among the participating MDBs to harmonize their sanctioning guidelines, as well as to seek a common approach to the scope of sanctions when dealing with corporate groups.[27] Moreover, cross-debarment has underscored the need for closer cooperation and exchange of information among the MDBs. Parallel or joint investigations between MDBs and with national authorities have already become more common.

Although it is premature at this juncture to talk about an established *droit commun* among the MDBs,[28] these developments certainly open up that possibility. There is significant congruence among the MDBs in the forms of misconduct they consider sanctionable and shared due process principles for the adjudication of cases. The upcoming publication of sanctions decisions by the World Bank Group will begin to create a jurisprudence to fill out the detailed contours of these general principles. To the extent that other MDBs choose to rely on such jurisprudence or may be willing to follow suit and publish their own decisions, a common body of law may emerge in this area among MDBs.

Harmonization beyond the Major MDBs

The agreement opened up the possibility of broadening the harmonization efforts to other IFIs. The World Bank Group and other participating MDBs have started working with smaller, regional MDBs to help them develop and implement anticorruption programs that will conform to the core principles. Some of these MDBs have expressed interest in participating in a cross-debarment regime and have indicated that they may unilaterally recognize cross-debarment decisions. Others have made participation in the cross-debarment regime a specific goal for their institution. Although work remains to be done before MDBs can be added to the cross-debarment regime, the addition of other MDBs would be a positive development that would further strengthen

---

27   The World Bank recently adopted comprehensive guidance for dealing with corporate groups that, among other things, allows for the derivative sanctioning of affiliated parties of a sanctioned party under certain circumstances. As a general matter, subsidiaries controlled by the sanctioned parties will be sanctioned as a routine matter to avoid their use as a vehicle for circumvention, while parent companies are sanctioned only if they were involved in the misconduct or bear some responsibility for allowing it to happen. In addition, the Bank will also generally sanction successors to the extent necessary to ensure that the ongoing business continues to be sanctioned. As the sanctioning processes continue to converge, the harmonized treatment of corporate groups has become a topic of significant discussion among the MDBs.

28   Laurence Boisson de Chazournes, *Partnerships, Emulation, and Coordination: Toward the Emergence of a* Droit Commun *in the Field of Development Finance*, in this volume.

deterrence, harmonization, and collaboration—key components in the fight against fraud and corruption.

There are also inchoate efforts to extend a degree of harmonization beyond the IFI community to United Nations (UN) agencies and even bilateral aid agencies. On February 19–20, 2008, at the first Roundtable of the Legal Harmonization Initiative (LHI), sponsored by the World Bank, the idea of the harmonization of approaches to fraud and corruption among major MDBs, several UN agencies, and bilateral aid agencies was floated for the first time. Although the LHI roundtable participants expressed openness to the idea in principle, they also agreed that reaching that level of harmonization would require considerable discussion and effort, given the wide disparities in institutional governance structures, operational models, policies, and practices, including on the basic question of how they define "corruption."

Since the LHI roundtable, harmonization has proceeded along a number of parallel "paths of least resistance." As discussed in this chapter, the major MDBs, which share similar business models and had roughly similar sanctions regimes, found common ground in cross-debarment largely outside the LHI framework. At the same time, as part of the LHI, the MDBs and key bilateral aid agencies successfully negotiated a framework for operating with sectorwide approaches and cofinancing situations that included some basic common understandings on the handling of fraud and corruption issues. The UN common system[29] has launched a process to harmonize sanctions processes that is at a fairly advanced stage.

In November 2010, the G20 issued an Anti-corruption Action Plan that called for increasing international cooperation in combating fraud and corruption among international organizations. Although the details of implementation remain under discussion, the action plan provides an important impetus for harmonization among MDBs and beyond.

Notwithstanding the significant challenges that need to be faced as the MDBs, the United Nations, and bilateral aid agencies deepen their harmonization, and the broader international community develops even more robust approaches to fraud and corruption more generally, there remains room to extend the dialogue on a more comprehensive approach to harmonization on integrity among international actors. We believe that the importance of the fight against corruption, the logic of harmonization, and the potential benefits that we have discussed in this chapter demand it.

---

29   The High Level Committee on Management adopted recommendations on vendor sanctions for consideration by the organizations of the United Nations system, including agencies, funds, and programs and the Model Policy Framework on Vendor Sanctions for Agencies of the United Nations System.

PART II

LEGAL OBLIGATIONS AND INSTITUTIONS OF DEVELOPING COUNTRIES: RETHINKING APPROACHES OF IFIS

The Rule of Law and Development
In Search of the Holy Grail

Michael Trebilcock

Recent empirical research on the relationship between the nature and quality of a country's institutions and the quality of its development outcomes purports to demonstrate, inter alia, that improvements in the rule of law are likely to have dramatic impacts on development outcomes. For example, according to Daniel Kaufmann, an improvement in the rule of law by one standard deviation from the current levels in Ukraine to the middling levels prevailing in South Africa would lead to a fourfold increase in per capita income in Ukraine in the long run.[1] Similarly, according to Dani Rodrik, Arvind Subramanian, and Francesco Trebi, an "increase in institutional quality" (measured largely in terms of the strength of private property rights and the rule of law) "of one standard deviation, corresponding roughly to the difference between measured institutional quality in Bolivia and South Korea, produces a 2 log-points rise in per capita incomes, or a 6.4-fold difference."[2]

Reflecting this view of the relationship between the rule of law and development, there has been a massive surge in development assistance since the 1990s for law reform projects in developing and transitioning economies involving investments of many billions of dollars.[3] There has also been a major resurgence of scholarly interest in the relationship between law and development.

Proponents of an optimistic view of the relationship between the rule of law, or law more generally, and development have made bold claims about the potentially beneficial impact of legal reforms. For example, in his influential book *The Other Path*, Hernando De Soto claims: "The legal system may be the main explanation in the difference in development that exists between industrialized countries and those that are not industrialized."[4] He also argues that "development is possible only if efficient legal institutions are available to

---

1   Daniel Kaufmann, *Governance Redux: The Empirical Challenge*, in *The Global Competitiveness Report 2003-2004* 137 (Xavier Sala-i-Martin ed., Oxford U. Press 2004).

2   Dani Rodrik, Arvind Subramanian, & Francesco Trebi, *Institutions Rule: The Primacy of Institutions over Geography and Integration in Economic Development*, 9 Journal of Economic Growth 141 (2004).

3   *See* David Trubek, *The Rule of Law and Development Assistance: Past, Present and Future*, in *The New Law and Economic Development: A Critical Appraisal* 74 (David Trubek & Alvaro Santos ed., Cambridge U. Press 2006).

4   Hernando De Soto, *The Other Path: The Invisible Revolution in the Third World* 185 (Basic Books 1989).

all citizens"[5] and that "the law is the most useful and deliberate instrument of change available to people."[6]

In contrast, various law skeptics doubt the ability of legal reformers to identify appropriate legal reforms and contend that legal reforms often face potentially insurmountable economic, political, and cultural obstacles. They also argue that legal reform is frequently irrelevant because informal alternatives to law are of overriding importance as social control mechanisms.[7] In this respect, skeptics point to the failure of the first law and development movement in the late 1950s to early 1970s—discussed in more detail later in this chapter—and argue that we may be condemning ourselves to repeating earlier mistakes by ignoring the lessons of history.

In examining the relationship of law to development, several questions must be addressed:

- What do terms such as "law," "legal institutions," and "the rule of law" connote?

- Do law and legal institutions in fact significantly determine a country's development prospects (given particular conceptions of the ends of development)?

- To the extent that they do, why do many countries have chronically poor laws, legal institutions, or adherence to the rule of law (or in Mancur Olson's terms, why are they "leaving big bills on the sidewalk")?[8]

- If a country has chronically weak legal infrastructure, legal institutions, or rule of law, what measures are important and feasible in a law reform strategy?

- What is the appropriate role for external actors in promoting rule of law reforms in developing countries?

The Definition of Law, Legal Institutions, and the Rule of Law

"Law" could connote an almost infinite number of areas of substantive law, from commercial and corporate law to tax law, family law, property law, contract law, and administrative law. Nobody possesses the requisite expertise across all these areas to judge whether a country's laws reveal deficiencies in one respect or another as evaluated against some conception of the outcomes of development efforts. Instead, this chapter focuses on the major classes of legal institutions, which include courts, police, prosecutors, correctional institu-

---

5   *Id.,* at 186.

6   *Id.,* at 187.

7   *See* Kevin Davis & Michael Trebilcock, *The Relationship between Law and Development: Optimists versus Skeptics,* 56 Am. J. Com. L. 895 (2008).

8   Mancur Olson, *Big Bills Left on the Sidewalk: Why Some Nations Are Rich, and Others Poor,* 10 J. Econ. Perspectives 3 (1996).

tions, specialized regulatory or law enforcement bodies, legal education institutions, and professional regulatory bodies, and examines the characteristics of these institutions with respect to various conceptions of the rule of law.

Problems of evaluation begin with widely divergent understandings of the concept of the rule of law, which, despite its fashionable preeminence in many development circles, has been the subject of long-standing normative debates and is highly contested terrain. According to Brian Tamanaha in an intellectual history of the rule of law, "there are almost as many conceptions of the rule of law as there are people defending it."[9] I (with Ron Daniels) have reviewed these debates in some detail in previous work.[10] For present purposes, suffice it to say that conceptions of the rule of law run the gamut from the deontological (protection of basic human rights) to the instrumental (protection of property rights and contracts to promote investment and growth). They also run from extremely "thick" conceptions that largely equate the rule of law with a just legal system, which in turn is largely elided with a just society, to very "thin" or formalistic conceptions that emphasize that laws should be publicly promulgated; be predictable in their application; apply to all citizens, including government officials; and be subject to some form of neutral adjudication in the event of disputes as to their interpretation or application.

Objections to thick conceptions of the rule of law point out that such notions largely deprive the rule of law concept of independent meaning by equating it with "justice" in all its manifestations—and hence with particular conceptions of the ends of development—rather than as a means of vindicating those ends.[11] Objections to thin conceptions of the rule of law point out that even grossly unjust or immoral societies, such as Nazi Germany or apartheid South Africa, might meet purely formalistic criteria while lacking any elements of basic civil and political rights.[12] Intermediate conceptions of the rule of law stress due process or natural justice values of the kind familiar to Western constitutional and administrative lawyers, as well as basic civil rights.[13]

It is important to identify the causal mechanisms that translate improvements in the quality of the rule of law into enhanced development outcomes. From an economic perspective, much of the literature emphasizes that protection of private property rights and enforcement of contracts translate into enhanced incentives to engage in productive investments and hence enhanced economic growth. The stability and predictability of a legal system are regarded as having similar effects. From a noninstrumental or deontological perspective, such as that adopted by Amartya Sen in *Development as Freedom*,

---

9   Brian Z. Tamanaha, *On the Rule of Law: History, Politics, Theory* 3 (Cambridge U. Press 2004).

10   Michael J. Trebilcock & Ronald J. Daniels, *Rule of Law Reform and Development: Charting the Fragile Path of Progress* 1–57 (Edward Elgar 2008).

11   *Id.*, at 23–25.

12   *Id.*

13   For an argument along these lines, *see* Tom Bingham, *The Rule of Law* (Allen Lane 2010).

an enhanced commitment to the rule of law may be justified as an end in it-self. The rule of law provides greater protections for the freedoms of concern to Sen, and their protection does not need to be justified by reference to in-strumental objectives but presumably legal institutions can still be empirically evaluated by how well these freedoms are in fact protected.[14]

The Relationship between the Rule of Law and Development

Recent empirical evidence is often advanced to support the claim that the quality of a country's commitment to the rule of law significantly, even dra-matically, affects its economic development prospects. However, this claim is not new. A version of this claim appeared in the 1960s in what became known as "the law and development movement." Based on an assumption that law is central to development, the movement's proponents believed that educat-ing developing countries' legal professionals would advance the countries' reform efforts.[15] The view did not endure; shortly after its inauguration, it was declared dead by two of its founders, David Trubek and Marc Galanter, in a widely cited paper,[16] in which they extensively critiqued, in a development context, the "model of legal liberalism" that motivated the initial movement.

According to Trubek and Galanter, the components of the liberal legalism paradigm are fivefold. First, society is made up of individuals, intermediate groups into which individuals voluntarily organize themselves, and the state. The state is the primary locus of supra individual control in society, and thus state action involves the coercion of individuals. Second, the state exercises its control over the individual through law—bodies of rules addressed uni-versally to all individuals similarly situated. Third, rules are consciously de-signed to achieve social purposes or effectuate basic social principles, which are for the society as a whole, not for limited groups within it. Fourth, when the rules made through this process are applied, they are enforced equally for all citizens, and in a fashion that achieves the purposes for which the rules were consciously designed. Fifth, the legal order applies, interprets, and changes universalistic rule. The courts have the principal responsibility for defining the effect of legal rules and concepts on individual and group behavior, and thus normally have the final say in defining the social meaning of laws. In this respect, the courts are the central institutions of the legal order. Finally, the be-havior of social actors tends to conform to the rules: officials are guided by the rules, not by personal, class, regional, or other bases of decision making; and a large number of the rules will be internalized by most of the population.

---

14   Amartya Sen, *Development as Freedom* (Anchor Books 2000).

15   World Bank, *Law and Development Movement*, available at <http://siteresources.worldbank .org/INTLAWJUSTINST/Resources/LawandDevelopmentMovement.pdf>.

16   David Trubek & Marc Galanter, *Scholars and Self-Estrangement: Some Reflections on the Crisis in Law and Development Studies in the United States*, 4 Wis. L. Rev. 1062 (1974).

However, according to Trubek and Galanter, this paradigm has little application or relevance to many, perhaps most, developing countries:

> The ethnocentric quality of liberal legalism's model of law in society is apparent. Empirically, the model assumes social and political pluralism, while in most of the Third World we find social stratification and class cleavage juxtaposed with authoritarian or totalitarian political systems. The model assumes that state institutions are the primary locus of social control, while in much of the Third World the grip of tribe, clan, and local community is far stronger than that of the nation-state. The model assumes that rules both reflect the interests of the vast majority of citizens and are normally internalized by them, while in many developing countries rules are imposed on the many by the few and are frequently honoured more in the breach than in the observance. The model assumes that courts are central actors in social control, and that they are relatively autonomous from political, tribal, religious, or class interests. Yet in many nations courts are neither very independent nor very important.[17]

This critique of the relevance of even a relatively thin conception of the rule of law to many developing countries has in turn attracted criticism. For example, Brian Tamanaha,[18] in a review of the paper by Trubek and Galanter, points out:

> One of the major sources of oppression and rapaciousness in developing countries today is authoritarian governments. The central premise of the liberal rule-of-law system is the protection of individuals from the tyranny of the government. Law-and-development theorists should be striving to devise ways in which the rule-of-law model can be adapted to local circumstances and nurtured into maturity, rather than expending the bulk of their efforts in tearing this model down.
>
> Informative though it was, the legal liberal paradigm elucidated by Trubek and Galanter was seriously misleading insofar as it implied that all the elements described were prerequisite to a rule-of-law system. Even the United States, as they observed, did not satisfy the description. Operating around the world today are many variations of the rule of law, coexisting with individualist-oriented as well as with communitarian-oriented cultures. It has always consisted more of a bundle of ideals than a specific or necessary set of institutional arrangements.
>
> A minimalist account of the rule of law would require only that the government abide by the rules promulgated by the political authority and treat its citizens with basic human dignity, and that there be access to a fair and neutral (to the extent achievable) decision maker or judiciary to hear claims or resolve disputes. These basic elements

---

17 *Id.*, at 1080–81.
18 Brian Tamanaha, *The Lessons of Law and Development Studies*, 89 Am. J. Intl. L. 470 (1995).

are compatible with many social-cultural arrangements and, not-withstanding the potential conflicts, they have much to offer to developing countries.[19]

Tamanaha also points out that the critique of liberal legalism developed by Trubek and Galanter (and other scholars) often leads to a "state law bad, folk law good" attitude, when in fact often "folk law is the culprit" in sanctifying various basic human rights abuses of, for example, women and ethnic or religious minorities.[20] This raises an important issue regarding the relative value of formal and informal rules and norms. For reformers, this is often a chicken versus egg problem: should informal rules come first and serve as the basis for formal rules and norms, or vice versa? Trubek and Galanter seem to assume that informal rules should precede and support formal norms, and recent research partially supports their assumption. Katharina Pistor, Antara Haldar, and Amrit Amirapu show that the status of women in society is relatively weakly associated with various rule of law indices and that in poor countries this association disappears altogether. They suggest that this occurs because the status of women in society is determined primarily by social norms about gender equality and these norms are only weakly affected by legal institutions.[21] In contrast, in the excerpt above, Tamanaha seems to suggest the opposite: formal rules can predominate over informal rules, even when they conflict with them. Similarly, scholars such as Richard McAdams have argued that formal law and legal institutions have the potential to shape and modify social norms over time[22]—that is to say, social or cultural norms and practices should not necessarily be viewed as a timeless given.

Reasons for the Chronically Poor Quality of the Rule of Law and Related Legal Institutions in Many Countries

Rule of law deficiencies are persistent and serious in many developing countries despite the widely claimed instrumental and intrinsic importance of the rule of law to development, and despite the fact that external donors have invested billions of dollars in rule of law reform initiatives in many developing countries. The World Bank's governance data on the status of the rule of law reported that only 3 out of 18 Latin American countries had positive rule of law ratings in 2008 (Chile, Costa Rica, and Uruguay). In sub-Saharan Africa only 6 out of 47 countries had positive rule of law ratings in 2008 (Botswana, Cape Verde, Mauritius, Namibia, the Seychelles, and South Africa). Ratings

---

19   *Id.,* at 476.

20   *Id.,* at 481, 484.

21   Katharina Pistor, Antara Haldar, & Amrit Amirapu, *Social Norms, Rule of Law, and Gender Reality,* in *Global Perspectives on the Rule of Law* 241 (James Heckman, Robert Nelson, & Lee Cabatongian ed., Routledge 2010).

22   *See* Richard McAdams, *The Origin, Development and Regulation of Norms,* 96 Mich. L. Rev. 338 (1997); Richard H. McAdams, *The Legal Construction of Norms: A Focal Point Theory of Expressive Law,* 86 Va. L. Rev. 1649 (2000).

were negative in 12 countries of the former Soviet Union in 2008. The countries of Eastern Europe present a far more positive picture, and Asia presents a mixed bag, with its huge diversity of countries, which vary enormously in size, colonial history, legal heritage, political ideology, and religious complexion. Notable exceptions to generally low rule of law ratings are Singapore and Hong Kong, SAR China. Over the course of the prior decade, few countries with weak ratings had significantly improved their score and some deteriorated further.

Although rule of law measures used by the World Bank in its governance database[23] are susceptible to methodological criticisms,[24] the general conclusion about the serious and persistent impediments to establishing the rule of law in developing countries is not unfounded. Many developing countries also perform poorly on a conception of the rule of law as encompassing the protection of various civil and political rights (as Amartya Sen's conception of development as freedom does),[25] and with respect to corruption.[26] Ratings on the rule of law, freedom, and corruption indices are often highly correlated.

This body of experience has led some scholars to question the value and sustainability of the entire rule of law reform enterprise. Recall that the postwar law and development movement was declared by some of its founders to be a failure by the mid-1970s.[27] The movement's most recent variant faces the risk of meeting the same fate. Indeed, according to Thomas Carothers,

> One cannot get through a foreign policy debate these days without someone proposing the rule of law as a solution to the world's troubles. The concept is suddenly everywhere—a venerable part of western political philosophy enjoying a new run as a rising imperative of the era of globalization. Unquestionably, it is important to live in peaceful, free, and prosperous societies. Yet its sudden elevation as a panacea for the ills of countries in transition from dictatorships or statist economies should make both patients and prescribers wary. The rule of law promises to move countries past the first, relatively easy phase of political and economic liberalization to a deeper level of reform. But that promise is proving difficult to fulfill.[28]

---

23   The World Bank defines the rule of law thus: "Rule of law captures perceptions of the extent to which agents have confidence in and abide by the rules of society, and in particular the quality of contract enforcement, property rights, the police, and the courts, as well as the likelihood of crime and violence." Daniel Kaufmann, Aart Kraay, and Massimo Mastruzzi, *World Bank Governance Indicators Project 2010*, available at <http://info.worldbank.org/governance/wgi/index.asp>.

24   See Kevin Davis, *What Can the Rule of Law Variables Tell Us about Rule of Law Reforms?* 26 Mich. J. Intl. L. 141 (2004).

25   *See* Freedom House, *Decline in Rule of Law Seen in New Data Released by Freedom House* (Jun. 26, 2007), available at <http://www.freedomhouse.org/template.cfm?page=70&release=521>.

26   See Transparency International, *Global Corruption Report 2008*, available at <http://www.transparency.org/news_room/in_focus/2008/gcr2008>.

27   *See* Trubek & Galanter, *supra* note 16.

28   Thomas Carothers, *The Rule of Law Revival*, 77 Foreign Affairs 95 (Mar./Apr. 1998).

In a similar vein, Yves Dezalay and Bryant Garth claim that

> the rule of law has become a new rallying cry for global missionaries. "Money doctors" selling competing economic expertises continue to be very active on the global plane, but the 1990s also witnessed a tremendous growth in rule doctors armed with their own competing prescriptions for legal reforms and new legal institutions at the national and transnational level. . . . So far the rule of law industry cannot claim too many successes in the latest campaign.[29]

According to Brian Tamanaha,

> For all but the most sanguine observers, the triumphalist confidence of the 1990s has dissolved. . . . Amidst this host of new uncertainties there appears to be wide-spread agreement, traversing all fault lines, on one point, and one point only: that the "rule of law" is good for everyone. . . . This apparent unanimity in support of the rule of law is a feat unparalleled in history. No other single political ideal has ever achieved global endorsement. . . . Notwithstanding its quick and remarkable ascendance as a global ideal, however, the rule of law is an exceedingly elusive notion. . . . If it is not already firmly in place, the rule of law appears mysteriously difficult to establish."[30]

Tamanaha, in a somewhat more pessimistic assessment of the effects of the law and development movement over the past fifty years, argues that the fundamental problem confronting rule of law reformers is that factors that influence law extend far beyond law itself. These factors include the history, tradition, and culture of a society; its political and economic system; the distribution of wealth and power; the degree of industrialization of the ethnic, linguistic, and religious compositions of the society; the level of education of the populace; the extent of urbanization; and the geopolitical surroundings. He calls this the "connectedness of law principle" and argues that discrete rule of law reform initiatives typically ignore or discount the many interconnections surrounding the formal and informal institutions and the broader social context.[31]

Even after adopting a relatively minimalist or procedural conception of the rule of law and an eclectic notion of the ends served by the rule of law, recent studies provide extensive evidence of how little we know about

---

29   Yves Dezalay & Bryant Garth, *Introduction*, in *Global Prescriptions: The Production, Exportation and Importation of a New Legal Orthodoxy* Vol. 1, 1 (Yves Dezalay & Bryant Garth ed., U. of Michigan Press 2002).

30   Tamanaha, *supra* note 9, at 3.

31   Brian Z. Tamanaha, *The Primacy of Society and the Failures of Law and Development: Decades of Stubborn Refusal to Learn*, Washington U. in St. Louis School of Law Faculty Research Paper Series No. 10-03-02 (Mar. 26, 2010).

promoting the rule of law in developing countries.[32] After reviewing the evidence, Carothers concludes:

> The rapidly growing field of rule of law assistance is operating from a very thin base of knowledge at every level—with respect to the core rationale of the work, the question of where the essence of the rule of law actually resides in different societies, how change of rule of law occurs, and what the real effects are of changes that are produced.[33]

In earlier work, Ron Daniels and I have hypothesized that the potential impediments that countries may encounter in implementing even a limited, procedural conception of the rule of law fall into four crude (and often overlapping) categories.[34]

Resource Constraints

The first of these impediments is technical or resource related. Despite political will on the part of their leadership and citizens, poor countries simply lack the financial, technical, or specialized human capital resources needed to implement good institutions generally, and legal institutions more specifically. This lack of resources impairs a country's development prospects (whatever one's conception of development) by making it poorer (in some relevant normative sense), which in turn further diminishes its ability to establish good institutions, hence creating a vicious downward spiral.

With respect to such resource-related impediments, the general orientation of reform requires more effective or efficient deployment of existing resources devoted to a country's legal system, a reordering of a country's domestic priorities and reallocation of resources from other areas of expenditure to the legal system, or the infusion of resources from external donors (in the form of financial assistance or technical advice and training and the like). Indeed, regarding the narrowly instrumental economic rationale for rule of law reform, governments lacking the necessary resources should be prepared to borrow the money required to fund the needed reforms and finance borrowing costs from future economic growth and increased tax revenues. However, other obstacles are likely to exist.

---

32 *See* Carothers, *supra* note 28, and Thomas Carothers, *The Problem of Knowledge*, in *Promoting the Rule of Law Abroad: In Search of Knowledge* 15 (Thomas Carothers ed., Carnegie Endowment for International Peace 2006); *Beyond Common Knowledge: Empirical Approaches to the Rule of Law* (Erik G. Jensen & Thomas C. Heller ed., Stanford U. Press 2003), especially Thomas Heller, *An Immodest Postscript*, in *id.*, 382.

33 Thomas Carothers, *The Problem of Knowledge*, in *Promoting the Rule of Law Abroad: In Search of Knowledge* 15, 27 (Thomas Carothers ed., Carnegie Endowment for International Peace 2006).

34 Trebilcock & Daniels, *supra* note 10. The following discussion is derived from this book.

Social-Cultural-Historical Constraints

Another category of impediments to reform relates to a set of social or cultural values, norms, attitudes, or practices that are inhospitable to even a limited procedural conception of the rule of law.[35] For example, Amir Licht, Chanan Goldschmidt, and Shalom Schwartz, in a recent paper in which they correlate scores on world value surveys with scores on rule of law, democracy, and corruption indices, argue that societies that accord higher weight to social embeddedness and hierarchy than to individual autonomy and egalitarianism exhibit lower commitments to the rule of law, democracy, and noncorrupt governance, although there is significant unexplained variance around the mean.[36] Whether culture is conceived of as a form of consciousness or as a form of lawlike social norms, the policy prescriptions needed to overcome this class of impediment are not nearly as obvious as in the case of technical or resource-related obstacles, nor is any impact likely to be immediate, dramatic, or predictable. In other words, changing culture, however conceived, may present at least as formidable a set of challenges as resource constraints to changing laws and legal institutions, particularly if the purpose is to change human behavior.[37]

An important historical perspective on the emergence of the rule of law is presented in recent works by Douglas North, John Wallis, and Barry Weingast[38] and by Weingast, the latter of which has parallels with path-dependence theories reviewed by Mariana Prado and me in a separate paper[39] and overlaps with political economy constraints, discussed below.[40]

According to North, Wallis, and Weingast, the most common social order throughout history is the limited-access order or natural state, which solves the problem of violence through rent creation, granting powerful individuals and groups valuable rights and privileges so that they have incentives to cooperate rather than to fight. The resulting rents, limits on competition, and limited access to organizations hinder long-term economic and political development of these societies. In contrast, open-access orders use competition and open access to organizations and institutions to control violence and are characterized by rent erosion and long-term growth.

---

35   *See* Rosa Ehrenreich Brooks, *The New Imperialism: Violence, Norms, and the Rule of Law*, 101 Mich. L. Rev. 2275 (2003); Amy Cohen, *Thinking with Culture in Law and Development*, 57 Buff. L. Rev. 511 (2009).

36   Amir N. Licht, Chanan Goldschmidt, & Shalom H. Schwartz, *Culture Rules: The Foundations of the Rule of Law and Other Norms of Governance*, 35 J. Comp. Econ. 659 (2007).

37   *See* Cohen, *supra* note 35.

38   Douglas North, John Wallis, & Barry Weingast, *Violence and Social Order: A Conceptual Framework for Understanding Recorded Human History* (Cambridge U. Press 2009).

39   Mariana Prado & Michael Trebilcock, *Path Dependence, Development, and the Dynamics of Institutional Reform*, 59 U. Toronto L.J. 341 (2009).

40   Barry Weingast, *Why Developing Countries Prove So Resistant to the Rule of Law*, in *Global Perspectives on the Rule of Law* 28 (James Heckman, Robert Nelson, & Lee Cabatingan ed., Routledge 2010). Much of the following discussion is drawn from this chapter.

The authors argue that the transition from a limited-access order to an open-access order is a "difficult process, and only two or two-and-a-half dozen states have successfully completed it." They divide the transition into two parts, the "doorstep conditions" and the transition proper. There are three doorstep conditions:

- Rule of law for elites
- The perpetual state (the creation of perpetually lived organizations)
- Consolidated control over violence and the military

The transition proper occurs when sufficient numbers of people become citizens in the sense that the state treats a large category of people impersonally and identically. At the same time, processes must begin that afford citizens access to organizations in both politics and economics, granting them the ability to compete as they wish in either system.

In a subsequent paper, Weingast emphasizes two core aspects of the rule of law. First, the impersonal aspects of law: the certainty or predictability of the law, including the absence of arbitrary actions by the state against individuals; transparency; and the requirement that the state treat individuals as citizens with equality before the law. Second, that the state be able to honor these aspects of the rule of law tomorrow, even if it experiences turnover in officials.

By this definition, natural states have substantial difficulties creating the rule of law. First, the rule of law contrasts with the typical natural state dominated by personal relationships. Second, natural states have difficulty creating the predictability necessary for the rule of law. Third, natural states often seem to act arbitrarily. Finally, and perhaps most important, natural states have great difficulty in providing credible enduring commitments.

According to Weingast, rule of law reforms virtually always fail for two reasons: violence and the absence of perpetuity. Transplanting open-access-order institutions—such as markets, elections, and legal systems—cannot create an open-access order. These reforms seek to dismantle the natural state systems of privilege and limited access, and therefore they threaten violence and disorder. Rather than making everyone better off, as the reformers intend, these reforms threaten to make everyone worse off. Also central to creating the rule of law is creating a perpetual state whose institutions, rules, and policies do not depend on the identity of current officials or dominant coalitions. The problem with natural states in the developing world is that almost not one is a perpetual state. Thus, in order to gain the rule of law, natural states must enter the transition from limited-access order to open-access order. Fragile natural states must become basic ones; basic natural states must become mature ones; and mature natural states must begin the transition with the doorstep conditions. Only at this stage of development are states capable of beginning to create the institutional and organizational basis for the rule of law.

Even though North, Wallis, and Weingast present an important historical approach to the relationship between culture and institutions, their argument seems rather deterministic and has a strong modernization theory flavor, somewhat akin to Walt Rostow's "stages of growth" theory.[41] There are good reasons to call attention to the path-dependence element of institutional development (which may have little to do with deep-seated cultural values), as discussed below. However, path dependent does not mean that societies are stuck in a phased trajectory and that they will not be able to evolve unless they follow all the steps in a prescribed sequence. Indeed, path dependence should not dissuade citizens and decision makers in developing countries from pursuing institutional reforms, acknowledging that change will be difficult and protracted, and outcomes unpredictable. A core element of path dependence is that there is no linearity: societies are complex, and change will be unpredictable. Thus, I do not subscribe to the sequence North, Wallis, and Weingast offer (basic natural states, mature natural states, open-access societies) because there are likely to be multiple equilibria, and progress will not be as linear and predictable as the authors suggest.[42]

Political Economy Constraints

A third class of potential impediments to the effective implementation of even a limited conception of the rule of law might be loosely characterized as political economy–based impediments. Here the lack of effective political demand for reforms, on the one hand, and vested supply-side interests, on the other, render reforms politically difficult to realize even if (by assumption) they would make most citizens better off in terms of their own values.

On the demand side, a procedurally oriented conception of the rule of law has many of the attributes of the public good—"everybody's business is nobody's business"—creating a major collective-action problem. In other words, diffuse citizen commitment to the rule of law is unlikely to translate into effective political mobilization for reforms. Moreover, one should not naively assume that all external constituencies are likely to benefit from rule of law reform; indeed, those who derive benefits from corruption, cronyism, favoritism, and the like in existing institutional arrangements and legal processes are likely to resist such changes.[43]

---

41   *See,* for a summary of the five stages of growth theory, Walt W. Rostow, *The Stages of Economic Growth: A Non-Communist Manifesto* 4–17 (3d ed., Cambridge U. Press 1990).

42   *See* Prado & Trebilcock, *supra* note 39.

43   *See* Daniel Kaufmann, *Rethinking Governance: Empirical Lessons Challenge Orthodoxy* (discussion draft, Mar. 2003), available at <http://papers.ssrn.com/sol3/papers.cfm?abstract _id=386904&download=yes>; Joel Hellman & Daniel Kaufmann, *The Inequality of Influence* (preliminary draft, Dec. 2002), available at <http://papers.ssrn.com/sol3/papers .cfm?abstract_id=386901&download=yes>; Karla Hoff & Joseph Stiglitz, *After the Big Bang? Obstacles to the Emergence of the Rule of Law in Post-Communist Societies,* 94 Am. Econ. Rev. 753 (2004).

Curtis Milhaupt and Katharina Pistor emphasize the importance of the demand side,[44] arguing that the economic literature implicitly considers only the supply of law in a given society, largely neglecting the role of demand. The authors suggest that because the relation between law and markets functions according to a continuous feedback loop, the causal connection runs both ways and there is "endogeneity" in the relationship. Law can play an important coordination function in markets, and it can enhance the credibility of state-supplied governance structures. Milhaupt and Pistor conclude that the demand for law as a governance device is likely to be affected by the extent to which potentially effective constituencies are allowed to participate in law making and law enforcement and to promote legal adaptations to changing economic and social conditions.

On the supply side are vested or incumbent interests in institutions or processes that do not comport even with a minimalist, procedurally oriented conception of the rule of law. For example, a corrupt or incompetent judiciary, public prosecution, police, correctional system, tax administration, or other specialized law enforcement, administrative, or regulatory agency, as well as a member of a private bar or legal education institution, is likely to resist reforms that threaten its interests.

The critical relationship between the rule of law and issues of political economy is insightfully articulated by José Maravall and Adam Przeworski:

> To develop a positive conception of the rule of law one must start with political forces, their goals, their organization and their context. It is not stability that distinguishes the rule of law but the distribution of power. When power is monopolized, the law is at most an instrument of the rule of someone. Only if conflicting political actors seek to resolve their conflicts by recourse to law does law rule. Rule of law emerges when self-interested rulers willingly restrain themselves and make their behaviour predictable in order to obtain sustained, voluntary cooperation of well-organized groups commanding valuable resources. In exchange for such cooperation, rulers will protect the interests of these groups by legal means . . .

> The difference between rule by law and rule of law lies in the distribution of power, the dispersion of material resources, the multiplication of organized interests; in societies that approximate the rule of law, no group becomes so strong as to dominate the others, and law, rather than reflect the interests of a single group, is used by the many. The rule of law is conceivable only if institutions tame or transform brute power. As organized interests multiply, a society will come closer to the rule of law, power will not be monopolized, and the law will not be used by the few against the many.[45]

---

44 Curtis J. Milhaupt & Katharina Pistor, *Law & Capitalism: What Corporate Crises Reveal about Legal Systems and Economic Development around the World* (U. of Chicago Press 2008).

45 José María Maravall & Adam Przeworski, *Introduction*, in *Democracy and the Rule of Law* 1, 2–4 (José María Maravall & Adam Przeworski ed., Cambridge U. Press 2003).

Stephen Holmes similarly argues:

> Why do people with power accept limits to their power? An even
> more pointed formulation is: why do people with guns obey peo-
> ple without guns? An economic twist is: why would the rich ever
> voluntarily part with a portion of their wealth? In legal theory, the
> parallel question runs: why do politicians sometimes hand power to
> judges? Why do politicians allow judges, who control neither purse
> nor sword, to overturn and obstruct their decisions and sometimes
> even to send office-holders to jail? . . . Societies may approximate
> the rule of law if they consist of a large number of power-wielding
> groups, comprising a majority of the population, and if none of them
> become so strong as to be able thoroughly to dominate the others.
> We may be able to loosen the grip of a few organized interests on
> power by forcing them to share political leverage with a variety of
> other groups. This is polyarchy; it is also rough justice, the only kind
> human beings will ever experience. Formulated differently, the bal-
> ancing of many partialities is the closest we can come to impartiality.
> This may not sound particularly ideal, but it is nevertheless histori-
> cally quite rare and very difficult to achieve.[46]

Legal Origins Constraints

Another explanation for the puzzle of differential legal performance is associated with the rapidly proliferating body of literature, principally in the financial
development field, that focuses on whether legal origins have influenced countries' financial development, with the assertion that legal origins are a major
determinant of rates of economic growth. In a widely cited paper in 1997,[47] followed by similar works, LaPorta, Lopez-De-Silanes, Shleifer, and Vishny (frequently referred to as LLSV),[48] assert a causal linkage between legal origins and
financial development and, indirectly, economic growth. This claim is largely
based on cross-country studies that purport to show that judicial systems based
on common law have developed more sophisticated financial institutions and
financial markets than those based on civil law. Among civil law jurisdictions,
the French civil law system has lagged behind others, including those of Germany and Scandinavia. The authors conclude that countries with more sophisticated financial markets generally recognize more extensive shareholder and
creditor rights and that common law jurisdictions are superior in these respects
to civil law jurisdictions, in particular to the system in France.

LLSV rely on two interrelated mechanisms through which legal origin influences finance. The political mechanism holds that (a) legal traditions differ

---

46   Stephen Holmes, *Lineages of the Rule of Law*, in *Democracy and the Rule of Law* 19, 24 (José María
     Maravall & Adam Przeworski ed., Cambridge U. Press 2003).

47   Rafael LaPorta, Florencio Lopez-De-Silanes, Andrei Shleifer, & Robert W. Vishny, *Legal Deter-
     minants of External Finance*, 52 J. Finance 1131 (1997).

48   Rafael LaPorta, Florencio Lopes-De-Silanes, & Andrei Shleifer, *The Economic Consequences of
     Legal Origins*, National Bureau of Economic Research Working Paper No. 13608 (2007).

in terms of the priority they attach to private property, compared with the rights of the state (or as the authors put it, "common law stands for the strategy of social control that seeks to support private market outcomes, whereas civil law seeks to replace such outcomes with state-desired allocations"); and (b) the protection of private contracting rights forms the basis of financial development. The adaptability mechanism stresses that (a) legal traditions differ in their formalism and ability to evolve with changing conditions; and (b) legal traditions that adapt efficiently to minimize the gap between the contracting needs of the economy and the legal system's capabilities will more effectively foster financial development than more rigid systems.

This literature[49] is persuasively critiqued by Kenneth Dam, *The Law-Growth Nexus: The Rule of Law in Economic Development*.[50] In this book, Dam points out that the regulation of shareholder and creditor rights in most jurisdictions (civil and common law) is a matter of relatively recent statutes and not common law or private law civil codes, and thus drawing sharp differences between civil and common law systems on this account is unwarranted.[51] Dam also notes that France enjoyed more rapid per capita economic growth than Britain from 1820 to 1998 as a whole; recent governance studies by the World Bank find legal origins to have a small-to-nonexistent impact on the quality of the rule of law or economic growth records, especially among poorer countries;[52] and the much broader governance measures employed by the World Bank provide a more helpful framework of analysis for an institutional reform agenda. In a similar vein, Gillian Hadfield, in "The Levers of Legal Design: Institutional Determinants of the Quality of Law,"[53] argues that the binary classification of legal systems as either common law or civil law obscures many institutional differences that do not closely track this binary categorization.

Based on recent comparative legal research with which I have been associated,[54] the performance of common law systems in former colonies that inherited these systems from their British imperial overseers varies markedly on numerous measures, including contemporary appraisals of the rule of law. Thus, variations in performance within legal families are often much greater

---

49   The empirical evidence that proponents and critics rely on is masterfully surveyed in a paper by Thorsten Beck & Ross Levine, *Legal Institutions and Financial Development*, in *Handbook of New Institutional Economics* 251 (Claude Ménard & Mary M. Shirley ed., Springer 2008).

50   Kenneth Dam, *The Law-Growth Nexus: The Rule of Law in Economic Development* 26–55 (Brookings Institution Press 2006).

51   *See* also Mark Roe, *Legal Origins, Politics and Modern Stock Markets*, 120 Harv. L. Rev. 460 (2006).

52   *See* Kaufmann, *supra* note 1.

53   Gillian Hadfield, *The Levers of Legal Design: Institutional Determinants of the Quality of Law*, 36 J. Comp. Econ. 43 (2006); *see* also Symposium, *Economics and Comparative Law*, 59 U. Toronto L.J. 179 (2009).

54   Ron Daniels, Michael Trebilcock, & Lindsey Carson, *The Legacy of Empire: The Common Law Inheritance and Commitments to Legality in Former British Colonies*, 59 Am. J. Comp. L. 111 (2011).

than variations between them. This suggests that many variables other than legal origins alone explain subsequent legal performance, in particular, I argue, the degree to which the British colonial authorities afforded representation to the indigenous population in legislative bodies, and the extent to which indigenous and British common law courts and animating values were integrated, thereby fostering the development of a localized common law jurisprudence.

A Brief Review of Rule of Law Reform Experience

I now turn to a brief review (elaborated on elsewhere)[55] of the efficacy of recent reforms to legal institutions in Latin America, Africa, Central and Eastern Europe, and Asia, relating these reform efforts to notions of path dependence that Mariana Prado and I have reviewed in a separate publication.[56]

Although path dependence in its purest form is constraining and deterministic, we are not prisoners of our past. Mariana Prado and I have argued that path dependence provides insights for those promoting institutional reforms. Indeed, the path-dependence literature provides a wealth of information for those promoting institutional reforms. First, the concepts of self-reinforcing mechanisms and switching costs, for instance, show that reforms in key institutional nodes of any system are likely to fail if they do not address both the nature and the scale of switching costs faced by internal and external actors engaged in or with these institutions. Second, to the extent that particular institutions have become embedded, over time, in a broader matrix of mutually reinforcing institutional interdependencies, nodal reform that ignores this fact is likely to be further compromised. Third, the concept of critical junctures shows that comprehensive or ambitious reforms in minimally functional institutions (or networks of institutions) during "normal times" can be disruptive and are likely to be strongly resisted by affected stakeholders. As path-dependence theory emphasizes, much institutional change will be incremental and will occur on the margins; indeed, attempting too much may be a recipe for achieving too little.

Judicial Reform

A prominent focus of rule of law reforms has been judicial reform such as reducing court backlogs, which are large and growing in many developing countries. Reform efforts to this end have involved improving court record keeping through enhanced information technology and more proactive case-management techniques. Complementary reform initiatives have often involved externally supported judicial training programs.[57] In some cases, these

---

55   *See* Trebilcock & Daniels, *supra* note 10.

56   *See* Prado & Trebilcock, *supra* note 39.

57   Trebilcock & Daniels, *supra* note 10.

initiatives have had a positive impact on court backlogs, although various scholars have noted that enhancing judicial capacity by increasing the volume of cases processed says little or nothing about the quality of judicial decision making.[58] Judicial corruption and incompetence are endemic in many developing countries, particularly at lower levels of the court systems and outside major urban centers. Reform efforts have barely penetrated these courts and are thus largely ineffective, because most citizens have contact (if any at all) only with courts at the lowest level of the system.[59]

One persistent challenge is that reforms often ignore self-reinforcing mechanisms at the individual level, where the belief systems or patterns of behavior on the part of internal and external actors may have adjusted to the former institutional arrangement and might not readily adapt to the new regime. These forms of adaptive behavior will likely increase the costs of moving to a new system because they will generate resistance to reforms akin to the "installed base problem" (for example, the resistance to moving from an imperial to a metric system of weights and measures).[60]

Legal Education

Individual belief systems or patterns of behavior are often reinforced by legal education. Historically, such education in many developing countries has focused heavily on rote learning and regurgitation on exams.[61] In Latin America, many public law schools suffer from overpopulation and too many part-time students and instructors.[62] Although private law schools have recently proliferated in many developing countries, they are of highly variable quality, ranging from internationally recognized law schools to those offering only part-time degrees or considered to be diploma mills. Legal education institutions in Central and Eastern Europe have historically been tightly controlled by the state, which has led to a standardized, inflexible, and increasingly inappropriate legal curriculum.[63] In some countries in this region, with the support of international nongovernmental organizations (NGOs) and other institutions,

---

58   *See* Heller, *supra* note 32.

59   *Id.*

60   The term "installed base" refers to early adopters of a technology, who will bear a disproportionate share of transient incompatibility costs and may therefore resist the adoption of a newer technology. The larger the installed base, the more inertia it will generate. Joseph Farrell & Garth Saloner, *Installed Base and Compatibility: Innovation, Product Preannouncements, and Predation*, 76 Am. Econ. Rev. 940 (1986).

61   Trebilcock & Daniels, *supra* note 10, at 307–31; Joseph Tome, *Heading South but Looking North: Globalization and Law Reform in Latin America*, Wis. L. Rev. 691 (2000); Cheng Han Tan et al., *Legal Education in Asia*, 1 Asian J. Comp. L. 17 (2006).

62   Stephen Meili, *Legal Education in Argentina and Chile*, in *Educating for Justice around the World: Legal Education, Legal Practice and the Community* 138, 142 (Louise G. Trubek & Jeremy Cooper ed., Aldershot 1999).

63   *See* George E. Glos, *Soviet Law and Soviet Legal Education in an Historical Context: An Interpretation*, 15 Rev. Socialist L. 227, 257 (1989); Susan Finder, *Legal Education in the Soviet Union*, 15 Rev. Socialist L. 197, 207 (1989).

efforts have been made to reform the curriculum to be more relevant to new economic, social, and political environments and to reduce or eliminate the ideological connection between law and the state that prevailed in the communist era.[64]

Legal education in Africa is extremely varied with respect to institutional support, funding, and curriculum development. South Africa, a relatively rich nation, has a considerable legal education infrastructure, but continues to suffer from underfunding and the low quality of historically black institutions. Many other African countries have much weaker legal education systems that contend with a serious lack of resources, including such basic resources as teaching and library materials. As in Latin America, many African law schools continue to emphasize rote learning, although significant efforts have been made recently to incorporate both clinical legal education and human rights dimensions into some law school curricula.[65] In many Asian countries, there are a large number of legal education institutions that are of widely variable quality, with a dramatic proliferation of these schools in China in particular.[66]

Resistance to legal reforms in many developing countries seems attributable in part to the vested interests of the professors, judges, and existing practitioners who seek to insulate themselves from curriculum changes or substantive or procedural reforms of the existing legal system, in part because these might entail a depreciation of their existing human capital and require investments in retraining and retooling. Lawyers who were trained and practice, adjudicate, or teach in a socially dysfunctional legal system and have made substantial investments in human capital in learning how to function in such a system are often not a progressive force for legal reform.

A more general problem with judicial reforms is that they do not account for relevant macroprocesses that connect what happens inside the courtroom with events that precede or succeed the courtroom proceedings (for example, the enforcement of judgments). In particular, recent rule of law reforms often neglect the most relevant law enforcement agency, the police force, despite the fact that historically in many countries the police have been viewed as a form of paramilitary organization, primarily dedicated to regime maintenance in

---

64   European Commission: Education and Training, available at <http://ec.europa.eu/education/index_en.htm>; Louis F. Del. Duca, *Cooperation in Internationalizing Legal Education in Europe—Emerging New Players*, 20 Penn. St. Intl. L. Rev. 9 (2001).

65   Manu Ndulo, *Legal Education in Africa in the Era of Globalization and Structural Adjustment*, 20 Penn. St. Intl. L. Rev. 489 (2002); Philip F. Iya, *From Lecture Room to Practice: Addressing the Challenges of Reconstructing and Regulating Legal Education and Legal Practice in the New South Africa*, Third World Legal Studies 141, 144, 151 (2000–03).

66   Tan et al., *supra* note 61; Mei-Ying Hung, *China's WTO Commitment on Independent Judicial Review: Impact on Legal and Political Reform*, 52 Am. J. Comp. L. 77 (2004); Vincent Cheng Tang, *Judicial and Legal Training in China: Current Status of Professional Development and Topics of Human Rights*, China-OHCHR National Workshop for Lawyers and Judges (2002), available at <http://www.icclr.law.ubc.ca/Publications/Reports/Beijing_August_2002.pdf> (citing the official China News Net Report on Chinese Legal Aid System Basically Formed, 600,000 People Aided in 5 Years, Sep. 29, 2002).

societies dominated by military or authoritarian governments.[67] This has made policing of secondary importance in many developing and transitional economies and has led incumbent political regimes to support or at least acquiesce in extensive human rights abuses by police forces, including torture, coerced confessions, indefinite detention without trial, and rampant corruption.[68]

In an attempt to deal with this abuse, modest efforts have been made in some countries to implement civilian police oversight mechanisms and reform criminal procedure laws.[69] These laws, at least in theory, enable courts to act as a check on these forms of abuse, through, for example, rules that deem evidence to be inadmissible when obtained illegally. However, in practice, courts in these countries have not been assertive monitors of abuses of public office, in part because of their historical subservience to the executive branch of government in terms of appointments, promotions, and resources.[70] Attempts at strengthening judicial independence through the creation of semiautonomous judicial councils to vet appointments and promotions and to maintain a disciplinary regime for judicial misconduct have often been met with fierce resistance from the executive and legislative branches of government, as well as the judiciary itself.[71]

Correctional Institutions

The problem of ignoring elements of the legal system, such as the police, in rule of law promotion strategies is replicated in penal reform efforts.[72] These reforms seek to improve correctional institutions in developing countries and transition economies while ignoring these institutions' relationship with the criminal justice system. Reform efforts in this context have focused on developing correctional institutions as professional public establishments, often through training programs for correctional personnel provided by international agencies and NGOs and the provision of paralegal advisory services to

---

67   Article 1 of United Nations Code of Conduct for Law Enforcement Officials, adopted by the General Assembly in 1979, GA Res. 34/169, UN GAOR, 34th Sess., Supp. No. 46, UN Doc. A/34/46 (1979); Rachel Nield, *Confronting a Culture of Impunity: The Promise and Pitfalls of Civilian Review of Police in Latin America*, in *Civilian Oversight of Policing: Governance, Democracy and Human Rights* 223 (Andrew Goldsmith & Colleen Lewis ed., Hart 2000).

68   Mercedes S. Hinton, *A Distant Reality: Democratic Policing in Argentina and Brazil*, 5(1) Crim. Justi. 75, 95 (2005); Paul Chevigny, *Defining the Role of the Police in Latin America*, in *The (Un) Rule of Law and the Underprivileged in Latin America* 49 (Juan E. Mendez, Guillermo O'Donnell, & Paulo Sergio Pinheiro ed., U. of Notre Dame Press 1999).

69   Colleen Lewis, *The Politics of Civilian Oversight: Serious Commitment or Lip Service?* in *Civilian Oversight of Policing: Governance, Democracy and Human Rights* 19 (Andrew Goldsmith & Colleen Lewis ed., Hart 2000).

70   Nield, *supra* note 67.

71   *See* Linn Hammergren, *Do Judicial Councils Further Judicial Reform? Lessons from Latin America*, Carnegie Endowment for International Peace Working Paper No. 28 (Apr. 2002).

72   Standard Minimum Rules for the Treatment of Prisoners, adopted by the First United Nations Congress on the Prevention of Crime and the Treatment of Offenders, held in Geneva in 1955, and approved by the Economic and Social Council by its resolution 663 C(XXIV) of July 31, 1957, and 2076 (LXII) of May 13, 1977.

inmates to advise them of their rights as prisoners relating to abuses suffered within correctional institutions and their related legal rights under the country's criminal justice system.[73] Some countries, especially in Latin America, have appointed official ombudsmen to investigate prisoners' complaints and report thereon to government, while in other countries (such as several in sub-Saharan Africa), pursuant to regional treaty commitments, official rapporteurs make periodic visits to correctional institutions and report publicly on conditions therein.[74]

Historically, the role of prisons in many countries was tied principally not to crime, punishment, or rehabilitation, but to suppressing political opposition and/or extracting labor from vast populations of captive workers (especially in the former Soviet Union). Severe prison overcrowding has been a chronic problem, leading to a very high incidence of infectious diseases such as HIV/AIDS and tuberculosis.[75] However, prison reform efforts focused on correctional institutions often ignore the fact that a significant source of the overcrowding problem in correctional institutions in many developing countries is the high percentage of inmates held on remand awaiting trial for often lengthy periods due to the inefficiencies in the broader criminal justice system. Where reforms to the criminal justice system have been undertaken, for example, providing judges with greater discretion to impose noncustodial forms of sentences, the judiciary has often shown a reluctance to invoke these powers, particularly in contexts of widespread public concern over high and rising violent-crime rates.[76] Thus, as with other reform efforts, penal reform efforts need to deal with the prison institution's relationship to the broader criminal justice system.

Corrections, dealing as it does with a small and marginalized subset of the population, is (perhaps more than any other institution) inextricable from the broader successes and failures of the wider rule of law reform. Penal reform depends, at least in part, on the efficiency of court processes, the effectiveness of law enforcement, the broader complex of social factors determining crime rates more generally, a vigorous legal bar willing to defend prisoners' rights, and a culture of human rights robust enough to conceptualize prisoners within its ambit.

---

73 *Penal and Prison Reform in Africa*, vols. 13–14 Political Risk Insurance Newsletter 5 (Apr. 2001).

74 The United Nations Latin American Institute for the Prevention of Crime and Treatment of Offenders, *ILANUD Activities in 2002 and 2003 Work Programme.*

75 *See* the *Introduction* to the *Draft Inter-American Declaration Governing the Rights and the Care of Persons Deprived of Liberty,* developed by the government of Costa Rica in conjunction with Penal Reform International; Centre for the Study of Violence and Reconciliation, *Annual Report 2001/2002* Criminal Justice Programme (2002), available at <http://www.csvr.org.za/docs/2001.pdf>.

76 Mark Ungar, *Prisons and Politics in Contemporary Latin America* 25 Hum. Rights Q. 909, 912 (2003).

Administrative Agencies

Other relevant institutional interconnections involve bureaucracy. In both developed and developing countries, important aspects of the administration of justice are vested in specialized law enforcement or administrative agencies that deal with matters as diverse as tax administration, public utilities regulation, environmental regulation, competition law enforcement, and election management bodies. These agencies are more easily detachable from the existing bureaucracy, entailing less complex or sweeping reforms that therefore may be less likely to suffer from path-dependence problems.

Tax administration is a specialized law enforcement or regulatory function that is weak in most developing countries and hence provides an important example of the challenges that these countries face.[77] Effective tax administration is of critical importance to all developing countries because a constrained ability to collect revenues legally due limits a government's ability to fund development priorities. In many countries, the gap between taxes nominally due and taxes actually collected is extremely large—often in the range of 40 percent—suggesting great potential for improved tax administration performance.

To improve the tax system, a number of developing countries have set up large taxpayer units (LTUs) with a view to building specialized and integrated expertise in tax assessment, given that LTUs are the source of much of the effective taxable capacity. In addition, a number of countries have also set up semiautonomous revenue agencies (SARAs), designed to ensure the fiscal autonomy of the organization and greater freedom in personnel policies and information technology development.[78] These reforms appear to have been successful in broadening the taxpayer base and increasing the percentage of taxes nominally due that are actually collected. However, the experience with SARAs over time has been mixed—typically, these agencies are initially successful in increasing tax collection, but their performance tends to decline in effectiveness, in some cases because of rampant corruption within the agency,[79] and in other cases because of increasing political interference from the ministry of finance or other executive arm of the government in personnel and assessment processes.[80] This trend suggests that the ability of these agencies to maintain themselves over time as "islands of virtue" in

---

77   Malcolm Gillis, *Tax Reform: Lessons from Postwar Experience in Developing Nations*, in *Tax Reform in Developing Countries* 492, 493 (Malcolm Gillis ed., Duke U. Press 1989); for examples from India, Indonesia, Mexico, Singapore, Spain, and the Philippines, *see* Arindam Das-Gupta & Dilip Mukherjee, *Incentives and Institutional Reforms in Tax Enforcement: An Analysis of Developing Country Experience* (Oxford U. Press 1998).

78   Trebilcock & Daniels, *supra* note 10, at 200–235.

79   Susan Rose-Ackerman, *Corruption and Government: Causes, Consequences, and Reform* 86 (Cambridge U. Press 1999) (showing that in tax reform, incentive schemes can be used only if levels of performance can be measured by external monitors).

80   Robert Taliercio, Jr., *Unsustainably Autonomous? Challenges to the Revenue Authority Model in Latin America Tax Agencies in Developing Countries* (World Bank 2001).

an otherwise corrupt or incompetent general public administration may be quite limited without complementary reforms, over time, of the surrounding institutional matrix.

Another similarly motivated example of reforms is the implementation of independent regulatory agencies (IRAs) for infrastructure sectors, such as telecommunications, electricity, and water. During the 1990s U.S.-style IRAs were created in many Latin American countries[81] to insulate regulatory decisions from electoral politics. To secure this insulation, IRAs were accorded a series of institutional guarantees of independence. For instance, in presidential systems, these guarantees would include fixed terms of office for commissioners, congressional approval of presidential nominations, and alternative sources of funds to ensure financial autonomy.[82] In the context of privatization of state-owned utility companies, this insulation was intended to provide a credible commitment by the government to existing rules and norms, theoretically protecting investors from arbitrary and unjustifiable subsequent modifications in the regulatory framework.

However, the establishment of U.S.-style IRAs has met with a series of obstacles.[83] In some cases, their creation was resisted by bureaucrats who were also opposed to privatization and a competitive environment in infrastructure services, thereby exemplifying high switching costs and the installed base problem. In other cases, the transfer of civil servants from the preexisting bureaucracy to the IRAs brought deeply embedded practices that are difficult to change, impairing some of the institutional innovations adopted by IRAs, such as those designed to insulate these agencies from political and electoral interests. This reality illustrates the difficulty of mitigating self-reinforcing mechanisms, especially when they are embedded in the institutional culture. Finally, some of the institutional guarantees of independence in these agencies were not effective due to the fact that they were operating in a different institutional matrix from the country of origin of the transplant. Thus, the creation of IRAs largely ignored the importance of institutional interconnections.

A related class of administrative agency is competition agencies.[84] About sixty mainly developing or transitioning countries have competition agencies that are fifteen years old or younger.[85] The World Bank reports that a 2000 sur-

---

81 Jacint Jordana & David Levi-Faur, *Hacia un estado regulador Latinoamericano? La difusión de agencias reguladoras autónomas por países e sectores* (2005). *See also* Giandomenico Majone, *The Rise of the Regulatory State in Europe*, 17 West Eur. Pol. 77 (1994) (discussing the European experience).

82 Warrick Smith, *Utility Regulators—the Independence Debate*, Public Policy for the Private Sector, note 127 (Oct. 1997), available at <http://rru.worldbank.org/documents/publicpolicyjournal/127smith.pdf>.

83 Mariana Mota Prado, *The Challenges and Risks of Creating Independent Regulatory Agencies: A Cautionary Tale from Brazil*, 41Vand. J. Transnatl. L. 435 (2008).

84 For a recent survey, *see* Michael Trebilcock & Edward Iacobucci, *Designing Competition Law Institutions: Values, Structure, and Mandate*, 41 Loy. U. Chi. L.J. 455 (2010).

85 A recent survey and analysis of the competition laws of 102 countries found mild prelimi-

vey found that, on average, competition agencies in industrial countries are 40 percent more effective than competition authorities in developing countries.[86] Surveys or evaluations of the experience of such agencies by the Competition Policy Implementation Working Group of the International Competition Network (ICN),[87] and the International Development Research Centre (Ottawa)[88] have identified a number of challenges in this regard.

First, many countries have borrowed heavily from developed countries in designing their respective laws, and the legislative framework does not address effectively the realities of the jurisdiction that these agencies are called upon to regulate. Some statutes fail to deal with important anticompetitive forms of conduct because of carve-outs or exceptions for industrial policy, political economy, or other reasons. Others are expansive in their scope, but fail to establish any set of priorities for the agency consistent with its resources and capabilities. Others do not provide for the compulsory *ex ante* notification of mergers, while others set notification thresholds so low that agencies are overwhelmed with merger notifications that they are not able to review effectively. In yet other cases, agencies are not invested with adequate investigative powers to unearth and eliminate anticompetitive conduct; they are unable to enforce compulsory disclosure laws successfully and lack powers to grant immunities to facilitate cartel investigations. In yet others, fines and other penalties are too low to induce effective deterrence or cannot be effectively enforced.

Second, young agencies commonly report a lack of cooperation and coordination of policy and effort from particular government ministries and other regulatory bodies in their attempt to enforce and promote competition policy, in part as a result of the recent introduction of competition laws without provisions that address prior conflicting legislation or sectoral regulatory regimes. In some cases, these problems have been partly mitigated by memoranda of understanding with other agencies as to respective roles and responsibilities.

Third, many agencies in developing countries face major obstacles in dealing with cross-border anticompetitive conduct, especially international cartels, and often lack formal and informal cooperative mechanisms with

---

nary support for the claim that competition law has a positive, albeit quite limited, effect on the intensity of competition within a nation. Much of the impact appears to be due to the strength of enforcement in particular areas rather than the scope of the substantive law, largely through reducing collusive practices. The study finds that merger or abuse of dominance law does not seem to enhance competition intensity. Keith N. Hylton & Fei Deng, *Antitrust around the World: An Empirical Analysis of the Scope of Competition Laws and Their Effects*, 74 Antitrust L.J. 271 (2007).

86   World Bank, *World Development Report 2002: Building Institutions for Markets* 141 (Oxford U. Press 2001).

87   International Competition Network, Implementation Working Group, *Lessons to Be Learnt from the Experiences of Young Competition Agencies* (May 2006).

88   Taimoon Stewart, Julilan Clarke, & Susan Joekes, *Competition Law in Action: Experiences from Developing Countries* (International Development Research Centre May 2007).

those countries' authorities that have more effective jurisdiction over potential wrongdoers.

Fourth, many agencies responding to the ICN survey pointed to numerous challenges relating to the interface between the competition authority and the judiciary and reported that cases often take years to process, partly as a result of a lack of specialized competence among public prosecutors, attorneys, and the local judiciary. An earlier ICN survey of competition agencies in developing and transition economies noted that

> the all but unanimous view expressed is that the judiciary is a major stumbling block in the path of effective competition enforcement—the judges do not understand competition law and are content to avoid the necessity to learn through diverting competition issues into a maze of esoteric administrative and procedural side-streets out of which the substantive matters at issue rarely emerge.[89]

Fifth, many new agencies suffer from extreme financial and human resource constraints that pose major challenges in priority setting, as well as political cronyism, which compromises the quality of key appointments. Developing and retaining specialized human capital within agencies and complementary educational and professional institutions are pressing challenges.[90]

Finally, the studies note the lack of a competition culture in many of the jurisdictions in which these new agencies operate, reflected in an unawareness of the rules of competition law among the business community, government agencies, nongovernment agencies, the media, the judiciary, and the general public. There is also a general ignorance of the overall responsibility to ensure that such rules are observed in the interest of competition and economic development. Many of these new agencies are operating in economies in transition from command to market-based economies, with major state-owned enterprises (SOEs) or recently privatized SOEs often operating in highly concentrated sectors. In many developing countries with long histories of state-led development policies and import substitution policies that severely restrict import competition and foreign investment, extensive state-owned enterprises and highly concentrated economic sectors are subject to extensive price, entry, and exit regulation, which implies that both within and outside government there are substantial vested interests that are antithetical to effective competition.[91] An earlier ICN report concluded:

---

89   International Competition Network Working Group, *Capacity Building and Technical Assistance: Building Credible Competition Authorities in Developing and Transition Economies* 35 (Jun. 23–25, 2003).

90   *See* Daniel Sokol, *The Development of Human Capital in Latin American Competition Policy*, in *Competition Law and Policy in Latin America* 13 (Eleanor Fox & Daniel Sokol ed., Hart 2009).

91   *See* Ignacio de Leon, *A Market Process Analysis of Latin American Competition Policy*, available at <http://papers.ssrn.com/sol3/papers.cfm?abstract_id=258959>.

> In the end, we have been persuaded that the over-arching challenge confronting competition authorities in developing and transition countries relates to their stature and standing within the ranks of key stakeholders or interest groups, as well as the public at large. In other words, all struggle to make themselves heard and it is this that constitutes the gravest challenge confronting competition authorities in these countries.[92]

I have reviewed elsewhere the empirical evidence on the efficacy of an instrumental (property rights/contract enforcement) conception of the rule of law and do not explore it here.[93] However, it is important to note here significant disconfirming evidence of the causal relationship between the rule of law and instrumental development outcomes, especially at relatively early stages of economic development. In particular, it is worth noting the so-called China enigma: over the past three decades China, has attracted enormous levels of domestic and foreign investment and recorded historically unprecedented growth rates, despite its mediocre rankings on conventional rule of law criteria.

Identifying Feasible Reform Strategies

Approaches to rule of law reforms that do not take into account adaptive behavior with respect to the particular institutional context, as well as mutually reinforcing effects among interdependent institutions, are unlikely to be successful. If one takes path dependence seriously, future reform strategies will be significantly constrained and shaped by the legacies of history. The lessons of path dependence lead to a conundrum because path dependence shows that isolated institutional reforms focused on microprocesses are likely to ignore both self-reinforcing mechanisms and institutional interdependencies, and are therefore often doomed to failure. However, systemwide ambitious reforms during "normal times" are also disruptive and likely to fail because of the serious switching costs that they are likely to entail (and the resistance that these will engender). Thus, despite institutional interdependencies, all-encompassing reforms are simply not feasible. This is true during normal times, and there seems to be evidence that even in postconflict societies (which may present more opportunities or at least greater urgency for change), all-encompassing reforms often achieve very limited success.[94]

Are reformers then left only with windows of opportunities (critical junctures) in which major reforms can be successfully implemented? Is there any

---

92 International Competition Network Working Group, *supra* note 89, at 74.

93 *See,* further, Michael Trebilcock & Paul-Erik Veel, *Property Rights and Development: The Contingent Case for Formalization,* 30 U. Pa. J. Intl. L. 397 (2008); Michael Trebilcock & Jing Leng, *The Role of Formal Contract Law and Enforcement in Economic Development,* 92 Va. L. Rev. 1517 (2006).

94 Marina Ottaway, *The Post-War "Democratic Reconstruction Model": Why It Can't Work,* Paper presented at United States Institute for Peace (2002).

way that reformers can take note of the lessons of path-dependence theory without being in a potentially eternal waiting period for the right moment? As Dani Rodrik puts it, "the challenge for the empirical literature on institutions is to explore these [path-dependent] patterns without falling into the trap of reductionism or of historical and geographical determinism."[95]

There are two potential (and complementary) strategies for dealing with this conundrum. First, reformers may be able to identify some institutions that can be more easily detached from a broader mutually reinforcing institutional matrix or be created de novo (such as semiautonomous revenue agencies, new constitutional or human rights courts or commissions, semi-independent regulatory agencies, or one-stop government agencies, like the Brazilian Poupatempo)[96] for issuing, for example, passports, driver's licenses, identification cards, and health cards, and providing alternative forms of dispute resolution.[97] This strategy may enable more ambitious stand-alone reforms that nevertheless have important showcase effects with lower switching costs or greater benefits than skeptics had assumed, although even here the experience with semiautonomous revenue and independent regulatory agencies suggests that these institutions are likely to be fragile in the absence of complementary reforms, over time, to the surrounding institutional matrix.

The second strategy is to reform existing institutions that are interconnected and mutually reinforcing by limiting reforms to certain core changes, followed in the future by complementary reforms to reinforce the initial efforts. This strategy implies that reforms should be incremental, which is quite different from many current reform practices that are either stand-alone or so sweeping as to be infeasible.

One of the lessons of path dependence is that we are not writing on a blank slate. It is true that in certain times, or at critical junctures—for example, the aftermath of economic collapse, civil war, or military invasion—the credibility and legitimacy of incumbent elites may be weakened, creating new political openings for marginalized constituencies.[98] At the same time, it is unlikely that all preexisting economic, social, and cultural factors that create

---

95   Dani Rodrik, *Feasible Globalizations*, KSG Working Paper Series RWP02-029, at 6-8 (2002), at <http://www.hks.harvard.edu/fs/drodrik/Research%20papers/Feasglob.pdf>. *See* also Dani Rodrik, *One Economics, Many Recipes: Globalization, Institutions, and Economic Growth* 153–92 (Princeton U. Press 2007); *see* also Francis Fukuyama, *Development and the Limits of Institutional Design*, in *Political Institutions and Development: Failed Expectations and Renewed Hopes* 21 (Natalia Dinello & Vladimir Popov ed., Edward Elgar 2007); Francis Fukuyama, *Statebuilding: Governance and World Order in the 21st Century* (Cornell U. Press 2004).

96   *See* Mariana Prado & Ana Carolina Charin, *Bureaucratic Reforms and Development: How Innovative Was the Poupatempo (Saving Time) Experience in Brazil?* (unpublished paper 2010) (copy on file with University of Toronto Faculty of Law).

97   *See* Heller, *supra* note 32; Mariana Prado, *Institutional Bypass: An Alternative to Development Reform* (unpublished paper 2010) (copy on file with University of Toronto Faculty of Law).

98   *See* Michael Trebilcock, *Journeys across the Divides*, in *The Origins of Law and Economics: Essays by the Founding Fathers* 422 (Francesco Parisi & Charles Rowley ed., Edward Elgar 2005).

costs for switching to new institutional regimes can be ignored[99] (as contemporary challenges to institutional reform in, for example, Iraq and Afghanistan exemplify). Not only should reformers recognize the importance of switching costs, but they should also be sensitive to the different kinds of switching costs associated with reform.[100]

First, in terms of political economy considerations, switching costs may be high for those who benefit from the institutional status quo[101] but may be mitigated by reforms that create or strengthen a countervailing political constituency that benefits.[102] Alternatively, vested interests may need to be "bought off" or grandfathered in some way to mute opposition. Second, switching costs may involve individual learning costs in adapting to a new regime (the "installed base" problem), although these can be lessened by state-sponsored public education programs and gradual processes of transition that avoid the need for abrupt adaptation to a new regime. Third, switching costs may reflect the scarcity of financial and human resources required to implement new institutional regimes, which can be alleviated by external financial and technical assistance. Finally, switching costs may include the disruption of deeply embedded cultural benefits or practices that are resistant to change.[103] Here, reforms that adapt traditional institutions (such as traditional forms of alternative dispute settlement or communal property rights) may moderate problems of cultural dissonance, and reforms implemented over time may lead to modifications in cultural belief systems.

In this respect, alternative dispute resolution (ADR) is a class of reforms that have shown significant promise, largely through demonstration effects. ADRs sometimes build on traditional or community-based forms of dispute settlement, such as adaptations of the Lok Adalat system in India, the Shalish system in Bangladesh, the Gacaca tribunals in Rwanda in the aftermath of years of civil war and genocide, the Casas de Justicia in Latin America, and alternative law groups in the Philippines.

---

99   This can be true even in postconflict societies; see Susan Rose-Ackerman, *Corruption and Post-Conflict Peace-Building*, 34 Ohio N.U.L. Rev. 405 (2008).

100 This section draws on the analysis developed in Ronald J. Daniels & Michael J. Trebilcock, *The Political Economy of Rule of Law Reform in Developing Countries*, 26 Mich. J. Intl. L. 99 (2004).

101 Resistance to reform can also be higher if there is uncertainty regarding the identity of potential beneficiaries. The uncertainty is higher in large-scale reforms. Dani Rodrik & Raquel Fernandez, *Resistance to Reform: Status Quo Bias in the Presence of Individual-Specific Uncertainty*, 81 Am. Econ. Rev. 1148 (1991).

102 How much instability these reforms should generate, that is, how much room for constant contestation would be good for future reforms, is a topic that deserves further research. For an insightful analysis, see Susan Rose-Ackerman, *Was Mancur a Maoist? An Essay on Kleptocracy and Political Stability*, 15 Eco. and Pol. 163 (2003).

103 *See*, for instance, how informal institutions for contract enforcement in the footwear industry resisted the changes brought by an open-trade regime when NAFTA was implemented in Mexico; Christopher Woodruff, *Contract Enforcement and Trade Liberalization in Mexico's Footwear Industry*, 26 World Development 979 (1998).

These ADRs have sought to marry indigenous methods of dispute settlement with broader rule of law norms such as equality before the law to
minimize cultural switching costs. In these cases, reformers have struggled to
navigate the difficult compromise between two sometimes conflicting models
of dispute resolution and the respective roles of the formal court system and
informal modes of dispute settlement. Despite these difficulties, these ADRs
have been shown to have a major benefit: they acknowledge and rely on
context-specific forms of institutional vindication or instantiation of rule of
law values, thereby reducing cultural switching costs and nurturing an increasingly robust domestic constituency for rule of law reforms over time. In
this sense, these reforms enable a broadly representative range of social, economic, and political interests to see that their concerns and values are aligned
with the promotion and preservation of the rule of law.

The Role of External Actors in Promoting Rule of Law Reform in Developing Countries

A tailored approach, overtly attentive to the domestic political context of the
countries in question, will enhance the likelihood of success of external efforts
at promoting rule of law reform in developing countries. If, as many have
persuasively argued, the rule of law is ultimately a political phenomenon,
such political attention only makes sense. In this regard, Daniels and I have
proposed a set of hypothetical political formulations with varying degrees of
support for rule of law reform that are useful in considering how reforms can
be sensitive to different political contexts.[104] These paradigmatic formations,
each of which can be related to real-life examples, will pose different kinds
of challenges for rule of law reformers and create a range of openings and
opportunities for an international role. Thus, the relative salience of each obstacle to reform discussed above will vary with each different formation (and
the almost infinite variations between them)—and with them, the role of the
international community.

The first stylized formation (Type I) is characterized by an environment of
broad political support for the rule of law. The state that Daniels and I envi-
sion has progressive-minded political leadership at the highest levels, strong
support from within the ruling party, and broad popular support for legal
reforms. The archetypal administration is that of Nelson Mandela in South
Africa, particularly in the early days after his election in 1994. Not only did
Mandela himself have a strong mandate, but public support for legal reform
was widespread as well. Another, perhaps more contentious, example is Lee
Kuan Yew, prime minister of Singapore from 1959 to 1990 and senior government minister thereafter, who was strongly committed to a highly competent,
meritocratic, noncorrupt public administration throughout his lengthy term
as prime minister, although the independence of the judiciary in cases involv-

---

104 Trebilcock & Daniels, *supra* note 10.

ing government officials has been more problematic. Additional examples include several countries in Central Europe following the collapse of the Soviet Union.

The second stylized formation (Type II) is more ambiguous in its support for rule of law reform. There is a strong desire for such reform at the highest political levels, but more systematic opposition from a variety of complex economic and social relationships operating below the political surface. This kind of opposition might be rooted, for instance, in an entrenched ideological orientation inconsistent with the rule of law, or in powerful public or private interests with a stake in a general state of lawlessness. These administrations will often be identifiable by the rise of a charismatic or prominent leader in a time of general political or economic turmoil. Somewhat ironic examples include Mikhail Gorbachev, Boris Yeltsin, and Vladimir Putin. At least in their early days, these leaders brought tremendous promise of reform, despite, among other problems, the meteoric rise of an oligarchic class of extraordinarily powerful organized criminals, rampant corruption, and the pervasive influence of communist ideology, which retained a not-insignificant degree of popular support.

The third stylized formation (Type III) is marked by a highly corrupt political leadership with strong incentives for maintaining the status quo and no predisposition to reform. In such states, there may be varying degrees of organized popular opposition in the form of NGO or other civil society activity, and there may be some degree of opposition from, or some tendency toward, or pockets of reform within, the leadership of some governing factions or government agencies. However, where the political leadership establishes any sort of lasting foothold, it will almost invariably have complex webs of support in military, administrative, or judicial branches of government, and often among some segments of the public. There are myriad examples of authoritarian and kleptocratic administrations to pick from, including the long-standing regime of Robert Mugabe as prime minister and then president of Zimbabwe, President Mobutu in Zaire, the Duvaliers in Haiti, and Saparmurat Niyazov, self-anointed "leader of the Turkmens," as president of Turkmenistan. Although these states will very often be undemocratic or authoritarian, it is not an absence of democracy per se but rather hostility to the rule of law that places an administration in this category. Governments with nominal election procedures in an otherwise repressive context may be hostile to rule of law reform—indeed, Mugabe is an example par excellence. More legitimate, popular elections may also produce governments hostile to many of the characteristics of the rule of law, as with the popular election of Yasser Arafat's Palestinian Authority in 1996.

There are several ways in which this trichotomy should be viewed as merely suggestive rather than exhaustive or definitive. First, the lines between these three categories are not strictly demarcated boundaries: states may slide in and out of each category as governments change policy and character over time. Moreover, ruling parties in any given state may have differing interests across different institutions and therefore support reform efforts in some institutions, and in some respects, but not in others. Second, there may be substantially different political formations within each category, with significant implications for rule of law reform prescriptions. The categories follow not the markings of democracy but rather those of the rule of law. Consequently, within each category, there are likely to be widely differing political contexts to which reformers (domestic and external) will have to be attentive when selecting appropriate strategies for reform. For instance, in states with authoritarian governments—even those generally in favor of reform—it may be difficult to pursue legal remedies against the state or its representatives in court proceedings (Singapore may be an example).

As one moves along the spectrum from Type I to Type III states, top-down, state-centric reform strategies become less feasible, and bottom-up, community-based reform strategies become a more promising option.

Type I States

In Type I states, where broad political and popular support for rule of law reform exists, the role of the international community should be focused most on alleviating resource constraints. Although sociocultural factors and various forms of vested interests may act as important barriers to reform, in these states, domestic governments, rather than the international community, will be best placed to address these concerns.

The preferred method of intervention in the most favorable (although admittedly rare) cases should be unconditional aid, again leaving to the domestic government the choice of reform priorities and strategies and sources of technical advice, unless for credible commitment and signaling purposes the recipient government requests conditionality. The "mallet"-like political pressure of accession conditions on membership in regional or multilateral economic or political associations will play little fruitful role, because the state is already generally politically aligned with the viewpoint of reformers. Similarly, because trade policy (preferences or sanctions) does not direct new resources to rule of law initiatives, it will be irrelevant in these circumstances. Due to their punitive nature, economic sanctions are entirely misplaced.

Although there is a case for conditional aid in more equivocal cases, it is important to emphasize that government policy may be fluid, and that strongly pro reform administrations can shift policies quickly, particularly when they come to power in a period of transition or during a key "constitutional moment." Donors must therefore be vigilant in monitoring the trajectory of Type I governments and enforcing conditions where appropriate—a historical weakness of development agencies.

The funding of nonstate drivers of rule of law reform such as local NGOs can play a role in these states, as it can in almost any situation. However, in these cases, NGOs that cooperate with, rather than oppose, government policies are likely to be more effective.

Type II States

In states with generally reform-minded political leadership but with a less secure political base and widespread opposition from vested interests within state agencies, including legal institutions and perhaps private sector parties who benefit from dysfunctional public institutions, a more diverse set of strategies will be necessary. In these cases, resources may be scarce, but international agencies or external donors cannot responsibly commit to unconditional aid. Even where high-level political leadership supports reform, increased aid flows to antagonistic public or legal institutions can be misdirected and wasted or used for regressive purposes. Governments truly committed to reform may agree to conditional aid that binds them to a policy and protects them from internal special interests. A case can be made for conditionality through accession or trade preferences on similar grounds. Also, there may be a good case for nonstate-led reforms through local NGOs or alternative law groups operating more independently than the state in institutional contexts in which independence of legal institutions is likely to be problematic.

Type III States

Governments unequivocally opposed to rule of law reform will rarely be sensitive to state-level pressure mechanisms such as trade or other economic sanctions and forms of conditionality attached to aid, debt relief, trade preferences, or accession to regional or multilateral economic or political associations. As Ernest Preeg argues in respect to U.S. sanctions (such as denial of most-favored-nation trading status) against China, "the basic reason why these unilateral economic sanctions are ineffective is that the foreign policy objective is to change the oppressive behavior of an authoritarian or totalitarian government, which constitutes a direct threat to its control if not survival."[105] Although U.S. sanctions in this instance were intended to stimulate democracy more than the rule of law, the point is the same.

In these cases, the role of nonstate actors should become a central aspect of rule of law reform efforts, with a particular focus on local and international NGOs developing reforms independent of state agencies and on providing financial and technical assistance to these groups. In China and Laos, NGOs have played an important role as de facto monitoring mechanisms for correctional institutions where the state has denied access to formal state-level monitoring channels. Properly designed and implemented nonstate dispute-resolution mechanisms, often based on traditional forms of community-based dispute settlement, can also be a vital element of access to justice in circumstances in which courts suffer from chronic backlog, corruption, or bias and hence a lack of legitimacy.

---

105 Ernest H. Preeg, *Feeling Good or Doing Good with Sanctions: Unilateral Economic Sanctions and the US National Interest* 201 (Center for Strategic and International Studies 1999).

Conclusion

States may evolve either negatively or positively from one stylized type to another in the foregoing typology, requiring the international community continually to reassess its rule of law reform promotion strategies and to readjust its menu of strategies accordingly. However, even acknowledging this fact, and acknowledging further that all desirable rule of law reforms cannot be realistically embarked upon simultaneously, if only because of resource constraints, even in the most favorable (Type I) political environments, issues of prioritization and sequencing will invariably arise. Although these issues must largely be resolved by domestic constituencies committed to rule of law reform, as must the particular forms of institutional vindication or instantiation of rule of law values, nurturing over time an increasingly robust domestic constituency for the rule of law that reflects a demand-side perspective requires that a genuinely representative range of social, economic, and political interests come to see that their concerns and values are compatible with the promotion and preservation of the rule of law.

In this respect, I (along with others) question the aptness of the relatively high priority that the international community has often accorded to formal judicial reform in the rule of law initiatives that it has promoted in developing countries in recent years.[106] This is often accompanied by a relative lack of attention to institutional reforms that are more likely to affect the day-to-day interactions of the citizenry with the legal system, such as police, prosecutors, and specialized law enforcement and administrative agencies, including agencies of government that issue, for example, passports, driver's licenses, identification cards, health cards, building permits, and business licenses.[107] These institutional reforms also would include access-to-justice initiatives such as informal community-based dispute-resolution mechanisms (often reflecting adaptations to and elaborations of traditional dispute-settlement mechanisms), through which more visible and immediate material benefits from successful institutional reform are likely to be experienced by a wide cross-section of the citizenry. Recent civil justice needs surveys of representative samples of the population in a number of developed countries[108] provide helpful examples of instruments for identifying the relative frequency and shortcomings of citizen interactions with state agencies.

---

106   *See* Carothers, *supra* note 28; Stephen Golub, *A House without Foundation*, in *Promoting the Rule of Law Abroad: In Search of Knowledge* 105 (Thomas Carothers ed., Carnegie Endowment for International Peace 2006); Bryant Garth, *Building Strong and Independent Judiciaries for the New Law and Development: Beyond the Paradox of Consensus Programs and Perpetually Disappointing Results*, 52 DePaul L. Rev. 383 (2002–03).

107   Famously described by Charles Reich as "the new property," Charles A. Reich, *The New Property*, 73 Yale L.J. 733 (1964); lack of effective access to which in many developing countries is equally famously described by Hernando De Soto in *The Other Path*, *supra* note 4, and is increasingly well documented in various reports in the World Bank's "Doing Business" surveys.

108   *See*, for example, Jamie Baxter, Michael Trebilcock, & Albert Yoon, *The Ontario Civil Needs Project: A Comparative Analysis of the 2009 Survey Data* (unpublished paper Aug. 27, 2010) (copy on file with University of Toronto Faculty of Law).

Although the success of institutional reforms in one context ultimately often depends, to an important extent, on complementary institutional reforms in other contexts,[109] not everything can be pursued at once. Judicial reforms (and reforms to legal education) are likely to have longer-term and less visible social payoffs to citizens at large and hence are less likely to engage their interest and support than other reforms noted above, given the many more pressing and immediate survival challenges citizens in developing countries often face. Thus, both domestic and international proponents of rule of law reform in developing countries face a hitherto underacknowledged challenge of rendering rule of law reform politically salient to most citizens of these countries. Strategic choices on sequencing are important in addressing this challenge.

---

109 *See* Rachel Kleinfeld, *Competing Definitions of the Rule of Law: Implications for Practitioners*, Carnegie Endowment for International Peace Working Paper No. 55 (2005).

Rethinking Justice Reform in Fragile and Conflict-Affected States

The Capacity of Development Agencies and Lessons from Liberia and Afghanistan

DEVAL DESAI, DEBORAH ISSER, AND MICHAEL WOOLCOCK

> *In order to truly address the problems afflicting post-conflict countries, donors must not settle for superficial, humbug solutions. Instead, they must presume that a problem they are encountering here is unique and idiosyncratic, presume it is incredibly complex and nuanced, and presume it is nowhere close to monolithic and that the symptoms in one part of the country or in one part of the world must stem from entirely different pathologies than those working to create the same symptoms in another part. At a minimum, such presumptions will force donors to do the foundational diligence that is truly necessary to accomplish sustainable change.*
>
> — Christiana Tah, minister of justice, Liberia[1]

Introduction: Justice and Conflict[2]

There is broad and growing recognition across a range of development actors that fragile and conflict-affected states (FCSs) pose particular development challenges; indeed, they are a key development challenge of the coming decade. Home to approximately 1.5 billion people, FCSs contain many of the world's poorest and most vulnerable. People in FCSs are more than twice as likely to be undernourished as those in other developing countries, more than three times as likely to be unable to send their children to school, twice as likely to see their children die before the age of five, and more than twice as likely to lack clean water. No low-income FCS has yet achieved a single Millennium Development Goal.[3]

---

1   From a presentation delivered by Christiana Tah to the World Bank's Law, Justice, and Development Week 2010 in Washington, DC. *See* Abdul Salam Azimi and Christiana Tah, *Justice Development Programming in Fragile and Conflict-Affected Areas: Perspectives of Two Leaders in Justice Administration,* 15 Justice and Development Working Paper Series 1, 12 (2011).

2   This chapter draws on Deval Desai & Caroline Sage, *Justice,* an Input Paper for the *World Development Report 2011* (Nov. 5, 2010), available at <http://wdr2011.worldbank.org/justice>, and presentations made by Minister of Justice Tah of Liberia, Chief Justice Azimi of Afghanistan, Michael Woolcock (World Bank), and Pablo de Greiff (International Center for Transitional Justice) at the World Bank's Law, Justice and Development Week, Washington, DC, November 2010.

3   World Bank, *World Development Report 2011: Conflict, Security and Development* 2–6 (World Bank 2011) ("WDR2011").

Multilateral development groups and organizations have highlighted FCSs in their recent strategies: the Organisation for Economic Co-operation and Development (OECD) Development Asisistance Committee (OECD-DAC) has convened the International Network on Conflict and Fragility (INCAF), which has developed a series of materials and guidance notes designed to improve involvement—or reduce the harm of "poorly-conceived involvement"—in these "most challenging [of] development situations." Such states "face severe development challenges such as lack of security, weak governance, limited administrative capacity, chronic humanitarian crises, persistent social tensions, violence or the legacy of civil war."[4] The United Nations Development Programme (UNDP),[5] the African Development Bank,[6] and the European Commission[7] have followed suit, seeking improved donor engagement in FCSs. Bilateral donors—including the British,[8] Dutch,[9] French,[10] and German governments[11]—have also taken clear positions on FCSs as a priority development challenge.

As development actors have directed their attention toward FCSs, there has been a concomitant burgeoning recognition of the importance of laws, norms, and justice institutions in meeting the particular challenges posed by such situations. The president of the World Bank, Robert Zoellick, has argued that "a fundamental prerequisite for sustainable development [in FCSs] is an effective rule of law," using this as a rallying cry for broader development engagement in justice reform in FCSs:

---

4   OECD-INCAF, About the Fragile States Principles, available at <http://www.oecd.org/document/40/0,3746,en_21571361_42277499_42283112_1_1_1_1,00.html>. See also OECD-DAC, Principles for Good International Engagement in Fragile States and Situations (Apr. 2007), available at <http://www.oecd.org/dataoecd/61/45/38368714.pdf>.

5   Executive Board of the United Nations Development Programme and of the United Nations Population Fund, Role of UNDP in Crisis and Post-conflict Situations, UN Doc. DP/2001/4 (2000), available at <http://www.undp.org/execbrd/pdf/dp01-4.PDF>.

6   African Development Fund, Strategy for Enhanced Engagement in Fragile States (Jan. 2008), available at <http://www.afdb.org/fileadmin/uploads/afdb/Documents/Policy-Documents/30736191-EN-STRATEGY-FOR-ENHANCED-ENGAGEMENT-IN-FRAGILES-STATES.PDF>.

7   European Commission, Communication from the Commission to the Council, the European Parliament, the European Economic and Social Committee and the Committee of the Region, Towards an EU Response to Situations of Fragility: Engaging in Difficult Environments for Sustainable Development, Stability and Peace, SEC (2007) 1417, available at <http://ec.europa.eu/europeaid/what/education/documents/eu_communication_situations_of_fragility_en.pdf>.

8   Department for International Development, Building Peaceful States and Societies: A DFID Practice Paper (2010), available at <http://www.dfld.,gov.uk/Documents/publications1/governance/Building-peaceful-states-and-societies.pdf>.

9   Ministry of Foreign Affairs (Development Cooperation), Our Common Concern: Investing in Development in a Changing World (2007), available at <http://www.minbuza.nl/dsresource?objectid=buzabeheer:32207&type=pdf>.

10   France Coopération, Fragile States and Situations of Fragility: France's Policy Paper (2007), available at <http://www.diplomatie.gouv.fr/en/IMG/pdf/EtatsFragiles-2.pdf>.

11   Federal Ministry for Economic Cooperation and Development, Development-Oriented Transformation in Conditions of Fragile Statehood and Poor Government Performance (2007), available at <http://www.oecd.org/dataoecd/4/38/43480415.pdf>.

> A legal order is a safeguard against the serious risk of criminalisation of the state. Corruption adds to fragility and undermines legitimacy. Abuse of state power destroys confidence, and ultimately the state's core purpose. Building the rule of law is also vital to public safety—poorly trained and paid police usually add to fragility by arming and empowering predators. In much of Afghanistan, the greatest security fear for businesspeople is kidnapping, often by the police.[12]

Most recently, this entreaty was taken up by *World Development Report 2011: Conflict, Security and Development* (hereafter WDR "2011"),[13] which tackles the development challenges presented by FCSs. Building on the work of North, Wallis, and Weingast, and others,[14] the WDR 2011 highlights justice as one of three key areas (the others being security and jobs) on which donors should focus in order to build effective and sustainable transitions out of situations characterized by endemic conflict and fragility.[15]

However, while legal, regulatory, and justice institutions are now seen as an important part of the solution to problems of conflict, fragility, and development, this recognition is not matched by a correspondingly clear sense of what should be done, how it should be done, by whom, in what order, or how success may be determined. Nor is this a new problem. The effort to forge theories and operational models on the role of justice initiatives in laying a path out of fragility must build on the experiences of the constituent fields of conflict and development: the former, a field that has been the domain of those engaged in rule of law reform as a component of state building in countries emerging from conflict,[16] the latter the domain of actors concerned primarily with economic growth. Both fields have struggled with a similar conundrum: on the one hand, there is a broad North-South, left-right consensus that justice, or rule of law, is key to achieving their respective goals; and on the other hand, a recognition that surefire ways of achieving rule of law remain elusive.[17]

---

12 Robert Zoellick, *Fragile States: Securing Development*, 50 Survival 67, 75–76 (2008).

13 *Supra* note 3.

14 *See* Douglass North, John Joseph Wallis, & Barry Weingast, *Violence and Social Orders* (Cambridge U. Press 2009). *See* also Douglass North, *Institutions, Institutional Change, and Economic Performance* 54 (Cambridge U. Press 1990) (claiming that the absence of a low-cost means of enforcing contracts is "the most important source of both historical stagnation and contemporary underdevelopment in the Third World"); Dani Rodrik, Arvind Subramanian, & Francesco Trebbi, *Institutions Rule: The Primacy of Institutions over Geography and Integration in Economic Development*, 9 J. Econ. Growth 131 (2004).

15 *Supra* note 3.

16 *See* Kirsti Samuels, *Rule of Law Reform in Post-conflict Countries: Operational Initiatives and Lessons Learnt*, World Bank Social Development Papers: Conflict Prevention and Reconstruction No. 37, 4–6 (2006), available at <http://siteresources.worldbank.org/INTCPR/Resources/WP37_web.pdf> (arguing that, save multilateral assistance to post-Soviet transition countries, the majority of rule of law work in FCSs has been carried out by USAID and the United Nations Department of Peacekeeping Operations).

17 Thomas Carothers, *Promoting the Rule of Law Abroad: The Problem of Knowledge*, Carnegie Paper No. 34, 6–7 (2003). *See* also Brian Tamanaha, *On the Rule of Law: History, Politics, Theory* 127–37 (Cambridge U. Press 2004); Rachel Kleinfeld, *Competing Definitions of the Rule of Law*,

This chapter contributes to the discourse of justice (or rule of law) reform in FCSs in the following way: while other critiques have focused on extremely important failings of planning, technique, and execution (such as inadequate donor coordination, a lack of readily available and appropriately skilled international personnel, and excessively curtailed time horizons),[18] this chapter seeks to *problematize the conceptual underpinnings of justice reform efforts*. This chapter begins by exploring the conceptual bases and corresponding operationalization of the two dominant paradigms of justice reform—that of rule of law linked to state building, and that of justice reform linked to economic growth. Using the examples of Liberia and Afghanistan, the chapter examines the shortcomings of these models. It explores a *lack of capacity*, not in the traditional sense of technical expertise on the part of actors in countries, but on the part of donors to understand those countries and contexts in which they are working and to support processes that lead to sustainable change. The chapter seeks not to lessen or discount the vital importance and legitimacy of national policymakers but to problematize donor action, arguing that failings in justice programs can often be traced to the predilection of development actors to treat challenges requiring fundamental changes in people's attitudes, perceptions, values, and behavior (as governance and legal reform invariably does) as variants on technical problems that focus on—in Minister Tah's words— "superficial, humbug solutions."[19]

The current convergence of the two fields—state building and development—may present an opportunity to rethink conceptual underpinnings of justice reform efforts at the nexus of conflict and development, leading to more successful operational approaches. The latter part of the chapter explores the dynamic that may ensue from a convergence of these two fields and offers ways to avoid mutual negative reinforcement of the two models that could result in "securitizing"[20] the approach of development actors, overemphasizing existential threats to development goals, and undermining broader considerations of the state-society compact on which the efficacy of any institutional reform effort ultimately turns.

---

in *Promoting the Rule of Law Abroad: In Search of Knowledge* 31 (Thomas Carothers ed., Carnegie Endowment for International Peace 2006). *See, generally, Promoting the Rule of Law Abroad: In Search of Knowledge* (Thomas Carothers ed., Carnegie Endowment for International Peace 2006); Richard E. Messick, *Judicial Reform and Economic Development: A Survey of the Issues*, 14 World Bank Research Observer 117 (1999); Samuels, *supra* note 16; and Stephan Haggard, Andrew MacIntyre, & Lydia Tiede, *The Rule of Law and Economic Development*, 11 Annual Rev. Pol. Science 205 (2008).

18   Samuels, *supra* note 16; World Bank: Report on Headline Seminar, Rule of Law in Fragile and Conflict-Affected Situations (Jul. 21, 2009), available at <http://siteresources.worldbank .org/EXTLICUS/Resources/511777-1224016350914/5474500-1257528293370/Final_Report _H3-Rule_of_Law_July_21_09.pdf>.

19   Azimi & Teh, *supra* note 1. *See, generally*, Lant Pritchett & Michael Woolcock, *Solutions When the Solution Is the Problem: Arraying the Disarray in Development*, 32(2) World Development 191 (2004).

20   Ole Waever, *Securitization and Desecuritization*, in *On Security* 46 (Ronnie Lipschutz ed., Columbia U. Press 1995).

The (In)capacity of Concepts and Models

The elevation of the rule of law to the status of a sine qua non for peace and development has occurred on two tracks that, although parallel, have remained largely discrete. One track emerged in the 1990s as the United Nations experienced an unprecedented demand for peace interventions, from Haiti to the Balkans, El Salvador to East Timor. As mission mandates took on ever more ambitious tasks of civilian administration, the justice components of those mandates quickly grew from police reform to reform of all components of the criminal and civil justice system. The fundamental importance of the rule of law to the project of post-conflict state building was set out by the secretary-general of the United Nations in 2004, in a document that embodies the paradigm that this chapter calls the "state-building" model. The document sets out a definition of the rule of law that equates it with a political system with substantive content—a state that generates, promulgates, and is ruled by laws that fulfill certain technical *and normative* criteria:

> [The rule of law] refers to a principle of governance in which all persons, institutions and entities, public and private, including the State itself, are accountable to laws that are publicly promulgated, equally enforced and independently adjudicated, and which are consistent with international human rights norms and standards. It requires, as well, measures to ensure adherence to the principles of supremacy of law, equality before the law, accountability to the law, fairness in the application of the law, separation of powers, participation in decision-making, legal certainty, avoidance of arbitrariness and procedural and legal transparency.[21]

The UNDP further defines the primary modality of the rule of law in its clear nexus with security and recurrence of conflict: "Conflicts may be caused by or result in the breakdown of law and order, or a collapse of state institutions. Preventive measures can be taken to help strengthen local capacity to prevent conflict occurring and to support the institutional structures that support dispute resolution and democratic governance. Strengthening the rule of law can be a critical tool for conflict prevention."[22] As a result, the UNDP takes a state-centric approach, placing national institutions at the center of its model: "the initial focus needs to be on building the capacity of national institutions and stakeholders to prevent and bring an end to violations, insecurity and impunity through their own capacity and resilience."[23] In this way, the rule of law, as a way of defining and constraining state power and of containing and managing disputes, is linked to the aims and ends of state building: the rule of law is intrinsically tied to the construction of a functioning state

---

21 The Rule of Law and Transitional Justice in Conflict and Post-conflict Societies: Report of the Secretary-General, at 4, UN Doc. S/2004/616 (2004).

22 UNDP Bureau for Crisis Prevention and Recovery, The Rule of Law in Fragile and Post-conflict Situations 1 (2009), available at <http://www.undp.org/cpr/documents/jssr/rol_concept_note_july09.pdf>.

23 *Id.*, at 7.

and—through its ability to contain conflict—is part of the establishment of a monopoly over violence. Consequently, justice interventions in this paradigm focus primarily on strengthening the capacity of state law-and-order institutions while bringing substantive laws into compliance with international human rights standards.

The second dominant approach to rule of law reform began even earlier, with origins commonly attributed to the law and development movement of the 1960s and 1970s. This "economic development" paradigm seeks to enhance the quality of the legal underpinnings deemed necessary to support inclusive economic growth. Most commonly associated with the World Bank but broadly reflecting neoclassical economic orthodoxy, this approach stresses the importance to growth of legal concerns such as property rights, contract enforcement, and judicial predictability and efficiency. This paradigm is distinct from the state-building one in terms of nomenclature: it uses the term "justice" to encapsulate a range of issues that would likely fall under the rubric of "rule of law reform" when considered by state-building actors. Its approach is also substantively distinct. While the Bank has long shared the United Nations' "belief that reconstructing countries devastated by warfare [is] an international responsibility,"[24] it has consistently used a strictly economic—rather than political—lens to examine the role of law and justice. According to Eugene Meyer, the first head of the World Bank:

> Prosperity, like peace, must . . . be viewed as indivisible. And even from the narrowest considerations of self-interest, each of us must be concerned with the economic development of the world as a whole. For we shall prosper individually only as we prosper collectively.
>
> But there are even larger considerations than material welfare which dictate our recognition of the world's essential unity. Economic distress is a prime breeder of war; it makes for a desperation from which aggression seems the only avenue of escape. . . . We are engaged in the first large-scale, practical implementation of the United Nations spirit. . . . Our endeavor is a concrete test of the capacity of nations to work cooperatively toward the solution of a specific common problem.[25]

The economic development paradigm consequently focuses predominantly on the role and functioning of justice institutions, many of which enable market activity, and the locus of which is generally the nation-state

---

24   World Bank, World Development Report 2011: Concept Note i (2010), available at <http://siteresources.worldbank.org/EXTWDR2011/Resources/6406082-1256239015781/WDR_2011_Concept_Note_0207.pdf>.

25   International Bank for Reconstruction and Development, First Annual Meeting of the Board of Governors: Proceedings and Related Documents 15–16 (World Bank 1946).

(given the mandate and history of the Bank and the fact that its members are states-parties).[26] Functioning legal frameworks and institutions may be seen as developmental goods in themselves, allowing people to uphold and exercise their rights.[27] More important, in this paradigm, they are also instrumental in realizing a range of other development goals: without justice, people cannot easily receive or access public goods and basic services, nor can they effectively access a range of markets.[28]

It is important to note that these two paradigms are, of course, stylized, and as such gloss over internal differences and pluralities among agencies and donors. There is both heuristic and narrative utility in boiling down the complex conceptual, political, and organizational underpinnings of these two broad approaches to justice reform as state building and economic development. Both the heuristic and narrative values can be seen in figure 1, which forms part of the Capstone Doctrine of the United Nations' Department for Peacekeeping Operations.[29] The Capstone Doctrine, which was devised by the UN Peacekeeping Best Practices Section, is an attempt to outline the fundamental principles and core objectives of peacekeeping in response to new challenges, as a revamp of the General Guidelines on UN Peacekeeping issued in 1995.[30] It thus forms both a useful analytical tool and a narrative around which to structure interventions, and clearly shows the division that actors have seen between state building and economic development.

---

26 Alvaro Santos, *The World Bank's Uses of the "Rule of Law" Promise in Economic Development*, in *The New Law and Economic Development: A Critical Appraisal* 253 (David M. Trubek & Alvaro Santos ed., Cambridge U. Press 2006). *See*, generally, Stephen Humphreys, *Theatre of the Rule of Law: Transnational Legal Intervention in Theory and Practice* 131–49 (Cambridge U. Press 2010). On the role of nonstate justice institutions, *see infra*; *see* also Varun Gauri, *How Do Local-Level Legal Institutions Promote Development?* World Bank Policy Research Working Paper 5108 (2009).

27 Amartya Sen, *What Is the Role of Legal and Judicial Reform in the Development Process?* 2 World Bank Legal Rev. 33 (2005).

28 *See*, generally, Amartya Sen, *Development as Freedom* (Oxford U. Press 2001); *see* also, on the importance of customary and formal law and norms to land market access, Klaus Deininger, *Land Policy Reforms*, in *Analyzing the Distributional Impact of Reforms: A Practitioners' Guide to Trade, Monetary and Exchange Rate Policy, Utility Provision, Agricultural Markets, Land, and Education* vol. 1, 213 (Aline Coudouel & Stefano Paternostro ed., World Bank 2005).

29 United Nations, Department for Peacekeeping Operations, *United Nations Peacekeeping Operations: Principles and Guidelines* (United Nations 2008) (hereafter "Capstone Doctrine").

30 Jean Marie-Guéhenno, Under-Secretary-General for Peacekeeping Operations, Remarks to the Fourth Committee of the General Assembly (Oct. 19, 2006), available at <http://www.un.org/en/peacekeeping/articles/article191006.html>.

Figure 1[31]

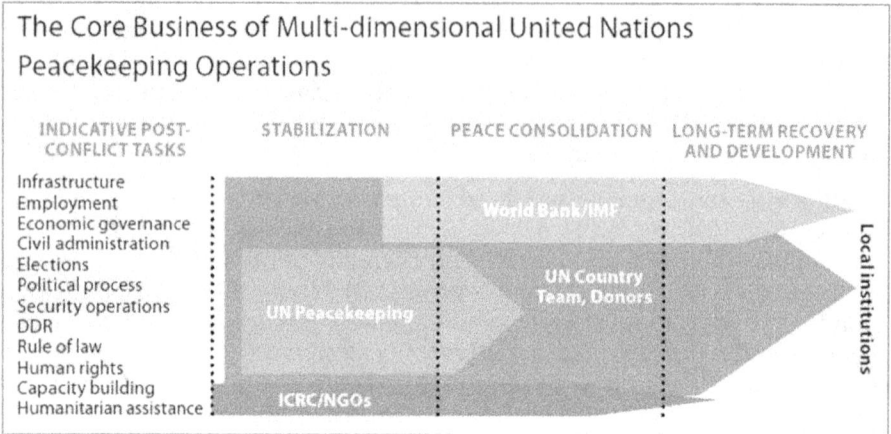

The Core Business of Multi-dimensional United Nations Peacekeeping Operations

| INDICATIVE POST-CONFLICT TASKS | STABILIZATION | PEACE CONSOLIDATION | LONG-TERM RECOVERY AND DEVELOPMENT |

Infrastructure
Employment
Economic governance
Civil administration
Elections
Political process
Security operations
DDR
Rule of law
Human rights
Capacity building
Humanitarian assistance

World Bank/IMF

UN Country Team, Donors

UN Peacekeeping

ICRC/NGOs

Local institutions

Models

While the paradigms highlighted here may differ in terms of stylized philosophical underpinnings, there are distinct similarities in the models[32] used to apply those underpinnings to real-world situations. This section examines four ways that these paradigms are translated into operational models that exhibit similar features and suffer from similar flaws: state-centrism, organizational isomorphism, short time frames, and linear trajectories of change. This analysis draws on two key arguments made by Pritchett and Woolcock[33] regarding conceptual failures of development practice. First, that the goal of much of development is "to ensure that the provision of key services . . . is assured by effective, rules based, meritocratic, and politically accountable public agencies—that is, something resembling Weberian bureaucracies."[34] Second, that the problems associated with realizing this objective are compounded by "skipping straight to Weber"; that is, an "attempt to remedy problems of 'inadequate services' by calling upon a centralized bureaucracy to supply a top-down and uniform public service," providing "a technical (supply) solution . . . implemented by an impersonal, rules driven, provider." In doing so, development actors give short shrift to a key link in the implementation chain, namely, those ongoing, face-to-face "interactions between citizens, the state, and providers" that

---

31   *Supra* note 29, at 23.

32   We acknowledge those who would seek to limit the use of the word "model" and draw a keen distinction between it and "ideology." *See* Joel M. Ngugi, *The World Bank and the Ideology of Reform and Development in International Economic Development Discourse*, 14 Cardozo J. Intl. & Comp. L. 313, 319–23 (2007). We use the term in a much more general sense here, as an attempt to refer to organizing logics that might be ascribed to families of intervention.

33   Pritchett & Woolcock, *supra* note 19, at 191.

34   *Id.,* at 192.

necessarily entail deep contextual knowledge, adaptive strategies, and engagement beyond institutional forms.[35]

State-Centrism

As established above, state-building and economic development practitioners generally place state institutions at the center of their justice reform work in FCSs (although the expressions of this can differ, with the former placing a greater emphasis on the monopoly over violence[36] and the latter engaging with aspects of institutions that support economic development and service delivery).[37] In general, there is good reason to support the tradition of political philosophy and policy that holds that state-backed formal institutions are a desirable means to a range of development ends, including security, political participation, and economic growth.[38] However, an exclusive focus on state institutions as the appropriate form promoting capable legal and regulatory institutions may miss the mark. In many FCSs, these institutions are either decimated or captured by political, criminal, or other interests, and may be inaccessible owing to economic, political, geographic, or linguistic factors. State institutions in such contexts characteristically lack infrastructure or institutional capacity, and can be remote, unaffordable, delayed, and seen as unfair, incomprehensible, and/or a foreign imposition, thus effectively denying legal protection to ordinary people. In many countries, customary systems operating outside the state regime are often the dominant form of regulation and site of dispute resolution. For example, in Sierra Leone about 85 percent of the population is predominantly governed by customary law; with a population of approximately 5 million people, the country had an estimated 125 legally trained personnel in 2003, 95 percent of whom were based in the capital, Freetown.[39] According to the Liberian minister of justice, in the aftermath of the ravaging civil war,

> [l]egal institutions barely functioned as many of the well educated and well trained citizens in law enforcement and the law fled the country in the 1990s. The few who remained in the country tried to provide a semblance of law and order, but were often threatened into submission, leaving citizens very distrustful of the formal legal system. Corruption among judges and other public officials became more prevalent than in the past, due to the fact that civil servants regularly received meager salaries several months in arrears. Ultimately, the formal justice system virtually collapsed and, consequently, most citizens (educated and uneducated) resorted to the

---

35   *Id.*, at 193.

36   UNDP, Evaluation of UNDP Assistance to Conflict-Affected Countries vii, 57 (2006), available at <http://www.undp.org/execbrd/pdf/f_EO_Conflict.pdf>.

37   *Supra* note 14.

38   *See,* generally, WDR 2011.

39   Paul James-Allen, *Accessing Justice in Rural Sierra Leone: A Civil Society Response,* Open Society Justice Initiatives: Legal Aid Reform and Access to Justice 57 (Feb. 2004).

informal justice system as a viable alternative. In a few instances, vigilante justice or mob violence prevailed.[40]

The existence of plural legal orders is not just a question of access; they may also be hotly contested political arenas with deep implications for the allocation of power, mechanisms of social accountability, governance structures, and the ethnic and ideological identity of the state. In Afghanistan, for example, efforts by the Kabul government to expand its reach to areas traditionally governed by nonstate justice systems—*jirgas* and *shuras*—have historically been met with hostile resistance that threatened state legitimacy and control.[41] In Liberia, while "progressive" voices call for the elimination of customary justice systems as a means of remedying the historical legacy of discrimination, many citizen users of customary justice consider the idea of a single (formal) justice system for all Liberians to be a further unwanted imposition of a Monrovia-based elite.[42] In such situations, external interventions that focus exclusively on state institutions are seen as—and indeed are—political choices with considerable consequences.

In recent years, the state-building approach has moved discursively to embrace the importance of nonstate justice systems.[43] The nature of this rhetorical engagement is, in its weaker form, disconnected; that is, nonstate justice systems are a "thing" to be engaged with, with strategies of engagement remaining ad hoc. In its stronger form, engagement is still underpinned by state-centrism; nonstate institutions are to be harmonized or embedded organizationally (through laws and structural reforms) and normatively (through the transmission and enforcement of human rights norms) into the state system.[44] Justice actors therefore focus on "entry points" for the transformation of such systems along a state-centric model.[45]

This trend has been mirrored in the literature on economic development. Recognition of the importance of nonstate systems has been rhetorical (e.g., accounting for them discursively as "alternative dispute resolution" alongside

---

40   Azimi & Tah, *supra* note 1, at 8–9.

41   Thomas Barfield, Neamat Nojumi, & J. Alexander Thier, *The Clash of Two Goods: State and Non-state Dispute Resolution in Afghanistan*, in *Customary Justice and the Rule of Law in War-Torn Societies* (Deborah H. Isser ed., USIP Press, forthcoming 2011).

42   Deborah H. Isser, Stephen C. Lubkemann, & Saah N'Tow, *Looking for Justice: Liberian Experiences with and Perceptions of Local Justice Options*, USIP Peaceworks No. 63 (Nov. 2009).

43   *See* Strengthening and Coordinating United Nations Rule of Law Activities: Report of the Secretary-General, at 11, UN Doc. A/63/226 (2008). *See*, generally, Ewa Wojkowska, *Doing Justice: How Informal Justice Systems Can Contribute* (UNDP Oslo Governance Centre 2006).

44   Deborah H. Isser, *The Problem with Problematizing Legal Pluralism*, in *Legal Pluralism and the Future of Development: Dialogues for Success* (Caroline Sage, Brian Tamanaha, & Michael Woolcock ed., Cambridge U. Press, forthcoming 2012).

45   Wojkowska, *supra* note 43.

other nonstate systems such as commercial arbitration).[46] In its more muscular state-centric form, the literature has pressed for harmonization and formalization as a means of providing economic goods: Hernando de Soto's call for the formalization of customary land rights as a means to develop an asset base for the poor can be seen in this light.[47]

Unless the conceptual underpinnings of both justice paradigms shift away from state institutions as the answer, these trends will run into the same problems as their orthodox antecedents: an overemphasis on particular *forms* rather than on the actual *functions* they are meant to perform. Rather than starting with predetermined notions of the "right" institutional formulation, an alternative conception of an array of justice institutions starts with an analysis of the prevailing justice needs of citizens; the ways in which the various institutions mediate power, rights, and accountability; and the process through which such institutions can be made to deliver justice more fairly and effectively. As Minister Tah puts it, assume that every situation is "unique and idiosyncratic," "incredibly complex and nuanced."[48]

Organizational Isomorphism

The second key feature underpinning both paradigms is the presumption that inputs, incentives, and information deemed successful by experts in one context will work in the same way elsewhere; or, put differently, that a particular organization's functionality (what it does) is a product of its design (what it looks like), thereby justifying the transplanting of best practices (e.g., a given country's constitution or commercial code) from one context to another. This phenomenon follows closely from the first feature: the assumption of state-centrism is itself a form of isomorphism. Isomorphism further encompasses the limited engagement with social context on the part of donors and derives from stylized views of the relationship between individual and society. An alternative approach is rooted in the notion that institutions are instead *intersubjectively constructed*; that is, communities build shared understandings through social interaction of what an institution is, what it does, and how it should be assessed and (where necessary) improved.[49] For example, in the context of Liberia, legalized notions of human rights—such as the right to a fair trial—while important, may not "automatically assuage the concerns and

---

46 *See,* for example, International Council on Human Rights Policy, *When Legal Worlds Overlap: Human Rights, State and Non-state Law* 3–5 (ICHRP 2009).

47 Hernando de Soto, *The Mystery of Capital: Why Capitalism Triumphs in the West and Fails Everywhere Else* (Basic Books 2000). *See* also Commission on Legal Empowerment of the Poor, *Making the Law Work for Everyone* vol. 1 (CLEP & UNDP 2008).

48 Azimi & Tah, *supra* note 1, at 12..

49 *See* Varun Gauri, Michael Woolcock, & Deval Desai, *Intersubjective Meaning and Collective Action in "Fragile" Societies: Theory, Evidence, and Policy Implications,* Policy Research Working Paper No. 5707, World Bank (2011).

distrust of a public that for so long has been alienated from the formal justice system" and that is looking for the meting out of justice.[50]

In FCSs, such isomorphism may render reform ineffectual; it may also lead to *increased* conflict. In Liberia, insistence on the best practice of prohibiting customary courts from handling serious crime has—in the absence of both sufficient capacity and a shared sense of what constitutes justice—led to impunity and mob justice, and has undermined the legitimacy of the fledgling democratic state.[51] To take land and justice as an example, there is a broad[52] (albeit nuanced and critiqued)[53] literature on the value of formalizing land rights that is rooted in concepts of legal certainty and access to justice. However, competing claims can be extremely difficult to regulate owing to the plurality of ways by which people conceive of land and land rights—for example, on a spectrum between communal and individual goods (indeed, for some disputants, it may be inconceivable that land be considered a good amenable to exchange). In a study regarding land privatization in Mongolia, a Mongolian pastoralist being interviewed regarding a murder in a fight over a campsite reflected: "This land ownership is the worst possible thing for livestock husbandry. Cropland can be privatized and protected, OK. Livestock husbandry must certainly not be settled. The climatic conditions are extremely difficult and changeable here. Therefore, pasture must be shared among herders and used in common . . . it must be left as it is and has been for hundreds of years."[54]

Short Time Frames

A related issue, stemming from the above point, is that reform is expected to take place within highly unrealistic time frames—three to five years being the limit of an electoral cycle and/or the (maximum) time a task manager may oversee a given project before moving on.[55] Imperatives to support projects meeting predetermined targets (such as the Millennium Development Goals) and to prioritize for support those projects that demonstrably work can mean

---

50   Azimi & Tah, *supra* note 1, at 9.

51   Isser, Lubkemann, & N'Tow, *supra* note 42.

52   *See* de Soto, *supra* note 47; Sebastian Galiani & Ernesto Schargrodsky, *Property Rights for the Poor: Effects of Land Titling*, Ronald Coase Institute Working Paper No. 7 (2009); Timothy Besley, *Property Rights and Investment Incentives: Theory and Evidence from Ghana*, 103 J. Pol. Econ. 903 (1995).

53   Deininger, *supra* note 28; Antara Haldar & Joseph Stiglitz, *The Dialectics of Law and Development: Analyzing Formality and Informality*, paper prepared for the Initiative for Policy Dialogue's China Task Force (2008), available at <http://policydialogue.org/files/events/Haldar_Stiglitz_dialectics_law_dev_1.pdf>; Klaus Deininger & Hans Biswanger, *The Evolution of the World Bank's Land Policy: Principles, Experience, and Future Challenges*, 14 World Bank Research Observer 247 (1999).

54   Maria Fernandez-Gimenez & Batjav Batbuyan, *Law and Disorder: Local Implementation of Mongolia's Land Law*, 35 Dev. and Change 141, 154–5 (2004).

55   Lant Pritchett, Michael Woolcock, & Matt Andrews, *Capability Traps? The Mechanisms of Persistent Implementation Failure*, Center for Global Development Working Paper No. 234 (2010).

rule of law projects face unwarranted expectations and, when they fail to meet them, suffer doubly when rival initiatives are lauded. As the WDR 2011 notes, attaining a one-standard deviation improvement in the rule of law (as measured by the World Bank's governance indicators) takes an average of 41 years in the 20 *fastest reforming* developing countries, let alone FCSs (where, in effect, the timescale for improvement is infinite, since their recent trajectory is inexorably downward). Such time frames are a daunting challenge not only to FCSs but also to donors and international agencies; embarking on crucial reforms whose realization, by their very nature, is likely to span multiple generations (let alone careers and budget cycles) suggests the need for an entirely different response framework.

Linear Trajectories of Change

A fourth problem, which characterizes the assessment of development projects more generally, is that change is presumed to take place along a linear trajectory, enabling relatively quick judgments to be made about project efficacy now and into the future.[56] In terms of political and legal reform, institutions change along trajectories that are likely to be anything but linear[57]—a more realistic view would characterize such change processes as "step-functions" (or "punctuated equilibriums": long periods of stasis followed by abrupt transformation) or "J-curves" (wherein things get worse before they get better). If this is so, it makes evaluating institutional reform efforts highly problematic: without knowing where a given project lies in its trajectory, it is highly likely that a false diagnosis (i.e., inaccurately declaring failure or success) will be rendered. In a world where time frames are short, patience is thin, uncertainty is high, and trajectories are unknown (or even unknowable), however, institutional reform projects that can *claim* to deliver clear and predictable results in a short time will be highly favored, privileging the familiar tropes of best practice. Care must be taken to shift the incentives for "superficial, humbug solutions" that reinforce cycles of bad projects in favor of engaging with complexity and basing projects on "foundational diligence."[58]

The cumulative upshot of these similarities is that both the state-building and the economic development approaches miss the interconnectedness of institutions and the social networks in which they are embedded. As a result, donor help is lopsided.[59] Fragile governments are called on to make complex and difficult trade-offs within unrealistic time frames, generating in the process outcomes that are less than satisfactory and that, through failing *in this*

---

56   Michael Woolcock, *Toward a Plurality of Methods in Project Evaluation: A Contextualized Approach to Understanding Impact Trajectories and Efficacy*, 1 J. Dev. Eff. 1 (2009).

57   Michael Woolcock, Simon Szreter, &Vijayendra Rao, *How and Why Does History Matter for Development Policy?* 47 J. Dev. Studs. 70 (2011).

58   Azimi & Tah, *supra* note 1.

59   *Id.*, at 12.

way, delegitimize the very idea of reform, erode the likelihood that pro-reform coalitions will be sustained over time, and stifle long-run organizational innovation and indigenous learning, thereby undermining the very possibility of more effective reform in this domain.

Ideas for Experimentation

Thus far, this chapter has sketched out the dynamics of the gradual convergence of two distinct and powerful paradigms for development interventions—state building and economic development—that both reinforce and undermine the best and worst in each other. This convergence is new and unusual: in Kennedy's[60] and Kennedy's[61] genealogies of development, paradigms or consensuses have tended to collapse under critique in particular "moments" rather than to converge and assimilate or mutate. How such convergence might affect the supranational and national spaces for justice reform is anybody's guess; however, it is safe to assume that, as others have said in the context of the convergence of paradigms in education, it will result in "nontrivial changes in the structure, culture and organization"[62] of such reform in FCSs.

It might thus be possible to sketch out the following dynamic between evolving concepts in rule of law/justice reform in FCSs: there is a move by development actors to engage in space that has traditionally been the domain of those engaged in state building. This brings a development lens to the causes and consequences of conflict: for example, the need to resolve underlying disputes, such as those over land or labor, which might otherwise spill over into conflict.[63] This broadening has the potential to enrich justice reform in FCSs. However, development actors moving into this space are simultaneously engaging with those who take a state-building approach, which requires the ability to adopt a security lens, a lens that underscores the state monopoly over force. This can lead to initiatives that undermine local institutions that may be fundamental to containing the spread of violence and that focus on law, order, and the control of deviance, with less consideration of rights and entitlements—that is, "legitimate" grievances, and control and oversight over state power.[64] Broader questions of the state legal architecture—the nature of a rule of law state—and state/citizens relationships tend to be ignored.

---

60   Duncan Kennedy, *Three Globalizations of Law and Legal Thought: 1850–2000*, in *The New Law and Economic Development: A Critical Appraisal* 19 (David Trubek and Alvaro Santos ed., Cambridge U. Press 2006).

61   David Kennedy, *The "Rule of Law," Political Choices, and Development Common Sense*, in *The New Law and Economic Development: A Critical Appraisal* 95 (David Trubek and Alvaro Santos ed., Cambridge U. Press 2006).

62   Martin Carnoy & Diana Rhoten, *What Does Globalisation Mean for Educational Change? A Comparative Approach*, 46 Comp. Ed. Rev. 1, 7 (2002).

63   WDR 2011, at xvi.

64   Desai & Sage, *supra* note 2; and *supra* notes 18 and 19, and accompanying text.

The first moves in this conceptual and policy reorientation are being made. We are starting to see a discursive engagement with nonstate justice at the policy level in the WDR 2011,[65] at the analytic level through the work of the Justice for the Poor program,[66] and at the operational level (discussions currently taking place around the next phase of the Afghanistan Justice Sector Reform Project envisage building links between state and nonstate institutions).[67] More broadly, emerging research on societal fragility[68] attempts to shift the locus of fragility from the state to society. It remains to be seen, however, whether such concepts will receive the fulsome embrace of reconceptualization or the minor recognition of marginal fixes at the institutional and/or operational level.

In the coming few years, donors will have to adapt to a new and rapidly changing conceptual terrain. They will have to acquire the capacity to react to changing concepts and to engage with the realities in the field.[69] Given the recondite, evolving, and dynamic nature of justice reform in FCSs, any prescriptions for donor policy or action are likely to prove unhelpful. This brave new world, however, will undoubtedly open up spaces for experimentation,[70] and actors will explore what works in this new space. In this spirit, let us conduct an early exploration of what this emerging space might look like through some modest sketches and brief suggestions that might support effective experimentation to underpin future efforts in this field, doing so through the lenses of *analysis*, *operations*, and *policy*.

The WDR 2011 is an appropriate frame for such efforts. The key findings of the WDR 2011 as regards justice in FCSs respond to the four problems with models outlined above:

- Exclusion of significant portions of the population (be that on the basis of ethnicity, religion, geography, etc.) from political voice, access to services, and economic opportunity establishes the conditions for triggering and

---

65 WDR 2011, at 155–6, 169, 260.

66 Sage, Tamanaha, & Woolcock, *supra* note 44. *See*, generally, Justice for the Poor website, at <http://web.worldbank.org/WBSITE/EXTERNAL/TOPICS/EXTLAWJUSTICE/EXTJUSFORPOOR/0,,menuPK:3282947~pagePK:149018~piPK:149093~theSitePK:3282787,00.html>.

67 As discussions are currently taking place, the nature of the project is in flux; this view represents that contained in World Bank, Afghanistan Justice Sector Reform Project: DRAFT Concept Note (2011) (copy on file with the authors).

68 World Bank, *Societal Dynamics and Fragility: Engaging Societies in Responding to Fragile Situations* (World Bank 2011).

69 We do not seek to diminish the importance of national policymakers to effective reform, and we stress that the arguments advanced in this chapter are inspired by the insights afforded to us by national policymakers from Afghanistan and Liberia.

70 We also appreciate the cautionary note in Aldous Huxley's eponymous novel, which painted a picture of a world organized to be the antithesis of local experimentation. Just as Huxley wrote of dystopian human homogeneity and highly stratified and rigid social structures and hierarchies, we, too, caution against the continued use by donors of presumptions of human homogeneity and of rigid human and social models: Aldous Huxley, *Brave New World* (HarperCollins 1998).

fueling conflict (requiring a response to state-centrism and organizational isomorphism).[71]

• Institutions, particularly nonstate institutions, that can mediate conflict and navigate and manage complex change are essential if societies are to emerge from cyclical conflict and endemic fragility (responding to *state-centrism* and, as a challenge to the idea of postconflict transitional moments, responding to short time frames).[72]

• The state-society compact needs to be broadened over time so that political settlements have broad-based legitimacy, which is a foundational requirement for a functioning rule of law (responding to short time frames).[73]

• Developing institutional capability and legitimacy is an inherently uneven (responding to linear trajectories of change) but endogenous process (responding to organizational isomorphism) that is generational in timescale (responding to short time frames).[74]

Implications for Analysis

Minister Tah provides clear guidance from the perspective of the daily realities faced by policymakers in the field. She highlights the importance of going beyond state-centrism and taking a holistic approach to available justice institutions in FCSs, outlining the tension between the expectations placed by the people on the government as a resolver of grievances[75] and the social fact that most citizens turn (at least initially) to nonstate institutions in their quest for justice.[76] She also stresses that what we have termed organizational isomorphism ("a cookie cutter approach")[77] remains inadequate: the particularities of FCSs—in the case of Liberia, a country where a "persistent traumatized population [routinely encounters] weakness in capacity-building programs due to lack of foundational preparedness of trainees and, most importantly, a disintegrated value system"[78]—suggests that there needs to be an enhanced appreciation of the importance of context as the foundation for effective engagement.

---

71   *See*, for example, WDR 2011, at 6, 13, 18.

72   *See*, for example, WDR 2011, at 119, 156.

73   *See*, generally, WDR 2011, at 193–97 (arguing that international support—rooted in local context—can help broaden state-society compacts, creating a double compact between state and citizen, and state and international community).

74   WDR 2011, at 251.

75   "The public . . . expects all grievances, past and present, to be redressed by the government with immediacy and without regard to resource limitations." Azimi & Tah, *supra* note 1, at 9.

76   "A public that for so long has been alienated from the formal justice system." Azimi & Tah, *supra* note 1, at 9.

77   *Id.*, at 12.

78   *Id.*, at 10.

As a result, donors need broad-based analytical capacity to try to make sense of complex, often fractured settings—in other words, to enable "a diligent inquiry into the deep[-]rooted causes that will guide an innovative and unique perspective."[79] The implication of these words is to appreciate the importance of justice beyond the narrowly defined "justice sector" to engage with a range of sources and drivers of societal stress, to which development initiatives themselves can contribute.[80]

Such capacity will allow donors to put the state into context and to be sensitive to nonlinearity in the evolution of the justice sector in FCSs. For example, trade-offs need to be made, such as between "the immediate release of those held in violation of their constitutional right to a speedy trial" per the demands of human rights advocates, and "the general public demands that the accused individuals remain incarcerated indefinitely to ensure that public safety is not compromised."[81] This will help build donor capacity to navigate transitional steps out of fragility, with an appreciation of the value of interim institutions and processes.[82]

This involves bringing to bear a much more plural set of expertise, disciplines, and methodologies than is the current norm (which disproportionately bears the imprint of lawyers, political scientists, and economists).[83] The disciplines that inform these might include the following:

- History, particularly the history of the dynamics and legacies of conflict. Chief Justice Azimi of Afghanistan noted the difficult legacy of the capacity and capability of judges that postinvasion Afghanistan inherited.[84] Minister Tah commented on the flight of trained legal personnel during the civil war.[85]

---

79   *Id.*, at 12.

80   The WDR 2011 supports this view, seeing justice as, in part, a set of "institutions required to address underlying disputes that contribute to violence": WDR 2011, at xvi.

81   Azimi & Tah, *supra* note 1, at 9.

82   Desai & Sage, *supra* note 2, at 5–6.

83   Yves Dezalay & Bryant Garth, *The Internationalization of Palace Wars: Lawyers, Economists, and the Contest to Transform Latin American States* 163–85, especially 163–76 (U. of Chicago Press 2002). *See*, generally, David Kennedy, *The Mystery of Global Governance*, 34 Ohio Northern U.L. Rev. 827 (2008).

84   "[W]ithin the judiciary over many years, all kinds of people were in office occupying the position of judge or court administrator. Most particularly, there were unqualified people and illegally appointed people. Personnel of the court system had been appointed during different political regimes, different governments, including the communist government, then the Mujahedeen government, then the Taliban government, then even after the Bonn Conference." Azimi & Tah, *supra* note 1, at 2.

85   "Legal institutions barely functioned as many of the well educated and well trained citizens in law enforcement and the law fled the country in the 1990s." Azimi & Tah, *supra* note 1, at 8.

- Psychology, noting Minister Tah's comments on psycho-social trauma[86] but also the ways in which perceptions of legitimacy, credibility, and effectiveness can vary among different actors, with serious consequences for the sustainability and efficacy of reform efforts.

- Sociology, to provide, for example, insights into the patterns of normative "disintegration" during periods of societal transition, the dynamics of conflict that accompany these transitions as power oscillates between different groups, and understandings of the conditions under which different aspects of people's identities become politically salient.[87]

- Anthropology, to generate, for example, a closer understanding of, and provide explanatory force for, the social role played by "trial by ordeal."[88]

- Communications (including drama and performance), especially between groups who have very different ways of making and interpreting knowledge claims (such as illiterate villagers and social scientists).[89]

Implications for Operations

Donor interventions in Liberia expect "the justice system to function today as any other justice system in the region and, in some instances, on international standards, without regard to cultural diversity, limited resources or consideration of the abyss from which the country has ascended."[90] If this situation is to change, donors must avoid organizational isomorphism and the presumption of linear trajectories of change, instead developing an understanding of the situation in which they are intervening before designing operations. For example, they need to be sensitive to long-run time horizons and the trade-offs that need to be made in the short term in order that a state-society compact might be built in the long term. Minster Tah's call provides an important framework for donor experimentation.

Operations need to be highly sensitive to the context of the situations in which they intervene. This is not a new observation.[91] However, this chapter's

---

86 "Security, rule of law, and the level of productivity in the country all depend on how well we address the psycho-social problems of the society and restore to the country the value system that was so badly damaged during the years of war." Azimi & Tah, *supra* note 1, at 10.

87 *See*, on the contribution of sociology to enriching legal understandings of norms and norm diffusion, Robert Ellickson, *Law and Economics Discovers Social Norms*, Yale Law School Faculty Scholarship Series Paper 407 (1998), available at <http://digitalcommons.law.yale.edu/fss_papers/407>. *See*, generally, on the importance of interdisciplinary approaches to studying and understanding social norms, Robert Axelrod, *An Evolutionary Approach to Norms*, 80 Am. Pol. Science Rev. 1095 (1986).

88 Azimi & Tah, *supra* note 1, at 10. On the potential role of ethnographic field research on this issue in Liberia, *see* Isser, Lubkemann, & N'Tow, *supra* note 42.

89 *Supra* notes 80 and 81.

90 Azimi & Tah, *supra* note 1, at 9.

91 *See*, for example, World Bank: Report on Headline Seminar, *supra* note 18; Rodrik, Subramanian, & Trebbi, *supra* note 14; Sage, Tamanaha, & Woolcock, *supra* note 44.

analysis of the two paradigms, coupled with Minister Tah's analysis, suggests three new ways to reconceptualize interventions:

- Levels of intervention: the limits of states in FCSs often (but not always[92]) coupled to settings of deep legal pluralism, imply that operations should be decentralized (including engagement with legal pluralism) rather than privileging state-centrism.

- Type of intervention: the nature of interventions designed to strengthen the operation of justice systems and institutions, especially at the local level, might be broadened in two ways. First, they might be targeted at specific issues underlying fragility at the social as well as the state level (e.g., to combat psycho-social trauma[93] among the Liberian population[94]). Second, they might be designed to shift social norms and expectations,[95] particularly through communication and education strategies[96] targeted at the public (e.g., "public education as to evidentiary standards"),[97] avoiding organizational isomorphism.

- Modality of intervention: given the contexts in which they occur, interventions need to have long time horizons[98] and modest aims, particularly because they need to be sensitive to policy trade-offs, avoiding short time frames and linear trajectories of change.

---

92 The Kosovo context, for example, was one of a state that retained significant formal capacity in spite of the conflict: Alexandros Yannis, *The UN as Government in Kosovo*, 10 Glob. Governance 67 (2004).

93 *See*, for example, Cheryl de la Rey & Ingrid Owens, *Perceptions of Psychosocial Healing and the Truth and Reconciliation Commission in South Africa*, 4 Peace & Conflict: J. of Peace Psychology 257 (1998). *See* also, for a critical perspective, Laurel Fletcher & Harvey Weinstein, *Violence and Social Repair: Rethinking the Contribution of Justice to Reconciliation*, 24 Hum. Rights. Q. 573, 638–9 (2002), which concludes that "a comprehensive community-based approach that includes the opinions and ideas of those whose lives have been most directly affected is critical," but that "international interventions should be implemented in the context of an ecological understanding of social repair."

94 Azimi & Tah, *supra* note 1, at 10, 12.

95 This builds on the work by Martha Nussbaum, Arjun Appadurai, and others on adaptive expectations: *see*, for example, Martha Nussbaum, *Women and Human Development: The Capabilities Approach* (Cambridge U. Press 2000); Arjun Appadurai, *The Capacity to Aspire: Culture and the Terms of Recognition*, in *Culture and Public Action* 59 (Vijayendra Rao & Michael Walton ed., World Bank 2004). *See* also Pablo de Greiff, Comments (World Bank's Law, Justice and Development Week, Nov. 2010) (on file with authors) (arguing that justice needs to engage with "adaptive preferences . . . the argument is that people who are under constant conditions of the prevision, in order to avoid constantly defeated expectations, adjust their preference forward, and that this has an impact on the way in which they participate in, among other things, economic activities").

96 *See*, for example, on community literature, theater, and radio, Milena Stefanova, Raewyn Porter, & Rod Nixon, *Leasing in Vanuatu: Findings and Community Dissemination on Epi Island*, 5(4) Justice for the Poor Briefing Note 1 (2010); Saumya Pant, Arvind Singhal, & Usha Bhasin, *Using Radio Drama to Entertain and Educate: India's Experience with the Production, Reception, and Transcreation of Dehleez*, 13 J. Dev. Comm. 52 (2002).

97 Azimi & Tah, *supra* note 1, at 9.

98 "[T]he transformation we so impatiently desire will occur over time." *Id.*

As a result, it might be useful to experiment with justice projects that seek to internalize norms in a particular social setting, that favor the provision of equitable spaces, or that support institutions engaging with a wide range of social fault-lines and fractures.[99]

Implications for Policy

Donors engaged in promoting justice in FCSs need to make context-sensitive policy. A first step in this direction could be to launch experimental programs that respond to the analytical and operational implications outlined in the preceding sections. Pilot programs and reports based on methodologies beyond the orthodox (historical analyses, for example) can provide an evidence base for effective, context-based policymaking that avoids state-centrism, organizational isomorphism, short time frames, and linear trajectories of change. For example, a donor might devise a strategy for engagement with nonstate systems, or might develop an holistic approach to avoid lopsided policy that supports one institution (such as the police) at the expense of the system as a whole.[100]

At the same time, however, donors need to ensure that counterparts in FCSs have the *capacity to engage* when determining policy and priorities. Afghanistan provides a cautionary tale. Chief Justice Azimi recounts that

> although the international community sought from us a list of our priorities, a plan for the future development of the judiciary and the priorities we wished to apply, we did not adequately express our needs. Up until only four years ago, we failed to specify what we needed, to set our priorities or to estimate the likely costs of those priorities. This led the international community to assume that everything was okay in the judiciary. Some simple donor-funded training programs were conducted from time to time, which seemed the best thing to be done; and donors were happy that these efforts were meeting our expectations.[101]

Donors thus need to rethink their engagement with the state, incorporating or reemphasizing building the state's policy expertise into their policy development practices.

Conclusion

The default assumption in most development work is that weak implementation systems are in large part a function of capacity constraints on the part of line ministries in recipient countries, and that as such performance can be best improved by engaging in various concrete activities—training sessions,

---

99   *See* Daniel Adler, Caroline Sage, & Michael Woolcock, *Interim Institutions and the Development Process: Opening Spaces for Reform in Cambodia and Indonesia*, Brooks World Poverty Institute Working Paper No. 86 (Mar. 2009).

100   Azimi & Tah, *supra* note 1, at 12.

101   *Id.*

policy change, infrastructure provision, organizational reform—designed to strengthen the prevailing structures and upgrade the skills of the agents working within them. Moreover, in a world of development assistance in which skepticism is high, time horizons are short, and resources are stretched, high-uncertainty issues such as enhancing justice in fragile and conflict-affected states generate multiple pressures for donors to show some form of short-term accomplishment; all too often, these pressures are relieved by pointing to changes in institutional form (what institutions look like)—laws passed, court-houses built, reporting procedures altered—as opposed to function (what they actually do), and by justifying actions on the basis that experts elsewhere have deemed them a best practice. Some of this work has been successful, but the considered assessment of most rule of law reform efforts, whether undertaken in the name of state building or economic development, is that, at best, much remains to be learned.

So understood, capacity deficits are as much a problem for international agencies as for FCSs themselves, and improving the effectiveness of justice initiatives therefore requires revisiting the theories and corresponding practices that inform current approaches.

Justice reform is best understood as an adaptive rather than (primarily) technical problem, one that requires a sustained commitment to understanding the idiosyncrasies of the context(s) in order to more correctly identify binding constraint problems and possible solutions. With this in mind, donors should seek to improve their capacity to broaden the range of groups with whom they engage at the operational level, the methodological base on which key decisions are made, and their willingness and ability to engage with actors beyond the state—and the formal justice sector itself—in the larger task of enhancing the quality and accessibility of justice for all.

International Norms and Standards Applicable to Situations of State Fragility and Failure

An Overview

Chiara Giorgetti[*]

State fragility and failure are best defined legally as the incapacity of a state to perform its obligations toward its citizens and toward the international community in general.[1] Fragile, failing, and failed states are characterized by an implosion of state structures, which results in the incapability of govern-

---

[*] Some of the ideas in this article are also developed in the author's book, *A Principled Approach to State Failure: International Community Actions in Emergency Situations* (Martinus Nijhoff 2010). The views expressed in this article are hers alone.

[1] Contemporary governance has resulted in a new standard of governance that has increased the overall responsibilities of each state. States must perform innumerable actions daily, directed at their own people, other states, and the international community. This requirement results in the obligation of each state to provide numerous goods and services, including protection, a functioning legal system, a working judiciary, an effective education system, health care, an efficient administration able to deliver goods and services, infrastructures, and the possibility of participating in the global economy. Moreover, the modern economic system requires each state to provide trade facilities, a financial market, communication systems, a road network, air connections, port access, and security. Further, any functioning contemporary state needs a large infrastructure to provide for the health and education of its citizens, as well as for terrestrial and aerial transport of people and goods. It needs to be able to support complicated financial and banking transactions, and must be able to support a functioning legal system. At the same time, the world has become more interdependent. The development of communication and the ease of travel have created a world society in which values, expectations, and political and economic views are broadly shared. Moreover, what happens in one part of the world can have immediate repercussions in other parts of the world and in a variety of domains, including financial transactions, environmental emergencies, health crises, and security risks. Further, the number of international conventions and bilateral and multilateral treaties has increased substantially. (The collection of the United Nations Treaty Series currently contains more than 158,000 bilateral and multilateral treaties deposited between 1946 and 2003, available at <http://treaties.un.org/Pages/Overview.aspx?path=overview/overview/page1_en.xml>.) However, certain states are unable to operate in this new system of increased responsibility, in terms of obligations toward other states, the international community, and their citizens. These states—often referred to as fragile, failing, or failed states—have become ineffective actors on the international stage, posing multiple problems for the international community as certain necessary obligations and required acts fail to be performed, weakening the entire system. One of these problems is that the rights of domestic populations are eroded. Health and other basic rights cannot be assured. As the failing of state sovereignty continues, the lack of respect for basic rights worsens, often giving rise to humanitarian crises. Another problem is that state failure has consequences in the international community. Failing and failed states are unable to perform their obligations toward the international community, for example, because they are unable to guarantee protection of their borders or airspace or are unable to address health emergencies.

mental authorities to perform their functions, including providing security, respecting the rule of law, exercising control, supplying education and health services, establishing commercial and banking systems, and maintaining economic and structural infrastructures.[2]

State fragility is multifaceted and can be depicted as a continuum, as the state becomes progressively less capable of performing its functions and slides deeper into the category of "failed." Complete state collapse is the ultimate, and rare, result; different stages of state fragility can be encountered along a continuum. A rigorous analysis of the legal implications, significance, and consequences of state fragility is—despite its importance—missing.[3]

The World Bank defines fragile states as states that are affected by conflict or have a country policy and institutional assessment (CPIA) index of 3.2 or below.[4] The CPIA index rates countries against sixteen criteria grouped into four clusters: economic management; structural policies; policies for social inclusion and equity; and public sector management and institutions.[5]

---

2   In particular, as Zartman describes, in fragile and failing sates, "as the decision-making center of the government, the state is paralyzed and inoperative: laws are not made, order is not preserved, and societal cohesion is not enhanced. As a symbol of identity, it has lost its power of conferring a name on its people and a meaning to their social action. As a territory, it no longer assures security and provisionment by a central sovereign organization. As the authoritative political institution, it has lost its legitimacy, which is therefore up for grabs, and so has lost its right to command and conduct public affairs. As a system of socioeconomic organization, its functional balance of inputs and outputs is destroyed; it no longer receives supports from, nor exercise controls over its people, and it no longer is even the target of demands, because its people know that it is incapable of providing supplies. No longer functioning, with neither traditional nor charismatic nor institutional sources of legitimacy, it has lost the right to rule." I. William Zartman, *Introduction: Posing the Problem of State Collapse*, in *Collapsed States: The Disintegration and Restoration of Legitimate Authority* 1, 5 (I. William Zartman ed., Lynne Rienner 1995) (internal citation omitted).

3   In fact, because definitions of what constitutes such states are, in general, informed by the analysts' definition of the state and their own views of the functions and role of the state, international law has not recognized and named the phenomenon of state failure and fragility. International law focuses on the creation and dissolution of a state, but has not focused on the evolution, changes, or temporary failures that may occur after a state is created. Furthermore, an agreed-upon definition of "fragility" or "failure" does not exist, with many actors criticizing the use of the terms "failing" and "failed" states. *See* Chiara Giorgetti, *A Principled Approach to State Failure: International Community Actions in Emergency Situations* (Martinus Nijhoff 2010).

4   Using 2005 data, for example, the CPIA of the following countries was less than 3.2: Albania, Angola, Azerbaijan, Bangladesh, Bosnia and Herzegovina, Burundi, Cambodia, Central African Republic, Chad, Comoros, Congo, Côte d'Ivoire, Democratic Republic of Congo, Djibouti, Dominica, Eritrea, The Gambia, Grenada, Guinea, Guinea-Bissau, Guyana, Haiti, Honduras, Indonesia, Kenya, Kiribati, Kyrgyz Republic, Lesotho, Mali, Mongolia, Mozambique, Nepal, Niger, Nigeria, Papua New Guinea, Republic of Yemen, Rwanda, São Tomé and Príncipe, Sierra Leone, Solomon Islands, Sudan, Tajikistan, Togo, Tonga, Vanuatu, Zimbabwe. *Id.*

5   World Bank, CPIA—Policies and Institutions for Environmental Sustainability, available at <http://go.worldbank.org/7NMQ1P0W10>. The World Bank created the Fragile States Initiative in 2003 to respond to state fragility. The Bank supports its initiative in this sector with the Post-Conflict Fund, the Low-Income Countries Under Stress Implementation Trust Fund, and other funds. *See* Rumu Sarkar, *International Development Law* 160 (Oxford U. Press 2009).

Fragility and conflict have repercussions on domestic populations. The World Bank estimates that one billion people live in countries affected by fragility and conflict; in these countries, poverty rates average 54 percent, compared with 22 percent for low-income countries as a whole. These countries are defined by weak political, legal, and economic institutions. The impact of warfare is also a protracted development challenge; achieving the Millennium Development Goals is difficult in fragile states.[6]

International law plays a central role in multiple aspects of state fragility, from defining the state and sanctioning its existence to—increasingly—regulating how to assist a state in postconflict rebuilding. In fact, as is discussed in this chapter, international norms and standards increasingly shape peacebuilding and state-building efforts in fragile and conflict-affected areas. At the urging of multilateral organizations and bilateral aid agencies, transnational benchmarks and prescriptions are applied to such diverse activities as framing constitutions; holding elections; establishing legislatures and courts; writing business, commercial, and tax laws; creating procurement arrangements; and reforming the security sector.[7]

The use of international standards and prescriptions in fragile states has substantially affected the form and conduct of emerging political and administrative institutions and, in turn, influenced reconstruction and development outcomes. In some instances, international benchmarking has helped fragile and conflict-affected areas develop transparent and effective governance and service-delivery arrangements. However, in other areas, no such arrangements exist or benchmarking has resulted in impositions that have impeded, rather than contributed to, achieving development objectives.[8]

---

6   World Bank, Fragile and Conflict-Affected Countries, available at <http://web.world bank.org/WBSITE/EXTERNAL/PROJECTS/STRATEGIES/EXTLICUS/0,,menuPK:511784~pagePK:64171540~piPK:64171528~theSitePK:511778,00.html>.

7   *See*, for example, Karin Von Hippel, *Democracy by Force: U.S. Intervention in the Post–Cold War World* (Cambridge U. Press 2000); Kirsti Samuels, *Post-conflict Peace-Building and Constitution-Making*, 6 Chi. J. Intl. L. 1 (2006); Sunil Bastian & Robin Luckham, *Introduction: Can Democracy Be Designed?* in *Can Democracy Be Designed? The Politics of Institutional Choice in Conflict-Torn Societies* 1, 5 (Sunil Bastian & Robin Luckham ed., Zed 2003); OSCE/ODIHR Draft Paper, International Standards and Commitments on the Right to Democratic Elections: A Practical Guide to Democratic Elections (Nov. 2002), available at <http://www.osce.org/odihr/elections/66040>; UNDP, Governance in Conflict Prevention and Recovery: A Guidance Note (Dec. 2009), available at <http://www.undp.org>; UNDP, Evidence Informed Policy in Post-conflict Contexts: Nepal, Peru and Serbia (Sept. 2009), available at <http://www.undp.org>; *Security Sector Reform in Challenging Environments* (Hans Born & Albrecht Scharbel ed., LIT Verlag 2009); and OECD DAC, Principles of Good International Engagement in Fragile States: Learning and Advisory Process on Difficult Partnerships (2006), available at <http://www.oecd.org/fs>. *See also The Role of International Law in Rebuilding Societies after Conflict— Great Expectations* (Brett Bowden, Hilary Charlesworth, & Jeremy Farrall ed., Cambridge U. Press 2009).

8   *See*, in general, *Governance in Post-conflict Societies: Rebuilding Fragile States* (D. Brinckeroff ed., Routledge 2007); J. Paul Dunne, *After the Slaughter: Reconstructing Mozambique and Rwanda*, 1(2) Economics of Peace and Security J. 38 (2006); Joanna MacRae, *Dilemmas of "Post"-Conflict Transition: Lessons from the Health Sector*, ODI Network Paper No. 12 (1995).

This chapter describes and examines the diverse ways in which international norms and standards influence state "rehabilitation," focusing on how they impact peace-building and state-building activities in fragile and conflict-affected areas. It also constructs an analytical framework to account for and evaluate the role of international law in reconstruction, development, and state-building activities.

Specifically, this chapter focuses on three sets of international norms and standards: those that constitute a framework that must be followed to regulate the creation or reestablishment of the state as a legal entity to reintegrate the fragile state into the international community; those that establish minimum standards of protection afforded to the individual; and those that guide the reconstruction of the domestic legal system.

The International Law Framework

The first sphere in which international law plays an obvious role in assessing and assisting fragile and conflict-affected states is the definition of statehood and sovereignty. These issues are explored below, first to provide an overview of the process of creating and recognizing postconflict states and then to examine relevant transitional arrangements for states that may provide useful alternatives in postconflict reconstruction.

How International Law Defines States: The Montevideo Convention

States are essentially a legal creation and are legal entities in international law. International law plays a fundamental role in defining states and in sanctioning their existence. The 1933 Montevideo Convention on the Rights and Duties of States embodies the commonly agreed-on definition of what a state is. Article 1 of the convention provides that "the state as a person in international law should possess the following qualifications: A permanent population; A defined territory; Government; and Capacity to enter into relations with other States." This latter criterion is often equated with independence. Any state, therefore, should possess these qualifications in order to be considered a state under international law. This definition is valid today, although it is challenged by state fragility.[9]

---

9   In reality, this definition is probably too static and does not reflect changes in statehood. Fragile and failing states often witness major shifts in population dynamics. Often, large portions of the population migrate outside the state border, as in Sudan and Somalia. Moreover, people may shift their allegiance from the central to the local level, as shown in Afghanistan and the Democratic Republic of Congo. However, neither of these changes alters the condition of a "state" when that condition has already been acquired. Similarly, fragile and failed states are often characterized by porous borders and the inability of a government to exercise territorial sovereignty. Their territory is often controlled by several groups and militias. Typically, the recognized government is capable of controlling only circumscribed areas around the capital. Examples include the Democratic Republic of Congo, whose government, for certain periods, controlled little territory outside the capital; Afghanistan, where the Taliban,

In reality, effective entities have existed that, for political reasons, were not recognized as states (for example, Rhodesia and Somaliland), while noneffective entities have been recognized as states (for example, Poland in World War II and Kuwait in 1990–91).[10] Nonetheless, the Montevideo criteria play an important initial role in assessing the viability of a new, postconflict state and should therefore be duly analyzed.

Relevant Peremptory Norms

In addition to providing an initial definition of state, international norms provide a framework of binding principles that guide postconflict reconstruction and affect the creation and establishment of states. In fact, the development of peremptory norms of international law guides the creation and reestablishment of conflict-affected states. Several norms are relevant.

Self-Determination

The principle of self-determination provides fundamental guidance in conflict-affected areas. It is recognized as a peremptory norm by several binding international instruments, as well as by decisions of the International Court of Justice.[11] The principle provides that peoples should be able to freely determine their own legal and political status within a given territory, particularly

---

and not the recognized government, controls most of the country; Sudan, where domestic rebel groups claim independence of parts of the southern territory; Somalia; Liberia; and Côte d'Ivoire. Further, one of the main characteristics of failed and failing states is a weak and ineffective government that does not and cannot provide for its people. However, during decolonization, several states gained independence even when there were no existing powers capable of exercising governmental functions. The Democratic Republic of Congo, for example, obtained its independence from Belgium on June 30, 1960, in the midst of internal fighting. A few days after independence, the Congolese Public Force mutinied, Belgian troops intervened, and one of the provinces, Katanga, announced secession from the main territory. However, the Democratic Republic of Congo was admitted to the United Nations in September 1960, as two different factions of government sought to be accepted at the UN as legitimate representatives. The independence of Guinea-Bissau from Portugal is another example. Although still under Portuguese rule, the African Party for the Independence of Guinea and Cape Verde declared independence unilaterally in 1973. A UN General Assembly vote in the same year denounced illegal Portuguese aggression and occupation, and discussed the issue of "illegal occupation by Portuguese forces" of the territory of Guinea-Bissau. Western states denied the existence of the necessary criteria for statehood, but GA Resolution 3061(XXVIII) accepted the "recent accession to independence of Guinea-Bissau," although its government controlled neither a majority of the population nor its main towns. Thus, as Higgins concludes, "statehood for purposes of UN admission, was attributed even when the new governments clearly lacked effective control." Rosalyn Higgins, *Problems and Process, International Law and How We Use It* 40 (Oxford U. Press 1994).

10   James Crawford, *The Creation of States in International Law* (2d ed., Oxford U. Press 2006).

11   For example, Article 1 of the UN Charter states the "purposes of the United Nations are . . . (2) to develop friendly relations among nations based on respect for the principle of equal rights and self-determination of peoples." Similarly, Article 55 of the UN Charter provides: "With a view to the creation of conditions of stability and well-being which are necessary for peaceful and friendly relations among nations based on the respect for the principle of equal rights and self-determination of peoples." *See* also UN Declaration on the Granting of Independence to Colonial Countries and Peoples, GA Res. 1514 (XV), UN GAOR, 15th Sess., Supp. No. 16, UN Doc. A/4684 (1961).

in relation to colonial territories. It played a fundamental role in the achievement of statehood at the end of the colonial period, and it reassumed relevance in the post–Cold War fragmentation that resulted in the establishment of many new states. It is still relevant today, especially in assessing the claims of minorities in postconflict situations such as Kosovo, Sudan, and Somalia.

Other international binding norms are also relevant in postconflict situations. The application of diverse binding norms, all simultaneously relevant, however, may create tension between principles and difficulties in their application. For example, the UN Charter endorses the principle of territorial integrity, by which the integrity of a territory of a member state is recognized as paramount.[12] Yet the principle of territorial integrity may be at odds with the principle of self-determination.

In general, it is recognized that the principle of self-determination applies as a matter of right only after a unit of self-determination has been determined, not just to any group of people desiring independence and self-government. As such, the principle applies to territories established and recognized as separate political units, including mandates, trusts, states, and other territories forming distinct political-geographical areas whose inhabitants have been arbitrarily excluded from government so as to have become "non-self-governing." Examples of the latter are Eritrea and Kosovo.[13] The difficulty is to define a non-self-governing territory precisely. The International Court of Justice sanctioned the validity of the unilateral declaration of independence of Kosovo from Serbia, finding that the declaration was not in violation of international law.[14]

The Use of Force

Article 2 of the UN Charter prohibits the threat or use of force against the territorial integrity or political independence of a state unless the threat is made or force is used in self-defense after an armed attack or is authorized by the Security Council under Chapter VII of the UN Charter to maintain international peace and security.

The international community has refused to accept the legal validity of acts derived by the illegal use of force. The tension between the principle of self-determination and the prohibition of the unlawful use of force is particularly relevant for conflict resolution and postconflict reconstruction. In

---

12 Article 2(4) of the UN Charter provides that "all Members shall refrain in their international relations from the threat or use of force against territorial integrity or political independence of any state, or in any other manner inconsistent with the Purposes of the United Nations."

13 *See* Crawford, *supra* note 10, at 126–27.

14 *Accordance with International Law of the Unilateral Declaration of Independence in Respect of Kosovo, Advisory Op.* (Jul. 22, 2010), available at <http://www.icj-cij.org/docket/index.php?p1=3&p2=4&k=21&PHPSESSID=76273a3bac6ddc533da3d2d44fc8e878&case=141&code=kos&p3=4>.

practice, this principle has not undermined actions by secessionist movements exercising their right to self-determination.

The tension is especially important when considering the legality of the use of force by external powers in conflict situations in accordance with or in violation of an applicable right to self-determination. The intervention of the international community in Kosovo is a case in point. In recent history, in fact, many critics have argued for the legality of "humanitarian interventions" as an exception to the prohibition of the use of force.

Humanitarian interventions are interventions by the international community or single actors therein to assist populations that suffer grave violations of human rights. Whether such interventions are approved by the United Nations and are therefore legal is of great importance to the process of postconflict reconstruction and the ability of multilateral and regional development partners to assist in that reconstruction. In Afghanistan, for example, following the Bonn Accords, the World Bank and other development agencies were able to reengage and assist in reconstruction and rebuilding. Conversely, the initial postconflict reconstruction efforts in Iraq encountered many difficulties. However, as the example of Somalia demonstrates, the legality of an intervention cannot completely guarantee local support.

State Recognition

State recognition is an international law issue that is relevant to the establishment of states. To enter fully into the international community, states must be recognized by other members of this community and thus by other states. It has been argued that recognition of a state by fellow states is in fact a requisite for statehood, "effectively forming an additional category to those stipulated in the Montevideo Convention."[15] Two main theories on the nature of recognition exist: is recognition of states by other states declaratory or constitutive? Although it is generally accepted that recognition is in principle declaratory (the Institut de Droit International expressly acknowledged that recognition has a declaratory effect and noted that the existence of a new state with all the legal effects attached to that existence would not be affected by the refusal of recognition by one or more states), recognition by other states is of great importance for the existence of states. For example, during the conflict in the former Yugoslavia, the recognition by some European Union members of the independent status of former constituent parts of the Socialist Federal Republic of Yugoslavia was crucial to ensure their viability. Similarly, in the Somalia crisis, withholding the recognition of the breakaway northern territory of Somaliland plays an important role in Somalia's existence.

Some authors think that only states that embrace democracy and human rights may effectively be recognized as members of the international

---

15   Higgins, *supra* note 9, at 41.

community.[16] This view is supported by the practice of states vis-à-vis the recognition of new states that were formerly part of the Soviet Union. In 1991, when the Soviet Union began to dissolve, the European Council issued a declaration containing guidelines on the recognition of new states in Eastern Europe and the Soviet Union establishing respect for democracy and human rights as a criterion for recognition.[17] A similar requirement was imposed on the former members of the Socialist Federal Republic of Yugoslavia by the Badinter Arbitration Commission, although the practice in this case is more complex.[18] At the moment, the practice of an additional requirement for recognition seems to have been imposed only on certain states.

Importantly, under international law, there is an established duty of collective nonrecognition of a state by other states if certain peremptory norms of international law have been violated, including the prohibition of the use of force and the principles of nondiscrimination and self-determination. Situations in which the duty of collective nonrecognition was exercised include South Africa–controlled Namibia, Rhodesia, Kuwait after the invasion by Iraq, Northern Cyprus, and East Timor.

Admission to International Organizations

International law plays an important role in the establishment of a state by regulating admission to international organizations. Article 4 of the UN Charter stipulates that only "peace-loving States" can be admitted to the United Nations. By doing so, it restricts admission to only those states that meet certain (minimal) legal requirements. Other international organizations include similar provisions. Of course, rules of admission vary in relation to each international organization. Under the World Bank Articles of Agreement, a country must join the International Monetary Fund (IMF) prior to becoming a member of the Bank. Membership in the International Development Association (IDA), the International Finance Corporation (IFC), and the Multilateral Investment Guarantee Agency (MIGA) is conditioned on membership in the International Bank for Reconstruction and Development (IBRD). Historically, this issue has been important for consideration of the admission of microstates.[19] The issue assumed renewed importance with the dissolution of Russia and Yugoslavia, especially for the admission of Yugoslavia itself and, more

---

16	*See*, in general, *Democratic Governance and International Law* (Gregory H. Fox & Brad R. Roth ed., Cambridge U. Press 2000).

17	Resolution of December 16, 1991, available at <http://207.57.19.226/journal/Vol4/No1/art6.html>.

18	*See* Sean D. Murphy, *Democratic Legitimacy and the Recognition of States and Governments*, in *Democratic Governance and International Law* 123 (Gregory H. Fox & Brad R. Roth ed., Cambridge U. Press 2000).

19	As Higgins concludes, citing, inter alia, the examples of Rwanda and Burundi, "statehood for purposes of UN admission, was attributed even when the new governments clearly lacked effective control." *See* Higgins, *supra* note 10.

recently, Kosovo.[20] Interestingly, Kosovo has been a member of the IMF—and thus the World Bank—since June 2009, although it has not yet become a member of the United Nations.

Rules relating to the admission of international organizations must be clear and detailed. Although the United Nations requires states to be "peace loving," Article 1 of the European Bank for Reconstruction and Development (EBRD) specifies that

> contributing to economic progress and reconstruction, the purpose of the Bank shall be to foster the transition towards open market-oriented economies and to promote private and entrepreneurial initiative in the Central and Eastern European countries committed to and applying the principles of multiparty democracy, pluralism and market economics.

States wishing to join the European Union must sign onto the 1950 European Convention for the Protection of Human Rights and Fundamental Freedoms. Member candidates are required to fulfill the 1993 Copenhagen criteria, which include

> stable institutions that guarantee democracy, the rule of law, human rights and respect for and protection of minorities; a functioning market economy, as well as the ability to cope with the pressure of competition and the market forces at work inside the Union; the ability to assume the obligations of membership, in particular adherence to the objectives of political, economic and monetary union.

An interesting question related to admission to international organizations is whether there is any value in sequencing admission between institutions by, for example, allowing admission to one organization as a stepping stone to joining more complex organizations. A possible sequencing could provide admission to the Organisation for Security and Co-operation in Europe (OSCE), then to the Council of Europe, and finally to the EU.

Forms of and Alternatives to Statehood

States are not univocal, but are complex and multiformed entities. Principles of international law are relevant when considering different forms of states and alternatives to statehood. Internally, states can be constructed in many different ways—they can be more or less centralized. Some states are federal states and are made up of rather independent territories. Other states guarantee a large amount of autonomy to certain parts of their territory, which can enjoy varying degrees of self-government.

---

20 IBRD Articles of Agreement, Article I, available at <http://web.worldbank.org
.WBSITE/EXTERNAL/EXTABOUTUS/0,,contentMDK:20049564~pagePK:43912~piPK:36602
,00.html#I2>. The term "World Bank" refers to the International Bank for Reconstruction and
Development (IBRD) and the International Development Association (IDA).

In postconflict situations, considering the different internal structures a state can enjoy is important in fostering durable peace. A certain degree of autonomy could be granted to encourage reconciliation between fighting groups in internal conflicts. The development of a "menu of options" could be used to propose diverse state structures during peace negotiations. This approach was used in Somalia in the mid-1990s; such a menu was developed with the assistance of the European Union, which envisaged confederation, federation, decentralized unitary state, and consociation as possible options for reaching a peace agreement. Although the process did not produce tangible results in Somalia, it could be used to foster peace in other conflict situations.[21]

Temporary or permanent alternatives to statehood could be used as transitional arrangements for postconflict situations. For example, many different arrangements exist vis-à-vis statehood. There are several dependencies, including U.S. and British territories (including the U.S. and British Virgin Islands and Puerto Rico), and French Overseas Departments and Territories (DOM/TOM, Départements d'outre-mer and territoires d'outre-mer). Ministates such as Monaco and San Marino have fostered close ties with bigger neighbors, many of which provide services, security, and defense. Other unusual sovereignty arrangements include the Holy See, which is the Episcopal jurisdiction of the Pope; the Palestinian Authority; and the Western Sahara.

Additionally, alternatives to statehood include mandates, trusteeships, colonies, international administrations, and other ad hoc solutions.

Historically, the League of Nations—and subsequently the United Nations—created mandate or trusteeship mechanisms to deal with non-self-governing territories and former colonies. The mandate system was established under the League of Nations after World War I; trusteeship agreements are characteristic of the post–World War II system. According to these arrangements, member states were to administer trust territories until their independence and under the supervision of the Trusteeship Council (Chapter XII, Article 73, of the UN Charter). Both arrangements were temporary and emphasized the priority of local interests and the obligations of the administrating states to guarantee and respect their well-being, with the objective of developing self-government or independence. Usually the administration of territories and trusteeships was taken up by former colonial powers. In very few cases, the United Nations directly took on the role of trustee. For example, in 1962–63, during the transition period from Dutch to Indonesian rule, the Netherlands and Indonesia requested that the Trusteeship Council administer New Jaya. Namibia is another example. In this case, because of South Africa's prolonged refusal to expedite the independence process of Namibia, the United Nations took over the administration of Namibia without the consent of the trustee state, South Africa, and created the Council for Namibia.

---

21 Von Hippel, *supra* note 7, at 86–89.

There are at present no trusteeship arrangements; because of the past record and colonial abuses, trusteeships are unlikely to return. However, some authors have suggested the use of some form of trusteeship to deal with state failure and to transfer the responsibility for states in disarray to the UN Trusteeship Council.[22] This proposal has created a lively debate; although it is widely agreed that a return of the UN Trusteeship Council is impossible, alternative arrangements for fragile states should be appropriately considered.[23] Any new arrangements must be based on the duty of states to cooperate and provide assistance to one another, and must be devoid of any colonial undertones.[24]

The United Nations has indeed engaged in territorial administration of postconflict territories—international territorial administration is not new. In fact, since its inception, the United Nations—and before it, the League of Nations—has been entrusted by its members with some form of temporary administration power for international territories in special circumstances. The League administered the Free City of Danzig from 1920 to 1939; the United Nations was to do the same for the planned Free Territory of Trieste in 1947 (the territory was never released for reasons unrelated to the United Nations).[25] The involvement of the United Nations in the administration of special territories has grown, especially during peace-keeping missions such as those in West Papua and Namibia.[26] Two more recent UN interventions pushed the nation-building role further, creating international authorities to administer territories in Kosovo and East Timor. Both efforts were directed at the creation of new states, and their mandates encompassed most traditional governance functions and included specific provisions for running current affairs. Both missions were temporary and directed at the reconstruction of an efficient administration for the creation of a politically viable autonomous entity.

The United Nations Interim Administration of Kosovo

In Kosovo, the General Assembly gave the power to the secretary-general "to establish in the war-ravaged province of Kosovo an interim civilian administration led by the United Nations under which its people could progressively enjoy substantial autonomy." In particular, Security Council

---

22 Gerald Helman & Steven Ratner, *Saving Failed States*, 89 Foreign Policy 3 (Winter 1993).

23 *See* Ruth Gordon, *Saving Failed States: Sometimes a Neocolonialist Notion*, 12 Am. U.J. Intl L. & Pol'y 903 (1997): *see also* Ralph Wilde, *International Territorial Administration: How Trusteeship and the Civilizing Mission Never Went Away* (Oxford U. Press 2008).

24 See Giorgetti, *supra* note 3, at 179–92.

25 *See* British–United States Zone, Allied Military Government, Official Gazette, Free Territory of Trieste, Trieste, 1947; Department of Legal Affairs, Headquarters Allied Military Government, British-U.S. Zone, Judicial Decisions and Legal Opinions on Matters of Jurisdiction Relating to the Free Territory of Trieste, 1951.

26 Bruce Jones with Feryal Cherif, Evolving Models of Peacekeeping: Policy Implications and Responses, External Study 11 (Center on International Cooperation, NYU undated).

Resolution 1244 (1999) authorized the United Nations Interim Administration in Kosovo (UNMIK) to

> Perform basic civilian administrative functions; Promote the estab-
> lishment of substantial autonomy and self-government in Kosovo;
> Facilitate a political process to determine Kosovo's future status; Co-
> ordinate humanitarian and disaster relief of all international agen-
> cies; Support the reconstruction of key infrastructure; Maintain civil
> law and order; Promote human rights; and Ensure the safe and un-
> impeded return of all refugees and displaced persons to their homes
> in Kosovo.

The same resolution, approved under Chapter VII of the UN Charter, authorized the deployment of the Kosovo Force (KFOR), a peace-keeping force
led by NATO. The mandate for UNMIK included a special representative of
the secretary-general for Kosovo, who presided over the work of the administration and facilitated the political process designed to determine Kosovo's future status. The special representative was appointed by the secretary-general
under the advice of UN member states. In June 1999, UNMIK set up the Joint
Interim Administrative Structure to reestablish and deliver central and municipal administrative services. In most municipalities, municipal assemblies
with presidents, deputies, chief executive officers, and mandatory committees
on policy and finance, communities, and mediation were elected by the end
of 2000.

UNMIK regulated several internal matters that included international
obligations. For example, the special representative adopted several regulations establishing customs and taxes and Regulation 1999/12, which
established an international postal service. Regulation 1999/20 created the
Banking and Payments Authority of Kosovo and included specific provisions for international technical cooperation. Regulation 2000/25 established
the administrative department of transport and infrastructure and included
special provisions for air transport directed at supervising and regulating
"air transport carriers, air transport system operations, including air traffic
and air transport facility construction and maintenance." UNMIK approved
a constitutional framework that established provisional institutions of self-
government for Kosovo, including an assembly and a government headed by
a prime minister. These institutions were created in tandem with the transfer
of administrative powers to them from UNMIK.

The United Nations Transitional Authority in East Timor

The United Nations mission in East Timor was based on a framework similar to the one developed in UNMIK. UN Security Council Resolution 1272
provides that the United Nations Transitional Authority in East Timor (UN-
TAET) "has overall responsibility for the administration of East Timor and is

empowered to exercise all legislative and executive authority, including the administration of justice." This 1999 resolution mandates UNTAET

> to provide security and maintain law and order throughout the territory of East Timor; to establish an effective administration; to assist in the development of civil and social services; to ensure the coordination and delivery of humanitarian assistance, rehabilitation and development assistance; to support capacity-building for self-government; to assist in the establishment of conditions for sustainable development.

UNTAET's mandate was subsequently elaborted upon in various resolutions. Regulations adopted in 1999–2001, including Regulation 2000/12, Provisional Tax and Custom Regimes, and Regulation 2001/30, Banking and Payment Authority, include specific provisions for international technical cooperation. East Timor became an independent country on May 20, 2002. On the same day, the United Nations Mission of Support in East Timor (UNMISET) succeeded UNTAET. UNMISET was established under UN Security Council Resolution 1410 (2002) with the aim of providing assistance to administrative structures of the now-independent East Timor.

UNMIK and UNTAET created substantial debate among international lawyers, some criticizing these efforts as too invasive and opportunistic, while others praised the decisive involvement of a usually hesitant international community.[27] For the purpose of this chapter, it is useful to remember that the international community can be involved at different levels and in different forms in postconflict reconstruction. Furthermore, in both UNMIK and UNTEAT, domestic legislation was enacted by following existing normative standards on issues as diverse as banking, taxes, and transportation. In the immediate future, the actions of the international community in Afghanistan and Iraq will provide material for consideration. Furthermore, different examples of internal structures of the state should be examined in fragile states.

International Law Ensures That the Basic Rights of Individuals Are Respected

Human rights can play a fundamental role in postconflict and fragile situations. The successful creation of an international legal regime for human rights is a great achievement of the international community, and its consequence for postconflict reconstruction is substantial. The relevance of human rights in international law has substantially increased in the past twenty years. States can no longer make sovereignty claims in defense of egregious rights abuses. As

---

27   For a summary of the debate, *see* Wilde, *supra* note 23.

Rosalyn Higgins argues, "there is now a yardstick against which the behavior of states may be judged and a point of reference for the individual in the assertion of his claim."[28] Human rights principles provide a framework that directs state behavior toward its domestic population. Individuals have acquired a large range of rights vis-à-vis their own governments, which cannot claim domestic sovereignty privileges. Importantly, the rights acquired by individuals from their governments derive from international legal conventions and institutions to which states have voluntarily consented.

Human rights principles provide important structure and support for individuals, particularly those living in unstable situations.

Basic Human Rights Provisions

In general, human rights principles provide a specific framework within which states must act toward their citizens; that framework must include certain specific freedoms and rights. Obligations to confer rights on individuals are enumerated by international binding agreements, principally concluded under the aegis of the United Nations. There are six main widely ratified human rights conventions: the Universal Declaration of Human Rights; the International Covenant on Civil and Political Rights; the International Covenant on Economic, Social and Cultural Rights; the Convention against Torture and Other Cruel, Inhuman or Degrading Treatment or Punishment; the Convention on the Elimination of All Forms of Discrimination against Women; and the Convention on the Rights of the Child.

The rights afforded by states to their populations in accordance with these treaties include the right to life, the right to equality, the right to religious freedom, the right to a fair trial, the prohibition of cruel and unusual punishment, the prohibition of child labor and of recruiting child soldiers, the right to work, and the right of equality for women in education and work. Historically, there has been a distinction between civil and political rights on one side and economic, social, and cultural rights on the other. Since the end of the Cold War, a new (third) wave of human rights has surged that includes the right to development and the right to a clean environment. Although these rights are still emerging, they are increasingly gaining international recognition. These rights provide a framework within which a state must act toward its citizens and guide strategies for assisting fragile states.

International and Regional Provisions

The United Nations Charter provides for the fulfillment of personal rights of individuals by promoting "higher standards of living, full employment, and conditions of economic and social progress and development" as well as "solutions of international economic, social, health, and related problems; and international cultural and educational cooperation" and "universal respect for,

---

28   Rosalyn Higgins, *Conceptual Thinking about the Individual in International Law*, 4 British J. Intl. Studies 24 (1978).

and observance of, human rights and fundamental freedoms for all without distinction as to race, sex, language, or religion" (Article 55). These obligations fall on each member state. In fact, each member of the organization pledges to take action to achieve these goals (Article 56). As such, the United Nations is an organizational structure made up of agencies and programs to monitor the development and implementation of these rights by each state.

At the same time, regional organizations—including the European Union, the African Union, and the Organization of American States—have been created in practically every region of the world (with the notable exception of Asia). These organizations also impose obligations on each of their members, including numerous individual civil and political rights, as well as economic and social rights and rights of protection for minorities. Importantly, these regional organizations include judicial organs, which interpret the content of states' human rights obligations and can, in certain circumstances, allow individuals to obtain redress from states for human rights violations. These mechanisms can be fundamental in conflict situations.

For example, the European Court of Human Rights heard several cases related to the Georgia-Russia and Cyprus conflicts.[29] Similarly, the Inter-American Court of Human Rights played an important in role in providing redress to victims of human rights abuses in Latin America.[30] The European Court of Human Rights can directly entertain individual complaints.[31]

Human Rights in Fragile and Conflict-Affected States

Ratification of international human rights instruments is important in fragile and conflict-affected states. As Helen Durham argues, treaty ratification can assist a state in reassembling domestic legal infrastructure and demonstrate public support for important international principles that can assist in easing conflict.[32] In postconflict and fragile states, treaty ratification can also

---

29 *See*, for example, *Cyprus v. Turkey* I & II (case no. 6780/74, joined with case. no. 6780/75); *Cyprus v. Turkey* (case no. 8007/77); *Georgia v. Russia* I (13255/07) (2007); *Georgia v. Russia* II (case no. 38263/08) (2008); and *Georgia v. Russia* III (case no. 61186/09). For a complete list, *see* <http://www.echr.coe.int/NR/rdonlyres/5D5BA416-1FE0-4414-95A1-AD6C1D77CB90/0/Requêtes_interétatiques_EN.pdf>. The complete case law of the court is available at <http://www.echr.coe.int/ECHR/EN/Header/Case-Law/Decisions+and+judgments/HUDOC+database/>.

30 Information about the Inter-American Court of Human Rights is available at <http://www.corteidh.or.cr/>.

31 *See* Article 34 of the European Human Rights Convention, as amended by Protocol 11 (stating, "The Court may receive applications from any person, non-governmental organisation or group of individuals claiming to be the victim of a violation by one of the High Contracting Parties of the rights set forth in the Convention or the Protocols thereto. The High Contracting Parties undertake not to hinder in any way the effective exercise of this right"), available at <http://www.echr.coe.int/NR/rdonlyres/D5CC24A7-DC13-4318-B457-5C9014916D7A/0/ENG_CONV.pdf>.

32 Helen Durham, *From Paper to Practice: The Role of Treaty Ratification Post-conflict*, in *The Role of International Law in Rebuilding Societies after Conflict* 177 (Brett Bowden, Hilary Charlesworth, & Jeremy Farrall ed., Cambridge U. Press 2009).

incorporate recognized international legal standards into national norms and practice. Furthermore, treaty ratification can foster a connection between international norms and local understandings of them, providing a link between the postconflict society and the international community. Additionally, ratification of international treaties may have a beneficial symbolic effect on countries that underwent conflict as a demonstration that they are now full-fledged participants in the international community. For example, in the aftermath of a vicious civil war, Liberia chose to sign, ratify, or access 103 treaties on a single day in 2005, an occasion that was celebrated by the UN secretary-general as "a landmark in Liberia's journey away from a difficult past and toward a more tenable future grounded in the rule of law, respect for human rights, and good democratic governance."[33] Aside from the symbolic importance of such gestures,[34] however, this issue raises important questions on the implementation of these treaties and the need for personnel and financial resources to support implementation. The ratification of international treaties is also a means of allowing fragile states to continue engagement with the international community in general, as well as with institutions like the World Bank.[35]

International Human Rights in Fragile States: Superiority vis-à-vis Contradictory Local Norms

International human rights principles can directly influence conflict and fragility in many ways. In signatory states, international human rights standards take precedence over any contradictory local or domestic norms. In certain cases, as in Kosovo, human rights standards are implemented through binding declarations of the international administrations, mandating the respect of international law over any other sources of norms. It is important to ensure that there is no confusion about the correct application of international law.

---

33 *Id.*, at 189.

34 Scholars have struggled to explain why states choose to ratify international human rights treaties and to assess the consequence of ratification. Oona Hathaway argues that although the countries that have ratified human rights treaties generally have a better human rights record than those that have not, noncompliance with treaty obligations appears common. She further argues that treaty ratification may in fact be associated with worse practices than otherwise expected. *See* Oona Hathaway, *Do Human Rights Treaties Make a Difference?* 111 Yale L.J. 1870 (2002). Alternatively, some scholars argue that the ratification of international human rights instruments has a positive impact on the enjoyment of human rights by domestic populations. Beth Simmons argues that evidence suggests that governments that have ratified the ICCPR are more likely than those that have not to reduce their interference in the free practice of religion. Ratified treaties have their strongest effects in countries that are neither stable democracies nor stable autocracies. For example, the CAT has had a more significant impact on transitioning countries than on stable ones. See Beth A. Simmons, *Mobilizing for Human Rights: International Law in Domestic Politics* 355–63 (Cambridge U. Press 2009).

35 Durham, *supra* note 32, at 189.

International Human Rights in Fragile States:
Restoration of Previously Restricted Rights

The implementation of international human rights is especially important in fragile states; international human rights norms can be instrumental in reviving previously restricted civil liberties and freedoms such as speech, expression, and religious exercise, which may have been a cause of conflict. As such, human rights principles have the potential to foster reconciliation, shorten conflict, and blunt recidivism. The extent to which these rights can be meaningfully implemented depends on the nature of the conflict and of postconflict institutions.

International Human Rights Norms Applicable Only in Fragile States

Certain human rights principles are specifically directed at guiding states' behavior in conflict situations. For example, certain basic human rights can never be derogated, even at times of public emergencies. Under the ICCPR, these basic rights include the right to life; the prohibition of slavery and of torture or cruel, inhuman, or degrading treatment or punishment; the freedom of thought, conscience, and religion; and the principle of nondiscrimination. Additionally, human rights law provides specific protections that can assist the reconciliation process. For example, Article 20 of the ICCPR prohibits war propaganda and the advocacy of national, racial, or religious hatred that constitutes incitement to discrimination, hostility, or violence. Such norms can be instrumental in supporting cease-fire and peace agreements.

International Human Rights and the International Community

Human rights principles have at times been criticized as Western based.[36] However, a detailed study of human rights principles and customary principles applicable in most states demonstrates the similarities of these norms. Furthermore, although cultural sensitivities intrinsically run through all international law considerations, the issue of human rights relativity seems at times to be an opportunistic argument to avoid compliance. For example, in Somalia, the International Committee of the Red Cross (ICRC) was able to translate and explain the main essential tenets of Article 3 of the Geneva Convention by depicting it using local and traditional norms.

Human Rights Approach

It is now common for donors and aid agencies to adopt a rights-based approach.[37] In 2003, UN secretary-general Kofi Annan requested all UN agencies to mainstream human rights in all their activities and programming.

---

36   *See,* for example, Michael A. Freeman, *Human Rights: An Interdisciplinary Approach* 101–55 (2d ed., Polity Press 2011).

37   For a position on human rights by the World Bank, *see* Ana Palacio, *The Way Forward: Human Rights and the World Bank* (2006), available at <http://web.worldbank.org/WB SITE/EXTERNAL/TOPICS/EXTLAWJUSTICE/0,,contentMDK:21106614~menuPK:445673 ~pagePK:64020865~piPK:149114~theSitePK:445634,00.html>.

In practice, this means that international human rights principles guide all phases of programming, including assessing, analyzing, planning, designing, implementing, monitoring, and evaluating any assistance program.[38] Under this approach, the priority of international agencies and donors is to ensure that human rights are respected. As such, rights holders and their entitlements are identified, as are the corresponding duty bearers and their obligations. Assistance is provided to fulfill rights and obligations. This approach can be useful when resolving existing conflict. For example, on issues related to competing claims for shared resources, the World Bank sponsored the independent World Commission on Dams, which held that recognition of rights and assessment of risk would provide the basis for negotiated decisions of dams and their alternatives.[39]

Electoral Assistance

There is an increasing emphasis on ensuring that transitional administrations and new governments respect basic human rights principles and minority protections. Several UN programs assist with and supervise the fair occurrence of elections. Under Resolution 51/31, the UN General Assembly pledged to support the efforts of governments to promote and consolidate new or restored democracies. The Electoral Assistance Division of the UN Department for Political Affairs received 363 official requests for electoral assistance between 1989 and 2005 and provided electoral services in 96 countries.[40] Similarly, the European Union undertook to promote human rights and democratization in non-EU countries: for example, the Cotonou Agreement, concluded with African, Caribbean, and Pacific countries, bases the allocation of a part of the European Development Fund (governance initiative) on the beneficiary countries' commitment to institutional reforms in several governance-related fields, including human rights, democracy, and the rule of law. Humanitarian aid, however, is not related to the beneficiary country's respect for human rights.[41]

Right to Democracy

Similarly, there has been an increasing emphasis on ensuring that new and postconflict states are democratic. As Anne Peters argues, citing Lebanon, Cambodia, Afghanistan, East Timor, and the Democratic Republic of Congo, "post-conflict regime-building with international support has always been

---

38 UNICEF, The Human Rights Based Approach: A Statement of Common Understanding, available at <http://www.unicef.org/sowc04/files/AnnexB.pdf>.

39 Office of the United Nations High Commissioner for Human Rights, Frequently Asked Questions on a Human Rights–Based Approach to Development Cooperation, available at <http://www.ohchr.org/Documents/Publications/FAQen.pdf>.

40 See Electoral Assistance Division, Overview Information, available at <http://www.un.org/Depts/dpa/ead/overview.html>.

41 See Communication from the Commission to the Council and the European Parliament of 8 May 2001—The European Union's Role in Promoting Human Rights and Democratization in Third Countries (2001).

democratic."[42] This concept entails that the running of the state must be decided through periodical, free elections that are open to the entire adult population and requires the state to act upon its obligations to grant internationally recognized human rights and provide a minimum standard of living and freedom that allows all its citizens to enjoy a productive, free, and dignified life. However, the claim that international law should require states to be democratic has been criticized on the grounds that such a requirement is externally imposed and can be a vehicle for neocolonialism.[43] Critics also argue that in situations of fragility and conflict, it is too difficult for external actors to maintain their neutrality and independence within the political discourse of a nascent state.[44]

International Transitional Justice

Human rights principles play a fundamental role in ensuring transitional justice in postconflict situations. Transitional justice seeks recognition for victims and promotes possibilities for peace, reconciliation, and democracy.

Transitional justice relates to the accountability of human rights abuses and humanitarian law violation in postconflict situations and can assist societies in transition in reestablishing cohesion and providing retribution, deterrence, historical recording, and understanding and closure to the victims of abuse. Transitional justice can take many forms, including international or national criminal prosecutions, truth commissions, reparations programs, gender justice, security system reform, and memorialization efforts.

Truth and reconciliation commissions, which were common in Latin America and in post-apartheid South Africa, are essentially locally driven processes. Their goal is to provide a historical account of what happened and foster reconciliation. Often, criminal prosecutions are exchanged for public confessions and acknowledgment by perpetrators of past wrongdoings. Truth commissions are often official state bodies whose members are highly respected individuals, including international law practitioners. They make recommendations to remedy abuse and to prevent its recurrence.

Increasingly, transitional justice has taken on a judicial aspect, with the creation of international or internationalized courts or tribunals and the use of domestic courts. International ad hoc tribunals include the Tribunal for the Former Yugoslavia (ICTY) and the Rwanda Tribunal (ICTR), which were created as organs of the United Nations acting in its Chapter VII capacity. They

---

42   Anne Peters, *Dual Democracy*, in *The Constitutionalization of International Law* 263, 276 (Jan Klabbers, Anne Peters, & Geir Ulfstein ed., Oxford U. Press 2009).

43   For a thorough discussion on the topic, *see Democratic Governance and International Law* (Gregory H. Fox & Brad R. Roth ed., Cambridge U. Press 2000).

44   For example, on the issue of humanitarian intervention, *see*, in general, Lea Brilmayer, *What Is the Matter with Selective Intervention?* 37 Ariz. L. Rev. 955 (1995) (analyzing interventions by the United States); Christine Gray, *International Law and the Use of Force* (Oxford U. Press 2004); and *Humanitarian Intervention: Ethical, Legal and Political Dilemmas* (J. L. Holzgrefe & Robert O. Keohane ed., Cambridge U. Press 2003).

prosecute war crimes, crimes against humanity, and crimes of genocide. The ICTY and ICTR are the first post-Nuremberg examples of international criminal tribunals and have been fundamental in the development of international criminal law and ensuring retribution. However, they have been criticized for being too expensive and too detached from local realities and for providing "too little, too late."[45]

Several hybrid tribunals have been created, including the Sierra Leone Special Court and the Cambodia Extraordinary Chambers, that blend domestic and international principles and personnel.

In 2002, the International Criminal Court (ICC) was created as a first permanent tribunal mandated to prosecute individuals for war crimes, crimes against humanity, and genocide committed in the territories of signature countries or by nationals of signature countries or in special situations approved by the UN Security Council. The ICC's 110 members do not include the United States, China, Russia, or India.[46] The court can act only when national courts are unwilling or unable to investigate or prosecute such crimes. At present, the ICC is investigating events in Uganda, the Democratic Republic of Congo, the Central African Republic, Kenya, Darfur (Sudan—referred by the Security Council), and Libya (also referred to the prosecutor by the Security Council).[47]

In situations of state fragility and conflict, mechanisms must be established to ensure that international transitional justice and the international community can play a fundamental role. The United Nations and other international actors are involved in providing and developing justice mechanisms, and it is important at this stage to assess all available instruments and lessons learnt so that prompt and targeted advice can be given in postconflict reconstruction efforts.

International Humanitarian Law

International humanitarian law is a distinct body of law that is important in fragile and conflict-affected states. In times of armed conflict, international human rights law and international humanitarian law apply in a complementary manner. Humanitarian law regulates the conduct of hostilities and establishes minimum protection for civilians and victims of conflict; it prohibits direct attacks against civilians and civilian infrastructures and mandates parties to take precautionary measures to avoid or minimize

---

45   *See* Mahnoush A. Arsanjani & W. Michael Reisman, *The Law-in-Action of the International Criminal Court*, 99 Am. J. Intl. L. 385 (2005); Robert D. Sloane, *Sentencing for the "Crime of Crimes": The Evolving "Common Law" of the International Criminal Tribunal for Rwanda*, 5 J. Intl. Crim. Just. 713 (2007); and, generally, Jens David Ohlin, *Applying the Death Penalty to Crimes of Genocide*, 99 Am. J. Intl. L. 747 (2005).

46   A list of the states that are parties to the Rome Statute can found at <http://www.icc-cpi.int/Menus/ASP/states+parties/>.

47   For a short overview of the cases, *see* <http://www.icc-cpi.int/Menus/ICC/Situations+and+Cases/>.

incidental injuries to civilians. Since 1999 (and as a consequence of the shames of Srebenica and Rwanda), the mandates of all UN peace-keeping missions and operations led by regional organizations such as the African Union and the EU include a specific authorization to provide civilian protection.[48] A 2001 report by the International Commission on Intervention and State Sovereignty argues that states have a "responsibility to protect" civilians in situations of grave human rights abuses.[49]

Human rights principles can play an important role in fragile states by ensuring minimum rights of all people, by providing redress—including by judicial proceedings—when those rights are violated, and by guiding actions of the fragile state.

International Law Provides Support and Models to Reestablish a Functioning Domestic Legal Order

In addition to providing a general legal framework to guide state rebuilding and guarantee basic rights to individuals, international norms play an important role in reconstructing a domestic legal system, including writing constitutions, establishing domestic institutions, and promulgating legal codes. Sources of models include international and comparative legal regimes and standards and norms developed by international organizations.

Development and Humanitarian Assistance Programs in Fragile States

In situations where a state cannot entirely provide for the needs and rights of its people, donor countries have established cooperation programs and agencies to provide economic and technical development assistance. In these situations, international organizations and foreign states often provide substantial budgetary and technical support for essential governmental activities. In some cases, international experts manage key internal functions of a government. Development projects can range from the delivery of healthcare services to the restructuring of the legal and judicial systems. These types of interventions have generally been pursued with the consent of the government where the interventions took place.

Development and humanitarian assistance include the delivery of food, mainly by the World Food Program (WFP) and Food and Agriculture Organization of the United Nations (FAO), and water, sanitation, and health products, mainly by the World Health Organization (WHO) and the United

---

48   *See* Siobhán Wills, *Protecting Civilians: The Obligations of Peacekeepers* (Oxford U. Press 2009).

49   Report of the International Commission on Intervention and State Sovereignty, the Responsibility to Protect (Dec. 2001), available at <http://www.iciss.ca/pdf/Commission-Report.pdf>.

Nations Children's Fund (UNICEF). Other international actors, national aid agencies, and NGOs participate with these organizations in the implementation and delivery of development and humanitarian programs.

In fragile states where a national government cannot control large parts of the country that it represents or in situations where a government is absent, the international community has tried to provide development and humanitarian assistance with the consent of the local authorities in control of the territories. For example, UNICEF implements vaccination campaigns with the support of local authorities.

In certain situations of fragility, international organization conduct in several areas of internal affairs has been extensive to the point that international organizations affect the conduct of national affairs. The extent of their influence is particularly relevant in cases of very weak governments. For example, in Somalia, which has been without a government since 1991, the international community has been involved in port and road rehabilitation, judicial and legal restructuring, health service delivery and vaccination, and education—including choosing curriculum and the language of instruction.

A special body, the Somalia Aid Coordination Body (SACB),[50] was formed in December 1993 and restructured in 2006 to coordinate and organize funding and projects to provide assistance to the people of Somalia by the organizations working on and in Somalia. It comprised donor countries, UN agencies and programs, and NGOs. The framework for the SACB was outlined in the Addis Ababa Declaration[51] and the Code of Conduct for International Rehabilitation and Development Assistance.[52] In practice, the SACB coordinated and controlled most of the aid given to Somalia; it developed and implemented policies and guidelines for interventions, and in many cases it is a veritable partial substitute for government action.[53]

The risks of over-influencing domestic constituencies and imposing solutions are real and must be attentively scrutinized.

In providing assistance to fragile and conflict-affected countries, international organizations and other donors often refer to settled norms of international law. This situation is particularly visible in the implementation of rule of law and governance projects.

Rule of Law Projects

The powerful notion at the heart of the rule of law principle is that nobody is above the law, which implies that all people are equal in front of the law, all

---

50   *See* Somalia Aid Coordination Body, *Handbook* (2001).

51   *Id.*, at 2.

52   *Id.*, at 10.

53   Working arrangements between the international aid community and responsible Somali authorities, Nairobi, June 1996. *See* UN Doc. A/51/315, available at <http://www.un.org/documents/ga/docs/51/plenary/a51-315.htm>.

laws are applied equally, and political power should be exercised in accordance with agreed-upon law. Cognizant of the fundamental role played by the rule of law in ensuring long-lasting political and economic recovery, several international donors have implemented projects directed at strengthening the rule of law in peace-keeping and postconflict operations.[54]

The UN Security Council has espoused the principle and the 2000 Millennium Declaration[55] lists the goal of strengthening respect for the rule of law as the first of its objectives. The importance of the rule of law is also recognized in the 2000 Report of the Panel on UN Peace Operations (the Brahimi Report).[56]

In their concrete application, rule of law programs normally include four areas: supporting, restructuring, and retraining a national police force; assisting in the reconstruction of correction facilities and training of its personnel; rebuilding, reopening, and ensuring the functioning of the national court system; and promoting the protection of human rights and creating a mechanism of transitional justice. The implementation of rule of law projects in postconflict situations, including in Haiti and Liberia, has been rather problematic.[57] In fact, efforts of the international community have been perceived as ineffective and, at times, partisan and unbalanced, giving the "winning side" the instruments to consolidate its power.[58]

Governance Projects

Governance projects have been similarly criticized. The World Bank and the United Nations were the first international organizations to study and expand the model of good governance as a development policy. For example, the work of the United Nations Environment Programme (UNDP) is directed at strengthening democratic governance. The UNDP is active in parliamentary development, electoral systems and processes, access to justice and human rights, access to information, decentralization and local governance and public administration, and civil service reform. Projects in this area include assistance in setting up effective parliamentary "structures, systems, processes and procedures," as well as providing training to parliamentarians; providing assistance for electoral processes and for the establishment of systems of justice and laws, including legal and judicial reforms such as "improving the structure, organization and administration of court systems; training judges, magistrate, lawyers and support personnel." In 2008, the UNDP provided US$1.4 billion

---

54 See Jeremy Farrall, *Impossible Expectations? The UN Security Council's Promotion of the Rule of Law after Conflict*, in *The Role of International Law in Rebuilding Societies after Conflict* 134 (Brett Bowden, Hilary Charlesworth, & Jeremy Farrall ed., Cambridge U. Press 2009).

55 UN Millennium Declaration, UN Doc. A/Res./55/2, available at <http://www.un.org/millennium/declaration/ares552e.htm>.

56 Report of the Panel on United Nations Peace Operations, UN Doc. A/55/305–S/2000/809 (Aug. 22, 2002), available at <http://www.un.org/peace/reports/peace_operations/>.

57 *Id.*, at 148–53.

58 *See*, in general, *The Role of International Law in Rebuilding Societies after Conflict: Great Expectations* (Brett Bowden, Hilary Charlesworth, & Jeremy Farrall ed., Cambridge U. Press 2009).

to programs fostering democratic governance in 129 countries. For example, it supported electoral reform efforts in Lebanon through national awareness campaigns and the publication and dissemination of draft law booklets in several languages to libraries, universities, and the public in general.

In both governance and rule of law projects, international institutions and donor countries play a role at the very core of the running of the state. This assistance is therefore invaluable in postconflict societies. Lessons learned from the field show that avoiding the pitfalls of perceived favoritism, overdue influence, and overpromising is particularly important in postconflict societies.[59]

Emergency Assistance and Special Programming by International Organizations in Fragile and Failing States

International assistance by international organizations is normally based on an official agreement between the international organization and the recipient country.[60] In some exceptional cases, however, some international organizations can act without the specific agreement of the host state. Two examples are important.

The WFP was established[61] by the United Nations and the FAO in 1963 to fight hunger[62] and provide emergency food aid and associated nonfood

---

59 For a critical overview, *see* Thomas G. Weiss & Ramesh Thakur, *Global Governance and the UN: An Unfinished Journey* (Indiana U. Press 2009), and Jörg Friedrichs, *Global Governance as the Hegemonic Project of Transatlantic Civil Society*, in *Criticizing Global Governance* 45 (Markus Lederer & Philipp S. Müller ed., Palgrave Macmillan 2005).

60 *See*, for example, UN GA Res. 46/182, UN GAOR, 46th Sess., Supp. No. 49, UN Doc. A/46/49 (1991), which created the Office for the Coordination of Humanitarian Affairs (OCHA) (stating, "The sovereignty, territorial integrity and national unity of states must be fully respected in accordance with the Charter of the United Nations. In this context, humanitarian assistance should be provided with the consent of the affected country and in principle on the basis of an appeal by the affected country"). Similarly, the General Assembly resolution establishing UNICEF provides that "the Fund in agreement with the Government concerned, shall take all measures as are deemed appropriate to ensure the proper distribution of supplies or other assistance it provides" and further requires UNICEF not to engage in activity in any country "except in consultation with, and the consent of, the government concerned." *See* GA Res. 57(I), UN GAOR, 1st Sess., UN Doc. A/64/Add.1 (1946). The UNDP operates under the same premises. *See* the Standard Basic Assistance Agreement (SBAA) between the Recipient Government and the UNDP, available at <http://www.undp.org/idp/docs/TemplateSBAA .doc>. *See* also Decision 1998/2, in Decision Adopted by the Executive Board during 1998, DP/1999/2 (Oct. 5, 1998), available at <http://www.undp.org/execbrd/pdf/dp99-2e.pdf>.

61 World Food Programme, General Regulations and General Rules, Article I (Nov. 2010 ed.), available at <http://one.wfp.org/aboutwfp/how_run/GeneralRegulations_E.pdf>.

62 The WFP performs both emergency and longer-term activities; namely, it provides food assistance in refugee crises and other emergencies; improves nutrition for the world's most vulnerable, and promotes longer-term self-reliance of poor people and communities. *See* World Food Programme, Operations, available at <http://www.wfp.org/operations/ introduction/index.asp?section=5&sub_section=1>. In order to carry out its mandate in situations of emergency, the WFP Executive Board established several program categories, including a Development Programme Category, for food aid programs and projects to support economic and social development; an Emergency Relief Program Category, for food assistance to meet emergency needs; a Protracted Relief Program Category for food

items and logistics support at the request of the UN secretary-general. In exceptional cases, assistance "shall be fully coordinated with the United Nations system and efforts of governments, intergovernmental and non-governmental organizations in the areas concerned."[63] Further, Article X provides that bilateral donors, UN agencies, and NGOs can request "WFP services for operations which are consistent with the purposes of WFP and which complement WFP's operations."[64]

Similarly, the Governing Council of the UNDP may, under special circumstances, grant power to the administrator to approve assistance on a project-by-project basis without a formal agreement with the host country. This arrangement has been used in Myanmar and Somalia.[65]

The possibility that certain international organizations may directly provide or ask for assistance without the need for an official agreement or request by the government may provide a useful instrument in situations of state fragility and failure because it allows international organizations to, essentially, bypass the obstacle of government absence or lack of control. The very possibility of such an instrument is especially significant and should be kept in careful consideration for actions in situations of state failure.

---

assistance to meet protracted relief needs; a Special Operations Program Category for interventions undertaken to rehabilitate and enhance transport and logistics infrastructure to permit timely and efficient delivery of food assistance, especially to meet emergency and protracted relief needs and to enhance coordination within the United Nations System and with other partners through the provision of designated common services. *See* World Food Programme, General Regulations and General Rules, General Rule II.2. Recent interventions by WFP include assistance to refugees and internally displaced persons, including in places like Cote d'Ivoire and Libya, and providing assistance to population hit by tropical storm Matthew in Nicaragua and by floods in the Gambia. *See* World Food Programme, Operations List, available at <http://www.wfp.org/operations/list>.

63   *See* World Food Programme, General Regulations and General Rules, Article IX, Eligibility for Assistance.

64   *Id.*, Article X, Requests for Assistance.

65   For example, in Myanmar, Governing Council Decision 1993/21, reaffirmed by the board in decision 1996/1, to authorize the administrator to approve project extensions on a project-by-project basis. *See* UNDP Governing Council Decision 1993/21 (stating that the Governing Council decides "that, until a country programme for Myanmar is considered at an appropriate time, all future assistance from the United Nations Development Programme and related funds to Myanmar should be clearly targeted towards programmes having grass-roots-level impact in a sustainable manner, as called for in the aforesaid decision 92/26, particularly in the areas of primary health care, the environment, HIV/AIDS, training and education, and food security; [. . . and] requests the Administrator to continue to approve assistance to Myanmar on a project-by-project basis and to present to the Governing Council a report on the status of approval and implementation of new projects and recommendations for future programming, for its review at its forty first session (1994)"), available at <http://www.mm.undp.org/Executive_board.html#96>. The same arrangement is valid for some UNDP projects in Somalia. *See also* Giorgetti, *supra* note 3, at 30–35.

International Conventional Norms of General Applicability

In addition to international standards applicable specifically to fragile states, several international norms can assist in strengthening the legal systems of postconflict countries and states coming out of fragility. These include laws, standards, and best practice on diverse issues such as establishing central bank and fiscal supervisory and regulatory structures and strengthening transparency and accountability institutions, such as anticorruption agencies, supreme audit institutions, parliamentary committees, and antinarcotics enforcement.

In general, specific obligations derive from treaties and conventions, which are sources of international law and are binding only on states that have expressly agreed to be bound. The number of international conventions and bilateral and multilateral treaties increased substantially between 1946 and 2006. International norms ensuing from international treaties include rules on contracts for the international sale of goods, regulation of sea resources and air space traffic, regulations on trade, intellectual property protection, and international telecommunication. Some of these treaties recognize the special challenges faced by developing countries. A specific body of the United Nations, the International Law Commission (ILC), congregates recognized international legal experts for the promotion of the progressive development and codification of international law. The ILC developed a draft of the Rome Convention establishing the ICC, the Vienna Convention on Consular Relations, and the Vienna Convention on the Succession of States in Respect of Treaties.

For example, the 2005 UN Convention against Corruption is a broadly ratified treaty with 140 parties. Its widely recognized principles have resulted in the introduction and implementation of concrete obligations in domestic legal systems. To foster compliance, a group of experts representing various legal systems and observers from several UN organizations developed a legislative guide for the implementation of the convention to assist states seeking to ratify and implement the convention by identifying legislative requirements and developing the necessary legislation.[66]

Similarly, the 1980 UN Convention on the International Sale of Goods (CISG) provides legal rules governing the formation of a commercial contract for the international sale of goods and sets forth the rights and obligations of the buyer and seller. The convention has 74 parties and includes remedies for breach of contract as well as other aspects of the selling contract.[67]

Many other examples exist. The World Trade Organization (WTO), with 153 members, provides legal ground rules for international commerce, with

---

66   The 300-page Legislative Guide is available at <http://www.unodc.org/unodc/en/treaties/CAC/legislative-guide.html>.

67   The text of the convention and an explanatory note are available at <http://www.uncitral.org/uncitral/en/uncitral_texts/sale_goods/1980CISG.html>.

the purpose of helping trade flow as freely as possible.[68] The Convention on International Aviation (Chicago Convention) includes norms regulating air space and overflight rights, air craft registrations, and safety.[69] The 1982 United Nations Convention on the Law of the Sea (UNCLOS) regulates the rights and responsibility of states in their use of the world's oceans and establishes guidelines for business, the environment, and the management of natural resources. UNCLOS defines territorial waters and extends the exclusive economic zone to 200 nautical miles, allowing coastal nations sole exploitation rights over all natural resources therein.[70]

Each of these widely ratified treaties includes general rules that could be applicable in postconflict situations and could assist in developing domestic norms and in their integration into the international economic system.

Uniform and Model Rules

Additionally, the United Nations has developed uniform and model rules that provide a framework for and examples of legislation to be included in domestic legal systems.

The UN Commission on International Trade Law (UNCITRAL) plays an important role in developing a legal framework to facilitate international trade and investment, two core economic issues in postconflict reconstruction. UNCITRAL has a mandate to prepare and promote the use and adoption of legislative and nonlegislative instruments. UNCITRAL has developed, through an international process involving a variety of participants, texts on international commercial arbitration and conciliation, international sale of goods and related transactions, security interests, insolvency, international payments, international transport of goods, electronic commerce and procurement, and infrastructure development.

UNCITRAL adopted model laws on the procurement of goods, construction, and services. These model laws cover topics such as international bidding rules, promotion of competition, and the fair and equal treatment of suppliers and contractors.[71] In 2003, UNCITRAL adopted a model law on privately financed infrastructure projects that includes rules governing the selection of the concessionaire, the implementation of the concession contract, and its duration, extension,

---

68 A short description of the WTO is available at <http://www.wto.org/english/thewto_e/whatis_e/tif_e/fact1_e.htm>.

69 The text of the Chicago Convention is available at <http://www.icao.int/icaonet/dcs/7300.html>.

70 The text of UNCLOS as well as a historical perspective of the convention is available at <http://www.un.org/Depts/los/convention_agreements/convention_overview_convention.htm>.

71 The text of these model laws is available at <http://www.uncitral.org/uncitral/en/uncitral_texts/procurement_infrastructure.html>.

and termination.[72] In 2002, UNCITRAL adopted a model law on international commercial arbitration that includes rules on key aspects of international arbitration that are recognized worldwide. The model law covers all stages of the arbitral proceedings. UNCITRAL also developed a model law on international credit transfers that covers issues such as obligation of sender, time of payment, and bank liability.[73] UNCITRAL's Guide on Secured Transactions provides assistance to states in developing modern secured transaction.[74]

The United Nations Office of Drug and Crime (UNODC) plays an important role in the development of model laws and rules. UNODC has created model provisions (for civil and common law systems) on money laundering, terrorist financing, preventive measures for and proceeds of crime (in collaboration with the IMF), a model terrorist financing bill, a model bill on money laundering, proceeds of crime and terrorist financing, a model mutual assistance in criminal matters bill, and a model extradition (amendment) bill (all for common law systems). For civil law systems, UNODC has created model legislation on money laundering, confiscation and international cooperation in relation to the proceeds of crime, a model law on drug trafficking and related offenses, and a model law on international cooperation (extradition and mutual legal assistance) with regard to illicit traffic in narcotic drugs, psychotropic substances, and precursors.[75]

Model laws are particularly important for fragile states because they can be immediately used and promote the unification of applicable rules and standards, thereby increasing recognition and easing implementation.

International Norms Developed by International Organizations

The use of recommendations, guidelines, and informal notes by the World Bank and other international organizations plays a role in developing generally applicable norms and standards.[76] These norms influence international law and have significant implications for national administrations and individuals, as well as for states.

In fact, relevant international norms are developed and spread by the work of international organizations themselves, importantly by the World

---

72   The text of the Model Legislative Provisions is available at <http://www.uncitral.org/uncitral/en/uncitral_texts/procurement_infrastructure/2003Model_PFIP.html>.

73   Available at <http://www.uncitral.org/uncitral/en/uncitral_texts/payments/1992Model_credit_transfers.html>.

74   2007 UNCITRAL Legislative Guide on Secured Transactions, available at <http://www.uncitral.org/pdf/english/texts/security-lg/e/final-final.clean.01-07-09.pdf>.

75   The texts of all these model laws are available at <http://www.imolin.org/imolin/en/model.html>.

76   Some scholars argue that this development can be framed as a new discipline of international law: global administrative law. *See,* for example, Benedict Kingsbury, Nico Krisch, & Richard B. Stewart, *The Emergence of Global Administrative Law,* 68 L. & Contemp. Probs. 15 (2005).

Bank, including on issues of environmental assessment, involuntary resettlement, and other social standards. In effect, as Galit Sarfaty argues,

> World Bank operational policies are becoming *de facto* global standards among other development banks as well as institutions engaged in project finance. For example, they serve as a model for the Equator Principles, a set of voluntary social and environmental guidelines that have been adopted by at least twenty-nine private banks.[77]

Further, the World Bank plays an important role in enforcing social and environmental standards in borrower countries, for example, by attempting to incorporate into domestic law provisions related to indigenous people through binding loan agreements.[78] Similarly, the IFC, part of the World Bank Group, applies environmental and social standards to all projects it finances to minimize adverse impacts for the communities.[79]

Other international organizations develop guidelines and recommendations that have an effect on the work. For example, the International Telecommunication Union adopts resolutions every year on issues such as the management of radio frequency and satellite orbits and terrestrial and satellite radio communication broadcasting that are accepted by its members. Similarly, recommendations of the International Labour Organization, the International Civil Aviation Organization, and the United Nations Educational, Scientific, and Cultural Organization (UNESCO) are often considered as norm setting by their members.[80]

International Norms Developed by Hybrid Intergovernmental Administration

Finally, norms developed by hybrid intergovernmental administration create international norms and standards that are relevant for fragile states.

For example, the Codex Alimentarius Commission includes members of FAO, WHO, and several NGOs and develops standards for food safety. Similarly, the Internet Corporation for Assigned Names and Numbers (ICANN), a public corporation that includes both NGOs and government representatives, regulates the internet address protocol.[81]

---

77 See Galit A. Sarfaty, *The World Bank and the Internationalization of Indigenous Rights Norms*, 114 Yale L.J. 1791 (2005).

78 *Id.*

79 The IFC's Policy on Social and Environmental Sustainability is available at <http://www.ifc.org/ifcext/sustainability.nsf/Content/SustainabilityPolicy>.

80 *See* Benedict Kingsbury & Lorenzo Casini, *Global Administrative Law Dimensions of International Organizations Law*, 6 Intl. Organizations L. Rev. 319 (2009).

81 Kingsbury, Krisch, & Stewart, *supra* note 76, at 22.

Conclusion

The abundance of international norms and standards that can have an impact on postconflict reconstruction is clear, but they are complex to assess given the multiplicity of sources. Two sets of norms are particularly relevant—those linked to sovereignty and those linked to human rights.

Several international norms and standards can frame and guide the reconstruction of a domestic legal system to reintegrate a fragile state into the international community. The sources of these norms are international treaties, model laws, and guiding principles developed by a variety of international organizations.

There is a growing tendency to request that countries adopt specific norms and standards, agreed to and shared by the international community. This development can be viewed as positive because it ensures minimum standards and a shared understanding of applicable principles. However, it can also be seen as an external imposition that may create resentment.

Legal Obligations and Institutions of Developing Countries

Rethinking Approaches to Forest Governance

ANNIE PETSONK[*]

The Failure of Efforts to Develop Global Governance of Forests

Confronting dramatic forest destruction, particularly in the tropics, U.S. president George H. W. Bush called for a global agreement to conserve forests at the 1990 Houston Economic Summit.[1] The attention given to forests at Houston prompted nations to raise the topic of a global forest agreement for consideration in the run-up to the United Nations Conference on Environment and Development (UNCED), the "Earth Summit" held at Rio in 1992. The topic of forests turned out to be one of the most contentious at Rio.[2] Sharp differences between developed and developing countries, and within the developed countries' and developing countries' negotiating groups, made the adoption of the first global nonbinding consensus on forests reached at UNCED seem to be a considerable advance at the time.[3] The Forest Principles[4] and Chapter 11 of the Rio Agenda 21[5] set forth overarching principles and an action plan for sustainable forest management. Although they were nonbinding, the hope was that they would provide a foundation for a future treaty establishing global norms for forest governance.

---

[*] The views expressed are entirely the author's, as is responsibility for any errors or omissions. For valuable insights on the topics covered, and for permission to cite works in progress, the author is grateful to Danae Azura, Thomas Blackburn, William Boyd, Daniel Dudek, Jason Funk, Alexander Golub, Steven Hamburg, Sarah Hoagland, Korinna Horta, Peter Jenkins, Andrew Long, Ruben Lubowski, Christina McCain, Christopher Meyer, Michael Oppenheimer, Stephan Schwartzman, Gustavo Silva-Chavez, Richard Stewart, Charlotte Streck, Jonathan Wiener, and Dan Zarin. The chapter is dedicated to Edward M. Petsonk, whose delight in the natural world remains my inspiration.

1   *White House Statement on the Forests for the Future Initiative* (Aug. 14, 1992), available at <http://bushlibrary.tamu.edu/research/public_papers.php?id=4675&year=1992&month=all>.

2   Personal knowledge of the author, who attended UNCED as a member of the U.S. delegation.

3   *See*, for example, Susan Braatz, *International Forest Governance: International Forest Policy, Legal and Institutional Framework* (Invited Paper, XIIth World Forestry Congress, Quebec City, 2003), available at <http://www.fao.org/DOCREP/ARTICLE/WFC/XII/1053-C5.HTM>.

4   The Forest Principles are the Non–Legally Binding Authoritative Statement of Principles for a Global Consensus on the Management, Conservation and Sustainable Development of All Types of Forest Adopted at UNCED, UN Doc. A/CONF.151/26 (1992), available at <http://www.un.org/documents/ga/conf151/aconf15126-3annex3.htm>.

5   Text available at <http://www.un.org/esa/dsd/agenda21/>.

293

After Rio, a range of activities took place under UN auspices aimed at strengthening the Rio principles and implementing an action plan, but the picture never sharpened into an international forest convention. Starting in 1995, the UN Commission on Sustainable Development (CSD), the Intergovernmental Panel on Forests (IPF), and the Intergovernmental Forum on Forests convened regularly to attempt to strengthen "soft-law" pronouncements on forest management into a binding "hard-law" forest convention.[6] But although the soft–law-hard-law progression succeeded in some other areas and generated broad momentum in favor of more environmental treaties, it failed to produce a forest convention.[7]

Proponents of a convention argued that existing instruments with legally binding commitments, such as the Convention on Biological Diversity (CBD),[8] did not cover all aspects of forest management and conservation; strengthening synergies between and among various instruments, binding and nonbinding, could fill gaps and address inadequacies; a legally binding instrument could be more effective in mobilizing funding; and binding obligations were needed in order to spur national implementation commitments and generate the in-depth monitoring and enforceability crucial to effective implementation of those commitments.[9] These arguments were similar to those that had been put forward in the late 1980s in favor of a convention on biological diversity.

By the late 1990s, concerns were being voiced about the CBD's effectiveness as well as the institutional and capacity-building demands that rapidly proliferating environmental treaties were placing on developing countries. Some critics began to question whether environmental negotiations had acquired a content-free momentum of their own.[10] Many in government doubted that coordinating forest policies across disparate forest types, economic drivers of deforestation, and geographical, cultural, and other differences would yield benefits significant enough to justify the endeavor.[11] More fundamentally, at national and subnational levels, many governments simply did not want to undertake the surrender of sovereignty that would ensue from signing a binding commitment to manage forests under a global governance treaty. Their unwillingness to participate was compounded by the turn of significant segments of civil society away from a global forest convention, and spurred by

---

6   The International Tropical Timber Agreement (ITTA) is perhaps the sole binding treaty exclusively focused on forests. Its coverage is not global and stemming forest destruction is not its primary objective.

7   Radoslav S. Dimitrov, *Hostage to Norms: States, Institutions and Global Forest Politics*, 5(4) Global Envtl. Politics 1, 10 (Nov. 2005).

8   UN Convention on Biological Diversity, 31. I.L.M. 818 (1992).

9   Braatz, *supra* note 3; Richard G. Tarasofsky, *The International Forestry Regime—Legal and Policy Issues* (International Union for the Conservation of Nature and Natural Resources and World Wide Fund for Nature 1995); Barbara M. G. S. Ruis, *No Forest Convention but Ten Tree Treaties*, 52(206) Unasylva 3 (2001).

10 Dimitrov, *supra* note 7.

11 *Id.*

concerns that a national government–based negotiation could undermine efforts to establish nationally recognized rights of indigenous peoples.[12] By February 2000, the most that nations could agree to was yet another institutional home for soft-law discussions, the United Nations Forum on Forests (UNFF).[13]

Since then, various talks under UN auspices have produced a loose "international arrangement" on forests comprising the UNFF, the Collaborative Partnership on Forests (CPF), and various other programs that seek to facilitate and coordinate sustainable forest management at national, regional, and global levels through nonbinding means.[14]

As efforts to achieve a global forest convention crumpled in early 2000, various commentators warned that failure to reverse the economic trends favoring continued destruction, rather than preservation, of forests, would diminish the effectiveness of the already weak basket of soft-law pronouncements.[15] But proponents of global forest governance failed utterly to comprehend the core ingredient missing from any such regime: a strategy that makes forests worth more alive than dead.[16]

Filling the Void: Six Efforts to Rebalance Forest Economics

In the governance vacuum left by the collapse of the global forest convention negotiations, efforts seeking to rebalance economic drivers of forest destruction focused on six areas:

---

12 *Id.; see* also David Humphreys, *Redefining the Issues: NGO Influence on International Forest Negotiations*, 4(2) Global Envtl. Politics 51 (May 2004).

13 *See* Dimitrov, *supra* note 7, and Braatz, *supra* note 3; *see* also David R. Downes, *Global Forest Policy and Selected International Instruments: A Preliminary Review*, in *Assessing the International Forestry Regime* 65 (Richard G. Tarasofsky ed., International Union for the Conservation of Nature and Natural Resources 1999).

14 Report of the World Summit on Sustainable Development, UN Doc. A/CONF.199/20 (2002); Braatz, *supra* note 3. *Cf. Progress or Peril? Partnerships and Networks in Global Environmental Governance: The Post-Johannesburg Agenda* (Charlotte Streck, Jan Martin Witte, & Thorsten Benner ed., Global Public Policy Institute 2003).

15 *See*, for example, Dimitrov, *supra* note 7.

16 Neither the international environmental governance framework of the Convention on Biodiversity nor the forestry regime has been able to achieve significant change in on-the-ground environmental outcomes. Andrew Long, *Global Climate Governance to Enhance Biodiversity and Well-Being: Integrating Non-state Networks and Public International Law in Tropical Forests*, 41 Environmental Law 95 (2011). As one commentator notes, nations have economic disincentives to participate in multilateral global forest governance because any resulting policy for sustainable forest management would reduce economic benefits from logging and from clearing forests for agriculture. According to one estimate, losing 1 percent of global forest cover would cost $47 billion, that is, nine times less than the commercial benefits from logging it. *See* Dimitrov, *supra* note 7. Talks under the auspices of the UNFF continued, post-2000, to try to develop financial and institutional modalities, with much debate about potential sources of funding (*see* Braatz, *supra* note 3), but the discussion remained stuck in the frame of a search for financial mechanisms to cover incremental costs of sustainable forest management—a frame that has proven cumbersome in the context of the Global Environmental Facility (GEF) and that never enabled the UNFF or related forums to formulate a strategy that could counteract the economic disparities that Dimitrov cites.

- Reform of international financial institution (IFI) forest-related policies
- Legal mechanisms for protecting indigenous forest-dependent peoples
- Creation of protected areas
- Legal frameworks for requiring the sharing of economic benefits derived from forests
- Programs for certifying products derived from sustainably managed forests
- Campaigns to combat illegal logging

These efforts have achieved varying degrees of success in particular forest areas and locales. That their success has varied is not surprising given the diverse drivers of deforestation across ecosystems and economies.

Reform of IFI Forest Lending Practices

In the late 1980s, coalitions "characterized by . . . professionalism, careful fact-finding, rigorous economic and legal analysis, and subtle political savvy"[17] began pressing multilateral development banks to reform their lending practices in light of the dramatically poor environmental performance of many development bank–funded undertakings, including lending policies that amped, rather than damping, the economics that made trees worth more dead than alive.[18] In response, the World Bank formulated its 1991 Forest Strategy. The strategy was prompted by estimates that deforestation was affecting tens of millions of hectares a year in the developing world; tropical rain forests were shrinking inexorably; and the Bank's lending activities had contributed to these trends.[19] The 1991 strategy was conservation oriented and sought to better define the relationships between and among biodiversity, climate, forests, and development. Eventually classified as an operational safeguard, the policy included something environmentalists had demanded: a ban on Bank financing of commercial logging in moist tropical forests.[20]

---

17   Zygmunt J. B. Plater, *Multilateral Development Banks, Environmental Diseconomies, and International Reform Pressures on the Lending Process: The Example of Third World Dam-Building Projects*, 9 B.C. Third World L.J. 169 (1989).

18   *See*, for example, Bruce Rich, *The Multilateral Development Banks, Environmental Policy, and the United States*, 12 Ecol. L.Q. 681 (1985); submission of Bruce Rich, Esq., on behalf of the Environmental Defense Fund, in Environmental Performance of the Multilateral Development Banks: Hearings before the Subcommittee on International Development Institutions and Finance of the House Committee on Banking, Finance, and Urban Affairs, 100th Cong., 1st Sess. (1987); Bruce Rich, *Funding Deforestation: Conservation Woes at the World Bank*, The Nation (Jan. 1989); Bruce Rich, *The Emperor's New Clothes—The World Bank and Environmental Reform*, 7 World Policy J. 305 (Spring 1990).

19   Uma Lele, et al. *The World Bank Forest Strategy: Striking the Right Balance* (World Bank 2000).

20   *Id.*

But even under the new strategy, deforestation continued at alarming rates, generating a new wave of criticism that Bank policies were exacerbating, not containing, economic trends favoring deforestation. Shortly after efforts to reach a global forest convention came to a close in early 2000, the Bank published an in-depth internal review that confirmed much of the activists' critique. The reviews determined that although the Bank's strategy

> diagnosed the problem of externalities, it did not provide financing mechanisms to address the divergent costs and benefits of conservation at the local and global levels. At the local and national levels, communities and governments, given other pressing imperatives and their limited ability to bear these costs, perceive the costs of conservation relative to their benefits to be higher than does the global community.[21]

The review also found, inter alia, that the strategy was too narrowly focused on microeconomic issues such as the length and price of timber concessions; it underestimated the powerful effect of globalization and economic liberalization on forest outcomes.[22] The result was that a number of tropical nations experienced the Bank's involvement in their forest sectors as a kind of pendulum, swinging from a deforestation-exacerbating lending phase in the mid- to late 1980s and early 1990s to a no-lending phase in the mid-1990s, and then to an adjustment lending phase in the late 1990s in which the Bank promoted growth in processing and related export industries, even though that drove deforestation and the attendant adverse impacts on forest-dependent poor people.[23]

In the aftermath of the failure of the global forest convention, and bolstered by the internal operational review, civil society organizations intensified their pressure on the Bank to revise its policies. In 2002 the Bank did so, adopting a revised forests strategy and Operational Policy (OP) 4.36—Forests, which sought to take into account, comprehensively, the impacts of activities, policies, and practices inside and outside the sector on forests and people who depend on forests for their livelihoods. The strategy was founded on three pillars: harnessing the potential of forests to reduce poverty in a sustainable manner; integrating forests more effectively into sustainable development; and protecting vital local and global environmental services and values.

To the dismay of some environmentalists, the 2002 strategy removed the outright prohibition of World Bank financing of commercial logging operations in primary moist tropical forests, replacing it with an approach of

---

21   *Id.*

22   The review also found that the Bank's forest policy failed to address governance issues and omitted important stakeholder perspectives that were crucial determinants of actual outcomes in the field. *Id.*

23   Madhur Gautam, et al., *Indonesia: The Challenges of World Bank Involvement in Forests* (World Bank Operations Evaluation Department 2000), available at <http://lnweb90.worldbank .org/oed/oeddoclib.nsf/DocUNIDViewForJavaSearch/749C3A7FE1D679C98525697 000785B5A>.

improved forest management with targeted conservation of critical natural habitats in all types of forests. But it also incorporated safeguards requiring World Bank–financed investment operations to comply with independent certification standards. The strategy represented a shift to "cautious reengagement," including selective engagement with forest-priority countries and a deliberate focus on partnerships such as the World Bank–World Wildlife Fund (WWF) Alliance, the Program on Forests (PROFOR), and Forest Law Enforcement and Governance (FLEG) initiatives, which entail coordination among client countries, donors, international nongovernmental organizations (NGOs), research institutions, and civil society.[24] A key element of the 2002 strategy was its focus on emerging opportunities for innovative financing—a recognition of the need for more proactive efforts to rebalance the economics of forests; this focus, in turn, helped prepare the Bank to play a facilitating role in the area of forest carbon (discussed below).

Legal Protection for Indigenous Peoples and Their Lands

From the late 1980s through the mid-1990s, while environmentalists were mounting the critique of multilateral development bank forest-destructive lending practices, social scientists and development activists were beginning to express concern about the impact of those practices on indigenous peoples. Indigenous peoples and activists on their behalf began to focus on two legal pathways: specific recognition, under national/domestic law, of indigenous lands,[25] and broad recognition, under public international law, of indigenous rights.

Both pathways were extremely controversial, and efforts to pursue them led to confrontations that turned violent on more than one occasion.[26] The pursuit itself spoke volumes about the deep mistrust between indigenous communities around the world and the governments that, from a public international law perspective, were assumed to represent them in international treaty negotiations. Time and again, real cases bore out the basis of that mistrust, leading indigenous groups and their supporters to denounce the multilateral negotiations on global forest governance[27] and redouble their efforts to pursue domestic and international recognition of indigenous rights.

Indigenous peoples all over the world had long valued lands differently than nonindigenous. As an indigenous leader stated so eloquently more than a century ago:

> Our land is more valuable than your money. As long as the sun shines and the waters flow, this land will be here to give life to men

---

24 *Forests Sourcebook: Practical Guidance for Sustaining Forests in Development Cooperation* (World Bank 2008).

25 *See*, for example, Stephan Schartzman, Ana Valéria Araújo, & Paulo Pankararu, *Brazil: The Legal Battle over Indigenous Land Rights*, 29(5) NACLA Report on the Americas 36 (1996).

26 *See*, for example, Scott Wallace, *Farming the Amazon*, National Geographic (Jan. 2007).

27 *See* Dimitrov, *supra* note 7.

and animals. We cannot sell the lives of men and animals. It was put here by the Great Spirit and we cannot sell it because it does not belong to us.[28]

Domestic legislation specifically recognizing indigenous rights to particular areas of land, such as formal demarcation of indigenous lands in the Brazilian Amazon, did not in and of itself alter the neoclassical economic view of the relative value of forests for exploitation as opposed to forests for conservation. But as anthropologist Stephan Schwartzman notes, "Where Indian lands begin is where deforestation ends."[29] A crucial stick in the West-conceived "bundle" of property rights is the right to exclude others. Legal recognition of the boundaries of indigenous lands provided indigenous peoples with an essential tool by which they could begin to rebalance the sharp difference in economic perception of land values between themselves and those seeking to exploit forestlands for private gain.

In Brazil in particular, the movement for legal recognition of indigenous land boundaries proved that if legal systems recognized indigenous peoples' land rights, then in order to protect the resource they valued so highly, the indigenous peoples would exercise and defend their right to exclude from their lands those who would destroy the forests. Under Brazil's constitution, indigenous peoples hold generic rights to the lands they have traditionally occupied, but prior to the movement for demarcation, the amount of lands formally recognized as indigenous was zero. Today, as a direct result of the demarcation movement, more than 20 percent of the Brazilian Amazon is formally recognized as indigenous lands.[30] Moreover, empirical evidence indicates that the legal demarcation of indigenous lands has been a powerful factor in Brazil's success in reducing deforestation. As Erika Yamada and Raul Telles do Valle report, although indigenous lands have been subjected to intensive deforestation pressures, Brazil's Instituto Nacional de Pesquisas Espaciais (INPE, National Institute for Space Research) estimates that deforestation in the roughly 1 million hectares of designated indigenous lands in the Amazon amounts to only about 2 percent of deforestation nationally; of the deforestation occurring in indigenous lands, more than 95 percent is due to external forces.[31]

As demarcation began to prove an effective tool, its effectiveness depended greatly on several variables, including the domestic gover-

---

28 Quoted in "The Story of Crowfoot's Encounter," Blackfoot Crossing Historical Park, available at <http://www.blackfootcrossing.ca/treaties.html>.

29 Quoted in Wallace, *supra* note 26.

30 *See* Biviany J. Garzón, *REDD in Indigenous Territories of the Amazon Basin: Will Indigenous Peoples Be Direct Beneficiaries?* (Instituto Socioambiental 2009), available at <http://www.theredddesk .org/resources/reports/redd_in_indigenous_territories_of_the_amazon_basin>.

31 Erika M. Yamada & Raul S. Telles do Valle, *Forest Activities in Indigenous Lands and Carbon Credits Ownership in Brazil* (Instituto Socioambiental 2009), available at <http://www.theredddesk .org/resources/reports/redd_in_indigenous_territories_of_the_amazon_basin>.

nance situation in the nation undertaking the legal demarcation.[32] To bolster the case for indigenous rights to lands even in the absence of strong national governance capacities, advocates simultaneously pursued a public international law declaration recognizing indigenous rights. Many industrial country governments opposed such a declaration, fearing that it would spawn fresh rounds of domestic litigation challenging national or federal sovereignty over indigenous lands. But after an extensive global campaign, the United Nations Declaration on the Rights of Indigenous Peoples was agreed on in 2007.[33] The declaration, while admittedly "soft law" and therefore not legally binding, is increasingly being referred to in a range of international and domestic legal settings, an important step toward accreting the legitimacy needed for it to play a significant role in the economic rebalancing that is so crucial for forest protection to go forward.[34]

---

32 *See*, for example, Wallace, *supra* note 26.

33 GA Res. 61/295, UN GAOR, 61st Sess., UN Doc. A/RES/61/295 (2007). United Nations Declaration on the Rights of Indigenous Peoples (UNDRIP) was adopted by 144 states. Eleven states—including the Russian Federation—abstained. Four—Australia, New Zealand, Canada, and the United States—voted against. All four have since clarified their position, with many qualifications. On December 16, 2010, at a tribal nations conference hosted by the White House, U.S. president Barack Obama announced that the United States is "lending support" to the UNDRIP, and the U.S. State Department issued a statement explaining what "lending support" means (it does not mean full endorsement). *See* Arctic Indigenous Peoples Secretariat, *Qualified UNDRIP Support* (Feb. 21, 2011), available at <http://ips.arcticportal.org/athabaskan/itemlist/tag/UNDRIP>, and U.S. Department of State, Announcement of U.S. Support for the United Nations Declaration on the Rights of Indigenous Peoples (Dec. 16, 2010), available at <http://www.state.gov/r/pa/prs/ps/2010/12/153027.htm>.

34 Of particular note in the forest context are Articles 26, 27, 28, 29.1, and 32 of the UNDRIP:

Article 26

1. Indigenous peoples have the right to the lands, territories and resources which they have traditionally owned, occupied or otherwise used or acquired.

2. Indigenous peoples have the right to own, use, develop and control the lands, territories and resources that they possess by reason of traditional ownership or other traditional occupation or use, as well as those which they have otherwise acquired.

3. States shall give legal recognition and protection to these lands, territories and resources. Such recognition shall be conducted with due respect to the customs, traditions and land tenure systems of the indigenous peoples concerned.

Article 27

States shall establish and implement, in conjunction with indigenous peoples concerned, a fair, independent, impartial, open and transparent process, giving due recognition to indigenous peoples' laws, traditions, customs and land tenure systems, to recognize and adjudicate the rights of indigenous peoples pertaining to their lands, territories and resources, including those which were traditionally owned or otherwise occupied or used. Indigenous peoples shall have the right to participate in this process.

Article 28

1. Indigenous peoples have the right to redress, by means that can include restitution or, when this is not possible, just, fair and equitable compensation, for the lands, territories and resources which they have traditionally owned or otherwise occupied or used, and which have been confiscated, taken, occupied, used or damaged without their free, prior and informed consent.

Creation of Protected Areas

In the aftermath of the failure to reach a global forest convention, conservation organizations focused many of their efforts on the creation of protected areas and the challenge of securing durable funding to support those areas. In parallel, another group of actors, namely, social movements in developing countries, which had protested large-scale fossil fuel extraction, opposed the construction of big dams, and contested illegal timber extraction, also began to broaden their focus in support of land protection.[35] In some cases, social movements and conservation organizations worked together to support the creation of networks and mosaics of legally recognized indigenous lands, strictly protected natural areas, and sustainable-use reserves.[36]

Typically, funding was sought from governments, private foundations, and to a much more limited extent, ecotourism. Given the erratic nature of government financing and how widely tourism fluctuates with business cycles, one innovation in financing of protected areas was the attempt to develop trust funds that would be large enough to be self-sustaining over time. For example, in 2002, the WWF, the Brazilian government, and other partners jointly launched the Amazon Region Protected Areas (ARPA) program, aimed at creating a system of well-managed preservation areas and sustainable-use

---

2. Unless otherwise freely agreed upon by the peoples concerned, compensation shall take the form of lands, territories and resources equal in quality, size and legal status or of monetary compensation or other appropriate redress.

Article 29

1. Indigenous peoples have the right to the conservation and protection of the environment and the productive capacity of their lands or territories and resources. States shall establish and implement assistance programmes for indigenous peoples for such conservation and protection, without discrimination.

[...]

Article 32

1. Indigenous peoples have the right to determine and develop priorities and strategies for the development or use of their lands or territories and other resources.

2. States shall consult and cooperate in good faith with the indigenous peoples concerned through their own representative institutions in order to obtain their free and informed consent prior to the approval of any project affecting their lands or territories and other resources, particularly in connection with the development, utilization or exploitation of mineral, water or other resources.

3. States shall provide effective mechanisms for just and fair redress for any such activities, and appropriate measures shall be taken to mitigate adverse environmental, economic, social, cultural or spiritual impact.

35   Stephan Schwartzman, et al., *Social Movements and Large-Scale Tropical Forest Protection on the Amazon Frontier: Conservation from Chaos*, 19 J. Env. Development 274 (2010).

36   *Id. See* also Stephan Schwartzman & Barbara Zimmerman, *Conservation Alliances with Indigenous Peoples of the Amazon*, 19(3) Conservation Biology 721 (Jun. 2005).

reserves based on rigorous scientific planning and careful public consultation.[37] ARPA received initial funding from the Global Environment Facility (GEF), through the World Bank, the German KfW Development Bank, and WWF-Brazil.[38] ARPA's first phase, from 2003 to 2009, established more than 62 million acres of new protected areas—an area about the size of the U.S. state of Wyoming.

ARPA provided timely support to the Brazilian Environment Ministry's broader vision, articulated by Minister of Environment Marina Silva[39] and embodied in Brazil's National Plan to Prevent and Control Deforestation, of major reductions in deforestation achieved in part through the creation of a large mosaic of significant protected areas and sustainable-use areas.[40] The national plan was of critical importance for many reasons, among the most important of which was the fact that the government of Brazil backed the plan with funding to implement it. The plan also provided a mechanism for coordinating efforts between and among those seeking to create protected areas and those seeking to help indigenous forest-dependent people gain legal recognition of their lands. The development of institutional capacities for undertaking such coordination is particularly important in order to reduce or at least manage gaps, conflicts, and duplication of efforts between and among these stakeholders. Early evidence of the plan's implementation indicates that the managed mosaic approach, embracing both legal recognition of indigenous lands and creation of protected areas, can be an effective strategy for forest governance; the effectiveness is dependent on funding and governance.[41]

Benefit-Sharing Agreements

In 1989, the National Institute of Biodiversity (InBio) was established in Costa Rica;[42] one of its earliest initiatives was the development of a bioprospecting partnership, with benefit sharing, with the Merck pharmaceutical company.[43] At the time, it was hoped that such arrangements could provide durable

---

37   See World Wildlife Fund, *Amazon Region Protected Areas (ARPA)*, available at <http://www.worldwildlife.org/what/wherewework/amazon/arpa.html>.

38   Fundo Brasileiro para a Biodiversidade (Funbio), *Solutions ARPA*, available at <http://site.funbio.org.br/teste_en/Whatwedo/Solucoes/Arpa.aspx>.

39   See, generally, Marina Silva, *The Brazilian Protected Areas Program*, 19(3) Conservation Biology 608 (Jun. 2005).

40   ARPA's second phase, from 2010 to 2013, seeks to create and improve management of an even larger set of new protected areas. A primary objective of this second phase is the implementation of complementary financing mechanisms to cover in perpetuity the recurring expenses of ARPA's large network of protected areas. See World Wildlife Fund, *supra* note 37.

41   See, for example, Taylor H. Ricketts et al., *Indigenous Lands, Protected Areas, and Slowing Climate Change*, 8(3) PLoS Biology (Mar. 2010).

42   Additional information about InBio is available at <http://www.inbio.ac.cr/en/inbio/inb_antec.htm>.

43   See, for example, Ana Sittenfeld & Annie Lovejoy, *Biodiversity Prospecting*, 6(4) Our Planet 20 (1994), and Ana Sittenfeld, *InBio-Merck Collaborative Biodiversity Research Agreement, Costa*

conservation financing by sharing royalties from patenting drugs and other products derived from biologically active molecules, particularly those found in tropical forested countries. This hope also formed the basis for significant portions of the Convention on Biological Diversity (CBD) agreed to at Rio in 1992.

Although some additional bioprospecting or benefit-sharing agreements were developed in the 1990s, the number and breadth of such arrangements increased significantly after 2000. A 2008 survey done for the CBD secretariat,[44] a database compiled by the World Intellectual Property Organization (WIPO),[45] and other research indicate benefit-sharing agreements (including model and actual agreements) in a wide range of countries, including Australia,[46] Brazil, Canada, China, Costa Rica, Czech Republic, Ethiopia, India, Kenya, Lebanon, Nigeria, Pakistan, Russian Federation, South Africa, Sri Lanka, Thailand, and the United States.[47]

Benefit sharing varies by sector, but according to the CBD review, CBD standards for best practice in benefit sharing have become widely accepted. Although unscrupulous and ill-informed companies continue to bypass these standards, the larger or more socially responsible companies today would not consider genetic resources freely available. Benefits typically include a mix

---

Rica, in *Partnerships for Change* 33 (Department of the Environment, UK 1994). *See*, generally, "Biodiversity Prospecting Publications," available at <http://www.inbio.ac.cr/en/inbio/inb_prosppubl.htm>.

44   Sarah Laird & Rachel Wynberg, *Access and Benefit-Sharing in Practice: Trends in Partnerships across Sectors*, CBD Technical Series No. 38 (Secretariat of the Convention on Biological Diversity 2008).

45   WIPO maintains a database of biodiversity-related access and benefit-sharing agreements. The database includes both model and actual agreements, as well as documents from a diverse group of industrial and developing countries; it is available at <http://www.wipo.int/tk/en/databases/contracts/list.html>.

46   *See*, for example, Australia's model biodiversity access agreements, available at <http://www.environment.gov.au/biodiversity/science/access/model-agreements/index.html>.

47   *See*, for example, Kurt Repanshek, *National Park Service Finalizes "Benefits-Sharing Agreement" That Could Benefit Parks* (Apr. 6, 2010), available at <http://www.nationalparkstraveler.com/2010/04/national-park-service-finalizes-benefits-sharing-agreement-could-benefit-parks5661>: "Park Service Director Jon Jarvis said the benefits-sharing agreement 'would not lead to commercialization of national parks, but could return some royalties to the parks that would be put to work on conservation issues. . . . Implementing these changes is not about commercializing the parks,' said Mr. Jarvis in a press release. 'This decision is about the public receiving some benefit from commercial projects that result from analysis of samples collected in national parks.' The decision does not change the existing strict NPS research permit process, which remain[s] separate from any benefits-sharing negotiations. The commercial use or sale of park specimens is still prohibited, as is damage to or the consumptive use of park resources. In other words, while a researcher or company might sign a benefits-sharing agreement with a specific park, it can't begin collecting specimens until it has obtained a permit to do so from the park. Those permits are not automatic just because a benefits-sharing agreement has been signed, the document states."

of monetary benefits, such as fees per sample, royalties, and licensing agreements, and nonmonetary benefits, such as training, capacity building, research exchanges, equipment, technology transfer, and joint publications.[48]

Although hopes for benefit-sharing agreements have been high, their ability to deliver durable compensation for the protection of forests has been uneven at best, for several reasons. Industry sectors have waxed and waned in their participation; for example, many pharmaceutical companies with natural product drug discovery programs in the 1990s had closed their programs by 2008.[49] Bureaucracies for implementing such agreements can be formidable, entailing years of applications for permits; bioprospecting companies regularly avoid some countries because of "national regulatory labyrinths."[50] Benefit sharing in some sectors is complicated by the long chain of connection between the gathering of a biological material and the sale of a consumer product. For example, in the seed industry, plant breeding is cumulative; product development may take place across several companies; companies may market intermediate products without sharing benefits; and if benefit sharing is triggered only when seeds are sold to farmers, benefits arising from the sale of foodstuffs to final consumers may not be shared.[51]

The CBD review found that in only a very few cases, such as in InBio-Merck, did bioprospecting partnerships include payments to support protected areas and local conservation activities, and that the most significant conservation benefits came from the discovery of new information that helps set conservation priorities. But, the review cautions, many nations initiating bioprospecting or benefit-sharing agreements tend to focus on future royalties, "which are unlikely to materialize."[52] So, although developments since 2000 have sought to regularize and increase the use of benefit-sharing arrangements, including the 2010 completion of the Nagoya Protocol on Access to Genetic Resources

---

48   Laird & Wynberg, *supra* note 44, at 117–18. For example, the U.S. Biotechnology Industry Organization (BIO) published voluntary guidelines for bioprospecting that encourage members to engage in benefit-sharing agreements with providers of their research specimens. Repanshek, *supra* note 47.

49   Laird and Wynberg note that stimulating increased demand for wild germplasm will require considerable effort from provider countries. They also note that Costa Rica, for example, has spent a lot of resources in developing an inventory and taxonomy of its biodiversity and "filling its shop window" for potential customers (users) and that some argue other countries should do likewise. At the same time, they implicitly caution nations not to raise high hopes. They quote a representative from the seed sector as saying: "Modern varieties are far more important to us. They contain more relevant genetic material than landraces or gene bank material. Maybe once in ten years we need to look at disease resistance or any other specific characteristic and need access to landraces and/or wild relatives. Modern varieties bring quality—wild products cannot be used directly and need a lot of work before they result in a product that can be sold." Laird & Wynberg, *supra* note 44, at 17.

50   *Id.*, at 25.

51   *Id.*, at 50–51.

52   *Id.*, at 30–31.

and the Fair and Equitable Sharing of Benefits Arising from Their Utilization to the Convention on Biological Diversity,[53] benefit sharing can be said at best to provide an occasional thumb on the scale balancing the economics of forest protection against the economics of forest destruction.

Combating Illegal Logging

Illegal logging for timber sale, land clearing, or other purposes has been discussed in many international institutions; the discussion became more heated following the collapse of the forest convention negotiations.[54] In 2002–04, human rights organizations focused on the role of timber in conflict areas.[55] A result was a group of initiatives seeking to combat illegal logging by using the power of timber-importing countries to reduce the demand for illegally logged timber, including timber logged in conflict areas. In 2003, the European Union launched its Forest Law Enforcement, Governance and Trade (FLEGT) Action Plan.[56] That same year, U.S. president George W. Bush launched a

---

53   The Nagoya Protocol on Access to Genetic Resources and the Fair and Equitable Sharing of Benefits Arising from Their Utilization to the Convention on Biological Diversity is an international agreement that aims to share the benefits arising from the utilization of genetic resources in a fair and equitable way, including by appropriate access to genetic resources and by appropriate transfer of relevant technologies, taking into account all rights over those resources and to technologies, and by appropriate funding, thereby contributing to the conservation of biological diversity and the sustainable use of its components. It was adopted by the Conference of the Parties to the Convention on Biological Diversity at its 10th meeting, October 29, 2010, in Nagoya, Japan. *See* <http://www.cbd.int/abs/>.

54   According to the UK-AID-financed organization Illegal Logging.Org, forums for discussing illegal logging have included the EU's FLEGT process, the regional Forest Law Enforcement and Governance (FLEG) conferences, the Asia Forest Partnership, International Tropical Timber Organization (ITTO), the Food and Agriculture Organization (FAO), the United Nations Forum on Forests (UNFF), the UN Economic Commission for Europe, the Ministerial Conference for the Protection of Forests in Europe (MCPFE), the CBD, the Convention on International Trade in Endangered Species (CITES), the Congo Basin Forest Partnership, the World Trade Organization's (WTO) Committee on Trade and Environment, and the Group of Eight, among others. *See* <http://www.illegal-logging.info/approach.php?a_id=252>.

55   *See,* for example, Global Witness, *Logging Off: How the Liberian Timber Industry Fuels Liberia's Humanitarian Disaster and Threatens Sierra Leone* (2002), available at <http://www.globalwitness.org/library/logging>; and Amnesty International, *Open Letter to Members of the United Nations Security Council* (Nov. 13, 2002), available at <http://www.theperspective.org/openlettertosecuritycouncil.html>.

56   FLEGT components include the negotiation of bilateral voluntary partnership agreements (VPAs) with producer countries, with licensing systems to identify legal products exported from partner countries and license them for import to the EU and deny entry to unlicensed products; capacity-building assistance to partner countries to set up licensing, improve enforcement, and reform laws; examination of EU member states' existing domestic legislation, and consideration of additional legislative options, to prohibit the import of illegal timber; encouragement of government procurement policies to limit purchases to legal (and sustainable) sources; encouragement of voluntary industry initiatives to control supply chains, and thereby exclude illegal products; and encouragement of financial institution scrutiny of flows of finance to the forestry industry. *See* EU FLEGT Overview at <http://illegal-logging.info/approach.php?a_id=119>.

presidential initiative against illegal logging.[57] A 2004 World Bank study[58] placing the market value of losses from illegal forest cutting at over US$10 billion per year heightened attention to the problem, as did a study done for the American Forest and Paper Association,[59] an industry trade group, that suggested that illegal harvesting was depressing forest product prices by 7–16 percent globally, and U.S. prices by 2–4 percent.

Both FLEGT and the president's initiative against illegal logging were premised on voluntary partnerships, and both were dependent on government funding.[60] Each made some progress, but as the Bush administration drew to a close, stronger action was clearly needed, because the financing, capacity building, and voluntary partnerships were not enough to counterbalance the gains from illegal logging.

In May 2008, the U.S. Congress enacted, and President Bush signed into law, the Food, Conservation, and Energy Act of 2008, which, by amending the Lacey Act, banned the import of illegally harvested wood and wood products.[61] In 2010, the European Union[62] followed suit. The laws are broad in scope and have led to at least one high-profile enforcement action. In November 2009, agents of the U.S. Fish and Wildlife Service executed a search warrant on Gibson Guitars of Nashville, Tennessee. The raid was based on an

---

57 *See* <http://georgewbush-whitehouse.archives.gov/infocus/illegal-logging/>.

58 *Sustaining Forests: A Development Strategy* 17 (World Bank 2004), available at <http://siteresources.worldbank.org/INTFORESTS/Resources/SustainingForests.pdf>.

59 Seneca Creek Associates & Wood Resources International, *"Illegal" Logging and Global Wood Markets: The Competitive Impacts on the U.S. Wood Products Industry*, study prepared for the American Forest and Paper Association (2004), available at <http://www.illegal-logging.info/uploads/afandpa.pdf>.

60 The Bush initiative sought partnerships in the Congo basin, the Amazon basin, and South/Southeast Asia, and was backed by initial funding of up to $15 million in 2003. *See* <http://georgewbush-whitehouse.archives.gov/infocus/illegal-logging/piail.html>. To date, only one FLEGT VPA has been concluded (with Ghana); *see* <http://ec.europa.eu/environment/forests/flegt.htm> (accessed Feb. 2011).

61 The Lacey Act makes it a crime to import fish or wildlife taken illegally under the rules of the country of origin. As amended in 2008 (P.L. 110-246, 16 U.S.C. 3372), the Lacey Act extends to plants and wood products, making it a violation of U.S. law to import, export, transport, sell, receive, acquire, or purchase in interstate or foreign commerce any plant, with some limited exceptions, taken in violation of the laws of a U.S. state or any foreign law that protects plants. The Lacey Act also makes it unlawful to make or submit any false record, account, or label for, or any false identification of, any plant. The prohibition makes it unlawful to import any product containing wood or plant material that was illegally taken. *See* U.S. Department of Agriculture Animal and Plant Health Inspection Service [Docket No. APHIS–2008–0119] Implementation of Revised Lacey Act Provisions, Notice, 74 Federal Register No. 169, at 45415-45417 (Sep. 2, 2009).

62 *See* Regulation (EU) No. 995/2010 of the European Parliament and of the Council of October 20, 2010, laying down the obligations of operators who place timber and timber products on the market. The legislation prohibits the sale of timber logged illegally under the rules of the country of origin, and requires companies to exercise due diligence to ascertain that the timber they sell in the EU was harvested legally. The regulation takes effect in 2013. Implementing regulations are being drafted; the full text of the regulation is available at <http://illegal-logging.info/uploads/l29520101112en00230034.pdf>.

affidavit and published reports alleging that Gibson was using rosewood and mahogany illegally harvested in Madagascar and shipped to the United States through Germany.[63] In 2010, the United States commenced action to seize the alleged illegally harvested wood.[64]

Closing markets to the products of illegal logging and stepping up the enforcement of such closures are certainly key elements in rebalancing the economics of forest destruction, particularly where high-value rare woods like mahogany are concerned. The effectiveness of the effort to combat illegal logging depends, however, in part on how broadly market closures are achieved; to date, they seem to be occurring primarily in industrial countries. Even within industrial countries, uneven enforcement could undermine the effectiveness of the bans. For example, the new EU law leaves it up to each member state to decide what penalties it will apply to those who trade in illegally harvested wood, raising the possibility that member states that choose to adopt weak penalties might become entrepots of illegal timber.[65]

Forest Certification

In the aftermath of the failure of efforts to achieve a global forest convention, interest in forest certification programs increased significantly.[66] Forest certification has been called a form of nonstate market-driven global governance that relies on consumer behavior, mediated through market preference, to influence forest management.[67] Forest certification programs seek to encourage consumers to choose certified forest products based on improved environmental performance and to encourage producers to go through the certification process in order to gain market share, price premiums, reputational advantage, or other benefits. Forest certification thus assumes that purchasers will prefer sustainably produced forest products and will demand them in the

---

63   Miller & Chevalier, *Gibson Guitar Raid* (Nov. 2009), available at <http://www .millerchevalier.com/Publications/MillerChevalierPublications?find=20504>.

64   E. Thomas Wood, *What the Feds Found at Gibson*, Nashville Post (Aug. 12, 2010).

65   The member states' penalties may include "fines proportionate to the environmental damage, the value of the timber or timber products concerned and the tax losses and economic detriment resulting from the infringement, calculating the level of such fines in such way as to make sure that they effectively deprive those responsible of the economic benefits derived from their serious infringements, without prejudice to the legitimate right to exercise a profession, and gradually increasing the level of such fines for repeated serious infringements" as well as immediate suspension of authorization to trade; however, there is no mandatory minimum penalty, so the deterrent value is unclear. *See* Reg. (EU) No. 995/2010, Article 19.

66   *See*, for example, Steven Bernstein & Benjamin Cashore, *Non-state Global Governance: Is Forest Certification a Legitimate Alternative to a Global Forest Convention?* in *Hard Choices, Soft Law: Combining Trade, Environment, and Social Cohesion in Global Governance* 33 (John Kirton & Michael Trebilcock ed., Ashgate Press 2004).

67   *See* Long, *supra* note 16, and Kelly Levin et al., *Can Non-state Governance "Ratchet-Up" Global Standards? Assessing Their Indirect Effects and Evolutionary Potential*, Rev. Eur. Community & Intl. Envtl. L. 1, 4–5 (2007).

marketplace with public education campaigns and the organization of buyer groups to educate and socialize retailers.[68]

Nearly 60 forest certification systems operate around the world,[69] ranging from those organized primarily by conservation advocates to those organized primarily by industry, with each side expressing concerns about the other's program.[70] Although several hundred million acres of forest have been certified, the Nature Conservancy estimates that the percentage of certified wood reaching global markets represents a very small fraction—less than 5 percent—of the international forest products trade.[71]

Why have these programs not captured more of the market for forest products? First, substantial investment in certification programs and chain of custody is necessary, making certified products often more expensive than their uncertified competitors. So, rather than balancing the scales against economic forces favoring deforestation, certification programs fundamentally depend on the willingness of purchasers and end consumers to pay higher prices for sustainably managed and verified products. Thus, market forces work against certification programs to a certain degree.

Second, although many efforts have been undertaken to create buyer groups, nonbinding voluntary certification programs are unable to deploy the tool that has been so effective in some other environmental fields at reducing leakage and addressing competitiveness, in effect counterbalancing economic incentives to engage in trade in environmentally harmful products. That tool is a ban on trade with nonparties in products that don't meet the environmental standard. Such bans are key elements of the Montreal Protocol on the Ozone Layer, the Basel Convention on Hazardous Wastes, and the Convention on International Trade in Endangered Species of Flora and Fauna.[72] But although unilateral bans on trade in illegally harvested wood products are being adopted and enforced,[73] applying such unilateral bans to trade on products

---

68   Bernstein & Cashore, *supra* note 66, at 38.

69   Nature Conservancy, *Forest Conservation and Responsible Trade* (2011), available at <http://www.nature.org/initiatives/forests/strategies/art22184.html>.

70   Bernstein and Cashore identify the Forest Stewardship Council (FSC) as a program organized primarily by NGOs, and identify as industry organized the American Forest and Paper Association's Sustainable Forestry Initiative program in the United States, the Canadian Standards Association program initiated with support from the Canadian Pulp and Paper Association (now the Forest Products Association of Canada), and the Pan European Forest Certification system, created by landowner associations that felt excluded from the FSC process. *See* Bernstein & Cashore, *supra* note 66, at 38.

71   Nature Conservancy, *supra* note 69.

72   *See* Carol A. Petsonk, *The Role of the United Nations Environment Programme (UNEP) in the Development of International Environmental Law*, 5 Am. U.J. Intl. L. & Policy 351 (1990).

73   The Gibson case illustrates the challenges faced by forest certification programs. Since 1996, Gibson's Nashville factory has held an FSC chain-of-custody certificate guaranteeing that all certified wood comes from legal sources, such as community-managed forests in Honduras and Guatemala. Gibson's factory and the guitars are subject to annual FSC inspection and were recertified in September 2008. Notwithstanding the FSC 2008 inspection and certifica-

that fail to meet voluntary nonstate forest certification programs would likely raise substantial issues under the rules of the multilateral trading system.[74]

Can Recognizing REDD+ in Carbon Markets Help?

A different lens through which to view the forest governance program is the concept of carbon markets as a countervailing force against the economic pressures that favor deforestation.[75] This section examines why the concept of carbon markets did not gain acceptance in the implementation of the 1997 Kyoto Protocol, traces the origin and evolution of the Reducing Emissions from Deforestation in Developing Countries (REDD) approach, and examines prospects for its future application.

Why Was Forest Carbon Largely Left Out of the Kyoto Protocol?

The demise of the global forest convention in early 2000 coincided with a crescendo in the negotiations on rules for implementing the Kyoto Protocol on Climate Change.[76] The protocol agreed to in 1997 placed binding caps on the greenhouse gas emissions of more than 30 industrial nations for the years

---

tion, published reports alleged that certain wood in Gibson's factory was illegally harvested from Madagascar, and the United States commenced the legal action discussed above following the 2008 amendment of the Lacey Act. *See* Miller & Chevalier, *supra* note 63. Gibson has since committed to ensure that all of the wood that it uses comes from FSC-certified or otherwise verified legal sources. *See* Rainforest Alliance, *Gibson Guitars Working with Rainforest Alliance on Wood Sourcing Legality* (Jul. 2010), available at <http://www.rainforest-alliance.org/newsroom/news/gibson-release-jul10>.

74   *Cf.* Duncan Brack, *Combating Illegal Logging: Interaction with WTO Rules* (Environment and Resource Governance Series IL BP 2009/1, Jun. 2009), available at <http://www.chathamhouse.org.uk/research/eedp/papers/view/-/id/754/>.

75   "The international community has lurched from one policy approach to another, throwing too little money and too many plans at the problem and hoping for the best, without any overall effort to forge a coherent, performance-based approach that addresses directly the structural tensions embedded in forest governance and the basic forces driving forest destruction. Explanations of the failure of global forest governance have focused on a variety of factors, including the tremendous variability in the forces driving deforestation, deep-seated conflicts over sovereignty and control of forest resources, and limited institutional and forest governance capacities at national and sub-national levels. . . . In short, efforts to frame tropical deforestation as a global problem have not translated into workable solutions in part because deforestation is not a unitary phenomenon amenable to easy generalization, much less global governance. Previous ways of seeing the problem, in other words, have not provided a sufficient foundation for effective governance, raising the important question of whether a climate policy approach to deforestation (a very different way of seeing the problem) will succeed where past efforts have failed." William Boyd, *Ways of Seeing in Environmental Law: How Deforestation Became an Object of Climate Governance*, 37 Ecol. L.Q. 843, 866 (2010). *See* also William Boyd, *Deforestation and Emerging Greenhouse Gas Compliance Regimes: Toward a Global Environmental Law of Forests, Carbon, and Climate Governance*, in *Deforestation and Climate Change: Reducing Carbon Emissions from Deforestation and Forest Degradation* 1 (Valentina Bosetti & Ruben Lubowski ed., Edward Elgar 2010).

76   Kyoto Protocol to the United Nations Framework Convention on Climate Change, UN Doc. FCCC/CP/1997/7/Add.1, December 10, 1997, 37 I.L.M. 22 (1998) (entered into force Feb. 16, 2005) (Kyoto Protocol).

2008–12, issued each nation an amount of emissions allowances equal to their emissions caps, gave nations flexibility to reallocate their emissions allowances among themselves in order to meet their obligations jointly, and authorized nations that reduced emissions below capped levels to save their surplus allowances for future use or transfer them to other nations.[77] This kind of emissions cap-and-trade system had been tested in the United States and proven very effective at reducing emissions of sulfur dioxide, a major cause of acid rain;[78] the Clinton-Gore administration advocated strongly for its inclusion in the Kyoto Protocol.

In the Kyoto negotiations, the United States also supported a New Zealand proposal for inclusion of provisions explicitly allowing developing nations voluntarily to take caps on emissions and participate in emissions trading. But the 77 developing countries and China solidly opposed the New Zealand proposal, citing the 1995 negotiating mandate for the protocol, in which nations had agreed that the protocol would result in no new commitments for developing countries.[79] A few developing countries, wanting to test the possibility of trading but not wanting to adopt a cap, did support the proposition that any developing country that voluntarily wished to could allow investors to develop projects in its territory that reduced emissions below what would have otherwise occurred and transfer the resulting "emissions offset" to industrial nations—an idea that became the protocol's clean development mechanism (CDM).[80]

The question of whether the CDM would recognize offsets from reduced deforestation was not dealt with at Kyoto in 1997. The resolution of that question, as well as other forest-related issues and carbon market issues, was pushed into negotiations that took place from 1998 to 2000 on rules elaborating the relatively spare prose of the Kyoto Protocol and clarifying its implementation. At talks in The Hague in late 2000, after an all-night session in which U.S. negotiators pressed for some recognition of forest carbon in the rules for implementing Kyoto's market mechanisms, the gray rainy dawn found exhausted American delegates sitting at an empty table. The Europeans, opposing any ambit for forests in carbon markets, had walked out. By the time the negotiations reconvened in the spring of 2001, newly elected U.S. president George W. Bush had renounced both Kyoto and his campaign pledge to cap carbon dioxide emissions. The United States wasn't coming back to the table.

---

77 Kyoto Protocol, Articles 3, 4, and 17.

78 U.S. Clean Air Act Amendments of 1990, Title IV, 42 U.S.C. Sections 7652 et seq. *See also* Andrew Aulisi et al., *From Obstacle to Opportunity: How Acid Rain Emissions Trading Is Delivering Cleaner Air* (Environmental Defense Fund 2000), available at <http://www.edf.org/documents/645_SO2.pdf>.

79 Conference of the Parties to the United Nations Framework Convention on Climate Change, Berlin, F.R.G., March 28–April 7, 1995, Addendum, Decision 1/CP.1, Section II(2)(b), FCCC/CP/1995/7/Add.1 (Jun. 6, 1995) (Berlin Mandate).

80 Kyoto Protocol, Article 12.

Why was the issue of including forests in carbon markets so controversial in the climate treaty talks?[81] The U.S. interest in it was a long-standing one. In the early 1990s, the Bush administration began to explore market-based policies for inclusion in the 1992 United Nations Framework Convention on Climate Change (UNFCCC) and advocated a "comprehensive approach" in which all greenhouse gases, their sources, and sinks—including forests—would be included.[82] President Bush also developed a "forests for the future initiative" to begin to address tropical deforestation in the field.[83] In the negotiations leading up to Kyoto and following the protocol's adoption, the Clinton administration maintained this position, expanding it to support binding caps on emissions, which the previous administration had eschewed, and broad opportunities for crediting forest carbon.

The European Union was much more cautious about both "market mechanisms" and forest carbon. The EU supported the idea of reallocation of targets among nations in a group (like the EU itself), but agreed to emissions trading only grudgingly, after the United States had offered to tighten the target that it would inscribe as its Kyoto commitment.[84] Many Europeans were skeptical that market mechanisms would work. Some objected to market mechanisms on moral grounds, arguing that emissions trading amounted to the sale of indulgences. Many Europeans were also skeptical about forest protection as an element of climate mitigation. They regarded forest protection as a moral obligation, and the history of failed initiatives in tropical forest conservation made them reluctant to consider the possibility that "forest sinks" would be durable enough to justify using them to offset increases in fossil fuel emissions. Consequently, proposals to bring forest protection into market mechanisms generated bitter and strong opposition from many Europeans.[85]

---

81   *See*, generally, Federica Bietta, *From the Hague to Copenhagen: Why It Failed Then and Why It Could Be Different*, in *Deforestation and Climate Change: Reducing Carbon Emissions from Deforestation and Forest Degradation* 27 (Valentina Bosetti & Ruben Lubowski ed., Edward Elgar 2010).

82   *See*, for example, Case No. 147516CU 5 P-5: Memo from Dick Stewart to Allan Bromley and List, *Work of the Task Force to Further Develop the "Comprehensive" and "Trading" Approaches to Possible Climate Change Agreement* (copy on file with George H. W. Bush Library).

83   *See White House Statement on the Forests for the Future Initiative, supra* note 1.

84   "Some of you here have, perhaps, heard from your home capitals that President Clinton and I have been burning up the phone lines, consulting and sharing new ideas. Today let me add this. After talking with our negotiators this morning and after speaking on the telephone from here a short time ago with President Clinton, I am instructing our delegation right now to show increased negotiating flexibility if a comprehensive plan can be put in place, one with realistic targets and timetables, market mechanisms, and the meaningful participation of key developing countries." Remarks as prepared for delivery for Vice President Al Gore, Kyoto Climate Change Conference (Dec. 8, 1997), available at <http://clinton2.nara.gov/WH/EOP/OVP/speeches/kyotofin.html>.

85   During the 2000 climate talks in The Hague, European environmentalists displayed an enormous banner reading "Don't SINK the Kyoto Protocol!" In their view, and in the view of some of their governments, allowing credit for uptake of carbon dioxide by forest sinks would give the United States an unfair advantage, because the United States was experiencing increases in its forest cover, whereas Europe's forest cover was thought to be relatively stable, with few opportunities for increasing forestlands.

Important at the time was the position of the Brazilian government. Brazil had supported, some might even say originated, the idea of the CDM. But in the late 1990s, the government of Brazil adamantly opposed including crediting of forest carbon in the CDM, arguing that such crediting would be tantamount to locking up Brazilian forests. European environmentalists opposed to forest carbon crediting pointed to the lack of good measurement data on tropical deforestation. Brazilian civil society representatives, attending the climate talks for the first time, realized that their government had taken a position on a crucial issue for civil society, namely, whether forest-dependent communities could be remunerated for protecting forests that mitigate climate change, without consulting with those communities to ascertain their views—and that this position also conveniently allowed their government to protect the confidentiality of data about the very high rates of deforestation nationwide.[86]

Origin and Evolution of REDD+

When the negotiations in The Hague fell apart in November 2000, these civil society representatives decided to commence broad consultation in Brazil with forest communities and others concerned about the Amazon. They also undertook an intensive examination of the objections to forest carbon crediting that had caused The Hague talks to founder and found that a main objection to the inclusion of forest carbon projects in the CDM was the high potential for leakage; that is, while trees might be protected in one place and credits awarded that avoided deforestation, the emission reductions might be negated if loggers simply increased tree cutting elsewhere.[87] Much of the acrimony in The Hague had been focused on whether to allow crediting for uptake of carbon dioxide by trees in forest sinks, whereas the problem that concerned the civil society representatives most was reducing deforestation and its attendant greenhouse gas emissions.

On the basis of their consultations and research, and working with forest scientists and anthropologists, this group crafted a new proposal that did not involve crediting for uptake by sinks. The group proposed that reductions in deforestation in developing countries be compensated through carbon markets and that the reductions be achieved at national scale over multiyear periods. They initially presented this "compensated reduction" proposal in 2003,[88] and published a key paper on it in 2005.[89]

---

86   Eli Kintisch & Antonio Regalado, *Cancun Delegates See the Trees through a Forest of Hot Air*, 330 Science 1597 (Dec. 17, 2010).

87   *Id.*

88   *See* Bernhard Schlamadinger et al., *Should We Include Avoidance of Deforestation in the International Response to Climate Change?* in *Tropical Deforestation and Climate Change* 53 (Paulo Moutinho & Stephan Schwartzman ed., Instituto de Pesquisa Ambiental da Amazônia 2005).

89   Márcio Santilli et al., *Tropical Deforestation and the Kyoto Protocol: An Editorial Essay*, 71(3) Climatic Change 267 (2005); *see* also Kintisch & Regalado, *supra* note 86.

The compensated reduction proposal addressed virtually all the key objections to forest carbon crediting. It tackled the issue of leakage from individual projects, because crediting would only occur for reductions achieved across large scales (at the national level). It provided a basis for addressing the issue of measurement, because the proposal could succeed only if governments made public their data about deforestation. In fact, the proposal triggered a flurry of activity among forest scientists, who began sharing their data and methodologies and demonstrating to governments that advances in remote sensing could provide a solid basis for implementing the compensated reduction proposal.[90] The proposal addressed the issue of durability, or permanence, by requiring that reductions be demonstrated over multiyear periods and through provisions suggesting that portions of reduction credits be held in reserve as insurance against forest fires and other disasters.[91] And, as one commentator observed,

> it reframed the issue from one focused on forests as carbon sinks—the dominant framing during the Kyoto Protocol discussions—to one focused on the forest sector as a source of emissions, thereby putting the problem in the same regulatory lexicon as fossil fuel emissions and smoothing the way for an integration into climate policy.[92]

More fundamentally, the compensated reduction proposal sought to provide what no previous efforts at forest governance had achieved: a powerful framework for rebalancing the economics of forest destruction in every forest ecosystem, in every nation around the world. At the Eleventh Conference of the Parties to the United Nations Framework Convention on Climate Change, held in Montreal, Canada, in late 2005, delegates from Papua New Guinea and Costa Rica, supported by delegates from developing countries from Central America, South America, and Africa working together in a Coalition for Rainforest Nations (CfRN), formally introduced the concept of compensating nations for reducing emissions from deforestation. Zeroing in on the fundamental issue of rebalancing, the group said:

> In the absence of revenue streams from standing forests, communities and governments in many developing nations have little incentive to prevent deforestation. As a consequence, communities must bear losses of the services from forests that are not currently valued economically, while globally, we all must assume the consequences of increased greenhouse gases in the Earth's atmosphere. It is

---

90 *See*, for example, Ruth DeFries et al., "Reducing Greenhouse Gas Emissions from Deforestation in Developing Countries: Considerations for Monitoring and Measuring," Report of the Global Terrestrial Observing System (GTOS), No. 46; Global Observation of Forest Cover–Global Observation of Land Dynamics (GOFC-GOLD), Report No. 26 (2006), available at <http://www.fao.org/gtos/pubs.html>; and Gregory P. Asner et al., *Condition and Fate of Logged Forests in the Brazilian Amazon*, 103 Proceedings of the National Academy of Science (PNAS), No. 34, at 12947–12950 (Aug. 22, 2006).

91 Santilli et al., *supra* note 89.

92 William Boyd, *Ways of Seeing in Environmental Law: How Deforestation Became an Object of Climate Governance*, 37 Ecol. L.Q. 843, 846 (2010).

estimated that tropical countries could reduce 1.5GtC emissions from tropical deforestation over ten years and generate billions of dollars in conservation and climate mitigation revenue. Without a more complete market valuation, standing forests cannot overcome the economic opportunity costs associated with their conservation . . . As developing nations, we are prepared to stand accountable for our contributions to global climate stability, provided international frameworks are appropriately modified, namely through fair and equitable access to carbon emissions markets.[93]

CfRN titled its intervention "Reducing Emissions from Deforestation in Developing Countries (REDD): Approaches to Stimulate Action."[94]

The effect of REDD on the climate treaty talks was dramatic. Nation after nation rose to speak in support of opening a discussion on the concept.[95] That in itself was remarkable, because inherent in the proposal was a greater degree of developing-country participation than the iron-clad division between industrial and developing countries embodied in the Berlin Mandate. But it was also remarkable in that the quiet eloquence of REDD broke through the acrimony that had encrusted forest issues since the collapse of The Hague meeting half a decade earlier.

Although REDD originated in the context of the climate treaty talks, it quickly began to exert a powerful gravitational pull on the forest governance debate. There were several reasons. The first was time horizons. Previous efforts at forest governance had failed to produce a framework that could deliver incentives for forest protection durably over the multidecade periods needed for forest conservation and sound forest management. REDD in carbon markets provided a way to match forest governance with greenhouse gas emissions management, a similarly long-term task requiring sustained durable investment over multidecade periods. Because demand for greenhouse gas emission reductions would continue far into the future, matching the two

---

93 UNFCCC, Submission by the Governments of Papua New Guinea and Costa Rica: Reducing Emissions from Deforestation in Developing Countries; Approaches to Stimulate Action, at 4-7 U.N. Doc. FCCC/CP/2005/MISC.1 (Nov. 11, 2005), available at <http://unfccc.int/resource/docs/2005/cop11/eng/misc01.pdf>.

94 *Id*. Although the World Bank began calling for such rebalancing as early as 2002, a framework for rebalancing was unlikely to emerge in the climate treaty talks unless championed by a substantial grouping of developing countries themselves. *Cf. Sustaining Forests: A World Bank Strategy* 8-9 (World Bank 2002), available at <http://siteresources.worldbank.org/INTFORESTS/214573-1113990657527/20632625/Forest_Strategy_Booklet.pdf>. ("There is a need for creative mechanisms to pay for the protection of forest environmental services of both local and global importance. It is highly unlikely that governments will be able to significantly scale down log extraction, unless the costs in terms of foregone revenue can be offset in some way. Moreover, very few countries would be prepared to borrow funds— from the World Bank or other sources—to finance forest protection as a substitute for forest production. We must therefore help foster new markets and payment systems for environmental services from forest ecosystems, and to interest developing countries in activities that will improve forest management and conservation.")

95 Personal knowledge of the author, who attended the conference as an observer.

problems offered the potential to exert a downward pressure on deforestation rates over a very long time horizon, giving those who would invest in forest carbon crediting an incentive to support improved forest governance over commensurately long times.

The second reason was scale. Prior to REDD, climate treaty talks had paid scant attention to the large role that deforestation played in global greenhouse emissions. Analyses of global emissions, and ranking of nations in terms of largest emitters, had typically considered only emissions from the combustion of fossil fuel. But the compensated reduction proposal prompted experts to take emissions from deforestation into account, with results that many experts found surprising. Although most climate policy experts knew that the largest and second-largest emitting nations were the United States and China, most didn't realize that numbers three and four were Indonesia and Brazil, with 70 percent or more of their national greenhouse gas emissions from deforestation.[96] Most experts also didn't realize that deforestation was responsible for an amount of emissions roughly comparable to the entire global transportation sector. But if deforestation emerged as a large component of the climate puzzle, deploying carbon markets in the service of compensating reductions in deforestation offered the opportunity to generate incentives for very large scale reductions in deforestation. No previous effort to improve forest governance had the potential to exert as broad a downward pressure on global deforestation rates.[97]

The third reason was urgency. Forest scientists were warning that if dramatic reductions in deforestation rates were not made swiftly, the world's native forests could simply disappear. Climate scientists were warning that without rapid early emission reductions, the goal of averting dangerous interference with the climate system—which many interpreted as warming more than 2 degrees Celsius above preindustrial levels—could be permanently foreclosed. REDD in carbon markets offered the possibility of spurring investment

---

96 Eveline Trines et al., *Integrating Agriculture, Forestry, and Other Land Use in Future Climate Regimes: Methodological Issues and Policy Options*, Climate Change Scientific Assessment and Policy Analysis WAB Report 500102 002, at 82 (Government of the Netherlands 2006), available at <http://www.pbl.nl/en/publications/2006/integrating_agriculture_forestry_and _other_land_use_climate_regimes.html>. *See* also Bryan Walsh, *Getting Credit for Saving Trees*, Time (Jul. 12, 2007). ("Pop quiz for all you global-warming experts: After China and the U.S., which country emits the greatest quantity of greenhouse gases per year? Answer high-tech Japan or industrial Germany, and you flunk. . . . It's rural Indonesia, which emits 3.3 billion tons of carbon dioxide annually—almost entirely from deforestation.")

97 This point was subsequently taken up in Europe, including in Nicholas Stern, *The Economics of Climate Change: The Stern Review* (Cambridge U. Press 2007), and Johan Eliasch, *Climate Change: Financing Global Forests—The Eliasch Review* (Earthscan 2008).

in cost-effective,[98] large-scale, immediately available[99] emission reductions, buying precious time for new low-carbon fossil fuel technologies to mature.[100] Although some critics feared, and continue to fear, that REDD could drive carbon prices down and crowd out more costly low-carbon energy technologies, subsequent analyses have demonstrated that REDD will not flood carbon markets as long as market actors are allowed to "bank," or save, surplus emission reductions,[101] and that bringing options for REDD into carbon markets could actually broaden the ambit for innovation in low-carbon fossil fuel technologies.[102]

The fourth had to do with equity. For fifteen years, "equity" in the climate talks had stood for the concept that industrial countries should go first and no new commitments should be introduced for developing countries. But the way that Papua New Guinea and Costa Rica presented REDD addressed a

---

98   Including a global program to reduce deforestation within a global carbon market system lowers the estimated total costs of a policy to achieve 535 ppmv of CO_2-equivalent concentrations in 2100 by up to 25 percent. Alternatively, a global REDD program could enable additional reductions of about 20 ppmv by 2100 with no added costs compared with an energy-sector-only policy. Valentina Bosetti, Ruben Lubowski, Alexander Golub, & Anil Markandya, *Linking Reduced Deforestation and a Global Carbon Market: Implications for Clean Energy Technology and Policy Flexibility,* Environment and Development Economics/FirstView Article (2011).

99   Early emissions reductions have particular value as a global insurance policy for maintaining climatic options in light of scientific uncertainty. Linking deforestation reductions to a market system in combination with credit banking also would encourage greater reductions in the near term, allowing targets to be met ahead of schedule. In addition to helping individual firms buffer against carbon market volatility, this has value at the global level in terms of enhancing flexibility to potentially tighten emission targets at lower cost in response to future scientific information, taking into account effects on technological innovation in the energy sector. *See* Bosetti et al., *supra* note 98.

100 Some of the concern over avoiding "flooding" has centered on concerns that REDD credits might reduce carbon prices and thus reduce incentives for the development and deployment of clean energy technologies. Recent research suggests that such effects are likely to be modest relative to the benefits of implementing ambitious climate policies and may actually slightly boost research and innovation within some energy technology sectors, including carbon capture and storage; *see* Bosetti et al., *supra* note 98. The flexibility provided by REDD could also grant firms some time to more efficiently schedule their long-lived capital investments in new technologies, such as carbon capture and storage. This could spur firms to invest in more research and development and then leapfrog to new technologies available in a few years' time rather than sinking costs into the technological options that are currently available. *See* Sabine Fuss, et al., *Options on Low-Cost Abatement and Investment in the Energy Sector: New Perspectives on REDD,* Environment and Development Economics/FirstView Article (2011); and Alexander Golub, *Options on REDD as a Hedging Tool for Post-Kyoto Climate Policy,* in *Deforestation and Climate Change: Reducing Carbon Emissions from Deforestation and Forest Degradation* 165 (Valentina Bosetti & Ruben Lubowski ed., Edward Elgar 2010).

101 *See* Pedro Piris-Cabezas, *REDD and the Global Carbon Market: The Role of Banking,* in *Deforestation and Climate Change: Reducing Carbon Emissions from Deforestation and Forest Degradation* 151 (Valenina Bosetti & Ruben Lubowski ed., Edward Elgar 2010); and Bosetti et al., *supra* note 98. *See* also Brian C. Murray, Ruben Lubowski, & Brent Sohngen, *Including International Forest Carbon Incentives in Climate Policy: Understanding the Economics,* Nicholas Institute for Environmental Policy Solutions Report 09-03 (2009).

102 Fuss et al., *supra* note 100.

different conception of equity, namely, the fact that many smaller tropical forest nations felt disempowered in the climate treaty talks because forest carbon projects had been shut out of the CDM. By framing their proposal as an issue of "fair and equitable access to carbon emissions markets," they put REDD at center stage in the climate treaty talks and opened a new way of thinking about issues in forest governance.

The fifth was community. Some policy experts had argued that market-based approaches could not work to protect tropical forests because unclear land tenure, including communal ownership of the forest resources, would make it difficult to tell who owned the carbon, hamper interactions with carbon markets, and expose the resources to destructive "free riding" and the classic "tragedy of the commons."[103] But new empirical analyses of common-pool resources and social-economic organization indicated that some variables seemed to enhance the chances that communities would self-organize in favor of sustainable management of jointly held resources.[104] These variables could encourage community members to work together to promote sustainability and thereby maximize the return to the overall community.[105]

REDD's proponents explicitly framed their intervention in terms of community,[106] and it quickly became clear that REDD, applied at the level of communally held forest resources, had the potential to connect many variables.[107] The question of legal recognition of land rights played a pivotal role. For example, the reason many indigenous peoples and rubber tappers in the

---

103 Garrett Hardin, *The Tragedy of the Commons*, 162 Science 1243 (1968).

104 *See*, for example, Elinor Ostrom, Roy Gardner, & James Walker, *Rules, Games and Common-Pool Resources* (University of Michigan Press 1994); and *People and Forests: Communities, Institutions, and Governance* (Clark C. Gibson, Margaret A. McKean, & Elinor Ostrom ed., MIT Press 2000). *See*, generally, Elinor Ostrom, *Governing the Commons: The Evolution of Institutions for Collective Action* (Cambridge U. Press, 1990), identifying common aspects of successful communally owned resource management:

   1. Clearly defined boundaries (effective exclusion of external unentitled parties)

   2. Rules on appropriation and provision of common resources are adapted to local conditions

   3. Collective choice allows most resource appropriators to participate in decision making

   4. Effective monitoring by monitors who are part of or accountable to the appropriators

   5. Graduated sanctions for resource appropriators who violate community rules

   6. Cheap and easily accessible mechanisms of conflict resolution

   7. The self-determination of the community is recognized by higher-level authorities

   8. In the case of larger common-pool resources, organization in the form of multiple layers of nested enterprises, with small local common-pool resources at the base level

105 *See* Bjorn Vollan & Elinor Ostrom, *Cooperation and the Commons*, 330 Science 923 (Nov. 12, 2010).

106 Submission by the Governments of Papua New Guinea and Costa Rica, *supra* note 93, at 4.

107 *See* Elinor Ostrom, *A General Framework for Analyzing Sustainability of Social-Ecological Systems*, 325 Science 419 (Jul. 24, 2009). Additional relevant variables include size of the resource system, predictability of system dynamics, and low mobility of the resource unit. *Id.*, at 421.

Amazon, particularly in Brazil, supported REDD —and a central reason that Brazil has at least some of the governance capacity necessary to control deforestation—is that the indigenous peoples and rubber tappers had largely won the struggle for legal recognition of their rights to the land on the forest frontier, and their communities and the government thus had greater capacity to connect with sensitively undertaken programs to reduce deforestation. In the fisheries sector, analyses indicated that imposing total allowable catch quotas for a given fishery resource in some instances led to widespread dumping of unwanted fish, misrepresentation of catches, and closure of the fishery; but assigning transferable fishery quotas and requiring neutral observers on board ships transformed the variables to favor communal restoration of the fishery to sustainability.[108] In a similar way, sensitively developed REDD programs had the potential to connect economic incentives for forest protection with communally held forest resources.

Thus, REDD evolved remarkably quickly in the global climate treaty talks. A series of UNFCCC technical workshops in 2006–08 explored questions of measurability, permanence, and baselines. REDD gained support from a broad range of developing countries. In 2007, the government of Brazil adopted a decree on climate change that, inter alia, established a domestic target of a 70 percent reduction in deforestation from historical average levels (1996–2005) by 2017.[109] Brazil's presentation of this plan exerted a major effect in the global discussion of REDD. China and India, having gone through a cycle of deforestation and having commenced reforestation, pressed to expand the concept of REDD to include forest management, and so the proposal evolved into REDD+. At the contentious Copenhagen Climate Conference in 2009, REDD made as much proress as, if not more than, any other single issue. And although disagreements remain over whether REDD should be applied exclusively at national levels or at subnational levels as well, the climate talks at Cancún, Mexico, in 2010 resolved most outstanding issues in terms of broad principles for the operation of REDD+, including such safeguards as explicit recognition of the UN Declaration on the Rights of Indigenous Peoples.

What Does the Future Look Like for REDD+?

As nations build on the framework of REDD+ and associated principles and develop the "robust and transparent" national forest-monitoring systems and rules "for measuring, reporting and verifying anthropogenic forest-related emissions" called for under the Cancún agreements,[110] they will try to reach

---

108 Colin W. Clark, *The Worldwide Crisis in Fisheries: Economic Models and Human Behavior* (Cambridge U. Press 2006).

109 Government of Brazil, Interministerial Committee on Climate Change, Decree No. 6263 of November 21, 2007, available at <http://www.uncsd2012.org/rio20/content/documents/National%20Plan%20on%20Climate%20Change%20Brazil.pdf>.

110 *See* Kintisch & Regalado, *supra* note 86.

agreement on approaches to formulating national baselines from which to credit REDD+ and to develop frameworks for the distribution of carbon market benefits, including approaches to compensating high-forest, low-deforestation countries for protecting forest stocks (an activity that yields no emission reductions and therefore is not susceptible to compensation directly in carbon markets).[111] Some nations have also proposed that they negotiate provisions to ensure that REDD+ delivers biodiversity and social benefits along with carbon benefits.[112]

REDD's original proponents anticipated its adoption as a freestanding protocol under the UNFCCC or a set of decisions under the Kyoto Protocol.[113] Efforts to implement such mechanisms are still going on; however, it may not be possible to reach agreement on a legally binding path forward under UNFCCC or Kyoto auspices before December 31, 2012, when the current Kyoto Protocol commitments expire. Certainly the failure of the United States to enact climate legislation has compounded the difficulty of reaching multilateral agreement in the near future. Consequently, it seems increasingly likely that there will be an interim period in which national, regional, state, and provincial carbon markets, operating separately but linked by the fungibility of carbon, play a principal role in addressing both climate change mitigation and forest governance.

This decentralized approach to carbon markets offers substantial opportunity for creativity and learning by doing, particularly with regard to bringing REDD+ into carbon markets, but it also entails substantial risks. Carbon markets that adopt weak criteria for the inclusion of REDD+ risk undermining the effectiveness of global efforts to combat climate change and entrenching constituencies in favor of those weak rules. Markets that adopt overly stringent criteria for the inclusion of REDD+ risk choking off the best near-term opportunity to obtain rapid, cost-effective, global-scale reductions in greenhouse gas emissions and improvements in forest governance. Bringing REDD+ into national, subnational, and regional emissions trading systems via programs that hew closely to the core elements needed for effective, high-integrity, linkable carbon markets[114] offers the best prospects for near-term climate mitigation that values and saves the world's remaining great forests and compensates the communities that depend on them.

---

111   Andre Cattaneo, *Incentives to Reduce Emissions from Deforestation: A Stock-Flow Approach with Target Reductions*, in *Deforestation and Climate Change: Reducing Carbon Emissions from Deforestation and Forest Degradation* 93 (Valentina Bosetti & Ruben Lubowski ed., Edward Elgar 2010).

112   *See*, for example, Michael Obersteiner et al., *Towards a Sound REDD: Ensuing Globally Consistent Reference Scenarios and Safeguarding Sustainability Co-benefits*, in *Deforestation and Climate Change: Reducing Carbon Emissions from Deforestation and Forest Degradation* 121 (Valentina Bosetti & Ruben Lubowski ed., Edward Elgar 2010); and Long, *supra* note 16 (proposal to require nonstate actor certification of sustainability of REDD forest carbon).

113   Submission by the Governments of Papua New Guinea and Costa Rica, *supra* note 93, at 8.

114   *See*, for example, Annie Petsonk, *"Docking Stations": Designing a More Open Legal and Policy Architecture for a Post-2012 Framework to Combat Climate Change*, 19 Duke J. of Intl. & Comp. L. 433 (2009).

IFIs can play a helping role, but they must tread lightly and cautiously in order to facilitate, rather than frustrate, the process. The World Bank's Forest Carbon Partnership Facility[115] has made an important start in this regard, but some critics think it has tried to do too much too fast. Moving forward, IFI efforts to assist nations with building capacity for REDD and REDD+ must be coordinated with broader IFI efforts to assist nations with carbon market readiness.

---

115 Benoit Bosquet, Stefano Pagiola, & André Aquino, *Preparing for REDD: The Forest Carbon Partnership Facility*, in *Deforestation and Climate Change: Reducing Carbon Emissions from Deforestation and Forest Degradation* 71 (Valentina Bosetti & Ruben Lubowski ed., Edward Elgar 2010).

PART III

INTERNATIONAL FINANCE AND THE CHALLENGES OF REGULATORY GOVERNANCE

Networks In(-)Action?

The Transgovernmental Origins of, and Responses to, the Financial Crisis

CHRIS BRUMMER

Most accounts seeking to examine the causes of the global financial crisis identify the culprit as the weak regulatory supervision in the United States. Certainly, the international financial crisis started on American shores, and its origins have been partially located in weak regulatory oversight and lax monetary policy: U.S. financial authorities substantially lowered interest rates to stimulate the economy following the collapse of the tech bubble and, inadvertently or otherwise, gave rise to speculative real estate lending practices for subprime borrowers. Mortgage and other types of loans were then bundled together before being sliced and diced to be sold off to financial institutions. In turn, these institutions restructured and engineered the risk inherent in these loans through an alphabet soup of complex financial instruments known as collateralized debt obligations or credit default swaps, bought and sold in largely unregulated over-the-counter markets. Other oversight mechanisms, such as those provided by credit rating agencies, also were lax. Burdened by powerful conflicts of interest and a privileged position in the market for their services, agencies provided scant scrutiny of the risks residing in the real estate on which the financial edifice had been constructed.

Yet U.S. rules and regulations were not the only ones that failed to predict the onset and spread of this crisis and subsequently to counter its ill effects. As this chapter discusses, a variety of international codes and standards were on the books and widely disseminated by international standard-setting bodies and transgovernmental networks of financial authorities, yet these were unable to foresee or prevent the crisis. As a result, the financial crisis seeped into the slipstream of the entire global economy. Following the crisis and in recognition of oversight failures, a considerable collection of international agenda- and standard-setting organizations were developed and the international regulatory community proceeded to set out various initiatives at breakneck speed to fill some of the prudential and supervisory gaps at not only national but international levels of regulatory cooperation and governance.

This chapter reviews some key international efforts launched to regulate global systemic risk. It first surveys the global regulatory architecture just prior to the crisis and the international approaches in place geared toward mitigating and addressing systemic risk. Despite a growing and evolving set of international financial standards, major lacunae pervaded transnational legislative initiatives touching sectors as diverse as banking, payment systems, accounting, and executive compensation. The chapter then highlights key co-ordination efforts undertaken by regulators in the wake of the crisis. Finally, it briefly outlines some criticisms of the evolving regulatory system and draws lessons for international financial law as a tool for combating global systemic risk.

Creating the Network: The First Steps of Global Financial Regulation

Perhaps the most important means of regulating credit risk in the decade leading up to 2008 was through the regulation of "capital" held by systemically important financial institutions, most importantly, banks. Capital represents, from a legal standpoint, "the portion of a bank's assets that have no associated contractual commitment for repayment."[1] It constitutes a cash (or liquid) cushion against which a bank can draw if its lending or investment decisions turn out poorly. Capital can thus provide a gauge to determine the prospective safety and soundness of a financial institution.

The first international accord geared toward regulating capital was devised in 1988 by the Basel Committee on Banking Supervision. Under the accord (widely referred to as "Basel I"), banks were required to meet two capital adequacy requirements, expressed in practice as meeting two ratios that measure the capital on a bank's books against the bank's risk-weighted assets. Although it was an important step forward in providing the first global standards for bank supervision, Basel I generated a variety of problems that became apparent as it was implemented. Most important, the risk-weighting system was somewhat arbitrary and failed to distinguish risks among creditors belonging to the same risk category. For example, because all commercial loans were weighted at 100 percent, a bank could earn greater returns by lending to a less-than-creditworthy corporation than to an established company with a better credit history.[2]

"Basel II," launched in 2004 and only partially implemented by banks by the time the crisis struck, spoke to these problems in part by adopting two broad methodologies—a standardized and an internal risk-based approach—to provide more tailored risk assessments. Under the standard approach, bank asset risk was determined by the rating assigned to the borrower or issuer in question. That is, where a borrower had a credit rating from a recognized rating agency (for example, Moody's or Standard & Poor's), the lending bank could use that rating as a basis of calculating the risk associated with that borrower. The higher the credit rating of the borrower, the lower the capital charges associated with the bank's assets.

---

1   Douglas J. Elliott, *Basel III, the Banks and the Economy* 3 (Brookings Inst. 2010), available at <http://www.brookings.edu/~/media/Files/rc/papers/2010/0726_basel_elliott/0726_basel_elliott.pdf>.

2   Daniel K. Tarullo, *Administrative Accountability and International Regulatory Networks* 23 (Nov. 4, 2008) (on file with author).

Critically, Basel II allowed the biggest international banks to use their own internal risk calculations as a basis for calculating capital charges under various iterations of the "internal ratings-based approach." In light of this, banks were allowed to develop their own empirical models, which were subject to regulatory approval, to measure and account for the credit risk on their books and to ensure that there was sufficient provision to protect against default by customers and clients of the bank.

In addition to regulating bank capital, international standards and codes sought to shore up the market infrastructure used by financial institutions in their transactional dealings with each other. Payment and settlement systems operated as the transmission channels for the transfer of cash and securities between financial market participants. The safety and soundness of market infrastructure mechanisms were thus seen as critical to assuring safety and soundness across the market. By 2001, the Committee on Payment and Settlement Systems (CPSS) had offered ten general principles setting out consensus on best practice for the operation of sound financial systems, as well as the role central banks should play in supervising systemically important institutions. The CPSS and the International Organization of Securities Commissions jointly developed a set of conceptual recommendations for securities settlement systems and clearinghouses.

In addition to international efforts aimed at regulating the conduct of international market participants, efforts were also geared toward helping investors better understand the financial health and stability of financial firms. Under fair value accounting methods adopted under U.S. generally accepted accounting principles and international financial reporting standards (IFRS), the assets of all companies, including financial institutions, are generally accounted for and priced in light of their current market value. In doing so, fair value differs substantially from approaches that focused on historic costs of assets, enabling firms to create hidden reserves on their balance sheets.

Network Shortcomings: International Standards and Codes Miss Their Mark

Despite the existence of standards and codes, just a few of which are discussed here, the international regulatory system failed to predict the onset of the crisis and stop its quick progression through the global financial system. As the dust has settled, a number of critical areas have been noted where coverage was either incomplete or nonexistent. A few examples are noted below.

Few international standards in place in 2008 addressed the web of financial institutions such as hedge funds, investment banks, and securities firms that grew during the previous decades to become central sources of credit in ways that rivaled and even eclipsed traditional deposit-taking institutions (that is, traditional "banks"). The Basel Agreements had limited implications for the shadow banking industry because such institutions were not deposit-taking banks as traditionally understood and defined by existing regulations.

This meant that in practice, national authorities could choose the extent to which the accords would apply to their local financial institutions—an outcome that led to varying regulatory approaches.

Not only did shadow banking largely escape the attention of the international regulatory community; so did the activities in which shadow banks participated. This was particularly the case with derivatives instruments such as credit default swaps and other types of esoteric credit derivative instruments, which allowed credit risk to be hedged and transacted off balance sheets, freeing financial institutions to take on more and greater risks in the expectation that these too could be engineered and sold into the financial markets.[3] The vast webs of transactions involving such instruments made locations of risk difficult to identify. When the web came undone, most vividly after the collapse of Lehman Brothers in 2008, the dissolution included institutions, such as AIG, that had taken substantial positions in the credit derivative market. No international best practice standards had been developed to address such instruments or the infrastructure supporting derivatives trading. As a result, derivatives such as credit default swaps were commonly traded off exchanges in most countries and escaped registration and disclosure obligations that would ordinarily apply in the case of most securities transactions.[4]

Fair value accounting, meanwhile, was not without its trade-offs and risks. Of perhaps greatest importance is procyclicality. Fair value accounting allows institutions to record excessively high values for their assets, such as derivatives contracts and mortgage-backed securities. High asset valuations in turn feed high recorded profits on investments, inflate bonuses for financial services executives, and lead to more irrational exuberance in a self-enforcing cycle.[5] When market cycles turn and markets crash, procyclicality can (and did) fuel irrational despair. Falling prices often activate margin calls by banks seeking to limit their own exposures to borrowers and in the process contribute to a downward spiral in market prices as securities are sold off into the market.[6]

The international community had failed to devise global rules to prevent institutions from becoming too large or too interconnected to fail. This gap was all the more notable given the proliferation of large universal banks and

---

3   Credit default swaps operate much like insurance contracts, whereby the credit risk of an obligation can be reduced by entering into an agreement with a counterparty, requiring that counterparty to pay for losses arising if there is a default on the obligation. In return for regular payments, the counterparty thus agrees to protect the obligation holder from losses arising if this obligation goes into default.

4   Michael Greenberger, University of Maryland School of Law, statement, *The Role of Derivatives in the Financial Crisis: Hearing before the Fin. Crisis Inquiry Comm'n* (2010), available at <http://www.michaelgreenberger.com/files/FCIC-Michael_Greenberger_Testimony.pdf>.

5   Adair Turner, *The Turner Review: A Regulatory Response to the Global Banking Crisis* 65 (Fin. Serv. Auth. 2009), available at <http://www.fsa.gov.uk/pubs/other/turner_review.pdf>.

6   Andreas Nölke, *The Politics of Accounting Regulation: Responses to Subprime Crisis*, in *Global Finance in Crisis: The Politics of International Regulatory Change* 43 (Eric Helleiner et al. ed., Routledge 2010).

the well-known collapse in the 1990s of the Bank of Credit and Commerce International, an event that writ large the regulatory challenges of winding down large and complex financial institutions. The absence of global rules on "too big to fail" as well as cross-border resolution meant that, in a globalized world, institutions were capable of reaching a size and breadth of activities that few regulators could have predicted a decade before, and whose failure could give rise to international contagion and deep uncertainty regarding how assets could and should be located and distributed upon insolvency. The 30 largest institutions around the world are deeply international, with 53 percent of their assets abroad, and have on average 1,000 subsidiaries, of which 68 percent operate abroad and 12 percent in offshore financial centers. By 2008, a number of international banks and financial institutions operated across the globe, including in developing countries, where their services provided key channels for local persons and businesses to access finance. The absence of international standards and codes on the regulation of bank size and cross-border resolution carries particular salience for regulators in developing countries, which may be especially vulnerable to financial services providers failing and repatriating their assets to their home-state jurisdictions.

Finally, oversight and surveillance of international financial standards were far from robust leading up to the 2008 financial crisis. Central to the global surveillance system administered by the International Monetary Fund (IMF) and the World Bank is the Financial Sector Assessment Program (FSAP). Under FSAP, the World Bank and the IMF assess a country's implementation of key financial standards deemed necessary for a stable financial system. However, FSAP suffered from a variety of weaknesses. Only those countries that were recipients of loans from the World Bank and the IMF were formally required to participate in the program. Thus, most countries, including the United States, never underwent surveillance of any sort. And when countries did participate, the data provided to international institutions was largely self-reported by national authorities—and depended on information provided by regulated financial entities that were themselves subject to little supervisory oversight.[7] The information gained by surveillance was published only with the permission of the inspected country; the monitored country thus had discretion as to whether information regarding its compliance could be shared with other regulators or market participants.

Networks in Action: Responses by the International Regulatory Community

In the wake of the financial crisis, many countries, including the United States, were spurred to reform their domestic regulatory systems as well as the international regulatory system. Taking the lead in coordinating at the global level

---

7   World Bank, *Financial and Private Sector Development—Financial Sector Assessment Program*, available at <http://lnweb90.worldbank.org/FPS/fsapcountrydb.nsf/FSAPexternalcountry reports?OpenPage&count=5000>.

was the Group of 20 (G20), which assumed from the Group of Seven (G7) the role as the leading agenda setter for international finance. In the organization's first leaders' summit, in Washington, DC, in 2008, heads of state tasked finance ministers with enhancing global financial regulation and promoting the integrity and stability of international financial markets. To carry out the mandate, working groups were established to make recommendations in areas as diverse as accounting and disclosure and prudential oversight while developing recommendations to dampen cyclical forces in the financial system. The Washington Summit's declaration contained a detailed action plan based in part on the principle that all financial markets, products, and participants—including shadow banking institutions—must be subject to prudential regulation. In London in 2009, the G20 published a Leaders Statement that went a step forward by committing to do whatever was necessary to strengthen global financial supervision and regulation. Participant countries laid out a framework for improving prudential regulation that included tackling a range of issues inadequately addressed in the previous regulatory order, such as hedge funds, credit derivatives, and executive compensation. The work in the wake of these two summits continued in Pittsburgh (2009) and Seoul (2010), and covered not only financial regulatory matters but also trade, currency, and monetary affairs. This section presents a general overview of some key financial market initiatives following the panic of 2008.

As the centerpiece of initial international regulatory efforts, broader wholesale reforms of capital ratios for banking regulatory purposes were introduced. First, the methodology for determining risk weightings of trading assets was tightened and made stricter.[8] Under the 2010 "Basel III" process, regulators shifted the focus of their gaze from the issue of risk weighting (the denominator in the ratio) to the capital requirements themselves (the numerator in the ratio), and then to the ratio itself. Under Basel III, banks are required to hold three times as much capital on reserve as compared with before the crisis, an effort to move banks toward making more risk-averse decisions and to force them to maintain a larger cushion of safety against sudden and longer-term losses. In addition, Basel III requires banks to hold more tier I capital, that is, better-quality capital, such as common equity. (Basel III raises the amount of common equity that must be held to 7 percent of assets from 2 percent by 2015.) In addition, banks are subject to an additional "conservation buffer" of 2.5 percent in times of strong economic growth, meaning in effect that a bank will need 7 percent common equity, 8.5 percent tier 1 capital, and 10.5 percent tier 2 capital to meet its capital requirements; if a bank cannot meet this threshold, it will not be able to pay dividends. Finally, a countercyclical capital buffer can be applied by regulators, requiring that banks hold more capital in times of growth as a check against procyclicality. Such a buffer is expected to be enforced up to the maximum of 2.5 percent.[9]

---

8   Elliott, *supra* note 1.

9   Felix Salmon, Reuters: Felix Salmon Blog, *Basel III Arrives*, <http://blogs.reuters.com/felix-salmon/2010/09/12/basel-iii-arrives/> (Sept. 12, 2010).

The Basel Committee introduced several new capital ratios alongside risk-weighted prudential requirements in order to enhance the stability of the global financial system. Banks must now satisfy a leverage ratio measuring tier I capital against total risk adjusted assets. The leverage ratio sets a back-stop on the amount of debt that a bank can take on. Two additional liquidity coverage ratios were introduced, mandating that financial institutions main-tain an "adequate level of assets that can be converted into cash to meet its liquidity needs" for short (30 calendar days) and long-term (up to a year) time horizons under a severe liquidity stress scenario specified by national banking supervisors.[10]

The international regulatory community also moved to better supervise institutions that in the past had often escaped scrutiny from banking regula-tors. In October 2010, the Financial Stability Board (FSB), an agenda-setting body launched from the Financial Stability Forum in the wake of the crisis, issued its report *Intensity and Effectiveness of SIFI Supervision*. The report rec-ommends that all "systemically important financial institutions" be subject to capital charges even more exacting than those spelled out in Basel III. The FSB also announced that it would "develop criteria for assessing which institu-tions pose global systemic risk" in order to help ensure consistent implemen-tation throughout the jurisdictions of its members.[11] As part of its work, the international community, in this case acting mainly under the auspices of the International Organization of Securities Commissions (IOSCO), has sought to create standards for the regulation of players formerly operating in the shadow banking system, notably hedge funds, that had in the run-up to the crisis largely escaped oversight.[12]

In May 2010, and in response to G20 agenda items calling for the stan-dardization and trading of derivatives instruments, the CPSS and IOSCO published the report *Guidance on the Application of the 2004 CPSS-IOSCO Rec-ommendations for Central Counterparties to OTC Derivatives CCPs* to promote consistent applications of existing standards so as to better address risks asso-ciated with clearing over-the-counter derivatives and bolster the effectiveness of central counterparties as risk-mitigating devices.[13] The CPSS and IOSCO also published *Considerations for Trade Repositories in OTC Derivatives Markets*, which lays out factors that trade repositories should consider in designing

---

10   Daniel Pruzin, *Basel Panel Issues Final Basel III Package; Version Contains New Liquidity Rule Details*, Intl. Bus. & Fin. Daily Online (BNA) (Dec. 17, 2010).

11   Fin. Stability Bd., *Progress since the Washington Summit in the Implementation of the G20 Recommendations for Strengthening Financial Stability* 8 (2010), available at <http://www.financialstabilityboard.org/publications/r_101111b.pdf> (hereinafter, 2010 Financial Stability Report).

12   Technical Comm., IOSCO, Hedge Funds Oversight (2009), available at <http://www.hedgefundlawblog.com/wp-content/uploads/2009/06/iosco-hedge-fund-regulation-report.pdf>.

13   Comm. on Payment and Settlement Sys. & Technical Comm. of the Int'l Org. of Securities Comm'ns, *Guidance on the Application of the 2004 CPSS-IOSCO Recommendations for Central Counterparties to OTC Derivatives CCPs* (2010), available at <http://www.bis.org/publ/cpss89.htm>.

and operating their services and relevant authorities should consider in regulating and overseeing trade repositories.[14]

Various efforts at improving transparency have been introduced for accounting standards. In 2009, the International Accounting Standards Board promulgated a new standard, IFRS 9, as part of the first phase of accounting reforms. IFRS 9 addresses the classification and measurement of financial assets; the second and third phases will address impairment and hedge accounting, respectively. The major advantage of IFRS is its simplicity and effectiveness at measuring financial instruments. IAS 39, the older accounting regime, categorized all assets according to four different asset categories. IFRS 9 requires all financial assets to be measured at either "amortized cost" or "fair value" after considering the business model of the entity for managing the financial asset and the contractual cash flow characteristics of the financial asset.[15] Amortized cost is less sensitive to market conditions than fair value, which can fluctuate based on market movements and can potentially depress the value of assets on the books in a depressed market.

At the level of surveillance, the IMF has approved making financial stability assessments a regular and mandatory part of its surveillance for members that host systemically important financial sectors. Previously, participation in an FSAP was voluntary for all IMF members. Now, however, FSAPs are mandatory for all countries determined to have systemically important financial sectors. Twenty-five jurisdictions were identified by the IMF in 2010 as having systemically important financial sectors, according to a methodology that evaluates both the size and the interconnectedness of each country's financial sector: Australia; Austria; Belgium; Brazil; Canada; China; France; Germany; Hong Kong SAR, China; Italy; Japan; India; Ireland; Luxembourg; Mexico; the Netherlands; the Republic of Korea; Russia; Singapore; Spain; Sweden; Switzerland; Turkey; the United Kingdom; and the United States.[16] Nearly 90 percent of the global financial system is represented by this group, as well as 80 percent of global economic activity.[17] It also includes 15 of the G20 member countries and more than half of the membership of the FSB. Each country will have to undertake an FSAP assessment every five years, and all can volunteer for more frequent surveillance. The methodology will be reviewed periodically to make sure it continues to include countries that are systemically important to the global financial system. Finally, peer reviews were launched by institutions such as the FSB to assist in evaluating the implementation or achievement of international regulatory objectives.

---

14   2010 Financial Stability Report, *supra* note 11, at 13.

15   PricewaterhouseCoopers, *Significant Changes to the Classification and Measurement of Financial Assets: IFRS 9 Financial Instruments* (Feb. 23, 2010), available at <http://www.pwc.com/us/en/alternative-investment/alerts/IFRS-9-financial-instruments.jhtml>.

16   *Id.*

17   *Id.*

New Networks Deconstructed: Criticisms Thus Far

As is clear from the analysis above, in the years immediately following the financial crisis, the international regulatory community can boast a staggering range of advances and achievements that strengthened the financial system more than most people, including many experts, realize.

It is worth noting, however, that like most regulatory reforms, global efforts are not without flaws. In my book *Soft Law and the Global Financial System: Rule Making in the 21st Century*, I elaborate potential progress and shortcomings in more depth; for the purposes of this chapter, I will outline three general complaints. Perhaps most important, various commentators have criticized the scope of the reforms. Although capital requirements have increased for certain derivatives-related trading, there are still no internationally recognized best practices with regard to disclosure requirements for derivatives instruments or under what conditions they should be registered and what institutions should be permitted to deal in them. Similarly, although regulation for particular regulatory matters and participants has improved, a variety of institutions, in particular hedge funds and private equity funds, have escaped scrutiny and international regulatory efforts. As such, risky transactions will potentially move from regulated sectors of the economy such as banking to less or unregulated sectors of the financial economy. Even where international standards have been developed, compliance with many of these standards remains beyond the scope of monitoring activities practiced by international financial institutions such as the World Bank and the IMF, as well as by market participants.

Other criticisms have focused on the belief that the rules emerging from international coordination efforts are not sufficiently strict. Some studies have suggested, for example, that the socially optimal amount of capital that banks should hold may be in excess of Basel III standards. Complicating matters further, these standards are not required to be implemented formally until 2019. In the interim, regulators permit compliance with Basel II's lower capital requirements, thus giving time for distressed financial institutions to improve their balance sheets or to game laxer requirements before they have to switch to the new regime. As many critics have argued, by 2019, the world may have experienced more financial crises, and measures responding to these crises may counteract Basel III's effectiveness in practice.

Finally, although the efforts mark important advances in initiating better regulatory cooperation, these efforts remain superficial in many sectors. Most commentators agree, for example, that the architecture for cross-border regulatory cooperation remains inadequate to deal with another financial crisis. The Basel Committee's work has identified the need for greater coordination in light of the failures of the crisis and calls on authorities to develop a framework for greater cooperation. Similarly, although the FSB initiatives have made important headway in developing capital standards for systemically important institutions, and the FSB is presumably on its way to generating standards for identifying such institutions, the FSB's work thus far provides no details on how such communication and cooperation should take place. A challenge is the difference and variety of global financial institutions with regard to their structures and activities and, by extension, the nature and degree of the risks they pose to the global financial system. Furthermore, many regulators do not have even the basic mandates or independence required to shut down distressed institutions that pose imminent systemic dangers, much less cooperate internationally, and as a result, collaboration will likely take years to implement.[18] Much of the remit is instead enjoyed by judges, who, unlike regulators, are unaccustomed to international coordination of their work. As a result, bankruptcy of a large financial institution would still cause many of the same dislocations and chaos as experienced in prior crises.

None of the issues addressed above poses insurmountable obstacles to success, and two to three years of regulatory effort in this regard is too short a time to formulate a definitive statement of failure. These are difficult and charged issues, often evidencing considerable domestic policy priorities, risk and cost allocations, and national interests. Challenges with few obvious solutions take time to resolve. The complexity of the process is further embedded in the dynamics and obstacles that inform most cross-border regulatory efforts, for example, in relation to international coordination between domestic agencies and tensions that may arise owing to domestic politics and interest.

First, at a fundamental level, financial authorities and stakeholders may be at odds regarding the role that the state should play in overseeing the market. For example, on the issue of executive compensation, prior to the 2009 G20 meeting in Pittsburgh, some national leaders, and with special vigor President Nicholas Sarkozy of France, called for international limits on the amount of pay a banker could earn. However, the notion of government-dictated compensation is anathema to U.S. conceptions of free market capitalism, and the U.S. government resisted any regulation of banker pay. Because of this deep difference in philosophy and competitive considerations, the international community opted for a compromise focusing not so much on pay but on the determination of pay and the alignment of incentives between executives and their firms.

Second, competitive considerations continue to inform virtually every element of regulatory decision making, even in the wake of the financial crisis. For example, the Volcker rule, which is part of the Dodd-Frank Wall Street Reform and Consumer Protection Act of 2010 (H.R. 4173), bars banks from dealing on their own account in speculative derivatives and (mortgage-backed) securities and in investing more than 3 percent of their capital in hedge funds and private equity. The Volcker rule was introduced as part of more extensive U.S. efforts to address the too-big-to-fail problem. However, it gained little traction among EU countries, including the United Kingdom, for reasons beyond differences in regulatory philosophies: European banks have historically adhered closely to a universal banking model that has allowed

---

18   2010 Financial Stability Report, *supra* note 11.

them to undertake a number of banking as well as investment banking activities and to thus compete fiercely with markets that constrain the activities of banks. By contrast, the United States, since the Great Depression, under the auspices of the Glass-Steagall Act, maintained regulatory walls between banking and investment banking, restrictions that were dismantled in 1999 owing to the pressures of competition on U.S. institutions from European firms. If adopted in Europe, the Volcker rule would force many highly profitable European banks to change their historical business model fundamentally. For U.S. banks, adjustment costs, although significant, are likely familiar and arguably less onerous overall.

Third, the perceived sovereignty costs accompanying stricter or more robust standards and institutional mechanisms can limit international coordination. International rules often undermine the ability of a government to act in the best interest of its local economy. Many countries have shied away from cross-border resolution and bankruptcy cooperation because binding rules on the matter could impair the ability of local institutions to determine when financial institutions are insolvent, as well as how the institutions are restructured or liquidated. Regulators could face considerable complexities and challenges in making determinations of when and how distressed financial institutions should be recognized as being insolvent. This particular challenge can be especially costly for countries where a distressed bank is a systemically important institution that serves as a primary source of capital. International rules could also diminish prospects for courts to decide on the best method for the disposition of assets to most optimally benefit local economic interests and protect local creditors.

International surveillance and monitoring of countries' compliance with best practices likewise generate considerable sovereignty costs. International standards exhibit their most powerful compliance pull when they are acknowledged by the market as being important and when both regulators and markets can evaluate a jurisdiction's compliance with them. Where surveillance is strong and information about lack of compliance with standards is shared with the market, firms in noncompliant countries may experience higher costs of capital, and governmental authorities may suffer reputational costs in the international community. As a result, many regulators from both developed and developing countries resisted efforts in 1999 to make the FSAP a formal requirement of membership in the IMF or to impose obligations on all countries to adhere to the standards. Countries did not wish to become subject to oversight where the quality of the regulatory oversight could be scrutinized both by the market and by the international community, and where their national constituents could face the economic costs associated with perceptions of higher risk. The 2008 crisis changed the calculation of many countries, especially as the economic costs of poor financial supervision became increasingly evident. That said, although the G20 has committed to participation, not every IMF member has, and the IMF has not taken every step possible to heighten market discipline and transparency with regard to compliance with international standards and leveraging market discipline.

Concluding Thoughts

The transgovernmental origins of the crisis shed light on the international regulatory community. Standards in place at the time of the crisis did little to prevent the crisis and, because of their weaknesses, channeled its internationally contagious reach. Efforts since the crisis have fallen short of ensuring that these shortcomings are fully addressed. That said, a number of critical advances and achievements have been made in the global regulation of systemic risk that, when fully implemented, will significantly improve the international financial system.

Some of the success stems from the fact that "systemic" risks are viewed or experienced as broadly shared.[19] And when actors internalize the costs of financial instability or decline, cooperation becomes much easier. Furthermore, unlike many other species of international economic law, agreements concerning international financial market regulation are not undergirded by treaties and are technically nonbinding. Thus, reneging on international regulatory commitments entails fewer legal consequences, which may induce some parties to come to the negotiating table—even though in some instances standards may be backed by a variety of disciplinary mechanisms. In contrast to hard law instruments that require domestic political processes and ratification procedures, international financial law can be operationalized largely through domestic administrative agencies.

The changes in international standards implemented since 2008 demonstrate that even when a strong demand for cross-border regulation arises, international financial law is no panacea, even with the conditions that make agreement possible and the qualitative features that can give it advantages in the coordination process. Standard setting is an arduous process that can be fraught by misaligned and antagonistic interests between national supervisory agencies and regulators. Therefore, agreement between financial authorities is not guaranteed, even when rules are not legally binding. Especially when issues could carry steep distributive and asymmetric consequences for interested parties by disadvantaging local market participants or binding the flexibility of governments to tailor solutions according to their policy preferences, gaps may persist throughout the regulatory architecture.

---

19   *See*, for example, Christopher Brummer, *How International Financial Law Works (and How It Doesn't)*, 99 Geo. L.J. 257, 322 (2011) (noting the implications of making the surveillance of international rules more robust); Christopher Brummer, *Why Soft Law Dominates Finance—and Not Trade*, 13 J. Intl. Econ. L. 623 (2010) (same).

Mitigating the Impact of Financial Crises on the Brazilian Capital Market

ALEXANDRE PINHEIRO DOS SANTOS[*]

Introduction

The recent international financial crisis highlighted the importance of continuing cooperation and exchange of information between all regulators of financial or capital markets and the need for supervision of the financial system as a whole from the perspective of financial stability. The crisis also showed that nonfinancial institutions can be equally relevant from the standpoint of systemic risk. A yet more far-reaching revelation was that markets and products can affect market stability and, therefore, should be supervised from that perspective.

In this sense, one of the challenges for regulators around the world is the abandonment of old ideas, such as notions that regulation stifles innovation; that self-regulation should prevail over state regulation; that investors and markets behave rationally; that qualified investors are always able to evaluate the products they acquire; that products and services for qualified investors do not need regulation and supervision; and that only the public markets should be strictly regulated.

The main objective of this chapter is to present an overview of the situation of Brazil in the recent financial crisis and the current conditions of the Brazilian capital market. The chapter spotlights the role of the Brazilian Securities Commission (Comissão de Valores Mobiliários, CVM), a federal agency established by Law 6385 of December 7, 1976.[1] CVM is headed by a chair and four commissioners, all of whom are appointed by the Brazilian president from among persons of good reputation and recognized competence in the field of capital markets. All board members must undergo a public hearing before the Senate; once confirmed, they serve for five years.

CVM's mandate is to regulate, supervise, oversee, and promote the securities market. In its institutional role, CVM ensures the regular and efficient operation of capital markets. In performing this mandate, CVM also develops a regulatory function in which it must observe not only national laws but also international standards of conduct, especially when it comes to the field of

---

[*] This chapter is based on the author's participation in the panel Mitigating the Impact of Financial Crises on Emerging Markets and Transition Economies, which was part of the event Law, Justice, and Development Week 2010, conducted by the World Bank in November 2010. This chapter represents the views of the author and not necessarily of the Brazilian Securities Commission (CVM).

[1] The statute is available at <http://www.planalto.gov.br/ccivil_03/Leis/L6385.htm> (in Portuguese).

capital markets as part of an increasingly globalized and interconnected financial system. Brazil actively participates in the Group of Twenty (G20), the Financial Stability Board (FSB), and the International Organization of Securities Commissions (IOSCO),[2] and adheres closely to the policies pursued by such bodies. CVM, faithfully observing the constitutionally sheltered tenets of market economics,[3] pursues an efficient securities market, which needs to be free, competitive, informed, and reliable. Such qualities depend on the adequate protection and harmonization of the interests of all players in the global financial system.

The basic principle that informs the actions of CVM is full and fair disclosure. The agency is inspired by the example of the U.S. Securities and Exchange Commission (SEC).

The regulatory system of the Brazilian capital market is essentially a rules-based system. However, CVM seeks to permanently encourage and make appropriate use of a system of self-regulation in Brazil,[4] a system that is both mandatory[5] and voluntary and that extends to the enforcement of market rules.[6] This support for self-regulation, however, does not prevent CVM from adopting an effective risk-based supervision system, whose inspiration includes the experience of the Financial Services Authority (FSA).[7] CVM usually conducts public hearings regarding its regulatory projects to obtain suggestions from market participants and other interested parties.

This standard of conduct enables CVM, despite its continued alignment with the international consensus on matters related to capital markets (which contributes considerably to the prevention of cross-border arbitrage), to issue rules that address in a balanced way the transnational perspective and the peculiarities of the country.

---

2   In 2011, CVM chair Maria Helena Santana was appointed chairwoman of IOSCO's Executive Committee. Additional information regarding this subject is available at <http://www.iosco.org/news/pdf/IOSCONEWS205.pdf>.

3   On the subject, see Article 170 of the Constitution of the Federative Republic of Brazil, available at <http://www.planalto.gov.br/ccivil_03/constituicao/constitui%C3%A7ao.htm> (in Portuguese).

4   This regulation is in line with the IOSCO Objectives and Principles of Securities Regulation, which are among the FSB Key Standards for Sound Financial Systems. The IOSCO Objectives and Principles of Securities Regulation are available at <http://www.iosco.org/library/pubdocs/pdf/IOSCOPD329.pdf>.

5   On the subject, see Article 17 of Law No. 6385, of December 7, 1976, available at <http://www.planalto.gov.br/ccivil_03/leis/L6385compilada.htm> (in Portuguese).

6   An example of state use of a self-regulatory role in the capital market is given in Article 49, paragraph 5, of CVM Instruction No. 461 of 2007, which provides that in relation to penalties for violations of rules under its jurisdiction, CVM may deduct those penalties that have already been imposed under a mandatory self-regulation. This document is available at <http://www.cvm.gov.br/asp/cvmwww/atos/Atos_Redir.asp?File=\inst\inst461consolid.doc> (in Portuguese).

7   For more information regarding this subject, see CVM Deliberation No. 521 of 2007 (as amended), available at <http://www.cvm.gov.br/asp/cvmwww/atos/Atos_Redir.asp?File=\deli\deli521consolid.doc> (in Portuguese).

Brazil, like other countries with a similar level of importance in the world, has experienced significant economic development in recent years and has not suffered severely from the effects of the recent crisis. One aim of this chapter is to highlight a few characteristics of the Brazilian scenario that may have made possible this relatively smooth path through the crisis and its aftermath. The chapter also discusses some trends and regulatory measures that were taken after the crisis to mitigate its impact and prevent further similar occurrences, with a particular focus on the capital market.

Economy and Performance of Brazil before the Financial Crisis

In recent years, the most important economic indexes in Brazil have behaved positively, and market participants expect that this will be the case for the coming years. For instance, Brazil's gross domestic product is expected to increase 4.5 percent in 2011; the country's inflation rate is under control; and the public debt is considered comfortable.[8]

Strong economic foundations, alongside the remarkable improvement in corporate governance practices adopted by publicly held companies, have boosted trading volume, market capitalization, and the number of IPOs, all of which have grown substantially in the past 10 years. Brazilian market capitalization jumped from US$225 billion in 2000 to US$1.5 trillion in 2010; the daily average trading of shares rocketed from US$348 million to more than US$3 billion. During the same period, the number of investors, especially individual investors, has increased markedly.

In terms of capital activities, almost all categories of products have grown substantially in the past decade. For instance, public offerings of equities totaled US$ 133 billion in 2010, more than double the 2009 figure. Even if the public offering of Petrobras, the largest Brazilian publicly held company, is excluded from the figure for 2010, the results remain positive. It is instructive to note the evolution of IPOs over the same period: at the beginning of the 2000s, there were no IPOs in Brazil; today, the Brazilian market is considered one of the most active. The total amount of IPOs reached about US$2.1 billion in the first quarter of 2011.

Collective investment vehicles such as funds and investment clubs have become significantly more popular. Investment funds have showed great diversity, with an emphasis on structured funds. Investment clubs have grown impressively, enrolling a larger number of small investors. The number of investment funds almost doubled in the past decade to more than 10,000, while the number of investment clubs grew tenfold. Today, there are more than 3,000. The market has been an effective option for financing Brazilian companies.

---

8   Additional information regarding this subject is available at <http://www.fazenda.gov
     .br/portugues/docs/perspectiva-economia-brasileira/edicoes/Economia-Brasileira-Em-Per
     pectiva-Mar-Abr11.pdf> (in Portuguese).

Several factors have allowed Brazil to recover rapidly after the recent crisis, even though the crisis affected the country in terms of the lack of global liquidity. First of all, the effects of the crisis in Brazil were short-lived. A second factor is that, before the crisis, the Brazilian economy was probably in its best shape in many years because of the implementation of economic reforms and the general growth in the global economy. Moreover, the Brazilian capital market was growing strongly without artificial incentives. In fact, the significant development of the Brazilian market in recent years is due mainly to a natural process of maturation. This is in stark contrast to what occurred in the early days of the Brazilian capital market, when tax relief was seen as central to the country's economy.

A third factor is the existence of a comprehensive, high-quality regulatory and oversight framework, with well-defined responsibilities between the Brazilian Central Bank and CVM. Basically, the Central Bank is responsible for prudential and systemic regulation, while CVM regulates conduct in the capital market. There is strong and increasing coordination between the two regulators, a development spurred by the fact that many institutions are subject to regulation by both the Central Bank and CVM. In terms of systemic risk, for example, the Central Bank has access to information within the capital market that is deemed necessary at the international level.

Modern rules and regulations, such as the law that restructured the Brazilian Payment System,[9] have prevented the sudden appearance, growth, and spread of risks in most segments of the Brazilian financial and capital market. Further, when risk does appear, this legislation provides tools to handle and reduce the exposure. The present Corporate Insolvency Law[10] also helped ensure stability within payment systems, because it recognizes collateral granted by market participants and also confirms netting agreements in case of insolvency.

Some current recommendations of the FSB are already in place in Brazil, thanks in large part to the conservative path followed by the Central Bank regarding the banking system. In practical terms, a mechanism already exists to deal with banks in distressed financial condition;[11] the leverage is lower than allowed in other jurisdictions; capital requirement is higher than that set out in Basel II;[12] and banks are required to consolidate the assets held through

---

9   Available at <http://www.planalto.gov.br/ccivil_03/Leis/LEIS_2001/L10214.htm> (in Portuguese).

10   Available at <http://www.planalto.gov.br/ccivil/_ato2004-2006/2005/lei/L11101.htm> (in Portuguese).

11   Since 1974, a statute has been in force that subjects financial institutions, including credit unions, to intervention or extrajudicial liquidation by the Central Bank (Law No. 6024, of March 13, 1974). The grounds include losses arising from mismanagement, violation of banking legislation, and violation by management of bylaws or statutory rules or of regulations from the Central Bank and the National Monetary Council.

12   National Monetary Council (CMN) Resolution No. 2099, of August 17, 1994, and its subsequent amendments, established the minimum capital and net assets requirements for the

offshore vehicles. Brazil supported proposals to revise the standards of international banking regulation that led to Basel III.[13]

Regarding the Brazilian capital market, the legal and regulatory framework helped the country avoid or at least reduce some weaknesses that may have contributed to the financial crisis. For example, Brazil adheres to the final beneficiary model[14] and the central counterparty solution,[15] and requires registration for almost all transactions in the capital market.[16] Even so, Brazil was affected to a limited extent by the financial crisis, which prompted the country to take regulatory measures to deal with the crisis as well as to make its system more resilient.

Regulation and Regulatory Trends in the Brazilian Capital Market

In 2008, CVM issued a rule (CVM Instruction No. 475 of 2008)[17] designed to improve the quantity and the quality of information rendered to investors by publicly held companies regarding financial and derivative instruments, including the requirement for a sensitivity analysis. Another important rule (CVM Instruction No. 480 of 2009),[18] which was adopted in 2009 and came into force in 2010, broadened transparency requirements and improved the quality of information provided by publicly held companies. Among the requirements of this latter rule is the duty of the issuer to disclose its compensation policy; its stock option programs; and the maximum, minimum, and average compensation paid to its directors and executive officers. The financial crisis provided notorious examples of why it is essential to clearly identify the remuneration given to directors and management. Indeed, an issuer's compensation policy provides valuable information about its incentives system. It is through its compensation packages that an issuer can encourage its managers to adopt a short-, medium-, or long-term outlook and to pursue goals set by

---

financial institutions authorized to operate in Brazil by the Central Bank. This document is available at <https://www3.bcb.gov.br/normativo/detalharNormativo.do?method=detalharNormativo&N=094163143> (in Portuguese).

13   Additional information regarding this subject is available at <http://www.anbima.com.br/mostra.aspx/?id=1000001316>.

14   CVM Instruction No. 122 of 1990 provides for the identification of final investors in transactions on stock exchanges. This document is available at <http://www.cvm.gov.br/asp/cvmwww/atos/Atos_Redir.asp?Tipo=I&File=\inst\inst122.doc> (in Portuguese).

15   A central counterparty is an institution that stands between operations and contracts, becoming the buyer for every seller and the seller for every buyer.

16   In this regard, it is worth mentioning that the Brazilian Clearing and Depository Corporation (CBLC), the Central Securities Depository (CSD) operated by BM&FBOVESPA S.A. (Bolsa de Valores, Mercadorias e Futuros), acts as the central counterparty in all transactions within that institution.

17   Available at <http://www.cvm.gov.br/asp/cvmwww/atos/Atos/inst/inst475.doc> (in Portuguese).

18   Available at <http://www.cvm.gov.br/asp/cvmwww/atos/Atos_Redir.asp?File=\inst\inst480consolid.doc> (in Portuguese).

the organization. For these reasons, and in line with the current level of international consensus on the need for a high level of transparency on pay and incentive programs,[19] CVM decided to specifically address the subject in Instruction No. 480. That instruction also requires the issuers to disclose, among other pieces of information, their corporate governance practices, their risk management and control policies, and the main risks they face.

In 2010, CVM Instruction No. 481 of 2009[20] entered into force, regulating public requests to exercise voting rights by proxy at meetings of publicly held companies and stipulating the information such companies must provide to shareholders before the meetings (e.g., the curriculum of candidates for positions in administration, the proposed remuneration of directors, and comments on a company's financial statements). Due to the increasing number of companies with dispersed ownership in Brazil, the regulation of these issues has grown increasingly important, especially if Brazil is to see a more efficient organization of the shareholders of large corporations.

In relation to public requests for proxies, Instruction No. 481 seeks to promote the participation (particularly through the Internet) of shareholders in decision-making processes. The instruction provides that shareholders representing more than 0.5 percent of capital may include candidates for the board or the supervisory board in the public requests made by the administration; companies that have an electronic system for proxy requests should allow shareholders with more than 0.5 percent of the capital to make their requests through this system; and companies that have not established an electronic system must bear a portion of the costs of public requests promoted by shareholders representing more than 0.5 percent of the capital, within certain limits. Instruction No. 481 also requires that all materials used in public requests for proxies, and information and documents relating to meetings, be made available to shareholders on the CVM website. This rule has significantly reduced the costs associated with the exercise of voting rights and facilitated the supervision of the business by shareholders.

Brazil has also tackled two other issues that are usually high on the agendas of regulators: OTC derivatives and collective-investment vehicles.

Most problems spawned by the recent crisis relate to markets and products that were previously unregulated, notably OTC derivatives, which are negotiated and settled directly between the parties. Regulators worldwide have been encouraged to adopt a series of measures to enhance transparency of the OTC market and thereby permit better management of the risks its participants encounter, and to enable closer monitoring of such markets. Some of these measures were present in the Brazilian market even before the crisis occurred.

---

19   On the topic, *see*, for example, G20 Leaders' Statement at Pittsburgh Summit, available at <http://www.g20.org/Documents/pittsburgh_summit_leaders_statement_250909.pdf>.

20   Available at <http://www.cvm.gov.br/asp/cvmwww/atos/Atos/inst/inst481.doc> (in Portuguese).

The vast majority of derivative instruments in Brazil are currently traded on the stock market, as opposed to the scenario commonly found in other economies, where many derivative instruments are traded in the OTC market. Moreover, even the transactions in Brazil's organized OTC market are subject to a registration procedure,[21] and financial institutions, which are normally the counterparties in this kind of transaction, are required to carry out these sorts of transactions only in organized markets.[22] Brazil also has rules for the approval of standards for derivative contracts by CVM.[23] In general, the Brazilian system is widely considered to be adequate to meet international standards,[24] and Brazil's experience can help inform the development of market infrastructure in other jurisdictions.

Notwithstanding the positive impact of such regulation, and in order to support an initiative by market institutions to establish an external body that would gather and consolidate information on operations carried out in all markets, in 2010 CVM issued Instruction No. 486.[25] This rule changed CVM Instruction No. 467 of 2008 and expressly authorized the creation of mechanisms for sharing information necessary for the success of the initiative.

Brazil's efforts to tackle collective-investment vehicles (more specifically, collective-investment funds) have been spurred by the international recognition that hedge funds need to be brought under regulation in those countries where they currently have the status of unregulated entities.

In Brazil, all investment funds (private equity, hedge funds, etc.) and their managers are registered with CVM. As a result, Brazil already enjoys a high degree of monitoring and transparency regarding transactions and portfolios.[26] Nonetheless, CVM is assessing further regulation in relation to certain issues, such as liquidity, suitability, the quality of assets, and conflict of interests, in addition to the certification of managers. CVM is also addressing securitization. CVM has recently reformed the substantive rules and statements regarding investment funds in receivables so as to ensure, among other things,

---

21   Currently, the rules on this matter are contained in CVM Instruction No. 461 of 2007 (as amended), available at <http://www.cvm.gov.br/asp/cvmwww/atos/Atos/inst/inst461consolid.doc> (in Portuguese).

22   It is worth mentioning that Provisional Measure No. 539 of July 26, 2011, established as a condition of validity of any derivative contract to carry out a registration procedure with institutions authorized to perform such activity by the Brazilian Central Bank or CVM. This document is available at <http://www.planalto.gov.br/CCIVIL_03/_Ato2011-2014/2011/Mpv/539.htm> (in Portuguese).

23   For more information regarding this subject, see CVM Instruction No. 467 of 2008 (as amended), available at <http://www.cvm.gov.br/asp/cvmwww/atos/Atos_Redir.asp?File=\inst\inst467consolid.doc> (in Portuguese).

24   On the topic, see, for example, G20 Leaders' Statement at Pittsburgh Summit, supra note 16.

25   Available at <http://www.cvm.gov.br/asp/cvmwww/atos/Atos/inst/inst486.doc> (in Portuguese).

26   These developments are consistent with the IOSCO Objectives and Principles of Securities Regulation, which are among the FSB Key Standards for Sound Financial Systems.

regular dissemination of information on the repurchase of loans and to establish a standard chart of accounts.

As regards the convergence of Brazilian standards with International Financial Reporting Standards (IFR), corporations' financial statements for the year 2010 already follow the new standards.

Among other regulatory issues under discussion at CVM is the issue of suitability. In 2009, the Committee for Regulation and Supervision of Financial Markets, Capital, Insurance and Private Pension Plans (COREMEC), whose members are CVM, the Central Bank, and other relevant Brazilian regulators, issued Resolution No. 7, recommending that COREMEC's members adopt rules that specify, for supervised institutions, the duty to verify the adequacy of financial products or services to meet the needs, interests, and objectives of clients or participants in benefits plans.[27]

COREMEC also approved in 2010 the results of a study conducted by its members about laws and regulations regarding the use of the work of rating agencies. The study indicated that risk ratings are used in industry regulations primarily for three purposes: for the identification or classification of assets or institutions; as a public offering of securities resulting from securitization transactions; and as a requirement of transparency. The Brazilian Central Bank, it should be noted, does not condone the use of such ratings for purposes of prudential regulation. COREMEC subsequently established a group, through its Resolution No. 14, whose main task is to evaluate the possibility of eliminating or mitigating references to credit ratings in the existing rules.[28] This is important because there is a perception that the use of such ratings can be interpreted as a stamp of approval from the regulator, which might discourage careful diligence in the selection of assets by financial institutions, asset managers, and institutional investors, ultimately increasing systemic risk.

This work is in line with the document issued by the FSB and submitted to the G20 meeting in Seoul in 2010, which outlines principles for reducing reliance on ratings in regulations and seeks to encourage market institutions to make their own risk analysis[29] (the G20 adopted these principles). A report on the results of the work is to be submitted to COREMEC by the end of 2011.

In addition to having discussions and adopting specific regulatory measures, CVM has been improving its relationship with other regulators whose performance contributes to the proper functioning of the market. Such cooperation will contribute to the prevention of problems such as those

---

27   This resolution is available at <http://www.bovespasupervisaomercado.com.br/090 701NotA.asp> (in Portuguese).

28   This resolution is available at <http://www.bcb.gov.br/pre/asimp/imagens/Delibera %E7%E3o_Coremec_14.pdf> (in Portuguese).

29   Available at <http://www.financialstabilityboard.org/publications/r_101027.pdf>.

that arose in the recent international crisis. For instance, CVM and the Brazilian Central Bank signed in 2010 a cooperation agreement that, among other improvements, enhanced the process of exchanging information between the two institutions during investigations of possible wrongdoing. CVM also signed in 2010 a technical cooperation agreement with the Department of Consumer Protection and Defense of the Brazilian Ministry of Justice for the exchange of information, improvement of regulatory activities, and monitoring and education related to capital market investors.

Better education of investors was also an objective of the National Strategy for Financial Education (Enef), an initiative of COREMEC that has the broad goal of strengthening the efficiency and robustness of the Brazilian financial system. Enef was introduced at the end of 2010 by Presidential Decree No. 7397.[30] Through targeted projects and coordinated actions, Enef aims to improve consumer understanding about financial products, promoting security in making investment decisions. It is hoped that the strategy will enable people to develop financial skills that help in identifying risks and opportunities of financial and capital markets.

Overview of Enforcement in the Brazilian Capital Market

In the aftermath of the financial crisis, the adoption of an appropriate enforcement policy by regulators of financial or capital markets is becoming increasingly important. In light of this, it may be of interest to outline the current enforcement activities of CVM and CVM's relationship with federal prosecutors and the federal police in Brazil.

Today, administrative investigations are conducted by public federal attorneys together with specialized investigators of CVM staff. This model was created in 2008, since when the investigation period has been reduced, with even the most complex procedures being concluded in about 10 months.[31]

Another important element that has contributed to the good performance of the Brazilian Securities Commission in its enforcement activities is the role played by the Committee for Settlements of Proceedings. This committee delivers opinions on proposals for settlement of administrative cases made by defendants or people under investigation prior to a final determination by CVM commissioners. The committee can even negotiate the terms of an agreement. The agreement that may be proposed to CVM is called *termo de compromisso* and clearly has its roots in the SEC's experience regarding settlements and consent decrees. Basically, a settlement may be concluded with CVM if the defendant or person under investigation undertakes to cease the practice

---

30 The decree is available at <http://www.planalto.gov.br/ccivil_03/_Ato2007-2010/2010/Decreto/D7397.htm> (in Portuguese).

31 For more information regarding this subject, see Julya Sotto Mayor Wellisch & Alexandre Pinheiro dos Santos, *A evolução do processo administrativo sancionador no âmbito da Comissão de Valores Mobiliários*, 48 Revista de Direito Bancário e do Mercado de Capitais 53 (2010).

of unlawful acts or activities and correct the irregularities, including indemnifying losses. The agreement is not subject to court approval.[32]

Furthermore, CVM, after participating in joint actions to prevent and stop unfair practices, signed cooperation agreements with the Federal Prosecutors Office, as well as with the Brazilian Federal Police Department. Many positive results have already been achieved, including the freezing of wrongdoers' assets and the beginning of criminal lawsuits related to insider trading. In 2011, CVM and the Federal Prosecutors Office obtained the first criminal conviction in Brazil for insider trading. Two former executives of Sadia S.A. were convicted by a court and sentenced to prison and a fine.[33] This case is particularly significant given that insider trading became a criminal offense in Brazil only in 2002. CVM and federal prosecutors have also entered into agreements with some potential lawbreakers to indemnify losses or to restrict activities in the capital market.

CVM's commitment to cooperation in enforcement is underscored by CVM's signing, in 2009, of the IOSCO Multilateral Memorandum of Understanding for Cooperation and Assistance.[34]

Conclusion

As this chapter has shown, Brazilian regulators, especially CVM, have adopted some important measures in the run-up to and the aftermath of the recent financial crisis. Those measures aim, inter alia, at creating more certainty, predictability, transparency, and efficiency in the Brazilian financial and capital markets. In that respect, they are likely to help prevent future similar crises.

Brazil's abiding concern to foster a healthy and predictable environment in the capital market has enhanced the credibility of the financial system as a whole, which in turn has promoted international recognition of the strength of the Brazilian economy.

---

32 For more information regarding this subject, see Julya Sotto Mayor Wellisch & Alexandre Pinheiro dos Santos, *O termo de compromisso no âmbito do mercado de valores mobiliários*, 53 Interesse Público 137 (2009).

33 The ruling was appealed.

34 Essentially, enforcement in the Brazilian capital market is in line with the IOSCO Objectives and Principles of Securities Regulation, which are among the FSB Key Standards for Sound Financial Systems.

Developments in Climate Finance from Rio to Cancun

Charlotte Streck and Thiago Chagas

International climate policy seeks to define solutions to mitigate climate change as well as adapt to the adverse effects of climate change by reducing greenhouse gas (GHG) emissions. Climate change has an impact on livelihoods, food security, and the economic output of countries. Research shows that in anomalously warm years, gross domestic product (GDP) goes down, particularly in developing countries.[1] Climate change is also associated with increasing water scarcity and declining water quality, warming and acidification of the world's oceans, a rise in the sea level (and associated coastal impacts), extreme weather events, climate-related impacts on public health, and additional threats to forest ecosystems and endangered species. Developing countries are likely to suffer disproportionally from these effects of global climate change.[2]

In the effort to alleviate the effects of climate change, international financial institutions can help developing countries cover the additional adaptation costs and support other mitigation efforts and equitable solutions while recognizing differences in historic responsibility, wealth, and capacities.[3] Climate finance has been a central issue in the development of the UN climate regime. There is consensus that mitigation pledges and commitments proposed so far fall short of the level of action required by science; in addition, countries are still far from any agreement on how to share the economic burden that enhanced mitigation actions demand.

Developing countries are reluctant to assume the additional costs for mitigating global problems that they consider the legacy of developed countries'

---

1   For an analysis of the relationship between development and climate change, *see World Development Report 2010: Development and Climate Change* ch. 1 (World Bank 2010), available at <http://siteresources.worldbank.org/INTWDR2010/Resources/5287678-1226014527953/WDR10-Full-Text.pdf>.

2   McKinsey Global GHG Abatement Cost Curve, Version 2.0 (Jan. 2009); Project Catalyst, *Project Catalyst Brief: Synthesis Paper* (Dec. 2009), available at <http://project-catalyst.info/images/1.%20Limiting%20global%20warming%20to%202%20degrees/Publications/3.%20Towards%20a%20global%20climate%20agreement/4-page%20briefing/091201%20SYNTHESIS%20Summary.pdf>.

3   Nicola Ranger, Alex Bowen, & Bob Ward, *Mitigation Climate Change through Reductions in Greenhouse Gas Emissions: Background*, in *Mitigating Climate Change through Reductions in Greenhouse Gas Emissions: The Science and Economics of Future Paths for Global Annual Emissions* 4 (Alex Bowen & Nicola Ranger ed., Grantham Research Institute on Climate Change and the Environment 2009), available at <http://www2.lse.ac.uk/GranthamInstitute/publications/Policy/docs/PBMitigatingBowenRangerDec09.pdf>.   **345**

patterns of industrialization and consumption. Consequently, developing countries tend to make climate change actions conditional on the availability of new and additional resources for global environmental action from developed countries.[4] Thus, a key ingredient in a successful international climate agreement is a robust institutional architecture through which to source, allocate, and disburse finance for climate change mitigation and adaptation actions to developing countries. The 2009 Copenhagen Accord[5] states that scaled-up, new, additional, predictable, and adequate funding, as well as improved access to this funding, must be provided to developing countries for, inter alia, adaptation to climate change. The accord describes the collective commitment, confirmed by the Cancun Agreements,[6] by developed countries to provide new and additional resources approaching $30 billion for 2010–12, increasing to $100 billion annually by 2020.[7]

Focusing on the sources and mechanisms that help finance developing-country climate change action under the international climate regime, this chapter offers an overview of the existing and evolving structures of financing climate change mitigation and adaptation. It is divided into five sections: a brief history of climate finance; a description of existing and future sources of finance; an examination of mechanisms that distribute climate finance; a summary of the key climate issues that need to be addressed going forward; and some concluding thoughts.

UNFCCC and Climate Finance

At the UN Conference on Environment and Development in Rio de Janeiro in 1992, countries adopted several key international legal instruments on the environment, including the United Nations Framework Convention on Climate Change (UNFCCC). According to Article 2, the objective of the UNFCCC is the "stabilization of greenhouse gas concentrations at a level that would prevent dangerous anthropogenic interference with the climate system." Although it does not establish emission reduction goals, the UNFCCC allows for further refinement and development of such goals through the adoption of protocols.

The agreement reached in 1992 was perceived by the signatory countries and the broader international community as an important political

---

4   The 1990 London Amendment of the Montreal Protocol, for example, expressly states that fund contributions "shall be additional to other financial transfers to" developing countries. *See* Report of the Second Meeting of the Parties to the Montreal Protocol on Substances That Deplete the Ozone Layer, UN Doc. UNEP/OzL.Pro.2/3 (Jun. 29, 1990), Annex II, Article 10, paragraph 6.

5   Decision 2/CP.15, Report of the Conference of the Parties on Its Fifteenth Session of the UN FCCC, UN Doc. FCCC/CP/2009/11/Add.1 (Mar. 30, 2010).

6   Decision 1/CP.16, UNFCCC, Report of the Conference of the Parties on Its Sixteenth Session, UN Doc. FCCC/CP/2010/7/Add.1 (Mar. 15, 2011) (Decision 1/CP.16).

7   Dollar amounts are in U.S. dollars.

accomplishment. Despite the lack of precise wording and obligations, the UNFCCC managed to set out key principles and supervisory instruments to stimulate progression. From an environmental perspective, however, it was clear that mitigation commitments under the UNFCCC needed to be strengthened if countries were to achieve any meaningful environmental outcome. With that in mind, parties built into the UNFCCC a review process to periodically assess the adequacy of commitments made under the regime. The first such review started with the so-called Berlin Mandate, a negotiating mandate that led to the creation and adoption of the Kyoto Protocol on December 11, 1997.[8]

The Kyoto Protocol contains a set of binding emissions targets for developed countries, the so-called Annex I countries.[9] These countries agreed to reduce their total greenhouse gas (GHG) emissions by an average of 5 percent compared to the level of 1990 between 2008 and 2012 (known as the first commitment period).[10] Non–Annex I countries are parties to the protocol that have not assumed any quantified GHG stabilization or reduction commitment. In fact, developing countries established as a precondition for their participation in the negotiations of the Berlin Mandate that no quantified targets for developing countries would be discussed at that moment.[11]

The UNFCCC Conference of Parties (COP) , which brings together on an annual basis all countries that are parties to the UNFCCC; and the COP Serving as the Meeting of the Parties to the Kyoto Protocol (CMP) have made several important decisions that elaborate and enhance the international climate regime. These include the adoption of the Marrakesh Accords, the Bali Action Plan (BAP), and the Cancun Agreements, as well as the negotiations of the Copenhagen Accord. The Marrakesh Accords elaborate the rules for accounting and trading mechanisms established under the Kyoto Protocol. The BAP, the Copenhagen Accord, and the Cancun Agreements signal (albeit slow) progress in the discussions on a future climate regime that pursues a more ambitious and inclusive effort to mitigate climate change.

The Marrakesh Accords constitute a set of decisions adopted initially by COP7 at the UN Climate Change Conference in 2001 in Marrakesh, and confirmed in 2005 by CMP1. These accords establish guidelines, modalities, and procedures related to the implementation of the Kyoto Protocol's flexible mechanisms, the treatment of land use, land-use change and forestry activi-

---

8   Kyoto Protocol to the United Nations Framework Convention on Climate Change, UN Doc. FCCC/CP/1997/7/Add.1 (Dec. 10, 1997), 37 I.L.M. 22 (1998) (entry into force Feb. 16, 2005) (Kyoto Protocol). As of this writing, 192 states and the European Union are parties to the Kyoto Protocol.

9   Forty-one industrialized countries are currently listed in Annex I to the convention. These include the members of the Organisation for Economic Co-operation and Development (OECD) and countries with economies in transition (the EITs), including the Russian Federation, the Baltic states, and several Central and Eastern European states.

10   Kyoto Protocol, Article 3(1).

11   *See* Clare Breidenich, et al., *The Kyoto Protocol to the United Nations Framework Convention on Climate Change*, 92 Am. J. Intl. L. 315 (1998).

ties, and accounting rules for assigned amount units (AAUs). The decisions made under the Marrakesh Accords were responsible for operationalizing the tools and instruments created under the Kyoto Protocol and enabled an early start of the clean development mechanism (CDM). The CDM is currently the only flexible mechanism under the Kyoto Protocol that allows for the participation of developing countries in efforts to reduce GHG emissions.

With the adoption of the BAP in 2007, international action moved to a two-track approach: the UNFCCC track and the Kyoto Protocol track. Parties to the Kyoto Protocol were negotiating on renewed quantified targets for developed countries under the Ad Hoc Working Group on Further Commitments for Annex I Parties (AWG-KP), which was established in 2005 pursuant to Article 3.9 of the Kyoto Protocol. The BAP charted the course for a new negotiating process by officially establishing the Ad Hoc Working Group on Long-Term Cooperative Action (AWG-LCA)—the second track—which brought the United States back into UN climate discussions.[12] Under the BAP, developing countries agreed to engage in climate change mitigation through voluntary nationally appropriate mitigation actions (NAMAs), supported by financial and technological assistance from industrialized countries in a measurable, reportable, and verifiable manner.

In 2009, the Copenhagen Accord was supported by 114 states but not adopted at the UN Climate Change Conference (COP15). The negotiations and the work of both the AWG-LCA and the AWG-KP were planned to culminate in concrete proposals for a comprehensive climate agreement for the period after 2012. There were high expectations that countries could achieve meaningful results in Copenhagen, including an agreement on a second commitment period for the Kyoto Protocol. However, what happened in Copenhagen did not live up to those expectations. Although the accord was not formally adopted, elements of the Copenhagen Accord did form the basis for decisions made at the UN Climate Change Conference in 2010 in Cancun (COP16).

The outcomes of the two negotiating tracks, along with other decisions, were adopted by the COP and the CMP in Cancun.[13] When preparing the decisions for adoption, the Mexican presidency of the COP/CMP combined all decisions into a package (the "Cancun Agreements"), thus bringing—at least nominally—the main outcomes of the two tracks under one umbrella. The Cancun Agreements reiterate that "the largest share of historical global emissions of greenhouse gases originated in developed countries and that, owing to this historical responsibility, developed country Parties must take the lead

---

12 Decision 1/CP.13, UNFCCC, Report of the Conference of the Parties on Its Thirteenth Session, UN Doc. FCCC/CP/2007/6/Add.1 (2007). The AWG-LCA had a mandate until COP15 in Copenhagen in 2009. The mandate was extended twice for a year: at COP15 and COP16.

13 The full range of decisions adopted by the COP and the CMP is available at <http://unfccc.int/meetings/cop_16/items/5571.php>.

in combating climate change and the adverse effects."[14] Importantly, both the COP and the CMP "[took] note" of the economy-wide emission reduction targets "to be implemented by" developed-country parties, referring to those submitted by them pursuant to the Copenhagen Accord.[15]

The evolution of the climate regime has been anchored in the principles laid down in Article 3 of the UNFCCC, in particular the principle of common but differentiated responsibilities.[16] Decisions adopted by the COP and the CMP underscore the obligation of developed countries to take the lead in combating global climate change and the fact that developing countries' commitments are conditioned on developed countries' effective implementation of their obligations related to financial resources and transfer of technology.

Thus, mobilizing investments for GHG reductions and climate change adaptation in developing countries has been—and still is—a crucial issue under the UNFCCC and the Kyoto Protocol.[17] Since the adoption of the UNFCCC in 1992, states have disputed by what means developed economies should help developing countries combat climate change. Under Article 4(2), UNFCCC industrialized countries and those with economies undergoing the transition to market economies should undertake to adopt policies and measures that will "demonstrate that developed countries are taking the lead in modifying longer term trends in anthropogenic emissions consistent with the objective of the Convention." The UNFCCC also includes a commitment to assist countries particularly vulnerable to the effects of climate change and to promote technology transfer. Article 4(7) makes developing-country action conditional on the effective implementation of commitments under the UNFCCC related to financing and the transfer of resources and technologies.[18]

Sources of Climate Finance

Limiting global warming to 2 degrees Celsius above preindustrial levels, as recommended by the Intergovernmental Panel on Climate Change (IPCC), and further lowering this target to 1.5 degrees Celsius, as requested by particularly vulnerable nations, will require developed and developing countries to

---

14 Decision 1/CP16, Section III(A), preamble.

15 *Id.*, at paragraph 36.

16 Article 3(1) of the convention provides that "the Parties should protect the climate system for the benefit of present and future generations of humankind, on the basis of equity and in accordance with their common but differentiated responsibilities and respective capabilities. Accordingly, the developed country Parties should take the lead in combating climate change and the adverse effects thereof."

17 United Nations Framework Convention on Climate Change, Article 2, opened for signature May 9, 1992, 1771 U.N.T.S. 107.

18 "The extent to which developing country Parties will effectively implement their commitments under the Convention will depend on the effective implementation by developed Country Parties of their commitment under the Convention relating to financial resources and transfer of technology." The UN Convention on Biological Diversity contains a similar provision in Article 20(4), 31 I.L.M. 818 (1992).

take significant steps to curb their emissions. Research indicates that in order to stabilize GHG concentrations at 450 parts per million (ppm), global carbon dioxide (CO_2) emissions must be confined to approximately 10 gigatonnes (Gt) per year after 2050.[19] Given current worldwide emissions of approximately 48 Gt per year, this target presents a considerable challenge, and reaching it is achievable only if vast amounts of investments for mitigation action are made over the coming decades, in both developed and developing countries. The actual amount of funding needed to stabilize global emissions and reach the targets is under debate.

Current commitments to mitigate climate change fall short both in ambition and in available financing. If the targets pledged at COP15 in Copenhagen are fully realized by 2020, nations will deliver only 60 percent of the emissions reductions needed to be on track to avoid dangerous climate change as defined by the IPCC. Under a business-as-usual scenario, the worldwide emissions trajectory is expected to reach 56 Gt of CO_2 equivalent by 2020. If the Copenhagen pledges are met, merely 5 Gt of emissions per year can be reduced or avoided by 2020.[20]

Studies show that both the additional $30 billion in fast-start financing and the annual $100 billion by 2020 stipulated by the Cancun Agreements are well below what is projected to be needed for the developing-country share of reducing global temperature to the agreed-upon target.[21] The World Development Report 2010 indicates that the international community is far from reaching the amount of funding that is needed to stabilize CO_2 concentrations at 450 ppm. The authors of that report conclude that in developing countries, mitigation action alone would require investments in the range of $140 to $175 billion per year until 2030, with "associated financing needs" of $265 to $565 billion. For adaptation, the estimated costs range from $30 to $100 billion per year.[22] These estimates represent an approximately twofold increase in the pledged $100 billion, and when compared to the current amount of funding committed under climate finance, a staggering twentyfold increase.

There is also reason to fear that pledged amounts are significantly higher than the amounts that will be disbursed, and it remains to be seen whether the amounts of $30 billion and $100 billion will be delivered. Data on climate funds shows that as of May 2011, about $28 billion was pledged by developed countries to climate funds, while only about $12.5 billion had

---

19   German Advisory Council on Global Change, *Climate Protection Strategies for the 21st Century; Kyoto and Beyond* (WBGU 2003, available at <http://www.gci.org.uk/Documents/wbgu_sn2003_engl.pdf> (accessed Apr. 24, 2011).

20   United Nations Environment Programme, *The Emissions Gap Report* (2010), available at <http://www.unep.org/publications/ebooks/emissionsgapreport/>.

21   *See*, for example, UNFCCC, Investment and Financial Flows to Address Climate Change— An Update, UN Doc. FCCC/TP/2008/7 (Nov. 26, 2008); Project Catalyst, *Scaling Up Climate Finance: Finance Briefing Paper* (Sep. 2009); and *World Development Report 2010: Development and Climate Change* (World Bank 2010).

22   *World Development Report 2010: Development and Climate Change* (World Bank 2010).

been deposited with these funds.[23] Of the amount disbursed by the climate funds, about 77 percent was spent on mitigation, while 21 percent was made available for adaptation.

Although the Cancun Agreements confirm the financing pledges announced in Copenhagen, they fail to provide insight into where "new and additional" financing will come from. There are many proposals on how resources could be mobilized, most of them lacking specificity or political agreement. Although contributions from public budgets are essential and will have to be scaled up, it is unlikely that climate change costs in the tens of billions of dollars annually could be covered through government contributions alone. There is also the risk that these public contributions are not as new and additional as promised. In addition, overreliance on national budgets may lead to donor country fatigue or may divert official development assistance from other areas.[24] Public funding must be complemented by revenue generation through new mechanisms, such as an internationally coordinated carbon tax, levies on bunker fuels or international aviation, or auctioning of AAUs.

Although most developing countries insist on public sector contributions by developed countries as the main form of finance, developed countries highlight the importance of private financing and market-linked mechanisms as funding sources. The proposals vary widely. China proposes that developed countries commit 0.5 percent of their total GDP to support projects addressing climate change in developing countries. India argues similarly and proposes a GDP-dependent contribution from Annex I parties of 0.3 to 1.0 percent; private financing would be a welcome but additional contribution. These targets are as vulnerable as current funding commitments, however, and enforcing them could be difficult, as the case of enforcing the Monterey development assistance target of 0.7 percent of gross national income has shown.[25] South Africa advocates a blend of sources, that is, Annex I public contributions, earmarked revenues from auctioning of allowances in developed countries, and the carbon market. Among developing countries, the most differentiated proposal comes from Mexico, which argues for a financing model under which all countries (except for the least developed ones) contribute in accordance with their historic responsibility, actual GHG quota, GDP, and population.[26]

---

23 *See* <http://www.wri.org/publication/summary-of-developed-country-fast-start-climate-finance-pledges>; and <http://www.climatefundsupdate.org/graphs-statistics/pledges-by-country> and <http://www.climatefundsupdate.org/graphs-statistics/deposits-by-country>.

24 Richard Doornbosch & Eric Knight, *What Role for Public Financing in International Climate Change Mitigation*, OECD Discussion Paper, SG/SD/RT (2008) 3.

25 During the International Conference on Financing for Development, which took place in 2002 in Monterrey, Mexico, rich countries reaffirmed their commitment to provide 0.7 percent of their gross national product to official development assistance.

26 UNFCCC, Submissions to the Ad Hoc Working Group on Long-Term Cooperative Action under the Convention (AWG-LCA), FCCC/AWGLCA/2009/MISC.1 (Mar. 13, 2009); UNFCCC, Submissions to the Ad Hoc Working Group on Long-Term Cooperative Action under the Convention (AWG-LCA), FCCC/AWGLCA/2008/MISC.2 (Aug. 14, 2008).

Annex I parties are generally less outspoken than non–Annex I parties on sources of funding. The European Union is open to various sources of funding proposals, including government contributions as a function of GHG emissions, GDP per capita, and other factors from all countries except the least developed ones and small island states; international auctioning of AAUs; and levies on international aviation and maritime transport. The EU Commission expects one-third of external mitigation funding to come from international crediting mechanisms, most likely carbon markets.[27] The most pronounced proposals come from Switzerland and Norway. Switzerland envisages a global carbon tax of US\$2 per tonne of carbon dioxide equivalent (tCO_2e) on all fossil fuel emissions; developing countries below a certain GDP per capita would be excluded.[28] Norway merges public funding sources with private-style sourcing by proposing international auctions of AAUs.[29] By mobilizing funds through the sale of international emission rights, this proposal follows the precedent of applying levies to market-based mechanisms under the Kyoto Protocol.

The Adaptation Fund, which is funded from 2 percent of the certified emissions reductions (CERs) that are generated by CDM project activities, is an example of a carbon market–based levy.[30] The fund has generated a total of \$130 million since the start of the CER monetization program in 2009.[31] Due to the genuinely international character of the fund, auctioning allowances would overcome problems related to relying on contributions from developed countries. The amount of allowances auctioned could be predefined by a number of allowances, by a fixed percentage of the total amount, or by a predefined revenue requirement.

However, in light of the uncertainty behind the scope, scale, governance, and timely implementation of new financing instruments, the UN High-Level Advisory Group on Climate Change Financing (AGF) stresses the importance of continued long-term budgetary contributions. Although the AGF acknowledges the tough fiscal realities that many developed countries face, it calls for an increase in the existing tax base, where possible, in order to increase the domestic revenue base and strengthen budgetary contributions to mitigation and adaptation action.[32]

---

27   European Commission, Council of Ministers and EU Council, Conclusions of the European Council, March 19 and 20 2009; Conclusions of the Council of Ministers, March 2, 2009; Communication of the European Commission of January 28, 2009, COM (2009) 39 final; Commission Staff Working Document of January 28, 2009, 102.

28   UNFCCC, Submissions to the Ad Hoc Working Group on Long-Term Cooperative Action under the Convention (AWG-LCA), FCCC/AWGLCA/2008/MISC.5 (Oct. 27, 2008).

29   Norway's submission on auctioning allowances is available at <http://unfccc.int/files/kyoto_protocol/application/pdf/norway_auctioning_allowances.pdf>.

30   CDM project activities in least-developed countries, as well as small-scale afforestation and reforestation project activities (regardless of their location), are exempt from channeling 2 percent of their CERs into the Adaptation Fund.

31   More information is available at <http://www.climatefundsupdate.org/listing/adaptation-fund>.

32   Report of the Secretary-General's High-Level Advisory Group on Climate Change Financing

Regardless of the final decisions on resource mobilization, a single financing mechanism will not be able to mobilize billions of dollars annually over a prolonged period of time. Climate finance will have to rely on a blend of funding sources, ranging from voluntary contributions from developed countries to international fund-raising mechanisms, the mobilization of private capital via carbon markets, and other mechanisms that facilitate direct investments in technologies, adaptation, and mitigation actions. Taking into account that a significant, if not the largest, share of the required resources will have to come from private sources, this financial mechanism should leverage and complement, not crowd out, private investments.

Studies indicate that multilateral development banks have been effective at using pledged public funds to leverage private investments. It is estimated that for every $10 billion of additional resources, multilateral development banks could deliver between $30 and $40 billion in grants and loans. It is also estimated that for every $1 of public funding, between $2 and $4 of additional private capital flows can be leveraged.[33] Investors will likely continue to expand their exposure to the development of renewable energy projects and energy efficiency. In the EU, estimates indicate that two-thirds of the necessary emissions reductions in the energy sector can be achieved by 2020 using low-cost energy efficiency measures, many of which are already commercially viable and therefore can be financed by private capital.[34] Private investments (equity and debt) in capital-intense low-carbon technologies that currently have lower rates on return than conventional high-carbon alternatives will be released only if carbon pricing delivers additional incentives or adequate public financing is provided.

Institutional Arrangements for Climate Finance

Existing UNFCCC financing mechanisms and their institutional arrangements are currently undergoing a reform that seeks to streamline operations, improve transparency, and respond to equity concerns. New market and nonmarket mechanisms are also being designed to increase the scope and participation of developing countries in the climate regime. This section provides an overview of the key UNFCCC mechanisms associated with mitigation and adaptation finance and recent developments in international negotiations.

(2010), available at <http://www.un.org/wcm/webdav/site/climatechange/shared/Documents/AGF_reports/AGF_Final_Report.pdf>.

33 *Id.*

34 European Commission, *Questions and Answers on the Communication Stepping Up International Climate Finance: A European Blueprint for the Copenhagen Deal*, MEMO/09/384 (2009), available at <http://europa.eu/rapid/pressReleasesAction.do?reference=MEMO/09/384&format=HTML&aged=1&language=EN&guiLanguage=en>.

Institutions under the UNFCCC and the Kyoto Protocol

Article 11 of the UNFCCC provides a mechanism for the provision of financial resources on a grant or concessional basis. The operation of such a mechanism is entrusted to one or more existing international entities that are accountable to and operate under the guidance of the COP. The COP will determine the mechanism's policies, program priorities, and eligibility criteria. Article 11.2 provides for an equitable and balanced representation of all parties within a transparent system of governance. The Kyoto Protocol clarifies that the implementation of commitments should take into account the need for adequacy and predictability in the flow of funds and the importance of appropriate burden sharing among developed-country parties.

According to the UNFCCC, developed-country parties provide (on a voluntary basis) financial assistance to developing parties through the Global Environment Facility (GEF), which is currently the sole operating entity of the UNFCCC's financial mechanism. During the negotiations of the UNFCCC, developing countries argued in favor of a new financial institution to support the efforts of developing countries. Prior to the adoption of the UNFCCC, developed countries had indicated that they would support a unified funding mechanism for all forthcoming conventions. They clearly wished to avoid the proliferation of funds proceeding from the proliferation of environmental treaties and envisioned the GEF as the financial mechanism for all future financial transfers for environmental projects with global impact. Developed countries thus linked their financial commitment to the acceptance of the GEF as *the* operating entity of a UNFCCC financing mechanism. Developing countries eventually agreed to the GEF as an interim financial mechanism; the UNFCCC COP specified that a permanent relationship between the GEF and the UNFCCC would be contingent on reforms that would ensure that the GEF would promote transparency, democracy, and universality of participation. Intense political negotiations led to a restructuring of the GEF and an upgrade from its interim status to the operating entity of the UNFCCC financial mechanism in 1994.

In November 2001, the COP invited the GEF, as the financial mechanism of the UNFCCC, to establish and operate two new funds related to the UNFCCC. With decision 7/CP.7, the GEF established a Special Climate Change Fund and a Least Developed Countries Fund. The Special Climate Change Fund finances activities, programs, and measures relating to climate change that are complementary to those funded by resources allocated to the climate change focal area of the GEF and by bilateral and multilateral funding. The Least Developed Countries Fund meets the agreed-upon full cost of preparing national adaptation plans of action.

In addition to the UNFCCC funds, a number of dedicated bodies have been created to serve the flexible mechanisms of the Kyoto Protocol. These include the Joint Implementation Supervisory Committee, the CDM Executive Board, and the Adaptation Fund Board, which decides on the allocation of finance raised by the CDM levy earmarked for financing adaptation. The

Adaptation Fund Board was created in 2007 by decision 1/CMP.3 to operate the Adaptation Fund. As the operating entity of the Adaptation Fund, the board is fully accountable to the CMP. On an interim basis and subject to review every three years, the GEF was invited to serve as secretariat to the board and the World Bank was invited to serve as trustee to the fund.

The GEF Trust Fund received $3.13 billion for the period 2006–10. This funding covered all operational areas and programs of the GEF, including climate change. Because this funding was too small to invest in large projects, the GEF focused on removing market barriers to replicating demonstration projects and creating enabling environments.[35] The GEF plays a unique role as the operating entity of the UNFCCC financial mechanism, but it has had limited success in channeling sufficient funding to address climate change.[36] GEF disbursements are slow and limited in scale, procedures are cumbersome, and its governance is burdened by an uneasy relationship between the COP and the GEF council. The GEF secretariat has recognized the need to change and has developed proposals on how to reform the GEF so it can better meet the challenges of a more substantial financial mechanism.[37] The call for new or reformed institutional arrangements reflects the increase in scope and complexity in the search for a financial mechanism that responds to a more comprehensive post-2012 climate deal.

At the COP16 in December 2010, parties to the UNFCCC agreed to establish a Green Climate Fund that is accountable to and operates under the guidance (rather than the direct authority) of the COP.[38] The trustee of this fund will be accountable to the 24-member Green Climate Fund Board, with equal representation from developed and developing countries, and supported by an independent secretariat. The World Bank serves as its interim trustee, subject to a review three years after the fund begins operations.[39] The further design of the fund was delegated to a 40-member transitional committee (15 members from developed countries, 25 from developing), which will be convened initially by the UNFCCC secretariat and is to submit its recommendations to the 17th COP (COP17) in December 2011.[40] The Cancun Agreements also established a standing committee to assist the COP in areas such as "improving coherence and coordination" among different finance channels and the measurement, reporting, and verification of finance. The committee's specific roles and functions are to be further defined.[41]

---

35 GEF, GEF Strategy to Enhance Engagement with the Private Sector, GEF/C.28/24 (May 10, 2006).

36 Gareth Porter, Neil Bird, Nanki Kaur, & Leo Peskett, *New Finance for Climate Change and the Environment* (Heinrich Boell Foundation & WWF Jul. 2008).

37 GEF , Future Strategic Positioning of the GEF, GEF/R.5/7/Rev.1 (Mar. 2, 2009).

38 Decision 1/CP.16, paragraph 102.

39 *Id.,* at paragraph 107.

40 *Id.,* at paragraphs 109–10 and Annex III, paragraph 1.

41 *Id.,* at paragraph 112.

Existing Market Mechanisms

The Kyoto Protocol added a new set of market-based mechanisms to the climate finance tools available for financing climate change mitigation. While the joint implementation mechanisms allow for the exchange of project-based emission reduction units among developed countries, the CDM authorizes the crediting of emissions reductions achieved by projects in developing countries by Annex I parties. CDM credits (CERs) result from projects that reduce emissions below a baseline. The baseline describes how the emissions would develop in the absence of CDM projects.[42] Acquiring CERs from CDM projects enables Annex I parties (and entities from such countries operating under an emissions cap) to achieve emissions reductions in a cost-efficient manner.

By 2009, the CDM market had reached combined transacted values of $20 billion.[43] Thirteen percent of the transactions were primary CER transactions: transactions between the project owners and the first buyers. The rest took the form of secondary transactions, where primary buyers sell their assets into the broader carbon market.[44] Driven by rules of the EU emissions-trading scheme, the majority of the demand for CERs has come from European buyers, mostly private sector. Within the private-industry sector, European utility companies are the largest investors in CERs.[45]

The CDM is undergoing a number of changes as a result of Article 9 of the Kyoto Protocol and CMP decisions related to the annual work carried out by the CDM executive board. Many decisions have been adopted in order to streamline the CDM approval process and enhance transparency of the executive board and its supporting panels, such as requests for the executive board to ensure consistency in its decision-making process and to improve communication channels with project developers.

Programmatic approaches are also gaining traction in the evolution of the CDM. Programs of activities (PoAs) are a special category within the CDM that allow subprojects to be added to a registered program over time, thus creating flexibility for initiatives that involve large amounts of small emissions reduction measures, such as the distribution of solar water heaters or the implementation of manure digesters across a large region. Under a PoA, the project developer needs to register only the general activity under the CDM, after which he or she can add subprojects over time, thus expanding the reach of the mechanism and reducing transaction costs. The programmatic

---

42   Decision 4/CMP.1, Annex II, paragraph 27, UNFCCC, Report of the Conference of the Parties Serving as the Meeting of the Parties to the Kyoto Protocol on Its First Session, UN Doc. FCCC/KP/CMP/2005/8/Add.1 (Mar. 30, 2006).

43   Alexandre Kossoy & Philippe Ambrosi, *State and Trends of the Carbon Market 2010* (May 2010), available at <http://siteresources.worldbank.org/INTCARBONFINANCE/Resources/State_and_Trends_of_the_Carbon_Market_2010_low_res.pdf>.

44   *Id.*

45   *Id.*

CDM approach is seen by many as a stepping stone to other forms of accounting for and incentivizing GHG reductions in developing countries.

Emerging Mechanisms

As part of the BAP, parties agreed to launch "a comprehensive process to enable the full, effective and sustained implementation of the Convention through long-term cooperative action, now, up to and beyond 2012." Parties decided to address, among other points, the following:

> 1.b enhanced national/international action on mitigation of climate change, including inter alia, consideration of . . .
>
> ii. nationally appropriate mitigation actions by developing country parties in the context of sustainable development, supported and enabled by technology, financing and capacity building, in a measurable, reportable and verifiable manner; . . .
>
> vii. ways to strengthen the catalytic role of the Convention in encouraging multilateral bodies, the public and private sectors and civil society, building on synergies among activities and processes, as a means to support mitigation in a coherent and integrated manner.[46]

Proposed financing approaches include crediting emissions reductions of NAMAs and an incentive mechanism to reduce emissions from deforestation. Both mechanisms seek to expand developing-country engagement beyond the project-based and offset design of the CDM to more comprehensive sectoral and/or national mitigation actions. NAMAs are generally understood as voluntary mitigation actions by non–Annex I countries in the context of sustainable development goals and objectives and that reduce emissions below business-as-usual levels.

In the course of 2010, 43 proposals for NAMAs were submitted by developing countries to the UNFCCC; these were officially incorporated into the Cancun Agreements. COP16 invited developing countries to submit information on NAMAs for which they seek international support, including estimated costs, emissions reductions, and the time frame for implementation.[47] Despite these initial submissions and provisions, the concept of NAMAs has remained largely undefined and may comprise a very diverse set of activities, ranging from capacity building to conventional command-and-control regulations to sectoral emissions-trading schemes in developing countries. However, some relevant elements of NAMAs can be distilled:

- NAMAs should be appropriate for the national circumstances and development needs of the developing country.
- NAMAs should promote the country's sustainable development.

---

46 See BAP, paragraphs 1(b)(ii) and 1(b)(iv).

47 Decision 1/ CP.16, paragraph 54.

- NAMAs are accessible to developed-country support (technology, finance, and capacity building).
- NAMAs will be subject to measurement, review, and verification (MRV) and recorded in a registry, thus facilitating the matching of these activities with the finance, technology, and capacity-building support available.

NAMAs will be subject to performance-based standards in order to assess whether mitigation actions are actually taking place. The Cancun Agreements state that domestically supported NAMAs will be "MRVed" domestically (following internationally agreed-upon guidelines), while internationally supported NAMAs will be subject to international MRV.[48] These provisions on MRV lead to the assumption that at least two categories of NAMAs will be developed: unilateral NAMAs implemented by developing countries with their own resources; and supported NAMAs implemented with international multilateral or bilateral support. The provisions in Cancun on the creation of a registry to record NAMAs and to match NAMAs with international finance seem to further support this assumption. Separate sections of the registry will record NAMAs for which no international finance has been provided and NAMAs that have been matched with international support.[49]

NAMAs will likely receive funding from international conventional channels, such as the Green Climate Fund, and from bilateral or multilateral financial institutions. These funds are normally transferred via donations and concessional loans under the official development assistance framework.

Parties are considering the creation of a third category of NAMAs (credited NAMAs), which could be partly financed via carbon markets. Credited NAMAs would allow developing countries to sell offsets arising from emissions reductions achieved below a pre-established crediting level. This mechanism would target private investors seeking to generate returns on their capital, as well as governments and industry looking for ways to ease international or domestic GHG compliance costs. Private capital would be deployed via debt or equity investments and through the use of contracts for the sale and purchase of offsets.

Within or outside the NAMA framework, sectoral plans and actions are being discussed that could help provide a comprehensive coverage of sectors and sources in developing countries. Sectoral approaches include sector-specific fund-based NAMAs (functioning under the framework of supported NAMAs, as described above), sectoral trading, and sectoral crediting mechanisms. An example of a sectoral crediting framework being designed (or debated) is the Reducing Emissions from Deforestation and Forest Degradation (REDD) mechanism.

REDD is an effort to create a financial value for the carbon stored in forests, offering incentives for developing countries to reduce emissions from

---

48   *Id.,* at paragraphs 61 and 62.
49   *Id.,* at paragraph 59.

forested lands and invest in low-carbon paths to sustainable development. REDD+ includes the role of conservation, sustainable management of forests, and enhancement of forest carbon stocks. In Cancun, an incentive mechanism was established to encourage REDD+ activities in developing countries.[50] These reductions are contingent on developed countries providing adequate and predictable financial, technical, and technological support.[51] With appropriate support, developing countries are also encouraged to develop a national REDD+ strategy; national and, if appropriate, subnational reference (emission) levels; a national or, if appropriate, interim subnational MRV system; and an information system on how social, legal, and environmental safeguards are being addressed and respected throughout the implementation of REDD+ activities.[52] The REDD+ decision recognizes implementation through a three-phase approach.[53] The AWG-LCA has been given a mandate to explore financing options for the full implementation of results-based actions, and a separate decision on market-based mechanisms is to be finalized at COP17 in Durban in 2011.[54]

The AWG-LCA negotiation text in the run-up to Cancun showed a variety of language and options around other sectoral approaches. Several cooperative sectoral approaches and sector-specific actions were considered to enhance the implementation of Article 4.1(c) of the UNFCCC, which obliges parties to promote the development, application, and diffusion of climate-friendly technologies in all relevant sectors, including energy, transport, industry, agriculture, forestry, and waste management. Particular focus was given to sector-specific issues related to international shipping and aviation and the agricultural sector. The Cancun Agreements contain few of those elements, however, showing considerable divergence of views among parties, in particular in relation to the voluntary nature of sectoral approaches and references to the principle of common but differentiated responsibilities.[55]

Unfinished Business

Although COP16 succeeded in bringing the derailed climate negotiations back on track, it left many thorny issues undecided. In addition to summarizing the main elements of a future framework for collaborative action on climate change, the Cancun Agreements contain an array of mandates, deadlines, and

---

50   *Id.,* at Section III(C) and Annex I.

51   *Id.,* at paragraphs 71 and 74.

52   *Id.,* at paragraph 71.

53   These are (a) development of national strategies or action plans, policies and measures, and capacity building, (b) implementation of national policies and measures and national strategies or action plans that could involve further capacity building, technology development, and transfer and results-based demonstration activities, and (c) results-based actions, fully measured, reported, and verified.

54   Decision 1/CP.16, paragraph 77.

55   *Earth Negotiations Bulletin,* vol. 12, no. 498 (Dec. 13, 2010).

work programs, setting an ambitious agenda for climate negotiators. This agenda includes both elaborating on the various new frameworks and mechanisms agreed upon and reaching consensus on the more contentious issues that COP16 did not (and was not expected to) see agreement on.

Mitigation commitments are further left unsettled. Although the COP "takes note" of the commitments made thus far by developed-country parties,[56] both the COP[57] and the CMP[58] urge parties to raise their commitments. What commitments are eventually agreed to will be a crucial question under discussion in the years to come. Developing countries have pushed for a second commitment period for the Kyoto Protocol. However, developed countries, in particular Japan and Canada, have expressed reluctance to agree to new commitments without participation from other main emitters. Another contentious issue with regard to the Kyoto Protocol and the UNFCCC is the legal form of a future climate agreement. In Cancun, parties merely agreed that the AWG-KP should aim to "complete its work" on considering further commitments for Annex I parties "as soon as possible,"[59] implicitly recognizing that there is no agreement on the horizon. The AWG-LCA simply concluded that there was a need to "continue discussing legal options."[60]

There is much to be done regarding funding. Although commitments on both fast-start[61] and long-term[62] finance were formally recognized and the Green Climate Fund was established at Cancun,[63] the question of how much money will come from what sources remains unanswered. This question becomes all the more cardinal as developing countries become dependent on the level of financial support provided by developed countries. This support includes the development and implementation of adaptation plans,[64] supported NAMAs,[65] and plans and activities to combat deforestation,[66] as well as bilateral and multilateral cooperation on technology development,[67] and strengthening endogenous capacities for fully implementing the UNFCCC.[68] Other outstanding issues include the governance of the Green

---

56   Decision 1/CP.16, paragraph 36.

57   *Id.*, at paragraph 37.

58   Decision 1/CMP.6, paragraph 4, UNFCCC, Report of the Conference of the Parties Serving as the Meeting of the Parties to the Kyoto Protocol on Its Sixth Session, UN Doc. FCCC/KP/CMP/2010/12/Add.1 (Mar. 15, 2011).

59   *Id.*, at paragraph 1.

60   Decision 1/CP.16, paragraph 145.

61   *Id.*, at paragraph 95.

62   *Id.*, at paragraph 98.

63   *Id.*, at paragraphs 102–11 and Annex III.

64   *Id.*, at paragraph 18.

65   *Id.*, at paragraph 52.

66   *Id.*, at paragraph 71.

67   *Id.*, at paragraph 116.

68   *Id.*, at paragraph 130.

Climate Fund, on issues such as membership, voting, secretariat, and trustee functions, and prioritization of funding and the role of civil society organizations.[69] Other contentious items left open for the ad hoc working groups include the elaboration and recommendation of new market-based[70] and non-market mechanisms, and the consideration of a second commitment period of caps for emissions from land-use activities.[71]

Conclusions

The international community has come a long way from the Kyoto Protocol's bipolar world, with its division into Annex I and non–Annex I countries. Yet the possibility of any meaningful climate treaty is slim without a deal between the United States and China. Even if these two countries come to an agreement, it is unlikely that a treaty will set legally binding carbon targets for all major emitters. Whether for cultural or constitutional reasons, a bottom-up approach in which international commitments follow domestic policies and bilateral arrangements is the preferred policy choice for most nations. A disaggregated climate agenda that deals with various items separately is clearly more manageable in its complexities than a treaty that establishes targets and accounting rules but does not consider today's wide range of national circumstances and capacities.

The world of Annex I (developed) versus non–Annex I (developing) countries no longer accommodates the principle of "common but differentiated" responsibilities very well. Today, many developing countries have assumed leadership in international climate negotiations and have acknowledged their responsibility by adopting (voluntary and domestic) emissions-reduction targets, such as Brazil's commitment to reduce deforestation, Mexico's pledge to stabilize emissions by 2050, and Chinese investments in energy efficiency and renewable-energy deployment.[72] Many more countries have engaged in a process of developing low-carbon development plans that show a path toward a new and sustainable form of development, decoupling economic growth and prosperity from ever-increasing GHG emissions.

Although international negotiators will continue to seek compromise in establishing targets and commitments, accounting and financing frameworks, governments, private actors, and civil society have started implementing climate solutions. Whoever leads and prevails in climate negotiations, progress in implementing climate solutions is of the upmost importance. National

---

69   *Id.,* at paragraph 109 and Annex III.

70   *Id.,* at paragraph 81.

71   Decision 2/CMP.16, paragraph 3, UNFCCC, Report of the Conference of the Parties Serving as the Meeting of the Parties to the Kyoto Protocol on Its Sixth Session, UN Doc. FCCC/KP/CMP/2010/12/Add.1 (Mar. 15, 2011).

72   *See* information available on Brazil, Mexico, and China in the official UNFCCC compilation of NAMAs, available at <http://unfccc.int/resource/docs/2010/sbsta/eng/l18.pdf>.

governments and multilateral institutions will be challenged to put in place regulations and incentive frameworks for reducing emissions as they adapt to a changing climate. The challenge is formidable, and time is running out.

By the same token, climate finance and the institutional arrangements underpinning it are likely to remain decentralized and fragmented. Many different funding sources (private and public), managing institutions (multilateral, bilateral, and national), and financing instruments (domestic or budgetary, international public mechanisms, and private investments and capital markets) will play a part in the near, medium, and long term. Although fragmentation poses the risk of inefficiencies and duplication of efforts, the UNFCCC will be able to step up to its role as a central coordinator and catalyzer of efforts, ensuring a reasonable degree of harmonization with respect not only to GHG accounting and monitoring methods but also to mobilization, allocation, and distribution of climate finance.

Governing a Fragmented Climate Finance Regime

Richard B. Stewart, Bryce Rudyk, and Kiri Mattes

International climate negotiations have increasingly focused on climate finance as a promising tool both to provide significant resources for mitigation and adaptation in developing countries and to promote the broader political bargain that needs to be reached between developed and developing states. At its meetings in Copenhagen in 2009 and Cancun in 2010, the United Nations Framework Convention on Climate Change (UNFCCC) Conference of Parties (COP) began to address some of the larger issues that climate finance presents, including the magnitude of funds required; the potential sources of these funds; and institutional structures for governance of some forms of climate finance. Most notably, developed-country commitments to provide long-term climate finance of $100 billion annually by 2020 formed a key component of the 2009 Copenhagen Accord.[1] These financial commitments were formalized in Cancun, where the COP also agreed to create a global Green Climate Fund (GCF) to manage a portion of the financial commitments.

These amounts and the institutions created by the UNFCCC are important, but represent only part of the story about global climate finance. The climate finance regime will necessarily include many different sources of finance, and mechanisms and institutions for generating, disbursing, and using these resources. The GCF will likely channel only public sources of funds, and only a portion of those. It will not deal with the significant amount of private finance that is needed, and it will not provide an accounting of the finance that flows through many different channels. It will not coordinate the domestic developed country emissions trading systems. It will not address issues of compliance or discharge a number of other key functions. Most notably, it will not set and oversee implementation of overall policy for climate finance and its role in the global climate change regime complex.

This chapter summarizes the emergence and current status of climate finance in international climate negotiations; sets forth the broad array of functions that global climate finance institutions must carry out; describes the institutions that are already in place; and outlines the agenda for future institution building that will be needed to implement an effective system of climate finance.

---

1   Dollar amounts are in U.S. dollars.

The Emergence of Climate Finance

Until recently, the focus of negotiations within the UNFCCC was on setting targets and timetables for reducing greenhouse gas (GHG) emissions. It was only when attempts to negotiate a second commitment period for the Kyoto Protocol started to stall that climate finance emerged as a viable alternative for progress in the global response to climate change.

Climate Finance in International Climate Negotiations

The obligation for developed countries to provide financial support for developing-country mitigation and adaptation is not new: the 1992 UNFCCC requires the Annex II developed countries (mainly the Organisation for Economic Co-operation and Development [OECD] countries) to provide "new and additional financial resources" to help developing countries mitigate their GHG emissions,[2] as well as meet the costs of adapting to the adverse effects of climate change.[3] However, raising and disbursing climate finance were largely ignored in the early years of the Framework Convention. By 2008, the Global Environment Facility (the entity designated to operate as the financial mechanism of the UNFCCC) had allocated just over $2.4 billion to developing countries for measures to address climate change.[4] Amounts flowing through other channels were similarly small, with Annex II countries reporting total flows of public funds of between $2 billion and $5 billion annually between 1999 and 2003.[5] At that time, there was no recognized field of "climate finance," and so funding projects with climate change objectives was generally subsumed within broader programs for official development assistance (ODA).

Conceptions of climate finance began to expand beyond the conventional notion of transfers of public funds, to the possibility of using private funds and markets, with the introduction of the Kyoto Protocol's flexibility mechanisms, in particular, the Clean Development Mechanism (CDM). Under the CDM, projects in developing countries that reduce emissions earn credits that can be traded and sold on international exchanges and used by industrial countries to meet their emission reduction targets under the Kyoto Protocol. Although the CDM was introduced to give developed countries flexibility in meeting their protocol targets, it has demonstrated how market mechanisms may be used to stimulate private investment in mitigation projects in

---

2   United Nations Framework Convention on Climate Change Article 4.3 (May 9, 1992), available at <http://unfccc.int/resource/docs/convkp/conveng.pdf>.

3   *Id.*, Article 4.4.

4   OECD-IEA, *Financing Climate Change Mitigation: Towards a Framework for Measurement, Reporting and Verification* (2009), available at <http://www.oecd.org/dataoecd/0/60/44019962.pdf>; UN Secretary-General's High-Level Advisory Group on Climate Change Financing (AGF), *Background Paper for First Meeting, 31st March 2010, Prepared by the Secretariat,* Annex 1, available at <http://www.usclimatenetwork.org/resource-database/high-level-advisory-group-on-climate-change-financing-agf-background-paper> ("AGF Background Paper").

5   OECD-IEA, *supra* note 4, at 16. Note, however, that these amounts do not include U.S. contributions, as these were only reported for the year 2001.

developing countries. Revenue from the sale of credits has generated between $3 billion and $10 billion annually since the CDM's inception.

Climate finance only seriously emerged on the UNFCCC negotiating agenda at the UN Climate Change Conference 2009 (COP15) in Copenhagen. Although COP15 was largely perceived as a failure due to the stalemate reached on emissions targets, climate finance was one area in which significant outcomes were reached. Negotiations in Copenhagen addressed the magnitude of financial transfers necessary to limit the increase in global mean temperature to 2 degrees Celsius, resulting in a commitment by developed countries to mobilize $10 billion annually for 2010–12, rising to $100 billion annually by 2020.[6]

Another important element of the Copenhagen Accord was its acknowledgment of the need to utilize a "wide variety of sources, public and private, bilateral and multilateral, including alternative sources of finance."[7] Following the accord's call to study these potential sources, the UN secretary-general convened a High Level Advisory Group on Climate Change Financing (AGF) in early 2010.[8]

The UN Climate Change Conference 2010 (COP16) in Cancun was hailed as a revival of the multilateral process, with agreement reached on a "balanced package" of outcomes.[9] Notably, the COP formalized developed countries' COP15 commitments of $30 billion in fast-start funding and $100 billion a year by 2020. It also established several new institutions in the climate finance landscape, including the GCF, a standing committee, and a registry for nationally appropriate mitigation actions (NAMAs).[10]

What Is Climate Finance?

"Climate finance" is a term with several definitions. Accordingly, any discussion is best prefaced by specifying what the term means.

There are two ways to quantify the amount of financial resources needed to address climate change: the "full cost" refers to the total cost of all investments and expenditures on projects that have some mitigation or adaptation

---

6   Decision 2/CP.15, Article 8, Copenhagen Accord, FCCC/CP/2009/11/Add.1. March 30, 2010.

7   Id., Article 7.

8   The AGF conveyed its final report to the secretary-general in November 2010. See AGF, Report of the Secretary-General's High-Level Advisory Group on Climate Change Financing (Nov. 5, 2010), available at <http://www.un.org/wcm/webdav/site/climatechange/shared/Documents/AGF_reports/AGF_Final_Report.pdf>.

9   The COP's main decision was based on matters negotiated within the Ad Hoc Working Group on Long-Term Cooperative Action (AWG-LCA). There are currently two negotiating tracks within the UNFCCC: the AWG-LCA and the Ad Hoc Working Group on Further Commitments for Annex I Parties under the Kyoto Protocol (AWG-KP).

10   Decision 1/CP.16, The Cancun Agreements: Outcome of the Work of the Ad Hoc Working Group on Long-term Cooperative Action under the Convention, FCCC/CP/2010/7/Add.1. March 15, 2011 ("Cancun Agreements").

objectives. "Incremental cost" is a concept derived from Article 4.3 of the UNFCCC, which requires developed countries (the Annex II countries) to provide financial resources to developing countries to meet the "agreed full incremental costs of implementing measures" under the Framework Convention. Although there is no settled methodology for operationalizing this notion of incremental cost, incremental cost generally refers to the additional cost of mitigation or adaptation in a project, compared with higher carbon alternatives or the alternative without targeting adaptation.[11] For example, a measure of full cost would include the full value of a developing country's investment in low-carbon-power-generating infrastructure. A measure of incremental cost would capture only the additional cost of investing in the low-carbon alternative relative to the higher emitting options available. Climate finance is generally understood as covering incremental costs.

Climate finance is increasingly understood to be drawn from multiple sources and to be provided in a variety of forms. Accordingly, climate finance includes, but is not limited to, domestic public funds, including bilateral transfers to foreign governments and to multilateral funds, as well as investments by multilateral financial institutions; purely private flows channeled through carbon markets; and hybrid finance, which includes various forms of assistance by international and domestic public financial institutions to ensure the economic viability of climate-related projects largely funded by private capital.

Conceptions of climate finance vary depending on whether climate finance is limited to resources originating in developed countries or include those originating in developing countries. For the purpose of negotiations within the UNFCCC, climate finance refers only to the provision of financial support by developed countries to developing countries. The Copenhagen Accord and Cancun Agreements retained this North-South conception of climate finance. This narrow definition of climate finance makes sense when considering international institutions and measures created under the UNFCCC, including mechanisms to build North-South trust.

An intermediate conception of climate finance includes all cross-border financial flows to support mitigation and adaptation in developing countries, including South-South flows of financial support by one developing country to another. These flows have become important because several non–Annex II countries now have relatively advanced economies and have become donors for climate-related projects in other developing countries, notwithstanding the lack of obligation under the UNFCCC to provide such assistance.[12] This intermediate definition is appropriate in considering all the international mechanisms for delivering climate finance to developing countries.

---

11   Project Catalyst, *From Climate Finance to Financing Green Growth Briefing Paper* 15 (Nov. 23, 2010), available at <http://www.project-catalyst.info/images/publications/101127_from _climate_finance_to_financing_green_growth_formated.pdf>.

12   China and the United Arab Emirates are two examples.

The broadest conception of climate finance includes domestic investment within developing countries. Cross-border flows represent only a fraction of the total amount that will ultimately be invested in climate-related projects and infrastructure in developing countries, with the bulk of funds being locally derived through domestic capital markets. Many of these flows would generally not be aimed at meeting the incremental costs of climate-sustainable projects relative to higher-carbon alternatives. Nonetheless, including these internal flows in discussions of climate finance is appropriate to ensure that incremental cost financing is used effectively to leverage domestic investment and that developing countries have correspondingly appropriate policies, institutional capacities, and incentives in place to promote effective investment in low-carbon development and adaptation measures.

Estimating Climate Finance Needs and Goals

Estimates of the finance required for global climate mitigation and adaptation have varied widely, depending on each estimate's methodology and political purpose. Determining the magnitude of funds that can be characterized as climate finance and that will flow through, and be governed by, various climate finance institutions is important to designing effective institutions.

Mitigation

One of the more influential studies of the need for international climate finance for mitigation was that released by Project Catalyst in mid-2009, which estimated that €55–80 billion was required annually between 2010 and 2020 to finance the incremental cost of abatement in developing countries.[13] At COP16 in Cancun, Project Catalyst released a study with revised figures, reflecting refinements in methodology, as well as the impact that the global financial crisis has had on the path of business-as-usual emissions.[14] This study estimates that $60 billion per annum will be required by 2020 to support mitigation investment in developing countries to move to a 2 degrees Celsius pathway. This estimate is further broken down by sector as set out in table 1.

---

13   Project Catalyst, *Financing Global Action on Climate Change: Finance Briefing Paper* 9 (Aug. 2009), available at <http://www.project-catalyst.info/images/2. %20Climate %20Finance/ Publications/4. %20Financing %20global %20action/090810 %20Financing %20global %20action %20on %20climate %20change %20- %20Bonn %20version %20- %20full.pdf>; Project Catalyst, *Financing Needs* 1 (Dec. 2009), available at <http://www.project-catalyst .info/images/2. %20Climate %20Finance/ Publications/2. %20Briefing %20papers %20on %20climate %20finance/20091203 %20Finance %20Needs %20Briefing.pdf>.

14   Project Catalyst's 2009 figures were based on the McKinsey Global GHG Abatement Cost Curve, Version 2.0, from January 2009. In August 2010, McKinsey released a revised version of the curve, Version 2.1, reflecting the lower path of bsuiness-as-usual emissions as a result of the impact of the global financial crisis. *See* McKinsey & Company, *Impact of the Financial Crisis on Carbon Economics, Version 2.1 of the Global Greenhouse Gas Abatement Cost Curve* (Aug. 2010).

Table 1. Sectoral Breakdown of Climate Finance Required for Mitigation by 2020[15]

Sector	$ per annum	Example of measures requiring support
Low-carbon power	18 billion	Support for feed-in tariffs, concessional finance, or support-enabling measures (such as grid updates) to stimulate investment in low-carbon-power-generation capacity
Energy efficiency	18 billion	Incremental cost support to assist with transaction costs, enhance the implementation of policy measures, and reinforce cost-positive measures
Land use	25 billion	Support countries in efforts to reduce deforestation, change land-use practices, and support alternative economic development

Adaptation

Reliably estimating future financing needs for adaptation has proved difficult. The methodology employed in studies has varied significantly, as have the resulting figures. One of the more widely cited studies was conducted by the UNFCCC Secretariat in 2007, which estimated that additional investments and financial flows of between $49 billion and $171 billion per annum would be required for adaptation by 2030, of which between $27 billion and $66 billion annually would be used in developing countries.[16] More recently, the Economics of Adaptation to Climate Change project, supported by the World Bank, estimated the annual cost for developing countries to adapt to climate change between 2010 and 2050 at between $70 billion and $100 billion at 2005 prices.[17] Although adaptation costs expressed as a percentage of gross domestic product are considerably higher in sub-Saharan Africa than in any other region, in absolute terms, East Asia and the Pacific will incur the greatest share of these costs.[18]

One reason that it is so difficult to estimate the costs of adaptation is the problem of distinguishing the portion of a project or measure attributable to enhancing resilience to climate change, as opposed to broader development

---

15 Project Catalyst, *supra* note 11, at 4–5.

16 UNFCCC, *Investment and Financial Flows to Address Climate Change* 99–123, paragraphs 371–473 (2007), available at <http://unfccc.int/resource/docs/publications/financial_flows.pdf>.

17 World Bank, *Economics of Adaptation to Climate Change, Synthesis Report* xxvii (2010), available at <http://climatechange.worldbank.org/sites/default/files/documents/EACCSynthesis Report.pdf>.

18 *Id.*, at xix.

and resource management objectives. This is particularly a problem for projects that aim to increase resilience of food production, transport, public health, and social services to more extreme weather and increased climate variability. The task may be less difficult for other types of projects, including those that create physical protections against erosion and rising sea levels and those that address increased salinity of drinking water. A further difficulty arises from the inherent uncertainty involved in trying to model future changes in climate, predicting the effects that these changes will have, and understanding how these effects may be addressed.[19]

Current Flows

There is no reliable aggregate accounting of climate finance at this time, but for North-South flows, one can estimate that in 2009 between $7.2 billion and $9.2 billion in both public and private funds flowed from developed to developing countries, as depicted in figure 1.

Figure 1. Estimated North-South Climate Finance 2009[20]

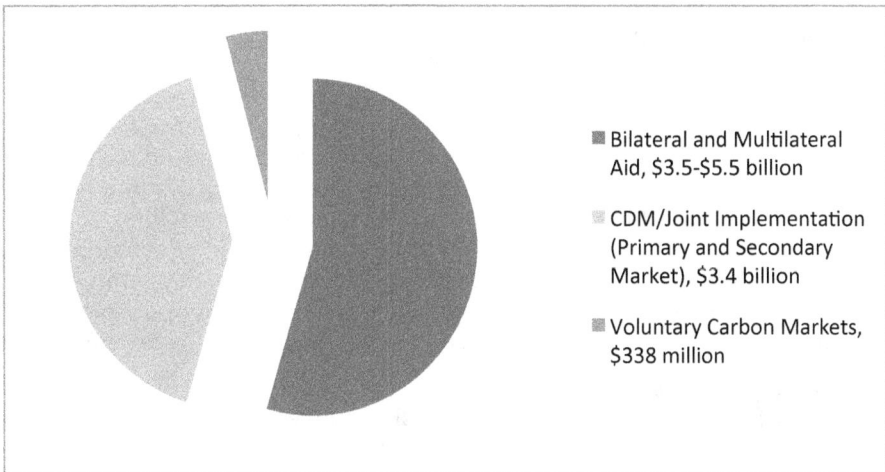

- Bilateral and Multilateral Aid, $3.5-$5.5 billion
- CDM/Joint Implementation (Primary and Secondary Market), $3.4 billion
- Voluntary Carbon Markets, $338 million

Scaling up from the current, relatively small amounts of climate finance to the $100 billion set out in the Cancun Agreements will require a new set of institutions. These institutions will need to manage this rapid scale-up and overcome many of the governance challenges that have plagued climate finance and ODA to date.

---

19   *Id.*, at xxi.

20   These figures are taken from different sources and should be read as a rough estimate only. Estimates of bilateral and multilateral aid are taken from the AGF Background Paper, Annex 1; the CDM/JI and voluntary carbon market estimates are taken from Alexandre Kossoy & Philippe Ambrosi, *State and Trends of the Carbon Market 2010* (May 2010), available at <http://siteresources.worldbank.org/INTCARBONFINANCE/Resources/State_and_Trends_of_the _Carbon_Market_2010_low_res.pdf>.

The Challenges in Creating Climate Finance Institutions

The challenges in creating an institutional regime for international climate finance cannot be overstated. The trend in negotiations away from centralized institutions for climate change toward a bottom-up fragmented regime is seen clearly in climate finance, where there is a proliferation of international climate financing sources and mechanisms and associated public and private institutions.

In many ways, this highly plural structure is desirable in order to access a wide variety of public and private sources and thereby raise finance in the amounts required. It also allows for experimentation with different climate finance sources, forms, and institutions, promoting competition to ensure that all aspects of climate mitigation and adaptation are funded effectively and sufficiently. Notwithstanding the rhetoric around the GCF, it is clear that no single global institution will emerge to raise, govern, disburse, and track all climate finance: this is not cause for lament. However, a pluralist regime does pose significant challenges.

At its core, the governance challenge in climate finance, not unlike in other areas of climate change and international law, is creating institutions that are both effective and seen as legitimate by all parties. Donors want confidence that financial resources are being used honestly, economically, and environmentally effectively. If available institutional channels do not meet these requisites, donor countries will either shift funding to other channels or not fulfill their financial commitments. Conversely, developing-country trust in the funding institutions will affect the extent to which these countries are willing and able to make transformative investments in both mitigation and adaptation. Such finance must help further the development goals of recipient countries and be provided on terms that allow recipients a significant say in the means by which financing is provided and the ends to which financing is devoted.

Discussions in the lead-up to Cancun, particularly regarding the establishment of the GCF, highlighted the division between developed and developing countries about appropriate governance structures for climate finance institutions. Developed countries have preferred existing Bretton Woods institutions such as the World Bank, in which voting is based on capital contributions, thereby favoring developed countries. Developing countries have preferred new institutions under the oversight of the UNFCCC COP, in which they form the majority. This division is a result of insufficient access to climate finance under the Global Environmental Facility (GEF) and a half-century of developing-country experience with ODA and foreign direct investment. Although climate finance is intended to be new and additional to ODA, it does not escape many of the issues that have created tension between donor and recipient countries, including the imposition of donor conditionality, lack of direct access, mismatched regulation and policies of implementing agencies, and lack of local ownership of projects.

Creating institutions that are both effective and widely accepted as legitimate for climate financing requires an understanding of governance challenges. Three main governance issues will shape how future climate finance institutions are structured: multiplicity of sources, forms, and channels; multiplicity of actors; and conditionality.

Multiplicity of Sources, Forms, and Channels

The broad dimensions of the climate finance regime become apparent when considering the multiplicity of sources from which funds will be drawn, the forms in which assistance will be provided, and the channels through which support will be disbursed.

Sources of finance may be broadly categorized as being either public or private in nature. Public sources are those that are derived from governments, with public funds predominantly provided through budgetary appropriations from developed countries (historically as part of their budget for ODA). Although such appropriations will continue as a source of public funds, the AGF has identified a number of other public sources that, it hopes, will be less susceptible to the vagaries of domestic budget processes. These potential additional sources include international and domestic emission trading system (ETS) allowance auctions, domestic carbon taxes, international bunker fuel (aviation and shipping) levies, an international financial transaction tax, redirected fossil fuel subsidies, and International Monetary Fund (IMF) Special Drawing Rights. Private sources of funds will be drawn from the interaction between carbon and offset markets. Hybrid financing can be provided through risk mitigation and return-enhancement instruments used by public international and domestic financial and regulatory institutions to leverage private investments.

Climate finance will be provided in a variety of forms, including grants, concessional debt, payments for services, novel de-risking mechanisms, and traditional foreign investment. These different forms of finance will enable support to be provided in a manner that best meets a project's needs. For example, the lack of potential private market mechanisms for adaptation means that adaptation will be primarily funded by public finance in the form of grants and concessional loans. Sectoral or large-scale offset projects with low to medium cost may be funded through offset markets, with funding acting as a "payment for the service" of reducing emissions. High-cost mitigation opportunities, such as carbon capture and storage (CCS) and renewable energy may require a combination of private venture capital, public research and development support, and favorable regulatory environments.

Finally, climate finance will be provided through a variety of channels. Channels may be climate-change specific, such as specialized bilateral and multilateral funds like the Adaptation Fund, the GCF, and the Climate Investment Funds, and, for private funds, the offset market. However, a significant volume of funds will also flow through nonspecific channels, such as World Bank portfolio funds and sovereign wealth funds.

This multiplicity of sources, forms, and channels and the hybrid nature of some of them will have distinct effects on the structure of climate finance institutions. Significant amounts of private funds will be leveraged by public finance through mechanisms such as loan guarantees, feed-in tariff top-ups, and investment, currency, and political risk guarantees. This intertwining of funds requires institutions that can process both public and private finance, for example, in the tracking of climate finance commitments and transfers or in the raising and disbursement of funds. Current institutions are almost exclusively dedicated to one type of finance, for example, the proposed GCF will likely manage only public finance, and organizations tracking climate finance generally consider only public forms of aid.

Multiplicity of Actors

Although only national governments are parties to the UNFCCC and negotiate emissions limitation targets and timetables, a broader scope of governmental, intergovernmental, and nongovernmental actors is involved in addressing climate change.

Governmental and intergovernmental involvement occurs at a number of different governance levels: international, regional, national, and subnational. A sample of the institutions in the variety of levels is set out in table 2.

Table 2. Selected Governmental Institutions in Climate Finance

International	UNFCCC, World Bank (Clean Investment Funds, Special Climate Change Funds), CDM, GEF, OECD Development Assistance Committee, Multilateral Environment Fund, International Renewable Energy Agency, International Maritime Organization, International Civil Aviation Organization, International Energy A, UN Development Programme (UNDP), UN Environmental Programme (UNEP)
Regional	EU ETS, Asian Development Bank (ADB), African Development Bank (AfDB), European Bank for Reconstruction and Development (EBRD), Inter-American Development Bank (IADB)
National	New Zealand ETS; Australian International Climate Forest Initiative; Japan's Hatoyama Initiative; Germany's International Climate Initiative; Indonesian Climate Change Trust Fund; Bangladesh Climate Change Resilience Fund; Brazil Amazon Fund; national implementing entities such as Senegal's Centre de Suivi Ecologique; national climate change departments and ministries
Subnational	Western Climate Initiative (Western U.S. states and Canadian provinces), New South Wales Greenhouse Gas Reduction Scheme

In addition to the large number of public actors sampled in table 2, private actors (organizations, corporations, and individuals) are also integral to climate finance institutions. Not only will a significant portion of finance come from private entities—through offset provisions in domestic emissions trading legislation, international transfer provisions under domestic carbon taxes, or private capital flows—but private organizations are also involved in some of the regime's institutional functions. A selection of these institutions is identified in table 3.

Table 3. Selected Nongovernmental Institutions in Climate Finance

Disbursement	Private investment banks
Monitoring and tracking	Aiddata.org, World Resources Institute, Heinrich Boll Stiftung, Overseas Development Institute, Climatefundsupdate.org, Project Catalyst
Policy setting	Regional Greenhouse Gas Initiative, international conservation NGOs, Deutsche Bank's GETFiT program

The challenge of developing and operating a successful regime of climate finance institutions involving such a multitude of actors across the various levels of governance is clear. The slothlike pace of the UNFCCC negotiations—with only 192 parties—suggests that a greater number of participants with different forms of constituencies might be paralyzing if they are all involved in a single institution.

There is movement toward disaggregating functions across multiple institutions for certain institutional functions. To ensure the broader necessary participation, this trend should continue, understanding that for some institutional functions, thematic areas, or regional groupings, it may not be possible or desirable to disaggregate beyond the international or regional level. A key factor in this implementation will be the recognition of which actors are necessary for any institutional function and the assurance that they have the ability to participate. For example, emissions trading systems are being created at the domestic or subnational level, but their offset policies will have a significant impact on developing countries. To date, there has been little developing-country involvement in the creation of domestically created offset regimes. Disaggregation must therefore be complemented by arrangements to ensure proper participation and promote consistency, direction, and accountability.

Conditionality

Conditionality (or the placing of conditions on financial flows) is, and will continue to be, an integral part of climate finance, particularly for private finance for mitigation. Mitigation finance to developing countries will be primarily delivered through the pay-for-performance model of the offset mechanisms attached to developed-country ETS. As these funds flow to offset increased emissions in the donor countries, strict oversight of the funded emissions reductions is necessary. As well, public and private development aid donors and concessional funders will want to set conditions on the use of their funds and have similarly strict supervision of outcomes. Currently, lacking international institutional channels, decisions on conditions for both of these types of activities occur within donor (very often developed) countries. This raises serious questions about the fairness and structure of the conditions.

Although applying conditions in climate finance is necessary, both ODA and earlier climate-related finance have been viewed antagonistically by recipient countries. In the GEF (the current operating entity of the UNFCCC), conditionalities are set and enforced in what is perceived as a one-sided fashion through the "contributor prerogative."[21] New disbursement institutions will need to be seen as legitimate in order to effectively design and implement conditions.

The Emerging Climate Governance Landscape for Climate Finance

The multiplicity of sources, forms, channels, and actors means that there will be a decentralized regime of climate finance institutions. Current and proposed institutions under the UNFCCC address only a subset of the necessary institutional functions. This section discusses the functions of the future climate finance regime.

Core Functions in a Climate Finance Regime

Six institutional functions are necessary in any future climate finance regime:

- Policy and rule making
- Securing commitments and raising funds
- Disbursing funds
- Promoting institutional coherence, coordination, and linkage
- Monitoring performance and securing accountability
- Compliance

This list is not definitive; the boundaries of these functions are far from clear.

What is certain is that no one institution is capable of performing all of these functions. Rather, these functions will be distributed across a variety of

---

21 Jacob Werksman, *From Coercive Conditionality to Agreed Conditions: The Only Future for Future Climate Finance*, in *Climate Finance: Regulatory and Funding Strategies for Climate Change and Global Development* 189 (Richard B. Stewart, Benedict Kingsbury, & Bryce Rudyk ed., New York U. Press 2009).

climate finance institutions. Further complexity is created by differences in the type of funding (public, private, hybrid); the type of measures being funded (mitigation or adaptation); and the specific category of activity funded within a given type of measures (for example, mitigation activities include renewable energy, energy efficiency, CCS, transport, and the Reducing Emissions from Deforestation in Developing Countries, REDD mechanism).

Policy and Rule Making

Policy and rule making is a pervasive function: it is a key component of meta-governance, which in the climate finance context includes such matters as setting overall climate finance targets and timetables, setting goals for different sources of funds, apportioning responsibility among states for the provision of funds, and prioritizing different types of measures for funding. This function extends to administrative and regulatory rule making, such as the formulation of accounting standards and reporting guidelines, and determining criteria for NAMAs seeking international support. To some extent, these functions will be carried out by all institutions within the climate finance regime: it is highly unlikely that any institution will exist without taking on some element of policy- and rule-making responsibility. However, there is also a need for setting overall priorities and steering and coordinating the activities of the many different institutions that make up the climate finance regime complex.

The UNFCCC COP provides the most obvious example of higher-level policy making in the current climate finance regime. The COP acts almost as a legislative body, making high-level decisions that establish the parameters of the international community's response to climate change. The COP is assisted in this function by the UNFCCC's two subsidiary bodies, the Subsidiary Body for Scientific and Technological Advice (SBSTA) and the Subsidiary Body for Implementation (SBI), which are concerned with administrative policy and rules for implementing the Framework Convention. Thus, for example, the SBI reviews financial assistance given to non–Annex I parties and provides advice to the COP regarding the Framework Convention's financial mechanism; the SBSTA undertakes technical work necessary for improving the guidelines for national communications and emissions inventories. However, the COP and its subsidiary bodies do not, and cannot, discharge some overall policy-making functions that encompass the entire climate finance regime complex: many institutions and activities fall outside the UNFCCC umbrella, and the number of these institutions will only grow with time.

Securing Commitments and Raising Funds

The mobilization of climate finance has traditionally been conceived of as a process of securing political commitments by developed countries to provide funds in an international forum, such as the UNFCCC; the subsequent generation of pledged amounts via domestic budgetary appropriations; and their transfer to developing countries through bilateral or multilateral mechanisms. However (as has been the case more generally with development aid), these pledges rarely translate into delivery of all the funds pledged. The objective of securing a reliable, predictable flow of funds tends to be compromised by the reality of domestic appropriation processes, which preclude donor countries making binding budgetary precommitments or, in many cases, delivering on pledges previously made.

The climate finance regime will increasingly rely on more innovative ways of raising funds, including the use of market mechanisms and new sources that are less vulnerable to domestic political cycles, such as the levy on CDM transactions that currently finances the Adaptation Fund. Although the AGF has identified innovative potential sources of funding outside domestic budget processes, including auctions of assigned amount units and international transport levies, many of these sources would still have to be administered domestically. Thus, a major challenge going forward will be finding a way to ensure that these funds, which will be collected by national agencies and institutions, are channeled into the international regime and delivered to developing countries.

The acts of raising funds and securing commitments will increasingly rely on hybrid strategies that use public funds and resources (including capital contributions or guarantees) as a means of leveraging larger flows of private finance. Multilateral development banks like the World Bank already play this leveraging role and will continue to do so, as will new public-private partnerships, such as the CP3 initiative being developed by the UK Department for International Development,[22] which aims to use public funds and private sector expertise to overcome traditional barriers to low-carbon investment in the developing world.

Disbursing Funds

Disbursing funds involves the application of funds raised to projects and programs for mitigation and adaptation and the allocation of resources across various thematic areas (for example, in the case of mitigation, thematic areas include energy efficiency, renewable energy, transport, CCS, and REDD). Institutional discussion and creation in climate finance have, to date, predominantly focused on disbursement institutions.

The receipt of funds by developing countries is often frustrated or delayed by the decisional requirements and review processes of disbursement institutions. These institutions, of course, need to ensure the efficient use and allocation of funds; ensure that institutions receiving funds have in place, and observe, arrangements for financial integrity; impose specific conditions on the use of funds, some of which are insisted on by donor countries; and monitor, review, and evaluate performance. However, with each of these disbursing funds having its own decision-making structures, procedures, and bureaucracies, the demands on recipient agencies can be overly onerous and serve as a barrier to accessing financial assistance. In reforming the current

---

22   Hugh Whelan, *CP3, UK/Asian Govt Climate Fund, Issues Mandate for Asset Manager as Part of UN$100bn Plan: P8/P80*, Responsible Investor (Feb. 16, 2011), available at <http://www .responsible-investor.com/home/article/cp3>.

disbursement institutions and designing future ones, a significant challenge will be to promote coordinated policy and regulations among disbursement institutions and between institutions and recipient countries.

Existing institutions carrying out disbursement of climate finance include a number that operate under the UNFCCC (namely, the Adaptation Fund and the GEF) and many more that operate outside the UNFCCC (especially through specialized multilateral and bilateral funds, multilateral development banks [MDBs], market mechanisms, and private investment).

Existing Disbursement Mechanisms under the UNFCCC. The GEF is an independent multilateral financial institution that provides grants to developing countries and countries with economies in transition for projects related to climate change, as well as other international environmental focal areas, including biodiversity, international waters, land degradation, the ozone layer, and persistent organic pollutants. The GEF has been designated to operate the UNFCCC financial mechanism,[23] under the control of the COP and subject to review every four years. GEF funding depends on voluntary contributions from donor countries (primarily UNFCCC Annex II countries) that follow predefined burden-sharing rules.

The GEF was initially established as a pilot program in 1991, with the objective of providing cofinance to developing countries and economies in transition for projects with global environmental benefits. The World Bank was appointed as trustee and administrator of the fund, and acted as an implementing agency, along with the UNEP and the UNDP, for projects cofinanced by the fund.[24]

Although the formal governance of the GEF has been structured in an effort to secure equitable representation (in particular, via the constituency system in the GEF Council, which divides seats equally between developed and developing countries), the GEF has been criticized as being unresponsive to developing-country concerns. Developing countries are particularly wary of the conditionalities that accompany grants of funds imposed by the fund's implementing agencies (which include the World Bank, the ADB, the AfDB, the UNDP, the UNEP, the EBRD, the IDB, the Food and Agriculture Organization of the United Nations, the International Fund for Agriculture and Development, and the UN Industrial Development Organization), which are viewed as informal avenues for developed countries to exert control over recipients.[25]

---

23   The "financial mechanism" is the mechanism by which funds are provided to developing
      countries under the convention.

24   For a detailed discussion of the GEF's establishment and subsequent reform, *see* Charlotte
      Streck, *The Global Environmental Facility — A Role Model for International Governance?* 2 Glob.
      Envtl. Pol. 71 (2001).

25   *See* discussion in Athena Ballesteros, et al., *Power, Responsibility and Accountability: Rethinking
      the Legitimacy of Institutions for Climate Finance* 12 (World Resources Institute 2010).

The Adaptation Fund was established under the Kyoto Protocol to finance concrete adaptation projects and programs in developing countries that are particularly vulnerable to the adverse effects of climate change. It is primarily funded through imposition of a 2 percent levy on CDM transactions and had collected approximately $110 million as of 2010.[26] The fund approved its first two projects for financing, in Senegal and Honduras, at the end of 2010, with the Senegalese project to be implemented by Senegal's Centre de Suivi Ecologique, the first certified national implementing entity (NIE) under the Adaptation Fund's pioneering arrangements for direct access to funds. Agencies from Jamaica and Uruguay have also been accredited as NIEs.

The Adaptation Fund is often heralded as a new model for climate finance governance. The fund's board is composed of a majority of members drawn from developing countries; it is hoped that this composition will address the historical power imbalance between donor and recipient countries and allow for a more equitable form of governance. It is also hoped that the fund's innovative procedures for enabling developing countries to have direct access to funds, via accredited NIEs, will increase financing opportunities for vulnerable developing countries and allow a greater sense of ownership of both the fund and the projects that it supports. Yet the fund has been subject to much criticism, in particular regarding the long period that elapsed between the time it was established in late 2001, through to the date it became operational in 2009, and then the first approval of projects in late 2010.

Existing Disbursement Mechanisms outside the UNFCCC. The World Bank, along with the AfDB, the ADB, the EBRD, and the IDB, manages the largest portfolio of non-UNFCCC climate funds, with approximately $8 billion of capital cumulatively committed to a range of climate-specific funds such as the Climate Investment Funds (CIF).[27] Donor countries have pledged $6.3 billion to the CIF, which comprises two trust funds: the Clean Technology Fund (CTF), for scaling up investments in low-carbon technologies; and the Strategic Climate Change Fund (SCF), to support programs testing innovative approaches to climate change.[28] In structuring the governance of these funds, the World Bank has attempted to address developing-country concerns, ensuring that the trust fund committee for each fund has equal representation from contributor and recipient countries.[29]

Aside from their roles in raising and administering climate-specific funds, the World Bank and other MDBs have had a huge impact (both positive and negative) on mitigation and adaptation activities through their wider

---

26   AGF Background Report, Annex I.

27   AGF Background Report, at 10.

28   OECD-IEA, *supra* note 4, at 23–24; World Bank, *Making the Most of Public Finance for Climate Action: The World Bank Group at Work*, Issues Brief No. 2 (May 2010), available at <http://climatechange.worldbank.org/climatechange/sites/default/files/documents/DCFIB %20 %232-web.pdf>.

29   *See* Climate Investment Funds website at <http://www.climateinvestmentfunds.org>.

portfolio lending activities. For the period between 1995 and 2005, approximately one-third of the World Bank's total lending went to sectors relevant to the mitigation of climate change. In the case of regional development banks over the same period, the share was about one-half.[30] For the 2009 financial year, the World Bank Group's total energy financing was $8.2 billion, of which $3.3 billion was loans for renewable energy (including hydro) and energy-efficiency projects and programs. The goal is for renewable and energy-efficiency loans to represent 50 percent of all energy financing by 2011.[31]

A relatively recent phenomenon is the formation of specialized bilateral and multilateral funds to fund mitigation and adaptation activities in developing countries. Examples of bilateral funds include Germany's International Climate Initiative and Australia's International Forest Carbon Initiative. An example of a multilateral fund is the Nordic Climate Facility.[32]

Another recent development is the establishment of national funds by donee countries. A number of developing countries have established nationally administered specialized funds for which international contributions are sought. Two prominent examples are Brazil's Amazon Fund, administered by the Brazilian National Development Bank, and Indonesia's Climate Change Trust Fund, administered by Indonesia's National Development Planning Agency.

Promoting Institutional Coherence, Coordination, and Linkage

A significant downside of a fragmented and dispersed regime for climate finance is the potential for inefficiency arising from the duplication of functions, the multiplication of transaction costs, and the pursuit of incompatible or mutually harmful objectives. Thus, a further function for climate finance institutions is to promote coherence among the activities of the various institutions; address overlaps, gaps, and conflicts among different programs; and promote compatibility and mutual reinforcement in the distributed administration of climate finance.[33] One challenge will be to identify opportunities for mutual reinforcement and synergies between different finance mechanisms, including linking different carbon markets to enhance overall efficiency; securing appropriate coupling between regulatory requirements and financial and other markets; and promoting synergies between different sources of

---

30 UNFCCC, *Review of the Experience of International Funds, Multilateral Financial Institutions and Other Sources of Funding Relevant to the Current and Future Investment and Financial Needs of Developing Countries,* Technical Paper, FCCC/TP/2007/4 (Nov. 21, 2007).

31 World Bank Issues Brief, *Climate Change,* available at <http://go.worldbank.org/BPY7 QIRNA0>.

32 For a comprehensive listing of bilateral and multilateral funds, *see* <http://www .climatefundsupdate.org> and <http://www.climatefinanceoptions.org>.

33 Robert O. Keohane & David G. Victor, *The Regime Complex for Climate Change* 19 (Harvard Project on International Climate Agreements, Discussion Paper 10-33, Jan. 2010), available at <http://belfercenter.ksg.harvard.edu/files/Keohane_Victor_Final_2.pdf>.

public, private, and hybrid finance and between international flows and domestic finance in developing countries. Further coordination challenges arise when the policies of a domestic or regional institution have an indirect (but significant) impact on third-party states and stakeholders. This is a particular problem in domestic and regional ETSs, where the scheme's rules and policies governing the recognition of offsets and the terms on which they may be traded have material repercussions for the developing countries in which offsets originate. Ideally, such institutions should incorporate some avenue by which developing countries can participate in, or at least be heard on, matters affecting their interests.

When the Framework Convention was first agreed on, the expectation was that the financial mechanism of the UNFCCC would encompass all flows of funds going to mitigation and adaptation and that the COP would be able to exercise control over these flows and their application. As it has turned out, the GEF (the operating entity designated to administer the financial mechanism) has not always been responsive to the views within the COP; in any event, a greater volume of climate funds now flows outside the UNFCCC than in it. A goal of the UNFCCC Standing Committee will be to assist the COP in exerting greater guidance and control over funds flowing both within and outside the UNFCCC.

As more national and regional carbon markets emerge, there will be important opportunities for developing broader and more efficient markets for mobilizing private flows of climate finance and directing them to the most advantageous uses by linking and integrating these different markets. The International Carbon Action Partnership (ICAP) was formed by countries and regions that have implemented, or are actively pursuing the implementation of, carbon markets through mandatory cap-and-trade programs, with a view to promoting linkage between current and emerging carbon markets at a global level. ICAP acts as a forum for sharing experience and knowledge and evaluating best practices, with the ultimate aim of enhancing the design of market-based mechanisms and ensuring their compatibility at an early stage of their development.[34]

Monitoring Performance and Securing Accountability

The monitoring function will primarily be exercised via the anticipated regime for measurement, review, and verification (MRV) of support provided and mitigation outcomes attained (in particular, for internationally supported NAMAs). There is some degree of overlap between the monitoring and compliance functions to the extent that monitoring can be characterized as a form of "soft compliance." However, monitoring can be viewed as a distinct function because it has broader objectives than pure compliance. Monitoring is a way of promoting transparency in the climate finance regime and ensuring accountability of both donor countries and recipients. When the results are

---

34   *See* ICAP website at <http://www.icapcarbonaction.com>.

suitably aggregated and reported, monitoring also enables some assessment to be made of the overall progress of the climate finance regime toward its stated objectives.

The main mechanism at present for monitoring developed-country support for mitigation and adaptation projects is national communications under the UNFCCC: Annex II parties are required to provide details of the funds they have provided in satisfaction of their obligations under Article 4 of the Framework Convention. The UNFCCC Secretariat publishes these reports and compiles information into a synthesis report; however, inconsistencies in reporting undermine the reliability of the resulting figures, as does the absence of reports from key contributors such as the United States.[35] The provision of bilateral aid for climate change–related projects is also captured by the OECD Development Assistance Committee's Credit Reporting Service, which requires OECD donors to apply the "Rio markers" to identify ODA that has been directed to projects with the primary objective of mitigation or adaptation.

Several civil society organizations have assumed an important role in monitoring the provision of public climate finance. Project Catalyst, the World Resources Institute, and climatefundsupdate.org are examples of organizations monitoring the extent to which developed countries are fulfilling their pledges to provide public funds, particularly since COP15 in Copenhagen.

Monitoring, measurement, review, and verification are all equally important for private financial flows and their application. Thus, under current arrangements in the CDM, the responsibility for ensuring both financial and environmental integrity rests with the executive board. Going forward, this function will likely be increasingly decentralized with the establishment of domestic ETSs: agencies in the European Union, the United States, and other OECD countries will have to develop and apply regulatory standards for determining the qualification of mitigation activities in other countries and the extent of emissions reductions achieved. Host countries will also play a role in determining whether mitigation activities qualify for recognition and in monitoring emissions reductions. Private firms or other intermediary institutions, including nonprofit and hybrid public-private institutions, may also play a role in the certification of projects and emissions reductions for the purpose of these market mechanisms.

Compliance

The compliance function is concerned with ensuring that parties meet their obligations with respect to the provision of funds and their application. The effectiveness of any future climate finance regime will depend, to a significant extent, on the existence of credible mechanisms that ensure that commitments to provide finance are met and that real and credible outcomes are achieved by application of these funds.

---

35   OECD-IEA, *supra* note 4, at 16.

There will not be one overall compliance mechanism for the climate finance regime; rather, a series of different mechanisms applicable to different sources and forms of funds will need to be developed. For example, it would not be politically feasible to require hard compliance for state commitments to provide funds through budgetary appropriations. Instead, the regime will rely on soft compliance measures, such as monitoring and publicizing state transfers of funds, and the exertion of political and moral pressure as the main mechanisms for encouraging states to follow through with their political pledges to provide funds.

At the other end of the spectrum, there is clearly a need for hard compliance mechanisms in the offset market to ensure the environmental integrity of credits being traded. An example of such a mechanism is the compliance regime, overseen by the CDM executive board, which regulates the issue of certified emission reductions from CDM projects. Contractual obligations and remedies will also play a prominent role in compliance for private flows of funds.

Of particular interest is the potential for crosscutting mechanisms that promote compliance by both states and private participants. One prominent proposal is for a system of buyer liability, under which liability for variations in the quality of carbon credits sold in a market would fall on the buyers. Drawing on the example of bond markets, the price of credits would depend on market expectations as to their integrity, which would be based on both the reputation of the sellers and information about their integrity in previous years. The emergence of credit-rating agencies, and fluctuations in price according to risk, would generate strong incentives for states and entities within states to comply with emission stabilization/reduction targets, without having to resort to unwieldy state-to-state compliance.[36]

New Climate Finance Institutions Emerging from Copenhagen and Cancun

Three new UNFCCC institutions were included in the Copenhagen Accord and the Cancun Agreements—the Green Climate Fund, the Standing Committee, and a NAMA registry. None of the three is yet operational or has had its mandate fully established. Thus, whether they are to fill the institutional deficits in climate finance remains an open question.

The Green Climate Fund

A significant outcome of COP16 at Cancun was the decision to establish the GCF, which will be designated as an operating entity of the financial mechanism of the UNFCCC.[37] The GCF was established primarily as a disbursement

---

36   *See*, in particular, Robert O. Keohane & Kal Raustiala, *Toward a Post-Kyoto Climate Change Architecture: A Political Analysis* (Harvard Project on International Climate Agreements, Discussion Paper 08-01, Jul. 2008), available at <http://belfercenter.ksg.harvard.edu/files/KeohaneFinalWebRevised4_09.pdf>.

37   Cancun Agreements, paragraph 102.

mechanism, responsible for managing some portion of the $100 billion per annum to be mobilized by developed countries, which it will use to support programs, policies, and other activities in developing countries using thematic windows.[38]

The GCF is to be governed by a board of twenty-four members with equal representation of developed and developing countries.[39] The World Bank will serve as interim trustee, subject to review three years after the fund's operationalization.[40] The more detailed design and modalities of the fund are to be determined by a transitional committee, comprising members possessing relevant expertise and skills, 15 of whom are drawn from developed countries and 25 of whom are from developing countries.[41] The aim is for this design process to be completed before the COP in Durban in December 2011.

The transitional committee's terms of reference include formulating rules of procedure for the GCF board; considering the types of financial instruments the funds will use; establishing mechanisms for independent evaluation of the fund's performance and ensuring financial accountability and the evaluation of activities supported by the fund; and arranging for stakeholder input and performance. One of the more difficult items in the transitional committee's mandate is to determine the legal and institutional arrangements for the fund's establishment and operation. In particular, the transitional committee will need to explore the possibilities for the fund's relationship with the COP and the arrangements by which they will interact. To the extent that the fund is an institution established by the COP, it may be inferred that the COP will have some considerable degree of control over its operation. However, although the Cancun decision speaks of the fund being "accountable to" and "under the guidance of" the COP, it is *not* "under the authority" of the COP, as most developing countries had desired. This suggests that the fund will retain some degree of independence and a separate institutional identity.

Another area of uncertainty is which implementing bodies will actually disburse the funds flowing through the GCF. One possibility is that a new implementing body will be established under the GCF. Alternatively, or in addition, funds may flow through one or more existing bodies that already administer and disburse climate finance. The Cancun decision establishing the fund makes no reference to the GEF, the Adaptation Fund, or other specific bodies, although it does provide that a "significant share of new multilateral funding for adaptation should flow through the Green Climate Fund." The transitional committee has been charged with considering how to ensure

---

38   Cancun Agreements, paragraph 102. The Cancun Agreements provide for a mitigation funding window and an adaptation funding window, with the possibility of further thematic windows being established at a later time.

39   Cancun Agreements, paragraph 103.

40   Cancun Agreements, paragraphs 104–07.

41   Cancun Agreements, paragraphs 109–11.

complementarity among the GCF and other bilateral, regional, and multilateral funding arrangements, an implicit acknowledgment by the COP of the plural nature of climate finance as well as the need for some degree of cooperation and coordination within this regime.

The Standing Committee

Another institution emerging from the conference at Cancun is the standing committee, established to assist the COP in exercising its functions with respect to the financial mechanism of the Framework Convention. The committee's composition, functions, and modalities for operation are yet to be determined; indeed, the process by which they will be determined is not at all clear. What is apparent is that the committee will seek to play a role in promoting institutional coordination and linkage, using the analytical framework discussed above. In particular, the standing committee is supposed to assist the COP with improving coherence and coordination in the delivery of climate financing, rationalization of the financial mechanism, mobilization of financial resources, and measurement, reporting, and verification of support provided to developing-country parties.[42]

The NAMA Registry

Another new institution, conceived in Copenhagen and formalized in Cancun, is the NAMA registry, which will record developing-country NAMAs seeking international support and facilitate the matching of these activities with the finance, technology, and capacity-building support available.[43] This registry will be maintained by the UNFCCC Secretariat. Countries will regularly submit information regarding developing-country NAMAs seeking international support (along with the estimated costs, emissions reductions, and anticipated time frame for implementation); developed-country support available for NAMAs; and developing-country support that has been provided.[44] The COP has agreed to develop modalities for facilitating support through the registry, which may include the development of some functional relationship with the financial mechanism and its operating entities (the GCF, the GEF, and the Adaptation Fund).[45]

The registry will involve a number of the institutional functions presented above. It will play an important role in monitoring, acting as a central repository for information regarding financial support available from developed countries and provided to NAMAs, as well as the outcomes achieved from the provision of that support. It will also play a coordination role to the extent that it facilitates the matching of available resources with NAMAs seeking international support.

---

42 Cancun Agreements, paragraph 112.

43 Cancun Agreements, paragraph 53.

44 Cancun Agreements, paragraphs 54, 55, 56, and 59.

45 Cancun Agreements, paragraph 57.

Future Regime Design Considerations

The emerging global climate finance regime, where finance will be drawn from a multitude of public and private sources and provided in a variety of forms, raises critical challenges for governance. Arrangements must be made to promote transparency and accountability in both the provision and the application of funds and to ensure that finance is applied effectively and efficiently. There is also a need to develop linkages between different sources of funds, including between public and private finance and among different markets and instruments. The regime must develop and operate within an overall framework that enables trust to grow between donor and recipient countries. There is no easy resolution to these issues: no single preexisting regime provides an appropriate model for the governance of climate finance, nor will a one-institution-fits-all approach be effective. This section provides a framework for future analysis by outlining some of the main institutional design criteria in the consideration of the new regime.

One versus Many Institutions

Climate finance will not be channeled through one centralized fund, nor will there be one single, overarching governing body; rather, the administration and governance of climate finance will be performed by a multitude of institutions that collectively make up the regime. The obvious concern with disaggregating administration and governance in this manner is that it is inefficient and will lead to an overall lack of coherence in strategies.

However, there are also advantages to having a more decentralized regime: for one, it enables more room for the development of bottom-up initiatives and the establishment of locally appropriate institutions. A more dispersed regime also allows for greater flexibility across different issues and greater adaptability of institutions over time.[46] Given the embryonic nature of climate finance, decentralization of functions enables institutional experimentation and learning and the potential for beneficial competition.

The flexibility of current arrangements enables immediate action to be taken by countries and other parties in order to meet emerging needs, sidestepping institutional inertia within the UNFCCC. A recent example of this is <http://www.faststartfinance.org>, a website for reporting commitments of fast-start finance and the details of projects financed by these funds. The website, which is administered by the UNDP, was launched by the Netherlands with the support of ten other countries in order to provide transparency around the provision of fast-start funds in the absence of any formal reporting mechanism.

Formal versus Informal Institutions

It is not always necessary to have an "institution" in the narrow sense of the word, that is, a formal organization with a physical location, staff, and

---

46   Keohane & Victor, *supra* note 33.

budget, charged with specific functions. In some fields, governance may be better served by the formulation of a set of shared coordinating norms, which can then act as an organizing principle for action among a network of actors. Thus, rather than tasking a single body with hierarchical oversight of conduct, a number of coequal institutions could agree on a set of external norms that would guide future actions in the field. The Millennium Development Goals are an example of a regime that focuses on coordinated norms and practices rather than a formal "peak" institution as the primary means of achieving international objectives.

One area in which the informal coordination approach could be adopted is in the disbursement of funds for climate-related purposes. Although a number of different multilateral bodies and bilateral funds will be responsible for disbursing funds, these transfers could be guided by a widely agreed-upon set of high-level principles dealing with issues such as prioritization between countries, distribution across thematic areas, and ultimate environmental objectives. In this way, the norms would play a critical role linking and coordinating the actions of a diverse range of actors. However, such an arrangement would have to be complemented by arrangements for transparency and monitoring.

New versus Existing Institutions

One point of continuing contention in negotiations is the extent to which climate finance should be administered by existing institutions, as opposed to new institutions created expressly for that purpose. The preference among developed countries is to avoid duplication and use existing channels of funding, rather than creating new climate finance bodies. This would mean a significant ongoing role for the World Bank and other MDBs that currently dominate the administration of climate funds that, it is argued, already have significant institutional expertise in the provision of climate finance.[47] By contrast, developing countries have generally been in favor of the creation of new institutions for climate finance, falling within the UNFCCC framework and answerable to the COP. This option is equated with greater control and more equitable representation of developing countries. It also reflects the developing world's distrust of the World Bank and other MDBs and is consistent with developing-country efforts to distinguish climate finance from development aid.[48]

Specialized Institutions for Public and Private Finance or Hybrid Approaches?

With finance flowing from both public and private sources, the question arises as to whether there should be separate institutions dedicated for public finance and for private finance, or whether there are opportunities to develop

---

47   Arunabha Ghosh, *Harnessing the Power Shift: Clean Technologies, Innovative Finance and the Challenge for Climate Governance* 28–29 (Oxfam Research Report, Oct. 6, 2010), available at <http://www.oxfam.org.uk/resources/policy/climate_change/downloads/harnessing-the-power-shift-climate-finance-061010.pdf>.

48   *Id.*, at 29–31.

institutions that deal with both. Presently, most institutions deal with only public or private funds, and these separate arrangements are likely to prevail in most cases: the issues that public and private sources raise tend to be very different, as are the mechanisms available for their governance.

However, there may be some opportunities for institutional convergence, particularly in the field of monitoring. For example, the relatively rigorous monitoring system developed under the CDM could be extended into the public arena as a means of ensuring the environmental integrity of projects and programs funded. Another opportunity is to develop institutions that specialize in using public funds and resources to leverage private climate finance.

What Is the Appropriate Level of Governance?

Different institutional functions can be best performed at different jurisdictional levels. Thus, an important design consideration is whether an institution should be situated at the international, regional, or domestic level. Generally, the preference in climate finance is for a bottom-up approach, where institutions are as localized as possible. Particularly when considering the disbursement of funds, there are strong arguments in favor of the devolution of control over funds to national agencies, which would enhance national ownership of projects; ensure the alignment of environmental policies with national priorities; enhance synergies between sectors and between mitigation, adaptation, and REDD; reduce the transaction costs associated with a burgeoning multilateral bureaucratic structure; and build national decision-making capacity.[49]

The bottom-up approach can be taken only so far, however, and there will be instances when local governance is not capable of dealing with the various externalities arising or of achieving the international objectives desired. The bottom-up approach is also limited by the lack of institutional capacity in some states. Developing nations are not a homogenous group, and there is wide variance in domestic capacity to effectively manage and apply large amounts of funding in a manner that will bring about real abatement and adaptation outcomes. Accordingly, while some nations already control the application of climate funds, the devolution of control over funds will be more gradual for others and only following measures directed at strengthening national institutions.[50]

Public versus Private Delivery of Institutional Functions

Another question is whether functions should be carried out by public or private institutions: the answer to this question does not always correspond

---

49   Benito Muller, *The Reformed Financial Mechanism of the UNFCCC: Post Copenhagen Architecture and Governance* 12 (ECBI Policy Brief, Apr. 2010), available at <http://www.oxfordclimate policy.org/publications/documents/ecbiRFM2final.pdf>; Luiz Gomez-Eceverri & Benito Muller, *Key Issues on Governance of Climate Change Finance, Based on the Proceedings of a Meeting at La Redoute, Bad Godesberg* 5 (ECBI Policy Brief, Aug. 9, 2009), available at <http://www .oxfordclimatepolicy.org/publications/documents/ecbiLaRedoute9August.pdf>.

50   Ballesteros et al., *supra* note 25, at 51.

with the public/private characterization of the funds in question. Thus, for example, while the raising and disbursement of private finance will largely take place through private channels, public institutions such as the CDM executive board may play a prominent role in the policy-making and regulatory function, in the monitoring of the mechanism, and in ensuring compliance. On the other hand, private institutions are increasingly stepping into voids of governance over public funds, particularly in the field of monitoring. Thus, for example, in the absence of adequate official data, organizations such as Heinrich Boll Stiftung, the Overseas Development Institute, and the World Resources Institute[51] have engaged in concerted efforts to compile and present data measuring the amounts of climate finance that are currently being provided. Private institutions will likely play a more formal role in the administration of public climate finance in the future, for example, as independent auditors verifying country reports of support provided and mitigation and adaptation outcomes achieved.

Conclusion

The challenges in creating appropriate institutions for climate finance within and outside the UNFCCC are significant and should occupy at least as much negotiating time as that dedicated to emissions limitations. Building institutions for climate finance will likely be more difficult than creating institutions for emissions reduction control. For emissions reduction, the core challenge is coming to political agreement. For climate finance, not only is there the challenge of reaching political agreement, but there are also significant organizational and technical issues that must be addressed.

Many functions of the climate finance regime are not currently being performed. Tracking commitments and flows—integral to building trust between the parties—is being handled in a noncomprehensive manner by a variety of public and private institutions. Domestic and regional emissions trading systems are being created in developed countries with little input from the developing countries that will participate in their offset mechanisms and little coordination with other trading systems. Bilateral and multilateral public climate funds continue to proliferate, targeting various thematic and regional areas with differing policy requirements.

There is clearly a need for rigorous thinking and action on the institutions necessary for climate finance. One need only consider the extensive and acrimonious debates that have surrounded the CDM to realize the importance of institutional design as we move to expand the flow of climate finance.

---

51   Athena Ballesteros, et al., *Summary of Developed Country "Fast-Start" Climate Finance Pledges* (Nov. 24, 2010), available at http://www.wri.org/publication/summary-of-developed-country-fast-start-climate-finance-pledges.

Index

www.ingramcontent.com/pod-product-compliance
Lightning Source LLC
Chambersburg PA
CBHW060956220326
41599CB00023B/3728